Exam 70-515: Web Applications Development with Microsoft .NET Framework 4

OBJECTIVE	CHAPTER	LESSON
1. DEVELOPING WEB FORMS PAGES		
1.1 Configure Web Forms pages.	Chapter 1	Lessons 2 and 3
1.2 Implement master pages and themes.	Chapter 2	Lessons 1 and 2
1.3 Implement globalization.	Chapter 6	Lesson 1
1.4 Handle page life cycle events.	Chapter 1	Lesson 1
	Chapter 3	Lesson 1
1.5 Implement caching.	Chapter 2	Lesson 3
1.6 Manage state.	Chapter 3	Lessons 2 and 3
2. DEVELOPING AND USING WEB FORMS CONTROLS		
2.1 Validate user input.	Chapter 5	Lesson 1
2.2 Create page layout.	Chapter 5	Lessons 2 and 3
2.3 Implement user controls.	Chapter 7	Lesson 1
2.4 Implement server controls.	Chapter 4	Lessons 1 and 2
	Chapter 7	Lesson 2
2.5 Manipulate user interface controls from code-behind.	Chapter 2	Lesson 1
	Chapter 4	Lessons 1 and 2
	Chapter 5	Lesson 2
3. IMPLEMENTING CLIENT-SIDE SCRIPTING AND AJAX		
3.1 Add dynamic features to a page by using JavaScript.	Chapter 9	Lesson 2
3.2 Alter a page dynamically by manipulating the DOM.	Chapter 9	Lesson 3
3.3 Handle JavaScript events.	Chapter 9	Lessons 2 and 3
3.4 Implement ASP.NET AJAX.	Chapter 9	Lesson 1
3.5 Implement AJAX by using jQuery.	Chapter 9	Lesson 3
4. CONFIGURING AND EXTENDING A WEB APPLICATION		
4.1 Configure authentication and authorization.	Chapter 13	Lesson 2
4.2 Configure providers.	Chapter 13	Lesson 1
4.3 Create and configure HttpHandlers and HttpModules.	Chapter 10	Lesson 1
4.4 Configure initialization and error handling.	Chapter 3	Lesson 1
	Chapter 8	Lesson 1
4.5 Reference and configure ASMX and WCF services.	Chapter 10	Lessons 2 and 3
4.6 Configure projects and solutions, and reference assemblies.	Chapter 1	Lesson 3
4.7 Debug a Web application.	Chapter 8	Lessons 1 and 2
4.8 Deploy a Web application.	Chapter 8	Lesson 3
5. DISPLAYING AND MANIPULATING DATA		
5.1 Implement data-bound controls.	Chapter 12	Lesson 2
5.2 Implement DataSource controls.	Chapter 12	Lesson 1
5.3 Query and manipulate data by using LINQ.	Chapter 11	Lessons 1 and 2
5.4 Create and consume a data service.	Chapter 10	Lessons 2 and 3
5.5 Create and configure a Dynamic Data project.	Chapter 12	Lesson 3
6. DEVELOPING A WEB APPLICATION BY USING ASP.NET MVC 2		
6.1 Create custom routes.	Chapter 14	Lesson 2
6.2 Create controllers and actions.	Chapter 14	Lesson 2
6.3 Structure an ASP.NET MVC application.	Chapter 14	Lesson 1
6.4 Create and customize views.	Chapter 14	Lesson 2

Exam Objectives   The exam objectives listed here are current as of this book's publication date. Exam objectives are subject to change at any time without prior notice and at Microsoft's sole discretion. Please visit the Microsoft Learning website for the most current listing of exam objectives:
http://www.microsoft.com/learning/en/us/exam.aspx?ID=70-515#tab2

Microsoft®

MCTS Self-Paced Training Kit (Exam 70-515): Web Applications Development with Microsoft® .NET Framework 4

Tony Northrup
Mike Snell

PUBLISHED BY
Microsoft Press
A Division of Microsoft Corporation
One Microsoft Way
Redmond, Washington 98052-6399

Library of Congress Control Number: 2010933008

ISBN: 978-0-7356-2740-6

4 5 6 7 8 9 10 11 12 13 QGT 6 5 4 3 2 1

Printed and bound in the United States of America.

Microsoft Press books are available through booksellers and distributors worldwide. For further information about international editions, contact your local Microsoft Corporation office or contact Microsoft Press International directly at fax (425) 936-7329. Visit our Web site at www.microsoft.com/mspress. Send comments to: tkinput@ microsoft.com.

Acquisitions Editor: Martin DelRe
Developmental Editor: Karen Szall
Project Editor: Rosemary Caperton
Editorial Production: Online Training Solutions, Inc.
Technical Reviewer: Kenn Scribner; Technical Review services provided by Content Master, a member of CM Group, Ltd.
Cover: Tom Draper Design

Body Part No. X17-21595

[2011-08-19]

For my partner, Chelsea Knowles
—TONY NORTHRUP

For my wife, Carrie Snell
—MIKE SNELL

Contents at a Glance

Contents

Chapter 6   Globalization and Accessibility   291

Chapter 8   Debugging and Deploying   387

Chapter 9   **Working with Client-Side Scripting, AJAX, and jQuery**   **453**

Chapter 10 Writing and Working with HTTP Modules and Web Services   551

Chapter 12 Working with Data Source Controls and Data-Bound Controls   685

Chapter 14 Creating Websites with ASP.NET MVC 2   831

What do you think of this book? We want to hear from you!

Microsoft is interested in hearing your feedback so we can continually improve our
books and learning resources for you. To participate in a brief online survey, please visit:

www.microsoft.com/learning/booksurvey/

Acknowledgments

We would like to thank the hardworking people at Microsoft Press, in particular Rosemary Caperton, for getting us involved and for her guidance on this work.

Many thanks also to Kathy Krause and her team at OTSI (*www.otsi.com*) for keeping the book on schedule and providing excellent editing suggestions. She left no stone unturned and made us both seem like better writers than we are.

Thanks also go to our fantastic technical editor, Kenn Scribner. He added a lot to this book by challenging our coding examples, working through the labs, getting the CD right, and helping ensure consistency. It was truly great to have such a strong technical editor on the team.

Finally, we would like to thank our families and friends for their patience and understanding during the long nights and weekends that are the writing process.

Introduction

This training kit is designed for developers who plan to take Microsoft Certified Technical Specialist (MCTS) exam 70-515, as well as for developers who need to know how to develop applications by using the Microsoft .NET Framework 4 and Microsoft ASP.NET. We assume that before you begin using this kit, you have a working knowledge of Windows and Microsoft Visual Basic or Microsoft Visual C#. The topics in this training kit cover what you need to know for the exam as described on the Skills Measured tab for the exam, which is available at *http://www.microsoft.com/learning/en/us/exam.aspx?ID=70-515&locale=en-us#tab2.*

By using this training kit, you'll learn how to do the following:

- Create a web application by using web server controls, event handlers, application state, and session state.
- Create websites that take advantage of master pages, themes, and cascading style sheets.
- Use the wide variety of controls that ship with ASP.NET, including those for validation, navigation, user input, data binding, and much more.
- Create user controls and custom web server controls.
- Create a web application that stores user-specific information and preferences.
- Develop accessible web applications that can be used by a global audience.
- Write rich Internet applications (RIAs) by using client script, Asynchronous JavaScript and XML (AJAX), and jQuery.
- Connect your web applications with data by using Microsoft ADO.NET, Microsoft Language-Integrated Query (LINQ) queries, LINQ to SQL, the Entity Framework, and more.
- Write template-driven, data-bound websites by using Dynamic Data in ASP.NET.
- Monitor, troubleshoot, and debug ASP.NET applications.
- Build service-oriented applications (SOAs) by using Hypertext Transfer Protocol (HTTP) handlers and modules, web services, and Windows Communication Foundation (WCF).
- Add authentication and authorization features to your application to improve security and add multiple access levels.
- Build websites based on the ASP.NET MVC 2 framework.

Refer to the objective mapping page in the front of this book to see where in the book each exam objective is covered.

Hardware Requirements

We recommend that you use a computer that is not your primary workstation to do the practice exercises in this book, because you will make changes to the operating system and application configuration.

To use the companion CD, you need a computer running Windows XP with Service Pack 3 (SP3), Windows Vista with SP2, Windows 7, Windows Server 2003 with SP2, Windows Server 2003 R2, Windows Server 2008 with SP2, or Windows Server 2008 R2. The computer must meet the following minimum requirements:

- Personal computer with at least a 1-GHz 32-bit (x86) or 64-bit (x64) processor
- At least 1 GB of RAM (x86 systems) or 2 GB of RAM (x64 systems)
- At least a 40-GB hard disk
- DVD-ROM drive
- Super VGA (800 x 600) or higher resolution video adapter and monitor
- Keyboard and Microsoft mouse or compatible pointing device

Software Requirements

The computer used with the companion CD-ROM should also have the following software:

- A web browser such as Windows Internet Explorer
- An application that can display PDF files, such as Adobe Acrobat Reader, which can be downloaded at *www.adobe.com/reader*
- Microsoft Visual Studio 2010 Professional, a trial version of which can be downloaded at *http://www.microsoft.com/visualstudio/en-us/products/2010-editions/professional*

These requirements will support use of the companion CD-ROM.

Using the Companion Media

The companion media (CD) included with this training kit contains the following:

- **Practice tests**   You can reinforce your understanding of programming with ASP.NET 4 by using electronic practice tests that you customize to meet your needs from the pool of lesson review questions in this book, or you can practice for the 70-515 certification exam by using tests created from a pool of 200 realistic exam questions, which give you many practice exams to ensure that you are prepared.
- **An eBook**   An electronic version (eBook) of this book is included for when you do not want to carry the printed book with you.

> **NOTE** **DIGITAL CONTENT FOR DIGITAL BOOK READERS**
>
> If you bought a digital-only edition of this book, you can enjoy select content from the print edition's companion media. Go to *http://go.microsoft.com/fwlink/?Linkid=206094* to get your downloadable content. This content is always up to date and available to all readers.

How to Install the Practice Tests

To install the practice test software from the companion CD to your hard disk, perform the following steps:

1. Insert the companion CD into your CD drive and accept the license agreement. A CD menu appears.

> **NOTE** **IF THE CD MENU DOES NOT APPEAR**
>
> If the CD menu or the license agreement does not appear, AutoRun might be disabled on your computer. Refer to the Readme.txt file on the CD for alternate installation instructions.

2. Click Practice Tests and follow the instructions on the screen.

How to Use the Practice Tests

To start the practice test software, follow these steps:

1. Click Start, click All Programs, and then select Microsoft Press Training Kit Exam Prep. A window appears that shows all the Microsoft Press training kit exam prep suites installed on your computer.

2. Double-click the lesson review or practice test you want to use.

> **NOTE** **LESSON REVIEWS VS. PRACTICE TESTS**
>
> Select the (70-515) Web Applications Development with Microsoft .NET Framework 4 *lesson review* to use the questions from the "Lesson Review" sections of this book. Select the (70-515) Web Applications Development with Microsoft .NET Framework 4 *practice test* to use a pool of 200 questions similar to those that appear on the 70-515 certification exam.

Lesson Review Options

When you start a lesson review, the Custom Mode dialog box appears so that you can configure your test. You can click OK to accept the defaults, or you can customize the number of questions you want, how the practice-test software works, the exam objectives to which you want the questions to relate, and whether you want your lesson review to be timed. If you are retaking a test, you can select whether you want to see all the questions again or only the questions you missed or did not answer.

After you click OK, your lesson review starts.

- **Article I**   To take the test, answer the questions and use the Next and Previous buttons to move from question to question.

- **Article II**   After you answer an individual question, if you want to see which answers are correct—along with an explanation of each correct answer—click Explanation.

- **Article III**   If you prefer to wait until the end of the test to see how you did, answer all the questions, and then click Score Test. You will see a summary of the exam objectives you chose and the percentage of questions you got right, both overall and per objective. You can print a copy of your test, review your answers, or retake the test.

Practice Test Options

When you start a practice test, you choose whether to take the test in Certification Mode, Study Mode, or Custom Mode:

- **Certification Mode**   Closely resembles the experience of taking a certification exam. The test has a set number of questions. It is timed, and you cannot pause and restart the timer.

- **Study Mode**   Creates an untimed test during which you can review the correct answers and the explanations after you answer each question.

- **Custom Mode**   Gives you full control over the test options so that you can customize them as you like. In all modes, the test user interface is basically the same but with different options enabled or disabled depending on the mode. The main options are discussed in the previous section, "Lesson Review Options."

When you review your answer to an individual practice test question, you see a "References" section that lists where in the training kit you can find the information that relates to that question and provides links to other sources of information. After you click Test Results to score your entire practice test, you can click the Learning Plan tab to see a list of references for every objective.

How to Uninstall the Practice Tests

To uninstall the practice test software for a training kit, use the Uninstall A Program option in Windows Control Panel.

Microsoft Certified Professional Program

Microsoft certifications provide the best method for proving your command of current Microsoft products and technologies. The exams and corresponding certifications are developed to validate your mastery of critical competencies as you design and develop, or implement and support, solutions with Microsoft products and technologies. Computer professionals who become Microsoft-certified are recognized as experts and are sought after industry-wide. Certification brings a variety of benefits to the individual and to employers and organizations.

> *MORE INFO* **ALL THE MICROSOFT CERTIFICATIONS**
>
> For a full list of Microsoft certifications, go to *www.microsoft.com/learning/mcp/default.asp*.

Errata and Book Support

We've made every effort to ensure the accuracy of this book and its companion content. If you do find an error, please report it on our Microsoft Press site at Oreilly.com:

1. Go to *http://microsoftpress.oreilly.com*.

2. In the Search box, enter the book's ISBN or title.

3. Select your book from the search results.

4. On your book's catalog page, under the cover image, you'll see a list of links. Click View/Submit Errata.

You'll find additional information and services for your book on its catalog page. If you need additional support, please email Microsoft Press Book Support at *tkinput@microsoft.com*.

Please note that product support for Microsoft software is not offered through the addresses above.

We Want to Hear from You

At Microsoft Press, your satisfaction is our top priority, and your feedback our most valuable asset. Please tell us what you think of this book at:

http://www.microsoft.com/learning/booksurvey

The survey is short, and we read every one of your comments and ideas. Thanks in advance for your input!

Stay in Touch

Let's keep the conversation going! We're on Twitter: *http://twitter.com/MicrosoftPress*

Preparing for the Exam

Microsoft certification exams are a great way to build your resume and let the world know about your level of expertise. Certification exams validate your on-the-job experience and product knowledge. Although there is no substitute for on-the-job experience, preparation through study and hands-on practice can help you prepare for the exam. We recommend that you augment your exam preparation plan by using a combination of available study materials and courses. For example, you might use the Training Kit and another study guide for your "at home" preparation, and take a Microsoft Official Curriculum course for the classroom experience. Choose the combination that you think works best for you.

CHAPTER 1

Introducing ASP.NET 4

The web development experience continues to evolve with Microsoft Visual Studio 2010 and Microsoft ASP.NET 4. The most important improvements are:

- Simplified deployment of applications, settings, and data.
- Easy redirection of search engine–friendly URLs to different pages.
- Cascading style sheet–friendly rendering for many controls.
- Applications that start up before the first user request.
- Extensible request validation for more flexible security.
- Easy setting of meta tags at run time.
- The ability to enable view state for individual controls to reduce page sizes.
- Static client IDs to allow web server controls to be reliably accessed from JavaScript.
- The inclusion of AJAX jQuery scripts in Visual Studio templates.
- Improved Language-Integrated Query (LINQ) capabilities for creation of strongly typed queries for collections and databases.
- Dynamic Data templates for rapid development of data-driven websites.
- Compressed session state data.
- A new Chart control for quick creation of interactive three-dimensional charts.
- Built-in ASP.NET MVC 2 for creation of layered applications that are easily testable.

With these new tools, you can build highly interactive, robust web applications more efficiently than ever. All of these enhancements were developed to give ASP.NET developers more control and increased confidence when building and deploying the next generation of websites.

This chapter introduces the basics of website development with ASP.NET. Lesson 1, "Understanding Web Communications," describes the key players in any website: the server, the browser (or client), and Hypertext Transfer Protocol (HTTP). This serves as a basis for understanding the architecture of all web communications. In Lesson 2, "Creating a Website and Adding New Webpages," you will learn the key components that make up an ASP.NET development site. Lesson 3, "Working with Web Configuration Files," describes how to configure the many aspects of an ASP.NET application.

Exam objectives in this chapter:

- Developing Web Forms Pages
    - Configure Web Forms pages.
    - Handle page life cycle events.
- Configuring and Extending a Web Application
    - Configure projects and solutions, and reference assemblies.

Lessons in this chapter:

Before You Begin

To complete the lessons in this chapter, you should be familiar with developing applications in Visual Studio by using Microsoft Visual Basic or Microsoft Visual C#. In addition, you should be comfortable with all of the following:

- The Visual Studio 2010 Integrated Development Environment (IDE)
- A basic understanding of Hypertext Markup Language (HTML) and client-side scripting
- Making assemblies available to other applications
- Working with Visual Studio projects, files, classes, and designers

 REAL WORLD

Tony Northrup

Visual Studio makes it easy to jump into web development. It's so easy, in fact, that many developers manage to create their first applications without understanding the fundamentals. This chapter is designed to save you time in the long run by teaching you the most critical web development fundamentals. Yes, you can create a working web application without understanding the difference between HTTP GET and HTTP PUT. However, at some point in your career (and perhaps at some point in this book) you're going to need to do some detailed troubleshooting, and if you don't have a solid background, that troubleshooting is going to take you much longer than it needs to.

Lesson 1: Understanding Web Communications

Like all client-server applications, web applications have two distinct components:

- **Client** Also known as the *front-end interface*, the web browser presents the user interface, accepts user input, and sends data to the server for processing.

- **Server** Also known as the *back end*, the web server responds to requests from clients for specific pages. It responds with an HTML page that includes instructions for how to generate the user interface.

The web browser (the client) and the web server communicate by using Hypertext Transfer Protocol (HTTP), a text-based network protocol assigned to TCP port 80. If the server has a certificate, the client and server can use HTTP Secure (HTTPS) to authenticate the server and encrypt communications. HTTPS is assigned to TCP port 443.

Communications typically follow these steps:

1. A user enters an address, such as *http://www.microsoft.com/*, into the web browser.

2. The web browser connects by using HTTP and sends a GET request, such as GET / (to retrieve the root page), to the web server.

3. The web server processes the requested page. This action might cause the server to return static HTML or image files, or it might execute ASP.NET code that performs workflow tasks or connects to a database.

4. The web server uses HTTP to send a response back to the web browser. If the request was processed successfully, the web server returns the HTTP status code 200, along with an HTML document. If the server cannot find the page, it returns the code 404. If the user requests an outdated or relocated page, the server returns the code 302 and the new URL so that the browser can access the correct page. This is known as *redirection*. Several other responses are possible as well, depending on the particular situation.

5. The user's web browser then processes the response by displaying the HTML page (if the code was 200), showing an error message (if the code was 404), or loading a different page (if the code was 302). Other server responses are similarly handled by the browser, depending upon the response.

This process is repeated each time the user clicks a button or link.

This lesson provides an overview of the responsibilities and boundaries of a web browser and a web server. You will also learn the basics of HTTP and how browsers and servers use it to process user requests.

After this lesson, you will be able to:

- Describe the web server's role in responding to requests for resources.
- Describe the web browser's role in submitting requests and presenting the response to the user.
- Examine HTTP communications to determine what is being sent between the client and server and whether the communications were successful.

Estimated lesson time: 20 minutes

The Web Server's Role

The web server provides the content and the web browser displays it to the user. At the simplest, a web server sends static files, such as static HTML or image files, through an HTTP connection to a web browser.

Modern web servers do far more, however. When a web server receives a request, some of the actions it takes are to:

1. **Verify that the request is structured legitimately.**   Sometimes, malicious clients send malformed web requests to compromise web servers. Web servers must be able to detect this and respond appropriately—usually by ignoring the request.

2. **Authenticate itself.**   If the server has a Secure Sockets Layer (SSL) certificate and the request was made with HTTPS, the web browser uses the certificate to authenticate the server. The web server will also encrypt all content before returning it to the web browser.

3. **Authenticate the user.**   If the content requires authentication, the web server verifies that the user has submitted credentials. If the user has not been authenticated, the web server redirects the user to an authentication form.

4. **Authorize the user.**   After the Web server authenticates the user, the web server verifies that the user is allowed to access the requested content.

5. **Determine how to handle a request.**   If the web browser requested static content or was simply determining whether cached content could still be used, the web server can directly respond. If the web browser requested an ASP.NET page, the web server must forward the request to ASP.NET.

6. **Handle errors.**   If a server cannot process the user's request, it provides error information to the web browser.

7. **Cache output.**   Web servers can cache output to improve the response time of subsequent requests. Web servers also provide caching information to web browsers, so browsers know how long to keep content cached.

8. **Compress output.**   Before returning a page to a web browser, a web server can compress the content to reduce the bandwidth required.

9. **Log access.**   Web servers typically record usage information for security and performance-monitoring purposes.

The Web Browser's Role

Despite the attention web browsers receive, their role is relatively simple:

1. **Send requests to the web server.**   If the user enters *http://www.microsoft.com*, the web browser resolves the www.microsoft.com Domain Name System (DNS) address, uses HTTP to connect to the server, and requests a page.

2. **Authenticate the server.**   If the server has an SSL certificate and the request was made with HTTPS, the web browser uses the certificate to authenticate the server and then decrypt future communications.

3. **Process the response.**   If the server has provided HTML, the browser retrieves embedded objects, such as images, videos, or animations referenced in the HTML. If the server has provided an error, redirection, or other response, the browser responds appropriately.

4. **Display HTML and embedded objects.**   Web browsers use HTML standards to determine how to display a webpage to the user. Because HTML can contain embedded objects, a web browser might have to display dozens of objects to render a single webpage.

5. **Run client scripts.**   Client scripts, such as those written in JavaScript, enable interactive and responsive pages without reloading the page.

Understanding the Role of HTTP

HTTP is a text-based communication protocol that is used to request webpages from a web server and send responses back to a web browser. When a webpage is requested, the browser sends a request to the web server. The request might look like the following.

```
GET /default.aspx HTTP/1.1
Host: www.northwindtraders.com
```

> **MORE INFO**   **HTTP/1.1 SPECIFICATION**
>
> For more information about the current HTTP standard (HTTP/1.1), see the specification at *http://www.w3.org/Protocols/rfc2616/rfc2616.html*.

The first word in the request is the command, often known as the *method*. In this case, the command is GET. The command is followed by the Uniform Resource Identifier (URI) of the resource to be retrieved. In this case, the URI is /default.aspx. Following the URI is the version of HTTP to be used to process the command. In this case, the HTTP version is HTTP/1.1.

The second line of the request (Host: *www.northwindtraders.com*) identifies the name of the website. Most web servers host multiple websites with a single IP address, and need to know the website's name to return the correct page. This process involves using host headers to identify the website that will handle the request.

HTTP supports other commands, as shown in Table 1-1. If a website has Distributed Authoring and Versioning (DAV) enabled, many more commands are available, including LOCK and UNLOCK.

TABLE 1-1 Common HTTP/1.1 Methods

HTTP METHOD	DESCRIPTION
GET	Gets an object, such as a webpage, from the server. A GET request for a specific URL (Uniform Resource Locator) retrieves the resource. For example, GET /test.htm retrieves the test.htm resource (typically a static file, but it could be generated dynamically).
POST	Sends data to the web server for processing. This is typically what happens when users enter data on a form and submit that data as part of their request, but it has other meanings when used outside the bounds of HTML forms.
HEAD	Retrieves the meta information for an object without downloading the page itself. HEAD is typically used to verify that a resource hasn't changed since the browser cached it.
OPTIONS	Used by client applications to request a list of all supported commands. You can use OPTIONS to check to see if a server allows a particular command, thus avoiding wasting network bandwidth trying to send an unsupported request.
PUT	Allows a client to directly create a resource at the indicated URL on the server. If the user has permission, the server takes the body of the request, creates the file specified in the URL, and copies the received data to the newly created file.
DELETE	Deletes a resource on the web server if the user has permission.
TRACE	Used for testing or diagnostics; allows the client to see what is being received at the other end of the request chain.
CONNECT	Reserved for use with a proxy that can dynamically switch to being a tunnel, such as with the SSL protocol.
DEBUG	Starts ASP.NET debugging. This command informs Visual Studio of the process to which the debugger will attach.

What Is Distributed Authoring and Versioning?

Distributed Authoring and Versioning (DAV) is a set of extensions to HTTP/1.1 that simplifies website development when work is being carried out in a team scenario. DAV is an open standard and is available on numerous platforms. DAV provides the ability to lock and unlock files and the ability to designate versions.

DAV is built directly on HTTP/1.1, so no other protocols, such as File Transfer Protocol (FTP) or Server Message Block (SMB), are required. DAV also provides the ability to query the web server for various resource properties such as file names, time stamps, and sizes. DAV also gives developers the ability to perform server-side file copying and moving. For example, you can use the HTTP GET and PUT commands to retrieve files from the web servers and save them to different locations, or you can use DAV's COPY command to tell a server to copy a file.

The communication from the web browser to the web server is referred to as a *request*. In ASP.NET, there is a Request object that is used to represent the web browser's communications to the web server. ASP.NET wraps the resource request in an object that can be queried in code. By wrapping the HTTP request in a programmable object, ASP.NET provides your code access to things such as the cookies associated with your site, the query string parameters passed with the URL, and the path to the requested resource, and allows you to work with other relevant request-based information.

The communication from the web server back to the web browser is wrapped in the Response object. You can use this object to set cookies, define caching, set page expiration, and more. When a web server responds to a request, it uses what it finds in the Response object to write the actual, text-based HTTP response, such as the following.

```
HTTP/1.1 200 OK
Server: Microsoft-IIS/6.0
Content-Type: text/html
Content-Length: 38
<html><body>Hello, world.</body><html>
```

The first line indicates the communication protocol and version information. It also includes the status code for the response and the reason that describes the status code. The status codes are three-digit numbers and are grouped as shown in Table 1-2.

EXAM TIP

Even if you don't memorize every status code, you'll need to know the five status code groupings in Table 1-2 to troubleshoot web development problems.

TABLE 1-2 Status Code Groups

STATUS CODE GROUP	DESCRIPTION
1xx	Informational: The request was received, and the server is continuing to process.
2xx	Success: The action was successfully received, understood, and accepted.
3xx	Redirect Command: The client must access a different resource instead.
4xx	Client Error: The request has a syntax error or the server does not know how to fulfill the request.
5xx	Server Error: The server failed to fulfill a request that appears to be valid.

In addition to the status code groups, HTTP/1.1 defines unique status codes and reasons. A reason is nothing more than a very brief description of the status code. Table 1-3 shows a list of common status codes and reasons.

TABLE 1-3 Common Status Codes and Their Reasons

STATUS CODE	REASON
100	Continue
200	OK
201	Created
300	Multiple Choices
301	Moved Permanently
302	Found
400	Bad Request
401	Unauthorized
403	Forbidden
404	Not Found
407	Proxy Authentication Required
408	Request Time-out
413	Request Entity Too Large
500	Internal Server Error
501	Not Implemented

The second line of the response indicates the type of web server (Server: Microsoft-IIS/6.0). The third line (Content-Type) indicates the type of resource that is being sent to the web browser as part of the response. This indicator is in the form of a Multipurpose Internet Mail Extensions (MIME) type. In this example (Content-Type: text/html), the file is an HTML text file. The MIME type is a two-part designator that is shown as type/subtype, in which the first part is the resource type (text, in this example) and the second part is the resource subtype (html, in this example). Some common MIME types are shown in Table 1-4.

TABLE 1-4 Common MIME Types

MIME TYPE	DESCRIPTION
text	Textual information. Subtypes include plain, html, and xml.
image	Image data. Subtypes are defined for two widely used image formats, jpeg and gif, and other subtypes exist as well.
audio	Audio data. Requires an audio output device (such as a speaker or headphones) for the contents to be heard. An initial subtype, basic, is defined for this type.
video	Video data. The subtype mpeg is often used. Typically, videos are not transferred directly, but are read from an embedded object, such as a JavaScript or Adobe Flash object.
application	Any binary data. The subtype octet-stream is typically used.

The next line is content length (Content-Length: 38 in this example). This simply indicates the size of the content (in "octets," or 8-bit bytes) that follows. After the Content-Length line, the response message is returned. The browser attempts to process the content based on its MIME type. For example, it interprets HTML for HTML MIME types and shows a picture for image MIME types.

Submitting Form Data to the Web Server

The HTML <form> tag can be used to create a webpage that collects data from the user and sends the collected data back to the web server. The form tag is nested inside the <HTML> tags. The form tags typically include information for the user in the form of text, and input tags for defining controls such as buttons and text boxes. A typical use of the <form> tag might look like the following.

```
<form method="POST" action="getCustomer.aspx">
    Enter Customer ID:
    <input type="text" name="Id">
    <input type="submit" value="Get Customer">
</form>
```

This example form prompts the user for a customer ID, displays a text box that collects the desired customer ID, and also displays a Submit button that initiates the sending of data to the web server. The method attribute of the form tag indicates the HTTP command (POST) to use when sending the request to the server. The action attribute is the relative URL of the page to which the request will be sent.

There are two HTTP commands that can be used to submit the form data to the web server: GET and POST. When the GET command is used, the form data is appended to the URL as part of the query string. The query string is a collection of key–value pairs, separated by an ampersand (&) character. The start of the query string is indicated by a question mark (?). The following provides an example.

```
GET /getCustomer.aspx?Id=123&color=blue
HTTP/1.1
Host: www.northwindtraders.com
```

In this example, a GET request is made to the web server for a webpage called getCustomer.aspx on the root of the website (indicated by the forward slash). The query string contains the form data following the question mark (?).

When the GET command is used to send data to the server, the complete URL and query string can be seen and modified in the address bar of the web browser, as shown in Figure 1-1. This allows users to easily bookmark or link to the results of the form, which is important for search pages. However, it's not a good choice for authentication pages, because the user's credentials would be visible in the URL. It's also not a good choice when the user needs to transfer large amounts of information, because when Windows Internet Explorer and Internet Information Services (IIS) are used, the limit for a query string is 1,024 characters (other browsers and server implementations also have limitations, although they might not limit the length to the values IIS and Internet Explorer use).

FIGURE 1-1 Returning form results by using a GET request shows the input in the address bar.

The POST command is a better choice for submitting credentials and large amounts of data. When the POST command is used, the data is placed into the message body of the request as follows.

```
POST /getCustomer.aspx HTTP/1.1
Host: www.northwindtraders.com

Id=123&color=blue
```

Using the POST command removes the input from the URL and overcomes size constraints. Instead, the data is hidden in the message body.

Sending data back to the server as part of your request is often referred to as a *postback* in ASP.NET. Although its name comes from the POST command, it is possible to perform a postback by using the GET command already described. An ASP.NET webpage contains a property called IsPostBack that is used to determine if data is being sent back to the web server or if the webpage is simply being requested.

 REAL WORLD

Tony Northrup

There's no better way to understand HTTP than to watch your own web browser's inner workings as you surf. Though you can find several free sniffer applications on the web, my favorite is Microsoft Network Monitor (available from *http://www.microsoft.com/downloads*). You can also purchase several browser add-ons that monitor HTTP within your browser session, including HttpWatch from *http://www.httpwatch.com/* and Fiddler from *http://www.fiddler2.com/*.

 Quick Check

1. What protocol is used to communicate between the web browser and the web server?
2. In ASP.NET, what does the Request object represent?
3. In ASP.NET, what does the Response object represent?

Quick Check Answers

1. HTTP is used for web browser and web server communication.
2. The Request object in ASP.NET wraps the communication from the web browser to the web server.
3. The Response object in ASP.NET wraps the communication from the web server to the web browser.

Exploring HTTP

In this practice, you explore HTTP by using Telnet, the terminal emulation application that is built into Windows.

EXERCISE 1   Starting and Configuring Telnet

In this exercise, you start the Telnet client and configure it to work with HTTP.

1. From the Windows Features Control Panel tool, add the Telnet Client feature.

2. Open a command prompt. You can do so by selecting Start | All Programs | Accessories | Command Prompt.

3. Start Telnet. In the command prompt window, enter the following command to start the Telnet client.

    ```
    Telnet.exe
    ```

4. Configure Telnet to echo typed characters. Enter the following command into the Telnet window, which will cause locally typed characters to be displayed as you type them.

    ```
    set localecho
    ```

    Telnet will respond with the following.

    ```
    Local echo on
    ```

5. Set carriage return and line feed to On. Enter the following command to instruct Telnet that it should treat the Enter key as a combination of carriage return and line feed.

    ```
    set crlf
    ```

    Telnet will respond with the following.

    ```
    New line mode - Causes return key to send CR & LF
    ```

6. Open a connection to a website. Enter the following command into the Telnet command window to open a connection to *www.bing.com* on TCP port 80, the default port for a web server.

    ```
    o www.bing.com 80
    ```

    Telnet responds with the following.

    ```
    Connecting To www.bing.com. . .
    ```

    Note that Telnet will not indicate that you are indeed connected.

7. Press Enter until the cursor moves to the next line or the top of the page. Usually you only need to press Enter one additional time.

8. Attempt to retrieve the default page. Enter the following lines. After typing the second line, press Enter two times to indicate the end of the message to the web server.

```
GET / HTTP/1.1
Host: www.bing.com
```

After you have pressed Enter two times, the Bing website will return an HTML page. Notice that the status code is 200, which means that the server was able to return the page without a problem. The message body contains HTML with a hyperlink to the new location.

9. Press Ctrl+] to return to the Telnet prompt. Repeat the process with *www.contoso.com*. This time, you should receive an HTTP 301 message, which redirects you to a different page.

10. Press Ctrl+] to return to the Telnet prompt. Repeat the process with *www.microsoft.com*. This time, you should receive an HTTP 200 message. If you examine the HTML, you'll notice that the web server returned an error message indicating that you did not provide a valid HTTP User-Agent header. Browsers use the User-Agent header value to indicate the browser's type and capabilities.

EXERCISE 2 Monitoring HTTP with Network Monitor

In this exercise, you use Network Monitor to examine HTTP communications.

1. Visit *http://www.microsoft.com/downloads* and search for Network Monitor. Download the latest version of the software and install it by using the default settings.

2. Restart your computer to ensure that the Network Monitor drivers are bound to your adapters.

3. Launch Network Monitor.

4. In Network Monitor, click the New Capture button. Then click Start.

5. Open Internet Explorer and visit your home page. Wait for the page to load.

6. In Network Monitor, click the Stop button.

Network Monitor recorded all the packets that Internet Explorer transmitted and received, and those packets are visible in the Frame Summary pane. Unfortunately, Network Monitor also recorded communications from other network applications.

7. To filter the Frame Summary to display only HTTP packets, type **HTTP** in the Display Filter pane, and then click Apply.

Network Monitor displays just the HTTP packets.

8. In the Frame Summary pane, select the first frame. In the Frame Details pane, expand the Http section. Notice the command that was transmitted (probably GET), the URI, and the host.

9. In the Frame Summary pane, select the HTTP response, which is probably the second frame. In the Http section of the Frame Details pane, notice the StatusCode (probably 200), the server, the command that was transmitted (probably GET), the URI, and the host.

10. Browse through the other requests and responses, which probably include requests for objects contained in the HTML page.

Lesson Summary

- The web server is responsible for accepting requests for a resource and sending the appropriate response.

- The web browser is responsible for displaying data to the user, collecting data from the user, and sending data to the web server.

- HTTP is a text-based communication protocol that is used to communicate between web browsers and web servers by using TCP port 80 by default.

- Secure HTTP (HTTPS) uses TCP port 443 by default.

- Each HTTP method indicates the desired action. The most common methods are GET and POST.

- The process of sending data to a web server from a browser is commonly referred to as a *postback* in ASP.NET programming.

- You can troubleshoot HTTP by using a sniffer such as Microsoft Network Monitor.

Lesson Review

You can use the following questions to test your knowledge of the information in Lesson 1, "Understanding Web Communications." The questions are also available on the companion CD in a practice test, if you prefer to review them in electronic form.

> **NOTE ANSWERS**
>
> Answers to these questions and explanations of why each answer choice is correct or incorrect are located in the "Answers" section at the end of the book.

1. From within an ASP.NET page, you need to run a section of code only if the user has previously loaded the page and is submitting data as part of a form. Which Page object property should you use?

    A. IsCallback

    B. IsReusable

    C. IsValid

    D. IsPostBack

2. You are troubleshooting a problem users have when submitting information with a form. The form data does not appear in the web browser's address bar, but you know the web server is receiving the form data. After capturing the web communications with a sniffer, which type of HTTP request should you examine to see the data the user submitted?

    A. PUT

    B. CONNECT

    C. POST

    D. GET

Lesson 2: Creating a Website and Adding New Webpages

Visual Studio creates the initial structure for your website automatically. However, the structure itself does nothing useful. To create a functional website, you will need to add ASPX pages and write Visual Basic or C# code to turn the ASPX pages into dynamic HTML pages.

This lesson shows you how to create a new website with Visual Studio, describes the contents of the default website, and teaches you how to add your own ASPX web forms.

> **After this lesson, you will be able to:**
> - Create a new website within Visual Studio.
> - Understand the various configuration options available when defining a new website.
> - Add new web forms to a website.
>
> **Estimated lesson time: 35 minutes**

Creating Websites

The Visual Studio project system allows you to define a new website project based on how you intend to access the site content hosted on the site's web server. You can create a web project connected to a file-system–based server on your computer, an IIS server, or an FTP server. The option that is right for your website project depends on how you want to run, share, manage, and deploy your project. The following describes each option in further detail:

- **File system** A file-system–based website stores all of the files for the website inside a directory of your choosing. When you debug the website, Visual Studio runs the lightweight ASP.NET development server that is included in Visual Studio. A file-system–based site is great when you want to run and debug your website locally but do not want to run a local IIS web server (or cannot due to security restrictions on your network).

- **FTP** An FTP-based website is useful when you want to connect to your site via FTP to manage your files on a remote server. This option is typically used when your website is hosted on a remote computer and your access to the files and folders on that server is through FTP.

- **HTTP** An HTTP-based website is used when you are working with a site deployed inside of IIS (either locally or on a remote server). This type of website might be configured at the root of the IIS web server or in a virtual directory that is configured as an application. Note that a remote server running IIS will need the WebDAV Publishing role service or Microsoft Front Page Server Extensions 2002.

Creating a Website Project

You can create a new website project directly from Visual Studio. The basic steps for doing so are as follows:

1. In Visual Studio, use the File menu to create a new website (File | New | Web Site). This launches the New Web Site dialog box, as shown in Figure 1-2. This dialog box contains properties for setting the website type, location, Microsoft .NET Framework version, and default programming language.

2. Select the website type, location, and default programming language.

3. You might also want to select the target framework for your project. New to Visual Studio 2010 is the ability to code against multiple versions of the .NET Framework. You can choose among versions 2.0, 3.0, 3.5, and 4. Unless you need to use an earlier version, you should always use 4.

4. When you have defined your website, click OK to finish setting it up. Depending on your type selection, you might be prompted to enter additional information.

FIGURE 1-2 The New Web Site dialog box.

You can also use Visual Studio to create an ASP.NET web application. Use the File menu to create a new project (File | New | Project), and then select ASP.NET Web Application or ASP.NET Empty Web Application. Web applications and websites function and perform similarly, but web applications differ from websites in several important ways. For example, with a web application:

- You can create an MVC application.
- Visual Studio stores the list of files in a project file (.csproj or .vbproj), rather than relying on the folder structure.
- You cannot mix Visual Basic and C#.
- You cannot edit code without stopping a debugging session.
- You can establish dependencies between multiple web projects.

- You must compile the application before deployment, which prevents you from testing a page if another page will not compile.
- You do not have to store the source code on the server.
- You can control the assembly name and version.
- You cannot edit individual files after deployment without recompiling.

Typically, website projects are the right choice when one developer will be creating and managing a website. Web application projects are better for enterprise environments with multiple developers and formal processes for testing, deployment, and administration.

Creating a File-System–Based Website

A file-system–based website runs locally on the ASP.NET web server that ships with Visual Studio. This option allows you to keep your development local until you are ready to publish code to a server for sharing. To create a file-system–based website, you use the New Web Site dialog box and select File System from the Web Location list box (see Figure 1-2). You then simply set a valid folder location for storing your website files locally on a hard drive.

Visual Studio creates the folder for your site and adds two content webpages (Default.aspx and About.aspx), their code-behind files, and a master file named Site.master, with a code-behind file. The default website template also creates the folder App_Data, as well as a configuration file called Web.config. When the website opens, Visual Studio displays the Default.aspx page in HTML Source view, where you can see the page's HTML elements. Figure 1-3 shows an example of the IDE after a new website has been created.

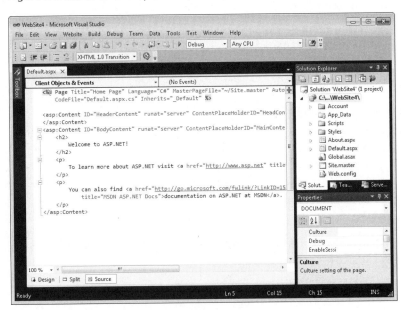

FIGURE 1-3 The structure of a newly created website.

CREATING A FILE-SYSTEM–BASED WEBSITE ON A SERVER

For learning and testing purposes, you should create websites on your local computer. However, in a production environment, you might need to create and update websites stored on remote servers, such as servers running Windows Server 2008 R2 and IIS 7.5.

IIS 7.5 does not support Front Page Server Extensions because it uses WebDAV natively. Therefore, you cannot use HTTP to create the website. However, you can create a file-system–based or FTP website. Of those two, the file-system–based website is preferred (the reasons for which are explained in the "Creating a Website with FTP" section later in this chapter).

To create a file-system–based website on a remote server running Windows Server 2008 R2, follow these high-level steps on the server:

1. Install .NET Framework 4 on the server (if it has not yet been installed).

2. Install IIS 7.5 with the ASP.NET role service.

3. After IIS is installed, open the IIS Manager. In the IIS Manager, create a new website that uses the ASP.NET 4 application pool.

4. Grant web developer user accounts NTFS Write permissions for the website folder.

5. From Windows Explorer, share the website folder. Grant web developer user accounts Change share permissions.

Then, on your development computer, follow these steps:

1. Use Windows Explorer to map a network drive to the shared folder.

2. Use Visual Studio to create a file-system–based website by specifying the drive letter of the WebDAV network drive.

When you debug or start without debugging from Visual Studio, it will run the website by using the lightweight ASP.NET development server that is included in Visual Studio. However, you can open the remote server's website by using Internet Explorer or another web browser, to verify that the site functions correctly on the website.

CREATING A FILE-SYSTEM–BASED WEBSITE WITH WEBDAV

The easiest way to publish a website to a server is to map a drive to the server. If firewall restrictions prevent you from mapping a drive, you can publish the website across HTTP by using WebDAV. On a server running Windows Server 2008 R2, follow the steps in the previous section to configure IIS, but do not share the folder by using Windows Explorer. Instead, configure WebDAV by following these high-level steps:

1. Add the WebDAV Publishing role service to IIS.

2. In the IIS Manager, add a WebDAV Authoring Rule to grant your user account access to Read, Write, and Source for the new website.

3. Enable WebDAV on the server.

4. On your client computer, map a network drive to the website's URL. You can do this from a command prompt by running the following command.

```
net use * http://<website_url>
```

5. On your client computer, use Visual Studio to create a file-system–based website by specifying the drive letter of the WebDAV network drive.

Creating a Website with HTTP

Most production websites and many development websites are hosted on computers running a version of Windows Server and IIS. IIS is not required when you are developing ASP.NET applications with Visual Studio, because Visual Studio includes a lightweight ASP.NET development server.

If you want to use IIS, you can publish files by using the file-system–based web location (described in the previous section) or the FTP web location (described in the next section). If the computer is running Windows 7, Windows Server 2008 (but not Windows Server 2008 R2), or earlier Windows operating systems, you can also create a website by using the HTTP web location type.

Before you can create a website by using HTTP, you must install the following Windows features:

- Internet Information Services\Web Management Tools\IIS 6 Management Compatibility \IIS 6 Metabase And IIS 6 Configuration Compatibility
- Internet Information Services\World Wide Web Services\Application Development Features\ASP.NET

To create a website that uses IIS running on your local computer, follow these steps:

1. Launch Visual Studio by right-clicking the application icon and clicking Run As Administrator.

2. In Visual Studio, use the File menu to create a new website (File | New | Website). This launches the New Web Site dialog box, as shown earlier in Figure 1-2.

3. Select the website type and default programming language.

4. Click the Web Location list, and then click HTTP.

5. Click the Browse button to open the Choose Location dialog box.

6. Click the Local IIS button.

7. Click the Create New Web Application button, type a name for your application, and then press Enter. Figure 1-4 shows a new web application being configured.

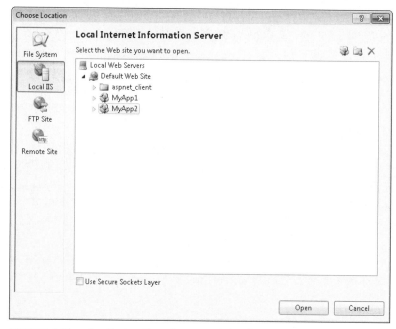

FIGURE 1-4 Choosing the location of a new website that will use IIS.

8. If you have an SSL certificate installed in IIS, select the Use Secure Sockets Layer check box.

9. Click Open.

10. Click OK.

Visual Studio creates a new web application on your local IIS server.

If you are connecting to a remote server, the remote server must have .NET Framework 4, ASP.NET, and Front Page Server Extensions installed and enabled. Microsoft does not support Front Page Server Extensions on IIS 7.5 and Windows Server 2008 R2. Therefore, you cannot create a new website that uses the HTTP deployment capabilities of Visual Studio on the most recent Microsoft server operating systems. If you receive the error message shown in Figure 1-5, create the website by using the file system or FTP.

FIGURE 1-5 Creating a new HTTP site requires Front Page Server Extensions.

Creating a Website with FTP

An FTP-based website is one that communicates with a remote server over FTP. This can be useful if you are using a hosting provider's server, communicating to it over FTP, and want to use Visual Studio to edit your files directly on the server. To create an FTP-based website project, first configure the web server as described in the "Creating a File-System–Based Website on a Server" section earlier in this chapter. Additionally, you must install the FTP Server role service on the server hosting the website.

When the server is properly configured, use Visual Studio to create a new website. In the New Web Site dialog box, from the Web Site Type drop-down list, select FTP. You then need to provide the FTP address for your site, such as *ftp://www.contoso.com*.

When you click OK in the New Web Site dialog box, you are prompted for a set of additional FTP parameters. This includes choosing between active and passive mode and selecting login credentials.

You should only use FTP when working with a web hosting provider that does not support file-system–based websites, WebDAV, or Front Page Server Extensions because, by default, FTP sends user credentials unencrypted. If you must use FTP, change your password regularly to minimize the potential impact of compromised credentials.

Website Solution Files

When a website is created, Visual Studio creates a solution file (.sln) and a hidden solution user options file (.suo). By default, these files are created in the My Documents\Visual Studio 2010 \Projects folder for websites. This is also true for those sites with actual root folders that are stored elsewhere. A solution file is an XML file that contains information such as the following:

- A list of the projects that are to be loaded into Visual Studio to make up the entire solution
- The default language for the solution
- A list of project dependencies
- Source control information, such as Microsoft Visual Studio Team Foundation Server
- A list of add-ins that are available

The solution user options file is a binary file that contains various user settings related to the IDE for the project. These files are not shared among developers (as a solution file would be). Settings in this file include the following:

- The task list
- Debugger break points and watch window settings
- Visual Studio window locations

Note that the solution files are not located in your website's folder because they are specific to Visual Studio and are not required in the deployed website. Also, a solution can contain many websites and Visual Studio projects, so it is best to keep the solution files in an independent folder. Some solution files also can be developer specific, meaning that developers might want to configure solution files based on their preferences.

A Visual Studio website also does not contain an associated project file. However, a Visual Studio web application does have a project file associated with it. Because it includes a project file, the web application is useful to developers who are building applications with Visual Studio and not just working with websites.

The Content of a Newly Created Website

If you create a website by using the default ASP.NET Web Site template, Visual Studio adds the default objects shown in Table 1-5. The order of the objects listed is the order in which you'll see them in the Visual Studio Solution Explorer window, which is the window in Visual Studio that you'll use to open and edit files, work with source control (if the appropriate bindings are established for the solution), and visualize the website's layout at a glance. If you don't see Solution Explorer, you can open it by using View | Solution Explorer.

TABLE 1-5 ASP.NET 4 Website Template Default Objects

OBJECT NAME	DESCRIPTION
Account	Contains user management forms for registering new users, logging in, and changing passwords
App_Data	Will contain application data files (.mdf and .xml files) if you access a local database
Scripts	Contains client-side JQuery JavaScripts used by some standard ASP.NET components
Styles	Contains the default site.css style sheet
About.aspx	The default About page
Default.aspx	The default page that appears when a user accesses your site without specifying a page in the URI
Global.asax	Code for Application and Session events, including Application.Start, Application.End, Application.Error, Session.Start, and Session.End
Site.master	Defines the header for the default site pages, including the menu structure
Web.config	The site configuration file

By right-clicking your site in Solution Explorer and clicking Add ASP.NET Folder, you can also add the folders in Table 1-6. These folders are protected by ASP.NET. If users attempt to browse to any of these folders (except App_Themes), they will receive an HTTP 403 Forbidden error.

TABLE 1-6 ASP.NET 4 Special Folders

FOLDER NAME	DESCRIPTION
App_Browsers	Contains custom browser definition files (.browser files) that ASP.NET uses to identify browsers and determine their capabilities. The .NET Framework includes a standard set of browser definition files in *<windir>*\Microsoft.NET\Framework*<ver>*\CONFIG\Browsers.
App_Code	Contains source code for classes (.cs, .vb, and .jsl files) that the developer intends to compile as part of the application.
App_Global-Resources	Contains resources (.resx and .resources files) that are compiled into satellite assemblies and have a global scope. Resource files are used to externalize text and images from your application code. This helps you support multiple languages and design-time changes without recompilation of source code.
App_Local-Resources	Contains resources (.resx and .resources files) that are scoped to a specific page, user control, or master page in an application.
App_Themes	Contains subfolders, each of which defines a specific theme (or look) for your site. A theme consists of files (such as .skin, .css, and image files) that define the appearance of webpages and controls.
App_Web-References	Contains web reference files (.wsdl, .xsd, .disco, and .discomap files) that define references to web services.
Bin	Contains compiled assemblies (.dll files) for code that the application requires to execute. Assemblies in the Bin folder are automatically referenced in your application.

Creating ASPX Pages

After your website has been created, the next step is to begin adding pages to the site. An ASP.NET page is also known as a *web form* and can be composed of a single file or a pair of files.

Single-File vs. Code-Behind Pages

An ASPX page always has two separate components: layout and code. The layout is expressed by using HTML, a formatting language that web designers specialize in. The code is written in ASP.NET, usually with Visual Basic .NET or C#, programming languages that web developers specialize in.

ASP.NET allows you to store both the layout and code in a single file, or to store them in separate files (a technique known as *code-behind*). If you are handling both the web design and web development roles, you might use the single-file method. If another individual will perform the layout work, or might in the future, code-behind is the preferred choice. If you are not sure, use the code-behind method, because it is easier to organize and more widely accepted in the development community.

The following code samples show a single-file web form that displays the current time. Note that the page is primarily standard HTML. The sections in bold are processed by ASP.NET on the server, however, and replace the ASP.NET Label control with the current time (as generated by the DateTime.Now.ToString static method) when the TimeLabel.Load event occurs.

Sample of Visual Basic Code

```
<%@ Page Language="VB" %>
<!DOCTYPE html PUBLIC "-//W3C//DTD XHTML 1.0 Transitional//EN" "http://www.w3.org/TR
/xhtml1/DTD/xhtml1-transitional.dtd">
<script runat="server">
Protected Sub TimeLabel_Load(ByVal sender As Object, ByVal e As System.EventArgs)
Handles TimeLabel.Load
    TimeLabel.Text = DateTime.Now.ToString
End Sub
</script>

<html xmlns="http://www.w3.org/1999/xhtml">
<head runat="server">
    <title>Single-File Web Form</title>
</head>
<body>
    <form id="form1" runat="server">
    <div>
        The time is:
        <asp:Label ID="TimeLabel" runat="server" onload="TimeLabel_Load"></asp:Label>
    </div>
    </form>
</body>
</html>
```

Sample of C# Code

```
<%@ Page Language="C#" %>
<!DOCTYPE html PUBLIC "-//W3C//DTD XHTML 1.0 Transitional//EN" "http://www.w3.org/TR
/xhtml1/DTD/xhtml1-transitional.dtd">
<script runat="server">
protected void  TimeLabel_Load(object sender, EventArgs e)
{
    TimeLabel.Text = DateTime.Now.ToString();
}
</script>

<html xmlns="http://www.w3.org/1999/xhtml">
<head runat="server">
    <title>Single-File Web Form</title>
</head>
<body>
    <form id="form1" runat="server">
    <div>
        The time is:
        <asp:Label ID="TimeLabel" runat="server" onload="TimeLabel_Load"></asp:Label>
    </div>
    </form>
</body>
</html>
```

Notice that the runat="server" attribute is defined in the script block. This indicates that the code contained within the script block will run on the server (and not on the client). On execution, ASP.NET will create server-side objects that contain this code as well as an instance of the Page class to contain the controls defined inside the page as instances of their type (System.Web.UI.WebControls.Label, for example).

By default, Visual Studio creates new ASP.NET web applications by using the code-behind structure. The following code samples show the same application written by using the code-behind technique. The ASPX file (code-behind.aspx) is as follows.

Sample of Visual Basic Code

```
<%@ Page Language="VB" AutoEventWireup="true" CodeFile="Code-behind.aspx.vb"
Inherits="Code_behind" %>

<!DOCTYPE html PUBLIC "-//W3C//DTD XHTML 1.0 Transitional//EN" "http://www.w3.org/TR
/xhtml1/DTD/xhtml1-transitional.dtd">

<html xmlns="http://www.w3.org/1999/xhtml">
<head runat="server">
    <title>Code-behind Web Form</title>
</head>
<body>
    <form id="form1" runat="server">
    The time is:
    <asp:Label ID="TimeLabel" runat="server" onload="TimeLabel_Load"></asp:Label>
</body>
</html>
```

Sample of C# Code

```
<%@ Page Language="C#" AutoEventWireup="true" CodeFile="Code-behind.aspx.cs"
Inherits="Code_behind" %>

<!DOCTYPE html PUBLIC "-//W3C//DTD XHTML 1.0 Transitional//EN" "http://www.w3.org/TR
/xhtml1/DTD/xhtml1-transitional.dtd">

<html xmlns="http://www.w3.org/1999/xhtml">
<head runat="server">
    <title>Code-behind Web Form</title>
</head>
<body>
    <form id="form1" runat="server">
    The time is:
    <asp:Label ID="TimeLabel" runat="server" onload="TimeLabel_Load"></asp:Label>
    </form>
</body>
</html>
```

Notice that the Visual Basic and C# code samples differ only by the page language in the first line of the file. Although each web form can only contain either Visual Basic or C#, you can have both a web form with Visual Basic and a web form with C# in the same website project (but not within a web application project). The code-behind file would be named code-behind.aspx.vb (for Visual Basic) or code-behind.aspx.cs (for C#).

Sample of Visual Basic Code

```
Protected Sub TimeLabel_Load(ByVal sender As Object, ByVal e As System.EventArgs)_
  Handles TimeLabel.Load
    TimeLabel.Text = DateTime.Now.ToString
End Sub
```

Sample of C# Code

```
public partial class Code_behind : System.Web.UI.Page
{
    protected void TimeLabel_Load(object sender, EventArgs e)
    {
        TimeLabel.Text = DateTime.Now.ToString();
    }
}
```

Notice that the code-behind layout file is almost identical to the single-file web form; it's missing only the <script> section. All of the code from the <script> section was moved into the code-behind file.

 REAL WORLD

Tony Northrup

Before ASP.NET, Microsoft's web development language was a scripting language called ASP (Active Server Pages). In ASP, you intermixed code and HTML freely, writing code in any part of a webpage that needed to be dynamic. In my mind, the single-file coding structure was introduced only to help ease the transition from ASP to ASP.NET. It has little practical use to today's .NET Framework developer.

Even if you don't work with a web designer, the code-behind structure is much easier for a web developer to maintain. You can make changes to ASPX pages without seeing code or even recompiling the application. On all but the simplest of webpages, storing code and layout in a single file would be overly cluttered.

When you reach Chapter 14, "Creating Websites with ASP.NET MVC 2," you'll discover that code-behind files aren't always used with model-view-controller (MVC). They're still available, and Visual Studio creates the code-behind file by default, but MVC's separation of presentation and logic limits the amount of code associated directly with ASPX files.

The Anatomy of an ASPX Page

A page in ASP.NET contains user interface layout information, code that executes on the server, and directives to both connect the layout with the code and to tell ASP.NET how the page should be processed. A standard ASP.NET page has an .aspx extension. A typical ASPX page includes three sections: page directives, code, and page layout. These sections are defined as follows:

- **Page directives**   This section is used to set up the environment and specifies how the page should be processed. This is where you can indicate an associated code file, a development language, a transaction, and more. A page directive resembles the following.

```
<%@ Page Title="Home Page" Language="C#" MasterPageFile="~/Site.master"
AutoEventWireup="true" CodeFile="Default.aspx.cs" Inherits="_Default" %>
```

- **Code**   This section contains code to handle events that execute on the server based on the ASP.NET page processing model. In single-file pages, the code is stored within one or more <script runat="server"></script> blocks. If you use a code-behind file, the code is stored in a separate file.

- **Page layout**   The page layout is written by using HTML that includes the HTML body, markup, and style information. The HTML body might contain HTML tags, Visual Studio controls, user controls, code, and simple text.

How to Create an ASPX Page

Follow these steps to create an ASPX page:

1. With a website open in Visual Studio, click the Website menu and then click Add New Item.

2. In the Add New Item dialog box (see Figure 1-6), in the Installed Templates list, select the programming language for the web form (such as Visual Basic or Visual C#).

FIGURE 1-6 Adding a new web form to your website.

3. In the middle pane, click Web Form, and then type a name for the web form.

4. To use a separate code-behind file, select the Place Code In Separate File check box.

5. You can opt to select the Select Master Page check box to select a page on which to base the look of your new web form. Master pages allow you to create a consistent look and feel for your entire website. We cover master pages in more detail in Chapter 2, "Using Master Pages, Themes, and Caching."

6. Click Add. If prompted, select a master page, and then click OK.

Website Compilation

Deploying an ASP.NET website can be as simple as copying your web application files to a web server. The first time a user (usually, the developer testing the deployment) opens a webpage, ASP.NET automatically compiles the application into an assembly and loads it into your site's application domain so that the request can be addressed. This can take a few seconds, slowing down any requests received before ASP.NET has finished compiling the application.

This model is referred to as *dynamic compilation*. It has several pros and cons, including the following:

- **Pro** Changes to a site file will result in an automatic recompilation of the resource. This allows for easier deployment.

- **Pro** The entire application does not need to be recompiled every time a change is made to a single page or component. This is great for large websites.

- **Pro** Pages that contain compilation errors do not prevent other pages in the website from running. This means that you can test websites that contain pages still in development.

- **Con** This model requires users who request pages before compilation is complete to take a compilation performance hit. That is, the first request for an uncompiled resource will be slower than subsequent requests.

- **Con** This model requires your source code to be deployed to the server. Default IIS settings protect the source code, reducing the risk of source code being downloaded by unauthorized users.

Visual Studio also allows you to precompile your website. When you do so, your entire site is compiled and error checked, and only the layout code and associated assemblies are deployed to the web server. Precompilation has the following pros and cons:

- **Pro** This model provides verification that all the pages and their dependencies can be compiled. This includes code, markup, and the Web.config file.

- **Pro** Performance for the first user requesting a resource is improved, because he or she is not required to take the compilation hit.

- **Con** Precompiled websites can be more difficult to deploy and manage, because you have to compile and then copy only the necessary files to the server (versus simply copying your code files to the server).

Quick Check

1. Where are solution files created by default?
2. Which ASP.NET page model separates layout from code?

Quick Check Answers

1. By default, solution files are created in the My Documents\Visual Studio 2010\ Projects folder.
2. The code-behind programming model separates user-interface layout markup from code.

Using Assemblies

The .NET Framework stores individual classes and entire libraries in assemblies. With ASP.NET, you might never have to think about assemblies; if you create stand-alone websites with custom classes, Visual Studio will automatically compile your custom classes along with your ASP.NET code the first time a user requests a page.

If you use a custom class from multiple applications (including both ASP.NET and Windows applications), you can choose to compile that class into a separate assembly. Then, you can reference that assembly from your Visual Studio projects by using the Add Reference dialog box.

When you reference an assembly, you can choose to store a copy of the class' assembly with every ASP.NET website that uses it, or you can store a single copy in the global assembly cache and have all applications access it from the central location. Typically, it is easier to manage assemblies and deploy websites when you store assemblies within the ASP.NET website folder structure.

You can view and manage the global assembly cache by opening the %windir%\assembly\ folder in Windows Explorer. You can automatically add signed assemblies to the global assembly cache by using a setup project. To manually add an assembly, copy it to the %windir%\assembly\ folder. To remove an assembly, right-click it in Windows Explorer and then click Uninstall.

PRACTICE **Creating a New Website and Adding a Page**

In this practice, you create a new website and explore its contents by using Visual Studio 2010. After that, you add a new webpage to the website.

ON THE COMPANION MEDIA

If you encounter a problem completing an exercise, you can find the completed projects in the samples installed from this book's companion CD. For more information about the project files and other content on the CD, see "Using the Companion CD" in this book's Introduction.

EXERCISE 1   Creating a New Website

In this exercise, you create a new, file-based website by using Visual Studio.

1. Start Visual Studio.

2. Create a file-based website. From within Visual Studio, select File | New | Web Site to open the New Web Site dialog box.

3. In the New Web Site dialog box, make sure the Web Site Type drop-down list box is set to File System. Click Browse to open the Choose Location dialog box. Then select File System, create the **%Documents%\Visual Studio 2010\WebSites\MyFirstSite** folder, and click Open. Click OK.

4. Explore the new website. In the Solution Explorer window (View | Solution Explorer), and notice the special folder called App_Data and the webpage called Default.aspx. Click the plus (+) sign beside the Default.aspx file to reveal its code-behind page.

5. In Windows Explorer, navigate to the actual folder that contains the solution file. This should be %Documents%\Visual Studio 2010\Projects\MyFirstSite. You can open this file and view it in Notepad. Also, notice that the actual web project files are not stored in this location.

6. Navigate to the folder containing your website files. This should be %Documents%\ Visual Studio 2010\WebSites\MyFirstSite. Here you can see your Default.aspx page, its code-behind file, the App_Data directory, and the Web.config file.

7. In Visual Studio, double-click the Default.aspx page in Solution Explorer. Then switch to Design view by selecting View | Designer.

8. From the toolbox, drag a Label control into the body of the Default.aspx page. In the Properties pane, change the ID to **TimeLabel**.

9. Click the Events button in the Properties pane. Double-click the Load event to create an event handler for the TimeLabel.Load event, which runs each time ASP.NET renders the TimeLabel control.

10. In the default TimeLabel.Load event handler, configure the TimeLabel control to display the current time by adding the following line of code.

```
Visual Basic
TimeLabel.Text = DateTime.Now.ToString
```

```
C#
TimeLabel.Text = DateTime.Now.ToString();
```

11. Next, compile the website. In Visual Studio, select Build | Build Web Site. Return to your website directory. Notice that it is unchanged. Visual Studio compiled your site but is hiding the results from you. Had this been a web application project, you would see a Bin directory and the compiled code placed in that directory.

12. View the Default.aspx page in a browser. In Visual Studio, select Debug | Start Without Debugging. After a moment, you should see the default webpage rendered with the current time displayed at the location where you dropped the Label control.

13. Use your browser to view the webpage source. Find the portion of the source HTML that displays the current time. Note that ASP.NET replaced the Label control with the current time, but did not modify the surrounding markup.

EXERCISE 2   Adding a New Webpage

In this exercise, you add a new webpage to the website that you just created.

1. Add a new webpage. In Visual Studio, from the Website menu, select Add New Item. In the Add New Item dialog box, select Web Form. In this case, set the page name to **Page2.aspx**. Next, clear the Place Code In Separate File check box and click Add.

2. Observe the result in Visual Studio. There should be no code-behind file for the file.

3. Edit Page2.aspx. As you did in the previous exercise, add a Label control named TimeLabel.

4. Create the TimeLabel.Load event handler, as you did in the previous exercise.

5. Add the code from the previous exercise to the TimeLabel.Load event handler in the <script> section to set TimeLabel.Text to the current time.

6. Run the page in a web browser and observe the results.

Lesson Summary

- You can use Visual Studio to publish websites to an IIS web server by using either HTTP or FTP. During development, you can test websites by using your local file system, without running a web server.

- You can create dynamic webpages by using ASPX web forms. ASP web forms separate the HTML layout from the .NET Framework code. Generally, you will store the HTML layout and the code in separate files, by using the code-behind technique. You do have the option of storing both the code and the HTML layout in a single file, however.

- ASP.NET automatically compiles a website the first time a user retrieves a webpage. To avoid any delay for the first several requests, you can precompile a website when publishing it.

Lesson Review

You can use the following questions to test your knowledge of the information in Lesson 2, "Creating a Website and Adding New Webpages." The questions are also available on the companion CD in a practice test if you prefer to review them in electronic form.

1. If you want to create a website on a remote computer running IIS 6.0 that does not have Front Page Server Extensions installed, which website type will you create?

    A. Remote HTTP

    B. File system

    C. FTP

    D. Local HTTP

2. Joe created a new website by using Visual Studio 2010, setting the website type to File, and setting the programming language to C#. Later, Joe received an elaborate webpage from his vendor, which consisted of the Vendor.aspx file and the Vendor.aspx.vb code-behind page. What must Joe do to use these files?

    A. Joe can simply add the files into the website, because ASP.NET 4 supports websites that have webpages that were programmed with different languages.

    B. The Vendor.aspx file will work, but Joe must rewrite the code-behind page by using C#.

    C. Both files must be rewritten in C#.

    D. Joe must create a new website that contains these files and set a web reference to the new site.

Lesson 3: Working with Web Configuration Files

You use Extensible Markup Language (XML) configuration files to store settings that control different aspects of an ASP.NET website. Most ASP.NET websites have a single XML Web.config file in the application's root directory; however, you can add Web.config files to any subfolder to change the behavior of that section of your website.

This lesson presents an overview of configuring websites by using configuration files.

> **After this lesson, you will be able to:**
> - Understand the configuration file hierarchy.
> - Use the graphical user interface (GUI) configuration tool to make changes to configuration files.
>
> **Estimated lesson time: 15 minutes**

Understanding the Configuration File Hierarchy

Configuration files allow you to manage the many settings related to your website. Each file is an XML file (with the extension .config) that contains a set of configuration elements. The elements define options such as security information, database connection strings, and caching settings. A site might actually be configured with multiple .config files. Therefore, it is important to understand how these files work together to establish and override various settings.

Configuration files are applied to an executing site based on a hierarchy. Generally, this means that there is a global configuration file for all sites on a server. This file, called Machine.config, is typically found in the %SystemRoot%\Microsoft.NET\Framework\<versionNumber>\CONFIG\ directory.

The Machine.config file contains settings for all .NET application types, such as Windows, Console, ClassLibrary, and web applications. These settings are global to the server. Some of the settings in the Machine.config file can be overridden by settings in Web.config files that are further down in the hierarchy, whereas other settings are more global in nature. The global ones are owned by the .NET Framework, so they are protected and cannot be over-ridden by the Web.config files.

The Machine.config file defines default settings for all sites running on a server, as long as another Web.config file further down the chain does not override any of these settings. To change settings for all websites on a computer, you can edit the root Web.config file, located in the same folder as the Machine.config file.

To change settings for an individual website, use the site-specific Web.config file located in the website's root folder. You can also add Web.config files to individual applications and folders within a website. Figure 1-7 shows the ASP.NET configuration hierarchy.

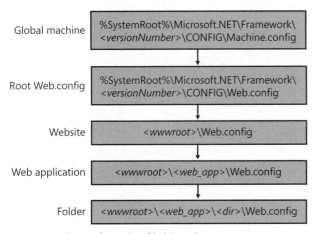

FIGURE 1-7 The configuration file hierarchy.

Processing the Configuration Files

When you initially run your web application, the ASP.NET runtime environment builds a cache of the configuration settings for your web application by flattening the layers of configuration files as follows:

1. ASP.NET retrieves the Machine.config file settings.

2. ASP.NET adds the settings from the root Web.config file to the cache, overwriting any conflicting settings that were created earlier when ASP.NET retrieved the Machine.config file.

3. If there is a Web.config file at the root of the website, ASP.NET reads this file into the cache, overwriting existing entries.

4. If there is a Web.config file at the web application level, ASP.NET reads it into the cache, also overwriting any existing settings. The resulting cache contains the settings for this website.

5. If you have subdirectories in your web application, each subdirectory can have a Web.config file that includes settings that are specific to the files and folders that are contained within the subdirectory. To calculate the effective settings for the folder, ASP.NET reads the website settings (steps 1–4), and then reads this Web.config file into the cache for this folder, overwriting (and thereby overriding) any existing settings.

Changes to .NET Framework 4 Configuration Files

All versions of the .NET Framework from 2.0 to 3.5 used the same configuration files. Because so much had changed since .NET Framework 2.0, Visual Studio 2008 SP1 created Web.config files for new web projects that were more than 125 lines long. This massive amount of XML made it difficult for developers to keep track of settings.

The .NET Framework 4 includes a new version of the Common Language Runtime (CLR), along with a new Machine.config file specific to .NET 4. The new Machine.config file includes the ASP.NET settings that earlier versions of Visual Studio had to add to individual Web.config files, allowing Visual Studio 2010 to create much simpler default Web.config files. As a result, your default Web.config files will only be about 40 lines.

Editing Configuration Files

Because they are XML files, the configuration files can be opened and modified with any text editor or XML editor. Visual Studio 2010 also provides the Web Site Administration Tool (WSAT), which can be used to modify many of the configuration file settings. You can access this tool by selecting Website | ASP.NET Configuration. The WSAT allows you to edit the following categories of the configuration files:

- **Security**   This setting allows you to manage users and configure permissions for your website.

- **Application Configuration**   This category is used to modify flexible, application-specific settings that function as application-wide constants. Figure 1-8 shows the Application tab of the WSAT.

- **Provider Configuration** The configuration file contains settings that allow you to specify the database provider to use for maintaining membership and roles, which you can tailor by using this WSAT feature.

FIGURE 1-8 The Application tab of the WSAT.

The WSAT lets you create and modify website settings that are not inherited. If a setting is inherited and cannot be overridden, the setting will be unavailable.

The IIS Manager included with IIS 7.5, as shown in Figure 1-9, allows you to edit many common ASP.NET configuration settings by using a GUI.

FIGURE 1-9 The ASP.NET settings in IIS 7.5.

PRACTICE **Modifying a Website Configuration**

In this practice, you use the WSAT to modify a website's configuration by enabling debugging on the website. After that, you view the changes in the Web.config file.

> ***ON THE COMPANION MEDIA***
>
> If you encounter a problem completing an exercise, you can find the completed projects in the samples installed from this book's companion CD. For more information about the project files and other content on the CD, see "Using the Companion CD" in this book's Introduction.

EXERCISE Creating the New Web.config File

In this exercise, you start Visual Studio and open the website created in the previous practice.

1. Open the MyFirstSite website from the previous practice.

> ***ON THE COMPANION MEDIA***
>
> Alternatively, you can open the completed Lesson 2 practice project in the samples installed from the companion CD.

2. Open the WSAT by selecting Website | ASP.NET Configuration.

3. Click the Application tab to display the application settings.

4. Click the Configure Debugging And Tracing link to open the page shown in Figure 1-10.

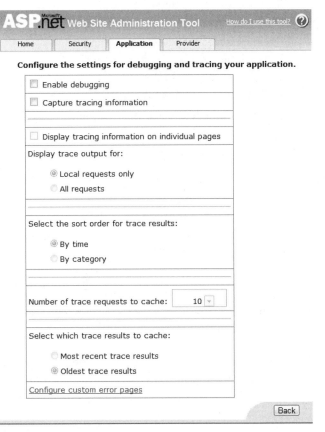

FIGURE 1-10 The Configure The Settings For Debugging And Tracing Your Application page.

5. Select the Enable Debugging check box to enable debugging for the current website. If you watch your browser closely, you'll see that selecting this check box performs a postback to the web server, which causes the WSAT to update the corresponding setting in the Web.config file.

6. Close the WSAT.

7. In Visual Studio, open the Web.config file. The new Web.config file will contain the following code (along with other unrelated settings).

```
<configuration>
    <system.web>
        <compilation debug="true" targetFramework="4.0" />
    </system.web>
</configuration>
```

Notice that the file contains the setting to set debug to true. This turns on debugging for the website.

Lesson Summary

- Websites are configured based on a hierarchy of XML configuration files, starting with the Machine.config file, followed by the Web.config file that is in the same folder. After that, you might have a Web.config file in the root of the website, in each web application, and in any subdirectory in a web application.

- The configuration files can be edited with a text editor, an XML editor, the WSAT, or the IIS Manager.

- The WSAT is used to add and modify the website settings.

Lesson Review

You can use the following questions to test your knowledge of the information in Lesson 3, "Working with Web Configuration Files." The questions are also available on the companion CD in a practice test, if you prefer to review them in electronic form.

> **NOTE ANSWERS**
>
> Answers to these questions and explanations of why each answer choice is correct or incorrect are located in the "Answers" section at the end of the book.

1. You want to make a configuration setting change that will be global to all web and Windows applications on the current computer. Which file do you change?

    A. Global.asax

    B. Application Web.config

    C. Machine.config

    D. Root Web.config

2. You want to make a configuration setting change that will affect only the current web application. Which file will you change?

    A. The Web.config file that is in the same folder as the Machine.config file

    B. The Web.config file in the root of the web application

    C. The Machine.config file

    D. The Global.asax file

Case Scenarios

In the following case scenarios, you apply what you've learned in this chapter. You can find answers to these questions in the "Answers" section at the end of this book.

Case Scenario 1: Creating a New Website

You are assembling a group of developers to create a new website for a company named Wide World Importers. Each developer will have Visual Studio 2010 installed on his or her mobile computer. Additionally, you have created a development server running Windows Server 2008 R2 to host different development versions of the website.

Each developer is creating an independent component of the website. You want each developer to be able to debug the web application independently, even when disconnected from your network. Additionally, you need to be able to evaluate stable versions of each developer's component of the website on your development server.

1. How can you allow developers to debug their components while disconnected from the network, and still be able to evaluate the entire site on your development server?

2. What types of websites will you create?

Case Scenario 2: Placing Files in the Proper Folders

You have created a new website for a company named Wide World Importers. The new site will use a third-party component called ShoppingCart.dll to process customer purchases. This component requires a Microsoft SQL Server 2005 Express Edition database. The database files are named Purchases.mdf (a data file) and Purchases.ldf (a transaction log file). In addition, you will add a new class file called ShoppingCartWrapper.vb or ShoppingCartWrapper.cs, which will be used to simplify the use of the ShoppingCart.dll component.

1. In what folder(s) will you place these files?

2. What is the benefit of using these locations?

Suggested Practices

To help you successfully master the exam objectives presented in this chapter, complete the following tasks.

Create a New Website by Using Visual Studio 2010

For this task, you should complete at least Practice 1. If you want a more well-rounded understanding of all of the website types, you should also complete Practice 2.

- **Practice 1** Become familiar with websites by creating a file-system–based website. Also create a local HTTP-based website and explore the differences.

- **Practice 2** You will need a remote computer with IIS, FTP, and Front Page Server Extensions installed. Create an FTP-based website and explore the options. Create a remote HTTP website and explore the options.

Add a Webpage to the Website

For this task, you should complete at least Practice 1. If you want a more well-rounded understanding of adding a webpage, you should also complete Practice 2.

- **Practice 1**   Create any type of website. Add a webpage that has a code-behind page. Add a webpage that does not have a code-behind page.
- **Practice 2**   Add another webpage, selecting a different programming language.

Program a Web Application

For this task, you should complete the previous two practices first.

- In a webpage that you have created, add code to test the IsPostBack property of the webpage and display a message if the webpage is posted back.

Examine Settings for a Web Application

For this task, you should complete all practices from the previous sections.

- Locate the Machine.config file and open it with Notepad.
- Explore the various settings that exist in the Machine.config file.
- Locate and open the Web.config file that exists in the same folder as the Machine.config file.
- Examine the settings that exist in this file.

Take a Practice Test

The practice tests on this book's companion CD offer many options. For example, you can test yourself on just the lesson review questions in this chapter, or you can test yourself on all the 70-515 certification exam objectives. You can set up the test so it closely simulates the experience of taking a certification exam, or you can set it up in study mode so you can look at the correct answers and explanations after you answer each question.

> **MORE INFO   PRACTICE TESTS**
>
> For details about all the practice test options available, see the "How to Use the Practice Tests" section in this book's Introduction.

CHAPTER 2

Using Master Pages, Themes, and Caching

Microsoft ASP.NET is designed to allow developers to focus on writing code while minimizing the time they spend on design elements such as layout, fonts, and colors. Because organizations tend to regularly change their design elements, it's important that those elements be separated from the code.

ASP.NET provides the ability to create master pages to separate the common elements, such as a logo and navigation, from the content of individual pages. Each master page represents a single file that controls the layout of all pages within a site. When you use master pages, your websites will be more consistent and easier to maintain.

To give you central control over aesthetics, including colors, fonts, and user interfaces, ASP.NET provides themes. Themes centralize the settings that define the appearance of a site, allowing you to change the look of every page on a site with one update. You can also switch between themes, allowing different users to have different experiences.

Though it will never directly add functionality to a website, caching is one of the most important features of ASP.NET. By properly implementing caching, you can improve the responsiveness of a site, reduce the processor utilization of your web server, and decrease the number of file system and database queries. Proper caching can allow you to get more out of less hardware, reducing server costs.

Exam objectives in this chapter:

- Developing Web Forms Pages
  - Implement master pages and themes.
  - Implement caching.
- Developing and Using Web Forms Controls
  - Manipulate user interface controls from code-behind.

Lessons in this chapter:

Before You Begin

To complete the lessons in the chapter, you should be familiar with developing applications with Microsoft Visual Studio by using Microsoft Visual Basic or Microsoft Visual C#. In addition, you should be comfortable with all of the following:

- The Visual Studio 2010 Integrated Development Environment (IDE)
- Hypertext Markup Language (HTML) and client-side scripting
- Creating a new website
- Adding web server controls to a webpage

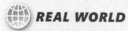 *REAL WORLD*

Tony Northrup

Master pages, themes, and caching weren't included in the original Microsoft .NET Framework. In fact, even with .NET 4 they're optional—any website can be created without using any of these components.

Microsoft added these capabilities because real-world developers demanded them. Take master pages—in theory, developers could include common components, such as a header and navigational controls, as user controls in every page on their sites. In practice, however, developers had a hard time maintaining sites after the initial release because some types of updates would require them to change every page on their site.

The performance gains you can get from caching used to be something developers thought about only after the site was completely functional. In 2010, however, Google made website performance a factor in their search results, meaning that reducing ASP.NET rendering time could increase the popularity—and profitability—of a website. You won't need to use caching while you're learning website development in a learning environment, but when you create real-world websites, you'll need every tool you have to improve website performance, and there's simply nothing more effective at reducing ASP.NET page generation time than caching.

Lesson 1: Using Master Pages

Windows applications have common elements to their user interface (UI). For example, if there is a menu bar, it's at the top of the window. Below that is a toolbar. Application status information appears at the bottom of the window. Because different applications tend to have these elements in the same places, it's easy for users to navigate within different applications.

Modern design applies the same philosophy to websites. Generally, websites have a logo at the top left of the page. A search box usually appears in the top middle or top right. Positioned below the logo and search box are navigation links. At the bottom of the page, below the page's unique content, users can find website copyright and contact information. By following these common guidelines, users can easily navigate your site the first time they visit it.

In ASP.NET, you can use master pages to provide a common structure to all pages in a site. Master pages isolate the common elements of a site's UI, such as the logo, search, and navigation, from each page's unique content. Individual ASPX pages you create are displayed within the master page when rendered for users. If you need to update part of the master page—such as copyright information in the page footer—you don't need to recompile individual pages.

This lesson describes how to create and use master pages in your applications.

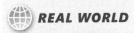

REAL WORLD

Tony Northrup

All websites require consistency. Before master pages were available, I used to create custom controls for every component that would be repeated throughout a website, including the logo, the navigation bar, and the page footer. That way, if I needed to change an aspect of one of the common components, I could make the change in one place and have it reflected throughout the site.

That worked great, unless I wanted to add or remove a component, or change the layout of the components. Then I'd have to go into every single webpage and make the change. After that, I'd have to test every page to make sure I hadn't made any mistakes.

Now master pages allow me to make centralized changes to the entire site by editing one file. It speeds up the development of content pages, too, because I don't have to worry about copying and pasting the structure for the shared controls. It's still important to test every page after making changes to the master, however.

Overview of Master and Content Pages

An ASP.NET master page defines the common layout of the pages in your site. Advantages of using master pages include the following:

- They allow you to centralize the common functionality of your pages so that you can make updates in just one place.

- They make it easy to create one set of controls and code and apply the results to a set of pages. For example, you can use controls on the master page to create a menu that applies to all pages.

- They give you fine-grained control over the layout of the final pages by allowing you to control how the placeholder controls are rendered.

- They provide object models that allow you to customize the master pages from individual content pages.

A master page is defined with the file extension .master. Master pages are very similar to regular ASPX pages. They contain text, HTML, and server controls; they even have their own code-behind files. One difference is that a master page inherits from the MasterPage class instead of the Page class. Another is that instead of an @ Page directive at the top of the page source, master pages contain an @ Master directive. Following this are the common things you would expect to see in the source code of an ASP.NET page such as <html>, <head>, and <form> elements. You can then embed your own source inside the master page, such as a company logo, navigation elements, and a footer.

You use master pages in conjunction with content pages. A content page contains page-specific content and inherits its shell from its master page. To enable pages to insert content into a master page, you must add one or more ContentPlaceHolder controls to the master page. This defines an area for content pages to add their page-specific text, HTML, and server controls.

At run time, master pages and content pages are processed as follows:

1. A user requests a page by typing the Uniform Resource Locator (URL) of the content page.

2. When the page is fetched, the @ Page directive is read. If the directive references a master page, the master page is read as well. If this is the first time the page has been requested, both pages are compiled.

3. The master page with the updated content is merged into the control tree of the content page.

4. The content of each Content control is merged into the corresponding ContentPlaceHolder control in the master page.

5. The resulting merged page is rendered to the browser as a single page.

Creating a Master Page

You create a master page through the Add New Item dialog box. You lay out a master page in a similar manner as you would any ASPX page. You can use tables, styles, controls, and so forth, to define your page. The following code shows a sample master page.

```
<%@ Master Language="C#" AutoEventWireup="true" CodeFile="Site.master.cs"
Inherits="SiteMaster" %>

<!DOCTYPE html PUBLIC "-//W3C//DTD XHTML 1.0 Strict//EN" "http://www.w3.org/TR/xhtml1
/DTD/xhtml1-strict.dtd">
<html xmlns="http://www.w3.org/1999/xhtml" xml:lang="en">
<head runat="server">
    <title></title>
    <link href="~/Styles/Site.css" rel="stylesheet" type="text/css" />
    <asp:ContentPlaceHolder ID="HeadContent" runat="server">
    </asp:ContentPlaceHolder>
</head>
<body>
    <form runat="server">
    <div class="page">
        <div class="header">
            <div class="title">
                <h1>
                    Contoso, Inc.
                </h1>
            </div>
            <div class="clear hideSkiplink">
                <asp:Menu ID="NavigationMenu" runat="server" CssClass="menu"
EnableViewState="false"
                    IncludeStyleBlock="false" Orientation="Horizontal">
                    <Items>
                        <asp:MenuItem NavigateUrl="~/Default.aspx" Text="Home"/>
                        <asp:MenuItem NavigateUrl="~/Products.aspx" Text="Products"/>
                        <asp:MenuItem NavigateUrl="~/Services.aspx" Text="Services"/>
                        <asp:MenuItem NavigateUrl="~/About.aspx" Text="About"/>
                        <asp:MenuItem NavigateUrl="~/Contact.aspx" Text="Contact"/>
                    </Items>
                </asp:Menu>
```

```
            </div>
        </div>
        <div class="main">
            <asp:ContentPlaceHolder ID="MainContent" runat="server"/>
        </div>
        <div class="clear">
        </div>
    </div>
    <div class="footer">
        Copyright <%=DateTime.Now.Year.ToString()%>, Contoso Inc.
    </div>
    </form>
</body>
</html>
```

In this example, the master page identifies a style sheet for the site, defines the top-level navigation for the site, and defines the site's footer. Notice the empty <title></title> tags in the <head> section. Pages that use this master sheet can specify the title by specifying the title attribute in the @ Page directive.

In addition, notice the ContentPlaceHolder controls. The first (here named HeadContent) is used to allow content pages to add information into the <head> section of the master page. For example, pages might add a page-specific <description> section. The second placeholder (here named MainContent) is used to define the actual page content. Figure 2-1 illustrates how this master page looks in Design view.

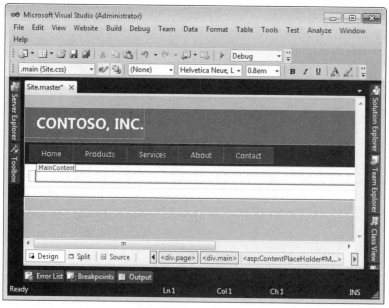

FIGURE 2-1 A master page in Design view.

Creating Content Pages

To add a content page to a Web Site project, select the Select Master Page check box in the Add New Item dialog box. To add a content page to a Web Application project, select Web Form Using Master Page from the Add New Item dialog box. Both methods allow you to select a master page for your ASPX page. Alternatively, you can associate an ASPX page to a master page by using the MasterPageFile attribute in the @ Page directive.

A content page provides the markup for the ContentPlaceHolder controls defined in a master page. When you create a new page and base it on a master page, Visual Studio provides you with an ASPX page that contains the content placeholder elements for the master page. You are then left to nest page-specific information inside the content placeholder controls.

The following page source demonstrates a content page derived from the master page defined earlier. Note that all text and controls must be within a Content control or the page will generate an error. Otherwise, the page behaves exactly like a standard ASP.NET page.

```
<%@ Page Language="VB" MasterPageFile="~/Site.master"
  AutoEventWireup="true" CodeFile="Login.aspx.vb" Inherits="Login"
  title="Contoso Login" %>

<asp:Content ID="HeaderContent" runat="server" ContentPlaceHolderID="HeadContent">
</asp:Content>
<asp:Content ID="BodyContent" runat="server" ContentPlaceHolderID="MainContent">
    <h2>
        Log In
    </h2>
    <p>
        Please enter your username and password.
        <asp:HyperLink ID="RegisterHyperLink" runat="server" EnableViewState="false">Register</asp:HyperLink> if you don't have an account.
    </p>
</asp:Content>
```

Notice that in the @ Page directive, the MasterPageFile attribute is set to the master page, Site.master. Inside this same directive is the title attribute. This allows you to set the actual title for the content page. This title will be used when the master page and content page are merged and output to the browser.

> **NOTE MASTER PAGE SETTINGS**
>
> In general, the master page structure has no effect on how you construct your content pages or program against them. However, in some cases, if you set a page-wide property on the master page, it can affect the behavior of the content page. For example, if you set the EnableViewState property on the content page to true but set the same property to false in the master page, view state is effectively disabled because the setting on the master page takes priority.

Attaching Master Pages to Content Pages

You can attach a master page to content pages by specifying a page directive or configuring the master page in a Web.config file. By default, Visual Studio configures the MasterPageFile property of the @ Page directive, as the following demonstrates.

```
<%@ Page Language="VB" MasterPageFile="~/MySite.Master" %>
```

You can also define a master page for a site, application, or folder by defining the masterPageFile property of the <pages> element in a Web.config file (note that the XML-based Web.config file is case sensitive). If you use this approach, all ASP.NET pages in the scope of the Web.config file that have Content controls are merged with the specified master page. If an ASP.NET page does not contain Content controls, the master page is not applied. The following shows an example of the <pages> element in a Web.config file.

```
<pages MasterPageFile="~/MySite.Master" />
```

 Quick Check

1. Which control is required when you are defining a master page?

2. Which control is required when you are implementing a content page?

Quick Check Answers

1. You must have at least one ContentPlaceHolder control defined per master page.

2. You place Content controls on content pages. One Content control is added to the page for each ContentPlaceHolder control identified by the master page.

Referencing Custom Master Page Properties, Methods, and Controls from Content Pages

You can leverage master pages to define application-specific settings on which content pages depend. For example, if many content pages need a user's login ID, you can set this value inside the master page and then make it available to content pages as a property of the master page. This saves you from having to look the value up or track it on all pages or in the session state.

The basic process to reference master page properties from a content page is as follows:

1. Create a public property in the master page code-behind file.

2. Add the @ MasterType declaration to the ASPX content page.

3. Reference the master page property from the content page by using the syntax Master.<*Property_Name*>.

The sections that follow describe this process in more detail. You can follow a similar process if you need to expose master page methods or reference properties of control values on the master page. In this way, you can map a property to a control's value.

REAL WORLD
Tony Northrup

Strive to minimize the dependencies between master and content pages. The fewer references you create between master and content pages, the fewer problems you'll encounter when you update them, and the easier it is to have different developers working on each.

Most websites require some interaction between the master and content pages, however. When a website requires a dependency, make the content page reference the master page, and not the other way around. Because you will have many different content pages for each master page, referencing methods, properties, or controls on content pages is bound to cause problems.

Though we don't discuss this in this book, you can use events to communicate between master and content pages. For example, if you need content pages to adjust their content based on the selection users make from a drop-down list on the master page, you could expose an event on the master page that is triggered when the user makes a choice. Then, content pages could subscribe to the event. In this way, the master page is sending messages directly to the content page— but the master page is not directly dependant on the content page. If another developer creates a content page and doesn't respond to the event, it won't cause a problem for the master page.

Creating a Public Property in the Master Page

Content pages can reference any public property declared in the master page code-behind file. For example, the following code sample defines the property SharedInfo in the master page code-behind file. In this example, the master page provides strong typing for the session variable, SharedInfo.

Sample of Visual Basic Code

```
Public Property SharedInfo() As String
  Get
    Return CType(Session("SharedInfo"), String)
  End Get
  Set(ByVal value As String)
    Session("SharedInfo") = value
  End Set
End Property
```

```csharp
public String SharedInfo
{
  get { return (String)Session["SharedInfo"]; }
  set { Session["SharedInfo"] = value; }
}
```

Session variables are an easy way to store user-specific information during a user's visit. Similarly, application variables store information that can be accessed by any user. Neither provides strong typing, however, which makes exposing them by using public properties a useful way to access these shared objects. For more information about session and application variables, refer to Chapter 3, "Handling Events and Managing State."

Connecting to Master Page Properties from Content Pages

You must add the @ MasterType declaration to the ASPX content page to reference master properties in a content page. This declaration is added just below the @ Page declaration. The following code demonstrates this.

```
<%@ Page Language="VB" MasterPageFile="~/Site.master"
  AutoEventWireup="true" CodeFile="Login.aspx.vb" Inherits="Login"
  title="Contoso Login" %>
<%@ MasterType VirtualPath="~/Site.master" %>
```

After you add the @ MasterType declaration, you can reference properties in the master page by using the Master class. For example, the following code sets the infoLabel control's Text property to the SharedInfo property exposed by the master page.

Sample of Visual Basic Code

```vb
infoLabel.Text = Master.SharedInfo
```

Sample of C# Code

```csharp
infoLabel.Text = Master.SharedInfo;
```

If you later change the master page associated with a content page, make sure you implement the same public properties to ensure that the content pages continue to function correctly.

If you are creating multiple master pages that might be referenced by the same set of content pages, you should derive all master pages from a single base class. Then specify the base class name in the @ MasterType declaration. This enables the content page to reference the same properties, regardless of which master page is being used.

Referencing Controls in the Master Page

In addition to properties, you can also reference and update controls in the master page from an individual content page. One way is to encapsulate the control's property in a property of the master page (as demonstrated earlier). This is often a clean solution, as the master page developer is exposing these properties on purpose and thereby creating a contract with the content pages.

The other means of referencing a control on the master page from a content page is through the Master.FindControl method. You need to supply this method with the name of the control you want it to find. This approach requires the content page to have knowledge of the master page. Master.FindControl returns a Control object, which you then need to cast to the correct control type. After you have this reference, you can read or update the object as if it were local to the content page.

The following code (which belongs in the Page_Load method of the content page) demonstrates this method by updating a Label control named Brand in the master page.

Sample of Visual Basic Code

```
Dim MyLabelBrand As Label = CType(Master.FindControl("LabelBrand"), Label)
MyLabelBrand.Text = "Fabrikam"
```

Sample of C# Code

```
Label MyLabelBrand = (Label)Master.FindControl("LabelBrand");
MyLabelBrand.Text = "Fabrikam";
```

In this example, a local variable named MyLabelBrand is set to reference a Label control on the master page. After you have this reference, you can use it to customize information in a master page's LabelBrand control.

Creating Nested Master Pages

Sometimes, web design might require multiple levels of master pages. For example, every single page on your site might have the same logo, search box, and copyright information. However, although pages within your online store might include navigation for product categories and a shopping cart link, pages within the community discussion section of your site would include forum navigation and links for user profile management. In this scenario, you could create a top-level master page for the logo, search box, and copyright information. You could then nest different master pages for the store and community sections of your website.

You can create a child master page from the Add New Item dialog box in Visual Studio by selecting the Select Master Page check box, as shown in Figure 2-2. You will then need to select the parent master page. Visual Studio will automatically specify the necessary declarations.

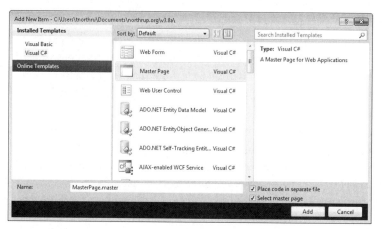

FIGURE 2-2 Declaring a child master page.

When nested, child master pages still use the .master extension. However, the child master pages also define the attribute MasterPageFile set in the @ Master declaration. This attribute points to the parent master page. The following example demonstrates a child master page with a parent master page named Site.master.

```
<%@ Master Language="C#" MasterPageFile="~/Site.master" AutoEventWireup="true"
CodeFile="CommunityMasterPage.master.cs" Inherits="Account_CommunityMasterPage" %>

<asp:Content ID="Content1" ContentPlaceHolderID="HeadContent" Runat="Server">
</asp:Content>
<asp:Content ID="Content2" ContentPlaceHolderID="MainContent" Runat="Server">
  <h2>Sub Department</h2>
  <asp:panel runat="server" id="panel1" backcolor="LightBlue">
    <asp:ContentPlaceHolder ID="ContentPlaceHolderSubDept" runat="server" />
  </asp:panel>
</asp:Content>
```

The child master page typically contains content controls that are mapped to content placeholders on the parent master page. In this respect, the child master page is laid out like any content page. However, the child master page also has one or more content placeholders of its own. This defines the areas where its content pages can put their content.

Dynamically Changing Master Pages

You define the master page in a content page's @ Page declaration. However, that doesn't mean you cannot switch to a different master page programmatically. Changing master pages allows you to provide different templates for different users. For example, you might give users a choice of different colors and styles (you can also do this with themes, as discussed in the next lesson). You could also use different master pages to format data for different browsers or different mobile devices.

To dynamically change master pages, follow these high-level steps:

1. Create two or more master pages with the same ContentPlaceHolder controls and public properties. Typically, you create one master page, copy it to create the second master page, and make any necessary modifications. Note that, from this point forward, you must make any changes to the ContentPlaceHolder controls or public properties to all master pages to ensure compatibility.

2. Provide a way for users to switch between master pages. (This step is optional.) If the master page should be the user's choice (for example, if color and layout are the primary differences), add links to your master pages to enable users to switch between pages. You need to define the current master page within the content page, however, so you can choose to store the setting in the Session variable or in another object that is accessible to both the master and content pages.

   For example, the following code can be called from a link or button on the master page to set a Session variable to the name of a different master page. After you define the master page within the content page, reload the page.

   Sample of Visual Basic Code

   ```
   Session("masterpage") = "~Master2.master"
   Response.Redirect(Request.Url.ToString)
   ```

   Sample of C# Code

   ```
   Session["masterpage"] = "~/Master2.master";
   Response.Redirect(Request.Url.ToString());
   ```

3. Define the master page in the content page's Page_PreInit method. Page_PreInit is the last opportunity you have to override the default master page setting, because later handlers (such as Page_Init) reference the master page. For example, the following code defines the master page based on the Session object.

   Sample of Visual Basic Code

   ```
   Sub Page_PreInit(ByVal sender As Object, ByVal e As EventArgs)
     If Not (Session("masterpage") Is Nothing) Then
       MasterPageFile = CType(Session("masterpage"), String)
     End If
   End Sub
   ```

   Sample of C# Code

   ```
   void Page_PreInit(Object sender, EventArgs e)
   {
     if (Session["masterpage"] != null)
       MasterPageFile = (String)Session["masterpage"];
   }
   ```

When you switch master pages, you need to make sure both pages define exactly the same content placeholder control names. Exercise 2 in this lesson's practice walks you through this process step by step.

In this practice, you create two different master pages. Each master page defines an alternative layout for the page. You then create a content page based on the master page. Finally, you add code to allow users to set their master page preference dynamically.

> **ON THE COMPANION MEDIA**
>
> If you encounter a problem completing an exercise, you can find the completed projects in the samples installed from this book's companion CD. For more information about the project files and other content on the CD, see "Using the Companion Media" in this book's Introduction.

EXERCISE 1 Creating Master Pages and a Content Page

In this exercise, you create a new ASP.NET website with two master pages and a content page.

1. Open Visual Studio and create a new website by using the ASP.NET Web Site template in either C# or Visual Basic.

2. Copy the Contoso logo to the root folder of your website from the the companion CD (\Sample Files\Chapter02\logo\Contoso.gif). Copy the style sheets (Site.css and Colorful-Site.css in the \Sample Files\Chapter02\Lesson1-Exercise1-Completed-CS\ Styles\ folder on the companion CD) to the Styles subfolder of your website.

3. Add a new master page to your website and name it **Professional.master**. In the <head> section, add a reference to the Site.css style sheet you copied. The reference will resemble the following.

   ```
   <link href="~/Styles/Site.css" rel="stylesheet" type="text/css" />
   ```

4. Purely for practice, add a menu bar to your master page and format it nicely. Make sure there is a content placeholder in the <head> section named **HeadContent**. Also verify that there is a content placeholder in the <body> section named **MainContent**. These are the same names used by the default Site.master page in the ASP.NET Web Site template; using the same names will allow you to manually change a page template without making other edits. Your page's structure should resemble the one in Figure 2-3, though it does not need to look exactly like it.

FIGURE 2-3 Creating the Professional.master page.

5. Save the Professional.master page. Then click File, and click Save Professional.master As. Save a second copy of the master page and name it **Colorful.master**. Change the style sheet reference from

```
<link href="~/Styles/Site.css" rel="stylesheet" type="text/css" />
```

to

```
<link href="~/Styles/Colorful-Site.css" rel="stylesheet" type="text/css" />
```

If you compare the Colorful-Site.css file to the Site.css file, you'll notice that in the Colorful-Site.css file the header and menu layout elements have a yellow background instead of a white background.

6. Add a new web form to your site and name it **Home.aspx**. In the Add New Item dialog box, select the Select Master Page check box, then click Add. In the Select A Master Page dialog box, select Professional.master. If you select the Professional.master file in Visual Studio, you can simply click the Website menu, click Add Content Page, and then rename the file **Home.aspx**.

7. Open Home.aspx in Design view, and create the page by following these steps:

  a. Verify that the content placeholders have the proper IDs: HeadContent and MainContent.

  b. Inside ContentPlaceholderMain, add a TextBox control and name it UserNameTextBox.

  c. Add a DropDownList control named SitePrefDropDownList.

  d. Add two ListItem elements to the DropDownList control, name them Professional and Colorful, and assign them the values Professional and Colorful. You can do so by clicking the smart tag in Design view and choosing Edit Items. This will launch the ListItem Collection Editor.

  e. Set the SitePrefDropDownList.AutoPostBack property to true.

  f. Add an OK Button control named OKButton.

Figure 2-4 shows how your page might now look in Design view.

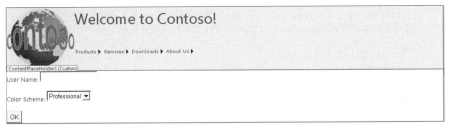

FIGURE 2-4 Defining a content page.

8. Build your project and open the resulting Home.aspx page in a browser. Verify that it displays correctly. Note that the page does not do anything yet; we will add code in the next exercise.

9. In Design view, double-click the OK button on the Home.aspx page to create and open the button's Click event handler. Add code to the ButtonSubmit_Click method to determine whether the user provided a value in the UserNameTextBox text box. If the user did, use the name he or she typed to define a Session variable named UserName and change the welcome message in the master page LabelWelcome accordingly. The following code demonstrates this.

Sample of Visual Basic Code

```
Protected Sub OKButton_Click(ByVal sender As Object, ByVal e As System.
EventArgs) Handles OKButton.Click
    If UserNameTextBox.Text <> [String].Empty Then
        Session("UserName") = NameTextBox.Text
        Dim welcome As Label = DirectCast(Master.FindControl("GreetingLabel"),
Label)
        welcome.Text = String.Format("Welcome, {0}!", Session("UserName"))
    End If
End Sub
```

Sample of C# Code

```
protected void OKButton_Click(object sender, EventArgs e)
{
    if (UserNameTextBox.Text != String.Empty)
    {
        Session["UserName"] = UserNameTextBox.Text;
        Label welcome = (Label)Master.FindControl("GreetingLabel");
        welcome.Text = String.Format("Welcome, {0}!", Session["UserName"]);
    }
}
```

10. Next, open the code-behind file for Professional.master. If you are using Visual Basic, add a Page.Load event handler. (For C# versions, the handler is provided for you by Visual Studio when the page source code is created.) In the Page.Load event handler, check to see if there is a Session variable named UserName. If there is, change the welcome message in the master page accordingly. The following code demonstrates this.

Sample of Visual Basic Code

```
Protected Sub Page_Load(ByVal sender As Object, ByVal e As EventArgs)
    If Session("UserName") IsNot Nothing Then
        GreetingLabel.Text = String.Format("Welcome, {0}!", Session("UserName"))
    End If
End Sub
```

Sample of C# Code

```
protected void Page_Load(object sender, EventArgs e)
{
    if (Session["UserName"] != null)
    {
        GreetingLabel.Text = String.Format("Welcome, {0}!",
Session["UserName"]);
    }
}
```

11. Open the About.aspx page. Using the source view, change the master page to Professional.master by editing the @ Page declaration and changing MasterPageFile to **~/Professional.master**. You can easily change the master page because the two ContentPlaceHolder server controls on the master page have the same IDs.

12. Build your project and open the Home.aspx page. Type your name in the NameTextBox control and then click OK. Verify that the page successfully changes GreetingLabel in the master page. Browse to the About.aspx page and then come back to the Home.aspx page. The page should pull your user name from session state. If you wait longer than 20 minutes before visiting another page, session state will expire and the user's name will no longer be available.

Note that you can add other pages by using the same Professional.master master page, and if the user has entered a name on the Home.aspx content page, the master page will display that name.

EXERCISE 2 Allowing Users to Dynamically Select Their Master Pages

In this exercise, you add functionality to a content page to change the master page dynamically in your code.

1. Continue editing the project you created in the previous exercise.

> **ON THE COMPANION MEDIA**
>
> Alternatively, you can open the completed Lesson 1, Exercise 1 project in the samples installed from the CD. For more information about the project files and other content on the CD, see "Using the Companion Media" in this book's Introduction.

2. Open Home.aspx in Design view. Double-click the drop-down list control to generate the default event handler. In the event handler, define the session variable, Template, by using the selected value. Then call Server.Transfer to reload the current page so that the updated master template can be used immediately. The following code demonstrates how to do this.

Sample of Visual Basic Code
```
Protected Sub DropDownListSitePref_SelectedIndexChanged( _
  ByVal sender As Object, ByVal e As System.EventArgs) _
  Handles DropDownListSitePref.SelectedIndexChanged
    Session("Template") = SitePrefDropDownList.SelectedValue
    Server.Transfer(Request.Path)
End Sub
```

Sample of C# Code
```
protected void DropDownListSitePref_SelectedIndexChanged(
    object sender, EventArgs e)
  {
    Session["Template"] = SitePrefDropDownList.SelectedValue;
    Server.Transfer(Request.Path);
  }
```

3. Add a Page_PreInit method to your code. In the Page_PreInit method, check to see if there is a Session variable named Template. If there is, use it to change the MasterPageFile object to the selected template's file name. The following code demonstrates this.

Sample of Visual Basic Code

```vb
Protected Sub Page_PreInit(ByVal sender As Object, _
  ByVal e As System.EventArgs) Handles Me.PreInit

  If Not (Session("Template") Is Nothing) Then
    MasterPageFile = String.Format("~/{0}.master", CType(Session("Template"),
String))
  End If

End Sub
```

Sample of C# Code

```csharp
protected void Page_PreInit(object sender, EventArgs e)
{
  if (Session["Template"] != null)
    MasterPageFile = String.Format("~/{0}.master", (String)Session["Template"]);
}
```

4. Build your application and then open the Home.aspx page. Click the Color Scheme list and then click Professional. The page automatically reloads because the DropDownList.AutoPostBack property is set to true. The newly loaded page has a yellow header because the page is now using the Colorful.master master page, which uses the Colorful-Site.css style sheet.

For additional practice, define the SitePrefDropDownList selection based on the Template session variable so that the user's selection is remembered when the page is reloaded.

Lesson Summary

- Master pages provide templates that you can use to create consistent webpages throughout an application.

- To use master pages, first create a master page and add site layout information and other common elements. Then add one or more ContentPlaceHolder controls to the master page.

- To add a content page to a Web Site project, add a Web Form and select the Select Master Page check box. To add a content page to a Web Application project, add a Web Form Using Master Page class. You then add content to the page inside the content area defined by the master page.

- To reference public properties in a master page, add the @ MasterType declaration to the content page and reference the property by using Master.<*Property_Name*>. To reference controls in a master page, call Master.FindControl from the content page.

- Nested master pages fit into the ContentPlaceHolder controls on a master page but can contain other content pages. To create a nested master page, add a master attribute to the @ Master page declaration and specify the parent master page.
- To programmatically change the master page from a content page, set the page's MasterPageFile property and reload the page by using Server.Transfer.

Lesson Review

You can use the following questions to test your knowledge of the information in Lesson 1, "Using Master Pages." The questions are also available on the companion CD in a practice test, if you prefer to review them in electronic form.

> **NOTE ANSWERS**
>
> Answers to these questions and explanations of why each answer choice is correct or incorrect are located in the "Answers" section at the end of the book.

1. Which of the following statements about referencing master page methods and properties is true? (Choose all that apply.)

   A. Content pages can reference private properties in the master page.

   B. Content pages can reference public properties in the master page.

   C. Content pages can reference public methods in the master page.

   D. Content pages can reference controls in the master page.

2. You are converting an existing web application to use master pages. To maintain compatibility, you need to read properties from the master page. Which of the following changes are you required to make to ASPX pages to enable them to work with a master page? (Choose all that apply.)

   A. Add an @ MasterType declaration.

   B. Add an @ Master declaration.

   C. Add a MasterPageFile attribute to the @ Page declaration.

   D. Add a ContentPlaceHolder control.

3. You need to change the master page of a content page at run time. In which page event should you implement the dynamic changing?

   A. Page_Load

   B. Page_Render

   C. Page_PreRender

   D. Page_PreInit

Lesson 2: Using Themes

Many applications target multiple groups of customers. For example, imagine a business-to-business site that you create for each of your partners to leverage. They, in turn, might want to leverage portions of your site for their customers. It doesn't take long to recognize the need for a different-looking version of the site for each of your partners. Each partner might want its own colors and styles. Partners might also need to change some of the graphics on the site if they intend to expose it to their customers. In this case, you need to create a separate theme for each of your partners.

An ASP.NET *theme* is a collection of styles, property settings, and graphics that define the appearance of pages and controls on your website. A theme can include *skin files*, which define property settings for ASP.NET web server controls; *cascading style sheet (.css) files* that define colors, graphics, the size and placement of controls, and the overall appearance of your site. You can easily create new themes to give your entire site a different look.

This lesson describes how to create and leverage ASP.NET themes.

> **After this lesson, you will be able to:**
> - Use themes to easily change the overall appearance of a website or all the sites in a domain.
> - Use themed skins to specify attributes for controls on a single page or an entire website.
> - Create a style sheet that defines the styles used throughout your site's theme.
> - Easily switch between themes for a page or a site, and programmatically base theme choice on a user preference selection.
>
> **Estimated lesson time: 35 minutes**

Themes Overview

The webpages that belong to the same website will invariably contain controls that have many properties in common across pages. These include properties for setting things such as background color, font size, foreground color, and other styles. You can manually set the properties for every control on every page in your site. However, that is time consuming, error prone (because you might overlook some settings), and difficult to change (because a change would have to sweep across your entire site). Instead, you can use ASP.NET themes.

Themes save you time and improve the consistency of a site by applying a common set of control properties, styles, and graphics across all pages in a website. Themes can be centralized, allowing you to quickly change the appearance of all the controls on your site from a single file. ASP.NET themes consist of the following set of elements:

- **Skins**   These are files with .skin extensions that contain common property settings for buttons, labels, text boxes, and other controls. Skin files resemble control mark-ups but contain only the properties you want to define as part of the theme to be applied across pages.

- **Cascading style sheets**   These are files with .css extensions that contain the style property definitions for HTML markup elements and other custom style classes. A style sheet is linked to a page, master page, or entire site. ASP.NET applies the styles to the page.

- **Images and other resources**   Images (such as a corporate logo) along with other resources can be defined inside a theme. This allows you to switch out the images when you switch themes for a site.

Not all of these items are required to define a theme. You can mix and match as necessary. The sections that follow further describe the use of themes and demonstrate how to implement them.

Creating a Theme

You create themes inside the special App_Themes ASP.NET folder. This folder is in your ASP.NET application root. The folder contains a separate folder for each theme in your site. You then add the corresponding skins, style sheets, and images to the theme folders. To define a theme for a single ASP.NET application, you can follow these steps:

1.   Add an App_Themes folder to your web application. In Visual Studio, right-click your website in Solution Explorer, click Add ASP.NET Folder, and then click Theme.

2.   Within the App_Themes folder, you define an individual folder for each theme in your application. For example, you could create theme folders named Red and Blue. The name you set for the folder is also the name of your theme. You use this name when referencing the theme.

   You can have multiple themes in a web application, as Figure 2-5 illustrates. ASP.NET automatically creates your first theme. To create additional themes, right-click the App_Themes folder in Solution Explorer, click Add ASP.NET Folder, and then click Theme.

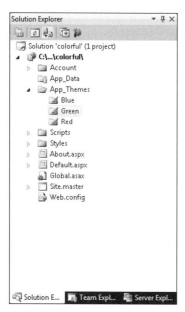

FIGURE 2-5 Creating multiple themes by adding subfolders to the App_Themes folder.

3. Next, you add skin files, style sheets, and images that make up your theme to your theme folder. Many times you define the first theme, copy it to the second, and then change the items as necessary.

4. The next step is to apply the theme to your site. You can do so at the individual page level by adding the Theme or StyleSheetTheme attribute to the @ Page directive and setting the attribute's value to the name of your theme (which is the folder name).

   Alternatively, you can apply the theme to an entire website or to individual applications and folders by adding the <pages theme="*themeName*"> element or the <pages styleSheetTheme="*themeName*"> element to the <system.web> section of a Web.config file. This will automatically apply the theme to all pages in your site.

> **NOTE THEME VS. STYLESHEETTHEME**
>
> If you use the StyleSheetTheme attribute, settings can be overridden because properties defined by StyleSheetTheme are applied before a page's control property set. If you use the Theme attribute, settings cannot be overridden because properties defined by Theme are applied after a page's properties.

Creating a Global Theme

ASP.NET also supports the concept of global themes. Global themes work exactly like standard themes; pages or applications must specify the theme by name. However, global themes are stored centrally and can be specified by any website running on a server. In this way, global themes only need to be maintained in one location on each server.

Instead of defining the theme in the *<application_root>*\App_Themes folder, you define a global theme in one of the following folders:

- **<iis_default_root>\Aspnet_client\System_web\<version>\Themes**   Use this folder for applications running in Internet Information Services (IIS). For example, for the current version of the .NET Framework, you would add your theme to the C:\inetpub\wwwroot\aspnet_client\system_web\4_0_30319\ folder.

- **%SystemRoot%\Microsoft.NET\Framework\<version>\ASP.NETClientFiles\Themes** Use this folder for file-system–based web applications.

Like standard themes, global themes must be contained in a folder with the name of the theme. You cannot use Visual Studio to directly create a global theme. However, you can create a theme for a web application and then move it to the global Themes folder.

Visual Studio does not recognize global themes; however, ASP.NET will apply your theme properly when you retrieve the page in the browser. If your application has a theme with the same name as a global theme, ASP.NET uses the application theme and ignores the global theme.

 Quick Check

1. In which folder should you place themes for an application?
2. In which folder should you place global themes for IIS websites?

Quick Check Answers

1. Place themes for an application in the App_Themes folder.
2. Place global themes in the *<iisdefaultroot>*\Aspnet_client\System_web*<version>* \Themes folder.

Creating a Skin File

Skin files serve to define default settings for server control appearance attributes. Each server control has attributes for things such as font, background color, width, height, and more. Many of these appearance attributes are common among the controls on your site. Both style sheets and skin files allow you to set these properties once and apply them to multiple places in your site.

A skin file differs from a style sheet in that the skin file uses the attributes of the actual control and not just a set of standard HTML style elements. In addition, skin files will be applied at the control level automatically by ASP.NET. Style elements, on the other hand, can be applied automatically only to HTML items. For ASP.NET controls, you must set the style class manually in your markup code.

You can add a skin file by following these steps:

1. In Solution Explorer, right-click your theme and then click Add New Item.

2. In the Add New Item dialog box, click Skin File. Type a name for your skin file (which always has a .skin extension), and then click Add.

Typically, you will create a separate skin file for every control type. However, you can embed skins for multiple controls in a single file.

Skin files contain two types of skins: default skins and named skins:

-   **Default skins**   A default skin automatically applies to all controls of the same type when a theme is applied to a page. A skin is considered a default skin if it does not have a SkinID attribute. For example, if you create a default skin for a Calendar control, the control skin applies to all Calendar controls on pages that use the theme. You cannot define multiple default skins for a single control type within a theme.

    Default skins are matched exactly by control type, so a Button control skin applies to all Button controls, but not to LinkButton controls, or to controls that derive from the Button object.

-   **Named skins**   A named skin is a control skin with a SkinID property set to a specific name value. Named skins do not automatically apply to controls by type. Instead, you explicitly apply a named skin to a control by setting the ASP.NET control's SkinID property (as you would a style sheet class). Creating named skins allows you to set different skins for different instances of the same control in an application.

The following is a default control skin for a Button control. It defines the foreground and background colors as well as font information.

```
<asp:Button runat="server"
  BackColor="Red"
  ForeColor="White"
  Font-Name="Arial"
  Font-Size="9px" />
```

Converting that default skin to a named skin is as easy as adding the SkinID attribute. For example, this named skin could be applied to Label controls.

```
<asp:Label runat="server"
  SkinId="Title"
  Font-Size="18px" />
```

Adding Images to Your Theme

Themes also allow you to switch out the images on your site. This is done through the skin file. To do this, you simply add a named skin of the Image control type to the skin file. You then set its SkinID appropriately.

For example, suppose you need to change the company logo for a site based on a specific theme. In this case, you would create a different theme for each company. Inside each theme's directory, you would add the appropriate image file. You could then create a skin file that contained the Image declaration as follows.

Company A's Skin File

```
<asp:Image runat="server"  SkinID="CompanyLogo"
  ImageUrl="~/App_Themes/Contoso/contoso.jpg" />
```

Company B's Skin File

```
<asp:Image runat="server" SkinID="CompanyLogo"
  ImageUrl="~/App_Themes/Fabrikam/fabrikam.jpg" />
```

Notice that in both skin files the SkinID is set to CompanyLogo. However, each defines a different logo file (ImageUrl). You can use this skin by first setting a page's Theme directive to either Contoso or Fabrikam (the name of the theme folder). You then add an Image control to the page and set its SkinId attribute appropriately. The following code shows an example.

```
<asp:Image ID="Image1" SkinID="CompanyLogo" runat="server" />
```

ASP.NET will then grab the correct company logo based on the skin file. If you switch themes, the logo will automatically switch as well.

Adding a Cascading Style Sheet to Your Theme

A cascading style sheet contains style rules that are applied to elements in a webpage. Cascading style sheet styles define how elements are displayed and where they are positioned on the page. Instead of assigning attributes to each element on your page individually, you can create a general rule that applies attributes whenever a web browser encounters an instance of an element or an element that is assigned to a certain style class.

To add a cascading style sheet to your website, right-click the name of your theme in Solution Explorer and select Add New Item. You can then select the Style Sheet item template. Here you define styles for HTML elements and your own custom style classes, which are those preceded by a dot (.).

The following are a few simple styles in a style sheet.

```
body
{
 text-align: center;
 font-family: Arial;
 font-size: 10pt;
}
.topNav
{
  padding: 0px 0px 0px 20px;
}
.header
{
  text-align: left;
  margin: 20px 0px 20px 0px;
}
.footer
{
  margin: 20px 0px 20px 0px;
}
```

When the theme is applied to a page, ASP.NET adds a reference to the style sheet to the head element of the page. In the HTML, this reference looks something like the following.

```
<link href="SiteStyles.css" rel="themeName/stylesheet" type="text/css" />
```

Visual Studio provides several tools for creating and managing styles in your application. These include the style builder, the style manager, IntelliSense in the style sheet, and more. Of course, style sheets are not reserved for just themes; style sheets can be used for any site, regardless of whether it uses a theme.

EXAM TIP

Cascading style sheets are not part of ASP.NET; they work for any type of website. They aren't specifically covered in the exam objectives and won't be covered in much detail in this book. However, cascading style sheets are a critical component of web design, and all web developers need to be familiar with them. There are many good topics and discussions on the Microsoft Developer Network *(http://msdn/microsoft.com)* regarding style sheets, including "Web Server Controls and CSS Styles" at *http://msdn.microsoft.com/library /h4kete56.aspx.*

Rules for Applying Themes

We've already looked at the ways in which you can apply themes to your pages or to the entire site. However, your site might have multiple, often conflicting, style definitions for the same set of controls. That is, you might have a standard style sheet, a theme, and actual styles defined directly on the controls. The definition that gets applied is determined by a standard precedence order followed by ASP.NET.

Within ASP.NET, attributes and elements take precedence in the following order (first to last):

1. Theme attributes in the @ Page directive
2. <pages theme="*themeName*"> elements in the <system.web> section of a Web.config file
3. Local control attributes
4. StyleSheetTheme attributes in the @ Page directive
5. <pages styleSheetTheme="*themeName*"> elements in a Web.config file

In other words, if you specify a Theme attribute in the @ Page directive, settings in the theme take precedence and override any settings you've specified directly for controls on the page. However, if you change the Theme attribute to use the StyleSheetTheme attribute, you have changed the precedence, and now control-specific settings take precedence over the theme settings.

For example, this directive applies a theme that would override control properties.

```
<%@ Page Theme="SampleTheme" %>
```

In other words, if SampleTheme specifies that Label controls use a red font, but you specify a blue font for a Label control, the labels appear with a red font.

The following directive changes the theme to a style sheet theme.

```
<%@ Page StyleSheetTheme="SampleTheme" %>
```

In this case, any changes you make to local control properties will override settings in the theme. Therefore, continuing the previous example, if SampleTheme specifies that Label controls are red but you override these to blue at the control level, the labels will show as blue. However, Label controls that do not have a color specified will appear as red.

You can also disable themes for a specific page by setting the EnableTheming attribute of the @ Page directive to false.

```
<%@ Page EnableTheming="false" %>
```

Similarly, to disable themes for a specific control, set the control's EnableTheming property to false.

Applying a Theme Programmatically

Themes are useful for centralized management of the styles in your application. You might create a second theme as you experiment with changing the look and feel of your site. However, you might also need to create multiple themes that get switched based on the identification or preference of the user.

To apply a theme programmatically, set the page's Theme property in the Page_PreInit method. The following code demonstrates how to set the theme based on a query string value; however, this works equally well if you use cookies, session state, or other approaches.

Sample of Visual Basic Code

```vb
Protected Sub Page_PreInit(ByVal sender As Object, ByVal e As System.EventArgs) _
  Handles Me.PreInit

  Select Case Request.QueryString("theme")
    Case "Blue"
      Page.Theme = "BlueTheme"
      Exit Select
    Case "Pink"
      Page.Theme = "PinkTheme"
      Exit Select
    Case Else
      Page.Theme = "GreenTheme"
      Exit Select
  End Select
End Sub
```

Sample of C# Code

```csharp
protected void Page_PreInit(object sender, EventArgs e)
{
  switch (Request.QueryString["theme"])
  {
    case "Blue":
      Page.Theme = "BlueTheme";
      break;
    case "Pink":
      Page.Theme = "PinkTheme";
      break;
    default:
      Page.Theme = "GreenTheme";
      break;
  }
}
```

To programmatically apply a style sheet theme (which works just like a theme but doesn't override control attributes), use the Page.StyleSheetTheme property.

Similarly, you can apply a skin to specific controls by setting the control's SkinID property in the Page_PreInit method. The following code shows how to set the skin for a control named Calendar1.

Sample of Visual Basic Code

```vb
Sub Page_PreInit(ByVal sender As Object, ByVal e As System.EventArgs) _
  Handles Me.PreInit

  Calendar1.SkinID = "BlueSkin"

End Sub
```

Sample of C# Code

```csharp
void Page_PreInit(object sender, EventArgs e)
{
  Calendar1.SkinID = "BlueSkin";
}
```

In this practice, you create a new website and define two themes for that site.

ON THE COMPANION MEDIA

If you encounter a problem completing an exercise, you can find the completed projects in the samples installed from this book's companion CD. For more information about the project files and other content on the CD, see "Using the Companion Media" in this book's Introduction.

EXERCISE   Creating and Applying a Theme

In this exercise, you create two local themes, one for each of two vendors. You then apply and test the themes. Finally, you add code to allow the user to dynamically change the theme of the site.

1. Open Visual Studio and create a new ASP.NET website named **ThemesLab** by using either C# or Visual Basic.

2. Add the App_Themes folder to your website. Right-click the site in Solution Explorer, click Add ASP.NET Folder, and then click Theme.

3. Create two theme folders. Name them **Contoso** and **Fabrikam**. To add the second theme, right-click the App_Themes folder, click Add ASP.NET Folder, and then click Theme.

4. Inside the Contoso theme folder, add the Contoso.gif logo from the samples installed from this book's CD. Then add the Fabrikam.gif logo to the Fabrikam theme.

5. Add a .skin file to the Contoso theme and name it **Logo**. Add skins for the logo Image, a TextBox control, and a Button control. Your skin file for Contoso should look as follows.

```
<asp:Image ImageUrl="~/App_Themes/Contoso/Contoso.gif"
  SkinID="Logo" runat="server" />

<asp:TextBox runat="server"
  BorderColor="Blue" BorderWidth="1pt" Font-Names="Arial" Font-Size="10pt"
  ForeColor="Brown" ></asp:TextBox>

<asp:Button runat="server"
  BorderColor="Blue" BorderWidth="1pt" Font-Bold="true"
  BackColor="White" ForeColor="DarkBlue" />
```

6. Repeat the same process for the Fabrikam theme, but use different colors. Your skin file for Fabrikam should look as follows.

```
<asp:Image ImageUrl="~/App_Themes/Fabrikam/Fabrikam.gif"
  SkinID="Logo" runat="server" />

<asp:TextBox runat="server"
  BorderColor="Orange" BorderWidth="1pt" Font-Names="Arial" Font-Size="10pt"
  ForeColor="Brown" ></asp:TextBox>

<asp:Button runat="server"
  BorderColor="DarkOrange" BorderWidth="1pt" Font-Bold="true"
  BackColor="DarkOrange" ForeColor="White" />
```

7. Add a style sheet to your Contoso theme and name it Style.css. Within the style sheet, define styles to set the default font family, size, and style for the HTML body and the CSS classes textBox and button. Your style sheet should resemble this:

```
body
{
    font-family : Tahoma;
    font-size : 10pt;
}

.textBox
{
  font-style: italic;
}

.button
{
  font-style: oblique;
  font-size: 30pt;
}
```

8. Copy this same style sheet to the Fabrikam folder, but change the font-family style to **Script** and the font-size style to **20pt**.

9. Open the Default.aspx page in Source view. Set the Theme property in the @ Page directive to **Fabrikam**.

10. Add the following controls within the <BodyContent> content placeholder:

   - **Image control** Set the SkinId to **Logo**.
   - **TextBox control** Set the CssClass to **textBox**. This control will get part of its style from the skin and part from the style sheet.
   - **Button control** Add a Button control to the page. Set the CssClass to **button**. This control will also get part of its style from the skin and part from the style sheet.

Your .aspx markup should look similar to the following (the Visual Basic @ Page directive is shown).

```
<%@ Page Theme="Fabrikam" Title="Home Page" Language="VB" MasterPageFile="~/
Site.Master" AutoEventWireup="true"
    CodeFile="Default.aspx.vb" Inherits="_Default" %>
<asp:Content ID="HeaderContent" runat="server" ContentPlaceHolderID="HeadConte
nt">
</asp:Content>
<asp:Content ID="BodyContent" runat="server" ContentPlaceHolderID="MainContent">
    <asp:Image ID="Image1" SkinID="Logo" runat="server" />
    <br />
    <asp:TextBox ID="TextBoxUname" runat="server"
      CssClass="textBox"></asp:TextBox>
    <br />
    <asp:Button ID="ButtonSubmit" runat="server" Text="Hello"
      CssClass="button" />
</asp:Content>
```

11. Run your Default.aspx page in a browser. You should see the full Fabrikam theme applied to the page. This includes the logo, skin, and style sheet. Figure 2-6 shows the page in a web browser. Close the page.

FIGURE 2-6 The Fabrikam theme applied to the Default.aspx page.

12. Next, remove the Theme attribute from the Default.aspx @ Page directive. Instead, add the Theme attribute to the <pages> element within <system.web> in the Web.config file, and set the theme to Contoso.

```
<pages theme="Contoso"/>
```

This should switch the site's theme. Run the application again. You should now see a new theme applied to the site, as shown in Figure 2-7.

FIGURE 2-7 The Contoso theme applied to the Default.aspx page via the Web.config file.

13. Finally, allow the user to switch themes at run time when he or she clicks the button. First, add an event handler to the button's click event that sets a Session variable to the theme that is not currently active. After setting the Session variable, reload the current page with Server.Transfer. Finally, add a PreInit event to the page that reads the theme from the session and applies it to the page. Your code should resemble the following.

```
Sample of Visual Basic Code
Protected Sub Page_PreInit(ByVal sender As Object, ByVal e As System.EventArgs)
Handles Me.PreInit
    If Session("theme") IsNot Nothing Then
        Page.Theme = DirectCast(Session("theme"), String)
    End If
End Sub

Protected Sub ButtonSubmit_Click(ByVal sender As Object, ByVal e As System.
EventArgs) Handles ButtonSubmit.Click
    If Page.Theme = "Contoso" Then
        Session("theme") = "Fabrikam"
    Else
        Session("theme") = "Contoso"
    End If
    Server.Transfer(Request.Path)
End Sub
```

Sample of C# Code

```csharp
public partial class _Default : System.Web.UI.Page
{
    protected void Page_PreInit(object sender, EventArgs e)
    {
        if (Session["theme"] != null)
        {
            Page.Theme = (string)Session["theme"];
        }
    }

    protected void ButtonSubmit_Click(object sender, EventArgs e)
    {
        string theme = Page.Theme;

        //switch themes
        if (theme == "Contoso")
        {
            Session["theme"] = "Fabrikam";
        }
        else
        {
            Session["theme"] = "Contoso";
        }
        Server.Transfer(Request.Path);
    }
}
```

Run the application and click the button a couple of times. Notice that the theme and style sheet change at run time. If you were to set the Page.Theme directly from the Button.Click event handler, the .NET CLR would throw an exception because you cannot set the page theme after the Page.PreInit event has been handled. For that reason, the code sample calls Server.Transfer to cause page processing to begin again.

Lesson Summary

- To create a theme, add an App_Themes subfolder to your application. Then, for each theme in your site, add a folder. The folder's name becomes the name of your theme.

- Themes can contain skin files, a style sheet, graphics, and other resources.

- You can apply a theme at the page level, at the site level (through the Web.config file), or at the individual control level.

Lesson Review

You can use the following questions to test your knowledge of the information in Lesson 2, "Using Themes." The questions are also available on the companion CD in a practice test, if you prefer to review them in electronic form.

> **NOTE ANSWERS**
>
> Answers to these questions and explanations of why each answer choice is correct or incorrect are located in the "Answers" section at the end of the book.

1. Which of the following theme applications will override an attribute that you specified directly on a control? (Choose all that apply.)

    A. A theme specified by using @ Page Theme="MyTheme"

    B. A theme specified by using @ Page StyleSheetTheme="MyTheme"

    C. A <pages theme="themeName"> element in the Web.config file

    D. A <pages styleSheetTheme="themeName"> element in the Web.config file

2. Which of the following is a valid skin definition inside a skin file?

    A. <asp:Label ID="Label1" BackColor="#FFE0C0" ForeColor="Red" Text="Label"></asp:Label>

    B. <asp:Label ID="Label1" runat="server" BackColor="#FFE0C0" ForeColor="Red" Text="Label"></asp:Label>

    C. <asp:Label runat="server" BackColor="#FFE0C0" ForeColor="Red"></asp:Label>

    D. <asp:Label BackColor="#FFE0C0" ForeColor="Red"></asp:Label>

3. You need to allow users to choose their own themes. In which page event should you specify the user-selected theme?

    A. Page_Load

    B. Page_Render

    C. Page_PreRender

    D. Page_PreInit

Lesson 3: Caching

ASP.NET caching stores frequently accessed data or whole webpages in memory, where they can be retrieved faster than they could be from a file or database. This helps to improve the performance and increase the scalability (in terms of number of users serviced) of a web application. As an example, if you have a product catalog in an e-commerce application, you might consider putting a lot of the catalog data into cache. Data that changes infrequently and is accessed by a lot of users is a good candidate for caching. The first access of this data would load it into the cache; subsequent requests would be served from the cache until the cache expires.

ASP.NET and the .NET Framework enable you to take advantage of caching without requiring you to write a lot of code to deal with the complexities of caching, such as cache expiration, updates, and memory management. There are two different types of caching in ASP.NET:

- **Application caching**   This represents a collection that can store any object in memory and automatically remove the object based on memory limitations, time limits, or other dependencies.
- **Page output caching**   This is ASP.NET's ability to store a rendered page, portion of a page, or version of a page in memory to reduce the time required to render the page in future requests.

This lesson covers both application caching and page output caching.

After this lesson, you will be able to:

- Use application caching to store frequently accessed data that takes a relatively long time to access.
- Use page output caching to improve the response time of page requests.

Estimated lesson time: 40 minutes

Application Caching

Application caching (also called *application data caching*) is the process of storing data (not pages) in a cache object. The cache object is available as a property of the Page object. It represents a collection class of type System.Web.Caching.Cache. The Page.Cache property actually uses an application-wide cache (not just a page-specific cache). This means that a single Cache object exists for your entire application; items in the Cache can be shared between user sessions and requests.

Using the Cache Object

You work with the Cache object as you would with Session or similar objects. You can assign items directly to the cache by giving them a name (key) and assigning them an object (value). You retrieve objects from the cache by checking for the key.

Always verify that an item is not null. If a value is null, that value either hasn't been cached or it has expired from the cache. If an item is null, you should retrieve it from the original source and, in most cases, place it into the cache.

The following code sample demonstrates how to cache and retrieve a String object with the Cache collection.

Sample of Visual Basic Code

```
Cache("Greeting") = "Hello, cache!"
If Cache("Greeting") IsNot Nothing Then
    Label1.Text = DirectCast(Cache("Greeting"), String)
Else
    Label1.Text = "Hello, world!"
End If
```

Sample of C# Code

```
Cache["Greeting"] = "Hello, cache!";
if (Cache["Greeting"] != null)
    Label1.Text = (string)Cache["Greeting"];
else
    Label1.Text = "Hello, world!";
```

You wouldn't normally cache a static string in your application; you'd more likely cache a file, a database query result, or other data that is shared and expensive to obtain. You can cache any object type, including your own custom types as long as they are serializable. However, just as you would from any generic collection, you must cast the object back to the correct type when you access it from the cache.

Inserting Items into the Cache

The previous example demonstrates that you can use the Cache object as you would Session or Application. You can access much more sophisticated functionality, however, by using the Insert method to add an item to the cache and control how that item gets removed from the cache. This functionality includes automatic removal based on a specific period of time, removal when a file changes, or removal when another cache object expires.

Insert has a number of overloads based on the many parameters you can set when adding an item to the cache. The following list outlines the parameters of the Cache.Insert method:

- **key** This is the name (as a String) that you'll use to access the cached object in the Cache collection. The key must be unique in the cache.
- **value** This is the data (as an Object) that you want to cache.

- **dependencies** A CacheDependency object identifies a file or a key to another item in the cache. When the file or related cached item is changed, this will trigger this cached object to be removed from the cache.

    If you cache a file, you should configure a dependency for the file so that it is removed from the cache after being modified. This helps ensure that your cache never becomes stale. You might also call the parameter onRemoveCallback to reload the cached item.

- **absoluteExpiration** This is the time (as a DateTime object) at which the object should be removed from the cache. This is absolute and therefore does not take into consideration whether the item has been recently accessed by a user. If you do not wish to use absolute expiration, you can set this property to System.Web .Caching.Cache.NoAbsoluteExpiration.

- **slidingExpiration** This is the time (as a TimeSpan object) after which the object should be removed from the cache if it has not been accessed by a user. Set this to System.Web.Caching.Cache.NoSlidingExpiration if you don't want to use it.

- **priority** This is a CacheItemPriority enumeration value that you can use to determine which objects are removed first when memory starts to run low (this process is called scavenging). Lower priority objects are removed sooner. The values for priority, from lowest (most likely to be removed) to highest (least likely to be removed) include the following:

    - Low
    - BelowNormal
    - Normal (Default is equivalent to Normal)
    - AboveNormal
    - High
    - NotRemovable

- **onRemoveCallback** This is an event handler that is called when the object is removed from the cache. This can be null if you don't want to specify a callback method.

Defining a Cache Dependency

A cache dependency links a cached item to something else such as a file or another item in the cache. ASP.NET monitors the dependency and invalidates the cache if the dependent item changes. The following code sample demonstrates how to make a cache dependency based on a file. If the file the cache is dependent upon changes, the object is removed from the cache.

Sample of Visual Basic Code

```
Cache.Insert("FileCache", File.ReadAllText("SourceFile.txt"), _
    New System.Web.Caching.CacheDependency(Server.MapPath("SourceFile.txt")))
```

Sample of C# Code

```
Cache.Insert("FileCache", File.ReadAllText("SourceFile.txt"),
    new System.Web.Caching.CacheDependency(Server.MapPath("SourceFile.txt")));
```

You can also create multiple dependencies for a single cached item. The following example demonstrates how to use an AggregateCacheDependency object to add an item to the cache that is dependent on both an item named CacheItem1 and a file named SourceFile.txt.

Sample of Visual Basic Code

```
Dim dep1 As CacheDependency = New CacheDependency(Server.MapPath("SourceFile.txt"))
Dim keyDependencies2 As String() = {"CacheItem1"}
Dim dep2 As CacheDependency = New System.Web.Caching.CacheDependency(Nothing, _
    keyDependencies2)
Dim aggDep As AggregateCacheDependency = New System.Web.Caching.
AggregateCacheDependency()
aggDep.Add(dep1)
aggDep.Add(dep2)
Cache.Insert("FileCache", File.ReadAllText("SourceFile.txt"), aggDep)
```

Sample of C# Code

```
System.Web.Caching.CacheDependency dep1 =
    new System.Web.Caching.CacheDependency(Server.MapPath("SourceFile.txt"));
string[] keyDependencies2 = { "CacheItem1" };
System.Web.Caching.CacheDependency dep2 =
    new System.Web.Caching.CacheDependency(null, keyDependencies2);
System.Web.Caching.AggregateCacheDependency aggDep =
    new System.Web.Caching.AggregateCacheDependency();
aggDep.Add(dep1);
aggDep.Add(dep2);
Cache.Insert("FileCache", File.ReadAllText("SourceFile.txt"), aggDep);
```

Setting an Absolute Cache Expiration

To cache an object for a set amount of time, pass the absoluteExpiration parameter to the Cache.Insert method. This parameter sets a time in the future at which your data should expire. The DateTime.Now object has a variety of methods for adding a specific number of minutes to the current time. The following example demonstrates this.

Sample of Visual Basic Code

```
Cache.Insert("FileCache", "CacheContents", Nothing, DateTime.Now.AddMinutes(10), _
    Cache.NoSlidingExpiration)
```

Sample of C# Code

```
Cache.Insert("FileCache", "CacheContents", null, DateTime.Now.AddMinutes(10),
    Cache.NoSlidingExpiration);
```

Setting a Sliding Cache Expiration

If you want your most frequently used cached objects to stay in your cache longer, you can specify a sliding expiration. A sliding expiration indicates the amount of time that must elapse between subsequent requests before an item is removed from the cache. Each time a new request comes in for an item, the sliding scale restarts.

You set a sliding expiration by passing a TimeSpan to the slidingExpiration parameter of the Insert method. The TimeSpan is the time after the last read request that the cached object will be retained. This example shows you how to keep an object in cache for 10 minutes after the last request.

Sample of Visual Basic Code

```
Cache.Insert("CacheItem7", "Cached Item 7", _
  Nothing, System.Web.Caching.Cache.NoAbsoluteExpiration, New TimeSpan(0, 10, 0))
```

Sample of C# Code

```
Cache.Insert("CacheItem7", "Cached Item 7",
  null, System.Web.Caching.Cache.NoAbsoluteExpiration, new TimeSpan(0, 10, 0));
```

Especially with a sliding cache expiration, it is possible that heavy usage will result in an item never being removed from the cache, preventing updates to the original object from being accessed. By defining an absolute expiration, you can be sure an object is eventually removed. When possible, add a cache dependency to your absolute and sliding cache expirations to immediately remove the cached object when the original is updated.

 Quick Check

1. How can you cause a cached object to be automatically invalidated after a specific amount of time?

2. Where is Cache data stored—in memory, on the hard disk, in a database, or on a state server?

3. What types of data can you store in the Cache collection?

4. What must you do before you use an object you retrieved from the Cache collection?

Quick Check Answers

1. Call the Cache.Insert method and provide a DateTime object for the absoluteExpiration.

2. The Cache object is stored in memory on the server.

3. You can store any serializable type of data in the Cache collection. However, when you retrieve the data, you must cast it to the correct type.

4. You must verify that the object is not null and then cast it to the correct type. If it is null, you must retrieve it from the original source rather than from the Cache.

Page Output Caching

After a web browser retrieves a page, the browser often keeps a copy of the page on the local computer. The next time the user requests the page, the browser simply verifies that the cached version is still valid, and then displays the cached page to the user. This improves the responsiveness of the site by decreasing the time required to load the page. It also reduces the load on the server because the server is not required to render a page.

Client-side caching requires that each individual user retrieve a dynamically generated version of your page. If one user visits your website 100 times, your web server only has to generate the page once. If 100 users visit your website once, your web server needs to generate the page 100 times.

To improve performance and reduce rendering time, ASP.NET also supports page output caching. With page output caching, ASP.NET can keep a copy of a rendered ASP.NET webpage in memory on the server. The next time a user requests it—even if it's a different user—ASP.NET can return the page almost instantly. If a page takes a long time to render (for example, if the page makes multiple database queries), this can significantly improve performance. If you have a lot of activity on your server, it can also increase your scalability, because resources used to retrieve data can be freed.

If your page shows dynamic information or is customized for individual users, you don't want the same version of the page sent from the cache to every user. Fortunately, ASP.NET gives you flexible configuration options to meet almost any requirement. You can even implement user controls to do partial-page caching while generating other portions of the page dynamically.

 REAL WORLD

Tony Northrup

Page output caching is the most effective way to reduce ASP.NET rendering time. After all, if the page output is cached, ASP.NET skips the rendering process entirely and just sends the HTML that it's already generated. If a page takes 0.5 seconds to generate, a single line of code to enable page output caching will improve the page's performance by 0.5 seconds.

In the real world, rendering time is just one component of website performance. On my personal ASP.NET website (*http://www.northrup.org*), ASP.NET takes about 0.01 to 0.02 seconds to generate most pages. I'm pretty proud of that, especially because the website is running on an old computer and every page requires multiple database queries. Yet, if you visit the site, pages won't appear nearly that quickly.

According to Google Webmaster Tools (*https://www.google.com/webmasters/tools/*), the average page on my site takes about 3.5 seconds to load. So the time it takes ASP.NET to query the database and generate my page is less than 1 percent of the page load time. Obviously, if I want to improve the performance of my website, I'll need to look elsewhere.

For most sites, the biggest factor in performance is actually network latency—the time it takes a packet to travel from the client to the server and back. Other than using a well-connected web hosting provider, there's not much you can do to improve network latency for public websites—after all, you don't have any control over how your users connect to the Internet.

Typically, the second biggest factor in website performance is the number of individual objects browsers need to load to display your page. Every image, style sheet, JavaScript, and Flash object on your page requires the web browser to send a separate Hypertext Transfer Protocol (HTTP) request across the Internet. Try to minimize the number of objects embedded in a page by combining multiple style sheets and JavaScripts and using text buttons and links instead of image links. If a browser needs to load more than six objects, consider distributing the objects between different hostnames to allow web browsers to request the files simultaneously—a process known as *parallelization*. For example, instead of loading all the thumbnails on a page from www.northrup.org, I load thumbnails from images1.northrup.org, images2.northrup.org, and images3.northrup.org.

The larger the files you're sending, the more your performance is limited by bandwidth. Bandwidth can be limited by either your server's Internet connection or the client's Internet connection, so your best bet is always to reduce the size of your webpages. Shorten your webpages, enable HTTP compression, minify your JavaScripts, and increase the compression of images, sounds, and videos.

Latency, embedded objects, and bandwidth are the biggest factors, but there are many smaller factors. Use a fast Domain Name System (DNS) provider and minimize the number of different hostnames. Whenever possible, enable client-side caching for the longest period of time possible. Link to your style sheet at the top of your webpage, and embed your analytics at the bottom. To get more tips and to performance-test your own site, visit *http://www.webpagetest.org/*.

Declaratively Configuring Caching for a Single Page

You can configure each ASP.NET page in your site to be cached independently. This gives you granular control over which pages get cached and how they get cached. You manage this by adding the @ OutputCache directive to the top of a page's markup. You can configure this directive by using the attributes shown in Table 2-1.

TABLE 2-1 OutputCache Attributes

ATTRIBUTE	DESCRIPTION
Duration	The number of seconds to cache the page. This is a required parameter.
Location	One of the OutputCacheLocation enumeration values, such as Any, Client, Downstream, Server, None, or ServerAndClient. The default is Any.
CacheProfile	The name of the cache settings to associate with the page. The default is an empty string ("").
NoStore	A Boolean value that determines whether to prevent secondary storage of sensitive information.
VaryByParam	A semicolon-separated list of strings used to vary the output cache. By default, these strings correspond to a query string value sent with Get method attributes, or a parameter sent by using the Post method. When this attribute is set to multiple parameters, the output cache contains a different version of the requested document for each combination of specified parameters. Possible values include none, an asterisk (*), and any valid query string or Post parameter name. Either this attribute or the VaryByControl attribute is required when you use the @ OutputCache directive on ASP.NET pages and user controls. A parser error occurs if you fail to include it. If you do not want to specify a parameter to vary cached content, set the value to none. If you want to vary the output cache by all parameter values, set the attribute to an asterisk (*).
VaryByControl	A semicolon-separated list of strings used to vary a user control's output cache. These strings represent the ID property values of ASP.NET server controls declared in the user control.
SqlDependency	A string value that identifies a set of database and table name pairs on which a page or control's output cache depends. Note that the SqlCacheDependency class monitors the table in a database that the output cache depends on, so that when items in a table are updated, those items are removed from the cache when table-based polling is used. When notifications (in Microsoft SQL Server) are used with the value CommandNotification, ultimately a SqlDependency class is used to register for query notifications with the computer running SQL Server.

ATTRIBUTE	DESCRIPTION
VaryByCustom	Any text that represents custom output caching requirements. If this attribute is given a value of browser, the cache is varied by browser name and major version information. If a custom string is entered, you must override the GetVaryByCustomString method in your application's Global.asax file.
VaryByHeader	A semicolon-separated list of HTTP headers used to vary the output cache. When this attribute is set to multiple headers, the output cache contains a different version of the requested document for each combination of specified headers.

The Location, CacheProfile, and NoStore attributes cannot be used in user controls (.ascx files). The Shared attribute cannot be used in ASP.NET pages (.aspx files).

The following example demonstrates how to cache a page for 900 seconds, regardless of the parameters passed to the page.

```
<%@ OutputCache Duration="15" VaryByParam="none" %>
```

If the page might display differently based on parameters, provide the names of those query string parameters in the VaryByParam attribute. The following example caches a different copy of the page for different values provided in the search or category query string parameters.

```
<%@ OutputCache Duration="15" VaryByParam="search;category" %>
```

If you want to invalidate a cache based on an ASP.NET control, you will need to identify the name that ASP.NET assigns to the control. You might think you can simply specify the control name for VaryByParam or VaryByControl, but ASP.NET generates more complex names.

To identify the ASP.NET-generated name for a control, first create your web form and add the control that you plan to vary by. Run the page and view the source in your web browser. Within the HTML source, find the control and make note of the name parameter. The following HTML source shows DropDownList and TextBox controls. The ASP.NET-generated names that you would need to specify as parameters for VaryByParam or VaryByControl are shown in bold.

```
<select name="ctl00$MainContent$ChoiceDropDownList" id="MainContent_ChoiceDropDownList">
    <option value="One">One</option>
    <option value="Two">Two</option>
    <option value="Three">Three</option>
</select>
<input name="ctl00$MainContent$UserNameTextBox" type="text" id="MainContent_
UserNameTextBox" />
```

Therefore, if you wanted to invalidate the cache if values in either field were changed, you would need to use the following OutputCache declaration.

```
<%@ OutputCache Duration="15"
    VaryByParam="ctl00$MainContent$ChoiceDropDownList;ctl00$MainContent$UserNameTextBox"
%>
```

Partial-Page Caching

To cache a portion of an ASP.NET webpage, move the portion of the page that you want to cache into an .ascx user control. Then, add the @ OutputCache directive to the user control. That user control will be cached separately from the parent page. For more information about user controls, refer to Chapter 7, "Creating Custom Web Controls."

Programmatically Configuring Caching for a Single Page

If you need to make run-time decisions about output caching, you can do so by using the Response.Cache object. The available programmatic methods do not correspond directly to the attributes provided by the @ OutputCache directive, but they provide basic functionality:

- **Response.Cache.SetExpires** Use this method to expire the page at a specific time. For example, you could specify DateTime.Now.AddMinutes(30) to expire the page in 30 minutes.

- **Response.Cache.SetCacheability** Use this method to specify an HttpCacheability enumeration value, such as HttpCacheability.Public (which enables caching at both the client and the server) or HttpCacheability.Server (which enables caching at the server but disables caching at the client).

- **Response.Cache.SetValidUntilExpires** Pass this method a true value to configure the cache to ignore cache-invalidation headers.

Using Substitution to Update Caches

Some pages might not be eligible for caching because they have simple elements that must be dynamically generated. As an alternative to creating separate user controls for the dynamic elements and configuring a different caching policy for those user controls, you can use substitution. ASP.NET provides two cache substitution techniques:

- **The Response.WriteSubstitution method** You add static placeholders to your page in places where dynamic content is required, and then use the Response.WriteSubstitution method to specify a method that replaces portions of a cached page with dynamically generated content. To specify the substitution method, call WriteSubstitution and pass a callback method with an HttpResponseSubstitutionCallback signature.

> **NOTE SUBSTITUTION WITH CACHED USER CONTROLS**
>
> You can't use substitution to update cached user controls where output caching is applied at the user control level.

- **The Substitution control** Substitution controls are similar to Label controls, but Substitution controls are exempt from output caching. The only useful property is Substitution.MethodName, which you use to specify the method that generates the content that is inserted at the location of the Substitution control. The method specified by MethodName must accept an HttpContext parameter and return a String. The String value is inserted into the response at the Substitution control location when the cached page is returned to the user. The following code demonstrates how to specify a substitution method that displays the current time in a Substitution control named Substitution1.

Sample of Visual Basic Code

```vb
Sub Page_Load(ByVal sender As Object, ByVal e As System.EventArgs)
  ' Specify the callback method.
  Substitution1.MethodName = "GetCurrentDateTime"
End Sub


' The Substitution control calls this method to retrieve the current date and
time.
' This section of the page is exempt from output caching.
Shared Function GetCurrentDateTime(ByVal context As HttpContext) As String
  Return DateTime.Now.ToString()
End Function
```

Sample of C# Code

```csharp
void Page_Load(object sender, System.EventArgs e)
{
  // Specify the callback method.
  Substitution1.MethodName = "GetCurrentDateTime";
}


// The Substitution control calls this method to retrieve the current date and
time.
// This section of the page is exempt from output caching.
public static string GetCurrentDateTime (HttpContext context)
{
  return DateTime.Now.ToString();
}
```

The AdRotator control also performs postcache substitution, by default, to constantly display new ads.

Programmatically Invalidating Cached Pages

Often you want to cache pages, but specific events might require you to stop using the cached page. For example, a page that displays results from a database query should only be cached until the results of the database query change. Similarly, a page that processes a file should be cached until the file is changed. Fortunately, ASP.NET gives you several ways to invalidate cached pages.

Determining Whether to Return a Cached Page Prior to Rendering

To directly control whether a cached version of a page is used or whether the page is dynamically regenerated, respond to the ValidateCacheOutput event and set a valid value for the HttpValidationStatus attribute. Then, from the Page.Load event handler, call the AddValidationCallback method and pass an HttpCacheValidateHandler object with your method.

The following example demonstrates how to create a method to handle the ValidatePage event.

Sample of Visual Basic Code

```
Public Shared Sub ValidatePage(ByVal context As HttpContext, _
  ByVal data As [Object], ByRef status As HttpValidationStatus)

  If Not (context.Request.QueryString("Status") Is Nothing) Then
    Dim pageStatus As String = context.Request.QueryString("Status")

    If pageStatus = "invalid" Then
      status = HttpValidationStatus.Invalid
    ElseIf pageStatus = "ignore" Then
      status = HttpValidationStatus.IgnoreThisRequest
    Else
      status = HttpValidationStatus.Valid
    End If
  Else
    status = HttpValidationStatus.Valid
  End If

End Sub
```

Sample of C# Code

```
public static void ValidateCacheOutput(HttpContext context, Object data,
  ref HttpValidationStatus status)
{
  if (context.Request.QueryString["Status"] != null)
  {
    string pageStatus = context.Request.QueryString["Status"];

    if (pageStatus == "invalid")
      status = HttpValidationStatus.Invalid;
    else if (pageStatus == "ignore")
      status = HttpValidationStatus.IgnoreThisRequest;
    else
      status = HttpValidationStatus.Valid;
  }
  else
    status = HttpValidationStatus.Valid;
}
```

Notice that this code sample uses logic to specify one of the HttpValidationStatus values to control how the page is cached:

- **HttpValidationStatus.Invalid**   This causes the cache to be invalidated so that the page is dynamically generated. The newly generated page is stored in the cache, replacing the earlier cached version.

- **HttpValidationStatus.IgnoreThisRequest** This causes the current page request to be dynamically generated without invalidating the previously cached version of the page. The dynamically generated page output is not cached, and future requests might receive the previously cached output.

- **HttpValidationStatus.Valid** This causes ASP.NET to return the cached page.

The following sample demonstrates how to configure your event handler (a method named ValidateCacheOutput) so that it is called when ASP.NET determines whether to use the cached version of the page.

Sample of Visual Basic Code

```
Protected Sub Page_Load(ByVal sender As Object, _
  ByVal e As System.EventArgs) Handles Me.Load

  Response.Cache.AddValidationCallback( _
    New HttpCacheValidateHandler(AddressOf ValidatePage), Nothing)

End Sub
```

Sample of C# Code

```
protected void Page_Load(object sender, EventArgs e)
{
  Response.Cache.AddValidationCallback(
    new HttpCacheValidateHandler(ValidateCacheOutput), null);
}
```

ASP.NET calls the method you specify when it determines whether to use the cached version of the page. Depending on how you set the HttpValidationStatus in your handler, ASP.NET will use a cached page or a new, dynamically generated version.

Creating a Cache Page Output Dependency

To create a cache page output dependency, call one of the following Response methods:

- **Response.AddCacheDependency** This makes the validity of a cached response dependent on a CacheDependency object.

- **Response.AddCacheItemDependency and Response.AddCacheItemDependencies** These make the validity of a cached response dependent on one or more other items in the cache.

- **Response.AddFileDependency and Response.AddFileDependencies** These make the validity of a cached response dependent on one or more files.

Configuring Caching for an Entire Application

You can configure output caching profiles that you can easily reference from pages in your application. This provides centralized configuration of output caching. To create a cache profile, add the <caching><outputCacheSettings><outputCacheProfiles> section to your Web.config file's <system.web> element, as the following sample demonstrates.

```
<caching>
  <outputCacheSettings>
    <outputCacheProfiles>
      <add name="OneMinuteProfile" enabled="true" duration="60"/>
    </outputCacheProfiles>
  </outputCacheSettings>
</caching>
```

Caching profiles support most of the same attributes as the @ OutputCache directive, including Duration, VaryByParameter, VaryByHeader, VaryByCustom, VaryByControl, SqlDependency, NoStore, and Location. Additionally, you must provide a Name attribute to identify the profile, and you can use the Enabled attribute to disable a profile if necessary.

After you create a cache profile, reference it from within a page by using the CacheProfile attribute of the @ OutputCache directive, as the following example demonstrates. You can override specific attributes on a per-page basis.

```
<%@ OutputCache CacheProfile="OneMinuteProfile" VaryByParam="none" %>
```

PRACTICE   **Using Page Output Caching to Improve Performance**

In this practice, you configure page output caching for a simple ASP.NET web application.

> **ON THE COMPANION MEDIA**
>
> If you encounter a problem completing an exercise, you can find the completed projects in the samples installed from this book's companion CD. For more information about the project files and other content on the CD, see "Using the Companion Media" in this book's Introduction.

EXERCISE   Enabling Page Output Caching

In this exercise, you enable page output caching for an ASP.NET webpage.

1. Open Visual Studio and create a new website called **CachedSite**, using the language of your preference.

2. Next, you will add controls to a page and enable output caching. To get started, open Default.aspx and add the following controls to the BodyContent ContentPlaceHolder.

    ■ A Label control named **ChosenLabel**.

- A DropDownList control named **ChoiceDropDownList**. Add three ListItem controls to the DropDownList (one for each choice).

- A Button control named **SubmitButton**.

Within BodyContent, your markup should resemble the following.

```
<asp:Label ID="ChosenLabel" runat="server" Text="Label"></asp:Label>
<br />
<asp:DropDownList ID="ChoiceDropDownList" runat="server">
    <asp:ListItem>One</asp:ListItem>
    <asp:ListItem>Two</asp:ListItem>
    <asp:ListItem>Three</asp:ListItem>
</asp:DropDownList>
<br />
<asp:Button ID="SubmitButton" runat="server" Text="OK" />
```

3. Add an event handler for the Button control's Click event. Add code to display the user's selected choice and the current time in the ChosenLabel control. The following code shows an example.

Sample of Visual Basic Code
```
Protected Sub SubmitButton_Click(ByVal sender As Object, _
  ByVal e As System.EventArgs) Handles ButtonSubmit.Click

  ChosenLabel.Text = String.Format("{0} at {1}", ChoiceDropDownList.
SelectedValue, _
    DateTime.Now.TimeOfDay.ToString())

End Sub
```

Sample of C# Code
```
protected void SubmitButton_Click(object sender, EventArgs e)
{
    ChosenLabel.Text = String.Format("{0} at {1}", ChoiceDropDownList.
SelectedValue,
        DateTime.Now.TimeOfDay.ToString());
}
```

4. Run the project from Visual Studio. Note that each time you choose a different item from the list and click the button, the name of the chosen item and the current time are displayed at the top of the page.

5. Return to Visual Studio and open the Default.aspx page in Source view. Add a page output cache directive to the top of the page so that the page is automatically cached for 10 seconds. Do not specify any dependencies. The following code sample demonstrates how to do this.

```
<%@ OutputCache Duration="10" VaryByParam="none" %>
```

6. Update the Web.config file to allow viewing of the Trace.axd file, which shows how long ASP.NET takes to render webpages. We can use this to determine whether the .NET Framework used a cached or uncached version of a page. Add the following line to the <system.web> section.

```
<trace enabled="true"/>
```

7. Run the page again in a web browser. Make a choice from the list and notice that the page updates correctly. Immediately make another choice from the list, and notice that the page name does not change and that it continues to display the previous time.

    Make note of the time, and repeatedly choose different pages from the list until 10 seconds have passed. After 10 seconds, notice that the page updates correctly and again shows the current time. This demonstrates that page output caching is working correctly; however, the caching prevents the form from functioning as intended.

8. Later in this exercise, you will change the OutputCache settings to invalidate the cache when the user selects a different value for ChoiceDropDownList. While you have the page open, view the HTML source in your browser. Make note of the name value for the drop-down list, which will resemble ctl00$MainContent$ChoiceDropDownList.

9. In your web browser, open Trace.axd at the root of the webpage. Examine the first request, and notice that the Trace Information section shows the time required for different phases of the page generation process, including Begin PreInit, Begin Load, and Begin Render. Return to Trace.axd and examine the second request. Notice that the Trace Information section is empty, indicating that the page was accessed from the cache rather than generated by ASP.NET.

10. Return to Visual Studio and open the Default.aspx page in Source view. Modify the page output cache to cache content for 20 seconds and vary the cache based on the DropDownList control. You must specify the name you identified in the HTML source. The following code sample demonstrates how to do this (though the name of your control might be different).

```
<%@ OutputCache Duration="20" VaryByParam="ctl00$MainContent$ChoiceDropDownList" %>
```

11. Run the page again in a web browser. Choose an item from the list, and notice the time displayed. Immediately choose another item from the list, and notice that the page updates correctly. Quickly choose the previous item from the list again.

    Because of the change you made to the OutputCache declaration, ASP.NET caches a separate version of the page for each value of the DropDownList control that you choose, and each expires 20 seconds after it is generated. Examine the results generated by Trace.axd to verify that some page requests were returned from cached results.

Lesson Summary

- You can use the Cache object to store data of any type. You can then access the cached data from other webpages in your application. The Cache object is an excellent way to reduce the number of database calls and file reads. Use the Cache.Add and Cache.Insert methods to add an object to the cache with a dependency to ensure that the cached object does not become stale.

- Page output caching stores a copy of a rendered page (or user control) in the server's memory. Subsequent requests for the resources are served from memory. Page output caching practically eliminates rendering time.

Lesson Review

You can use the following questions to test your knowledge of the information in Lesson 3, "Caching." The questions are also available on the companion CD in a practice test, if you prefer to review them in electronic form.

> **NOTE** **ANSWERS**
>
> Answers to these questions and explanations of why each answer choice is correct or incorrect are located in the "Answers" section at the end of the book.

1. You are creating an ASP.NET webpage that displays a list of customers generated by a database query. The user can filter the list so that only customers within a specific state are displayed. You want to maximize the performance of your web application by using page output caching. You want to ensure that users can filter by state, but you are not concerned about displaying updates to the list of customers because the customer list doesn't change very frequently. Which declarative @ OutputCache attribute should you configure?

   A. VaryByParam

   B. VaryByHeader

   C. SqlDependency

   D. VaryByCustom

2. You need to programmatically configure page output caching. Which object would you use?

   A. Request

   B. Response

   C. Application

   D. Server

3. You want to cache an object but have it automatically expire in 10 minutes. How can you do this?

   A. Directly define the Cache item.

   B. Call Cache.Get.

   C. Call Cache.Insert.

   D. Cast DateTime.Now.AddMinutes(10) to the Cache type.

4. Which tool can you use to create a cache dependency? (Choose all that apply.)

   A. An HTTP header

   B. A file

   C. A time span

   D. A registry key

   E. Another object in the Cache

Case Scenarios

In the following case scenarios, you apply what you've learned about how to implement master pages, themes, and caching. If you have difficulty completing this work, review the material in this chapter before beginning the next chapter. You can find answers to these questions in the "Answers" section at the end of this book.

Case Scenario 1: Providing Consistent Formatting for an External Web Application

You are an application developer working for Humongous Insurance. You are responsible for updating an external web application based on user requests. Currently, the web application's primary uses are:

- Enabling subscribers to search for and identify providers.
- Providing a reference for subscribers who need to know what is and isn't covered.
- Enabling subscribers to contact customer service representatives with questions.
- Providing portals to subscribers to enable them to read updates about Humongous Insurance and general health care topics.

You have a backlog of email from users. Although you have quite a few positive messages, today you are reading through the negative messages to identify ways to update the application to better serve users. Following is the text of email received from users:

- As I browsed the site, I felt like I was visiting several different sites. The layout of the page changed, and the logo is even different on some pages.

- Awful. There are so many different fonts that it looks like a ransom note. Why does every page look different? Get an editor.

- Nice website, but the colors are awful.

Answer the following questions for your manager:

1. How can you provide a consistent layout for the site?

2. How can you address the concerns about the inconsistency of fonts?

3. How can you ensure that a developer does not set the incorrect font on a control?

4. How can you enable users to change the colors of the website?

Case Scenario 2: Improving the Performance of a Public Website

You are a developer for Contoso, Ltd, a video rental company. Fortunately, the company's website has been getting busier and busier. Currently, both the web server and the back-end database are hosted on a single computer. Unfortunately, you've discovered that the server that runs the site and database isn't powerful enough to meet peak demand. During the busiest hours, you discover that processor utilization is very high.

You discuss the problems with other people at your organization. Following is a list of company personnel interviewed and their statements:

- **Dariusz Korzun, Database Administrator**   I did some analysis on the SQL Server database performance as you asked. The biggest problem is that when a user clicks on a movie genre on the website, such as comedy or drama, your application performs a very processor-intensive query to find the appropriate movies. I've optimized the indexes already, so there's nothing we can do besides upgrading the server or querying the database less often.

- **Wendy Richardson, IT Manager**   The company is doing well, but we don't have any budget to upgrade the server. So find a way to make the application more efficient.

Answer the following questions for your manager:

1. Is there a way you can use the application Cache object to improve performance?

2. How can you make sure stale cache information isn't sent to users after the company adds new movies?

3. Each page on the website is personalized with the current users' preferences. Is there a way you can use page output caching to improve performance?

Suggested Practices

To help you successfully master the exam objectives presented in this chapter, complete the following tasks.

Implement Master Pages and Themes

For this task, you should complete Practices 1, 2, and 4 to gain experience in using master pages and themes. Practice 3 shows you how to create pages formatted for mobile devices, and you should complete it if you are interested in client-specific rendering. Practice 5 helps you understand how themes can be used with custom controls, which is important to test if you create custom controls that other developers use.

- **Practice 1** Using a copy of the most recent web application you created, implement a master page model and convert your existing ASPX pages to content pages.

- **Practice 2** Using a copy of the most recent web application you created, create multiple master pages and give users the option of switching between master pages based on their layout and color preferences.

- **Practice 3** Create a web application that detects the client device and switches master pages based on the client type. For traditional web browsers, display a navigation bar on the left side of the screen. For mobile clients, consider displaying all content in a single column.

- **Practice 4** Using a copy of the most recent web application you created, add a theme to configure all controls with consistent colors.

- **Practice 5** Create a custom control and experiment with setting the attributes by using themes.

Implement Caching

For this task, you should complete Practices 1 and 2 to learn more about application caching.

- **Practice 1**   Using the most recent real-world ASP.NET web application you created that accesses a database, use the Cache object to store a copy of database results. View the Trace.axd page before and after the change to determine whether caching improves performance.

- **Practice 2**   Using the most recent real-world ASP.NET web application you created, enable output caching as thoroughly as possible without forcing users to experience outdated content.

Take a Practice Test

The practice tests on this book's companion CD offer many options. For example, you can test yourself on just the lesson review questions in this chapter, or you can test yourself on all the 70-515 certification exam objectives. You can set up the test so it closely simulates the experience of taking a certification exam, or you can set it up in study mode so you can look at the correct answers and explanations after you answer each question.

> **MORE INFO**   **PRACTICE TESTS**
>
> For details about all the practice test options available, see the "How to Use the Practice Tests" section in this book's Introduction.

CHAPTER 3

Handling Events and Managing State

The biggest difference between Windows and web applications is not the user interface; it's the life cycle. Users open a Windows application and work with it for hours at a time, and when they close it, the application has the opportunity to save their data. Web requests are much more short term. A user might request one page from your website and never return. Even if a user spends hours on your site, each individual request requires controls and objects to be created and finally destroyed.

Because pages and controls must be created for every user request, you must understand the Microsoft ASP.NET page life cycle in order to build pages efficiently and respond to user input reliably. ASP.NET provides different events for each major stage in the life cycle, and you can respond to any of them. Add controls too late in the page life cycle, and you will lose your themes, skins, and stored data. Handle the wrong control event, and your user interface won't behave correctly.

Because ASP.NET destroys any objects you've created within a page after the page is rendered, objects you create won't be available during the user's next request. ASP.NET provides several ways to persist data between requests:

- **View state**   With view state, data is stored within controls on a page. For example, if view state is enabled and you set the value of a Label control, ASP.NET will retain the custom value between requests.

- **Hidden fields**   As with the view state approach, a hidden field is stored as a field on a page. The view state technique and hidden fields only work for multiple requests to a single page.

- **Session state**   With session state management, data is stored for use within any page in a user's visit. For example, if a user provides a name, your application could retain it for the rest of the user's visit by storing it in session state.

- **Cookies**   With cookies, data is stored on the user's computer. Your application can ask a user's browser to store data in a file and send it back to the website with each request. Unlike session state, cookies can be accessed across different visits.

- **Query strings** With query strings, data is stored in a URL. If you need to store information about a page so that the link can be bookmarked or shared, add it to the query string. Users can easily edit query strings, however.

- **Application state** When application state is used, data is stored on a server that is accessible by any page running within the application. Application state can be accessed from different users' sessions, but it is lost if the application is restarted.

To build efficient and reliable web applications, you must understand when to use each of these state management techniques. The first lesson of this chapter describes the ASP.NET life cycle and shows you how to handle page and control events. The second and third lessons describe how to use client-side and server-side state management to store your application data.

Exam objectives in this chapter:

- Developing Web Forms Pages
  - Handle page life cycle events.
  - Manage state.

Lessons in this chapter:

Before You Begin

To complete the lessons in the chapter, you should be familiar with developing applications with Microsoft Visual Studio by using Microsoft Visual Basic or Microsoft Visual C#. In addition, you should be comfortable with all of the following:

- The Visual Studio 2010 Integrated Development Environment (IDE)
- Hypertext Markup Language (HTML) and client-side scripting
- Creating a new website
- Adding web server controls to a webpage

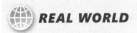

REAL WORLD

Tony Northrup

Visual Studio makes it so easy to handle events that many developers don't really understand them. You can double-click a button in the Visual Studio designer and write some code that runs when the user clicks it. Technically, you're handling an event, even though you don't need to understand how the event works. It's nice that Visual Studio is beginner friendly, but what happens when you need to add a button to a page at run time, modify one of the button's properties before the button is displayed, or programmatically change the button's HTML?

ASP.NET exposes every step of the webpage creation process by using events, and when you understand those steps and how to handle the events, you can do anything. Literally—anything. You can move view state information to the bottom of a form. You can intercept the user's request and alter or redirect the request, tricking ASP.NET into thinking that the request came from a different browser. You can even wait until ASP.NET has completely rendered the page, and then edit the HTML before sending it back to the user.

In the real world, developers are never on the job for more than a couple of months before they encounter challenges that require weaving code into non-default events. I don't expect you to memorize every event (though it wouldn't hurt for the exam), but you do need to be familiar with the various page and control events so that you know what you can do with ASP.NET when you finally encounter that seemingly insurmountable challenge.

Lesson 1: Understanding the ASP.NET Life Cycle and Handling Events

Pages, and the controls on them, have a life cycle. At different stages in the life cycle, ASP.NET raises events. For each event, you can create methods that run code to customize the behavior of pages and controls.

This lesson describes the life cycle of ASP.NET webpages and controls. You will learn how to respond to user interactions, such as the click of a button. You will also learn how to customize the page life cycle to alter the page layout at run time.

The ASP.NET Application Life Cycle

It is important to have a solid understanding of the life cycle of an ASP.NET application when you are working with server-side state management. This life cycle defines how the application server starts and stops your application, isolates it from other applications, and executes your code.

In production environments, ASP.NET applications run within a web server. The web server is usually Internet Information Services (IIS) hosted on a recent version of Windows Server, such as Windows Server 2008 R2, which includes IIS 7.5. The following stages constitute the application life cycle of an ASP.NET application running on IIS 7.5:

1. A user first makes a request for a page in your site.

2. The request is routed to the processing pipeline, which forwards it to the ASP.NET runtime.

3. The ASP.NET runtime creates an instance of the ApplicationManager class. The ApplicationManager instance represents the Microsoft .NET Framework domain that will be used to execute requests for your application. An application domain isolates global variables from other applications and allows each application to load and unload separately as required.

4. After the application domain has been created, an instance of the HostingEnvironment class is created. This class provides access to items inside the hosting environment, such as directory folders.

5. ASP.NET creates instances of the core objects that will be used to process the request. This includes HttpContext, HttpRequest, and HttpResponse objects.

6. ASP.NET creates an instance of the HttpApplication class (or an instance is reused). This class is also the base class for a site's Global.asax file. You can use this class to trap events that happen when your application starts or stops. When ASP.NET creates an instance of HttpApplication, it also creates the modules configured for the application, such as the SessionStateModule.

7. Finally, ASP.NET processes requests through the HttpApplication pipeline. This pipeline also includes a set of events for validating requests, mapping URLs, accessing the cache, and more. These events are of interest to developers who want to extend the Application class, but they are outside the scope of this book.

Responding to Application Events

The HttpApplication class provides several events that you can handle to perform actions when ASP.NET raises certain events at the application level. These include actions such as initializing variable values when your application starts, logging requests to your application, handling application-level errors, and more. ASP.NET raises these events based on your application starting, stopping, handling a request, and so on; the events do not work on a per-user level.

You handle the event for the stage of the application life cycle you intend to intercept. Events are mapped automatically if you follow the Application_ naming structure. The following list shows the method you would add to the Global.asax file (described next) and when ASP.NET raises the event:

- **Application_Start**   The Start event is raised when your application is started by IIS (usually as the result of a user request). This event is useful for initializing variables that are scoped at the application level.

- **Application_End**   The End event is raised when your application stops or shuts down. This event is useful if you need to free application-level resources or perform some sort of logging.

- **Application_Error**   The Error event is raised when an unhandled error occurs and rises up to the application scope. You could use this event to perform worst-case, catch-all error logging.

- **Application_LogRequest**   The LogRequest event is raised when a request has been made to the application. You can use this event to write custom logging information regarding a request.

- **Application_PostLogRequest**   The PostLogRequest event is raised after the logging of a request has completed.

These are just the most commonly used Application events. Others include Application_BeginRequest, Application_EndRequest, ResolveRequestCache, and many others. These events map to the application processing pipeline. For more information about other events, look up the HttpApplication class in the MSDN library and read "INFO: Application Instances, Application Events, and Application State in ASP.NET" at *http://support.microsoft.com/kb/312607*.

You can implement these events by adding a Global.asax file, also known as the Global Application Class, to your project. Visual Studio does not create a code-behind file for it by default. Instead, it has a script block that you use to add code for these events. Visual Studio 2010 automatically creates a Global.asax file for you when you use the ASP.NET Web Site template to create a website. If you use the ASP.NET Empty Web Site template, follow these steps to create the Global.asax file:

1. Open your website in Visual Studio. In Solution Explorer, right-click your website project file and select Add New Item to open the Add New Item dialog box.

2. In the Add New Item dialog box, select the Global Application Class item, and then click Add to add the file to your project.

Visual Studio will add a Global.asax file to your project. The file already contains stubbed-out method signatures for Application_Start, Application_End, and Application_Error. It also includes method signatures for Session_Start and Session_End. These are described later in this lesson.

The following code shows an example of a Global.asax file. In this example, the application-level variable *UsersOnline* is defined at application start. The variable is incremented when a new user comes to the site and starts a session. The variable is decremented when a session ends. (The session end code is only called for InProc session state management, which is covered in Lesson 3, "Using Server-Side State Management."

Sample of Visual Basic Code

```vb
<%@ Application Language="VB" %>
<script runat="server">
    Sub Application_Start(ByVal sender As Object, ByVal e As EventArgs)
        Application("UsersOnline") = 0
    End Sub

    Sub Session_Start(ByVal sender As Object, ByVal e As EventArgs)
        Application.Lock()
        Application("UsersOnline") = CInt(Application("UsersOnline")) + 1
        Application.UnLock()
    End Sub

    Sub Session_End(ByVal sender As Object, ByVal e As EventArgs)
        Application.Lock()
        Application("UsersOnline") = CInt(Application("UsersOnline")) - 1
        Application.UnLock()
    End Sub
</script>
```

Sample of C# Code

```csharp
<%@ Application Language="C#" %>
<script runat="server">
    void Application_Start(object sender, EventArgs e)
    {
        Application["UsersOnline"] = 0;
    }

    void Session_Start(object sender, EventArgs e)
    {
        Application.Lock();
        Application["UsersOnline"] = (int)Application["UsersOnline"] + 1;
        Application.UnLock();
    }

    void Session_End(object sender, EventArgs e)
    {
        Application.Lock();
        Application["UsersOnline"] = (int)Application["UsersOnline"] - 1;
        Application.UnLock();
    }
</script>
```

Writing and Reading Application State Data

You can read and write application-level state data by using the Application collection (an instance of the HttpApplicationState class). Because multiple webpages might be running simultaneously on different threads, you must lock the Application object when making calculations and performing updates to application-level data. For example, the following code locks (and later unlocks) the Application object for a single thread before incrementing and updating an application-level variable.

Sample of Visual Basic Code

```
Application.Lock()
Application("PageRequestCount") = CInt(Application("PageRequestCount")) + 1
Application.UnLock()
```

Sample of C# Code

```
Application.Lock();
Application["PageRequestCount"] = ((int)Application["PageRequestCount"]) + 1;
Application.UnLock();
```

If you don't lock the Application object, it is possible for another page to change the variable between the time that the process reads the current value and the time it writes the new value. This could cause a calculation to be lost. You do not need to lock the Application object when initializing variables in Application_Start. Whenever possible, you should use the Cache object instead. Caching is discussed in Chapter 2, "Using Master Pages, Themes, and Caching."

The values of an Application variable are of the Object type. Therefore, when you read them, you must cast them to the appropriate type. There is no need to lock a variable for a read, because multiple threads can read the same data without causing any problems.

Understanding the Life Cycle of an ASP.NET Webpage and Its Controls

The page life cycle starts when a user requests a webpage through a browser. The web server then processes the page through a series of stages before returning the results to the user's browser. These processing stages define the life cycle of a webpage. Figure 3-1 shows a high-level overview of the page processing life cycle.

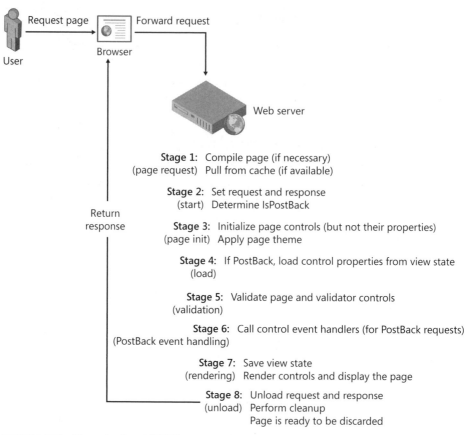

Request page → Browser → Forward request

User

Web server

Return response

Stage 1: Compile page (if necessary)
(page request) Pull from cache (if available)

Stage 2: Set request and response
(start) Determine IsPostBack

Stage 3: Initialize page controls (but not their properties)
(page init) Apply page theme

Stage 4: If PostBack, load control properties from view state
(load)

Stage 5: Validate page and validator controls
(validation)

Stage 6: Call control event handlers (for PostBack requests)
(PostBack event handling)

Stage 7: Save view state
(rendering) Render controls and display the page

Stage 8: Unload request and response
(unload) Perform cleanup
Page is ready to be discarded

FIGURE 3-1 The life cycle of an ASP.NET page.

When a webpage is requested, the server creates objects associated with the page, along with all of its child control objects, and uses these to render the page to the browser. When the final stage is complete, the web server destroys these objects to free up resources to handle additional requests. This allows the web server to handle more requests from more users.

Page Life Cycle Events

As ASP.NET processes a page through its stages, various events are raised for the page and its related controls. You write code to handle these events and thus respond to various actions related to the processing of a page.

For example, you might want to write code that gets called when a page is first loaded (stage 4) to determine whether the user is requesting the page or posting back to the server. The first time a user requests a page, you often need to initialize controls and their data. You usually do not need to do this when the form posts back, however.

It's also important to know the order in which events are called, so that your code runs in the proper sequence. Table 3-1 contains an ordered list of the more common events that are triggered when a page is processed by ASP.NET.

TABLE 3-1 Page Life Cycle Events

EVENT	DESCRIPTION
PreInit	This is the first real event you might handle for a page. You usually use this event only if you need to set values such as master page or theme.
	This event is also useful when you are working with dynamically created controls for a page without a master page. You should create the controls inside this event.
Init	This event fires after each control has been initialized. You can use this event to change initialization values for controls.
	If you need to dynamically add controls to a content page, use this event.
InitComplete	This event is raised after all initializations of the page and its controls have been completed.
PreLoad	This event fires before view state has been loaded for the page and its controls and before postback processing. This event is useful when you need to write code after the page is initialized but before the control view state has been re-established.
Load	The page is stable at this time; it has been initialized and its state has been reconstructed. Code inside the page load event usually checks for postback and then sets control properties appropriately.
	The page's load event is called first. Then the load event for each child control is called in turn (and then the load events for their child controls, if any). This is important to know if you are writing your own user or custom controls.
Control (postback) event(s)	ASP.NET now calls any events on the page or its controls that caused the postback to occur. This might be a button's click event, for example.
LoadComplete	At this point all controls are loaded. If you need to do additional processing at this time, you can do so here.
PreRender	This event allows final changes to the page or its control. It takes place after all regular postback events have taken place. This event takes place before ViewState is saved, so any changes made here are saved.

(continued)

EVENT	DESCRIPTION
SaveStateComplete	Prior to this event, the view state for the page and its controls is set. Any changes to the page's controls at this point or beyond are ignored. This event is useful if you need to write processing that requires the view state to be set.
Render	This is a method of the page object and its controls (not an event). At this point, ASP.NET calls this method on each of the page's controls to get its output.

The Render method generates the client-side HTML, Dynamic Hypertext Markup Language (DHTML), and script that are necessary to properly display a control on the browser.

This method is useful if you are writing your own custom control. You override this method to control output for the control. |
| Unload | This event is used for cleanup code. You can use it to manually release resources, a process that is rarely necessary. |

EXAM TIP

Know your page and control life cycle events for the exam (and for the real world). You'll need to know which events to handle to perform common tasks such as dynamically adding controls, changing master pages, and altering HTML output after controls have been rendered. Complete the practices at the end of this chapter to get more experience working with different life cycle events.

Adding Controls at Run Time

You can add controls to a form at run time by handling the Page.PreInit event (if you are not using master pages) or the Page.Init event (if you are using master pages and you are adding the control to a content page). If you add controls in Init or Load, you will need to manually call the Control.ApplyStyleSheetSkin method.

To add controls to a form, follow these high-level steps:

1. Add a Panel control to your ASPX page where you would like the controls to appear. You can also use a PlaceHolder control.

2. In the Page.PreInit or Page.Init event handler, create an instance of the control.

3. Set the control's properties. If you need to access the controls from another method, be sure to set the ID property.

4. Add event handlers for the control, if necessary.

5. Add the control to the Panel.Controls collection.

The instances you create in Page_Load or Page_Init will not be available in event handlers. Therefore, you will need to find the controls in the Panel.Controls collection and cast them to the right type.

The following code sample demonstrates how to add a Label, TextBox, and Button control to a form that contains a Panel control named Panel1; add an event handler for the Button.Click event; and then access each control from the event handler.

Sample of Visual Basic Code

```vb
Protected Sub Page_Load(ByVal sender As Object, ByVal e As System.EventArgs) _
    Handles Me.PreInit
    ' Create instances of the controls
    Dim FeedbackLabel As New Label()
    Dim InputTextBox As New TextBox()
    Dim SubmitButton As New Button()

    ' Assign the control properties
    FeedbackLabel.ID = "FeedbackLabel"
    FeedbackLabel.Text = "Please type your name: "

    SubmitButton.ID = "SubmitButton"
    SubmitButton.Text = "Submit"

    InputTextBox.ID = "InputTextBox"

    ' Create event handlers
    AddHandler SubmitButton.Click, AddressOf SubmitButton_Click

    ' Add the controls to a Panel
    Panel1.Controls.Add(FeedbackLabel)
    Panel1.Controls.Add(InputTextBox)
    Panel1.Controls.Add(SubmitButton)
End Sub

Protected Sub SubmitButton_Click(ByVal sender As Object, ByVal e As EventArgs)
    ' Create an instance of Button for the existing control
    Dim SubmitButton As Button = DirectCast(sender, Button)

    ' Update the text on the Button
    SubmitButton.Text = "Submit again!"

    ' Create the Label and TextBox controls
    Dim FeedbackLabel As Label = DirectCast(Panel1.FindControl("FeedbackLabel"), Label);
    Dim InputTextBox As TextBox = DirectCast(Panel1.FindControl("InputTextBox"), TextBox);
    ' Update the controls
    FeedbackLabel.Text = String.Format("Hi, {0}", InputTextBox.Text)
End Sub
```

Sample of C# Code

```csharp
protected void Page_Load(object sender, EventArgs e)
{
    // Create instances of the controls
    Label FeedbackLabel = new Label();
    TextBox InputTextBox = new TextBox();
    Button SubmitButton = new Button();

    // Assign the control properties
    FeedbackLabel.ID = "FeedbackLabel";
    FeedbackLabel.Text = "Please type your name: ";

    SubmitButton.ID = "SubmitButton";
    SubmitButton.Text = "Submit";

    InputTextBox.ID = "InputTextBox";

    // Create event handlers
    SubmitButton.Click += new System.EventHandler(SubmitButton_Click);

    // Add the controls to a Panel
    Panel1.Controls.Add(FeedbackLabel);
    Panel1.Controls.Add(InputTextBox);
    Panel1.Controls.Add(SubmitButton);
}

protected void SubmitButton_Click(object sender, EventArgs e)
{
    // Create an instance of Button for the existing control
    Button SubmitButton = (Button)sender;

    // Update the text on the Button
    SubmitButton.Text = "Submit again!";

    // Create the Label and TextBox controls
    Label FeedbackLabel = (Label)Panel1.Findcontrol("FeedbackLabel");
    TextBox InputTextBox = (TextBox)Panel1.FindControl("InputTextBox");

    // Update the controls
    FeedbackLabel.Text = string.Format("Hi, {0}", InputTextBox.Text);
}
```

To run that code by using a content page that has a master page assigned, change Page_Load to Page_Init.

Control Life Cycle Events

Controls, such as Button and TextBox, share a common life cycle with the Page class. Each server control, including Init, Load, Render, and Unload, goes through the same life cycle as a page. A control's event occurs during the same event for its parent, so when a page executes the load event, it then does so for each child control. Each child control that contains other child controls also executes the load event for each child control.

It is important to note that this synchronized event execution is true for all controls added to the page at design time. Those added dynamically during code execution will not have their events execute in a similar sequence to that of the page object. Instead, when they are added to the page dynamically, the controls' events are executed sequentially until the events have caught up to the current stage of their container (typically the executing page).

Creating Event Handlers

Controls in ASP.NET have default events that are usually handled by the application developer. For example, the Page object's default event is Load, and the Button object's default event is the Click event. Inside the Visual Studio page designer, you can attach an event handler for the default event of a control by simply double-clicking the design surface for the given control. For example, if you double-click a page, Visual Studio creates the Page_Load event stub in the code-behind file and then opens it for you. You can do the same for other controls you add to a page. Simply double-click a Button or TextBox to generate a default event handler in your code-behind file.

This double-click method works throughout Visual Studio. However, the Visual Basic .NET and C# designers differ when it comes to defining event handlers for other, non-default events.

ADDING A VISUAL BASIC .NET EVENT HANDLER

In Visual Basic .NET, you use two drop-down lists to define your events. This is a carryover from previous versions of Visual Basic. In the first drop-down list, you select an object on the page. The second drop-down list is then used to generate the event handler. The following steps walk you through this process. Here you add the event handler Page_Init.

1. Inside the Visual Studio Solution Explorer, right-click a webpage and select View Code. This opens the code-behind file without inserting any code.

2. In the code-behind file, select the object drop-down list from the upper-left part of the page and click Page Events, as shown in Figure 3-2.

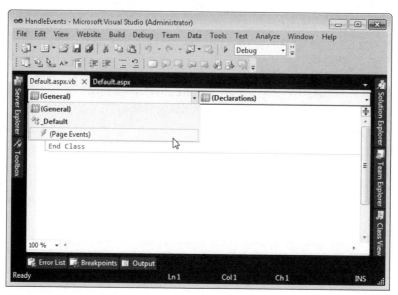

FIGURE 3-2 Selecting the object that contains the event you want to handle.

3. Select the event drop-down list from the upper-right part of the page. Notice that all the events for the page are listed. Those events that are already handled on the page are listed in bold. Select the Init event, as shown in Figure 3-3.

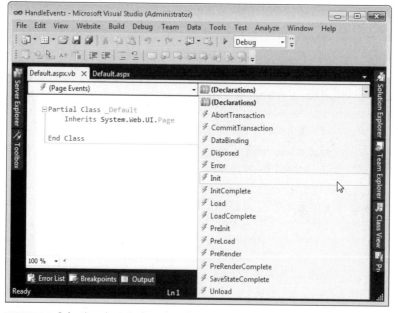

FIGURE 3-3 Selecting the Init event handler for a Visual Basic. NET webpage.

4. Next, Visual Studio generates the following event stub for you. You can then add code inside this event that will be executed when this event is fired.

```
Protected Sub Page_Init(ByVal sender As Object, ByVal e As System.EventArgs) _
    Handles Me.Init


End Sub
```

ADDING A C# EVENT HANDLER

The code editor for C# also has an event handler drop-down list. However, it only contains access to events you have already provided handlers for. The C# environment provides a tool for wiring up control events, but it does not provide such a tool for the Page events. For these, you have to code the event handler manually. Follow these steps to add the Init event handler to a C# webpage:

1. Right-click a webpage from Solution Explorer and choose View Markup to open the design code (HTML) for a page. Verify that the page's AutoEventWireup property is set to true in the @ Page directive (this is the default). This simply means that the runtime will automatically connect the event handlers it finds in your code that match the common form of Page_*EventName*.

2. Next, right-click the same page and click View Code to open the code editor with the page's code-behind file loaded. From within the partial class brackets, add the handler code as shown in the following code block. This code will automatically be connected to the page's Init event at compile time.

```
private void Page_Init(object sender, EventArgs e)
{

}
```

Handling events issued from individual controls in C# is a little easier. You are not required to recall the signature of each event. Instead, you can use the Property window for a control to generate an event stub in your code-behind file. The following procedure walks you through defining a Click event for a Button control.

1. Open a page in Design view. From the Toolbox, add a Button control to the page.

2. Select the Button control and view its properties (right-click and select Properties).

3. In the Properties window, click the Events icon (the yellow lightning bolt). This changes the Properties window to the events view. Figure 3-4 shows an example.

4. From here, you locate the event you want to handle and double-click it in the Properties window. This will open the code-behind page and insert the event handler stub code.

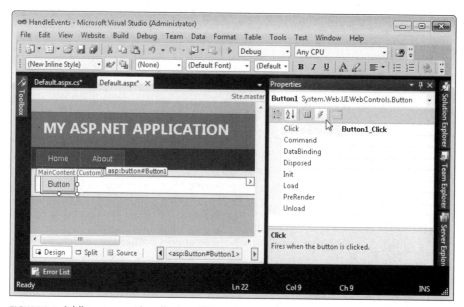

FIGURE 3-4 Adding an event handler to a C# server control.

Controlling Automatic Postback

Some web server controls always cause a postback when a specific event occurs. For example, the Button control's Click event always causes the browser to submit the form to the web server, initiating a postback. However, if a user selects a choice on a DropDownList, it does not post back to the server by default.

For instance, the TextBox contains a default event called TextChanged. By default, the TextChanged event does not cause an automatic postback, so nothing happens on the server the moment the user changes text. The event is not lost, however. Instead, ASP.NET raises the event during the next postback, which usually occurs when the user clicks a button.

When working with controls that have events that do not cause automatic postbacks to the server, it is important to understand when these events are raised. Recall the webpage life cycle defined in Table 3-1. Any postponed event (an event triggered by a user that does not cause an automatic postback) executes before the actual event that caused the postback. For example, if the text is changed in a TextBox and a Button is clicked, the Button click causes a postback, but the TextChanged event of the TextBox executes and then the Click event of the Button executes.

The AutoPostBack property for a control is used to change whether that control's default event causes an automatic postback to the server. Set AutoPostBack to true to turn a postponed event to one that causes an immediate postback. You can do so in the Properties window, by using code, or by adding the AutoPostBack="True" attribute to the web server control element in Source view. Figure 3-5 shows how to set AutoPostBack to true for a check box by using the Properties window. If the user were to change the state of that check box, the results would immediately be sent to the server.

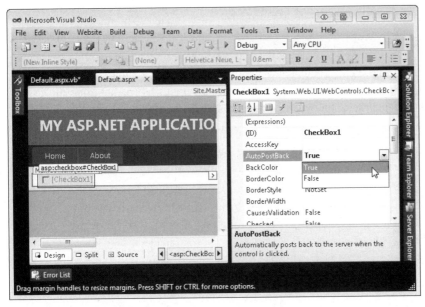

FIGURE 3-5 Setting AutoPostBack to true.

PRACTICE **Exploring the Webpage Life Cycle Events**

In this practice, you explore the webpage life cycle to gain an understanding of the events and when they are triggered.

ON THE COMPANION MEDIA

If you encounter a problem completing an exercise, you can find the completed projects in the samples installed from this book's companion CD. For more information about the project files and other content on the CD, see "Using the Companion Media" in this book's Introduction.

EXERCISE 1   Configuring Webpage Event Handlers

In this exercise, you configure event handlers for some of the webpage and server control events. You then run the webpage to display the order in which these events are fired by ASP.NET.

1. Open Visual Studio and create a new website called **LifeCycleEvents** by using your preferred programming language. This practice assumes that you are using the code-behind model (and not the single-page model).

2. Open the code-behind file for the Default.aspx page.

3. Add a Page.Load event handler to the page (the handler is there by default in C#). Recall that the Visual Basic process for this is different than the one for C# (see "Creating Event Handlers," earlier in this lesson).

4. In the Page.Load event handler, add code that will write to the Output window in Visual Studio through the System.Diagnostics.Debug class. The following code provides an example.

Sample of Visual Basic Code
```
Protected Sub Page_Load(ByVal sender As Object, _
   ByVal e As System.EventArgs) Handles Me.Load

   System.Diagnostics.Debug.WriteLine("Page_Load")

End Sub
```

Sample of C# Code
```
protected void Page_Load(object sender, EventArgs e)
{
    System.Diagnostics.Debug.WriteLine("Page_Load");
}
```

5. Add event handlers for the PreInit, Init, PreRender, and Unload events. In each, place a call to Debug.Write. Each call should write out the respective event name associated with the handler. These additional handlers should look like the following.

Sample of Visual Basic Code
```
Protected Sub Page_PreInit(ByVal sender As Object, _
   ByVal e As System.EventArgs) Handles Me.PreInit

    System.Diagnostics.Debug.WriteLine("Page_PreInit")
End Sub

Protected Sub Page_Init(ByVal sender As Object, _
   ByVal e As System.EventArgs) Handles Me.Init

    System.Diagnostics.Debug.WriteLine("Page_Init")
End Sub
```

```vb
Protected Sub Page_PreRender(ByVal sender As Object, _
  ByVal e As System.EventArgs) Handles Me.PreRender

    System.Diagnostics.Debug.WriteLine("Page_PreRender")
End Sub

Protected Sub Page_Unload(ByVal sender As Object, _
  ByVal e As System.EventArgs) Handles Me.Unload

    System.Diagnostics.Debug.WriteLine("Page_Unload")
End Sub
```

Sample of C# Code

```csharp
protected void Page_PreInit(object sender, EventArgs e)
{
    System.Diagnostics.Debug.WriteLine("Page_PreInit");
}

protected void Page_Init(object sender, EventArgs e)
{
    System.Diagnostics.Debug.WriteLine("Page_Init");
}

protected void Page_PreRender(object sender, EventArgs e)
{
    System.Diagnostics.Debug.WriteLine("Page_PreRender");
}

protected void Page_Unload(object sender, EventArgs e)
{
    System.Diagnostics.Debug.WriteLine("Page_Unload");
}
```

6. Run the web application in Debug mode (click the Start Debugging button on the standard toolbar). You might receive a prompt stating that the website cannot be debugged until you enable debugging in the Web.config file. Allow Visual Studio to enable debugging, and click OK to continue. The Default.aspx page should be displayed in a browser window.

7. In Visual Studio, locate the Output window (View Output). You should see the results of the Debug.WriteLine calls at the bottom of the Output window, as shown in Figure 3-6. Notice the order in which the events fired.

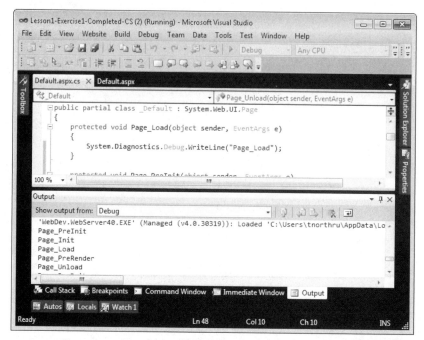

FIGURE 3-6 The Output window in Visual Studio showing the order in which the page events fired.

8. Reload the webpage in your browser. Notice that all the same events are processed again.

EXERCISE 2 Using Postback

In this exercise, you configure a web form that allows a user to either log on with a user name and password or to access the site as a guest by using an email address. If the user chooses to log on as a registered user, he or she should be prompted for both a user name and a password. If the user chooses to log on as a guest, he or she should be prompted for an email address only.

1. Open Visual Studio and create a new website by using the ASP.NET Web Site template and your preferred programming language. This practice assumes that you are using the code-behind model (and not the single-page model).

2. Create a second content page named **Home.aspx**.

3. Remove any existing controls from your Default.aspx page. Then add the following controls:

   - A DropDownList named **UserTypeDropDownList**. Add two items to the DropDownList with the text **Registered User** and **Guest**.

   - A Label named **UserNameLabel**.

   - A TextBox named **UserNameTextBox**.

   - A Label named **PasswordLabel**. Set PasswordLabel.Text to **Password:**.

   - A TextBox named **PasswordTextBox**.

   - A Button named **LogonButton**.

Though the layout isn't important, your form should resemble Figure 3-7.

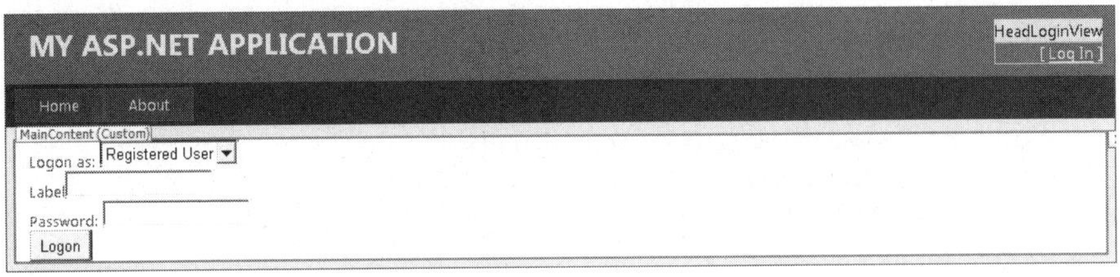

FIGURE 3-7 The sample form in Design view.

4. When the user clicks the Button, the form should check the credentials and redirect the client to Home.aspx. You will need to handle the Button.Click event to respond to the button click, so double-click the Button in the designer to create the event handler. Then call Response.Redirect to have the browser visit Home.aspx instead. In practice, you would add code to log the user on in this event handler.

Sample of Visual Basic Code

```
Protected Sub LogonButton_Click(ByVal sender As Object, _
    ByVal e As System.EventArgs) Handles LogonButton.Click

    Response.Redirect("Home.aspx", False)
End Sub
```

Sample of C# Code

```
protected void LogonButton_Click(object sender, EventArgs e)
{
    Response.Redirect("Home.aspx", false);
}
```

5. You need to change the labels and hide the password prompt if the user is visiting as a guest. You can do this from the Page.Load event handler. Within the event handler, determine whether Registered User or Guest is selected in UserTypeDropDownList. Depending on the choice, configure the controls in the form:

   - If the user is a guest, set PasswordLabel.Visible and PasswordTextBox.Visible to false. Also, set UserNameLabel.Text to **E-mail address:** and LogonButton.Text to **Visit**.

   - If the user is registered, set PasswordLabel.Visible and PasswordTextBox.Visible to true. Also, set UserNameLabel.Text to **Username:** and LogonButton.Text to **Logon**.

Your code will resemble the code shown on the following page.

Sample of Visual Basic Code

```vb
Protected Sub Page_Load(ByVal sender As Object, ByVal e As System.EventArgs)
Handles Me.Load
    If UserTypeDropDownList.SelectedValue = "Guest" Then
        PasswordLabel.Visible = False
        PasswordTextBox.Visible = False
        UserNameLabel.Text = "E-mail address: "
        LogonButton.Text = "Visit"
    Else
        PasswordLabel.Visible = True
        PasswordTextBox.Visible = True
        UserNameLabel.Text = "Username: "
        LogonButton.Text = "Logon"
    End If
End Sub
```

Sample of C# Code

```csharp
protected void Page_Load(object sender, EventArgs e)
{
    if (UserTypeDropDownList.SelectedValue == "Guest")
    {
        PasswordLabel.Visible = false;
        PasswordTextBox.Visible = false;
        UserNameLabel.Text = "E-mail address: ";
        LogonButton.Text = "Visit";
    }
    else
    {
        PasswordLabel.Visible = true;
        PasswordTextBox.Visible = true;
        UserNameLabel.Text = "Username: ";
        LogonButton.Text = "Logon";
    }
}
```

6. The Page.Load event is only processed when the browser requests a page. If you were to run the page in its current state, nothing would happen when the user selected Guest from the drop-down list. To force the browser to submit the form when the user changes the selected item in the UserTypeDropDownList, set UserTypeDropDownList.AutoPostBack to true. You can do this from Design view—select the drop-down list, view the Properties window, and set the value of AutoPostBack to true.

7. Run the webpage. With Registered User selected, notice that the user name and password text boxes appear. Type a user name and password, and then click Logon. Notice that the Button.Click event handler redirects the browser to Home.aspx.

8. Return to the Default.aspx page. Click the drop-down list and select Guest. Notice that the web browser immediately submits the form to the server, which causes the Page.Load method to run again. Because the user has now selected Guest, the Page.Load method hides the password text box. If you select Registered User, ASP.NET makes the password text box visible again.

Lesson Summary

- An ASP.NET page has a defined life cycle that determines how ASP.NET will process the page, call events, and connect data to the page.
- A server control is a control that you program by writing server-side code to respond to events from the control.

Lesson Review

You can use the following questions to test your knowledge of the information in Lesson 1, "Understanding the ASP.NET Life Cycle and Handling Events." The questions are also available on the companion CD in a practice test, if you prefer to review them in electronic form.

> **NOTE ANSWERS**
>
> Answers to these questions and explanations of why each answer choice is correct or incorrect are located in the "Answers" section at the end of the book.

1. In which file should you write code to respond to the Application_Start event?

    A. Any ASP.NET server page with an .aspx extension

    B. Web.config

    C. Global.asax

    D. Any ASP.NET server page with an .aspx.vb or .aspx.cs extension

2. You need to log data to a database when a user's session times out. Which event should you respond to?

    A. Application_Start

    B. Application_End

    C. Session_Start

    D. Session_End

3. You notice that clicking a CheckBox does not cause an automatic postback. You need the CheckBox to automatically post back so you can update the webpage based on server-side code. How do you make the CheckBox cause an automatic postback?

    A. Set the AutoPostBack property to true.

    B. Add JavaScript code to call the ForcePostBack method.

    C. Set the PostBackAll property of the webpage to true.

    D. Add server-side code to listen for the click event from the client.

4. You need to dynamically create an instance of a TextBox server control in a page. You do not use master pages. Based on the recommended best practices, in which page event would you create the server control to ensure that the view state is properly reconnected to the control on postback?

   A. PreInit

   B. Init

   C. Load

   D. PreRender

Lesson 2: Using Client-Side State Management

If your application needs to scale to thousands of users, then you should strongly consider using the client for storing application state. Removing this burden from the server frees up resources, allowing the server to process more user requests. ASP.NET provides several techniques for storing state information on the client. These include the following:

- **View state**   ASP.NET uses view state to track values in controls between page requests. You can also add your own custom values to the view state.

- **Control state**   Control state allows you to persist information about a control that is not part of the view state. This is useful to custom control developers. If view state is disabled for a control or the page, the control state will still function.

- **Hidden fields**   Like view state, HTML hidden fields store data without displaying that data to the user's browser. This data is presented back to the server and is available when the form is processed.

- **Cookies**   A cookie stores a value in the user's browser. The browser sends this value with every page request to the same server. Cookies are the best way to store state data that must be available for multiple webpages on a website.

- **Query strings**   A query string is a value that is stored at the end of a URL. These values are visible to the user through his or her browser's address bar. Use query strings when you want a user to be able to use email or instant messaging to store state data within a URL.

In this lesson, you will first learn when to choose client-side over server-side state management. Then you will learn how to implement all of the client-side state management techniques just listed: view state, control state, hidden fields, cookies, and query strings.

Choosing Client-Side or Server-Side State Management

State management information, such as user name, personalization options, or shopping cart contents, can be stored either on the client or on the server. If the state management information is stored on the client, the client submits the information to the server with each request. If the state management information is stored on the server, the server stores the information, but tracks the client by using a client-side state management technique. Figure 3-8 illustrates both client-side and server-side state management techniques.

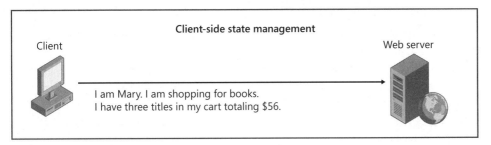

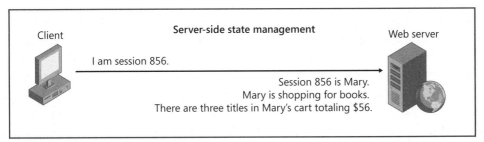

FIGURE 3-8 Client-side state management stores data on the client, whereas server-side state management requires the server to store the data.

Storing information on the client has the following advantages:

- **Better scalability**   With server-side state management, each client that connects to the web server consumes memory on that server. If a website has hundreds (or thousands) of simultaneous users, the memory consumed by storing state management information can become a limiting factor. Pushing this burden to the clients removes that potential bottleneck and frees the server to use its resources to serve more requests.

- **Support for multiple web servers**   With client-side state management, you can distribute incoming requests across multiple web servers (or a web farm). In this scenario, each client provides all the information any web server needs to process a request. With server-side state management, if a client switches servers in the middle of the session, the new server does not necessarily have access to the client's state information (because it is stored on a different server). You can use multiple servers with server-side state management, but you need either intelligent load balancing (to always forward requests from a client to the same server) or centralized state management (where state is stored in a central database to which all web servers have access).

Storing information on the server has the following advantages:

- **Better security**   Unless you digitally sign information stored on a client, users can change client-side state management information. Therefore, you should never use client-side state management to store confidential information such as passwords, access levels, or authentication status.

> **MORE INFO**   **DIGITAL SIGNATURES**
>
> You can digitally sign data by adding a private key to it (such as a password), generating a hash, and including the hash with the data you store on the client. When clients submit the data and the hash, add the private key to the data and re-generate the hash to verify that the data has not been modified. For more information about generating hashes, refer to the documentation for the System.Security.Cryptography namespace on MSDN. ASP.NET view state automatically hashes data to help reduce the chance of data modification.

- **Reduced bandwidth**   If you store large amounts of state management information, sending that information back and forth to the client can increase bandwidth utilization and page load times, especially when clients have low upstream bandwidth (as is common with home and wireless networks). Instead, you should store large amounts of state management data (say, more than 1 KB) on the server.

The choice you make for managing application state should be decided based on these trade-offs. If you are writing an application with relatively few users and high security requirements, you might consider implementing server-side state. If you want to maximize for scalability but potentially slow down requests across slower connections, you should rely on a heavy mix of client-side and server-side state management.

Of course, there is also persisted state, or data stored in the database. You need to factor this into your decision, too. You can decide to store all user information in the database and thus rely on it for state management. However, this often puts too much pressure on your database server. In this case, it is best to store real, transactional data in the database and rely on other techniques for managing more transient state data.

View State

View state is a mechanism used by ASP.NET to store user-specific request and response data between page requests. View state data is not stored by the server. Instead, it is saved into the page's view state and sent in the page's response back to the user. When the user makes the next request, the view state is returned with his or her request. When the page processes, ASP.NET pulls the view state from the page and uses it to reset the property values of the page and its controls. This allows ASP.NET to have all the object data between requests without having to store it on the server. The result is a more scalable web server that can handle more requests.

Unless it is disabled, view state is part of every ASP.NET page. As an example, suppose a user requests a webpage that allows users to edit their own profile information. When processing the user's request on the server, your application might have to go out to a database and get the user's profile information. Your application then uses this information to set the property values of the data entry fields on the page. When this page is sent to the user, these property value settings are wrapped up and stored in the view state. When the user then clicks a button to submit his or her changes to the server, the user also sends back the view state as part of the postback. ASP.NET uses this view state information to again set the property values of the server controls on the page back to what they were, as part of the request. It then checks to see if any of these values were modified by the user as part of the postback request. Next, suppose there is an issue with processing the page on the server, and therefore the server must return the same page back to the user. In this case, it again wraps the server control state (including any data changed by the user) back into the view state and sends it back to the client. You do not have to write this code; the ASP.NET view state client-side state management feature takes care of it.

The Page.ViewState property provides a dictionary object for retaining values between multiple requests for the same page. This object is of the type StateBag. When an ASP.NET page is processed, the current state of the page and its controls is hashed into a string and saved in the page as an HTML hidden field called __ViewState. If the data is too long for a single field (as specified in the Page.MaxPageStateFieldLength property), ASP.NET performs view state chunking to split it across multiple hidden fields. The following code sample demonstrates how view state adds data as a hidden form field within a webpage's HTML.

```
<input type="hidden" name="__VIEWSTATE" id="__VIEWSTATE"
  value="/wEPDwULLTEzNjkxMzkwNjRkZAVvqsMGC6PVDmbCxBlPkLVKNahk" />
```

Notice that the view state values are hashed, compressed, and encoded for Unicode implementations. This provides better optimization and more security than just simple HTML hidden fields.

The sections that follow describe how to work with ASP.NET view state. For most scenarios, it can be taken for granted. However, you might need to secure your view state data, disable view state data to increase performance, or add your own custom values to the view state.

View State Security Considerations

You need to be aware that view state can be tampered with, because it is simply a hidden field in the user's browser. Of course, you should analyze your application to better understand what risks you might face. An Internet application that works with private, personal information has a higher security risk than an internal application that solves simple problems without using private (or secret) information.

The view state also includes a message authentication code (MAC). This MAC is used by ASP.NET to determine if the view state has been tampered with. This helps ensure security in most situations without having to go to a fully encrypted view state. For most situations, you can rely on the fact that view state and MAC are base64 encoded and then hashed before being sent to the user's browser.

If you do have very sensitive information that is stored in the view state between page requests, you can encrypt it by using the ViewStateEncryptionMode property of the Page object. This will secure the view state but will also decrease the overall performance of the page processing, due to the encrypting and decrypting of data. It will also increase the size of the data being sent between the browser and server.

To enable view state encryption for your entire site, you set a value in your website configuration file. The viewStateEncryptionMode attribute of the pages element can be set to Always in the Web.config file. This tells ASP.NET to always encrypt your view state information for the entire site. An example of this setting in the configuration file is as follows.

```
<configuration>
  <system.web>
    <pages viewStateEncryptionMode="Always"/>
  </system.web>
</configuration>
```

Alternatively, you can control view state encryption at the page level. This is useful for scenarios in which sensitive information is confined to a single page or set of pages in your site. To do so, you again set the ViewStateEncryptionMode attribute to Always. However, you do so inside the individual page's directive section. The following is an example.

```
<%@ Page Language="C#" AutoEventWireup="true" ViewStateEncryptionMode="Always"%>
```

Because view state supports encryption, it is considered the most securable method of client-side state management. Encrypted view state is secure enough for most security requirements; however, it is more secure to store sensitive data on the server and not send it down to the client.

Disabling View State Data

View state is enabled by default for your page and all of the controls on the page. This includes controls, such as the Label and Literal controls, that you might never need to include as part of view state. Because view state data is sent back and forth between browser and server, you should always minimize the amount of view state data to improve performance. For websites that are only accessed from a local network, the view state size might not be a big concern. View state size is a concern for Internet websites and even intranet websites that might be accessed across slow connections, especially if a page includes more than 10 controls.

You can (and should) minimize the amount of data that gets stored and passed with the view state by disabling view state for controls and entire pages whenever possible. At the page level, you can control view state by enabling and disabling Page.EnableViewState and Page.ViewStateMode. For controls, use Control.EnableViewState and Control.ViewStateMode.

The ViewStateMode property is new in the .NET Framework 4. The ViewStateMode property of a page or a control has an effect only if the EnableViewState property is true. By default, Page.EnableViewState is True and Control.ViewStateMode is Inherit, which causes the control to use the page's view state. Therefore, if you don't change ViewStateMode, EnableViewState controls it entirely.

If you set EnableViewState to false, view state is disabled for the page or control, regardless of the value of ViewStateMode. If EnableViewState is set to true, you can set ViewStateMode to disable view state. Because ViewStateMode can inherit the page's setting, you should always leave EnableViewState set to true and use ViewStateMode to control view state.

To disable view state for all controls on a page, simply set Page.ViewStateMode to Disabled. You can then selectively re-enable view state for specific controls by setting each control's ViewStateMode property to Enabled. Essentially, ViewStateMode allows you to opt in to view state, whereas EnableViewState requires you to opt out.

Table 3-2 shows how to configure these properties to accomplish different goals.

TABLE 3-2 View State Settings

	PAGE. ENABLE VIEWSTATE	PAGE. VIEWSTATE MODE	CONTROL. ENABLE VIEWSTATE	CONTROL. VIEWSTATE MODE
Disable view state for a page, but enable it for a specific control	True	Disabled	True	Enabled
Disable view state for a page and disable it for a specific control	True	Disabled	False	Disabled or Inherit
Enable view state for a page, but disable it for a specific control	True	Enabled	False	Disabled
Enable view state for a page and for a control	True	Enabled	True	Enabled or Inherit

You can also disable view state in a Web.config file, by adding the following configuration entry to the <system.web> section.

```
<configuration>
  <system.web>
    <pages enableViewState="false">
  </system.web>
</configuration>
```

For a moderately complex form with 20 controls, view state could easily be 10 KB. Across a low-bandwidth connection, that 10 KB would result in about two additional seconds of delay when the user submits the form. That's enough to be very frustrating to users. With more complex forms, view state can be more than 40 KB, which is enough to delay a page response from a user with a typical cable modem by a full second. For that reason, you should do everything you can to minimize the amount of view state data.

> **NOTE** **COMPRESSING VIEW STATE DATA**
>
> ASP.NET does not provide a way to automatically compress view state data. However, if you enable dynamic HTTP compression by using GZip on your web server, the view state data will be compressed with the rest of the page. If you're determined to compress view state data without compressing the entire webpage, you can override the Page.SavePageStateToPersistenceMedium and Page.LoadPageStateFromPersistenceMedium methods, which serialize and deserialize view state data in each page. Within your overriding methods, use the System.IO.Compression.GZipStream to compress and decompress the view state data.

Reading and Writing Custom View State Data

You can use view state to add and retrieve custom values that you need to persist between page requests. Such a value doesn't have to be part of a control—it can be simply something you want to embed in the page to be returned as part of the next request. Adding a value to the view state collection is an efficient and secure way to accomplish this task.

Reading and writing these collection values is as straightforward as working with the Dictionary collection. The following code demonstrates simple calls to write data into the view state and retrieve it from the collection.

Sample of Visual Basic Code
```
'writing to view state
Me.ViewState.Add("MyData", "some data value")

'read from view state
Dim myData As String = CType(ViewState("MyData"), String)
```

Sample of C# Code

```csharp
//writing to view state
this.ViewState.Add("MyData", "some data value");

//read from view state
string myData = (string)ViewState["MyData"];
```

Adding data to the view state is great when you need the information to be passed back to the server as part of the page post. However, the content of the view state is for that page only. The view state does not transfer from one webpage to another (as a cookie does). Therefore, it is useful only for temporarily storing values between requests to a single page.

You can store a wide variety of object data inside the view state. You are not limited to just string values as you are with cookies. Instead, any data that can be serialized can be embedded in the view state. This includes classes in the .NET Framework that are marked serializable as well as classes that you write and mark serializable. The following code shows an example of storing a DateTime object instance inside the ViewState without converting it to a string.

Sample of Visual Basic Code

```vb
' Check if ViewState object exists, and display it if it does
If (Me.ViewState("lastVisit") IsNot Nothing) Then
    Dim lastVisit As DateTime = CType(Me.ViewState("lastVisit"), DateTime)
    Label1.Text = lastVisit.ToString()
Else
    Label1.Text = "lastVisit ViewState not defined!"
End If

' Define the ViewState object for the next page view
Me.ViewState("lastVisit") = DateTime.Now
```

Sample of C# Code

```csharp
// Check if ViewState object exists, and display it if it does
if (ViewState["lastVisit"] != null)
    Label1.Text = ((DateTime)ViewState["lastVisit"]).ToString();
else
    Label1.Text = "lastVisit ViewState not defined.";

// Define the ViewState object for the next page view
ViewState["lastVisit"] = DateTime.Now;
```

> **NOTE MOVING VIEW STATE**
>
> ASP.NET places view state information at the top of the form. Some people are concerned that this might impact their search engine rankings, based on the idea (which is unfounded, in my opinion) that search engines weigh HTML at the beginning of a webpage more highly than HTML at the bottom of the webpage. If you decide to move your view state data to the bottom of the page, you can do so by overriding the Page.Render method. Then use string manipulation techniques to move the hidden view state field from the top of the form to the bottom of the form, just before the </form> markup.

View State and Control State

Recall that you can disable view state for a given control. This can be problematic for control developers. If you write custom controls (see Chapter 7, "Creating Custom Web Controls"), you might need view state–like behavior that cannot be disabled by a developer. ASP.NET provides control state for just this purpose.

Control state allows you to store property value information that is specific to a control. Again, this state cannot be turned off and therefore should not be used in lieu of view state.

To use control state in a custom web control, your control must override the OnInit method. Here you call the Page.RegisterRequiresControlState method, passing an instance of your control to this method. From there, you override the SaveControlState method to write out your control state and the LoadControlState method to retrieve your control state.

 Quick Check

1. How do ASP.NET web forms remember the settings for controls between user requests?

2. Is the view state lost if a user refreshes a webpage? What if the user uses email to send a URL to a friend?

Quick Check Answers

1. View state, which is enabled by default, is used to embed control property values to be sent to the client and back again to the server.

2. View state is embedded inside the HTML of a single instance of a webpage displayed in the user's browser. It is lost and rewritten when a user refreshes his or her page. If the URL is copied and sent to another user, the view state does not go along. Instead, when new users request the page, they get their own view state instance.

Hidden Fields

As discussed, ASP.NET view state uses HTML hidden fields to store its data. Hidden fields in HTML are simply input fields that are embedded in a page's HTML, not displayed to the user (unless the user chooses to view the page's source), and then sent back to the server on the page post.

ASP.NET provides a control that allows you to create your own custom hidden fields in a manner similar to the one you would use to create and use other ASP.NET controls. The HiddenField control allows you to store data in its Value property. You add HiddenField controls to your page the way you would any other control, by dragging them from the Toolbox.

Like view state, hidden fields only store information for a single page. Therefore, they are not useful for storing session data that is used between page requests. Unlike view state, hidden fields have no built-in compression, encryption, hashing, or chunking. Therefore, users can view or modify data stored in hidden fields.

To use hidden fields, you must submit your pages to the server by using HTTP POST (which happens in response to a user pressing a submit button). You cannot simply call an HTTP GET (which happens if the user clicks a link) and retrieve the data in the hidden field on the server.

Cookies

Web applications often need to track users between page requests. These applications need to ensure that the user making the first request is the same user making subsequent requests. This type of common tracking is done with what are called cookies.

A *cookie* is a small amount of data that you write to the client to be stored and then passed with requests to your site. You write persistent cookies to a text file on the client machine. These cookies are meant to survive even if the user shuts down the browser and reopens it at a later time. You can also write temporary cookies to the memory of the client's browser. These cookies are used only during the current web session. They are lost when the browser closes.

Again, the most common use of cookies is to identify a single user as he or she visits multiple webpages within your site. However, you can also use cookies to store state information or other user preferences.

Figure 3-9 illustrates how a web client and a server use cookies. First (step 1), the web client requests a page from the server. Because the client has not visited the server before, it does not have a cookie to submit. When the web server responds to the request (step 2), the web server includes a cookie in the response; this cookie is written to the user's browser or file system. The web client then submits that cookie with each subsequent request for any page on the same site (steps 3 and 4, and any future page views).

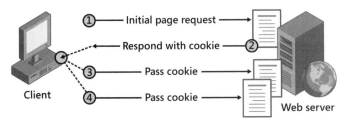

FIGURE 3-9 Web servers use cookies to track web clients.

> **NOTE ASP.NET SESSIONS AND COOKIES**
> By default, ASP.NET uses cookies to track user sessions. If you have enabled session state, ASP.NET writes a cookie to the user's browser and uses this cookie to identify his or her server session.

Cookies are the most flexible and reliable way of storing data on the client. However, users can delete cookies on their computers at any time. You can set cookies to have long expiration times, but that does not stop users from deleting all their cookies and thus wiping out any settings you might have stored in them. In addition, cookies do not solve the issue of a user moving from computer to computer (or from computer to mobile device). In these cases, users' preferences do not always go along with them. Therefore, if you allow a lot of personalization for users of your site, you need to allow the users to log on and reset their cookies. Doing so should then re-enable their customizations, assuming that you have them stored elsewhere.

Reading and Writing Cookies

A web application creates a cookie by sending it to the client as a header in an HTTP response. Of course, ASP.NET makes writing to and reading from the cookie collection a relatively straightforward task.

To add a cookie to the cookies collection and have it written out to the browser, you call the Response.Cookies.Add method. The Cookies property of the Page.Response property is of the type HttpCookieCollection. You add instances of HttpCookie to this collection. The HttpCookie object simply contains a Name property and a Value property. The following code shows how you might add an item to the cookies collection.

```
Response.Cookies.Add(New HttpCookie("userId", userId))
```

To retrieve a cookie sent back by the web browser, you read the values in the Request.Cookies collection. The following shows an example of this code.

```
Request.Cookies("userId").Value
```

As a larger example, the following sample code in a Page_Load event handler demonstrates both defining and reading cookie values by setting a cookie named lastVisit to the current time. If the user already has the cookie set, the code displays in the Label1 control the time the user last visited the page.

Sample of Visual Basic Code

```
' Check if cookie exists, and display it if it does
If Not (Request.Cookies("lastVisit") Is Nothing) Then
    ' Encode the cookie in case the cookie contains client-side script
    Label1.Text = Server.HtmlEncode(Request.Cookies("lastVisit").Value)
Else
    Label1.Text = "No value defined"
End If


' Define the cookie for the next visit
Response.Cookies("lastVisit").Value = DateTime.Now.ToString
Response.Cookies("lastVisit").Expires = DateTime.Now.AddDays(1)
```

Sample of C# Code

```
// Check if cookie exists, and display it if it does
if (Request.Cookies["lastVisit"] != null)
    // Encode the cookie in case the cookie contains client-side script
    Label1.Text = Server.HtmlEncode(Request.Cookies["lastVisit"].Value);
else
    Label1.Text = "No value defined";

// Define the cookie for the next visit
Response.Cookies["lastVisit"].Value = DateTime.Now.ToString();
Response.Cookies["lastVisit"].Expires = DateTime.Now.AddDays(1);
```

The first time the user visits the page in the previous example, the code displays "No value defined" because the cookie has not yet been set. However, if you refresh the page, it displays the time of the first visit.

Note that the code sample defines the Expires property for the cookie. You must define the Expires property and set it for the time period you would like the client to store the cookie if you want the cookie to persist between browser sessions. If you do not define the Expires property, the browser stores the cookie in memory and the cookie is lost if the user closes his or her browser.

To delete a cookie, you overwrite the cookie and set an expiration date in the past. You cannot directly delete cookies because they are stored on the client's computer.

> **NOTE VIEWING AND TROUBLESHOOTING COOKIES**
>
> You can use Trace.axd to view cookies for every page request. For more information, see Chapter 8, "Debugging and Deploying."

Controlling Cookie Scope

Cookies should be specific to a website's domain or a directory within that domain. The information in cookies is typically specific to that site and is often private. For this reason, a browser should not send your cookie to another site. By default, browsers will not send your cookie to a website with a different host name (although, in the past, vulnerabilities in browsers have allowed attackers to trick a browser into submitting another website's cookie).

You have control over a cookie's scope. You can either limit the scope to a specific directory on your web server or expand the scope to the entire domain. The scope of your cookie determines which pages have access to the information embedded in the cookie. If you limit the scope to a directory, only pages in that directory will have access to the cookie. You control cookie scope on a per-cookie basis. To limit the scope of a cookie to a directory, you set the Path property of the HttpCookie class. The following shows sample code for doing just that.

Sample of Visual Basic Code

```
Response.Cookies("lastVisit").Value = DateTime.Now.ToString
Response.Cookies("lastVisit").Expires = DateTime.Now.AddDays(1)
Response.Cookies("lastVisit").Path = "/MyApplication"
```

Sample of C# Code

```
Response.Cookies["lastVisit"].Value = DateTime.Now.ToString();
Response.Cookies["lastVisit"].Expires = DateTime.Now.AddDays(1);
Response.Cookies["lastVisit"].Path = "/MyApplication";
```

With the scope limited to the application's /MyApplication path, the browser submits the cookie to any page in the /MyApplication folder. Pages outside of this folder do not get the cookie, even if they are on the same server.

To expand the scope of a cookie to an entire domain, set the Domain property of the HttpCookie class. The following code demonstrates this.

Sample of Visual Basic Code

```
Response.Cookies("lastVisit").Value = DateTime.Now.ToString
Response.Cookies("lastVisit").Expires = DateTime.Now.AddDays(1)
Response.Cookies("lastVisit").Domain = "contoso.com"
```

Sample of C# Code

```
Response.Cookies["lastVisit"].Value = DateTime.Now.ToString();
Response.Cookies["lastVisit"].Expires = DateTime.Now.AddDays(1);
Response.Cookies["lastVisit"].Domain = "contoso.com";
```

Setting the Domain property to contoso.com causes the browser to submit the cookie to any page in the contoso.com domain. This might include those pages that belong to the sites *www.contoso.com*, *intranet.contoso.com*, or *private.contoso.com*. Similarly, you can use the Domain property to specify a full host name (such as *www.contoso.com*), limiting the cookie to a specific server.

Storing Multiple Values in a Cookie

The size of your cookie is dependent on the browser. Each cookie can be up to 4 KB in length. In addition, you can typically store up to 20 cookies per site. This should be more than sufficient for most sites. However, if you need to work around the 20-cookie limit, you can store multiple values in a single cookie by setting the cookie's name and its key value. The key value is usually not used when storing just a single value. However, if you need multiple values in a single named cookie, you can add multiple keys. The following code shows an example.

Sample of Visual Basic Code

```
Response.Cookies("info")("visit") = DateTime.Now.ToString()
Response.Cookies("info")("firstName") = "Tony"
Response.Cookies("info")("border") = "blue"
Response.Cookies("info").Expires = DateTime.Now.AddDays(1)
```

Sample of C# Code

```
Response.Cookies["info"]["visit"] = DateTime.Now.ToString();
Response.Cookies["info"]["firstName"] = "Tony";
Response.Cookies["info"]["border"] = "blue";
Response.Cookies["info"].Expires = DateTime.Now.AddDays(1);
```

Running this code sends a single cookie to the web browser. However, that cookie is parsed to form three values. ASP.NET then reads these three values back in when the cookie is submitted back to the server. The following shows the value sent to the web browser.

```
(visit=4/5/2006 2:35:18 PM)  (firstName=Tony)  (border=blue)
```

Cookie properties, such as Expires, Domain, and Path, apply for all the values within a single cookie. You cannot control these at the individual key value. Rather, they are controlled at the cookie (or name) level. You can access the individual values of a cookie by using Request.Cookies in the same way you define the values (using both name and key).

Query Strings

Query strings appended to URLs are commonly used to store variable values that identify specific context for a requested page. This context might be a search term, page number, region indicator, or something similar.

Query strings are set off from the URL with a question mark (?) followed by the query string term (or parameter name), an equal sign (=), and the value. You can append multiple query string parameters by using the ampersand (&). A typical query string might look like the following real-world example.

```
http://support.microsoft.com/Default.aspx?kbid=315233
```

In this example, the URL identifies the Default.aspx page. The query string contains a single parameter named kbid. The value for that parameter is set to 315233. In this example, the query string has one parameter. The following example shows a query string with multiple parameters. In this real-world URL, the language and market are set as parameters and the search term for searching the Microsoft.com website is set as a parameter.

```
http://search.microsoft.com/results.aspx?mkt=en-US&setlang=en-US&q=hello+world
```

Values sent to your page via the query string can be retrieved on the server through the Page.Request.QueryString property. Table 3-3 shows how you would access the three values in the preceding query string example.

TABLE 3-3 Sample Query String Parameter Access

PARAMETER NAME	ASP.NET OBJECT CALL	VALUE
mkt	Request.QueryString["mkt"]	en-US
setlang	Request.QueryString["setlang"]	en-US
q	Request.QueryString["q"]	hello world

Query strings provide a simple but limited way to maintain state information between multiple pages. For example, they provide an easy way to pass information from one page to another, as you would want to do when passing a product number from a page that describes a product to a page that adds the item to a user's shopping cart. However, some browsers and client devices impose a 2,083-character limit on the length of the URL. Another limitation is that you must submit the page by using an HTTP GET command so that query string values will be available during page processing. You also need to be aware that query string parameters and values are visible to the user in his or her address bar, and users often directly modify query string parameters.

> **IMPORTANT** **ALWAYS VALIDATE USER INPUT**
>
> You should expect users to modify data in your query strings. For that reason, you must always validate data retrieved from a query string.

One big advantage of query strings is that their data is included in bookmarks and in URLs sent by email. In fact, query strings are the only way to enable a user to include state data when copying and pasting a URL to another user. For that reason, you should use query strings for any information that uniquely identifies a webpage, even if you are also using another state-management technique.

> **IMPORTANT   PRACTICAL QUERY STRING CHARACTER LIMITS**
>
> Many browsers have 2,083-character limits on URLs, but you'll start to have problems with much shorter URLs if users send them by plaintext email or instant messaging. To allow a URL to be sent by email, limit the length to 70 characters (including the *http://* or *https://*). To allow a URL to be sent through instant messaging, limit the length to 400 characters.

REAL WORLD

Tony Northrup

Although only the most sophisticated users are comfortable modifying cookies or hidden fields, many casual users know how to change query strings. For example, the first interactive ASP.NET application I wrote allowed a user to rate pictures on a scale from 1 to 10, and the user's rating was submitted as a query string value. If the user rated a picture 7, the query string might read page.aspx?pic=342&rating=7. One day I noticed a picture with a rating above 100—a clever user had manually changed the query string to include a very large value, and my application had added the rating to the database without validation. To fix the problem, I added code to reject any request with a rating of more than 10 or less than 1.

A common mistake I see is that developers use query strings to allow users to navigate search results but do not validate the query strings properly. Often, query strings for search results have query strings for the search terms, the number of results per page, and the current page numbers. If you don't validate the query string, the user can set the number of results per page to a huge number, such as 10,000. Processing thousands of search results can take several seconds of your server's processing time and cause your server to transmit a very large HTML page. This makes it very easy for an attacker to perform a denial-of-service attack on your web application by requesting the search page repeatedly.

Don't ever trust values from a query string; they must always be validated.

Adding Query String Parameters to a URL

To create your own query string parameters, you modify the URL for any hyperlink a user might click. This is a simple process, but always getting it right can be time-consuming. In fact, there are no tools built into the .NET Framework to simplify the creation of query strings. You must manually add query string values to every hyperlink that the user might click.

For example, if you have a HyperLink control with NavigateUrl defined as page.aspx, you can add the string ?user=mary to the HyperLink.NavigateUrl property so that the full URL is page.aspx?user=mary.

To add multiple query string parameters to a page, you need to separate them with ampersands (&). For example, the URL page.aspx?user=mary&lang=en-us&page=1252 passes three query string values to page.aspx: user (with a value of mary), lang (with a value of en-us), and page (with a value of 1252).

Reading Query String Parameters in Your Page

To read a query string value, access the Request.QueryStrings collection just as you would access a cookie. To continue the previous example, the page.aspx page could process the "user" query string by accessing Request.QueryStrings("user") in Visual Basic or Request.QueryStrings["user"] in C#. For example, the following code displays values for the user, lang, and page query strings in the Label1 control.

Sample of Visual Basic Code

```
Label1.Text = String.Format("User: {0}, Lang: {1}, Page: {2}", _
    Server.HtmlEncode(Request.QueryString("user")), _
    Server.HtmlEncode(Request.QueryString("lang")), _
    Server.HtmlEncode(Request.QueryString("page")))
```

Sample of C# Code

```
Label1.Text = string.Format("User: {0}, Lang: {1}, Page: {2}",
    Server.HtmlEncode(Request.QueryString["user"]),
    Server.HtmlEncode(Request.QueryString["lang"]),
    Server.HtmlEncode(Request.QueryString["page"]));
```

```
//C#
Label1.Text = "User: " + Server.HtmlEncode(Request.QueryString["user"]) +
    ", Lang: " + Server.HtmlEncode(Request.QueryString["lang"]) +
    ", Page: " + Server.HtmlEncode(Request.QueryString["page"]);
```

> **SECURITY ALERT**
>
> You should always encode cookie or query string values by using Server.HtmlEncode before displaying the value in an HTML webpage to any user. Server.HtmlEncode replaces HTML code with special characters that a web browser cannot process. For example, Server.HtmlEncode replaces a < sign with &lt. If you display the value in a browser, the user sees the < sign, but the browser does not process any HTML code or client-side scripts.
>
> To provide extra protection, the runtime throws a System.Web.HttpRequestValidationException if it detects HTML or client-side scripting in a query string. Therefore, you cannot pass HTML code in a query string. This can be disabled by an administrator, however, so you should not rely on it for protection.

In this practice, you use different client-side state management techniques to track the number of pages a user opens. It helps you gain a better understanding of how each of the techniques works.

> **ON THE COMPANION MEDIA**
>
> If you encounter a problem completing an exercise, you can find the completed projects in the samples installed from this book's companion CD. For more information about the project files and other content on the CD, see "Using the Companion Media" in this book's Introduction.

EXERCISE 1   Storing Data in View State

In this exercise, you explore how data is stored in the view state and returned to the server during page processing.

1. Open Visual Studio and create a new ASP.NET website named **ClientState** in either C# or Visual Basic.

2. Add a second page to the project. Name this page **Default2.aspx**.

   a. Add a label named **Label1** to the page.

   b. Add a hyperlink control named **HyperLink1** to the page. Set the property HyperLink1.NavigateUrl to Default.aspx. This will access the other page without sending view state to that page.

   c. Add a button control named **Button1** to the page. This control will be used to submit the page back to the server.

3. Open the Default.aspx page. Add the same set of controls to this page, as follows:

   a, Add a label named **Label1** to the page.

   b. Add a hyperlink control named **HyperLink1** to the page. Set the property HyperLink1.NavigateUrl to Default2.aspx. This will access the other page without sending view state to that page.

   c. Add a button control named **Button1** to the page. This control will be used to submit the page back to the server.

4. Inside the Page_Load method for both Default.aspx and Default2.aspx, add code to store the current number of user clicks in the view state object. Also, add code to display the number of times a user has clicked inside the Label control. The following code sample demonstrates what this code would look like.

Sample of Visual Basic Code

```vb
Protected Sub Page_Load(ByVal sender As Object, _
  ByVal e As System.EventArgs) Handles Me.Load

    If (ViewState("clicks") IsNot Nothing) Then
      ViewState("clicks") = CInt(ViewState("clicks")) + 1
    Else
      ViewState("clicks") = 1
    End If

    Label1.Text = "ViewState clicks: " + CInt(ViewState("clicks")).ToString
End Sub
```

Sample of C# Code

```csharp
protected void Page_Load(object sender, EventArgs e)
{
    if (ViewState["clicks"] != null)
    {
        ViewState["clicks"] = (int)ViewState["clicks"] + 1;
    }
    else
    {
        ViewState["clicks"] = 1;
    }

    Label1.Text = " ViewState clicks: " + ((int)ViewState["clicks"]).ToString();
}
```

5. Build the website and visit the Default.aspx page. Click the button several times and verify that the clicks counter increments.

6. Click the hyperlink to load the Default2.aspx page. Notice that the counter value is not passed to this page. It is lost because a different page is opened.

7. Click the hyperlink to return to Default.aspx. Notice that the counter is again reset, demonstrating that switching between pages loses all view state information.

EXERCISE 2   Storing Data in a Hidden Field

In this exercise, you add a HiddenField control and use it to store client-side state.

1. Continue editing the project you created in the previous exercise. Alternatively, you can open the completed Lesson 2, Exercise 1 project in the samples installed from the CD.

2. Open the Default.aspx page in Source view. Add a HiddenField control and name it **HiddenField1**.

3. Open the code-behind file for Default.aspx. Edit the code in the Page_Load method to remove the existing code and instead store the current number of user clicks in the HiddenField1 object. As before, display the clicks in the Label control. The following code demonstrates this.

Sample of Visual Basic Code

```
Protected Sub Page_Load(ByVal sender As Object, _
  ByVal e As System.EventArgs) Handles Me.Load

    Dim clicks As Integer = 0
    Integer.TryParse(HiddenField1.Value, clicks)
    clicks += 1
    HiddenField1.Value = clicks.ToString

    Label1.Text = "HiddenField clicks: " + HiddenField1.Value
End Sub
```

Sample of C# Code

```
protected void Page_Load(object sender, EventArgs e)
{
    int clicks = 0;
    int.TryParse(HiddenField1.Value, out clicks);
    clicks++;
    HiddenField1.Value = clicks.ToString();

    Label1.Text = "HiddenField clicks: " + HiddenField1.Value;
}
```

Notice that HiddenField.Value is a String. This requires converting data to and from the String type, which you could do with int.TryParse or Int.Parse. This makes it less convenient and more error-prone than other methods of storing data.

4. Build your website and visit the Default.aspx page. Click the button several times and verify that the clicks counter increments.

   Notice that if you browse to other pages, the HiddenField value is lost.

5. View the source of the Default.aspx page in your browser (right-click anywhere within the browser's content area and then select View Source). In the source, notice that the hidden field value is displayed in plaintext.

EXERCISE 3   Storing Data in a Cookie

In this exercise, you use a cookie to track user clicks.

1. Continue editing the project you created in the previous exercise. Alternatively, you can open the completed Lesson 2, Exercise 2 project in the samples installed from the CD.

2. In the Page_Load method for both Default.aspx and Default2.aspx, add code to retrieve the current number of clicks from a cookie named clicks. Also add code to increment the number of clicks and store the new value in the same cookie. Display the clicks in the Label control. The following code demonstrates this.

Sample of Visual Basic Code

```vb
Protected Sub Page_Load(ByVal sender As Object, _
  ByVal e As System.EventArgs) Handles Me.Load

    ' Read the cookie clicks and increment
    Dim cookieClicks As Integer
    If Not (Request.Cookies("clicks") Is Nothing) Then
        cookieClicks = Integer.Parse(Request.Cookies("clicks").Value) + 1
    Else
        cookieClicks = 1
    End If

    ' Save the cookie to be returned on the next visit
    Response.Cookies("clicks").Value = cookieClicks.ToString

    Label1.Text = "Cookie clicks: " + cookieClicks.ToString

End Sub
```

Sample of C# Code

```csharp
protected void Page_Load(object sender, EventArgs e)
{
    // Read the cookie clicks and increment
    int cookieClicks;
    if (Request.Cookies["clicks"] != null)
    {
        cookieClicks = int.Parse(Request.Cookies["clicks"].Value) + 1;
    }
    else
    {
        cookieClicks = 1;
    }

    // Save the cookie to be returned on the next visit
    Response.Cookies["clicks"].Value = cookieClicks.ToString();

    Label1.Text = "Cookie clicks: " + cookieClicks.ToString();
}
```

3. Build the website and visit the Default.aspx page. Click the button several times and verify that the clicks counter increments.

4. Click the hyperlink to load Default2.aspx. Notice that the counter is not reset; you can browse to any page on the same site and read or update the cookie.

EXERCISE 4 Storing Data in a Query String

In this exercise, you use a query string to track user clicks.

1. Continue editing the project you created in the previous exercise. Alternatively, you can open the completed Lesson 2, Exercise 3 project in the samples installed from the CD.

2. In the Page_Load method for both Default.aspx and Default2.aspx, add code to retrieve the current number of clicks from a query string parameter named clicks. Also add code to increment the value of clicks and store the new value back in the query string via the Hyperlink1.NavigateUrl. Display the value of clicks in the Label control. The following code demonstrates how to do this.

Sample of Visual Basic Code

```
Protected Sub Page_Load(ByVal sender As Object, _
    ByVal e As System.EventArgs) Handles Me.Load

    If Not IsPostBack Then
        ' Read the query string
        Dim queryClicks As Integer
        If Not (Request.QueryString("clicks") Is Nothing) Then
            queryClicks = Integer.Parse(Request.QueryString("clicks")) + 1
        Else
            queryClicks = 1
        End If

        ' Define the query string in the hyperlink
        HyperLink1.NavigateUrl += "?clicks=" + queryClicks.ToString

        Label1.Text = "Query clicks: " + queryClicks.ToString
    End If
End Sub
```

Sample of C# Code

```
protected void Page_Load(object sender, EventArgs e)
{
    if (!IsPostBack)
    {
        // Read the query string
        int queryClicks;
        if (Request.QueryString["clicks"] != null)
        {
            queryClicks = int.Parse(Request.QueryString["clicks"]) + 1;
        }
        else
        {
            queryClicks = 1;
        }

        // Define the query string in the hyperlink
        HyperLink1.NavigateUrl += "?clicks=" + queryClicks.ToString();

        Label1.Text = "Query clicks: " + queryClicks.ToString();
    }
}
```

3. Build the website. Visit the Default.aspx page and click the hyperlink to load Default2.aspx. Notice that the counter is incremented as values are passed back and forth between the pages by using the query string.

4. Click the hyperlink several times to switch between pages. Notice that the URL includes the number of clicks, and it is visible to the user.

5. In your browser address bar, change the number of clicks to **100**, and then press Enter. Notice that ASP.NET increments the number of clicks to 101.

6. In your browser address bar, change the number of clicks to **Hello**, and then press Enter. Notice that ASP.NET throws an unhandled exception, demonstrating that non-numeric values will never be successfully processed.

If the user bookmarks the link and returns to the page later, or even uses the same URL on a different computer, the current clicks counter is retained. The user can also modify the URL to cause the change to display an incorrect number of clicks. With query strings, you can bookmark or send webpages by email and have the state information stored in the URL. However, you must include the query string in any link the user might click on the page, or the information will be lost.

Lesson Summary

- Use client-side state management when scalability is the top priority. Use server-side state management when data must be better protected or when bandwidth is a significant issue.

- ASP.NET uses view state by default to store information about controls in a web form. You can add custom values to view state by accessing the ViewState collection.

- Use control state when a custom control cannot function with view state disabled.

- Use hidden fields to store data in forms when view state is disabled. Hidden field values are available to users as plaintext in the HTML.

- On the client, cookies store data that the web browser submits with every webpage request. Use cookies to track users across multiple webpages.

- Query strings store small pieces of information in a hyperlink's URL. Use query strings when you want state management data to be bookmarked, such as when displaying multiple pages of search results.

Lesson Review

You can use the following questions to test your knowledge of the information in Lesson 2, "Using Client-Side State Management." The questions are also available on the companion CD in a practice test, if you prefer to review them in electronic form.

> **NOTE** ANSWERS
>
> Answers to these questions and explanations of why each answer choice is correct or incorrect are located in the "Answers" section at the end of the book.

1. You need to store a user's user name and password as he or she navigates to different pages on your site, so that you can pass those credentials to the server. Which type of state management should you use?

   A. Client-side state management

   B. Server-side state management

2. You need to track nonconfidential user preferences when a user visits your site, to minimize additional load on your servers. You distribute requests among multiple web servers, each running a copy of your application. Which type of state management should you use?

   A. Client-side state management

   B. Server-side state management

3. You are creating an ASP.NET webpage that allows a user to browse information in a database. While the user accesses the page, you need to track search and sorting values. You do not need to store the information between visits to the webpage. Which type of client-side state management would meet your requirements and be the simplest to implement?

   A. View state

   B. Control state

   C. Hidden fields

   D. Cookies

   E. Query strings

4. You are creating an ASP.NET website with dozens of pages. You want to allow the user to set user preferences and have each page process the preference information. You want the preferences to be remembered between visits, even if the user closes the browser. Which type of client-side state management meets your requirements and is the simplest to implement?

   A. View state

   B. Control state

   C. Hidden fields

   D. Cookies

   E. Query strings

5. You are creating an ASP.NET web form that searches product inventory and displays items that match the user's criteria. You want users to be able to bookmark or send search results in email. Which type of client-side state management meets your requirements and is the simplest to implement?

   A. View state

   B. Control state

   C. Hidden fields

   D. Cookies

   E. Query strings

Lesson 3: Using Server-Side State Management

Often, it is just not practical to store your state on the client. Your state might be more involved and thus too large to be transmitted back and forth. Perhaps you have state that needs to be secured and even encrypted and should not be passed around a network. Additionally, you might have state that is not client specific but global to all the users of your application. In all of these scenarios, you still need to store state. If the client is not the right choice, you must look to the server for a state management solution.

ASP.NET provides two ways to store state on the server and thus share information between webpages without sending the data to the client. These two methods are referred to as *application state* and *session state*. Application state information is global to the application and is available to all pages, regardless of the identity of the user requesting the page. Session state is a user-specific state that is stored by the server. It is available only to pages accessed by a single user during a visit to your site. This lesson explores these two server-side state management techniques.

After this lesson, you will be able to:

- Use application state to store and share information that is accessible to all webpages in a website.
- Use session state to store user-specific information on the server and share that information across pages within your site.

Estimated lesson time: 30 minutes

Application State

Application state in ASP.NET is a global storage mechanism for state data that needs to be accessible to all pages in a web application. You can use application state to store information that must be maintained between requests for pages. Again, application state is optional; it is often not required. You should consider it a form of application-level caching of data that is too time consuming to obtain on each request.

You store application state in an instance of the HttpApplicationState class that is provided through the Page.Application property. This class represents a key–value dictionary, where each value is stored and accessed by its key (or name). You can add to and read from the application state from any page on the server. However, keep in mind that the state is global and accessible by all pages executing on your server.

After you have added application-specific information to the application state, the server manages it. This state stays on the server and is not sent to the client. Application state is a great place to store information that is not user specific but that is global in nature. Because it is stored in the application state, all pages can access data from a single location in memory, rather than keeping separate copies of the data or reading it every time a page is requested.

Data stored in the Application object is not permanent; it will be lost any time the application is restarted. In particular, IIS might restart your ASP.NET application at any point. In addition, the application is also restarted if the server is restarted. To work within this constraint, you should understand how to read, write, and sometimes persist application state by using the application events described later in this lesson.

Session State

Most web applications need to store user-specific data between individual requests. For example, if a user is going through a multistep process to register for your site, you might want to temporarily store this data between pages until the user has completed the process. Of course, Windows applications do this all the time. These applications run in a process that remains running on the client during a user session. Therefore, they can simply store this data in memory on the client. ASP.NET applications have a disadvantage: they share a server process and do not own a process on the client. Lesson 2 already explored how you can rely on the client machine to store this type of data between requests. However, this is often not practical. Often, the data is too large or requires additional security. In these cases, you can use the shared ASP.NET process to store this data in memory, on the server. This is referred to as *session state* in ASP.NET.

Session state can be considered similar to application state. The big difference is that session state is scoped to the current browser (or user) session and only available to that session (and not the entire application). Each user on your site then has his or her own isolated session state running in your application's process on the server. This state is available to different pages as the user makes subsequent requests to the server. Session state is, however, lost if the user ends his or her session (or times out). In most cases, however, session state is not needed between sessions. Data that is needed from one session to another should be persisted in a data store.

By default, ASP.NET applications store session state in memory on the server. However, they can be configured to store this information in client-side cookies, on another state server, or inside a Microsoft SQL Server database. These other options support centralized session management for web farm scenarios in which multiple web servers run a single website.

Reading and Writing Session State Data

You store user-specific session state in the Session object. This is an instance of the HttpSessionState class and represents a key–value dictionary collection. Items are added, updated, and read in a similar manner as working with any .NET dictionary collection.

The following code demonstrates how to write to and read from the Session object. In this example, each time a user requests a page the time is written into his or her Session instance. The last time the user requested the page for the session is also displayed in a label control. Although this code performs a similar function to the ViewState in Lesson 2, the Session object is available to any page the user visits.

Sample of Visual Basic Code

```vb
' Check if Session object exists, and display it if it does
If (Session("lastVisit") IsNot Nothing) Then
    Label1.Text = Session("lastVisit").ToString()
Else
    Label1.Text = "Session does not have last visit information."
End If


' Define the Session object for the next page view
Session("lastVisit") = DateTime.Now
```

Sample of C# Code

```csharp
// Check if Session object exists, and display it if it does
if (Session["lastVisit"] != null)
{
    Label1.Text = ((DateTime)Session["lastVisit"]).ToString();
}
else
{
    Label1.Text = "Session does not have last visit information.";
}
// Define the Session object for the next page view
Session["lastVisit"] = DateTime.Now;
```

> **NOTE SESSION STATE AND COOKIES**
>
> If the user's browser allows cookies, ASP.NET writes a cookie to the client's computer to track the session. This cookie is called ASP.NET_SessionId and contains a random 24-byte value. Requests submit this cookie from the browser, and ASP.NET maps the cookie's value to the session on the server. Situations in which cookies are disallowed are addressed in the upcoming "Configuring Cookieless Session State" section.

Disabling Session State

If you don't use session state, you can improve performance by disabling it for the entire application. You do so by setting the sessionState mode property to Off in the Web.config file. The following shows an example.

```xml
<configuration>
  <system.web>
    <sessionState mode="off"/>
  </system.web>
</configuration>
```

You can also disable session state for a single page of an application by setting the EnableSessionState page directive to false. You can also set the EnableSessionState page directive to ReadOnly to provide read-only access to session variables for the page. The following code sample shows how to set a page directive to disable session state for a single page.

```
<%@ Page Language="C#" AutoEventWireup="true" CodeFile="Default.aspx.cs"
  Inherits="_Default" EnableSessionState = "False"%>
```

> **NOTE STORING VALUES IN SESSION STATE**
>
> Values stored in Session must be serializable.

Configuring Cookieless Session State

By default, session state uses cookies to track user sessions. This is the best choice for the vast majority of applications. All modern web browsers support cookies. However, users can turn them off. Therefore, ASP.NET allows you to enable cookieless session state.

Without cookies, ASP.NET tracks sessions by using the URL, embedding the session ID in the URL after the application name and before any remaining file or virtual directory identifier. For example, the following URL has been modified by ASP.NET to include the unique session ID lit3py55t21z5v55vlm25s55.

```
http://www.example.com/s(lit3py55t21z5v55vlm25s55)/orderform.aspx
```

You enable cookieless sessions through the Web.config file. Set the cookieless attribute of the sessionState element to true. The following example shows a Web.config file that configures an ASP.NET application to use cookieless sessions.

```
<configuration>
  <system.web>
    <sessionState cookieless="true"
      regenerateExpiredSessionId="true" />
  </system.web>
</configuration>
```

Responding to Session Events

Often you will want code to run when a user initiates a session or when a session is terminated. For example, you might want to initialize key variables when a session starts, or you might want to do some user-specific logging.

You can trap session events by using the Global.asax file (as discussed in the previous section). There are two special events that ASP.NET provides for responding to session activities:

- **Session_Start** Raised when a new user requests a page on your site and thus begins a new session. This is a good place to initialize session variables.
- **Session_End** Raised when a session is abandoned or expires. This event can be used to log information or free per-session resources.

Again, to implement these events, you use the Global.asax file as discussed in Lesson 1, in "Responding to Application Events."

Choosing a Session State Mode

Memory on the server is not always the best or most scalable place to store session state. For example, you might have a load-balanced server farm that routes requests between web servers based on server load. In this case, you cannot guarantee that a user will always be routed to the same server, and thus you might lose his or her session information. One solution to this issue is a smarter load balancer that allows for "sticky" sessions that assign users to servers and keep them there throughout a session. However, this can also be problematic if a server fails or if you need to take one down.

Fortunately, ASP.NET provides a few different session management modes for your application. These modes are configurable. You can, for example, start out by using an in-memory (InProc) mode and, as your site grows, switch session state to a database or a state server. ASP.NET provides the following session storage options:

- **InProc**   Stores session state in memory on the web server. This is the default mode. It offers much better performance than using the ASP.NET State Service or storing state information in a database server. However, it is limited in load-balanced scenarios where you might make a performance trade-off to increase scalability. The InProc mode is a good choice for simple applications. However, applications that use multiple web servers or that persist session data between application restarts should consider using the StateServer or SQLServer modes.

- **StateServer**   Stores session state in a service called the ASP.NET State Service. This ensures that session state is preserved if the web application is restarted and also makes session state available to multiple web servers in a web farm. ASP.NET State Service is included with any computer set up to run ASP.NET web applications; however, the service is set up to start manually by default. Therefore, when configuring the ASP.NET State Service, you must set the startup type to Automatic.

- **SQLServer**   Stores session state in a SQL Server database. This ensures that session state is preserved if the web application is restarted and also makes session state available to multiple servers in a web farm. On identical hardware, the ASP.NET State Service outperforms SQLServer. However, a SQL Server database offers more robust data integrity and reporting capabilities. In addition, many sites run their SQL Server databases on powerful hardware. You will want to performance-test for your scenario.

- **Custom**   Enables you to specify a custom session state storage provider. You also need to implement (code) the custom storage provider.

- **Off**   Disables session state. You should disable session state if you are not using it, to improve performance.

REAL WORLD

Tony Northrup

For the exam, you must understand every different form of state management, including session state.

In the real world, developers use two technologies for state in large-scale applications: cookies and databases. When a user visits a site, the site gives that user a permanent cookie that uniquely identifies the user. Cookies are also used to store preference choices (such as the number of search results per page) that the user makes without logging in. Everything else is stored in a database. With each page request, the web server uses the cookie to look up the user's information in the database, including shopping cart and account information. If users are willing, have them create logons so that you can re-assign them the same cookies if they log on from a different computer.

Why aren't Application and Session state as useful as they sound? The problem is that either can disappear at any point. You could write code that responds to the Application.End and Session.End events to save important data to a database, and then handle Application.Start and Session.Start to read it back in. However, ASP.NET can't call Application.End and Session.End if an application or server shuts down unexpectedly (and in the real world, they shut down regularly). Additionally, users often walk away from the computer for longer than your Session time-out. They expect their shopping carts to still be there when they return in an hour, a day, or a week—but Session state just isn't designed for long-term data storage.

Configuring Session State Modes

You can specify which mode you want ASP.NET session state to use by assigning SessionStateMode enumeration values to the mode attribute of the sessionState element in your application's Web.config file. Modes other than InProc and Off require additional parameters, such as connection-string values. You can examine the currently set session state by accessing the value of the System.Web.SessionState.HttpSessionState.Mode property in code.

The following example shows settings in a Web.config file that cause the session state to be stored in a SQL Server database identified by the specified connection string.

```
<configuration>
  <system.web>
    <sessionState
        mode="SQLServer"
        cookieless="true"
        regenerateExpiredSessionId="true"
        timeout="30"
        sqlConnectionString="Data Source=MySqlServer;Integrated Security=SSPI;"
        compressionEnabled="true"
        stateNetworkTimeout="30"/>
  </system.web>
</configuration>
```

Configuring session state for an application is typically the responsibility of the systems administrators who are responsible for hosting and supporting your application. For example, a systems administrator might initially configure a web application on a single server by using the InProc mode. Later, if the server gets too busy or requires redundancy, the systems administrator might add a second web server and configure an ASP.NET state service on a separate server. The administrator would then modify the Web.config file to use the StateServer mode. Fortunately, the session state mode is transparent to your application, so you won't need to change your code.

ASP.NET 4 introduces the compressionEnabled attribute, as demonstrated in the previous code sample. When you enable compression, ASP.NET uses the GZip algorithm to reduce the size of session state data before storing it. It will only be useful if session state is large, and it should only be used on web servers that can handle a small amount of additional processor utilization, because compression will consume a few additional processor cycles.

 Quick Check

1. Which typically consumes more server memory: application state or session state?

2. Which might not work if a user has disabled cookies in his or her web browser: application state or session state?

Quick Check Answers

1. Session state tends to use much more memory than application state because application state is shared among users, whereas session state exists on a per-user basis.

2. Session state, by default, won't work if a web browser that supports cookies has cookies disabled. Application state is not user-specific, though, and does not need to be tracked in cookies. Therefore, application state works regardless of the cookies setting.

In this practice, you use different server-side state management techniques to track the number of pages a user has opened.

> **ON THE COMPANION MEDIA**
>
> If you encounter a problem completing an exercise, you can find the completed projects in the samples installed from this book's companion CD. For more information about the project files and other content on the CD, see "Using the Companion Media" in this book's Introduction.

EXERCISE 1   Storing Data in the Application Object

In this exercise, you create two pages that link to one another. Each time a user accesses the site, the application variable will be incremented and displayed on the page. This demonstrates how to add custom values to the Application object and how to use the Global.asax file.

1. Open Visual Studio and create a new ASP.NET website. Name the site **ServerState**. Select either C# or Visual Basic as your programming language for the site.

2. Add a new page to the site and name this page **Default2.aspx**.

3. Open the Default.aspx page in Source view.

   a. Add the text Default Page 1 to the page.

   b. Add a label to the page and name it **Label1**.

   c. Also add a HyperLink control to the page and name it **HyperLink1**.

   d. Set the HyperLink1.NavigateUrl property to Default2.aspx.

4. Open Default2.aspx in Source view.

   a. Add the text Default Page 2 to the page.

   b. Add a label to the page and name it **Label1**.

   c. Also add a HyperLink control to the page and name it **HyperLink1**.

   d. Set the HyperLink1.NavigateUrl property to Default.aspx.

5. Open then Global.asax file. Add code to the Application_Start method to initialize an Application variable named *clicks* as follows.

   Sample of Visual Basic Code
   ```
   Sub Application_Start(ByVal sender As Object, ByVal e As EventArgs)
       Application("clicks") = 0
   End Sub
   ```

   Sample of C# Code
   ```
   void Application_Start(object sender, EventArgs e)
   {
       Application["clicks"] = 0;
   }
   ```

6. In the Page_Load method for both Default.aspx and Default2.aspx, add code to increment the number of clicks in the Application object. Don't forget to lock the application object before updating the value. Then add code to display the value in LabelApplicationClicks. The following code demonstrates this.

Sample of Visual Basic Code

```
Protected Sub Page_Load(ByVal sender As Object, _
  ByVal e As System.EventArgs) Handles Me.Load

    Application.Lock()
    Application("clicks") = CInt(Application("clicks")) + 1
    Application.UnLock()

    Label1.Text = String.Format("Application clicks: {0}",
Application("clicks").ToString())
End Sub
```

Sample of C# Code

```
protected void Page_Load(object sender, EventArgs e)
{
    Application.Lock();
    Application["clicks"] = ((int)Application["clicks"]) + 1;
    Application.UnLock();

    Label1.Text = string.Format("Application clicks: {0}",
Application["clicks"].ToString());
}
```

7. Build your website and visit the Default.aspx page. Click the hyperlink several times to switch between pages and verify that the click counter increments.

8. As an optional step, open the same page from a different browser window. If you do, you will notice that the click count includes the clicks you made from the first browser, because the Application object is shared among all user sessions.

9. Restart the web application and visit the same page again. Notice that the click count is reset; the Application object is not persisted between application restarts.

EXERCISE 2   Storing Data in the Session Object

In this exercise, you explore the use of the Session object.

1. Continue editing the project you created in the previous exercise. Alternatively, you can open the completed Lesson 3, Exercise 1 project in the samples installed from the CD.

2. Open the Global.asax file. Add code to the Session_Start method to initialize a session variable named *session_clicks*. This variable should be set to zero when the session is first initiated. The following shows an example.

Sample of Visual Basic Code

```
Sub Session_Start(ByVal sender As Object, ByVal e As EventArgs)
    Session("session_clicks") = 0
End Sub
```

Sample of C# Code

```csharp
void Session_Start(object sender, EventArgs e)
{
    Session["session_clicks"] = 0;
}
```

3. Open Default.aspx in Source view. Add a new Label control under the existing one. Name this control **Label2**. Do the same for Default2.aspx.

4. In the Page_Load method for both Default.aspx and Default2.aspx, add code to increment the number of clicks for the user's session. Also, add code to display the value in Label2. The following code shows how your Page_Load event should now look (the new code is shown in bold).

Sample of Visual Basic Code

```vb
Protected Sub Page_Load(ByVal sender As Object, _
  ByVal e As System.EventArgs) Handles Me.Load

    Application.Lock()
    Application("clicks") = CInt(Application("clicks")) + 1
    Application.UnLock()

    Label1.Text = String.Format("Application clicks: {0}", _
Application("clicks").ToString())

    Session("session_clicks") = CInt(Session("session_clicks")) + 1
    Label2.Text = String.Format("Session clicks: {0}", _Session("session_
clicks").ToString())

End Sub
```

Sample of C# Code

```csharp
protected void Page_Load(object sender, EventArgs e)
{
    Application.Lock();
    Application["clicks"] = ((int)Application["clicks"]) + 1;
    Application.UnLock();

    Label1.Text = string.Format("Application clicks: {0}",
Application["clicks"].ToString());

    Session["session_clicks"] = (int)Session["session_clicks"] + 1;

    Label2.Text = string.Format("Session clicks: {0}", Session["session_
clicks"].ToString());
}
```

5. Build your website and visit the Default.aspx page. Click the hyperlink several times to switch between pages and verify that both the Application and Session click counters increment.

6. From a different browser, open the same page. Notice that the Application click count includes the clicks you made from the first browser, because the Application object is shared among all user sessions. However, the Session click counter includes only clicks made from one browser.

7. Restart your web server. If you are running locally, you can right-click the server instance in the system tray and choose Stop. If you are running in IIS, open the IIS Manager and start and stop the server. Now visit the same page again. Notice that both click counts are reset; the Application and Session objects are not persisted between application restarts.

Lesson Summary

- You can use the Application collection to store information that is accessible from all webpages but is not user specific. To initialize Application variables, respond to the Application_Start event in your Global.asax file.

- You can use the Session collection to store user-specific information that is accessible from all webpages. To initialize Session variables, respond to the Session_Start event in your Global.asax file. You can store session information in the server's memory by using the InProc session state mode, store it in an ASP.NET State Service server by using the StateServer mode, store it in a database by using the SQLServer mode, implement your own custom session state storage by using the Custom mode, or turn session state off completely.

Lesson Review

You can use the following questions to test your knowledge of the information in Lesson 3, "Using Server-Side State Management." The questions are also available on the companion CD in a practice test, if you prefer to review them in electronic form.

> **NOTE** ANSWERS
>
> Answers to these questions and explanations of why each answer is correct or incorrect are located in the "Answers" section at the end of the book.

1. You need to store state data that is accessible to any user who connects to your web application and ensure that it stays in memory. Which collection object should you use?

    A. Session

    B. Application

    C. Cookies

    D. ViewState

2. You need to store a value indicating whether a user has been authenticated for your site. This value needs to be available and checked on every user request. Which object should you use?

   A. Session

   B. Application

   C. Cookies

   D. ViewState

3. Your application is being deployed in a load-balanced web farm. The load balancer is not set up for user server affinity. Rather, it routes requests to servers based on their load. Your application uses session state. How should you configure the SessionState mode attribute? (Choose all that apply.)

   A. StateServer

   B. InProc

   C. Off

   D. SqlServer

Case Scenarios

In the following case scenarios, you apply what you've learned about how to implement and apply ASP.NET state management. If you have difficulty completing this work, review the material in this chapter before beginning the next chapter. You can find answers to these questions in the "Answers" section at the end of this book.

Case Scenario 1: Selecting the Proper Events to Use

You are an application developer for Fabrikam, Inc. You are creating an application that allows managers within your company to create custom forms that their employees can use for data entry.

When a user requests a custom form, your application needs to query a database to determine the types and locations of different controls. Your application then needs to create the controls for your page dynamically, based on that information.

Answer the following questions for your manager:

1. In what event handler should you place code to dynamically create the controls? Why?

2. Where should you place code to set properties of the controls? Why?

Case Scenario 2: Remembering User Credentials

You are an application developer for Contoso, Ltd., a business-to-business retailer. You are writing an e-commerce web application that retrieves inventory and customer data from a back-end database server. Recently, your marketing department has received requests from customers to provide enhanced account-management capabilities. Your manager asks you to interview key people and then come to his office to answer his questions about your design choices.

Interviews

Following is a list of company personnel you interviewed and their statements:

- **Marketing manager** "We recently had a session with our most important customers to identify potential areas of improvement. One of the comments that we heard frequently was that they want a way to log on to our website and view past order information. I know I hate having to log on to websites every time I visit the webpage, so if we could remember their logon information, I think the customers would be happier."

- **Development manager** "This seems like a fair request; however, we need to keep security in mind. Don't do anything that would allow an attacker to steal a user's session and view his or her orders."

Questions

Answer the following questions for your manager.

1. What state management mechanism would you use to remember a user's logon credentials?

2. How can you reduce the risk of a user's credentials being stolen?

3. How should you store information about previous orders?

Case Scenario 3: Analyzing Information for Individual Users and for All Users

You are an application developer working for Fabrikam, Inc., a consumer web-based magazine. Recently, your marketing department personnel requested the ability to see a snapshot of what users are doing on the website in near–real time. Additionally, they would like to display advertisements to those users based on the content viewed in the current session. Finally, they would like the ability to analyze multiple different articles that users viewed during a given visit.

You discuss the needs with the marketing manager, who says, "We have great tools for analyzing website logs, but we often want to know what's happening on the site in real time so that we can make instant decisions. For example, if we post a new article, we'd like to see how many users are currently viewing that page. Also, I think we can better cater our advertisements to customer needs by analyzing a user's path through our website. Is there any way to track what a user does during a visit to our site?"

Answer the following questions for your manager:

1. How can you present data for all users, to be analyzed by the marketing department?

2. How can you analyze and track an individual user through the site?

Suggested Practices

To help you master the ASP.NET state management exam objectives presented in this chapter, complete the following tasks.

Respond to Application and Session Events

For this task, you should complete Practices 1 and 2 to understand how to respond to application and session events. If you are interested in the real-world behavior of these events, complete Practice 3 as well.

- **Practice 1** Using a web application that you previously developed, add code to initialize variables in the Application.Start event. Add code to release resources in the Application.End event.

- **Practice 2** Using a web application that you previously developed, add code to initialize variables in the Session.Start event. Add code to release resources in the Session.End event.

- **Practice 3** Using a publically available ASP.NET website, add code to the Application.Start, Application.End, Session.Start, and Session.End events that logs the occurrence of each. Leave the application running for several days, and then examine the logs to determine how frequently Application.End and Session.End failed to run for the corresponding Application.Start and Session.Start.

Create Event Handlers for Pages and Controls

For this task, you should complete Practices 1 and 2 to get a better understanding of how to handle page and control events.

- **Practice 1** Explore the non-default events that are available in each control. Experiment by enabling AutoPostBack on controls that have it disabled by default.

- **Practice 2** With a master page assigned, attempt to dynamically add a TextBox and a Button control to a content page in the Page.PreInit event handler. Note the exception that occurs. Move the code to the Page.Render event handler, and notice that the application runs, but input in the TextBox control is not available when you click the button, because view state does not work. Move the code to the Page.Init event handler, and verify that the controls work properly. Finally, move the code to the Page.Load event handler.

Manage State by Using Client-Based State Management Options

For this task, you should complete Practice 1 to get a better understanding of how to implement control state. Complete Practices 2 and 3 to explore how real-world websites use cookies.

- **Practice 1** Create a custom control and implement control state management.

- **Practice 2** View your Temporary Internet Files folder (typically located in C:\Users \<*username*>\AppData\Local\Microsoft\Windows\Temporary Internet Files). Examine cookies that websites have stored on your computer and open the files in a text editor to view the information they contain.

- **Practice 3** Disable cookies in your web browser. Visit several of your favorite websites to determine whether the website behavior has changed.

Manage State by Using Server-Based State Management Options

For this task, you should complete all of Practice 1 to get experience using the Application objects. Complete Practices 2 and 3 to gain experience working with user sessions.

- **Practice 1** Using a web application that you previously developed, add real-time application activity analysis functionality described in Case Scenario 2 so that you can open a webpage and view which pages users are currently viewing.

- **Practice 2** Using a web application that you previously developed, enable website personalization by using the Session object. Allow a user to set a preference, such as background color, and apply that preference to any page the user might view.

- **Practice 3** Disable cookies in your web browser and visit the web application you created in Practice 2. Attempt to set a preference and study how the application responds. Think about how an application might determine whether a browser supports sessions and what to do if the browser does not support sessions.

Maintain State by Using Database Technology

For this task, you should complete Practices 1 and 2 to understand how to configure state management to function in environments with multiple web servers hosting a single site.

- **Practice 1** Configure a web application to use a SQL state server.

- **Practice 2** Configure a web application to use the ASP.NET State Service.

Take a Practice Test

The practice tests on this book's companion CD offer many options. For example, you can test yourself on just the lesson review questions in this chapter, or you can test yourself on all the 70-515 certification exam objectives. You can set up the test so it closely simulates the experience of taking a certification exam, or you can set it up in study mode so you can look at the correct answers and explanations after you answer each question.

> **MORE INFO   PRACTICE TESTS**
>
> For details about all the practice test options available, see the "How to Use the Practice Tests" section in this book's Introduction.

CHAPTER 4

Using Server Controls

Server controls, such as Label, TextBox, and Button, are a fundamental concept of Microsoft ASP.NET development. In previous chapters, you created server controls (both by using the designer and at run time), modified their properties, and responded to events such as Button.Click.

In this chapter, you will more thoroughly explore server controls that you have already worked with, and you will work with server controls that have not previously been introduced, including the Table, Image, Calendar, and Wizard controls.

> **NOTE CONTROL COVERAGE**
>
> There are many controls in ASP.NET. This chapter covers a large sample of the standard controls. If you are looking for information on a specific control and cannot find it here, please look in this book's index, because controls such as Validation, Data, Asynchronous JavaScript and XML (AJAX), and others are covered in their respective chapters. Additionally, third-party developers have created hundreds of specialized controls, which you can find by searching the Internet.

Exam objectives in this chapter:

- Developing and Using Web Forms Controls
    - Implement server controls.
    - Manipulate user interface controls from code-behind.

Lessons in this chapter:

Before You Begin

To complete the lessons in the chapter, you should be familiar with developing applications with Microsoft Visual Studio by using Microsoft Visual Basic or Microsoft Visual C#. In addition, you should be comfortable with all of the following:

- The Visual Studio 2010 Integrated Development Environment (IDE)
- Hypertext Markup Language (HTML) and client-side scripting
- Creating a new website
- Adding web server controls to a webpage

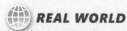

REAL WORLD

Tony Northrup

Looking back through my web developer career, I realize that I should have used web server controls more often. See, I'm an old-school developer, back from the days when you had to produce raw HTML as if you were writing to a console. I never really broke out of that habit, and I still regularly author my pages by using raw HTML instead of using an appropriate web server control.

This decision, made out of stubbornness, has caused me to waste many hours of development time maintaining my own code. If I had used a Label control instead of a Literal control with raw HTML, I could take advantage of the improvements to ASP.NET simply by upgrading the Microsoft .NET Framework. Now, when I update my existing web applications to take advantage of the newest HTML standards and guidelines, I'll have to dig through raw HTML. Debugging those changes will be difficult, too, because I won't have the .NET Framework making sure I close all my tags properly.

Learn from my mistake. Master the web server controls built into ASP.NET 4. If you need something more specific (such as a control that allows you to display a JavaScript advertisement), find one that another developer has created, or create one yourself, as described in Chapter 7, "Creating Custom Web Controls."

Lesson 1: Exploring Common Server Controls

ASP.NET includes many web server controls. In fact, with each new release, the number, power, and flexibility of these controls all increase. The broad range of controls available gives developers the tools they need to create applications that provide great user experiences. Not all of the controls will be covered in this book. However, the .NET Framework object model ensures that controls share a similar programming model. Thus, the experience this chapter gives you with a small sampling of the total will give you the knowledge you need to work with all of them.

This lesson covers many of the basic, standard web server controls you will use for your applications. Lesson 2 covers some of the more advanced or specialized controls in ASP.NET. Later chapters cover even more specialized controls on topics such as data-bound controls, validation, navigation, AJAX, site membership, and more.

After this lesson, you will be able to:

- Use the following web server controls:
    - Label
    - Literal
    - TextBox
    - CheckBox
    - RadioButton
    - DropDownList
    - ListBox
    - Button
- Use HTML controls when you do not need the advanced features of web server controls.

Estimated lesson time: 45 minutes

Web Server Controls

ASP.NET provides programmers with a set of web server controls for creating webpages. These controls provide more functionality and a more consistent programming model than HTML server controls. Web server controls are based on .NET Framework classes, typically inherited from the WebControl class. Unlike HTML controls, web server controls are not part of the HTML standard. However, ASP.NET renders web server controls as standardized HTML. In other words, if you use the Image web server control, ASP.NET renders it using the <img> HTML markup tag.

A web server control is able to provide more functionality than an HTML control because it is not tied to a single HTML tag element. Instead, web server controls typically render many HTML tags and might also include client-side JavaScript code. They also have the ability to detect the web browser's capabilities and render the appropriate HTML based on those capabilities. This allows ASP.NET web server controls to use a specific browser to its fullest potential. The programmer is also relieved from dealing with the actual HTML and instead works with the web server control to define the appropriate functionality for the page. This allows developers to use controls that would otherwise require very complex HTML, such as the Calendar, Wizard, Login, and GridView controls.

Adding Web Server Controls by Using Source View

In previous chapters, you added web server controls by dragging them from the Toolbox in the Visual Studio designer. You can also add them to a webpage by using Source view:

1. Open the webpage in Visual Studio.

2. Click the Source tab at the bottom of the webpage.

3. In the Source view of the webpage, type the web server control element and its attributes (see Figure 4-1). Alternatively, you can drag a control from the Toolbox directly into the page source.

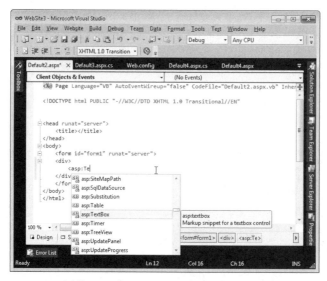

FIGURE 4-1 Adding a web server control to a page in Source view.

Note that web server controls must be located within an HTML form element that has the runat="server" attribute defined.

Setting Web Server Control Properties

Most web server controls inherit from the WebControl class. All web server controls must contain a unique (at the page level) ID attribute value to provide a way to programmatically reference the control. The other attributes and properties of a web server control are used to control the look and behavior of the control. Table 4-1 lists the frequently used attributes and properties that all web server controls have in common.

TABLE 4-1 Common Web Server Control Properties

PROPERTY	DESCRIPTION
AccessKey	The keyboard shortcut key. AccessKey can specify a single letter or number that the user can press while holding down Alt. For example, specify Q if you want the user to press Alt+Q to access the control.
BackColor	The background color of the control, which can be set by using standard HTML color identifiers, such as red or blue, or RGB values expressed in hexadecimal format (#ffffff).
BorderColor	The border color of the control, which can be set by using standard HTML color identifiers, such as black or red, or RGB values expressed in hexadecimal format (#ffffff).
BorderWidth	The width of the control's border in pixels. BorderWidth is not fully supported for all controls in browsers earlier than Windows Internet Explorer 4.0.
BorderStyle	The border style, if there is any. Possible values are NotSet, None, Dotted, Dashed, Solid, Double, Groove, Ridge, Inset, and Outset.
CssClass	The cascading style sheets class to assign to the control.
Style	A list of all cascading style sheet properties that are applied to the specified HTML server control.
Enabled	An attribute that disables the control when set to false. This dims the control and makes it inactive. It does not hide the control.
EnableTheming	The default is true, which enables themes for this control.
EnableViewState	The default is true, which enables view state persistence for the control.
Font	An attribute that contains subproperties that you can declare by using the property-subproperty syntax in the opening tag of the web server control element. For example, you can make a web server control's text italic by including the Font-Italic attribute in its opening tag.
ForeColor	The foreground color of the control. ForeColor is not fully supported for all controls in browsers earlier than Internet Explorer 4.0.
Height	The control's height. The Height property is not fully supported for all controls in browsers earlier than Internet Explorer 4.0.

(continued)

PROPERTY	DESCRIPTION
SkinID	The skin to apply to the control.
TabIndex	The control's position in the tab order. If this property is not set, the control's position index is 0. Controls with the same tab index can be tabbed according to the order in which they are declared in the webpage. This feature was introduced in Internet Explorer 4.0.
ToolTip	The text that appears when the user points to a control. The ToolTip property does not work in all browsers.
Width	The width of the control. The possible units are Pixel, Point, Pica, Inch, Mm, Cm, Percentage, Em, and Ex. The default unit is pixels.

In practice, you should define appearance attributes—such as the background color, border width, and font—in a style sheet, rather than on individual controls. For example, if you set the font individually for every control and later decide to use Times New Roman instead of Arial, you would need to update the properties of every control in your application. If you instead use a style sheet, you can update the appearance of all controls from within a single file. For more information about style sheets, refer to Chapter 2, "Using Master Pages, Themes, and Caching."

You can set the values of the of web server control properties by setting their attributes in Source view, by setting their properties in Design view, or by setting their properties programmatically in code. This section examines all three methods.

Upgrading from Earlier Versions of ASP.NET

ASP.NET 4 includes many improvements to the HTML rendering engine for web server controls to comply with the latest HTML standards. If you have an existing application written for ASP.NET 3.5 or earlier, and you upgrade it to ASP.NET 4, you will probably never notice a difference in your web browser.

If you do experience a problem with how controls render in ASP.NET 4, you can revert to the ASP.NET 3.5 rendering engine by defining the controlRenderingCompatibilityVersion property of the <pages> element in your Web.config file to 3.5. The following code sample demonstrates this.

```
<system.web>
  <pages controlRenderingCompatibilityVersion="3.5"/>
</system.web>
```

Visual Studio automatically adds this element to the Web.config file of any ASP.NET application it upgrades to ASP.NET 4. To make sure you take advantage of the rendering improvements in ASP.NET 4, you should set the value to 4.0 (or simply remove it) and test the application thoroughly.

If you need to programmatically determine whether a specific control is rendered with the ASP.NET 3.5 or ASP.NET 4 engine, check the Control.RenderingCompatibility property. Most web server controls derive from Control, so they make this read-only property available.

Some controls require you to turn on more advanced, cascading style sheet–friendly rendering: FormView, Login, PasswordRecovery, and ChangePassword. By default, ASP.NET renders these controls inside a <table> HTML tag to provide formatting. Typically, this works well, but using tables for formatting is considered an outdated technique. If you would prefer to use cascading style sheets to format the output from these controls, set the RenderOuterTable property to false.

The Label Control

The Label control displays text at a specific location on a webpage by using the properties that the control has been assigned. Use the Label control when you need to use server-side code to change the label's text or another one of its properties. If you simply need to display static text, do not use the Label control, because it requires processing on the server and increases the amount of data sent back and forth between the server and client. Instead, define your static text by using standard HTML.

In forms, labels are used as captions for user input controls. For example, you might create a Label control and set Label.Text to "Username: ". You could then place a TextBox control to the right of the Label control so that the user would know to enter his or her user name in the text box.

Because Label controls are often associated with user input controls, you can link keyboard shortcuts assigned to label controls to user input controls. In this way, if a user presses a keyboard shortcut (such as Alt+T), the web browser will set the focus to the user input control associated with the Label control. Keyboard shortcuts are useful for speeding user input when users are competent with a keyboard. More importantly, they're required for accessibility reasons; not all users are able to use a mouse to select controls.

To associate a Label control with a user input control and allow the user to access the user input control with a keyboard shortcut, follow these steps:

1. Add a Label control and a user input control, such as a TextBox, CheckBox, or ListBox control.

2. Set the Label.AccessKey property to the keyboard shortcut.

3. Set the Label.Text property, and underline the key used as the keyboard shortcut. For example, if the label should have Username on it and the keyboard shortcut is Alt+U, you would set Label.Text to "<u>U</u>sername". The HTML markup for underlining text is <u>. The browser will render the Label as "Username", and users familiar with keyboard shortcuts will recognize the underline convention that indicates the associated keyboard shortcut.

4. Set the Label.AssociatedControlID property to the ID of the input control to set focus to it when the user presses the keyboard shortcut.

Figure 4-2 shows how to associate user name and password Label controls with TextBox controls. Notice that Visual Studio automatically converts the <u> HTML markup tag to <u>. This process is known as *HTML character entity reference replacement* and is performed so that the angle brackets are not confused with actual HTML tags.

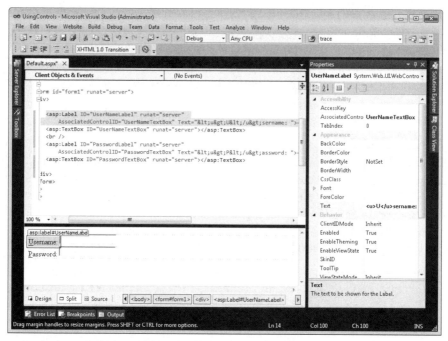

FIGURE 4-2 Associating a Label control with a TextBox control.

You can set the value of the label's Text property in two ways. As shown above, you can define the Text property. Alternatively, you can nest text between the opening and closing elements as follows.

```
<asp:Label ID="UsernameLabel" runat="server" >Username: </asp:Label>
```

You can also set the value of the Text property from code. If you change the Text property in code, the new value will override what is set on the page inside the designer. The following shows an example of this code.

Sample of Visual Basic Code

```
Label1.Text = "Some Text"
```

Sample of C# Code

```
Label1.Text = "Some Text";
```

The Literal Control

Use the Literal control when you want to add raw HTML to a page, without requiring ASP.NET to provide any additional processing. At first glance, the Literal control seems very similar to the Label control. However, Literal does not inherit from WebControl, as Label does. Additionally, the Literal control does not add any HTML elements to the webpage, whereas the Label is rendered as a <span> tag. This means that the Literal control does not have a style property, and you therefore cannot apply styles to its content.

The Literal control is useful when you need to add text to the output of the page dynamically (from the server) but do not want to use a Label. If your text is static, you can simply add it to the markup of the page (you do not need a Label or a Literal control). The Literal control contains the Mode property, which is used to specify any particular handling of the content of the Text property. The modes available and their descriptions are shown in Table 4-2.

TABLE 4-2 The Literal Control's Mode Properties

MODE	DESCRIPTION
PassThrough	The Text content is rendered as is. This includes HTML markup and script. These items are output to the page and processed by the browser as HTML and script, respectively.
Encode	The Text content is HTML encoded; that is, any HTML markup or script is actually treated like text and not HTML or script. Select this mode if you might display user input.
Transform	The Text content is converted to match the markup language of the requesting browser, such as HTML, Extensible Hypertext Markup Language (XHTML), Wireless Markup Language (WML), or Compact Hypertext Markup Language (cHTML). If the markup language is HTML or XHTML, the content is passed through to the browser. For other markup languages, invalid tags are removed.

As an example, consider a webpage with three Literal controls, one for each Mode property setting. Suppose the following code is added to the code-behind page to demonstrate the use of the Literal control and the effect of the Mode property.

Sample of Visual Basic Code

```
Protected Sub Page_Load(ByVal sender As Object, _
  ByVal e As System.EventArgs) Handles Me.Load

  Literal1.Text = "This is an <font size=7>example</font> &_
    <script>alert(""Hi from Literal1"");</script>"
  Literal2.Text = "This is an <font size=7>example</font> &_
    <script>alert(""Hi from Literal2"");</script>"
  Literal3.Text = "This is an <font size=7>example</font> &_
    <script>alert(""Hi from Literal3"");</script>"
  Literal1.Mode = LiteralMode.Encode
```

```
    Literal2.Mode = LiteralMode.PassThrough
    Literal3.Mode = LiteralMode.Transform
End Sub
```

Sample of C# Code

```csharp
protected void Page_Load(object sender, EventArgs e)
{
    Literal1.Text =@"This is an <font size=7>example</font>"+
      @"<script>alert(""Hi from Literal1"");</script>";
    Literal2.Text =@"This is an <font size=7>example</font>"+
      @"<script>alert(""Hi from Literal2"");</script>";
    Literal3.Text =@"This is an <font size=7>example</font>"+
      @"<script>alert(""Hi from Literal3"");</script>";
    Literal1.Mode = LiteralMode.Encode;
    Literal2.Mode = LiteralMode.PassThrough;
    Literal3.Mode = LiteralMode.Transform;
}
```

Figure 4-3 shows the rendered output of the Literal control when the webpage is displayed. The alert message was displayed twice: once for Literal2, which uses the PassThrough mode, and once for Literal3, which uses the Transform mode. Note that this is a security risk if you are setting the Text property of the Literal control dynamically from user input. However, the encoded version of the Literal control encodes the HTML and script and displays it to the browser window.

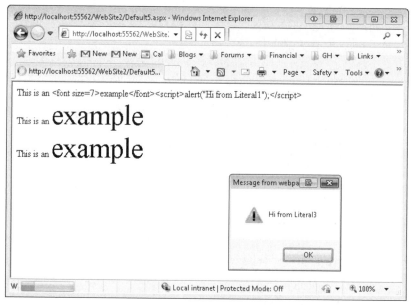

FIGURE 4-3 Literal controls rendered by using different Mode settings.

The TextBox Control

The TextBox control is used to collect information from a user. The control's Text property gets or sets the contents of the TextBox control. As with the Label control, you can set the Text property as an attribute, in between the opening and closing of the tag, or from code.

The TextBox control contains a TextMode property that you can set to SingleLine (the default), MultiLine, or Password. The SingleLine value allows the user to enter a single line of text. The Password value creates a single-line text box that masks the values entered by the user as they are entered. The MultiLine value allows the user to enter multiple lines of text. You use this value in conjunction with the Columns and Rows properties to provide a large TextBox for the user to enter a large amount of data. The Columns property sets the width of the TextBox in terms of the number of characters on a line. The Rows property sets the maximum height of a multiline TextBox in terms of the number of lines a user should be able to see at one time. Figure 4-4 shows an example of defining a multiline TextBox control by using the Properties window in Visual Studio.

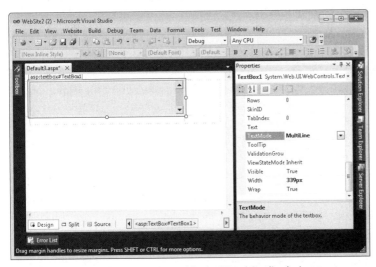

FIGURE 4-4 A multiline TextBox control in the Visual Studio designer.

The TextBox control also has a MaxLength property that limits the number of characters that can be entered by a user. This helps constrain the user's entry to what you can store in a database field. The Wrap property (whose default value is true) automatically continues the text on the next line when the end of the TextBox width is reached, instead of scrolling the text to the left.

The TextBox control contains the TextChanged event. This can be trapped by the server to respond when the user has changed the text of a TextBox. This event does not automatically trigger a postback, and it would probably annoy users to wait for a response after entering input into a TextBox. Instead, include a Button in the form to initiate the postback, and handle the TextBox.TextChanged event when you need to run code after users have updated specific fields.

The CheckBox Control

The CheckBox control allows users to easily make yes-or-no choices. The CheckBox control's Text property specifies its caption. Use the TextAlign property to specify on which side of the check box the caption appears. The Checked property is used in your code to both set and get the status of the CheckBox control.

The CheckedChanged event is raised when the state of the CheckBox control changes. By default, the AutoPostBack property of the CheckBox control is set to false. This means that changing the checked state does not cause a postback. However, the CheckChanged event will still be raised when another control causes a postback. You might set AutoPostBack to true if you need to respond immediately to the user's selection, however.

EXAM TIP

If you need to create groups of CheckBox controls, consider using the CheckBoxList control. The CheckBox control provides more granular layout control, but the CheckBoxList control is easier to use when binding with data.

The RadioButton Control

If you think of the CheckBox control as a yes-or-no question, you can think of the RadioButton control as multiple choice. The RadioButton control (named after the series of buttons on a car radio that allows you to select only one station at a time) prompts the user to select one from a list of mutually exclusive RadioButton controls in a group. This is useful when you are asking a user to select a single item from a group of items.

To group multiple RadioButton controls together, specify the same GroupName for each RadioButton control in the group. ASP.NET ensures that the selected radio button is exclusive within the group. Typically, you should set RadioButton.Checked to true for one of the RadioButton controls, to set the default.

Instead of adding multiple RadioButton controls, you can add a single RadioButtonList control, and then add list items for the desired choices. Figure 4-5 shows an ASPX page in Visual Studio with two sets of RadioButton controls; Payment Type is implemented by using individual RadioButton controls, and Shipping Type is implemented by using a RadioButtonList.

The RadioButton control's Text property specifies its caption. The TextAlign property is used to specify the side on which the caption appears. You determine which button is selected in your code by reading the Checked property of each control. The RadioButton control also exposes the CheckedChanged event so that your application can respond when a user clicks a radio button. This event does not automatically cause a postback to the server.

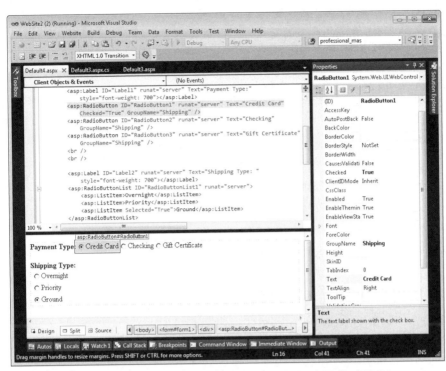

FIGURE 4-5 Using RadioButton and RadioButtonList with the Visual Studio designer.

The DropDownList Control

Like the RadioButton control, a DropDownList requires the user to select one of multiple choices. Whereas the RadioButton control displays all the options on the screen at all times, the user needs to click the DropDownList to view different options. Hiding non-default options makes the DropDownList better suited for longer lists of options, such as a user's country.

When you use the Visual Studio designer to add a DropDownList control, it prompts you to manually add the items to the list. Choose the default option by setting the item's Selected property to true. If you do not select an option, most browsers will automatically select the first item.

You can populate the list of choices in a DropDownList by calling the DropDownList.Items.Add method and passing it either a string or an instance of ListItem. The following code sample demonstrates using a for loop to add a list of years to a DropDownList, and then selecting the 85th item in the list if the form is not in postback.

Sample of Visual Basic Code

```vb
For i As Integer = 1900 To DateTime.Now.Year - 1
    BirthYearDropDownList.Items.Add(i.ToString())
Next

If Not IsPostBack Then
    BirthYearDropDownList.SelectedIndex = 85
End If
```

Sample of C# Code

```csharp
for (int i = 1900; i < DateTime.Now.Year; i++)
{
    BirthYearDropDownList.Items.Add(i.ToString());
}

if (!IsPostBack)
{
    BirthYearDropDownList.SelectedIndex = 85;
}
```

Figure 4-6 shows the DropDownList generated by this code sample.

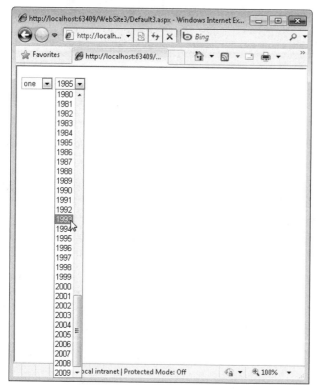

FIGURE 4-6 Using the DropDownList control to select from a large number of choices.

Handle the DropDownList.SelectedIndexChanged event to run code when the user selects a different option, or simply examine the DropDownList.SelectedValue property during postback to access the option the user selected as a String.

The ListBox Control

Like multiple CheckBox controls or a single CheckBoxList control, a ListBox control allows the user to select zero or more from multiple choices. Whereas the CheckBox control displays all the options on the screen at all times, the ListBox control provides a scrollbar for displaying more options than would otherwise fit in the space.

By default, a ListBox allows the user to select only one option at a time. Typically, if a user can only select one option, you should use a DropDownList instead. To allow users to select multiple options, set ListBox.SelectionMode to Multiple.

Figure 4-7 shows a ListBox control in use, with the SelectionMode set to Multiple. Note that selecting multiple options requires the user to hold down the Ctrl key when clicking—a trick most users are not aware of. Because of this, graphical user interface design best practices recommend using a CheckBoxList instead when a user must be able to select multiple choices, or a DropDownList when a user must select only a single choice.

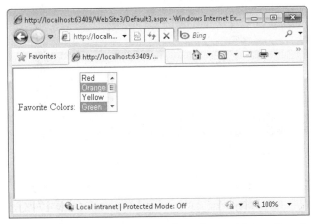

FIGURE 4-7 Using the ListBox control to select multiple options from a large number of choices.

The Button Control

The Button control displays a button on the webpage that a user can click to trigger a postback to the web server. A Button control can be rendered as a submit button (default) or a command button. A submit button simply performs a postback to the server. As you have done in earlier chapters, you can run code when a user submits a form by handling the button's Click event. In Visual Studio, simply double-click a Button in the designer to create the event handler.

Most of the time, you will create a Button.Click event handler to run code when a user clicks a button. If your form has multiple buttons that perform similar functions, such as navigation buttons that move back, up, or forward, you might find it more efficient to handle the Button.Command event instead. The Command event makes it easy to write a single method that handles the clicks of multiple buttons.

You define a button as a command button by assigning a value to its CommandName property and handling the Button.Command event. For example, Figure 4-8 shows three buttons that have unique CommandName properties but use the same Button.Command event handler.

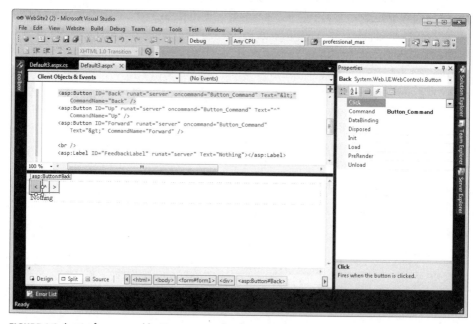

FIGURE 4-8 A set of command buttons on a webpage.

When a user clicks one of the command buttons, its Command event is called on the server. Because all three buttons in this example call the same event handler, the event handler must determine which button the user clicked by examining the e.CommandName parameter, which contains the value of the Button.CommandName property. The following code updates a Label based on which button the user clicked.

Sample of Visual Basic Code

```
Protected Sub Button_Command(ByVal sender As Object, _
                    ByVal e As System.Web.UI.WebControls.CommandEventArgs) _
                Handles Forward.Command, Up.Command, Back.Command
    Select Case e.CommandName
        Case "Back"
            FeedbackLabel.Text = "Back"
            Exit Select
        Case "Up"
            FeedbackLabel.Text = "Up"
            Exit Select
```

```
        Case "Forward"
            FeedbackLabel.Text = "Forward"
            Exit Select
    End Select
End Sub
```

Sample of C# Code

```csharp
protected void Button_Command(object sender, CommandEventArgs e)
{
    switch (e.CommandName)
    {
        case "Back":
            FeedbackLabel.Text = "Back";
            break;
        case "Up":
            FeedbackLabel.Text = "Up";
            break;
        case "Forward":
            FeedbackLabel.Text = "Forward";
            break;
    }
}
```

You can also use the CommandArgument property of the Button control to provide additional information about the command to perform. This property is also available from the CommandEventArgs object.

The Button control also contains a CausesValidation property. This property, set to true by default, causes page validation to be performed when a Button control is clicked. Set the CausesValidation property to false when you want the Button control to bypass page validation. Reset and help buttons are examples of buttons that typically bypass validation. See Chapter 5, "Input Validation and Site Navigation," for more details on page validation.

Browsers render the Button control as an ordinary button. If you need the power of the Button control but prefer the browser to render it as a hyperlink or an image, use the LinkButton or ImageButton control. Those controls behave like buttons, but additionally expose properties for defining the link or image.

HTML Server Controls

An HTML server control allows you to define actual HTML inside your ASP.NET page but work with the control on the server through an object model provided by the .NET Framework. Each HTML control is defined inside your page by using standard HTML tag syntax. This means they use the <input />, <select />, <textarea />, and similar tags. By default, these HTML tags are not connected to any server control. Therefore, it can be difficult to use them from the server in that there are no instances of related controls with properties and methods. Instead, you can simply access the tag values through the Page.Request.Form collection. This model is fine for very simple pages and was the only model for classic Active Server Pages (ASP), the precursor to ASP.NET.

Alternatively, you can apply the attribute runat="server" to these control tags, in which case ASP.NET will parse the HTML tag into a related, server-side object that provides properties and methods designed to work with that particular tag. This can make your programming experience much easier. In addition, ASP.NET uses view state to automatically maintain state for these items between calls.

In most cases, you should use the more powerful web server controls. Consider using HTML server controls in only these cases:

- When you are migrating existing, classic ASP pages over to ASP.NET.
- When the control needs to have custom client-side JavaScript attached to its events.
- When the web page has a lot of client-side JavaScript that is referencing the control.

> **MORE INFO**   **HTML AND WEB SERVER CONTROLS**
>
> For more information about the differences between HTML server controls and web server controls, go to *http://msdn.microsoft.com/en-us/zsyt68f1.aspx*.

Creating HTML Server Controls in Source View

One of the best uses for HTML server controls is for converting classic ASP pages over to a .NET Framework model. The classic ASP page typically contains <input /> tags nested inside a <form /> tag. Consider the following classic ASP webpage.

Classic ASP Webpage

```
<html>
    <head><title>Customer Page</title></head>
    <body>
        <form name="Form1" method="post" action="update.asp" id="Form1" >
            <input type="text" name="CustomerName"
                id="CustomerName" >
            <input type="submit" name="SubmitButton"
                value="Submit" id="SubmitButton" >
        </form>
    </body>
</html>
```

This page contains a form with a text box and a submit button. The user can type a customer name and click the submit button to send the entered data back to the update.asp page on the web server by using an HTTP POST command. This page can be converted to use ASP.NET HTML server controls and thus simplify the programming model on the server. Consider the following code. It represents the same page converted to ASP.NET.

Converted ASP.NET Webpage

```html
<html>
    <head><title>Customer Page</title></head>
    <body>
        <form name="Form1" method="post" id="Form1" runat="server">
            <input type="text" name="CustomerName"
                id="CustomerName" runat="server" >
            <input type="submit" name="SubmitButton"
                value="Submit" id="SubmitButton" runat="server">
        </form>
    </body>
</html>
```

Notice that the only changes were to add the runat="server" attribute to each control and the form tag. This attribute tells ASP.NET to create server control instances for each of these items. ASP.NET removes the runat attribute when rendering the page for the browser. In addition, the action attribute was removed from the form tag, because with ASP.NET you typically send the data back to the same page.

You must define the ID attribute value for every tag that you add the runat="server" attribute to. The value of this ID attribute becomes the name of the control instance in your code. Visual Studio automatically adds a default ID attribute when you add an HTML control.

If you decide that you no longer need to program an HTML server control in server code, you should convert it back to a plain HTML element. Each HTML server control in a page uses resources, so it is good practice to minimize the number of controls that the ASP.NET page needs to work with on the server. To do so, open the page in Source view, and then remove the runat="server" attribute from the control's tag. If the HTML element is referenced by client-side script, verify that ASP.NET has not changed its ID attribute in the rendered HTML.

Creating HTML Server Controls in the Designer

The HTML server controls are grouped together in the Toolbox of the Visual Studio designer. You can simply drag these controls onto your form. To create an HTML server control by using the Visual Studio designer, follow these steps:

1. Open an ASP.NET page inside the designer.

2. In the Toolbox, click the HTML tab to expose the HTML controls (see Figure 4-9).

3. Drag an HTML element to either the Design or the Source view of the webpage.

4. Convert the HTML element to a server control by setting the runat attribute. In Source view, add the runat="server" attribute (see Figure 4-9). Note that Figure 4-9 shows an HTML button followed by the Button web server control.

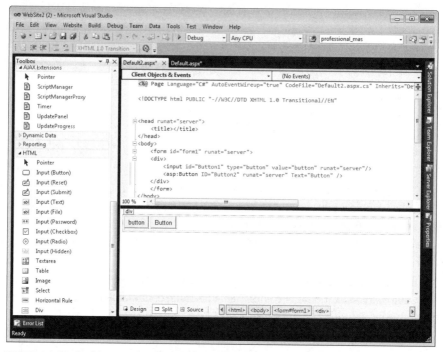

FIGURE 4-9 Setting the runat attribute of an HTML server control.

 **REAL WORLD**

Tony Northrup

For rapid development and easy manageability, always choose server controls over HTML controls. In the real world, however, you often don't need the power, or the performance overhead, of server controls. If you're creating an AJAX form, for example, the client does all the work, and controls might never be processed by the server. In those circumstances, you can still use server controls. You'll get better real-world performance out of HTML controls, however.

PRACTICE **Working with Web Server Controls**

In this practice, you work with the web server controls that are defined in this chapter.

ON THE COMPANION MEDIA

If you encounter a problem completing an exercise, you can find the completed projects in the samples installed from this book's companion CD. For more information about the project files and other content on the CD, see "Using the Companion Media" in this book's Introduction.

EXERCISE Adding Controls to the Webpage

In this exercise, you create a webpage that allows the user to generate a list of names, select a shipping type, and select multiple destinations.

1. Open Visual Studio and create a new website called **WebServerControls**.

2. Create a new page without a master page and edit it in Design view.

3. Drag a Label to the page, and set the Text property to **Name:**. To its right, drag a TextBox control, and set the ID property to **NameTextBox**. To its right, drag a Button control, set the Text property to **Add**, and set the ID property to **AddButton**.

4. On the next line, drag a Literal control to the page, and set the Text value to **Shipping Type:**. Below that, drag a RadioButtonList control to the page. Add three items, with the Text properties set to **Standard**, **Priority**, and **Urgent**. (To create a new line in the Visual Studio designer, simply place the cursor after the last control and press the Enter key.) Set the ID value to **ShippingTypeRadioButtonList**.

5. On the next line, drag a Literal control to the page, set the Text value to **Destinations**, and set the ID value to **DestinationsLiteral**. Below that, drag a CheckBoxList control to the page, and set the ID value to **DestinationsCheckBoxList**.

6. On the next line, drag a Button control to the page, set the ID to **ShipButton**, and set the Text to **Ship**. Below that, drag a Label control to the page, set the ID value to **ShippingConfirmationLabel**, and clear the default Text value.

    Your form should now resemble Figure 4-10.

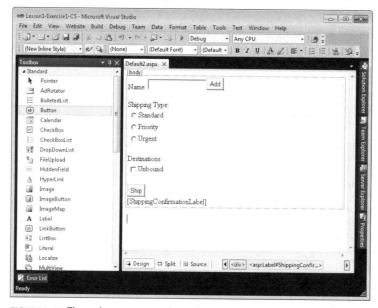

FIGURE 4-10 The web server controls on the page.

7. Now you will write code to add any text typed in the Name box to the Destinations-CheckBoxList. Double-click the Add button to create an event handler for Button.Click, and then write the necessary code.

```
Protected Sub AddButton_Click_
  (ByVal sender As Object, ByVal e As System.EventArgs) _
    Handles AddButton.Click

    If Not (NameTextBox.Text = [String].Empty) Then
        DestinationsCheckBoxList.Items.Add(Server.HtmlEncode(NameTextBox.Text))
        NameTextBox.Text = Nothing
    End If
End Sub
```

Sample of C# Code

```
protected void AddButton_Click(object sender, EventArgs e)
{
    if ( !(NameTextBox.Text == String.Empty))
    {
        DestinationsCheckBoxList.Items.Add(Server.HtmlEncode(NameTextBox.Text));
        NameTextBox.Text = null;
    }
}
```

8. Now you will write code to display the shipping type and destinations in Shipping-ConfirmationLabel when the user clicks the Ship button. Return to Design view, double-click the Ship button, and then write the necessary code.

Sample of Visual Basic Code

```
Protected Sub ShipButton_Click_
  (ByVal sender As Object, ByVal e As System.EventArgs) _
    Handles ShipButton.Click

    If (ShippingTypeRadioButtonList.SelectedValue = [String].Empty) OrElse _
      (DestinationsCheckBoxList.SelectedValue = [String].Empty) Then
        ShippingConfirmationLabel.Text = "You must select a shipping type and at
least one destination."
    Else
        ShippingConfirmationLabel.Text = _
          String.Format("Using {0} shipping to:<br>", _
    ShippingTypeRadioButtonList.SelectedValue)
        For Each li As ListItem In DestinationsCheckBoxList.Items
            If li.Selected Then
                ShippingConfirmationLabel.Text += li.Value + "<br>"
            End If
        Next
    End If
End Sub
```

Sample of C# Code

```csharp
protected void ShipButton_Click(object sender, EventArgs e)
{
    if ((ShippingTypeRadioButtonList.SelectedValue == String.Empty)
        || (DestinationsCheckBoxList.SelectedValue == String.Empty))
    {
        ShippingConfirmationLabel.Text = "You must select a shipping type and at
least one destination.";
    }
    else
    {
            ShippingConfirmationLabel.Text =
        string.Format("Using {0} shipping to:<br>",
ShippingTypeRadioButtonList.SelectedValue);
        foreach(ListItem li in DestinationsCheckBoxList.Items)
        {
            if (li.Selected)
            {
                ShippingConfirmationLabel.Text += li.Value + "<br>";
            }
        }
    }
}
```

9. Run the web application. Add several names, and note that the AddButton.Click event handler successfully adds an item to the CheckBoxList. Select different shipping options, and note that you can only select one radio button at a time. Select one or more of the check boxes, and then click the Ship button. Notice that the ShipButton.Click event handler successfully reads the selected values.

10. Open the page in Design view. Select the TextBox control and set its MaxLength property to **12** to restrict user input.

11. Run the page and type in the TextBox control. Notice that you cannot type more than 12 characters into the control.

12. In your web browser, view the page source. Notice that the Label control, which you used to display the Name prompt, is surrounded by a <span> element. Notice that the Literal controls do not have this element.

Lesson Summary

- A server control is a control that you can program by writing server-side code to respond to events from the control. Server controls contain the runat="server" attribute and must exist within a form that has the same runat attribute.

- The Label control displays text at a specific location on the webpage by using the properties that have been assigned to the Label control.

- The Literal control returns text without any additional processing and is useful when you need to return raw HTML.

- The TextBox control collects text from the user.

- The CheckBox control prompts the user to select or clear a check box to choose true or false.

- The RadioButton control prompts the user to select between mutually exclusive RadioButton controls in a group.

- The DropDownList control prompts the user to select one of many different options. The non-default options are hidden until the user clicks the list.

- The ListBox control prompts the user to select zero or more of many different options. Options are shown in a scrolling list.

- The Button control displays a button on the webpage that can be clicked to trigger a postback to the web server. For similar functionality with a different presentation, you can use the LinkButton or ImageButton controls.

- HTML server controls are useful when you need to migrate a classic ASP webpage to ASP.NET, or when you are working with a server control and you need to write a lot of associated client-side JavaScript.

Lesson Review

You can use the following questions to test your knowledge of the information in Lesson 1, "Exploring Common Server Controls." The questions are also available on the companion CD in a practice test, if you prefer to review them in electronic form.

> **NOTE ANSWERS**
>
> Answers to these questions and explanations of why each answer choice is correct or incorrect are located in the "Answers" section at the end of the book.

1. To add an HTML server control to a webpage, you must drag an HTML element from the Toolbox to the webpage and then perform which of the following tasks?

   A. Add the attribute run="server" to the control element in Source view.

   B. Double-click the HTML element to convert it to an HTML server control.

   C. Add the attribute runat="server" to the control element in Source view.

   D. Select the HTML element in Design view and set the RunAt property to true in the Properties window.

2. You are creating a web form that displays a stock chart. Users can choose from three different sizes for the chart: small, medium, and large. How could you implement the user interface? (Choose all that apply. Each answer forms a complete solution.)

   A. Add a RadioButtonList control.

   B. Add three RadioButton controls. Set the GroupName property of all controls to ChartSize.

   C. Add a CheckBoxList control.

   D. Add three CheckBox controls. Set the GroupName property of all controls to ChartSize.

3. You are creating a webpage that has several related buttons, such as Fast Forward, Reverse, Play, Stop, and Pause. You want to create a single event handler that processes the postback from these Button controls. Which of the following should you do to handle the event while writing the least amount of code? (Choose all that apply. Each answer forms part of the complete solution.)

   A. Handle the Button.Command event.

   B. Handle the Button.Load event.

   C. Define the Button.CommandName property of all controls to PlaybackControl.

   D. Define the Button.CommandName property so that each control has a unique value.

Lesson 2: Exploring Specialized Server Controls

It was not long ago that creating something as basic as a calendar on a webpage was a time-consuming task involving the creation of HTML tables with a hyperlink on each date. You might have also created JavaScript to process the selection of a date. With ASP.NET, common tasks such as creating a calendar involve simply dragging a feature-rich control on your webpage.

The previous lesson covered some of the more basic controls used to build webpages. There are, of course, many more controls available. This lesson covers some of the more specialized web server controls: Table, Image, ImageButton, ImageMap, Calendar, FileUpload, Panel, MultiView, Wizard, and Xml.

After this lesson, you will be able to:

- Use the following web server controls:

  - Table, TableRow, and TableCell
  - Image
  - ImageButton
  - ImageMap
  - Calendar
  - FileUpload
  - Panel
  - MultiView
  - View
  - Wizard
  - Xml

Estimated lesson time: 60 minutes

The Table, TableRow, and TableCell Controls

Tables arrange data in a grid format. In the early years of the web, developers used tables to lay out web pages. Today, however, the HTML <div> and <span> markups have replaced the table as the preferred method for HTML layout. Now, you only need to rely on tables for displaying data in a grid, such as a spreadsheet.

HTML provides the <table> tag for defining a table, the <tr> tag for creating a row, and the <td> tag for defining a column in the row. ASP.NET provides the Table control for creating and managing tables. Like its HTML counterpart, the Table control can be used to display static information on a page. However, the Table control's real power comes from the ability to programmatically add TableRow and TableCell controls from your code at run time. If you only need to display static information, consider using the HTML tags instead.

EXAM TIP

There is also an HtmlTable control. It can be created from the HTML <table> tag by adding the runat="server" attribute to the tag and assigning an ID to the tag. However, the Table control is easier to use because it provides a programming model that is consistent with the TableRow and TableCell controls.

Again, the Table control is the right choice when you need to programmatically add rows and cells to a table at run time. The rows are added by using the TableRow control and the cells are added by using the TableCell control. You add these rows and cells in a manner similar to the way you would dynamically create other controls on a page. Like other dynamically created controls, rows and cells must be re-created when the page posts back to the server. If you need the table to survive postback, consider using the Repeater, DataList, or GridView control.

The Table control contains a Rows collection property, which is a collection of TableRow controls. It is used to add and access the rows of your table. The TableRow control, in turn, contains a Cells collection property (also known as a collection association). This property represents a collection of TableCell controls. These are the actual cells (or columns) within a single row.

The Table, TableRow, and TableCell controls all inherit from the WebControl class. This class provides base properties such as Font, BackColor, and ForeColor. If you set these properties at the Table level, you can override them in TableRow instances, and in turn, the TableRow settings can be overridden in the TableCell instances.

Adding Rows and Cells Dynamically to a Table Control

Visual Studio provides a designer for adding rows and cells to Table controls on your page. You access this design tool from the Table control's Rows property in the Properties window. Similarly, you can use the designer to add cells to individual rows, as shown in Figure 4-11.

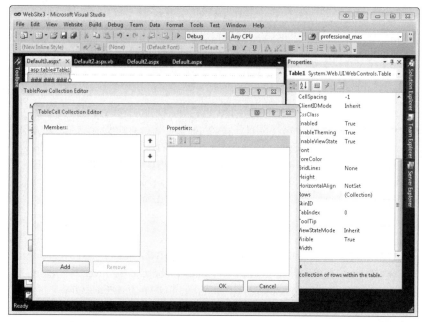

FIGURE 4-11 The TableCell collection editor in Visual Studio.

If you simply needed to add static rows and cells, it would be more efficient to simply use an HTML table. The real power of the Table control, however, is being able to work with it from your code. The following steps show how to dynamically add TableCell and TableRow objects to an existing Table control.

1. From the Toolbox, drag a Table control onto your page.

2. Open the code-behind file for the page, and add a Load event to the page.

3. Inside the Load event, write a for loop to create five new rows in the table.

4. Inside this loop, add another for loop to create three columns for each row.

5. Inside this loop, modify the TableCell.Text property to identify the row and column. The following code provides an example.

Sample of Visual Basic Code

```vb
Protected Sub Page_Load(ByVal sender As Object, _
  ByVal e As System.EventArgs) Handles Me.Load

    Table1.BorderWidth = 1
    For row As Integer = 0 To 4
      Dim tr As New TableRow()
      For column As Integer = 0 To 2
        Dim tc As New TableCell()
        tc.Text = String.Format("Row:{0} Cell:{1}", row, column)
        tc.BorderWidth = 1
        tr.Cells.Add(tc)
      Next column
      Table1.Rows.Add(tr)
    Next row
End Sub
```

Sample of C# Code

```csharp
protected void Page_Load(object sender, EventArgs e)
{
  Table1.BorderWidth = 1;
  for (int row = 0; row < 5; row++)
  {
    TableRow tr = new TableRow();
    for (int column = 0; column < 3; column++)
    {
      TableCell tc = new TableCell();
      tc.Text = string.Format("Row:{0} Cell:{1}", row, column);
      tc.BorderWidth = 1;
      tr.Cells.Add(tc);
    }
    Table1.Rows.Add(tr);
  }
}
```

In the code example, notice that the code starts by setting the BorderWidth property of the Table control to 1, which causes the Table to have a line around its outside edges. The TableCell objects also have their BorderWidth set to 1, which causes each TableCell to be outlined as well. Although this demonstrates how to programmatically change table properties, in practice you should use cascading style sheets to format your tables. When the webpage is displayed, it will look like the page shown in Figure 4-12.

Row:0 Cell:0	Row:0 Cell:1	Row:0 Cell:2
Row:1 Cell:0	Row:1 Cell:1	Row:1 Cell:2
Row:2 Cell:0	Row:2 Cell:1	Row:2 Cell:2
Row:3 Cell:0	Row:3 Cell:1	Row:3 Cell:2
Row:4 Cell:0	Row:4 Cell:1	Row:4 Cell:2

FIGURE 4-12 A webpage demonstrating how to dynamically create TableRow and TableCell controls.

The Image Control

The Image control can be used to display an image on a webpage. Again, this control should be used when you need to manipulate the properties of the control in server-side code. If you simply need to embed a static image on your page, you can use the HTML <img> tag. In fact, when the Image control is rendered to a page, it generates an <img> element.

The Image control inherits directly from the WebControl class. The ImageMap and ImageButton controls inherit directly from the Image control.

The Image control is represented as the <asp:Image> element in the source and has no content embedded between its opening and closing tags. Therefore, you can write this element as a singleton (closing the tag with /> instead of using a separate closing tag). It is important to understand that the *image itself* is not embedded in the webpage; instead, when the browser encounters the <img> element with the href attribute, the browser initiates a separate request for the image from the server.

The Image control's primary property, ImageUrl, indicates the path to the image that is downloaded from the browser and displayed on the page. This property maps directly to the src attribute" of the <img> element in HTML. Some additional properties to consider when working with the Image control are as follows:

- **AlternateText**   The Image control also contains a property called AlternateText. You can set this property to display a text message in the user's browser when the image is not available or the browser is set to not render the image. Most browsers display the AlternateText as a tooltip when a user points to the image, and AlternateText is important for helping users with special accessibility requirements navigate your page. For link images, assign AlternateText a value that describes the link. For content images, assign AlternateText a value that describes the image itself to help image search engines properly index your site.

- **ImageAlign**   The ImageAlign property of the Image control can be set to NotSet, Left, Right, Baseline, Top, Middle, Bottom, AbsBottom, AbsMiddle, or TextTop. These settings specify the alignment of the image in relation to the other objects on the webpage.

- **DescriptionUrl**   The DescriptionUrl property is an accessibility feature that is used to provide further explanation of the content and meaning of the image when nonvisual page readers are being used. This property sets the longdesc attribute of the <img> element that is generated. This property should be set to the Uniform Resource Locator (URL) of a page that contains details of the image in text or audio format.

- **GenerateEmptyAlternateText**   Setting the GenerateEmptyAlternateText property to true will add the attribute alt="" to the <img> element that the Image control generates. From an accessibility perspective, any image that does not contribute to the meaning of the page, such as a blank image or a page-divider image, should always carry this attribute; it causes the nonvisual page readers to simply ignore the image.

The following code provides an example of a web page with an Image control. An image file called Whale.jpg is inside a folder called Images. An HTML page called WhaleImageDescription.htm, which contains a description that can be used by nonvisual page readers, was also created. The following code demonstrates setting the Image control's properties programmatically inside the page's code-behind file.

Sample of Visual Basic Code

```
Protected Sub Page_Load(ByVal sender As Object, _
  ByVal e As System.EventArgs) Handles Me.Load

  Image1.ImageUrl = "~/images/whale.jpg"
  Image1.DescriptionUrl = "~/WhaleImageDescription.htm"
  Image1.AlternateText = "This is a picture of a whale"
End Sub
```

Sample of C# Code

```csharp
protected void Page_Load(object sender, EventArgs e)
{
  Image1.ImageUrl = "~/images/whale.jpg";
  Image1.DescriptionUrl = "~/WhaleImageDescription.htm";
  Image1.AlternateText = "This is a picture of a whale";
}
```

The ImageButton Control

The Image control does not have a Click event. In situations in which a Click event is necessary, you can use ImageButton or ImageMap instead. These controls allow you to treat an image like a clickable button. In addition, you can retrieve the x-coordinate and y-coordinate of the user's click. This is useful for determining where on the image the user has clicked. You can use this information on the server to perform different actions, depending on the area clicked by the user.

The ImageButton control is used to display a clickable image on a webpage that can be used to perform a postback to the web server when the image is clicked. This control generates an <input type="image"> element when rendering to HTML.

The ImageButton control is represented as an <asp:ImageButton> element in Source view and has no content, so you can write this element as a singleton element. As with the Image control, the ImageButton control's primary property, ImageUrl, indicates the path to an image that can be downloaded from the browser and displayed. This property maps directly to the src attribute of the <input> element in HTML. Because the ImageButton inherits from the Image control, it also contains the AlternateText, DescriptionUrl, and ImageAlign properties.

The ImageButton control has a Click event and a Command event that function like these same events do for the Button control. The second argument of the Click event has a data type of ImageClickEventArgs, which lets you retrieve the x-coordinate and y-coordinate of the user's click.

In the following example, a webpage was created and an ImageButton control was added to the page. This control uses an image that is both red and blue (redblue.jpg). The following code was added to the code-behind page to show how the ImageButton control's properties can be set programmatically and the Click event can be implemented.

```
Partial Class ImageControl
  Inherits System.Web.UI.Page

  Protected Sub Page_Load(ByVal sender As Object, _
    ByVal e As System.EventArgs) Handles Me.Load

    ImageButton1.ImageUrl = "~/images/redblue.jpg"
    ImageButton1.AlternateText = _
      "This is a button. The left side is red. The right is blue."
  End Sub

  Protected Sub ImageButton1_Click(ByVal sender As Object, _
    ByVal e As System.Web.UI.ImageClickEventArgs) Handles ImageButton1.Click

    ImageButton1.AlternateText = _
      String.Format("Button Clicked at {0},{1}", e.X, e.Y)
  End Sub
End Class
```

Sample of C# Code

```
public partial class ImageButton_Control : System.Web.UI.Page
{
  protected void Page_Load(object sender, EventArgs e)
  {
    ImageButton1.ImageUrl = "~/images/redblue.jpg";
    ImageButton1.AlternateText =
      "This is a button. The left side is red. The right is blue.";
  }
  protected void ImageButton1_Click(object sender, ImageClickEventArgs e)
  {
    ImageButton1.AlternateText =
      string.Format("Button Clicked at {0},{1}", e.X, e.Y);
  }
}
```

This code sets the ImageButton control properties in the Page_Load event handler. In the ImageButton1_Click event handler, the x-coordinate and y-coordinate are retrieved and placed into the AlternateText property. In this example, you can use this information to determine the area (or color) on which the user clicked and make a decision accordingly.

The ImageMap Control

The ImageMap control is used to display a clickable image that can be used to post form information back to the web server when the image is clicked. This control differs from the ImageButton control in that the ImageMap control allows you to define regions or "hot spots" that cause a postback, whereas clicking anywhere on an ImageButton causes a postback.

The ImageMap control generates an <img usemap="#myMap"> element in HTML. In addition, a <map name="myMap"> element with nested <area> elements is also created when the HTML is rendered.

The ImageMap control inherits directly from the Image control class. As with the Image control, the ImageMap control's primary property, ImageUrl, indicates the path to the image that can be downloaded from the browser and displayed. This property maps directly to the src attribute of the <img> element in HTML. Because the ImageMap inherits from the Image control, it also contains the AlternateText, DescriptionUrl, ImageAlign, and GenerateEmptyAlternateText properties.

In Source view, the ImageMap control is represented as an <asp:ImageMap> element and has nested hot spot elements that can be CircleHotSpot, RectangleHotSpot, and PolygonHotSpot elements.

The ImageMap control has a Click event that functions like the Click event for the ImageButton control. The second argument of the Click event has a data type of ImageMapEventArgs, which lets you retrieve the PostBackValue of the associated hot spot that the user clicked.

Working with HotSpot Classes

A hot spot is a predefined area on an image that can be clicked to perform an action. Hot spots can be created to define areas on the image that are displayed by the ImageMap control. You can define many overlapping areas, with each layer based on the HotSpot definition order. The first HotSpot defined takes precedence over the last HotSpot defined. The classes that inherit from the HotSpot base class are the CircleHotSpot, RectangleHotSpot, and PolygonHotSpot. Table 4-3 contains a list of HotSpot properties.

TABLE 4-3 HotSpot Properties

PROPERTY	DESCRIPTION
AccessKey	The keyboard shortcut for a HotSpot. You can place only a single character into this property. If this property contains C, for example, a web user can press Alt+C to navigate to the HotSpot.
AlternateText	The text that is displayed for a HotSpot when the image is unavailable or renders to a browser that does not support images. This also becomes the tooltip.
HotSpotMode	The behavior of the HotSpot when it is clicked. This can be NotSet, Inactive, Navigate, or PostBack.
NavigateUrl	The URL to navigate to when a HotSpot object is clicked.
PostBackValue	The string that is passed back to the web server and is available in the event argument data when the HotSpot is clicked.
TabIndex	The tab index number of the HotSpot.
Target	The target window or frame that displays the webpage and that is linked to the HotSpot.

Understanding the HotSpotMode Property

The HotSpotMode property is used to specify how the HotSpot behaves when it is clicked. You can specify the HotSpotMode on either the HotSpot or the ImageMap control. If you set the HotSpotMode on both the HotSpot and the ImageMap, the HotSpot takes precedence. This means that you can specify the HotSpotMode on the ImageMap control to set a default HotSpot behavior, but the HotSpotMode of the HotSpot must be set to NotSet to inherit the behavior from the ImageMap.

Specifying Navigate for the HotSpotMode causes the HotSpot to navigate to a URL when clicked. The NavigateUrl property specifies the URL to which to navigate.

> **NOTE   HOTSPOTMODE DEFAULT**
>
> **If ImageMap and HotSpot have their HotSpotMode properties set to NotSet, the HotSpot defaults to Navigate.**

Specifying PostBack for the HotSpotMode causes the HotSpot to generate a postback to the server when the HotSpot is clicked. The PostBackValue property specifies a string that is passed back to the web server in the ImageMapEventArgs event data when the HotSpot is clicked and the Click event is raised.

Specifying Inactive for the HotSpotMode property indicates that the HotSpot does not have any behavior when it is clicked. This is used to create an inactive HotSpot region within a larger active HotSpot, thus allowing you to create complex HotSpot zones within an ImageMap control. You must specify the inactive HotSpot before you designate the active HotSpot in the ImageMap control.

The following code presents an example of a webpage that contains a Label and ImageMap control. The ImageMap control is set to use a stoplight image (red, yellow, and green). The following code was added to the code-behind page to show how the ImageMap control's properties can be set programmatically and how the Click event can be implemented to display the HotSpot that is clicked.

Sample of Visual Basic Code

```vb
Partial Class HotSpotVb
  Inherits System.Web.UI.Page

  Protected Sub Page_Load(ByVal sender As Object, _
    ByVal e As System.EventArgs) Handles Me.Load

    ImageMapStopLight.ImageUrl = "~/images/stoplight.jpg"
    ImageMapStopLight.AlternateText = "Stoplight picture"
    ImageMapStopLight.HotSpotMode = HotSpotMode.PostBack

    Dim redHotSpot As New RectangleHotSpot()
    redHotSpot.Top = 0
    redHotSpot.Bottom = 40
    redHotSpot.Left = 0
    redHotSpot.Right = 40
```

```
    redHotSpot.PostBackValue = "RED"
    ImageMapStopLight.HotSpots.Add(redHotSpot)

    Dim yellowHotSpot As New RectangleHotSpot()
    yellowHotSpot.Top = 41
    yellowHotSpot.Bottom = 80
    yellowHotSpot.Left = 0
    yellowHotSpot.Right = 40
    yellowHotSpot.PostBackValue = "YELLOW"
    ImageMapStopLight.HotSpots.Add(yellowHotSpot)

    Dim greenHotSpot As New RectangleHotSpot()
    greenHotSpot.Top = 81
    greenHotSpot.Bottom = 120
    greenHotSpot.Left = 0
    greenHotSpot.Right = 40
    greenHotSpot.PostBackValue = "GREEN"
    ImageMapStopLight.HotSpots.Add(greenHotSpot)
  End Sub

  Protected Sub ImageMapStopLight_Click(ByVal sender As Object, _
    ByVal e As System.Web.UI.WebControls.ImageMapEventArgs) _
  Handles ImageMapStopLight.Click

    Label1.Text = String.Format("You clicked the {0} rectable.", e.PostBackValue)
  End Sub
End Class
```

Sample of C# Code

```
public partial class HotSpotControl : System.Web.UI.Page
{
  protected void Page_Load(object sender, EventArgs e)
  {
    ImageMapStopLight.ImageUrl = "~/images/stoplight.jpg";
    ImageMapStopLight.AlternateText = "Stoplight picture";
    ImageMapStopLight.HotSpotMode = HotSpotMode.PostBack;

    RectangleHotSpot redHotSpot = new RectangleHotSpot();
    redHotSpot.Top = 0;
    redHotSpot.Bottom = 40;
    redHotSpot.Left = 0;
    redHotSpot.Right = 40;
    redHotSpot.PostBackValue = "RED";
    ImageMapStopLight.HotSpots.Add(redHotSpot);

    RectangleHotSpot yellowHotSpot = new RectangleHotSpot();
    yellowHotSpot.Top = 41;
    yellowHotSpot.Bottom = 80;
    yellowHotSpot.Left = 0;
    yellowHotSpot.Right = 40;
    yellowHotSpot.PostBackValue = "YELLOW";
    ImageMapStopLight.HotSpots.Add(yellowHotSpot);

    RectangleHotSpot greenHotSpot = new RectangleHotSpot();
    greenHotSpot.Top = 81;
```

```
        greenHotSpot.Bottom = 120;
        greenHotSpot.Left = 0;
        greenHotSpot.Right = 40;
        greenHotSpot.PostBackValue = "GREEN";
        ImageMapStopLight.HotSpots.Add(greenHotSpot);

    }
    protected void ImageMapStopLight_Click(object sender, ImageMapEventArgs e)
    {
        Label1.Text = string.Format("You clicked the {0} rectangle.", e.PostBackValue);
    }
}
```

In the sample code, clicking a HotSpot on the ImageMap causes a postback of the PostBackValue to the server. ImageMapEventArgs contains the PostBackValue. Inside the Click event, the PostBackValue is placed into the Text property of the Label control. Figure 4-13 shows the page after the image has been clicked.

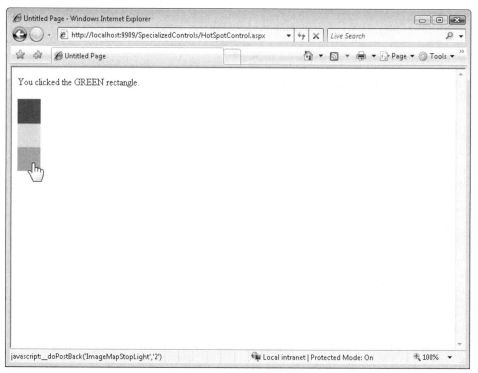

FIGURE 4-13 The rendered ImageMap displaying the PostBackValue message in the Label after the image hot spot was clicked.

The Calendar Control

The Calendar control allows you to display a calendar on a webpage. The calendar can be used when asking a user to select a date or series of dates. Users can navigate between years, months, and days. The Calendar control is a complex, powerful web server control that you can use to add calendar features to your page.

The Calendar control is represented as an <asp:Calendar> element in Source view. It can contain style elements to change the look of the control. When rendered to a user's browser, the control generates an HTML <table> element and uses a set of associated JavaScript scripts provided by ASP.NET.

The Calendar control can be used to select a single date or multiple dates. The SelectionMode property controls this. It can be set to one of the following settings:

- **Day**   Allows selection of a single date
- **DayWeek**   Allows the selection of either a single date or a complete week
- **DayWeekMonth**   Allows selection of single date, a complete week, or the whole month
- **None**   Does not allow you to select any date

The Calendar control contains many additional properties that can be used to adjust the format and behavior of this control. Table 4-4 contains a list of the Calendar properties and their associated descriptions.

TABLE 4-4 Calendar Properties

PROPERTY	DESCRIPTION
Caption	The text that is rendered in the Calendar.
CaptionAlign	The alignment of the caption: Top, Bottom, Left, Right, or NotSet.
CellPadding	The space between each cell and the cell border.
CellSpacing	The spacing between each cell.
DayHeaderStyle	The style to be applied to days of the week.
DayNameFormat	The format for the names of the days of the week: FirstLetter, FirstTwoLetters, Full, Short, Shortest.
DayStyle	The default style for a calendar day.
FirstDayOfWeek	The day of the week to display in the first column of the Calendar control.
NextMonthText	The text to be displayed in the next month navigation control; > is the default. This navigational control is only displayed if ShowNextPrevMonth property is true.

(continued)

PROPERTY	DESCRIPTION
NextPrevFormat	The tool that sets the format of the next and previous navigation controls. This can be set to CustomText (the default), FullMonth (for example, January), or ShortMonth (for example, Jan).
NextPrevStyle	The style to be applied to the next and previous navigation controls.
OtherMonthDayStyle	The tool that specifies the style for days on the calendar that are displayed and are not in the current month.
PrevMonthText	The text to be displayed in the previous month navigation control, which by default is <. This navigational control is only displayed if the ShowNextPrevMonth property is true.
SelectedDate	The date selected by the user.
SelectedDates	A collection of DateTime values that represents all of the dates that were selected by the user. This property contains only a single date if the SelectionMode property is set to CalendarSelectionMode.Day, which allows only single date selection.
SelectedDayStyle	The style of the selected day.
SelectionMode	A value that indicates how many dates can be selected. This value can be Day, DayWeek, DayWeekMonth, or None.
SelectMonthText	The text displayed for the month selection column. The default value is >>.
SelectorStyle	The style for the week and month selectors.
SelectWeekText	The text of the week selection in the week selector.
ShowDayHeader	An indicator that determines whether the day header should be displayed.
ShowGridLines	An indicator that determines whether grid lines should be displayed.
ShowNextPrevMonth	An indicator that determines whether the next and previous month selectors should be displayed.
ShowTitle	An indicator that determines whether the title should be displayed.
TitleFormat	A tool that sets the format for displaying the month (Month), or the month and year (MonthYear).
TitleStyle	The style for the title.
TodayDayStyle	The style of today's date.
TodaysDate	Today's date.

PROPERTY	DESCRIPTION
UseAccessibleHeader	A control that, when set to true, generates <th> for day headers (the default), or, when set to false, generates <td> for day headers, to be compatible with version 1.0 of the .NET Framework.
VisibleDate	Specifies the date that identifies which month to display in the Calendar control's header area.
WeekendDayStyle	The style of weekend days.

The Calendar control also exposes a few events with which to work. The primary event, SelectionChanged, is triggered after a user selects a date on the control. The SelectionChanged event causes a postback when the user selects a new date. Inside the event handler, you access the selected dates via the SelectedDates property. The SelectedDate property simply points to the selected date in the SelectedDates collection.

The VisibleMonthChanged event also causes a postback when the user selects a different month to be viewed. You can handle this event if you need to respond when the user changes months in the control.

The Calendar control is typically used as a date picker control. However, it can also be used to display a schedule. The trick to using the Calendar control to display scheduled items and special days such as holidays is to make the control large enough to display text in each day. You can then add Label controls (or other controls) to the Cell object's Controls collection in the DayRender event handler. The Calendar control's DayRender event triggers when each day is being readied for output. This is not a postback but an event that fires on the server as the control renders its HTML. This allows you to add text or controls to the day being rendered.

The following code example shows how a Calendar control can be used to display a schedule. In this example, a webpage was created and a Calendar control was added to the page. The following code was added to the code-behind page (within the page's partial class) to show how the Calendar control's properties can be set programmatically and the Calendar control events can be used to render individual days.

Sample of Visual Basic Code

```
Private scheduleData As New Dictionary(Of DateTime, String)(5)

Protected Sub Page_Load(ByVal sender As Object, ByVal e As EventArgs) Handles Me.Load
    ' Load the schedule (which would be read from a database)
    scheduleData.Add(New DateTime(2011, 1, 9), "Vacation Day")
    scheduleData.Add(New DateTime(2011, 1, 18), "Budget planning meeting")
    scheduleData.Add(New DateTime(2011, 2, 5), "Conference call")
    scheduleData.Add(New DateTime(2011, 2, 10), "Meet with art director")
    scheduleData.Add(New DateTime(2011, 2, 15), "Vacation day")

    Calendar1.Caption = "Personal Schedule"
    Calendar1.FirstDayOfWeek = System.Web.UI.WebControls.FirstDayOfWeek.Sunday
    Calendar1.NextPrevFormat = NextPrevFormat.ShortMonth
```

```
        Calendar1.TitleFormat = TitleFormat.MonthYear
        Calendar1.ShowGridLines = True
        Calendar1.DayStyle.HorizontalAlign = HorizontalAlign.Left
        Calendar1.DayStyle.VerticalAlign = VerticalAlign.Top
        Calendar1.DayStyle.Height = New Unit(75)
        Calendar1.DayStyle.Width = New Unit(100)
        Calendar1.OtherMonthDayStyle.BackColor = System.Drawing.Color.Cornsilk
        Calendar1.TodaysDate = New DateTime(2011, 1, 1)
        Calendar1.VisibleDate = Calendar1.TodaysDate
    End Sub

    Protected Sub Calendar1_SelectionChanged(ByVal sender As Object, ByVal e As EventArgs) _
        Handles Calendar1.SelectionChanged

        ActionLabel.Text = String.Format("Selection changed to: {0}", _
      Calendar1.SelectedDate.ToShortDateString())
    End Sub

    Protected Sub Calendar1_VisibleMonthChanged_
      (ByVal sender As Object, ByVal e As MonthChangedEventArgs) _
        Handles Calendar1.VisibleMonthChanged

        ActionLabel.Text = String.Format_
      ("Month changed to: {0}", e.NewDate.ToShortDateString())
    End Sub

    Protected Sub Calendar1_DayRender(ByVal sender As Object, ByVal e As DayRenderEventArgs) _
        Handles Calendar1.DayRender

      If scheduleData.ContainsKey(e.Day.[Date]) Then
          Dim lit As New Literal()
          lit.Text = "<br />"
          e.Cell.Controls.Add(lit)

          Dim lbl As New Label()
          lbl.Text = DirectCast(scheduleData(e.Day.[Date]), String)
          lbl.Font.Size = New FontUnit(FontSize.Small)
          e.Cell.Controls.Add(lbl)
      End If
    End Sub
```

Sample of C# Code

```
private Dictionary<DateTime, string> scheduleData = new Dictionary<DateTime,string>(5);

protected void Page_Load(object sender, EventArgs e)
{
    // Load the schedule (which would be read from a database)
    scheduleData.Add(new DateTime(2011, 1, 9), "Vacation Day");
    scheduleData.Add(new DateTime(2011, 1, 18), "Budget planning meeting");
    scheduleData.Add(new DateTime(2011, 2, 5), "Conference call");
    scheduleData.Add(new DateTime(2011, 2, 10), "Meet with art director");
    scheduleData.Add(new DateTime(2011, 2, 15), "Vacation day");

    Calendar1.Caption = "Personal Schedule";
```

```
        Calendar1.FirstDayOfWeek = FirstDayOfWeek.Sunday;
        Calendar1.NextPrevFormat = NextPrevFormat.ShortMonth;
        Calendar1.TitleFormat = TitleFormat.MonthYear;
        Calendar1.ShowGridLines = true;
        Calendar1.DayStyle.HorizontalAlign = HorizontalAlign.Left;
        Calendar1.DayStyle.VerticalAlign = VerticalAlign.Top;
        Calendar1.DayStyle.Height = new Unit(75);
        Calendar1.DayStyle.Width = new Unit(100);
        Calendar1.OtherMonthDayStyle.BackColor = System.Drawing.Color.Cornsilk;
        Calendar1.TodaysDate = new DateTime(2011, 1, 1);
        Calendar1.VisibleDate = Calendar1.TodaysDate;
}

protected void Calendar1_SelectionChanged(object sender, EventArgs e)
{
        ActionLabel.Text = string.Format("Selection changed to: {0}",
            Calendar1.SelectedDate.ToShortDateString());
}

protected void Calendar1_VisibleMonthChanged(object sender,
    MonthChangedEventArgs e)
{
        ActionLabel.Text = string.Format("Month changed to: {0}",
            e.NewDate.ToShortDateString());
}

protected void Calendar1_DayRender(object sender, DayRenderEventArgs e)
{
        if (scheduleData.ContainsKey(e.Day.Date))
        {
            Literal lit = new Literal();
            lit.Text = "<br />";
            e.Cell.Controls.Add(lit);

            Label lbl = new Label();
            lbl.Text = (string)scheduleData[e.Day.Date];
            lbl.Font.Size = new FontUnit(FontSize.Small);
            e.Cell.Controls.Add(lbl);
        }
}
```

This code adds dates to the calendar and then sets the Calendar control properties, such as style and size, in the Page_Load event handler. In the Calendar1_DayRender event handler, the Date and Cell of the day that is being rendered are available. If a special date is found, a Label is created that contains the special date, and it is added to the Cell object's Controls collection. When the webpage is displayed, the special dates are rendered on the Calendar control, as shown in Figure 4-14.

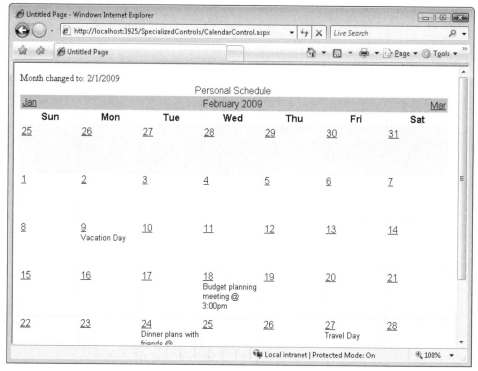

FIGURE 4-14 The rendered Calendar control displaying a schedule.

The FileUpload Control

The FileUpload control is used to allow a user to select and upload a single file to the server. The control displays as a text box and Browse button. The user can either type a file name and path into the text box or click the Browse button and select a file.

The FileUpload control is represented as an <asp:FileUpload> element in Source view. It has no content nested within its opening and closing tags, so you can write this element as a singleton element. This control generates an <input type="file"> element when rendered as HTML to a browser.

The FileUpload control does not cause a postback to the web server. After selecting a file, the user needs to cause a postback by using a different control, such as a Button. The postback causes the file to be uploaded to the server as posted data. At the server, the page code does not run until the file is uploaded to server memory.

The following properties give you flexible ways to access the uploaded file:

- **FileBytes**   The file is exposed as a byte array.
- **FileContent**   The file is exposed as a stream.
- **PostedFile**   The file is exposed as an object of type HttpPostedFile. This object has properties, such as ContentType and ContentLength.

You need to examine any file that is uploaded to determine whether it should be saved; you can examine characteristics such as the file name, size, and Multipurpose Internet Mail Extensions (MIME) type, which specifies the type of file that is being uploaded. When you are ready to save the file, you can use the SaveAs method on the FileUpload control or the HttpPostedFile object.

You can save the file in any location for which you have permission to create files. By default, the requireRootedSaveAsPath attribute of the httpRuntime configuration element in the Web.config file is set to true, which means that you need to provide an absolute path to save the file. You can get an absolute path by using the MapPath method of the HttpServerUtility class and passing to the method the tilde (~) operator, which represents the application root folder.

The maximum size of the file that can be uploaded depends on the value of the MaxRequestLength attribute of the httpRuntime configuration element in the Web.config file. If a user attempts to upload a file that is larger than the MaxRequestLength, the upload fails.

SECURITY ALERT

The FileUpload control allows users to upload files but makes no attempt to validate the safety of the uploaded files. The control does not provide a means to filter the file types that can be uploaded by a user, but you can examine the file characteristics, such as the file name and extension, as well as the ContentType, after the file has been uploaded.

Although you can provide client-side script to examine the file that is being submitted, remember that client-side validation is a convenience for the honest user. A hacker can easily strip the webpage of client-side code to bypass this validation.

In this example, a webpage was created and a FileUpload control was added to the page. In addition, a Button was added to the webpage so that the user can submit the file to the web server via postback. A folder called Uploads was added to the website . The following code was added to the code-behind page to show how the FileUpload control's properties can be set programmatically and a file can be uploaded and saved.

Sample of Visual Basic Code

```vb
Protected Sub Button1_Click(ByVal sender As Object, _
    ByVal e As System.EventArgs) Handles Button1.Click

    If (FileUpload1.HasFile) Then
        Label1.Text = _
          String.Format("File Length: {0}<br />File Name: {1}<br />MIME Type: {2}", _
            FileUpload1.FileBytes.Length,
            FileUpload1.FileName,
            FileUpload1.PostedFile.ContentType)
        FileUpload1.SaveAs( _
        MapPath("~/Uploads/" + FileUpload1.FileName))
    Else
        Label1.Text = "No file received."
    End If
End Sub
```

Sample of C# Code

```csharp
protected void Button1_Click(object sender, EventArgs e)
{
    if (FileUpload1.HasFile)
    {
        Label1.Text =
          string.Format("File Length: {0}<br />File Name: {1}<br />MIME Type: {2}",
          FileUpload1.FileBytes.Length,
          FileUpload1.FileName,
          FileUpload1.PostedFile.ContentType);
        FileUpload1.SaveAs(
          MapPath("~/Uploads/" + FileUpload1.FileName));
    }
    else
    {
        Label1.Text = "No file received.";
    }
}
```

The webpage is shown in Figure 4-15. When a file is selected and the Submit button is clicked, the code checks to see if a file has been uploaded. If a file has been uploaded, information about the file is placed into the Label control for display. The file is then saved to the Uploads folder. The website requires an absolute path, and MapPath performs the conversion from the relative path supplied to an absolute path. Finally, the file is saved.

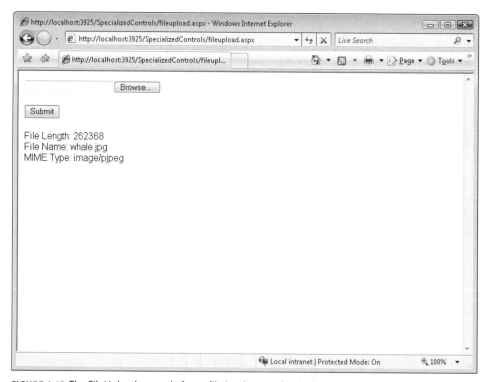

FIGURE 4-15 The FileUpload control after a file has been uploaded.

The Panel Control

The Panel control is used as a control container. It can be useful when you need to group controls and work with them as a single unit. A common example is the need to display and hide a group of controls. Panel controls are also useful for control developers who are creating features such as tabs or show/hide toggles.

In Source view, the Panel control is represented as an <asp:Panel> element. This element can contain many controls nested within it. These controls are considered to be contained by the Panel. In HTML output, the Panel control generates a <div> element inside the browser.

There are a few properties that you need to be aware of when working with the Panel control:

- **BackImageUrl** Used to display a background image in the Panel control
- **HorizontalAlignment** Sets the horizontal alignment of the controls that are in the Panel
- **Wrap** Specifies whether items in the Panel automatically continue on the next line when a line is longer than the width of the Panel control
- **DefaultButton** Specifies the button that is clicked when the Panel control has focus and the user presses Enter on his or her keyboard

As an example, consider a page with a Login form. You might want to provide a button that allows a user to turn off the visibility of (hide) this form. The following shows the markup of the ASPX source.

```
<body>
    <form id="form1" runat="server">
    <div>
        <asp:Button ID="ButtonShowHide" runat="server" Text="Login: hide form"
            width="200" onclick="ButtonShowHide_Click"/>
        <asp:Panel ID="Panel1" runat="server" BackColor="Beige" Width="200">
            <asp:Label ID="Label1" runat="server" Text="User name: "></asp:Label>
            <br />
            <asp:TextBox ID="TextBox1" runat="server"></asp:TextBox>
            <br />
            <asp:Label ID="Label2" runat="server" Text="Password: "></asp:Label>
            <br />
            <asp:TextBox ID="TextBox2" runat="server"></asp:TextBox>
            <br />
            <asp:Button ID="ButtonLogin" runat="server" Text="Login" />
        </asp:Panel>
    </div>
    </form>
</body>
```

The code to show and hide this form is straightforward. You need to handle the toggle button's Click event and set the Visible property of the Panel control appropriately. The following code demonstrates this.

Sample of Visual Basic Code

```
Protected Sub ButtonShowHide_Click(ByVal sender As Object, _
  ByVal e As System.EventArgs) Handles ButtonShowHide.Click

  Panel1.Visible = Not Panel1.Visible
  If Panel1.Visible Then
    ButtonShowHide.Text = "Login: hide form"
  Else
    ButtonShowHide.Text = "Login: show form"
  End If

End Sub
```

Sample of C# Code

```
protected void ButtonShowHide_Click(object sender, EventArgs e)
{
  Panel1.Visible = !Panel1.Visible;
  if (Panel1.Visible)
  {
    ButtonShowHide.Text = "Login: hide form";
  }
  else
  {
    ButtonShowHide.Text = "Login: show form";
  }
}
```

The example webpage is shown in Figure 4-16. Clicking the Logon: Hide Form button hides the Panel and all of its controls, and clicking again displays the Panel and its controls.

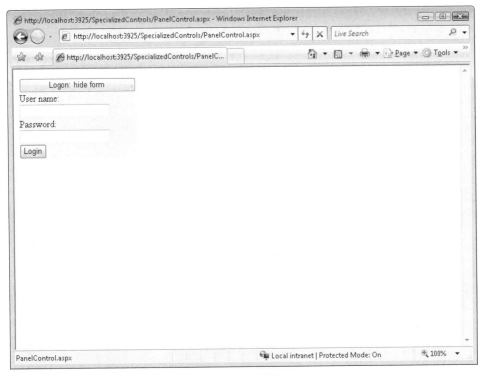

FIGURE 4-16 A Panel control with a button to toggle visibility.

The MultiView and View Controls

Like the Panel control, the MultiView and View controls are also container controls; that is, they are used to group other controls. Again, this is useful when you want to treat and manage a group of controls as a single unit. A MultiView exists to contain other View controls. A View control must be contained inside a MultiView. The two controls are meant to work together. The MultiView is meant to contain many child View controls. It allows you to hide one and then show another View to the user. The MultiView control is also used to create wizards, where each View control in the MultiView control represents a different step or page in the wizard.

MultiView and View do not generate any direct HTML elements when they are rendered, because these controls are essentially server-side controls that manage the visibility of their child controls. In Source view, the MultiView control is represented as an <asp:MultiView> element, and the View control is represented as an <asp:View> element nested inside a MultiView.

You can use the ActiveViewIndex property or the SetActiveView method to change the View programmatically. If the ActiveViewIndex is set to -1, no View controls are displayed. If you pass an invalid View or a null (Nothing) value into the SetActiveView method, an HttpException is thrown. Note that only one View control can be active at a time.

As an example, consider a user registration webpage in which you need to walk a user through the process of registering with your site. You could use a single MultiView control and three View controls to manage this process. Each View control represents a step in the process. An example of the page's layout is shown in Figure 4-17.

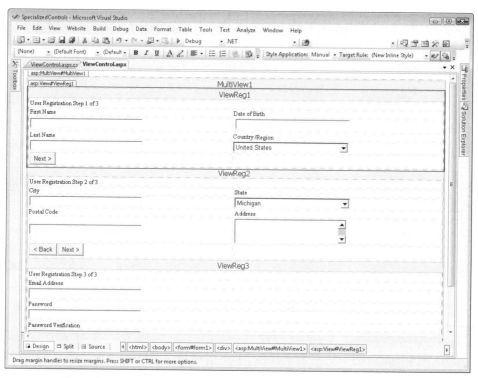

FIGURE 4-17 The MultiView and View control example webpage.

To manage the page in this example, the buttons on the page are set as command buttons. When a user clicks a button, the CommandName property of CommandEventArgs is checked to determine which button was pressed. Based on this information, the MultiView shows (and thereby hides) another View control. The following is an example of the code-behind page.

Sample of Visual Basic Code

```
Partial Class ViewControlVb
    Inherits System.Web.UI.Page

  Protected Sub Page_Load(ByVal sender As Object, _
    ByVal e As System.EventArgs) Handles Me.Load
```

```
      MultiView1.ActiveViewIndex = 0
    End Sub

    Protected Sub Button_Command(ByVal sender As Object, _
      ByVal e As CommandEventArgs)

      Select e.CommandName
        Case "Step1Next"
          MultiView1.ActiveViewIndex = 1
        Case "Step2Back"
          MultiView1.ActiveViewIndex = 0
        Case "Step2Next"
          MultiView1.ActiveViewIndex = 2
        Case "Step3Back"
          MultiView1.ActiveViewIndex = 1
        Case "Finish"
          'hide control from user to simulate save
          MultiView1.ActiveViewIndex = -1
      End Select
    End Sub
End Class
```

Sample of C# Code

```csharp
public partial class ViewControl : System.Web.UI.Page
{
  protected void Page_Load(object sender, EventArgs e)
  {
    MultiView1.ActiveViewIndex = 0;
  }

  protected void Button_Command(object sender, CommandEventArgs e)
  {
    switch (e.CommandName)
    {
      case "Step1Next":
        MultiView1.ActiveViewIndex = 1;
        break;
      case "Step2Back":
        MultiView1.ActiveViewIndex = 0;
        break;
      case "Step2Next":
        MultiView1.ActiveViewIndex = 2;
        break;
      case "Step3Back":
        MultiView1.ActiveViewIndex = 1;
        break;
      case "Finish":
        //hide control from user to simulate save
        MultiView1.ActiveViewIndex = -1;
        break;
    }
  }
}
```

When the webpage is displayed, the first step is displayed to the user. When he or she clicks Next, the processing returns to the server and the Button_Command event is fired. The page changes to another View control based on the results of this event. Figure 4-18 shows the MultiView example in action.

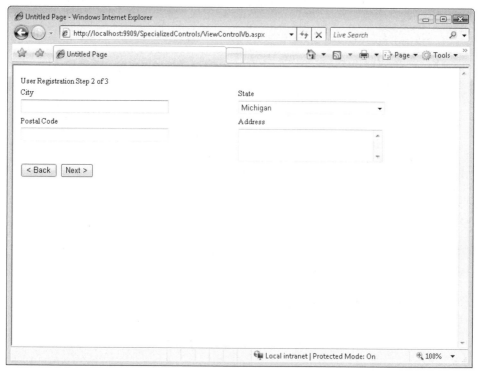

FIGURE 4-18 The MultiView control is used to switch between the View controls on the server.

The Wizard Control

The Wizard control is a complex control that is used to display a series of WizardStep controls to a user, one after the other, as part of a user input process. The Wizard control builds on the MultiView and View controls presented previously. It provides functionality to ensure that only one WizardStep control is visible at a time and provides the ability to customize most aspects of the Wizard and WizardStep controls. The most significant use of the Wizard control is to prompt the user for a large amount of data by breaking the data into logical chunks, or steps. The Wizard control presents the user with steps that can be validated, either at the end of the process or in between each step. You certainly can accomplish the same result by using separate webpages for each logical chunk of data, but the wizard consolidates the data collection process into a single webpage.

The Wizard control contains a header area that can be customized to display information specific to the step with which the user is currently engaged. The Wizard control also contains a sidebar area that can be used to quickly navigate to steps in the control. You can also programmatically control which step is displayed; you are not constrained to navigating through the steps in a linear fashion.

The built-in navigation capabilities determine which buttons are displayed based on the StepType value. The BaseWizardStep class contains the StepType property, which can be set to one of the following WizardStepType enumeration values:

- **WizardStepType.Auto** This renders navigation buttons based on the location of the step within the WizardSteps collection property of the Wizard control. This is the default.

- **WizardStepType.Complete** This is the last step to appear. No navigation buttons are rendered.

- **WizardStepType.Finish** This is the final data collection step; the Finish and Previous buttons are rendered for navigation.

- **WizardStepType.Start** This is the first step to appear; only the Next button is rendered.

- **WizardStepType.Step** This is a step between the Start and the Finish steps. The Previous and Next buttons are rendered.

In the following example, a wizard gives users the ability to select options on a vehicle. In a real vehicle selection scenario, many more options would, of course, be available. This, in turn, would dictate simplifying the option selection for the user (and thus justifying the use of the Wizard control).

To create the form for this example, you add a Wizard control to a webpage. Inside the Wizard control are WizardStep controls, one for each selection step, as follows: Exterior, Interior, Options, and Summary. The Exterior selection step contains three RadioButton controls for selection of a red, blue, or black exterior. The Interior selection step contains two RadioButton controls for selection of leather or cloth seats. The Options selection step contains CheckBox controls for selection of AM/FM radio, heated seats, and an air freshener. The Summary step contains a Label control that is populated with the selections that were made in the previous steps. In Figure 4-19, the populated WizardStep controls were cut out of Visual Studio and put in a single graphic for you to view.

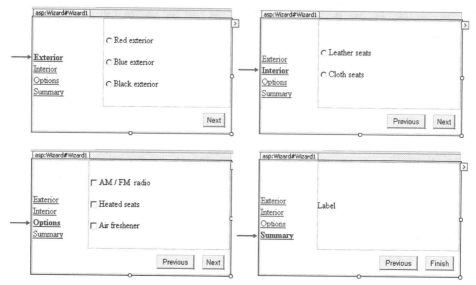

FIGURE 4-19 The WizardStep controls populated with the controls to be displayed to the user.

After the WizardStep controls were created and each step was populated, code was added to the code-behind page to populate the Label control in the Summary step. Also, code was added to the Form_Load event handler to assure that the Wizard control starts at the first step, and finally, code was added to the Wizard1_FinishButtonClick event handler to display the results. The code-behind page is as follows.

Sample of Visual Basic Code

```vb
Protected Sub Page_Load(sender As Object, e As EventArgs)
    If Not IsPostBack Then
        Wizard1.ActiveStepIndex = 0
    End If
End Sub


Protected Sub Wizard1_FinishButtonClick(sender As Object, e As
WizardNavigationEventArgs)
    Wizard1.Visible = False
    Response.Write(String.Format("Finished<br />{0}", Label1.Text))

End Sub


Protected Sub Wizard1_NextButtonClick(sender As Object, e As WizardNavigationEventArgs)
    If Wizard1.WizardSteps(e.NextStepIndex).Title = "Summary" Then
        Dim sb As New StringBuilder()

        For Each ws As WizardStep In Wizard1.WizardSteps
            For Each c As Control In ws.Controls
                If TypeOf c Is CheckBox Then
                    Dim cb As CheckBox = DirectCast(c, CheckBox)
                    If cb.Checked Then
                        sb.AppendFormat("{0}<br />", cb.Text)
```

```
            End If
         End If
      Next
   Next
   Label1.Text = sb.ToString()
End If
End Sub
```

Sample of C# Code

```csharp
protected void Page_Load(object sender, EventArgs e)
{
    if (!IsPostBack)
    {
        Wizard1.ActiveStepIndex = 0;
    }
}

protected void Wizard1_FinishButtonClick(object sender,
    WizardNavigationEventArgs e)
{
    Wizard1.Visible = false;
    Response.Write(string.Format("Finished<br />{0}", Label1.Text));
}

protected void Wizard1_NextButtonClick(object sender,
        WizardNavigationEventArgs e)
{
    if (Wizard1.WizardSteps[e.NextStepIndex].Title == "Summary")
    {
        StringBuilder sb = new StringBuilder();

        foreach (WizardStep ws in Wizard1.WizardSteps)
        {
            foreach (Control c in ws.Controls)
            {
                if (c is CheckBox)
                {
                    CheckBox cb = (CheckBox)c;
                    if (cb.Checked)
                    {
                        sb.AppendFormat("{0}<br />", cb.Text);
                    }
                }
            }
        }
        Label1.Text = sb.ToString();
    }
}
```

When the webpage is displayed, the user sees the first step (Exterior). The user can go from step to step, and on the final step, click Finish. In the Summary step, the Label control displays the current selections. After the user clicks Finish, the Wizard control is hidden and the summary information is displayed.

The Xml Control

The Xml control is used to display the contents of an XML document. This control is useful if your data is stored in XML and you need to execute an Extensible Stylesheet Language (XSL) transformation. The data can then be rendered for display to a user by using the Xml control.

The XML document to be displayed is specified by setting either the DocumentSource property or the DocumentContent property. The DocumentSource property accepts a string that specifies the location of an XML file to be loaded into the control. The DocumentContent property accepts a string that contains actual XML content.

The TransformSource property accepts an optional string that contains the location of an XSL transformation file to apply to the XML document. The Transform property accepts a Transform object that can be used to perform the transformation as well. The Xml control also contains the TransformArgumentList property, which is used to pass arguments to the XSL transformation.

In the following example, an Xml control is used to display the contents of an XML file after an XSL transformation is applied. This XML file and the XSL transformation file are as follows.

XML File: ProductList.xml

```
<?xml version="1.0" encoding="utf-8" ?>
<ProductList>
  <Product Id="1A59B" Department="Sporting Goods" Name="Baseball" Price="3.00" />
  <Product Id="9B25T" Department="Sporting Goods" Name="Tennis Racket" Price="40.00" />
  <Product Id="3H13R" Department="Sporting Goods" Name="Golf Clubs" Price="179.00" />
  <Product Id="7D67A" Department="Clothing" Name="Shirt" Price="12.00" />
  <Product Id="4T21N" Department="Clothing" Name="Jacket" Price="45.00" />
</ProductList>
```

XSL Transformation File: ProductList.xsl

```
<?xml version="1.0" encoding="utf-8" ?>
<xsl:stylesheet version="1.0"
xmlns:xsl="http://www.w3.org/1999/XSL/Transform"
xmlns:msxsl="urn:schemas-microsoft-com:xslt"
xmlns:labs="http://labs.com/mynamespace">
  <xsl:template match="/">
    <html>
      <head>
        <title>Product List</title>
      </head>
      <body>
        <center>
          <h1>Product List</h1>
          <xsl:call-template name="CreateHeading"/>
        </center>
```

```xml
      </body>
    </html>
  </xsl:template>
  <xsl:template name="CreateHeading">
    <table border="1" cellpadding="5">
      <tr >
        <th bgcolor="yellow">
          <font size="4" >
            <b>Id</b>
          </font>
        </th>
        <th bgcolor="yellow">
          <font size="4" >
            <b>Department</b>
          </font>
        </th>
        <th  bgcolor="yellow">
          <font size="4" >
            <b>Name</b>
          </font>
        </th>
        <th  bgcolor="yellow">
          <font size="4" >
            <b>Price</b>
          </font>
        </th>
      </tr>
      <xsl:call-template name="CreateTable"/>
    </table>
  </xsl:template>
  <xsl:template name="CreateTable">
    <xsl:for-each select="/ProductList/Product">
      <tr>
        <td align="center">
          <xsl:value-of select="@Id"/>
        </td>
        <td align="center">
          <xsl:value-of select="@Department"/>
        </td>
        <td>
          <xsl:value-of select="@Name"/>
        </td>
        <td align="right">
          <xsl:value-of select="format-number(@Price,'$#,##0.00')"/>
        </td>
      </tr>
    </xsl:for-each>
  </xsl:template>
</xsl:stylesheet>
```

For the webpage related to this example, an Xml control is added to the page. The following code was added to the code-behind file to display the XML file after the XSL transformation is applied.

Sample of Visual Basic Code

```
Protected Sub Page_Load(ByVal sender As Object, _
  ByVal e As System.EventArgs) Handles Me.Load

  Xml1.DocumentSource = "~/App_Data/ProductList.xml"
  Xml1.TransformSource = "~/App_Data/ProductList.xsl"
End Sub
```

Sample of C# Code

```
public partial class XmlControlVb : System.Web.UI.Page
{
    protected void Page_Load(object sender, EventArgs e)
    {
       Xml1.DocumentSource = "~/App_Data/ProductList.xml";
       Xml1.TransformSource = "~/App_Data/ProductList.xsl";
    }
}
```

When the webpage is displayed, the XML and XSL files are loaded. The resulting transformation is shown in Figure 4-20.

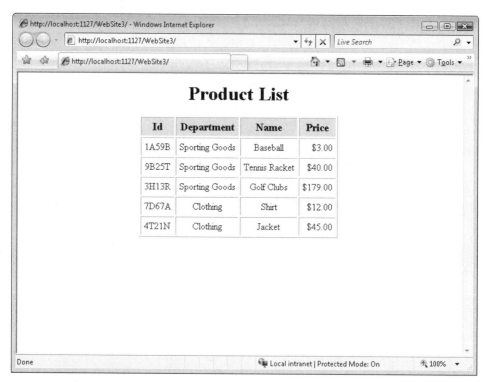

FIGURE 4-20 The result of applying the XSL transformation to the XML file.

Quick Check

1. What control provides the best implementation of a schedule of specific dates?

2. You want to create a webpage that prompts the user to input lots of data, and you want the data input to be spread across multiple screens. What is the best control to use to implement this solution on a single webpage?

3. Your customer wants her company's home page to contain an image of the world and require users to click their specific countries. This redirects the users to the websites for their respective countries. What control will you use?

Quick Check Answers

1. The Calendar control provides the best implementation of a schedule of specific dates.

2. The Wizard control is the best control to use.

3. The ImageMap control should be used.

PRACTICE   Working with Specialized Web Controls

In this practice, you use the specialized web controls that have been defined in this lesson to create a webpage that allows users to select an office by using a map and select a date for the office to be serviced.

> **ON THE COMPANION MEDIA**
>
> If you encounter a problem completing an exercise, you can find the completed projects in the samples installed from this book's companion CD. For more information about the project files and other content on the CD, see "Using the Companion Media" in this book's Introduction.

EXERCISE   Creating the Website and Adding Controls

In this exercise, you create a website and add controls to the site. You then add code to the code-behind page to initialize the Wizard control and the ImageMap hot spots. You also write code to display a summary after the wizard has completed its actions.

1. Open Visual Studio and create a new website by using your preferred programming language. Create a new webpage without a master page.

2. Add a Wizard control to the webpage. From the Wizard Tasks menu, select Add/Remove WizardSteps.

3. Use the collection editor to define three wizard steps. Set their Title properties to the following (in order): **Select Office**, **Service Date**, and **Summary**. Figure 4-21 shows an example. When complete, close the WizardStep Collection Editor.

FIGURE 4-21 The WizardStep Collection Editor.

4. Add a new folder to your project. Right-click the project node in Solution Explorer and select New Folder. Rename the folder **Images**.

5. Add the Floorplan.png file to the Images folder by dragging it to Solution Explorer from Windows Explorer. This file is available in the sample code installed from this book's CD.

6. In Design view, select the Wizard control. Use the Properties window to set the Width property to **475px** and the Height property to **350px**.

7. In Design view, click the Select Office link in the Wizard control to ensure that this is the current, selected step in the designer.

8. Add an ImageMap control to this step (drag from the Toolbox). Set its ID to **OfficeImageMap**. Set its ImageUrl property to point to the Floorplan.jpg file.

9. Under the ImageMap control, type **Office Selected:**. After this text, add a Label control with the **OfficeSelectedLabel** ID, and clear its Text property. Your ASPX source for this WizardStep control should look like the following, example.

```
<asp:Wizard ID="Wizard1" runat="server" Height="350px" Width="475px">
    <WizardSteps>
        <asp:WizardStep runat="server" title="Select Office">
            <asp:ImageMap ID="OfficeImageMap" runat="server"
                ImageUrl="~/Images/Floorplan.png">
            </asp:ImageMap>
            <br />
            Office Selected:
            <asp:Label ID="OfficeSelectedLabel" runat="server"></asp:Label>
        </asp:WizardStep>
        <asp:WizardStep runat="server" title="Service Date">
        </asp:WizardStep>
        <asp:WizardStep runat="server" Title="Summary">
        </asp:WizardStep>
    </WizardSteps>
</asp:Wizard>
```

10. In Design view, click the Wizard control's Service Date link to make this the active step. Inside this step, add the text **Select Service Date:**. Under this text, add a Calendar control, and set the ID to **ServiceDateCalendar**. Your ASPX source for this step should look like the following.

ASPX Source: Service Date

```
<asp:WizardStep runat="server" title="Service Date">
    Select Service Date:
    <br />
    <asp:Calendar ID="ServiceDateCalendar" runat="server"></asp:Calendar>
</asp:WizardStep>
```

11. Next, in Design view, click the Summary link in the Wizard control to make this the active step. In this step, add a Label control and set its ID to **SummaryLabel**, its Height to **200,** and its Width to **250**. Clear its Text value. Your ASPX source for this step should look like the following.

ASPX Source: Summary

```
<asp:WizardStep runat="server" Title="Summary">
    <asp:Label ID="SummaryLabel" runat="server" Height="200px" Width="250px">
    </asp:Label>
</asp:WizardStep>
```

12. From the Wizard Tasks menu, choose AutoFormat. Click Professional, and then click OK.

13. Open the webpage's code-behind file. If you are using Visual Basic .NET, add a Page_Load event handler.

14. In the Page_Load event handler, add an if statement that tests whether the webpage is being posted back to the server.

   a. Inside the false portion of the if statement (when the request is not a postback), add code to set the ActiveStepIndex of the Wizard control to the first WizardStep (0).

   b. In the same block, add code to set the HotSpot mode of the ImageMap to perform a postback (OfficeImageMap.HotSpotMode = HotSpotMode.PostBack).

   c. Finally, create a function that returns a RectangleHotSpot instance and takes the appropriate parameters. Add code to call this function and add the resulting RectangleHotSpot instance to the ImageMap control. Table 4-5 shows the dimensions of the various office hot spots.

TABLE 4-5 RectangularHotSpot Values

POSTBACKVALUE	LEFT	TOP	RIGHT	BOTTOM
Cubicle A	0	0	123	105
Cubicle B	124	0	262	105
Cubicle C	263	0	382	105
Cubicle D	258	164	382	286
Cubicle E	135	164	257	286
Cubicle F	0	164	134	286

15. Create an OfficeImageMap_Click event handler in the code-behind page. Add code to this event to place the PostBackValue from the ImageMap event arguments into the OfficeSelectedLabel control.

16. Create an event handler for the Wizard1_FinishButtonClick event in the code-behind page. In this event, add code to hide the Wizard control, and write a thank-you message to the user.

17. Create an event handler for the Wizard control's ActiveStepChanged event. Add code to this method to find out whether the active step is the summary step. If the summary step is the current step, populate the SummaryLabel control with a message that shows the current selection summary. Your final code-behind page should resemble the following example.

Sample of Visual Basic Code

```vb
Protected Sub Page_Load(ByVal sender As Object, ByVal e As System.EventArgs)_
  Handles Me.Load
    If Not IsPostBack Then
        Wizard1.ActiveStepIndex = 0
        OfficeImageMap.HotSpotMode = HotSpotMode.PostBack
        OfficeImageMap.HotSpots.Add(GetHotSpot("Cubicle A", 0, 0, 123, 105))
        OfficeImageMap.HotSpots.Add(GetHotSpot("Cubicle B", 124, 0, 262, 105))
        OfficeImageMap.HotSpots.Add(GetHotSpot("Cubicle C", 263, 0, 382, 105))
        OfficeImageMap.HotSpots.Add(GetHotSpot("Cubicle D", 258, 164, 382, 286))
        OfficeImageMap.HotSpots.Add(GetHotSpot("Cubicle E", 135, 164, 257, 286))
        OfficeImageMap.HotSpots.Add(GetHotSpot("Cubicle F", 0, 164, 134, 286))
    End If
End Sub


Private Function GetHotSpot _
    (ByVal name As String, ByVal left As Integer, ByVal top As Integer, _
        ByVal right As Integer, ByVal bottom As Integer) As RectangleHotSpot

    Dim rhs As New RectangleHotSpot()

    rhs.PostBackValue = name
    rhs.Left = left
    rhs.Top = top
    rhs.Right = right
    rhs.Bottom = bottom

    Return rhs
End Function


Protected Sub OfficeImageMap_Click(ByVal sender As Object, _
  ByVal e As System.Web.UI.WebControls.ImageMapEventArgs) _
  Handles OfficeImageMap.Click

    OfficeSelectedLabel.Text = e.PostBackValue
End Sub


Protected Sub Wizard1_FinishButtonClick(ByVal sender As Object, _
  ByVal e As System.Web.UI.WebControls.WizardNavigationEventArgs) _
  Handles Wizard1.FinishButtonClick

    Wizard1.Visible = False
    Response.Write("Thank you! Your request is being processed.")
End Sub


Protected Sub Wizard1_ActiveStepChanged(ByVal sender As Object, _
  ByVal e As System.EventArgs) Handles Wizard1.ActiveStepChanged
    If Wizard1.ActiveStep.Title = "Summary" Then
        SummaryLabel.Text = String.Format_
  ("Summary Info:<br />Room: {0}<br />Delivery Date: {1}", _
        OfficeSelectedLabel.Text, _
  ServiceDateCalendar.SelectedDate.ToShortDateString())
    End If
End Sub
```

Sample of C# Code

```csharp
protected void Page_Load(object sender, EventArgs e)
{
    if (!IsPostBack)
    {
        Wizard1.ActiveStepIndex = 0;
        OfficeImageMap.HotSpotMode = HotSpotMode.PostBack;

        OfficeImageMap.HotSpots.Add(GetHotSpot("Cubicle A", 0, 0, 123, 105));
        OfficeImageMap.HotSpots.Add(GetHotSpot("Cubicle B", 124, 0, 262, 105));
        OfficeImageMap.HotSpots.Add(GetHotSpot("Cubicle C", 263, 0, 382, 105));
        OfficeImageMap.HotSpots.Add(GetHotSpot("Cubicle D", 258, 164, 382,
286));
        OfficeImageMap.HotSpots.Add(GetHotSpot("Cubicle E", 135, 164, 257,
286));
        OfficeImageMap.HotSpots.Add(GetHotSpot("Cubicle F", 0, 164, 134, 286));
    }
}

private RectangleHotSpot GetHotSpot(string name, int left,
    int top, int right, int bottom)
{
    RectangleHotSpot rhs = new RectangleHotSpot();

    rhs.PostBackValue = name;

    rhs.Left = left;
    rhs.Top = top;
    rhs.Right = right;
    rhs.Bottom = bottom;

    return rhs;
}

protected void OfficeImageMap_Click(object sender, ImageMapEventArgs e)
{
    OfficeSelectedLabel.Text = e.PostBackValue;
}

protected void Wizard1_FinishButtonClick(
    object sender, WizardNavigationEventArgs e)
{
    Wizard1.Visible = false;
    Response.Write("Thank you! Your request is being processed.");
}

protected void Wizard1_ActiveStepChanged(object sender, EventArgs e)
{
    if (Wizard1.ActiveStep.Title == "Summary")
    {
        SummaryLabel.Text = string.Format
("Summary Info:<br />Room: {0}<br />Delivery Date: {1}",
            OfficeSelectedLabel.Text,
ServiceDateCalendar.SelectedDate.ToShortDateString());
    }
}
```

18. Run the webpage and test it.

- Try clicking each room on the floor plan and observe the results.
- Click the Service Date link or click Next to display the Calendar control. Select a date.
- Click the Summary link or click Next to display a summary of your selections.
- Click Finish to see the thank-you message.

Lesson Summary

- The Table, TableRow, and TableCell controls provide ways to format tabular and graphical information that is displayed on a webpage.
- The Image control is used to display an image on a webpage.
- The ImageButton control is used to display a clickable image that can be used to cause a postback to the web server when the image is clicked.
- The ImageMap control is used to display a clickable image that can be used to cause a postback to the web server with different results, depending on where the user clicks the image.
- The Calendar control displays a calendar for a month the user chooses, and allows the user to select dates and move to the next or previous month.
- The FileUpload control is used to display a TextBox and Browse button that allows a user to either type a file name and path or click Browse and select a file and path.
- The Panel control is a control container and is useful for controls that you want to display and hide as a group.
- The View control is a control container designed to work with the MultiView control that is useful for controls that you want to display and hide as a group.
- The MultiView control contains a collection of View controls; the MultiView control provides behavior that allows you to switch between View controls.
- The Wizard control is a complex control that is used to display a series of WizardStep controls to a user, one after the other.
- The Xml control is used to display XML data to a user.

Lesson Review

You can use the following questions to test your knowledge of the information in Lesson 2, "Exploring Specialized Server Controls." The questions are also available on the companion CD in a practice test, if you prefer to review them in electronic form.

> **NOTE ANSWERS**
>
> Answers to these questions and explanations of why each answer choice is correct or incorrect are located in the "Answers" section at the end of the book.

1. Which of the following represents the best use of the Table, TableRow, and TableCell controls?

    A. Creating and populating a table in Design view

    B. Displaying data in a grid format

    C. Creating a table of static images stored in a folder on your site

    D. Providing layout for dynamically generated controls

2. Your graphics department just completed an elaborate image that shows the product lines that your company sells. Some of the product line graphics are circular, others are rectangular, and others are complex shapes. You want to use this image as a menu on your website. What is the best way to incorporate the image into your website?

    A. Use ImageButton and use the x-coordinate and y-coordinate that are returned when the user clicks to figure out what product line the user clicked.

    B. Use the Table, TableRow, and TableCell controls, break the image into pieces that are displayed in the cells, and use the TableCell control's Click event to identify the product line that was clicked.

    C. Use the MultiView control and break up the image into pieces that can be displayed in each View control for each product line. Use the Click event of the View to identify the product line that was clicked.

    D. Use an ImageMap control and define hot spot areas for each of the product lines. Use the PostBackValue to identify the product line that was clicked.

3. You are creating a website that collects a lot of data from your users. The data collection spreads over multiple webpages. When the user reaches the last page, you need to gather all of the data, validate it, and save it to the database. You notice that it can be rather difficult to gather the data that is spread over multiple pages, and you want to simplify the development of this application. What control should you use to solve this problem?

    A. The View control

    B. The TextBox control

    C. The Wizard control

    D. The Panel control

Case Scenarios

In the following case scenarios, you apply what you've learned about server controls in this chapter. If you have difficulty completing this work, review the material in this chapter before beginning the next chapter. You can find answers to these questions in the "Answers" section at the end of this book.

Case Scenario 1: Determining the Type of Controls to Use

You are creating a new webpage that collects customer data. This webpage needs to capture customer names and addresses, along with an indicator of which customers are active. You also need to display several vertical market categories and give the data entry personnel the ability to place each customer into all matching categories. You also prompt the data entry personnel for the quantity of computers that the customer has, based on several ranges, such as 0–5, 6–50, 51–250, 251–1,000, and 1,001 or more.

- Define the type of controls that you will use and indicate why.

Case Scenario 2: Determining How to Prompt for Data

You are creating a new webpage that will be used to price a car insurance policy. There are many factors that go into pricing the policy, but the customer information can be placed into the following categories:

- Location
- Vehicles
- Other drivers
- Accident history
- Motor vehicle violations

You are concerned that a prospective customer might leave the site before all of the information is entered.

- List some of the ways that you can prompt the user for this information in an organized fashion, keeping the displayed prompts to a minimum so that the customer does not feel inundated with too many prompts.

Case Scenario 3: Implementing a Calendar Solution

You are a training provider who is creating a website that will be used to schedule training contractors to work at different locations. The application will prompt the user for the contractor information and the training class dates. The user can view a schedule that shows all of the training classes and which contractors are scheduled for specific times. Also, a contractor can log in and see the training classes that have been assigned to him or her.

1. Where can you use the Calendar control in this solution?
2. Would you need to use a Table control?

Suggested Practices

To help you master the Implement Server Controls exam objective presented in this chapter, complete the following tasks.

Implement Server Controls

Reading about different server controls is not enough to give you the experience you need to work with them in the real world. To gain this experience, complete all three practices.

- **Practice 1**   Visit your favorite e-commerce website. Recreate the checkout page by using web server controls.

- **Practice 2**   Create a webpage that displays a picture that the user uploads from his or her computer. Use the Image and FileUpload controls.

- **Practice 3**   Create a checkout form that prompts the user for both a billing address and a shipping address. For the shipping address, provide a radio button that prompts the user to use his or her billing address or enter a different shipping address. If the user chooses to enter a different shipping address, use a MultiView control to display text boxes that prompt for the required information. If the user chooses to use the billing address, display the billing address in a Label contained within a different View.

Take a Practice Test

The practice tests on this book's companion CD offer many options. For example, you can test yourself on just the lesson review questions in this chapter, or you can test yourself on all the 70-515 certification exam objectives. You can set up the test so it closely simulates the experience of taking a certification exam, or you can set it up in study mode so you can look at the correct answers and explanations after you answer each question.

> **MORE INFO   PRACTICE TESTS**
>
> For details about all the practice test options available, see the "How to Use the Practice Tests" section in this book's Introduction.

CHAPTER 5

Input Validation and Site Navigation

W hen you need users to enter data, such as a user name or address, it's important to give them quick and precise feedback about any mistakes they make. For example, if a user forgets to type his or her city, you shouldn't simply reject the input with a generic message. Instead, you should provide a descriptive message and highlight the field the user needs to edit. You can speed the process by validating the input before the user clicks a button to submit it to the server; Microsoft ASP.NET automatically generates client-side JavaScript to perform client-side validation. For security reasons, you also need to validate the input at the server. ASP.NET can handle many types of server-side validation automatically, too.

Another hallmark of a usable and robust web application is solid navigation. You need to know how to move the user from page to page based on a request, based on postback information, and based on the overall context of the user's actions. In addition, users expect to be able to navigate through a website as they see fit. You need to be able to manage the application as users move through it.

Web Parts are components of a webpage that can be personalized and rearranged. You can use Web Parts to improve a site's consistency while still allowing users to customize content to their specific needs. You can exchange information between Web Parts, allowing preferences that are set in one Web Part to propagate to others.

Exam objectives in this chapter:

- Developing and Using Web Forms Controls
    - Validate user input.
    - Create page layout.

Lessons in this chapter:

Before You Begin

To complete the lessons in the chapter, you should be familiar with developing applications with Microsoft Visual Studio by using Microsoft Visual Basic or Microsoft Visual C#. In addition, you should be comfortable with all of the following:

- The Visual Studio 2010 Integrated Development Environment (IDE)
- A basic understanding of Hypertext Markup Language (HTML) and client-side scripting
- Creating a new website
- Adding web server controls to a webpage

 **REAL WORLD**

Tony Northrup

In the real world, it's the end user who judges you. You might write the most manageable code with unbelievably thorough comments, but if the users hate using your website, you can't consider it a success.

This chapter covers three technologies that can greatly improve the usability and likeability of your websites. Input validation might sound like a security feature, and it is, but because it provides useful and immediate feedback to users, it's also a usability feature.

Naturally, proper navigation can make your site easier to use, but try to see the site through the user's eyes and not through your developer's eyes. Users don't care about the technical structure of the site; instead, your navigation should reflect how users access the site.

Finally, Web Parts allow you to create highly customizable websites. Internet users rarely care to customize a website, however, so Web Parts are best used on intranet applications. In particular, you should only use Web Parts when users will spend all day within an application and are willing to learn how to customize it.

Lesson 1: Performing Input Validation

In this lesson, you will learn how the validation framework operates and how you can use the validation controls that are included in ASP.NET to perform input validation.

Understanding the Validation Framework

A common problem for developers is ensuring that data entered by users is valid. That problem is made more difficult when the application exists in a web browser. When the data is sent from the browser to the server, you need to make sure that the data is valid. In addition, users expect some feedback and assistance entering valid data before they spend the time sending it to the server for a response. Fortunately, ASP.NET has a built-in data validation framework for handling this scenario. It provides a straightforward way to accomplish both client-side and server-side validation with minimal coding.

Client-side validation is a convenience to users, but it is not a security feature. It improves performance by checking the data at the browser before sending the data to the server. This avoids unnecessary communication with the server. Client-side validation isn't a security feature because a malicious user could easily bypass the client-side validation. Only server-side validation can improve security. Fortunately, ASP.NET makes it easy to build both client-side and server-side validation into webpages.

Adding Validation Controls to Your Page

Validation controls are found in the Visual Studio Toolbox. You add them to a webpage the same way you add other controls. The following are the basic steps for using a validation control on a webpage:

1. Open a webpage in Design view, and open the Visual Studio Toolbox. Add the input controls that require validation, such as TextBox and RadioButtonList controls.

2. Navigate to the Validation tab of the Toolbox. Drag the desired validation control next to (or near) the control you intend to validate. For example, you might drag a RequiredFieldValidator control next to a TextBox control to ensure that a user enters data in the text box.

3. Next, you set the ID property of the validation control (from Source view or in the Properties window). To enhance your code's readability, use a name for the control that is similar to the field it validates. For example, if you are validating a TextBox control named NameTextBox, you might name the validator NameTextBoxValidator.

4. The next step is to set the validation control's ControlToValidate property to the control being validated.

5. Set the ErrorMessage property to something that will be meaningful to the user. The value set as the ErrorMessage will be displayed to users as assistance when they try to submit the form with invalid data. This message is typically put into a ValidationSummary control on the page.

6. Set the Text property of the validation control to display a message to the user at the validation control location if validation fails. If you plan to display validation error messages in a ValidationSummary control, set the Text property to a short string such as an asterisk (*). Keeping this short minimizes the space that is required by the validation control but still offers a visual cue to the user that something is wrong with the item.

7. If you do not display the full error message in the Text property, set the validation control's tooltip property to be the same as or similar to the ErrorMessage property. This value will display when the user points to the validation control's text after validation fails.

8. Set the Display property to None to prevent the display of the Text property if validation fails. If you want to display the Text property, set Display to Static to leave a blank space where the error message will appear prior to validation. Otherwise, set Display to Dynamic to reformat the ASP.NET output around the Text if validation fails.

9. Optionally, add a ValidationSummary control to display all the validation error messages in one location after the user has triggered page-level validation by clicking a submit button. This is especially useful in scenarios in which the webpage is crowded with other controls, and displaying the validation error message next to the invalid control presents a difficult layout situation. Typically, you should place the ValidationSummary either near the submit button or at the top of the page. When the ShowMessageBox property is set to true, the ValidationSummary control will display a pop-up message with the validation errors in lieu of, or in addition to, displaying the validation errors on the webpage.

> **NOTE** **SETTING VALIDATION CONTROL COLOR**
> Use themes to configure validation control text to appear in red. Themes were discussed in Chapter 2, "Using Master Pages, Themes, and Caching."

Server-Side Validation

The validation controls work in concert with the Page object, the base class for your webpage. ASP.NET uses the Page class and the validation controls together to ensure that data coming from the client is still valid when it gets to the server.

The Page class has a Validators property that contains a collection of all the validation controls defined on the page. The Page class also has a Validate method. You call this method to ask the page to check each of the validation controls and determine if anything on the page is not valid.

ASP.NET calls the Validate method automatically after the page's Load event handler method executes. Therefore, after the page has loaded, you can find out if the page is indeed valid on the server. To do so, check the Page.IsValid property (set by the Validate method). This Boolean property is only true if all validation controls have completed their processing correctly. Although the IsValid property is set automatically, you need to check the IsValid property in every event handler to determine whether the code should run; that is, your code will still execute when IsValid is set to false unless you tell it not to.

Client-Side Validation

ASP.NET writes client-side validation code for you when you simply use the validation controls on your page. ASP.NET renders the controls, along with their JavaScript, to the page. This JavaScript executes as users enter and leave the focus of the controls on your page. Client-side validation is turned on by default. You can turn it off for specific validation controls by setting the EnableClientScript property to false.

Again, when the user leaves the focus of a control (uses the Tab key or otherwise navigates away from a control), the client-side validation for that particular control fires. If validation fails, the validation control's Text property is displayed to the user.

You can also use the Focus method of a control to set the focus to a specific control when your page is loaded. The Focus method adds client-side JavaScript code that executes at the browser to set focus to the appropriate control. In addition to the new Focus method, a validation control has a similar property called SetFocusOnError. You can set this property to true to cause the invalid control to automatically receive focus. In this way, a user does not leave the control until the control has valid data. This property is set to false by default.

Determining When to Cause Validation

Client-side validation is considered a convenience for users. Its primary benefit is that it prevents a page from being posted back to the server until all client-side validation has successfully occurred. Sometimes this can be a problem.

For example, suppose a user wants to click a cancel or help button, and the page is not in a valid state. The default behavior of these buttons is to attempt a postback to the server. However, if the page is not valid, clicking the button will trigger client-side validation and will not cause a postback to the server.

To avoid this, set the CausesValidation property to false for controls that should bypass validation. For example, if you have a button called ButtonReset that triggers a reset on the page, you can set it to cause a postback even when the page is not valid by setting ButtonReset.CausesValidation to false.

Using Validation Groups

Often you do not want to treat your entire page as a single entity that is validated as a whole. Instead, you might want to break up sections of the page and have them validated independently. This is especially true for long data entry forms with multiple sections. You might not want the entire page's validation to fire when only submitting a single section of the page. Fortunately, ASP.NET allows for this scenario.

The validation controls in ASP.NET provide the ValidationGroup property. This property can be assigned a string value to specify a section of your page (or a group of controls to validate as a single unit). This property exists on the validation controls and on the controls that cause a postback. When a control performs a postback, the validation controls that have a matching ValidationGroup property value are validated. This allows for these controls to validate as a unit.

When you process the postback on the server, the IsValid property on the Page object only reflects the validity of the validation controls that have been validated. By default, these are the validation controls that are in the same ValidationGroup, but you can call a validation control's Validate method to add that control to the set of controls on which the IsValid property reports.

There is also an overload method to the Page object's Validate method. This overload accepts a string that is used to specify the ValidationGroup to validate. This overload is executed when a postback that causes validation occurs. The Page object also has a GetValidators method that accepts a string containing the name of the ValidationGroup. This method returns the list of validation controls in the specified ValidationGroup.

Understanding the RequiredFieldValidator Control

The RequiredFieldValidator control is used to ensure that the user has entered a value into a control (excluding white space). The other validation controls do not require a value to be entered. Therefore, you will frequently need to use RequiredFieldValidator with one of the other controls to achieve the desired validation.

The RequiredFieldValidator control provides the property called InitialValue. It is used when the control that you are validating defaults to an initial value and you want to ensure that the user changes this value. For example, if you set some default text in your control, you can set the InitialValue property to this text to ensure that it is not a valid user input. As an example, consider a drop-down list for selecting a state on an address entry form. The drop-down list might contain a value that is an instruction to the user, such as "Select a state . . . ." In this case, you want to ensure that the user selects a state and not this value. You can use the InitialValue of the RequiredFieldValidator control to manage this scenario.

Using the CompareValidator Control

The CompareValidator control performs validation by using comparison operators such as greater than and less than to compare the data entered by a user with a constant you set or a value in a different control.

The CompareValidator control can also be used to verify that the data entered into a particular control is of a certain data type, such as a date or a number. To use the control for this purpose, you set the Type property to a valid data type. ASP.NET will then validate that the user's input can be cast into a valid instance of the specified type. If all you intend is a data type check, you can also set the Operator property to DataTypeCheck. Figure 5-1 shows the Type property being set from the Properties window for a CompareValidator control.

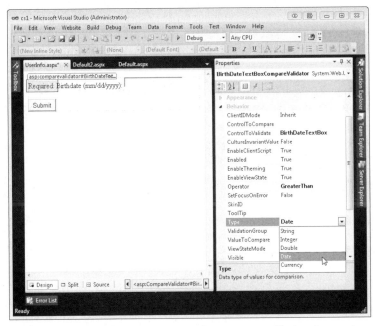

FIGURE 5-1 The CompareValidator control being set to verify that the user has entered a date value.

The CompareValidator control uses the ValueToCompare property to set a constant that is used to perform a comparison. For example, you might want to make sure that the user enters a birth date greater than 1900. You could do so by setting the ValueToCompare property to 1/1/1900. You would then set the Operator property of the control. This property defines how to perform the comparison and can be set to Equal, NotEqual, GreaterThan, GreaterThanEqual, LessThan, LessThanEqual, or DataTypeCheck. In the case of the birth date example, you would set this value to GreaterThanEqual. If you select DataTypeCheck, you can leave ValueToCompare blank, because ASP.NET simply verifies that the input is in the correct format.

You can also use the ControlToCompare property to define another control that is used to perform the comparison. In this case, you are doing a comparison from one control to the next. For example, if you are asking a user to enter a range of dates, you would want the second defined date to be later than the first. You could use a CompareValidator control to perform this check. You would set its ControlToValidate property to the second date entry text box, and its ControlToCompare property to the first date entry text box. You would then set the Operator property to LessThanEqual.

Using the RangeValidator Control

You often need to ensure that a value entered by a user is within a predefined range of acceptable values. For example, you might want to create a webpage that shows sales for the current year, through a specific date. You would then want to verify that the user has entered a date value that is within the range of the current year. To do so, you can use the RangeValidator control.

The RangeValidator control verifies that user input is within a specified range of values. This control has two very specific properties for managing the range of acceptable values: MinimumValue and MaximumValue. These properties work as their name indicates. The RangeValidator control also uses the Type property to determine the data type of the user's input.

If you want the user to enter a date in the past from the current calendar year, you would set the Type property to Date. You would then set the MinimumValue and MaximumValue properties programmatically on the server to represent the current year. The following code shows an example of what this might look like.

Sample of Visual Basic Code

```
Protected Sub Page_Load(ByVal sender As Object, _
  ByVal e As System.EventArgs) Handles Me.Load

  RangeValidatorSalesDate.MinimumValue = "1990"()

  RangeValidatorSalesDate.MaximumValue = _
    DateTime.Now.Year.ToString()

End Sub
```

Sample of C# Code

```
protected void Page_Load(object sender, EventArgs e)
{
  if (!IsPostBack)
  {
    RangeValidatorSalesDate.MinimumValue = "1990";
    RangeValidatorSalesDate.MaximumValue =
      DateTime.Now.Year.ToString();
  }
}
```

Using the RegularExpressionValidator Control

The RegularExpressionValidator control performs its validation based on a regular expression. A *regular expression* is a series of pattern-matching codes that you can use to identify and change simple and complex character sequences. The control uses the ValidationExpression property to contain the regular expression that is compared to the data that is to be validated. The data is validated if it matches the regular expression.

The regular expression language is complex, and Microsoft does not identify an understanding of the language as an exam objective, so this book will not teach its details. Fortunately, however, Visual Studio does have several predefined regular expressions from which to choose. For example, you might simply need to confirm that a user has entered a valid Internet email address. You can do so by selecting the button next to the ValidationExpression property in the Properties window. When you do this, you open the Regular Expression Editor dialog box shown in Figure 5-2.

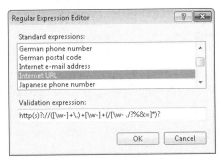

FIGURE 5-2 The Regular Expression Editor dialog box used for selecting predefined regular expressions for a RegularExpressionValidator control.

> **MORE INFO   REGULAR EXPRESSIONS**
>
> For more information about regular expressions, including tutorials and sample regular expressions, refer to the following sites:
>
> *http://www.regexlib.com/*
>
> *http://www.regular-expressions.info/*

The CustomValidator Control

Even with the robust set of validation controls provided by ASP.NET, you still might find yourself having another validation need. Luckily, there is the CustomValidator control. You can use it to create your own validation and have that validation run alongside the other validation on a page. The CustomValidator control performs validation-based code that you write. You can use JavaScript to write validation code that will be executed on the client side; you can also write server-side validation code by using your preferred Microsoft .NET Framework language.

Custom Client-Side Validation

Client-side validation provides users with immediate feedback when they are working with your page. If you intend to write custom validation and are using other client-side validation, you should consider writing the JavaScript necessary for your custom validation scenario. Your custom validation JavaScript needs to participate in the data validation framework that the other validation controls use. Following this framework ensures that your custom validation controls work alongside the other validation controls.

The first step in writing your custom client-side validation is to define a JavaScript function inside your webpage HTML source (not the code-behind). This function must have the following method signature.

```
function ClientFunctionName(source, arguments)
```

You can name your function to suit your needs. However, the parameters should follow the standard shown here. Your function will be automatically called by the data validation framework after it is attached to a CustomValidator control. When the function is called, the source parameter will contain a reference to the validation control that is performing the validation. The arguments parameter is an object that has a property called Value; this property contains the data to be validated by your client-side function.

Next, you need to write your validation logic. This logic should evaluate arguments.Value and determine if it is valid or not. After you have determined this, you set the arguments.IsValid property to true (valid) or false (invalid).

Finally, you attach your client-side function to a CustomValidator control by setting the ClientFunctionName property of the CustomValidator control to the name of your validation function.

Consider an example. Suppose you need custom validation for managing password rules at the client level. Your requirement might be that passwords must be between 6 and 14 characters in length and must contain at least one uppercase letter, one lowercase letter, and one numeric character. Suppose that your page includes a TextBox control for entering a new password, a Button control for submitting the password change, a ValidationSummary control for showing the long error message, a RequiredFieldValidator control to ensure that the user has typed a password, and a CustomValidator control for validating the actual password. Your webpage source might look as follows.

```
<%@ Page Language="VB" AutoEventWireup="false" CodeFile="NewPassword.aspx.vb"
Inherits="NewPassword" %>

<!DOCTYPE html PUBLIC "-//W3C//DTD XHTML 1.0 Transitional//EN" "http://www.w3.org/TR/
xhtml11/DTD/xhtml11-transitional.dtd">

<html xmlns="http://www.w3.org/1999/xhtml">
<head id="Head2" runat="server">
    <title>Change Password</title>
</head>
<body style="font-family: Arial">
    <form id="form1" runat="server">
    <div>
    <table width="400">
        <tr><td colspan="2" style="font-size: x-large">Change Password</td></tr>
        <tr>
            <td colspan="2">
                <asp:ValidationSummary ID="ValidationSummary1" runat="server" />
            </td>
        </tr>
        <tr>
```

```
                <td width="190" align="right" valign="middle">New password:</td>
                <td width="210" valign="middle">
                    <asp:TextBox ID="NewPasswordTextBox" runat="server"
TextMode="Password"></asp:TextBox>
                        <asp:RequiredFieldValidator ID="RequiredFieldValidatorPassword"
                          runat="server" ErrorMessage="Please enter a valid password" text="*"
                          ToolTip="Please enter a valid password"
                          ControlToValidate="NewPasswordTextBox"></asp:RequiredFieldValidator>

                        <asp:CustomValidator ID="NewPasswordCustomValidator" runat="server"
                            Text="*" ToolTip="Password must be between 6-14 characters and
include 1 capital letter, 1 lowercase letter, and 1 number"
                            ErrorMessage="Password must be between 6-14 characters and include 1
capital letter, 1 lowercase letter, and 1 number"
                            ControlToValidate="NewPasswordTextBox"
                            ClientValidationFunction="ValidatePassword"></asp:CustomValidator>
                </td>
        </tr>
        <tr>
            <td></td>
            <td><asp:Button ID="ButtonSubmit" runat="server" Text="Submit" /></td>
        </tr>
    </table>
    </div>
    </form>
</body>
</html>
```

The next step is to add client-side validation code to the webpage source. You can do so before the <body> tag on the page. The following provides an example JavaScript function called ValidatePassword. Notice that the function signature matches the one defined by the data validation framework. Also notice the setting of arguments.IsValid.

Sample of Validate Password Client-Side Validator

```
<script language="javascript" type="text/javascript">
    function ValidatePassword(source, arguments) {
        var data = arguments.Value.split('');
        //start by setting false
        arguments.IsValid = false;

        //check length
        if(data.length < 6 || data.length > 14) return;

        //check for uppercase, lowercase, and number
        var uc = false; var lc = false; var num = false;
        for (var c in data) {
            if (data[c] >= 'A' && data[c] <= 'Z') {
                uc = true;
            } else if (data[c] >= 'a' && data[c] <= 'z') {
                lc = true;
            } else if (data[c] >= '0' && data[c] <= '9') {
                num = true;
            }
            if (uc && lc && num) {
```

```
                    arguments.IsValid = true;
                    break;
            }
        }
    } </script>
```

The final step is to set the CustomValidator control's ClientValidationFunction property to the function name ValidatePassword. You can then run the webpage to test the example. When the TextBox control loses focus, the custom client-side validation is executed, as shown in Figure 5-3.

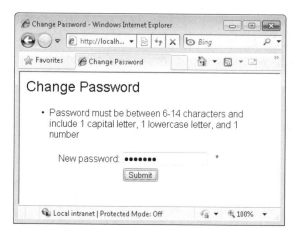

FIGURE 5-3 The client-side validation causes the ValidationSummary control to display the error message.

Custom client-side validators are typically used only for complex validations that cannot be done with a regular expression. For example, you might use a custom client-side validator on a user registration page to query a web service to verify that a user name is not already taken without requiring the page to post back to the web server. This simple example is only intended to demonstrate how to connect the JavaScript function with the ASP.NET CustomValidator.

Custom Server-Side Validation

The CustomValidator control can work client side, server side, or both. To implement server-side validation with the CustomValidator control, handle its ServerValidate event. This server-side event can be trapped in your code-behind file to execute code that you write. You provide an event handler for the specified CustomValidator control the same way you would for any other control. Server-side validation provides the same two types of parameters that you use for client-side validation: source provides access to the source validation control, and args provides the args.Value property for checking the data that should be validated. You also use the args.IsValid property to indicate validation success or failure. The following code shows the password example using the ServerValidate event to perform server-side validation.

Sample of Visual Basic Code

```vb
Protected Sub NewPasswordCustomValidator_ServerValidate( _
  ByVal source As Object, _
  ByVal args As System.Web.UI.WebControls.ServerValidateEventArgs) _
  Handles CustomValidatorNewPassword.ServerValidate

    Dim data As String = args.Value
    ' Start by setting false
    args.IsValid = False

    ' Check length
    If data.Length < 6 OrElse data.Length > 14 Then
        Return
    End If

    ' Check for uppercase, lowercase, and numeric
    Dim uc As Boolean = False
    Dim lc As Boolean = False
    Dim num As Boolean = False
    For Each c As Char In data
        If Char.IsUpper(c) Then
            uc = True
        ElseIf Char.IsLower(c) Then
            lc = True
        ElseIf Char.IsNumber(c) Then
            num = True
        End If

        If uc AndAlso lc AndAlso num Then
            'must be valid
            args.IsValid = True
            Exit For
        End If
    Next
End Sub
```

Sample of C# Code

```csharp
protected void NewPasswordCustomValidator_ServerValidate(object source,
  ServerValidateEventArgs args)
{
    string data = args.Value;
    // Start by setting false
    args.IsValid = false;

    // Check length
    if (data.Length < 6 || data.Length > 14) return;

    // Check for uppercase, lowercase, and numeric
    bool uc = false; bool lc = false; bool num = false;
    foreach (char c in data)
    {
        if (char.IsUpper(c))
        {
            uc = true;
        }
```

```
    else if (char.IsLower(c))
    {
        lc = true;
    }
    else if (char.IsNumber(c))
    {
        num = true;
    }

    if (uc && lc && num)
    {
        //must be valid
        args.IsValid = true;
        break;
    }
  }
}
```

The server-side validation you write does not need to provide exactly the same validation as that of the client-side code. For example, the custom client-side script for a CustomValidator control that validates a five-character customer ID might simply test to ensure that five characters are provided within the acceptable range (and are uppercase and lowercase as required). The server-side validation might perform a database query to ensure that the customer ID is that of a valid customer in the database.

 Quick Check

1. Which validation control can be used to determine whether data that is entered into a TextBox control is of type Currency?

2. What control can be used to display all validation errors on a page inside a pop-up window?

Quick Check Answers

1. You can use the CompareValidator control to do a data type check. Set its Operator property to DataTypeCheck and its Type property to Currency.

2. The ValidationSummary control can be used to show a summary of validation error messages for a page. The control can also be used as a pop-up browser window.

PRACTICE   **Working with Validation Controls**

In this practice, you create a webpage that simulates user registration with a site. This page will contain TextBox controls for the user to enter a name, email address, password, and password confirmation.

The following are the validation rules for the page:

- All fields must contain data.

- The user name field must be between 6 and 14 characters in length. These characters can be uppercase, lowercase, numeric, or underscores.

- The user's email address should be in valid email address format.

- The password and confirm password fields will be 6 to 14 characters. The user's password must contain at least one uppercase letter, one lowercase letter, and one number (as described in the custom validation control example earlier in this chapter).

ON THE COMPANION MEDIA

If you encounter a problem completing an exercise, you can find the completed projects in the samples installed from this book's companion CD. For more information about the project files and other content on the CD, see "Using the Companion Media" in this book's Introduction.

EXERCISE Creating the Website and Adding Controls

In this exercise, you create the website and add the user input controls.

1. Open Visual Studio and create a new ASP.NET Empty Web Site.

2. Add a new web form named **userreg.aspx** without a master page. In design view, add the words **User Registration** to the top of the page.

3. On separate lines, add the data entry field descriptions: **User name:**, **Email:**, **Password:**, and **Confirm password:**.

4. Add a TextBox control to each description. Name the TextBox controls **UserNameTextBox**, **EmailTextBox**, **PasswordTextBox**, and **ConfirmPasswordTextBox**.

5. Set the TextMode property of PasswordTextBox and ConfirmPasswordTextBox to **Password**.

6. Add a Button control under the text boxes. Set the Text property of the Button control to **Register**.

7. All of the TextBox controls require user input. Therefore, you will add a RequiredField-Validator after each TextBox control. Name each of these controls relative to the field it validates. For each of the RequiredFieldValidator controls, set the ControlToValidate property to the TextBox that is being validated. Set the ErrorMessage and ToolTip properties to **Your user name is required**, **Your email is required**, **A password is required**, and **You must confirm your password**, as appropriate. Set the Text property to an asterisk ().

8. Next, you will define validation for the UserNameTextBox control. The user name field must be between 6 and 14 characters in length. These characters can be uppercase, lowercase, numeric, or underscores.

9. To process this rule, you will use a RegularExpressionValidator control. Add one next to the UserNameTextBox control and set the ControlToValidate property to **UserNameTextBox**.

10. Set the Text property to an asterisk; set the ErrorMessage and ToolTip properties to **Please use only letters and numbers with no spaces**. Finally, set the ValidationExpression property to the regular expression **\w{6,14}**. The UserNameTextBox control should look similar to the following.

```
<asp:RegularExpressionValidator ID="RegularExpressionValidator1" runat="server"
    ControlToValidate="UserNameTextBox"
    ErrorMessage="Please use only letters and numbers with no spaces"
    ToolTip="Please use only letters and numbers with no spaces"
    ValidationExpression="\w{6,14}">*</asp:RegularExpressionValidator>
```

11. The field you need to validate next is the user's email address. To do so, you will use another regular expression validation control. Add it next to the EmailTextBox control. Set its Text, ToolTip, ControlToValidate, and ErrorMessage properties. Use the Properties window to set the control's ValidationExpression property. Select Internet Email Address from the list of available regular expressions.

12. The next control you need to add validation to is the PasswordTextBox control. You will use the custom validation example defined earlier in the chapter.

    a. To start, add a CustomValidator control next to the PasswordTextBox control.

    b. Set the ControlToValidate property to **PasswordTextBox**.

    c. Set the Text property to an asterisk (*).

    d. Set the ErrorMessage and ToolTip properties to **Please enter 6-14 characters, including at least 1 uppercase letter, 1 lowercase letter, and 1 number**.

    e. Set the ClientValidationFunction property to **ValidatePassword**.

    f. Below the head section of the HTML source, add the code from the "Sample of Validate Password Client-Side Validator," listing shown earlier in this lesson.

    g. Add the ServerValidate event handler for the CustomValidator control to your code-behind page. In this method, add the code from the "Custom Server-Side Validation" section earlier in this lesson.

13. The final validation you need to do is to ensure that both the password and confirm password fields contain the same data. To do so, start by adding a CompareValidator control next to the ConfirmPasswordTextBox control.

    a. Set the ControlToValidate property to **ConfirmPasswordTextBox**.

    b. Set the ControlToCompare property to **PasswordTextBox**.

    c. Set the Text property to *.

    d. Set the ErrorMessage and ToolTip properties to **Both password fields must match**.

14. Finally, add a ValidationSummary control to the top of the webpage. This will be used to display the long error messages when the user submits the form.

The completed webpage is shown in Figure 5-4.

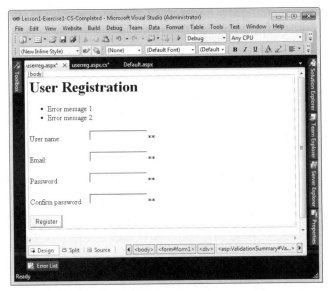

FIGURE 5-4 The completed webpage containing all validation controls.

15. Run the webpage.

16. Before entering any information into the TextBox controls, click Register. Verify that the RequiredFieldValidators are displayed by noting the errors that are displayed in the ValidationSummary control and by hovering your pointer over each of the asterisks to see each tooltip.

17. Test the user name validation by typing fewer than six characters into the TextBox-UserName control and clicking Register. Note the validation error. Also, try typing 15 or more characters. Next, type 10 characters into the field but use an invalid character such as the apostrophe ('). Finally, type valid data into the text box to ensure that the validation control works properly.

18. Test the email field by entering an invalid email address. Finally, test with a valid email address.

19. Test the password field for the appropriate input by trying to input fewer than 6 characters or more than 14 characters. Also, attempt a password that is all lowercase, all uppercase, or all numeric. Notice that special characters, such as the plus sign (+), minus sign (-), and percent sign (%), are allowed in the password, but not required. Finally, attempt to enter a valid password.

20. Test the confirmation password by typing a confirmation password that does not match the password. Test again with a matching password.

Lesson Summary

- The data validation framework provides a set of validation controls that bind to one or more web controls to perform validation of the data that is typed into those web controls.
- The ASP.NET validation controls provide both client-side and server-side validation.
- You can disable client-side validation by setting the EnableClientScript property to false.
- The validation controls available in ASP.NET include CustomValidator, CompareValidator, RangeValidator, RegularExpressionValidator, and RequiredFieldValidator.
- The ValidationSummary control can be added to a webpage to provide a summary of the validation errors on the webpage and as a pop-up message.
- The RegularExpressionValidator control is used to specify validation patterns.
- The CustomValidator control allows you to provide your custom client-side and server-side code to perform input validation.
- The Page.Validate method can be explicitly called to force validation.
- You can query a webpage's IsValid property to verify that the page is valid before running code. In fact, if you depend on validated inputs from the user, you must check this yourself in your code. ASP.NET won't invalidate the page for you if there is invalid input. (That is, ASP.NET won't throw an exception or notify you in any other way than the IsValid property.)

Lesson Review

You can use the following questions to test your knowledge of the information in Lesson 1, "Performing Input Validation." The questions are also available on the companion CD in a practice test, if you prefer to review them in electronic form.

> **NOTE ANSWERS**
>
> Answers to these questions and explanations of why each answer choice is correct or incorrect are located in the "Answers" section at the end of the book.

1. You need to validate a vendor ID entered by a user. The valid vendor IDs exist in a database table. How can you validate this input?

   A. Provide a RegularExpressionValidator control and set the ValidationExpression property to /DbLookup{code}.

   B. Provide a RangeValidator control, and set the MinValue property to DbLookup(code) and the MaxVaue property to DbLookup(code).

   C. Provide a CustomValidator control with server-side code to search the database for the code.

   D. Provide a CompareValidator control and set the compare expression to the name of a server-side function that performs a database lookup of the code.

2. You have created a webpage that contains many controls that are validated by using validation controls. This page also contains Button controls that perform postbacks. You disabled all of the client-side validation and noticed that when you clicked any of the Button controls, the code in the Click event handler was executing even when some of the controls did not have valid data. How can you best solve this problem to ensure that code is not executed when invalid data exists?

   A. In the Click event handler method for each of your Button controls, test the webpage's IsValid property and exit the method if this property is false.

   B. In the Load event handler method of the webpage, test the webpage's IsValid property and exit the method if this property is false.

   C. Re-enable the client-side script to disable postback until valid data exists.

   D. Add the runat="server" attribute to all of the validation controls.

3. You have created an elaborate webpage that contains many validated controls. You want to provide a detailed message for each validation error, but you don't have space to provide the detailed message next to each control. What can you do to indicate an error at the control and list the detailed error messages at the top of the webpage?

   A. Set the Text property of the validator control to the detailed message and set the ErrorMessage property to an asterisk. Place a ValidationSummary control at the top of the webpage.

   B. Set the ErrorMessage property of the validator control to the detailed message and set the Text property to an asterisk. Place a ValidationSummary control at the top of the webpage.

   C. Set the ToolTip property of the validator control to the detailed message and set the ErrorMessage property to an asterisk. Place a ValidationSummary control at the top of the webpage.

   D. Set the ToolTip property of the validator control to the detailed message and set the Text property to an asterisk. Place a ValidationSummary control at the top of the webpage.

Lesson 2: Performing Site Navigation

Seamless navigation from one webpage to another is what makes a collection of webpages feel like a web application. Developers must consider when and how to move a user between pages. This movement should seem automatic and planned, with the user in control. When setting up navigation, developers need to consider how to handle navigation following post-backs and how to allow a user to navigate within the site.

When a page performs a postback, web applications typically end up posting data to the webpage that originated the request. However, there are scenarios in which an application might post data from one webpage to another. Developers also need to consider where the application will navigate to as a result of a particular postback.

All websites have some form of user navigation control. The sites that stand out are those that provide easy-to-use navigation. Of course, you as the developer need to provide this navigation. You must determine what happens as the result of user-driven navigation—especially when a user is in the process of a transaction such as the purchase of a product.

This lesson covers tools for users to navigate your site and techniques that developers can use to transfer requests between pages.

> **After this lesson, you will be able to:**
> - Determine the correct method for navigating a user from one page to another in your site depending on your needs.
> - Redirect users to pages by using both client-side and server-side methods.
> - Use the SiteMap web server control to display a representation of a site's navigation structure inside the SiteMapPath, Menu, and TreeView navigation controls .
>
> **Estimated lesson time: 40 minutes**

Is Page Navigation Necessary?

Page navigation is the process of moving between one actual page of your website and another. However, with controls such as the Wizard control and technologies such as Asynchronous JavaScript and XML (AJAX), you can embed a lot of functionality inside a single actual page in your site. In this way, navigation takes on a new meaning. You are no longer moving between pages. Rather, you are moving around on your page. You might do so from the client, and you might do so as a response from a postback to the server.

Embedding all the controls and data collection for a particular process on a single page can make your work easier. Instead of moving data from page to page or storing it in the database or on the server, you can rely on the page itself to manage the entire process. Of course, these solutions are not always suitable for each data collection scenario. Therefore, it is important to know what is involved when doing page-to-page navigation.

Choosing a Method to Navigate Pages

There are many ways to navigate from one page to another in ASP.NET. It's helpful to first identify these ways and then examine each in detail. The following are the methods for page-to-page navigation in an ASP.NET site:

- **Client-side navigation** Client-side code or markup allows a user to request a new webpage. Your client code or markup requests a new webpage in response to a client-side event, such as the click of a hyperlink or the execution of JavaScript as part of a button click.
- **Cross-page posting** A control and form are configured to post back to a webpage that is different than the one that made the original request.

- **Client-side browser redirect**   Server-side code sends a message to the browser, informing the browser to request a different webpage from the server.
- **Server-side transfer**   Server-side code transfers control of a request to a different webpage.

Client-Side Navigation

One of the easiest ways to allow navigation to a different webpage is to provide a HyperLink control on the form and set the NavigateUrl property to the desired destination. The HyperLink control generates an HTML anchor tag, <a>. The NavigateUrl property is placed into the href attribute of the <a> element. The following example shows both the source of a HyperLink control and its rendered HTML.

HyperLink Control: Source

```
<asp:HyperLink ID="HyperLink1"
  runat="server" NavigateUrl="~/NavigateTest2.aspx">Goto NavigateTest2</asp:HyperLink>
```

HyperLink Control: Rendered HTML

```
<a id="HyperLink1" href="NavigateTest2.aspx">Goto NavigateTest2</a>
```

In this example, if this control is placed on a webpage called NavigateTest1.aspx, and the HyperLink control is clicked, the browser simply requests the NavigateTest2.aspx page. This means that no data is posted to NavigateTest2.aspx. If NavigateTest2.aspx requires data, you need to find a way to get the data to the page. One way to do this is to embed the data in the query string in the NavigateUrl property of the HyperLink control.

Another means of forcing client-side navigation is through JavaScript. In this case, you write code to perform webpage navigation by changing the document object's location property to a new URL. The document object represents the webpage in client-side JavaScript; setting its location property causes the browser to request the webpage defined by the location property's value.

The following example contains an HTML button element with a bit of client-side JavaScript to request a new page when the button is clicked.

```
<input id="Button1" type="button"
       value="Goto NavigateTest2"
       onclick="return Button1_onclick()" />
```

Notice that the onclick event is configured to call the client-side method, Button1_onclick. The JavaScript source for the Button1_onclick method is added into the <head> element of the page as follows.

```
<script language="javascript" type="text/javascript">
function Button1_onclick() {
  document.location="NavigateTest2.aspx";
}
</script>
```

Once again, the NavigateTest2.aspx page is requested, and no data is posted back to the web server. Of course, you could send data into the function as part of a parameter and then append that data to the query string of the request.

Cross-Page Posting

Cross-page posting is frequently the best choice in a scenario in which data is collected on one webpage and processed on another webpage that displays the results. In such a scenario, a Button control typically has its PostBackUrl property set to the webpage to which the processing should post back. The page that receives the postback receives the posted data from the first page for processing. This page is referred to as the *processing page*.

The processing page often needs to access data that was contained inside the initial page that collected the data and that delivered the postback. The previous page's data is available inside the Page.PreviousPage property. This property is set only if a cross-page post occurs. If the PreviousPage property is set to Nothing (null in C#), no cross-page posting occurred. You can access the controls found in the previous page by using the FindControl method of the PreviousPage property (which is a NamingContainer).

In the following example, a webpage called DataCollection.aspx contains a TextBox control called TextBox1 and a Button control that has its PostBackUrl set to ~/ProcessingPage.aspx. When the data collection page invokes the processing page, it executes server-side code to pull the data from the data collection page, encode it by using HtmlEncode, and then put it inside a Label control. The code to do so is as follows.

Sample of Visual Basic Code

```
Protected Sub Page_Load(ByVal sender As Object, _
   ByVal e As System.EventArgs) Handles Me.Load

  If Page.PreviousPage Is Nothing Then
    LabelData.Text = "No previous page in post"
  Else
    LabelData.Text = _
      Server.HtmlEncode(CType(PreviousPage.FindControl("TextBox1"), TextBox).Text)
  End If

End Sub
```

Sample of C# Code

```
protected void Page_Load(object sender, EventArgs e)
{
    if(Page.PreviousPage == null)
    {
        LabelData.Text = "No previous page in post";
    }
    else
    {
        LabelData.Text =
            Server.HtmlEncode(((TextBox)PreviousPage.FindControl("TextBox1")).Text);
    }
}
```

Accessing Posted Data as Strongly Typed Data

You can also provide access to cross-page posted data through strongly typed properties on the page. This eliminates the need to call FindControl and execute the type casting calls. You first define the public property (or properties) on your data collection page, and then you set the PreviousPageType directive on the processing page to point to the data collection page. ASP.NET does the remaining work to provide you with the properties that the strongly typed Page.PreviousPage object supports.

In the following example, the DataCollection.aspx page performs a cross-page postback to ProcessingPage.aspx. However, it first defines a public property called PageData, as follows.

Sample of Visual Basic Code

```
Public ReadOnly Property PageData() As String
  Get
    Return TextBox1.Text
  End Get
End Property
```

Sample of C# Code

```
public string PageData
{
  get { return TextBox1.Text; }
}
```

As in the previous example, the DataCollection.aspx page also contains a Button control on which the PostBackUrl property has been set to "~/ProcessingPage.aspx".

To access the newly created PageData property for the processing page, you need to set the PreviousPageType directive in the ProcessingPage.aspx page. This directive is added after the Page directive in the page's source and looks like the following.

```
<%@ PreviousPageType VirtualPath="~/DataCollection.aspx" %>
```

The DataCollection.aspx page contains a Label control that is populated from the PageData property. The following code demonstrates this.

Sample of Visual Basic Code

```
Protected Sub Page_Load(ByVal sender As Object, _
  ByVal e As System.EventArgs) Handles Me.Load

  If Page.PreviousPage Is Nothing Then
    LabelData.Text = "No previous page in post"
  Else
    LabelData.Text = _
      PreviousPage.PageData
  End If

End Sub
```

Sample of C# Code

```csharp
protected void Page_Load(object sender, EventArgs e)
{
    if (PreviousPage == null)
    {
        LabelData.Text = "No previous page in post";
    }
    else
    {
        LabelData.Text =
            PreviousPage.PageData;
    }
}
```

Note that you might find that IntelliSense does not show the PageData property when you code this example. Simply build the page that causes the data type of the PreviousPage property to be set, and the PageData property will be visible to IntelliSense.

Client-Side Browser Redirect

Often you need to redirect a user to another page based on the result of his or her request or postback to the server. For example, a user might click a Submit Order button on your page. After processing the order successfully, you might then want to redirect the user to an order summary page. The Page.Response object contains the Redirect method for doing just that.

The Redirect method can be used in your server-side code to instruct the browser to initiate a request for another webpage. The redirect is not a postback; to the web server, the client behaves as if the user clicked a hyperlink.

Consider the following example code. Here the SubmitOrder.aspx page contains a Button control that performs a postback to the server. After that postback has processed, a call is made to redirect the user to the OrderDetails.aspx page.

Sample of Visual Basic Code

```vb
Protected Sub ButtonSubmit_Click(ByVal sender As Object, _
  ByVal e As System.EventArgs) Handles ButtonSubmit.Click

    Response.Redirect("~/OrderDetails.aspx")

End Sub
```

Sample of C# Code

```csharp
protected void ButtonSubmit_Click(object sender, EventArgs e)
{
    Response.Redirect("~/OrderDetails.aspx");
}
```

The redirect is accomplished by sending an HTTP response code of 302 to the browser along with the URL of the page to which to redirect. The address that is displayed in the browser is updated to reflect the new URL location. Note that this comes at the cost of performing an extra call to the server.

The PreviousPage property does not get populated when you are using the Redirect method. To access data from the original page, you need to resort to traditional methods of passing data, such as placing the data into cookies or session state variables or passing the data in the query string.

Server-Side Transfer

You can use server-side transfers to cause ASP.NET to process a different webpage without requiring a new request from the browser. For example, if the browser requests page1.aspx, and page1.aspx calls Page.Server.Transfer("page2.aspx"), ASP.NET will process page2.aspx—even though the browser's address bar still shows page1.aspx.

Similar to the redirect example discussed in the previous topic, you execute a Transfer call from the server. This is typically the result of a postback. As an example, suppose you have a page called OrderRequest.aspx, and this page contains a button for submitting an order. When an order is submitted, your code on the server might transfer the entire request to another page called OrderProcessing.aspx. The following shows an example of making this method call.

Sample of Visual Basic Code

```
Protected Sub Button1_Click(ByVal sender As Object, _
  ByVal e As System.EventArgs) Handles Button1.Click

  Try

    Server.Transfer("~/OrderProcessing.aspx", False)
  Catch ex As System.Threading.ThreadAbortException
    'Ignore Server.Transfer exception
  End Try

End Sub
```

Sample of C# Code

```
protected void Button1_Click(object sender, EventArgs e)
{
  try
  {
    Server.Transfer("~/OrderProcessing.aspx", false);
  }
  catch (System.Threading.ThreadAbortException ex)
  {
    // Ignore Server.Transfer exception
  }
  }
}
```

Notice that the code sample catches a ThreadAbortException after calling System.Transfer. While you should typically avoid handling exceptions without processing them, calling Server. Transfer always results in the .NET Framework throwing a ThreadAbort Exception. The code works if you do not catch the exception; however, the uncaught exception incurs a slight performance penalty.

The Transfer method has an overload that accepts a Boolean parameter called preserveForm. You set this parameter to indicate whether you want to keep the form and query string data. You can also access the PreviousPage property during a transfer (just as you would with cross-page posting). If the page you transfer to throws an unhandled exception, processing will return to the original page.

 **REAL WORLD**

Tony Northrup

n the real world, many classes aren't as useful as they seem. For example, the SiteMap class (discussed next) doesn't use the industry standard format that search engines accept when you submit a site map. Therefore, you still need to write code to generate a separate site map for search engines. Server.Transfer, however, is actually far more useful than it might initially appear.

Server.Transfer allows you to switch to a different ASPX page without the user knowing. This means that you can create multiple ASPX pages (and their code-behind files) for a single page, allowing you to present users with a single webpage that appears in several completely different formats.

Imagine that you're creating a retail website that sells movies on DVDs and music on CDs. You might have a single Product.aspx page that displays any product that the website sells, but you also might want to display movie previews and reviews for the DVDs, and audio previews and band information for the CDs. You don't have to create a single page for both layouts; within Product.aspx, look up whether the product is a DVD or CD, and then use Server.Transfer to process the request with a product type–specific page, such as ProductDVD.aspx or ProductCD.aspx. Put any common components in a master page. For times when the user attempts to look up a product in the database that does not exist, you can also use Server.Transfer to redirect the user to an HTTP 404 File Not Found error page.

The real power of Server.Transfer is that it allows you to separate how webpages appear to users from the internal structure of the site.

Using the Site Map Web Server Control

Thus far you have seen how to help push users from page to page by using both client-side and server-side techniques. Another key component of any website is a solid navigational structure for users. Users need to be able to navigate to the various features and functionality provided by your application. ASP.NET provides controls to help you both manage the navigational structure of your site and provide the display of that structure to users.

You can manage and document your site structure by using a *site map*. A site map in ASP.NET is an XML file that contains the overall structure and hierarchy of your site. Site maps are used to populate ASP.NET navigation controls, such as the Menu, SiteMapPath, and TreeView controls, with your site's page hierarchy. You create and manage this file. This gives you control over which pages are top-level pages, which pages are nested pages within that top level, and any pages to which users will not be allowed to navigate.

You can add a site map to your application by right-clicking your website and selecting Add New Item | Site Map. A site map is an XML file with the extension .sitemap. You add nodes to the site map by adding <siteMapNode> elements. Each of these elements has a title attribute that gets displayed to the user, a url attribute to define the page to which to navigate, and a description attribute for defining information about the page. A .sitemap file (typically named Web.sitemap) for a small order-entry site might look as follows.

```xml
<?xml version="1.0" encoding="utf-8" ?>
<siteMap xmlns="http://schemas.microsoft.com/AspNet/SiteMap-File-1.0" >
  <siteMapNode url="~/Default.aspx" title="Home"  description="">
    <siteMapNode url="~/Catalog.aspx" title="Our Catalog"  description="">
      <siteMapNode url="~/ProductCategory.aspx" title="Products"  description="" />
      <siteMapNode url="~/Product.aspx" title="View Product"  description="" />
    </siteMapNode>
    <siteMapNode url="~/Cart.aspx" title="Shopping Cart"  description="" />
    <siteMapNode url="~/Account.aspx" title="My Account"  description="">
      <siteMapNode url="~/SignIn.aspx" title="Login"  description="" />
      <siteMapNode url="~/PassReset.aspx" title="Reset Password"  description="" />
      <siteMapNode url="~/AccountDetails.aspx" title="Manage Account"  description="">
        <siteMapNode url="~/Profile.aspx" title="Account Information"  description="" />
        <siteMapNode url="~/OrderHistory.aspx" title="My Orders"  description="">
          <siteMapNode url="~/ViewOrder.aspx" title="View Order"  description="" />
        </siteMapNode>
      </siteMapNode>
    </siteMapNode>
    <siteMapNode url="~/AboutUs.aspx" title="About Us"  description="" />
    <siteMapNode url="~/Privacy.aspx" title="Privacy Policy"  description="" />
    <siteMapNode url="~/ContactUs.aspx" title="Contact Us"  description="" />
    <siteMapNode url="~/MediaKit.aspx" title="Media Relations"  description="" />
  </siteMapNode>
</siteMap>
```

The site map defines the hierarchy and navigational structure of your site. It determines which pages involve subnavigation of the outer top-level navigation. It also determines which pages are left out of your direct navigation. In this example, that might include pages for checkout, shipping, and credit card processing. You do not want users to navigate directly to these pages. Rather, you want them to start with the shopping cart and use the navigation techniques discussed previously to move through the buying process.

Using the SiteMap Class

The SiteMap class provides programmatic access to the site navigation hierarchy from within your code-behind page. Its two primary properties are RootNode and CurrentNode, and both return SiteMapNode instances. The SiteMapNode object represents a node in the site map and has the Title, Url, and Description properties. To access nodes in the hierarchy, you can use the SiteMapNode instance's ParentNode, ChildNodes, NextSibling, and PreviousSibling properties. For example, the following code snippet can be used to navigate to the webpage that is listed as the parent webpage in the Web.sitemap file.

Sample of Visual Basic Code

```vb
Protected Sub Button1_Click(ByVal sender As Object, _
  ByVal e As System.EventArgs) Handles Button1.Click

  Response.Redirect(SiteMap.CurrentNode.ParentNode.Url)

End Sub
```

Sample of C# Code

```csharp
protected void Button1_Click(object sender, EventArgs e)
{
  Response.Redirect(SiteMap.CurrentNode.ParentNode.Url);
}
```

Displaying Site Map Information to Users

Of course, the site map information is just an XML file. To display this information, you need to put a navigational control on a webpage. This control can take a site map file or a SiteMapDataSource control as its data source and display information accordingly.

A SiteMapDataSource control is simply a control designed to provide you with programmatic access to a site map file. This control can also be used by the navigation controls to provide a source for their data. You can use a SiteMapDataSource control by dragging it onto your page. It will automatically connect with the site map file you have defined for your site.

There are a couple of attributes you can use to configure the SiteMapDataSource control. The first is ShowStartingNode. You can set this value to false if you do not want the user to see the root node in your site map file. The second is StartingNodeOffset. This is useful if you are creating a sub-navigational control and only want to show parts of the navigation. You can set this to the node at which you want to start. The following shows this control added to a page.

```
<asp:SiteMapDataSource ID="SiteMapDataSource1" runat="server"
  StartingNodeOffset="0" ShowStartingNode="False" />
```

Like the site map file, the SiteMapDataSource control does not have a visual representation to the user. Instead, it manages access to your site map data. To show the data to the user, you must add a navigational control and connect it to the SiteMapDataSource control. There are three main navigational controls available in ASP.NET: Menu, TreeView, and SiteMapPath.

The Menu control is used to show the structure of your site in a menulike format. It allows users to navigate both from the top level and to child levels within your site. There are many attributes that allow you to manage the Menu control; many of them have to do with the style and layout of the control. Two attributes to be aware of are DataSourceId and Orientation. You use the DataSourceId attribute to set the data source for the control. You can set it to the ID of a SiteMapDataSource control on your page. Orientation allows you to set the menu to be displayed vertically or horizontally. The following shows the markup source for a Menu control.

```
<asp:Menu ID="Menu1" runat="server" DataSourceID="SiteMapDataSource1"
  MaximumDynamicDisplayLevels="5" Orientation="Horizontal">
</asp:Menu>
```

Figure 5-5 shows a Menu control that uses the site map defined earlier. Notice that this Menu control is expanded for the My Account child items.

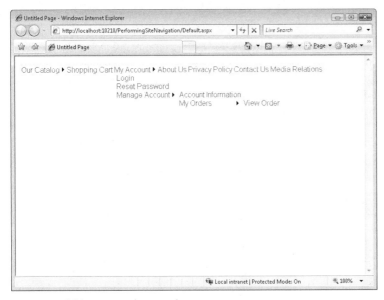

FIGURE 5-5 A Menu control on a webpage.

The TreeView control shows your site structure in a collapsible tree format. It allows the user to navigate to the hierarchy of your site and then select an item and navigate to the selected page. It works with the SiteMapDataSource control the same way the Menu control does. Figure 5-6 shows the same site map file shown in a TreeView control.

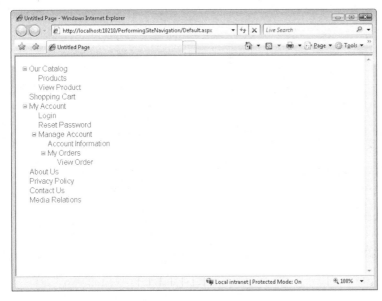

FIGURE 5-6 A TreeView control on a webpage.

The last navigational control, SiteMapPath, allows the user to see his or her current location within the site along with the path of pages followed to get there. This is often referred to as the *breadcrumb trail* of site navigation. This is useful if users navigate deeply into your site and need to work their way back up.

The SiteMapPath control can be added to a page or a master page file. It automatically picks up the site map file; you do not need to configure a data source. It then associates the site map with the actual page being requested by the user. Based on this information, it provides navigation back up to the parent page of the shown child page. Figure 5-7 shows a SiteMapPath for the Profile.aspx page in the site map XML file example defined earlier.

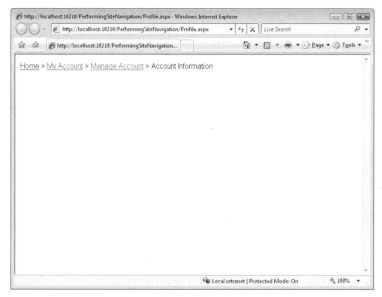

FIGURE 5-7 A SiteMapPath control on a webpage.

 Quick Check

- Which method of navigation requires the most communication between the browser and the web server?

Quick Check Answer

- Client-side browser redirect requires the most communication because it is a server-side method that tells the browser to request a new page, thus causing multiple calls to the server.

In this practice, you create the basis for the navigation of a web application for managing customers and their calls.

EXERCISE Creating the Web Application Project

In this exercise, you create the web application project. You also add a site map XML file and configure the layout of the navigation controls on the Default.aspx page.

1. Open Visual Studio and create a new ASP.NET Empty Web Site project called **WorkingWithSiteNavigation** by using your preferred programming language.

2. Add a site map file to the website by right-clicking the project in Solution Explorer and selecting Add New Item. Select the Site Map item from the Add New Item dialog box. Leave the name of the file as Web.sitemap.

3. Add a set of <siteMapNode> elements to the site map. Each node should represent a page in your fictitious customer service application. Your site map XML file should look as follows.

```xml
<?xml version="1.0" encoding="utf-8" ?>
<siteMap xmlns="http://schemas.microsoft.com/AspNet/SiteMap-File-1.0" >
  <siteMapNode url="Default.aspx" title="Home"  description="">
    <siteMapNode url="SearchCustomers.aspx" title="Search Customers"
        description="">
      <siteMapNode url="CustomerDetails.aspx" title="Customer Details"
        description="" />
    </siteMapNode>
    <siteMapNode url="NewCustomer.aspx" title="New Customer"  description="" />
    <siteMapNode url="CallLog.aspx" title="Log Call"  description="" />
    <siteMapNode url="ReportsList.aspx" title="Reports"  description="">
      <siteMapNode url="ReportIssues.aspx" title="Issues By Priority"
        description="" />
      <siteMapNode url="ReportCalls.aspx" title="Customer Call Report"
        description="" />
      <siteMapNode url="ReportActivities.aspx" title="Activities Report"
        description="" />
    </siteMapNode>
  </siteMapNode>
</siteMap>
```

4. Open the Site.master page. Remove the default Menu control.

5. Add two SiteMapDataSource controls to the page. You can do so from the Toolbox in the Data section. Configure one SiteMapDataSource control to not show the first node in the source data; name this node **MenuSiteMapDataSource**. Configure the second to show all of the site map data; name this node **TreeSiteMapDataSource**. These controls should look as follows.

```
<asp:SiteMapDataSource ID="MenuSiteMapDataSource"
    ShowStartingNode="false" runat="server" />
<asp:SiteMapDataSource ID="TreeSiteMapDataSource" runat="server" />
```

6. Add a Menu control to the master page. Configure this control to use the menu data source control. Set its display to show menu items horizontally across the top of the page by setting the Orientation property to Horizontal. Your control's configuration might look as follows.

```
<asp:Menu ID="Menu1" runat="server" DataSourceID="MenuSiteMapDataSource"
    Orientation="Horizontal">
</asp:Menu>
```

7. Add a TreeView control to the master page. Set the DataSourceId attribute to TreeSiteMapDataSource. This control should look as follows.

```
<asp:TreeView ID="TreeView1" runat="server" DataSourceID="TreeSiteMapDataSource">
</asp:TreeView>
```

8. Add a SiteMapPath control to the master page. You can use the default settings.

9. Finally, add a content page to the site: CustomerDetails.aspx. Be sure to specify Site.master as the master page. Add some content to the page. Optionally, put each of the navigation controls in a <div> tag, specify a class for each <div> tag, and then edit the Site.css style sheet to provide formatting for the navigation bar. The completed project from the companion CD demonstrates basic layout using <div> tags.

10. Right-click the Default.aspx page and select Set As Start Page.

11. Run the web application to display the Default.aspx page. Your page should resemble the one shown in Figure 5-8.

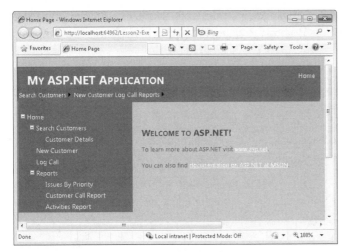

FIGURE 5-8 The CustomerDetails.aspx webpage with all the navigation controls.

12. Click the Customer Details link on both the Menu and TreeView controls, and notice that they both open the same page.

Lesson Summary

- There are multiple ways to use code to allow users to navigate from page to page in your site. You can write both client and server code to do so.

- You can send the entire processing of a page over to another page by using the server-side Page.Server.Transfer method. This is useful if you want to hide the file name of the processing page or run different pages for a single user request.

- You can create a site map XML file to represent the navigational structure of your website. You can display this information by using the Menu, TreeView, and SiteMapPath controls.

Lesson Review

You can use the following questions to test your knowledge of the information in Lesson 2, "Performing Site Navigation." The questions are also available on the companion CD as a practice test, if you prefer to review them in electronic form.

> **NOTE ANSWERS**
>
> Answers to these questions and explanations of why each answer is correct or incorrect are located in the "Answers" section at the end of the book.

1. Which of the following server-side methods of the HttpServerUtility class can be used to navigate to a different webpage without requiring a round trip to the client?

   A. Redirect

   B. MapPath

   C. Transfer

   D. UrlDecode

2. Which control automatically uses the Web.sitemap file to display site map information to a user on a webpage?

   A. Menu

   B. TreeView

   C. SiteMapDataSource

   D. SiteMapPath

3. You want to provide an Up button for your webpages that users can click to navigate one level higher on your website. You want to define the hyperlink programmatically by using the site map. Which class can you use to access the site map content to accomplish this?

   A. SiteMapPath

   B. SiteMapDataSource

   C. SiteMap

   D. HttpServerUtility

Lesson 3: Using Web Parts

Many webpages are collections of components. These components work as self-contained bits of functionality. For example, examine your favorite news site—it probably has a navigation bar to the left, a title bar at the top, at least one column of news, and a footer. Additionally, many news and portal sites provide customized, optional components, such as weather reports and stock quotes.

ASP.NET Web Parts give you the ability to provide your users with control over the components that appear on a webpage. With Web Parts, users can minimize or completely close groups of controls. So if they want to see a weather report on your page, they can add a weather component—or they can close it to save room for other content. You can also provide a catalog of Web Parts to enable users to add groups of controls wherever they want on a page.

This lesson describes how to create and use ASP.NET Web Parts.

What Are Web Parts?

Web Parts are components of predefined functionality that can be embedded in a webpage. They have a centralized framework, management structure, and customization model. These components of functionality can be added to and removed from pages by both site designers and individual users. They can even be moved around on a page to fit the individual needs of users.

Figure 5-9 shows an example of a Web Part page. Notice that the individual Web Parts have client-side menus that enable users to control them.

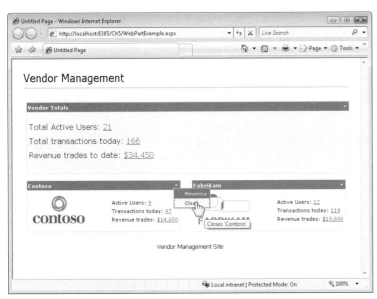

FIGURE 5-9 Web Parts generate client-side menus to enable customization.

You can also use a CatalogZone control to add a catalog to your Web Part page. A catalog allows users to add Web Parts to and remove them from the zones defined on your page. Figure 5-10 shows the same page in edit mode. Here users are given a list of Web Parts from which to choose. They can add these components to the defined zones on the page.

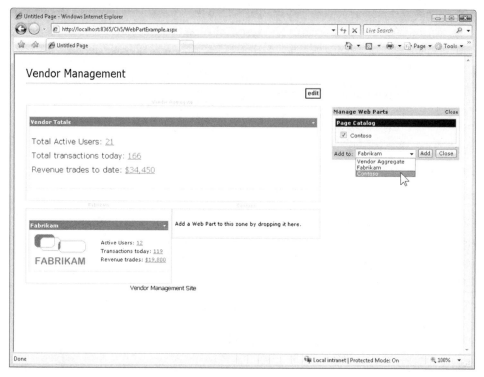

FIGURE 5-10 You can use a CatalogZone control to enable users to add Web Parts on demand, without writing any code.

Web Part pages and sites can provide users with several customization options. This is great when you are developing bits of functionality that will be deployed to a wide audience. Some common Web Parts you might create include the following:

- A list of recent news articles relating to your organization
- A calendar showing upcoming events
- A list of links to related websites
- A search box
- Picture thumbnails from a photo gallery
- Site navigation controls
- A blog

- News articles pulled from a Really Simple Syndication (RSS) feed
- Local weather information retrieved from a web service
- Stock market quotes and graphs

Any control can act as a Web Part, including standard controls and custom controls. Adding Web Parts to a page doesn't necessarily require writing any code, because you can do so entirely with the Visual Studio designer.

> **NOTE   SOURCES FOR WEB PARTS**
>
> Several sites on the Internet offer free Web Parts that you can download and add to your site.

The WebParts Namespace

ASP.NET includes many Web Parts; there are 13 controls in the designer Toolbox alone. These controls and classes can be found inside the System.Web.UI.WebControls.WebParts namespace. Many of these classes are discussed in depth in later sections. The following list provides a high-level overview of the most important WebParts classes.

- **WebPartManager**   The WebPartManager control is required on every page that includes Web Parts. It does not have a visual representation. Rather, it manages all the Web Part controls and their events on the specified page.
- **CatalogPart**   The CatalogPart control provides the user interface (UI) for managing a group of Web Parts that can be added to a Web Part page. This group is typically sitewide (and not just specific to a certain page).
- **PageCatalogPart**   The PageCatalogPart control is similar to the CatalogPart control. However, PageCatalogPart only groups those Web Parts that are part of a specific page. If a user closes certain Web Parts on the page, he or she can use the PageCatalogPart control to return them to the page.
- **EditorPart**   The EditorPart control allows users to define customizations, such as the modification of property settings, for the specified Web Part.
- **DeclarativeCatalogPart**   The DeclarativeCatalogPart control allows you to declare Web Parts that should be available to add to a page or to the entire site.
- **WebPartZone**   The WebPartZone control is used to define an area on your page in which Web Parts can be hosted.
- **EditorZone**   The EditorZone control provides an area on the page where EditorPart controls can exist.
- **CatalogZone**   The CatalogZone control defines an area in which a CatalogPart control can exist on the page.

Defining Web Part Zones

You add Web Parts to a page by placing them in zones. *Zones* define areas on the page in which Web Parts can be placed by a user or added by a developer. A zone has a width, height, and placement on the page. You can add one, many, or no Web Parts to a single zone. Figure 5-11 shows the zones defined by the Web Part page shown in the previous two figures.

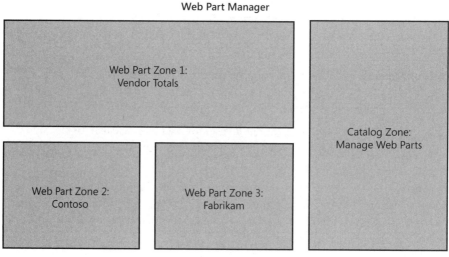

FIGURE 5-11 Zone definition for the example Web Part page.

Zones also allow you to set common styles for the Web Parts that are placed within the zone. This is called the Web Part's *chrome*. The chrome includes the Web Part's header style, the menu styles, outline borders, content styles, edit mode style, and more. Web Parts added to a zone take on the styles defined by that zone's chrome. Of course, you can define the common zone style definitions by using a skin, as described in Chapter 2.

You create Web Part zones by using the WebPartZone control. Again, this control defines an area on the page that contains (or can contain) Web Parts. This control also includes the HeaderText attribute. This attribute is used to define the text displayed to the user when the page (and zone) is in edit mode. Look closely at Figure 5-10 for an example of this text being displayed above the zone.

As an example, consider the top zone in Figure 5-9, shown earlier. To define this zone, you add a WebPartZone control to your page. To place Web Parts inside this zone, you have to add the ZoneTemplate control inside the WebPartZone. The ZoneTemplate control lets you add other ASP.NET controls to the zone and combine them into actual Web Parts. (This is discussed later in this lesson.) The following markup shows an example.

```
<asp:WebPartManager ID="WebPartManager1" runat="server">
</asp:WebPartManager>

<asp:WebPartZone ID="WebPartZoneVendor" runat="server"
  HeaderText="Vendor Aggregate" style="width: 650px; height: auto">
  <ZoneTemplate>

    <!--Add  content to the zone-->

  </ZoneTemplate>
</asp:WebPartZone>
```

Notice that the markup also contains the definition for the WebPartManager control. This control is required of every Web Part page. It does not have a visual representation; it is used by ASP.NET to manage the Web Parts on the page.

Creating Web Parts

There are three principal methods for creating ASP.NET Web Parts that can be managed by the WebPartManager inside your webpages. The first is to create a standard user control; the second (and simplest) is to use an existing ASP.NET control (such as Label) to define your Web Part; and the third is to create your own custom control and derive it from the WebPart class. This section covers the first two methods. The latter, custom controls, is covered in Chapter 7, "Creating Custom Web Controls." The custom control method does offer the most granular control over your Web Parts, but it is also the most time-consuming and complicated method. The other two methods offer a simpler approach that can be built on for most Web Part scenarios.

Building Web Parts with User Controls

Web Parts are defined inside the zones on your page. They can be added to the zones at design time or run time, or they can be configured to be there by the user. To create a Web Part based on a user control, you simply need to add the user control to a Web Part zone. The ASP.NET Web Part model takes care of the rest. For example, notice that in Figure 5-9 (shown earlier) the two bottom Web Parts (Contoso and Fabrikam) are similar. These could be defined by a single user control, and thus this user control could have two instances on the page. To use a user control (on any ASP.NET page), you must first register it with the page. This is done by adding the @ Register directive for the control near the top of the page. The following line of code provides an example.

```
<%@ Register src="VendorWebPart.ascx" tagname="VendorWebPart" tagprefix="uc1" %>
```

After the control is registered, you then add it to a Web Part zone. You can do so by nesting it inside the ZoneTemplate declaration. The following markup shows the VendorWebPart user control added to a Web Part zone.

```
<asp:WebPartZone ID="WebPartZone2" runat="server" HeaderText="Fabrikam"
  style="width: 350px; float: left; height: auto;">

  <ZoneTemplate>
    <uc1:VendorWebPart ID="VendorWebPart1" runat="server" title="Fabrikam" />
  </ZoneTemplate>

</asp:WebPartZone>
```

Notice the addition of the title attribute to the user control definition. This tells the Web Part what title to display according to the Web Part's chrome style setting.

Creating a Web Part Control from an Existing ASP.NET Control

You can also create a Web Part simply by inserting a standard ASP.NET control inside a <ZoneTemplate> element. The Web Part manager will take care of the rest. For example, the top section of Figure 5-9 shows a single Web Part titled Vendor Totals. This Web Part was created by using a Label control. The Label control then nests other controls inside it. These controls define the actual contents of the Web Part, whereas the Label control is simply the container. The following code shows this example.

```
<asp:WebPartZone ID="WebPartZone1" runat="server"
  HeaderText="Vendor Aggregate" style="width: 700px; height: auto">
  <ZoneTemplate>
    <asp:Label ID="Label3" runat="server" Text="" title="Vendor Totals">
      <div style="margin-top: 12px; margin-bottom: 20px;
        line-height: 30px; font-size: 12pt">
        Total Active Users: <a href="#">21</a>
        <br />Total transactions today: <a href="#">166</a>
        <br />Revenue trades to-date: <a href="#">$34,450</a>
      </div>
    </asp:Label>
  </ZoneTemplate>
</asp:WebPartZone>
```

Enabling Users to Arrange and Edit Web Parts

The Web Parts on your page can be displayed to the user in several different ways. The mode of display is dependent on what the user is doing with the Web Parts and the hosting page at the time. For example, if the user is simply viewing the Web Parts on a page, the display mode is browse and the user sees the Web Part as it appears in this mode. Of course, there are other modes with other display properties.

You change the display mode of the Web Parts on a page by using the WebPartManager control. You do so by setting its DisplayMode property in your code-behind file. Table 5-1 shows the valid property values for DisplayMode.

TABLE 5-1 Web Part Display Modes

DISPLAY MODE	DESCRIPTION
BrowseDisplayMode	This is the standard way in which users browse webpages. This is the default mode.
DesignDisplayMode	This mode enables users to drag Web Parts to different locations.
EditDisplayMode	Like design mode, edit mode enables users to drag Web Parts. Additionally, users can select Edit from the Web Parts menu to edit the title, size, direction, window appearance, and zone of Web Parts by using AppearanceEditorPart and LayoutEditorPart controls. To use this mode, you must add an EditorZone control to your webpage, and then add either AppearanceEditorPart or LayoutEditorPart, or both.
CatalogDisplayMode	This mode enables users to add additional Web Parts that you specify by using a CatalogZone control. This mode is available only after you add a CatalogZone to your webpage.
ConnectDisplayMode	This enables users to manually establish connections between controls by interacting with a ConnectionZone control. For example, Web Parts can be linked to show summary and detail information for the same report. This mode is available only after you add a ConnectionZone control to the page. For more information about Web Parts connections, see the "Connecting Web Parts" section later in this lesson.

As an example, consider the screen shown in Figure 5-10. You can see that the page is in a different display mode. Here the user has clicked the Edit button under the Vendor Management text to change the mode of the page. To enable this, the developer first set up the page with a CatalogZone control. The following code shows the markup of the layout of the CatalogZone control.

```
<asp:CatalogZone ID="CatalogZone1" runat="server" HeaderText="Manage Web Parts">

  <ZoneTemplate>
    <asp:PageCatalogPart ID="PageCatalogPart1" runat="server">
    </asp:PageCatalogPart>
  </ZoneTemplate>

</asp:CatalogZone>
```

The next step is to put the page into this display mode when the user clicks the Edit button. The following shows the code for the button's click event, and assumes that you added a string named mode with a value of browse to view state the first time the page loaded.

Sample of Visual Basic Code

```vb
Protected Sub ButtonEdit_Click(ByVal sender As Object, _
  ByVal e As System.EventArgs) Handles ButtonEdit.Click

  Dim mode As String = CType(ViewState("mode"), String)

  'switch modes
  If mode = "browse" Then
    ViewState("mode") = "edit"
    ButtonEdit.Text = "Done"
    WebPartManager1.DisplayMode = WebPartManager1.SupportedDisplayModes("Catalog")
  Else
    ViewState("mode") = "browse"
    ButtonEdit.Text = "Edit"
    WebPartManager1.DisplayMode = WebPartManager1.SupportedDisplayModes("Browse")
  End If

End Sub
```

Sample of C# Code

```csharp
protected void ButtonEdit_Click(object sender, EventArgs e)
{

  string mode = (string)ViewState["mode"];

  //switch modes
  if (mode == "browse")
  {
    ViewState["mode"] = "edit";
    ButtonEdit.Text = "Done";
    WebPartManager1.DisplayMode = WebPartManager1.SupportedDisplayModes["Catalog"];
  }
  else
  {
    ViewState["mode"] = "browse";
    ButtonEdit.Text = "Edit";
    WebPartManager1.DisplayMode = WebPartManager1.SupportedDisplayModes["Browse"];
  }

}
```

Notice that in the code, the display mode is set by using the SupportedDisplayModes collection. Also notice that in this case, the display mode is being set inside the ViewState (in PageLoad) and then passed to the page. Of course, there are other display modes, as defined in Table 5-1. This lesson's practice will walk you through the creation of a page that allows a user to switch between the various display modes.

Connecting Web Parts

One of the most powerful features of the Web Parts tool set is the ability to build connections between Web Parts. To understand the possibilities, imagine building an internal application to manage employee payroll. You could have:

- A main Web Part so you can browse employee data.
- A Web Part that displays a chart of the selected employee's overtime pay.
- A Web Part that shows a pie chart illustrating how payroll, benefits, stock options, and pension fit into the employee's overall compensation.
- A Web Part that compares the employee's pay to that of employees in the same position.

With Web Parts connections, the user can select an employee file and have all the other Web Parts automatically update with that employee's information. Naturally, the user analyzing the data would have the ability to add, remove, and rearrange Web Parts.

Connections are also useful for consumer-oriented websites. For example, if you are building a portal site, you might have Web Parts that display localized information based on the user's postal code, including the weather, local news, and the cafeteria menu. Rather than requiring the user to specify his or her postal code for each individual Web Part, all Web Parts can connect to a specialized Web Part that stores the users' postal code.

Creating a Static Connection

Connections can be either static or dynamic. If a connection is static, you (as the developer) establish the connection during the development process, and it cannot be changed by the user. Static connections are permanent and cannot be deleted by users.

Static connections typically involve a provider and one or more consumer Web Parts. The provider provides the connection data. The consumer receives the provider data. You define providers and consumers by using the attribute-based programming model of the .NET Framework. To create a static connection between Web Parts, you can follow these basic steps:

1. Create a provider Web Part. A provider Web Part can derive from the WebPart class, or you can create it as a user control. You must create a public method inside your provider with the ConnectionProvider attribute attached to it. This method should return the value that the consumer will receive. The following code shows the code-behind file for a user control provider Web Part that contains a TextBox control and a Button control.

Sample of Visual Basic Code

```
Partial Class Provider
  Inherits System.Web.UI.UserControl

  Dim _textBoxValue As String = ""

  <ConnectionProvider("TextBox provider", "GetTextBoxValue")> _
  Public Function GetTextBoxValue() As String
    Return _textBoxValue
  End Function
```

```
    Protected Sub Button1_Click(ByVal sender As Object, _
        ByVal e As System.EventArgs) Handles Button1.Click
        _textBoxValue = TextBoxProvider.Text
    End Sub

End Class
```

Sample of C# Code

```csharp
public partial class Provider : System.Web.UI.UserControl
{
    string _textBoxValue = "";

    [ConnectionProvider("TextBox provider", "GetTextBoxValue")]
    public string GetTextBoxValue()
    {
        return _textBoxValue;
    }

    protected void Button1_Click(object sender, EventArgs e)
    {
        _textBoxValue = TextBoxProvider.Text;
    }

}
```

2. Create a consumer Web Part. A consumer Web Part can derive from the WebPart class, or it can be a user control. You must create a public method with the ConnectionConsumer attribute that accepts the same type that the provider's ConnectionProvider method returns. The following code demonstrates a consumer Web Part user control.

Sample of Visual Basic Code

```vbnet
Partial Class Consumer
    Inherits System.Web.UI.UserControl

    <ConnectionConsumer("TextBox consumer", "ShowTextBoxValue")> _
    Public Sub ShowTextBoxValue(ByVal textBoxValue As String)
        LabelConsumer.Text = textBoxValue
    End Sub

End Class
```

Sample of C# Code

```csharp
public partial class Consumer : System.Web.UI.UserControl
{
    [ConnectionConsumer("TextBox consumer", "ShowTextBoxValue")]
    public void ShowTextBoxValue(string textBoxValue)
    {
        LabelConsumer.Text = textBoxValue;
    }
}
```

3. Create a webpage with a WebPartManager control. Add at least one WebPartZone container.

4. Add your provider and consumer Web Parts to WebPartZone containers. The following markup shows the preceding user controls added to the page.

```
<asp:WebPartZone ID="WebPartZoneProvider" runat="server"
  Height="400px" Width="300px">
  <ZoneTemplate>
    <uc1:Provider ID="Provider1" runat="server" title="Provider" />
    <uc2:Consumer ID="Consumer1" runat="server" title="Consumer" />
  </ZoneTemplate>
</asp:WebPartZone>
```

5. The next step is to add connection information to the WebPartManager markup. In this case, you add a <StaticConnections> element that includes a WebPartConnection control to declare the connection between the provider and consumer.

   The WebPartConnection control must have an ID attribute, an attribute to identify the provider control (ProviderID), an attribute to identify the provider method (Provider-ConnectionPointID), an attribute to identify the consumer control (ConsumerID), and an attribute to identify the consumer method (ConsumerConnectionPointID). The following markup demonstrates this.

```
<asp:WebPartManager ID="WebPartManager1" runat="server">
  <StaticConnections>
    <asp:webPartConnection
      ID="conn1"
      ProviderID="Provider1"
      ProviderConnectionPointID="GetTextBoxValue"
      ConsumerID="Consumer1"
      ConsumerConnectionPointID="ShowTextBoxValue" />
  </StaticConnections>
</asp:WebPartManager>
```

Note that you should have one WebPartConnection control for each pair of connected controls.

Exercise 3 in this lesson's practice walks you through the process of creating controls that connect to each other and configuring them in a webpage.

EXAM TIP

For the exam, you should know exactly how to establish a static connection, which attributes you must assign to each method, and what you must add to the ASPX page source.

Enabling Dynamic Connections

Dynamic connections can be established by users. You enable these by adding a ConnectionsZone control to the webpage.

To enable dynamic connections that a user can create or break, follow these steps:

1. Create a page with a provider and consumer connection, as described in the previous section.

2. Optionally, establish a static connection between the provider and consumer, as described in the previous section. This acts as a default connection that will always be there, but that users can modify by adding a new, dynamic connection.

3. Add a ConnectionsZone control to the webpage.

4. Add a control to enable the user to enter connect mode, as described in "Enabling Users to Arrange and Edit Web Parts" earlier in this lesson.

Establishing Dynamic Connections Among Web Parts

When a user views your page, he or she can enter connect mode and use the ConnectionsZone control to edit connections. To edit a connection as a user, follow these steps:

1. Switch the display mode of the page to connect mode.

2. On the Web Parts menu for either the provider or the consumer, select Connect from the menu, as shown in Figure 5-12.

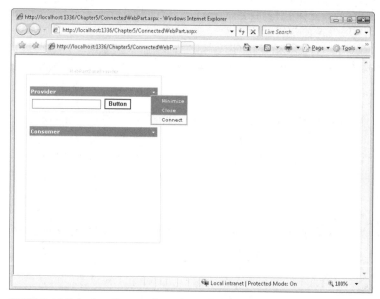

FIGURE 5-12 Selecting Connect from the Web Parts menu to edit the connection.

3. The ConnectionsZone object appears, as shown in Figure 5-13.

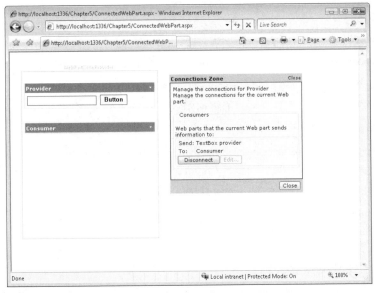

FIGURE 5-13 Using the ConnectionsZone control to dynamically establish a connection.

4. If there is an existing connection, click Disconnect to break the current connection. Then, click Create A Connection To A Consumer, select the consumer, and click Connect, as shown in Figure 5-14.

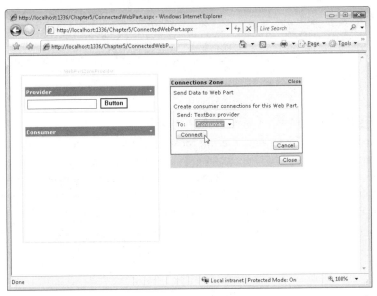

FIGURE 5-14 Clicking Connect to establish a dynamic connection between Web Parts.

5. When you are done editing connections, click Close. The Web Parts are connected, just as if you had connected them statically.

Personalizing Web Parts

Web Parts support personalization. *Personalization* allows changes to the layout to be stored for each user so that the user sees the same layout the next time he or she goes to the page. Web Parts personalization relies on client-side cookies. It uses these cookies to look up settings in the ASPNETDB SQL Server database. Typically, when you store personalized settings, you will also want to authenticate users by using either Windows or Forms authentication. This is not required, however.

> **MORE INFO** **USER AUTHENTICATION**
>
> For more information about user authentication, see Chapter 13, "Implementing User Profiles, Authentication, and Authorization."

Enabling Personalization for Custom Controls

By default, personalization automatically stores the location and other personalized Web Parts settings as described in the "Enabling Users to Arrange and Edit Web Parts" section earlier in this chapter. You can also store custom data in the personalization database to enable controls to remember information about users. To do so, you define a public property on the control. You then add the Personalizable attribute, as the following simplified code demonstrates.

Sample of Visual Basic Code

```
<Personalizable()> _
Property PostalCode() As String
  Get
    Return _postalCode
  End Get

  Set(ByVal value As String)
    _postalCode = value
```

```
  End Set
End Property
```

Sample of C# Code

```csharp
[Personalizable]
public string PostalCode
{
  get
  {
    return _postalCode;
  }

  set
  {
    _postalCode = value;
  }
}
```

Enabling Shared Personalization

Web Parts personalization is enabled by default, and authenticated users of a Web Parts page are able to personalize pages for themselves without any special configuration. However, individual or user-scoped personalization changes are visible only to the user who made them. If you want to provide webmasters (or any user) with the power to make personalization changes that affect how everyone sees Web Parts, you can enable shared personalization in your application's Web.config file.

Within the <system.web> section of the configuration file, add an <authorization> section, and within that, add an <allow> element to specify which user or users have access to shared personalization scope, as the following example shows.

```
<authorization>
  <allow verbs="enterSharedScope" users="SomeUserAccount"
    roles="admin"  />
</authorization>
```

The specified user or users now have the ability to edit a page in shared personalization scope so that the changes they make are visible to all users.

Disabling Personalization for a Page

You can also disable personalization for a page, which is useful if you want to take advantage of personalization on some pages but not on others. To disable personalization on a page, set the WebPartManager.Personalization.Enabled attribute to false. The following markup shows an example.

```
<asp:webPartManager ID="webPartManager1" runat="server">
  <Personalization Enabled="False" />
</asp:webPartManager>
```

In this practice, you create a webpage that uses Web Parts. You then expand the page capabilities to enable users to customize the page, and then add controls that communicate with each other.

> **ON THE COMPANION MEDIA**
>
> If you encounter a problem completing an exercise, you can find the completed projects in the samples installed from this book's companion CD. For more information about the project files and other content on the CD, see "Using the Companion Media" in this book's Introduction.

EXERCISE 1 Creating a Webpage with Web Parts

In this exercise, you create a webpage that uses Web Parts.

1. Open Visual Studio and create a new ASP.NET Web Site named **MyWebParts** by using either C# or Visual Basic.

2. Create a new web form without a master page, and name it **Default2.aspx**. In Solution Explorer, right-click the new page and then click Set As Start Page. Now edit it in Source view. From the Toolbox, on the WebParts tab, drag a WebPartManager control onto the page. This control isn't visible to users, but it must appear before any Web Part controls or the runtime throws an exception.

3. From the Toolbox, on the WebParts tab, drag four WebPartZone controls to the page. Set the IDs for these to **TopWebPartZone**, **LeftWebPartZone**, **CenterWebPartZone**, and **BottomWebPartZone**. Then set the HeaderText property for the zones to **Top Zone**, **Left Zone**, **Center Zone**, and **Bottom Zone**, respectively. Also, set the layout styles to display appropriately (which, in the real world, should be done with a style sheet). Your markup code should look as follows.

```
<html xmlns="http://www.w3.org/1999/xhtml">
<head runat="server">
    <title>My Web Part Page</title>
</head>
<body>
    <form id="form1" runat="server">

    <asp:WebPartManager ID="WebPartManager1" runat="server">
    </asp:WebPartManager>

    <div style="width: 700px">

      <asp:WebPartZone ID="WebPartZoneTop" runat="server"
        HeaderText="Top Zone" style="width: 700px; height: auto">
      </asp:WebPartZone>

      <asp:WebPartZone ID="WebPartZoneLeft" runat="server"
```

```
                    HeaderText="Left Zone" style="width: 300px; float: left; height: 300px">
            </asp:WebPartZone>

            <asp:WebPartZone ID="WebPartZoneCenter" runat="server"
              HeaderText="Center Zone"
              style="width: 400px; float: right; height: 300px">
            </asp:WebPartZone>

            <asp:WebPartZone ID="WebPartZoneBottom" runat="server"
              HeaderText="Bottom Zone" style="width: 700px; height: auto;">
            </asp:WebPartZone>

        </div>

      </form>
  </body>
  </html>
```

Your page, in Design view, should look similar to the one shown in Figure 5-15.

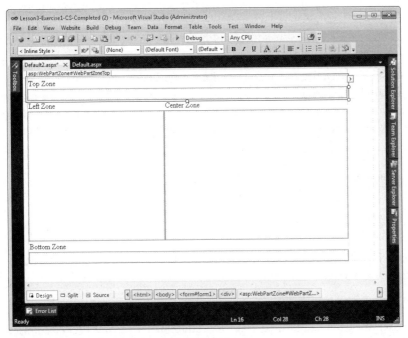

FIGURE 5-15 The webpage zones in Design view.

4. Add two new web user controls to your website by right-clicking the website in Solution Explorer and choosing Add New Item. Name the new controls **CalendarWebPart** and **LogoWebPart**. These will serve as simple Web Part examples. Add a Calendar control to the CalendarWebPart user control. Add an image to the LogoWebPart control.

These custom controls serve as examples only. A real Web Part could do something more like display the weather or query a database.

5. Open Default2.aspx in Design view. Drag the LogoWebPart user control from Solution Explorer to the Top Zone WebPartZone container. Next, drag CalendarWebPart to the Left Zone WebPartZone container.

6. Enable Windows authentication by editing the Web.config file. In the <system.web> section, remove the existing <authentication> definition. Then add the following code to the <system.web> section to enable Windows authentication.

```
<authentication mode="Windows">
</authentication>
```

You can use Web Parts personalization with either Forms or Windows authentication. Although Forms authentication is the better choice for Internet applications, Windows authentication requires less configuration, which makes it better suited to this demonstration.

7. Run your application in a browser. The first time you do so, it might take a little longer than expected to start, because Visual Studio is adding the ASPNETDB database to your project. Notice that your two controls appear on the page. Click the menu button in the upper-right corner of each control, and experiment with minimizing and closing the Web Parts. Notice that if you close a control you cannot reopen it without clearing the personalization data. Also notice that both Web Parts are currently labeled Untitled.

8. Return to Visual Studio and open Default2.aspx in Design view. To give the Web Parts meaningful display names, you need to edit the Title property. Click the instance of CalendarControl, view the properties, and notice that the title is not displayed. To edit the Title property, you must manually add it to the source code, as shown here.

```
<asp:WebPartZone ID="WebPartZoneLeft" runat="server"
  HeaderText="Left Zone" style="width: 300px; float: left; height: 300px;">
  <ZoneTemplate>
    <uc2:CalendarWebPart ID="CalendarWebPart1" runat="server"
      title="Calendar" />
  </ZoneTemplate>
</asp:WebPartZone>
```

9. Create a title for both the CalendarControl and LogoControl instances. Save the page and view it in a web browser again to verify that the title appears.

EXERCISE 2   Enabling Users to Customize Web Parts

In this exercise, you extend an existing Web Parts application to enable user customization.

1. Continue editing the project you created in the previous exercise. Alternatively, you can open the completed Lesson 3, Exercise 1 project in the samples installed from the CD.

2. Open Default2.aspx in Source view. Inside the center zone, add a ZoneTemplate control. Next, create a simple Web Part by placing a Label control inside the ZoneTemplate control. Finally, nest a DropDownList control inside the Label control. Set the ID property to **DropDownListModes**, and set the AutoPostBack property to true. Your markup should look as follows.

```
<asp:WebPartZone ID="WebPartZoneCenter" runat="server"
  HeaderText="Center Zone" style="width: 400px; float: right; height: 300px;">
  <ZoneTemplate>
    <asp:Label ID="Label1" runat="server" Text="" title="Edit Page">
      <asp:DropDownList ID="DropDownListModes"
        runat="server" AutoPostBack="true">
      </asp:DropDownList>
    </asp:Label>
  </ZoneTemplate>
</asp:WebPartZone>
```

3. If you are using Visual Basic, edit the Default2.aspx @ Page declaration to set the AutoEventWireup attribute to true. This is set to true by default in C#. This demonstrates the proper @ Page declaration.

```
<%@ Page Language="VB" AutoEventWireup="true" CodeFile="Default.aspx.vb"
  Inherits="_Default" %>
```

4. Create a Page_Init event handler in your code-behind file. In the Page_Init method (which is automatically called when the page is created), add an event handler so that ASP.NET calls the GenerateModeList method, which you create in the next step, during the InitComplete event. The following code demonstrates this.

Sample of Visual Basic Code
```
Sub Page_Init(ByVal sender As Object, ByVal e As EventArgs)
 AddHandler Page.InitComplete, AddressOf GenerateModeList
End Sub
```

Sample of C# Code
```
void Page_Init(object sender, EventArgs e)
{
 Page.InitComplete += new EventHandler(GenerateModeList);
}
```

5. Next, add a using directive for the System.Web.UI.WebControls.WebParts namespace. Then define the GenerateModeList method, which is called during the InitComplete event. In the event handler, write code to populate the DropDownListModes control by using the SupportedDisplayModes property of the WebPartManager control. Be sure to select the correct item in the list based on the current mode. The following sample code demonstrates this.

Sample of Visual Basic Code

```vb
Protected Sub GenerateModeList(ByVal sender As Object, ByVal e As EventArgs)

  Dim _manager As WebPartManager = _
    WebPartManager.GetCurrentWebPartManager(Page)
  Dim browseModeName As String = webPartManager.BrowseDisplayMode.Name

  DropDownListModes.Items.Clear()

  ' Fill the drop-down list with the names of supported display modes.
  For Each mode As webPartDisplayMode In _manager.SupportedDisplayModes

    Dim modeName As String = mode.Name

    ' Make sure a mode is enabled before adding it.
    If mode.IsEnabled(_manager) Then
      Dim item As ListItem = New ListItem(modeName, modeName)
      DropDownListModes.Items.Add(item)
    End If

  Next

  ' Select the current mode
  Dim items As ListItemCollection = DropDownListModes.Items
  Dim selectedIndex As Integer = _
    items.IndexOf(items.FindByText(_manager.DisplayMode.Name))

  DropDownListModes.SelectedIndex = selectedIndex
End Sub
```

Sample of C# Code

```csharp
protected void GenerateModeList(object sender, EventArgs e)
{
  WebPartManager _manager = WebPartManager.GetCurrentWebPartManager(Page);
  String browseModeName = WebPartManager.BrowseDisplayMode.Name;
  DropDownListModes.Items.Clear();

  // Fill the drop-down list with the names of supported display modes.
  foreach (WebPartDisplayMode mode in _manager.SupportedDisplayModes)
  {
    String modeName = mode.Name;
    // Make sure a mode is enabled before adding it.
    if (mode.IsEnabled(_manager))
    {
      ListItem item = new ListItem(modeName, modeName);
      DropDownListModes.Items.Add(item);
    }
  }

  // Select the current mode
  ListItemCollection items = DropDownListModes.Items;
  int selectedIndex = items.IndexOf(items.FindByText(_manager.DisplayMode.Name));
  DropDownListModes.SelectedIndex = selectedIndex;
}
```

6. Add the event handler for the DropDownListModes.SelectedIndexChanged event. Then write code to set the current mode to the mode selected from the list, as the following code demonstrates.

Sample of Visual Basic Code

```
Protected Sub DropDownListModes_SelectedIndexChanged(ByVal sender As Object, _
  ByVal e As EventArgs) Handles DropDownListModes.SelectedIndexChanged

  Dim manager As WebPartManager = _
    WebPartManager.GetCurrentWebPartManager(Page)
  Dim mode As WebPartDisplayMode = _
    manager.SupportedDisplayModes(DropDownListModes.SelectedValue)

  If Not (mode Is Nothing) Then
    manager.DisplayMode = mode
  End If

End Sub
```

Sample of C# Code

```
protected void DropDownListModes_SelectedIndexChanged(object sender, EventArgs e)
{
  WebPartManager manager =
    WebPartManager.GetCurrentWebPartManager(Page);

  WebPartDisplayMode mode =
    manager.SupportedDisplayModes[DropDownListModes.SelectedValue];

  if (mode != null)
    manager.DisplayMode = mode;
}
```

7. Run your website and open Default2.aspx in Windows Internet Explorer. (Other browsers might not provide complete functionality.) Notice that your two controls appear on the page. Click the drop-down list and select Design. Then drag your controls from one zone to another. Click the list again and return to browse mode.

8. Return to Visual Studio and to your page in Design view. Remove the center zone control and replace it with a <div> tag that uses the same style. Keep the drop-down control. Underneath it, add an EditorZone control. Then add an AppearanceEditorPart control and a LayoutEditorPart control to the EditorZone control. The following shows an example of the markup.

```
<div style="width: 395px; float: right; height: auto; padding-left: 5px">
  <asp:DropDownList ID="DropDownListModes" runat="server" AutoPostBack="true"
    OnSelectedIndexChanged="DropDownListModes_SelectedIndexChanged">
  </asp:DropDownList>

  <asp:EditorZone ID="EditorZone1" runat="server">
    <ZoneTemplate>
```

```
            <asp:AppearanceEditorPart ID="AppearanceEditorPart1" runat="server" />
            <asp:LayoutEditorPart ID="LayoutEditorPart1" runat="server" />
          </ZoneTemplate>
        </asp:EditorZone>
      </div>
```

9. Run your application in Internet Explorer. Click the drop-down list and select the newly added item, Edit. Next, click the menu button in the upper-right corner of the calendar control and select Edit. Notice that the EditorZone, AppearanceEditorPart, and LayoutEditorPart controls appear. Experiment with the controls to change their appearance and layout. Notice that adding this capability didn't require writing any other code; you simply needed to add the controls to the page. The WebPartManager control detects the presence of the EditorZone control and automatically enables edit mode.

10. Return to Visual Studio and open your page in Source view. Next, add a CatalogZone control below the EditorZone control. Now add a DeclarativeCatalogPart control into the CatalogZone control.

11. Add the WebPartsTemplate tag inside the DeclarativeCatalogPart control. This enables you to add controls to the catalog. Next, add your LogoControl and CalendarControl controls to the CatalogZone control. This adds the controls to the catalog. The following code provides an example.

```
<asp:CatalogZone ID="CatalogZone1" runat="server">
  <ZoneTemplate>
    <asp:DeclarativeCatalogPart ID="DeclarativeCatalogPart1" runat="server">
      <WebPartsTemplate>
        <uc1:LogoWebPart ID="LogoWebPart1" runat="server" title="Logo" />
        <uc2:CalendarWebPart ID="CalendarWebPart1" runat="server"
          title="Calendar" />
      </WebPartsTemplate>
    </asp:DeclarativeCatalogPart>
  </ZoneTemplate>
</asp:CatalogZone>
```

12. Run your web application in Internet Explorer. Click the drop-down list and select the newly added catalog mode. The catalog zone you created appears and shows the available controls. Select the logo control, select a zone from the drop-down list, and then click Add. Continue experimenting with the control; switch back to browse mode when you are done.

EXERCISE 3   Creating Connected Web Parts

In this exercise, you extend an existing application to enable connected Web Parts.

1. Continue editing the project you created in the previous exercise. Alternatively, you can open the completed Lesson 3, Exercise 2 project in the samples installed from the CD.

2. Create three new web user controls as follows:

- **GetName**   Add a Label control with the text **Please type your name**. Add a TextBox control named **NameTextBox**. Then add a Button control named **SubmitButton** and labeled **Submit**.

- **GreetUser**   Add a Label control named **GreetingLabel**.

- **ShowNameBackwards**   Add a Label control named **BackwardsLabel** with the text **Enter name to see it spelled backwards**.

3. Open the code-behind file for the GetName control. Add code to capture the text the user types in the TextBoxName control when he or she clicks Submit.

4. Next, add the System.Web.UI.WebControls.WebParts namespace to the control. Create a public method named GetUserName, and set the ConnectionProvider attribute. In this method, return the name the user typed. This control provides the user's name as data to the consumer controls. The following shows an example.

```vb
Sample of Visual Basic Code
Partial Class GetName
    Inherits System.Web.UI.UserControl

    Private _name As String = String.Empty

    Protected Sub SubmitButton_Click_
  (ByVal sender As Object, ByVal e As System.EventArgs) _
          Handles SubmitButton.Click
        _name = NameTextBox.Text
    End Sub

    <ConnectionProvider("User name provider", "GetUserName")> _
    Public Function GetUserName() As String
        Return _name
    End Function
End Class
```

```csharp
Sample of C# Code
private string _name = string.Empty;

protected void SubmitButton_Click(object sender, EventArgs e)
{
    _name = NameTextBox.Text;
}

[ConnectionProvider("User name provider", "GetUserName")]
public string GetUserName()
{
    return _name;
}
```

5. Open the code-behind file for the GreetUser control. Add the System.Web.UI.WebControls. WebParts namespace to the code-behind file, and then create a public method named GetName and set the ConnectionConsumer attribute. This control reads the user's name from the GetName control (after the user is connected) and displays it to the user as part of a greeting.

6. Create the GetName method so that it accepts a string and uses it to create a greeting by using the Label control, as the following code demonstrates.

Sample of Visual Basic Code

```
Partial Class GreetUser
    Inherits System.Web.UI.UserControl

    <ConnectionConsumer("User name consumer", "GetName")> _
    Public Sub GetName(ByVal Name As String)
      GreetingLabel.Text = "Welcome, " + Name + "!"
    End Sub

End Class
```

Sample of C# Code

```
public partial class GreetUser : System.Web.UI.UserControl
{
  [ConnectionConsumer("User name consumer", "GetName")]
  public void GetName(string Name)
  {
    GreetingLabel.Text = "Welcome, " + Name + "!";
  }

}
```

7. Open the code-behind file for the ShowNameBackwards control. Add the using statement for the System.Web.UI.WebControls.WebParts namespace. Then create a public GetName method as you did for GreetUser. You can use a similar definition for the ConnectionConsumer attribute. Inside this method, write code to reverse the order of the user's name and display it in the LabelBackwards control, as the following code demonstrates.

Sample of Visual Basic Code

```
Partial Class ShowNameBackwards
    Inherits System.Web.UI.UserControl

    <ConnectionConsumer("User name consumer", "GetName")> _
    Public Sub GetName(ByVal Name As String)
        Dim NameCharArray As Char() = Name.ToCharArray()
        Array.Reverse(NameCharArray)
        BackwardsLabel.Text = "Your name backward is: " & _
  New String(NameCharArray)
    End Sub
End Class
```

Sample of C# Code

```csharp
public partial class ShowNameBackwards : System.Web.UI.UserControl
{
    [ConnectionConsumer("User name consumer", "GetName")]
    public void GetName(string Name)
    {
        char[] NameCharArray = Name.ToCharArray();
        Array.Reverse(NameCharArray);
        BackwardsLabel.Text = "Your name backward is: " +
            new string(NameCharArray);
    }
}
```

8. Open the Default2.aspx page you created in Design view, and add the GetName, GreetUser, and ShowNameBackwards controls to the bottom zone. Specify titles for each control, as shown here.

```
<asp:WebPartZone ID="WebPartZoneBottom" runat="server"
  HeaderText="Bottom Zone" style="width: 700px; height: auto;">
  <ZoneTemplate>
    <uc3:GetName ID="GetName1" runat="server" title="Enter Name" />
    <uc4:GreetUser ID="GreetUser1" runat="server" title="Greeting" />
    <uc5:ShowNameBackwards ID="ShowNameBackwards1" runat="server"
      title="Backwards Name" />
  </ZoneTemplate>
</asp:WebPartZone>
```

9. Open Default2.aspx in Source view. Within the WebPartManager control, add a <StaticConnections> element. Within the <StaticConnections> element, add two WebPartConnection controls that declare the connections between the GetName provider and the GreetUser and ShowNameBackwards consumers.

The WebPartConnection control must have an ID attribute, an attribute to identify the provider control (ProviderID), an attribute to identify the provider method (Provider-ConnectionPointID), an attribute to identify the consumer control (ConsumerID), and an attribute to identify the consumer method (ConsumerConnectionPointID). The following markup demonstrates this.

```
<asp:webPartManager ID="webPartManager1" runat="server">
  <StaticConnections>
    <asp:webPartConnection
      ID="WebPartConnection1"
      ProviderID="GetName1"
      ProviderConnectionPointID="GetUserName"
      ConsumerID="GreetUser1"
      ConsumerConnectionPointID="GetName"
    />
    <asp:webPartConnection
      ID="WebPartConnection2"
      ProviderID="GetName1"
      ProviderConnectionPointID="GetUserName"
```

```
        ConsumerID="ShowNameBackwards1"
        ConsumerConnectionPointID="GetName"
    />
  </StaticConnections>
</asp:webPartManager>
```

10. Run Default2.aspx in your web browser. In the GetName control, type your name, and then click the button. Your name appears in the other two controls.

Lesson Summary

- Web Parts are controls that you create by using either custom controls that implement the Web Part class or standard user controls and ASP.NET controls. Web Parts are also managed by ASP.NET, which allows users to close, minimize, edit, and move them.

- To add Web Parts to a page, add a WebPartManager control to the top of the page, add WebPartZone containers to the page, and then add controls to the WebPartZone containers.

- To enable users to edit or rearrange Web Parts, you change the DisplayMode property of the WebPartManager control on your page.

- Web Parts can be connected so that they can share data. You connect them by defining both provider and consumer Web Parts, using the attribute-based programming model. In addition, you configure the connections between Web Parts by adding a <StaticConnections> element to the WebPartManager control.

Lesson Review

You can use the following questions to test your knowledge of the information in Lesson 3, "Using Web Parts." The questions are also available on the companion CD as a practice test, if you prefer to review them in electronic form.

> **NOTE ANSWERS**
>
> Answers to these questions and explanations of why each answer choice is correct or incorrect are located in the "Answers" section at the end of the book.

1. Which of the following can be a Web Part? (Choose all that apply.)

    A. A control based on the Web User Control template

    B. A standard Label control

    C. A type derived from WebPart

    D. A master page

2. Which of the following are required to enable users to change the title of a Web Part? (Choose all that apply.)

   A. LayoutEditorPart

   B. EditorZone

   C. CatalogZone

   D. AppearanceEditorPart

3. You have developed a webpage with many different Web Part components. Some Web Parts are enabled by default, and you want to give the user the ability to display others. Which classes should you use? (Choose all that apply.)

   A. LayoutEditorPart

   B. DeclarativeCatalogPart

   C. CatalogZone

   D. AppearanceEditorPart

4. You have created a Web Part control that prompts the user for personalization information, including his or her name, region, and preferences. You want other controls to be able to read information from this control to customize the information they display. How should you modify your Web Part to enable other Web Parts to connect to it?

   A. Create a method that shares the user's information, and add the ConnectionConsumer attribute to that method.

   B. Create a method that shares the user's information, and add the ConnectionProvider attribute to that method.

   C. Create a public property that shares the user's information, and add the Connection-Consumer attribute to that method.

   D. Create a public property that shares the user's information, and add the Connection-Provider attribute to that method.

Case Scenarios

In the following case scenarios, you apply what you've learned about input validation, site navigation, and Web Parts. If you have difficulty completing this work, review the material in this chapter before beginning the next chapter. You can find answers to these questions in the "Answers" section at the end of this book.

Case Scenario 1: Determining the Proper Validation Controls to Implement on a User Name

You are an application developer for Humongous Insurance. You are developing a new customer service portal. The first page users go to allows them to create a website account, which you then link to their customer information in your internal database.

On the registration page, the user must enter a valid email address, password, and account number. The password must be between 6 and 14 characters and contain at least one uppercase letter, one lowercase letter, and one number.

1. Which validation controls will you implement on the email address text box?
2. Which validation controls will you implement on the password text box?
3. Which validation controls will you implement to validate the account number?

Case Scenario 2: Implementing a Site Map

You are an application developer for Humongous Insurance. You are creating a website that customers can browse to answer frequently asked questions. To allow users to browse different categories of help, you want to create a menu that contains a tree view of the locations to which the user can navigate. You also want to display a breadcrumb path to show users the path to the page, allowing them to quickly navigate to higher levels.

- Which navigation controls will you use?

Case Scenario 3: Meeting Customization Requirements for an Internal Insurance Application

You are an application developer for Humongous Insurance. Six months ago, you released version 1.0 of a new .NET Framework web application that internal staff uses to perform several critical tasks, including:

- Looking up customer information when a subscriber calls.
- Managing the list of in-network physicians.
- Identifying subscribers who are behind on payments.
- Analyzing claims to identify areas of high cost.

Since the release of your application, you've been focused on fixing bugs. However, the application is now very stable, and you are beginning discussions with users to determine future features. At this stage, your manager would like you to meet with some users, analyze their requests, and determine how feasible these features might be when using the .NET Framework.

Interviews

Following is a list of company personnel who were interviewed, and their statements:

- **Accounts Receivable Manager** We have about two dozen employees in accounts receivable who are primarily responsible for chasing down subscribers who are behind on their payments. Your current application works great; however, it doesn't meet everyone's needs equally. To clarify, we have different groups for people responsible for corporate accounts, public sector accounts, small business accounts, and individual subscribers. Depending on the group, these employees want to see different information on the page. If possible, I'd like to enable users to customize pages and have those preferences remembered for each time they go to the page.

- **Underwriter** I'm responsible for analyzing claims and determining how we need to adjust prices to cover the cost of claims. I primarily use your application's reporting features. I love them—all I ask is that you make them more flexible. Right now, if I select a type of claim, I can see a chart of how the costs for that type of claim have changed over time. I'd like to be able to view that chart, but also view whether the claim is regional in nature, and whether specific types of organizations have more of that type of claim than others. Right now, I have to open different windows to see these different reports. I'd like them all to appear on a single page when I click a claim type.

Questions

Answer the following questions for your manager.

1. How can you provide the personalization capabilities requested by the Accounts Receivable Manager?

2. How can you enable different components to communicate with each other, as described by the Underwriter?

Suggested Practices

To successfully master the input validation and site navigation exam objectives presented in this chapter, complete the following tasks.

Validate User Input

For this task, you should complete Practices 1 and 2. Complete Practice 3 to obtain extra experience with the CustomValidator control.

- **Practice 1** Create a new webpage that collects data from users. Practice adding the validation controls to restrict data entry to valid entries.

- **Practice 2** Disable all client-side validation and test server-side validation.

- **Practice 3** Add at least one CustomValidator control, and supply client-side and server-side validation code.

Create Page Layout

For this task, you should complete Practices 1 through 5 to gain experience with using navigation and Web Parts.

- **Practice 1**   Configure some HyperLink controls to navigate to different webpages on the same website, and configure other HyperLink controls to navigate to a webpage on a different website.

- **Practice 2**   Add navigation controls to an existing website.

- **Practice 3**   Using the Web Parts page you created in the Lesson 3 exercises, open the webpage by using a browser other than Internet Explorer. Notice that ASP.NET renders the Web Part controls differently.

- **Practice 4**   Using the Web Parts page you created in Lesson 3, Exercise 3, expand the connected control capabilities so that the user's name is stored persistently.

- **Practice 5**   Using the Web Parts page you created in Lesson 3, Exercise 3, remove the static connections from Default.aspx. Then add a ConnectionsZone control to the page. View the page and use the ConnectionsZone control to manually establish the connections among the GetName, GreetUser, and ShowNameBackwards controls.

Take a Practice Test

The practice tests on this book's companion CD offer many options. For example, you can test yourself on just the lesson review questions in this chapter, or you can test yourself on all the 70-515 certification exam objectives. You can set up the test so that it closely simulates the experience of taking a certification exam, or you can set it up in study mode so that you can look at the correct answers and explanations after you answer each question.

> **MORE INFO**   **PRACTICE TESTS**
>
> For details about all the practice test options available, see "How to Use the Practice Tests" in this book's Introduction.

CHAPTER 6

Globalization and Accessibility

M any websites are developed for a single language and culture. However, these web-sites are often accessed by people living in different countries and speaking different languages. Website developers often ignore this potentially larger audience. Microsoft ASP.NET allows you to expand your reach to this audience by externalizing your site's text into separate, localized files called resource files.

A resource file is created for each language and culture that your site supports. ASP.NET determines the requested language and culture from the user's request and checks your site to see if it supports the request. If it does, ASP.NET will process the appropriate resources and render your page in the requested language. If it does not, ASP.NET will pick up your default resource file and return the response with that information.

If you want your site to be accessed by the widest variety of users, you must include support for accessibility. This means that you must support the many different display types and input devices that can be used to access your site. When you implement accessibility, the additional features typically benefit all users of your site.

ASP.NET provides several features to help you with both globalization and accessibility. This chapter covers these important topics from the perspective of an ASP.NET web developer.

Exam objectives in this chapter:
- Developing Web Forms Pages
    - Implement globalization.

Lessons in this chapter:

Before You Begin

To complete the lessons in this chapter, you should be familiar with developing applications with Microsoft Visual Studio by using Microsoft Visual Basic or Microsoft Visual C#. In addition, you should be comfortable with all of the following:

- The Visual Studio 2010 Integrated Development Environment (IDE)
- Using Hypertext Markup Language (HTML) and client-side scripting
- Creating ASP.NET websites and forms

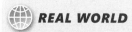
REAL WORLD

Mike Snell

Most web applications I have written, seen, or played a part in were written for a single-language, single-culture audience. In nearly all cases, globalization was either an afterthought or never even a consideration. I have seen many of these applications continue just fine for years, until they need to support another language. Companies are bought, others merge, or new markets are explored. If you have had a similar experience, you know that converting a single-language application to one that supports globalization requires no small amount of tedious work.

It's also true that implementing globalization at the start is much easier than it is after the application has been around for a while. Given this fact, and the ease with which ASP.NET applications can support globalization, I suggest that nearly all enterprise solution developers consider globalization from the start. Even if you have no current plans to translate an application, this step will pay off in the future. If you are writing an enterprise, mission-critical application, globalization should be assumed; if you are writing commercial software, it is an absolute imperative.

Lesson 1: Configuring Globalization and Localization

Many web application developers are asked to support users in a variety of cultures who speak different languages. These developers might be writing intranet applications for multinational companies, public websites for global audiences, or other web applications that need to reach a wide audience. For these reasons, ASP.NET provides the infrastructure to create web applications that automatically adjust formatting and languages according to the user's preferred language and culture.

This lesson describes how you use these features to create web applications suitable for a broad audience.

About ASP.NET Resources

To display an ASP.NET page in one of several different languages, you could prompt the user for his or her preferred language, and then write if-then statements to update the text of your page. However, that would be a complex, time-consuming chore that would require the person translating the website to know how to write code. Clearly this is not an effective solution. Instead, you need to externalize the items requiring translation and allow your code to connect to these items at run time. This allows a nontechnical translator to work without having to touch the code. It also saves you from introducing any errors that might creep into your code from the addition of language support.

ASP.NET uses resource files to support multiple languages. A *resource file* contains a language-specific set of text for a page or for an entire site. Your code accesses a resource file based on the user's requested language in his or her machine settings or browser settings. If a resource file exists for the requested language, ASP.NET uses it and thus renders your site in the language specified. If no resource file exists for the request, ASP.NET uses the default language setting for the site.

There are two types of resources in ASP.NET: local and global. *Local resources* are those specific to a page. *Global resources* are shared throughout the site. Most globalized ASP.NET applications take advantage of both. The sections that follow elaborate on each of these types of resources.

Using Local Resource Files

A local resource is specific to a single webpage and should be used for providing a version of a webpage in a different language. Local resources must be stored in the special App_LocalResources folder. This is either a subfolder of your site or a subfolder inside any folder containing webpages. If your site contains many folders, you might have an App_LocalResources subfolder in each folder of your site.

Each local resource file is page specific. Therefore, it is named by using the page name plus the .resx extension, as in *PageName*.aspx.resx. For example, to create a resource file for the Home.aspx page, you would create a file called Home.aspx.resx. This becomes the default base resource file for the Home.aspx page. ASP.NET uses this default resource file if it cannot find a match for the user's requested language-culture setting.

You create language-specific versions of the resource file by copying the original file and renaming it to include the specific language information, as in *PageName*.aspx.*languageId*.resx. For example, a Spanish version of the Default.aspx page could be named Default.aspx.es.resx ("es" is the abbreviation for Spanish). A German file could be named Default.aspx.de.resx ("de" represents German).

> **NOTE** **LANGUAGE AND CULTURE ABBREVIATIONS**
>
> You can find a list of language and culture identifications by searching the Microsoft Developer Network (MSDN) for "National Language Support (NLS) API Reference" or by going to *http://msdn.microsoft.com/en-us/goglobal/bb896001.aspx*.

Culture-Specific Local Resources

In ASP.NET development, the term *culture* refers to regional language and formatting differences. For example, English spoken in the United States is slightly different than the English spoken in England, Australia, or other parts of the world. Each country or region might also have different standards for currency, date, and number formatting. For example, in the United States, numbers are written in the following format: 12,345.67. In parts of Europe, the comma and period are used differently, and the same number is written as 12.345,67.

When a request specifies a culture, the Microsoft .NET Framework will adjust formatting as needed. That is, if you are formatting data as a date and the request defines both language and culture, the .NET Framework will know to format the data according to the request. You do not have to do anything additional in your code or resource files.

If, however, you need to translate differently based on culture, you should add a culture designation to your resource file. This is useful if there are different dialects you need to support, such as the difference between English in the United States and Great Britain, or the difference between Spanish in Mexico and Spain.

You add a culture designation to your resource by naming the file as follows: *PageName*.aspx.*languageId-cultureId*.resx. As an example, a Spanish (es) resource file designated for Mexico (mx) could be named as follows: Home.aspx.es-mx.resx. If you have defined resource files for both es and es-mx, ASP.NET uses the es-mx file for users requesting from Mexico; all other Spanish-speaking cultures receive the Home.aspx.es.resx file.

Examining the Contents of a Resource File

An ASP.NET resource file is an XML file that includes a set of key-value pairs for defining resources. The keys are unique and are used to define and reference the resource. The value, of course, is what is returned for the key. For example, the following markup shows the XML inside a resource file for defining a resource string to be used to set a page's title property.

```
<data name="PageResource1.Title" xml:space="preserve">
    <value>Customer Lookup</value>
</data>
```

In this example, the key (name) of the resource is PageResource1.Title, and the value is Customer Lookup. Visual Studio provides a tool for editing resource files so that you do not have to manually edit the XML. However, you can always open a .resx file inside the XML editor if you need to.

Generating Local Resources

You can use Visual Studio to automatically generate the default version of your local resource file. Doing so extracts the page and control elements into a resource file, which can save you time and effort. Note that resources are only generated for controls on the page (and not text outside of controls). To automatically generate a resource file by using Visual Studio, follow these steps:

1. Open your webpage (markup) in Visual Studio.

2. From the Tools menu, select Generate Local Resource. This causes Visual Studio to perform the following tasks:

   ■ Create the App_LocalResources folder (if necessary).

   ■ Generate an XML-based local resource file for the webpage in the App_LocalResources folder. This file contains resource settings for page elements (such as the title) and control properties (such as Text, ToolTip, Title, Caption, and other string-based properties).

> **NOTE MANUAL CREATION OF RESOURCE FILES**
>
> You can also manually create a resource file. You first define the folder to store the file (App_LocalResource) and then right-click and select Add New Item. You then select the Resource File template.

As an example, consider the web form shown in Figure 6-1. This page contains TextBox, Calendar, and Button controls. Notice the option to Generate Local Resource shown on the Tools menu.

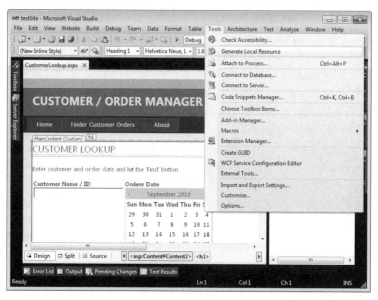

FIGURE 6-1 Generating a resource file directly from an ASPX page.

Generating a resource file for the page shown in Figure 6-1 externalizes the key string properties of the controls on the page into a .resx file. This file can be opened and edited by using Visual Studio's resource file editor. Figure 6-2 shows the generated, default resource file (CustomerLookup.aspx.resx) open inside Visual Studio. Notice that the Find button's Text property string value was set automatically based on the value defined in the markup.

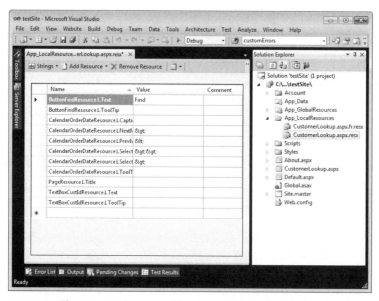

FIGURE 6-2 The generated resource file opened in the Visual Studio resource editor.

Remember, you can also work with the .resx file in an XML editor. Each key-value pair is an XML <data> element with a name that matches the named element on the page. The following shows an example of the Find button's Text property resource inside the XML.

```
<data name="ButtonFindResource1.Text" xml:space="preserve">
    <value>Find</value>
</data>
```

Localizing Text Outside of Controls

Recall that Visual Studio did not generate resources for all the text on the page. Rather, it only generated a resource for those items that were string properties of controls. Refer back to Figure 6-1. Notice that there are several text items on the page that were not externalized as resources. These items were not externalized because the text was not defined inside a control. ASP.NET needs to attach resources to controls so that it can associate the control and resource file through code running on the server. This is something you need to consider when creating your pages. If the text on your page requires resource-based localization, it is best to encapsulate that text inside a control.

You have a couple of options for doing so. ASP.NET includes the <asp:Localize> control to assist with localizing text. This control renders no markup to the page. It only works to localize text that is typically outside of a control. You can also use an <asp:Label> control. This control will provide you with additional markup options and works in a similar manner. The following shows an example of a text element on the page that uses the <asp:Localize> control.

```
<asp:Localize ID="LabelTitle" runat="server" Text="Customer Lookup"
  meta:resourcekey="LabelTitleResource1"></asp:Localize>
```

Attaching Controls and Resources Implicitly

When Visual Studio generates a resource file, it also automatically changes your markup to attach each page element with an associated resource. To do so, it adds the meta:resourcekey markup as an attribute of a specific control. This tells ASP.NET to look up the value for this item from the resource file by using the specified resource key (the name of the data element in the .resx XML). This is referred to as *implicit localization* because it is based on matching resources defined with the naming pattern *Key.Property*, where Key is the control name and Property is the property of the control on which to match (as in ButtonFind.Text or ButtonFindResource1.Text).

The following markup shows an example of the Find button's markup after the Text property was externalized into an implicit resource.

```
<asp:Button ID="ButtonFind" runat="server" Text="Find" CssClass="submitButton"
  meta:resourcekey="ButtonFindResource1" />
```

Notice that this markup still has a value defined for the Text property. This is to aid you at design time when laying out the page. Notice also that this markup contains the meta:resourcekey key set to ButtonFindResource1. ASP.NET will use this key to look up resources in the specified .resx file and match on any properties that might be set inside the resource file as meta:resourcekey. *<propertyName>* or ButtonFindResource1.Text. If it finds a property match, it will replace that control's property value with the value found in the resource file.

You can use this same method and naming convention when manually defining resources and attaching them to your markup. This is important, because you often will add or change controls on a webpage after you have generated the resource file. Visual Studio does not try to automatically keep the resource file in sync. Therefore, you typically generate resource files as one of the last steps of the development process. This becomes even more important as you build up different resource files for different languages and cultures. A change to your page in this case results in a change to each of the many resource files associated with the page.

Attaching Controls and Resources Explicitly

The implicit model discussed previously matches control property values to resources automatically (based on the *Key.Property* convention). However, you can also write markup to match a control's property to a resource explicitly. The following markup shows an example of matching the Text property with the ButtonFindResource1.Text resource.

```
<asp:Button ID="ButtonFind" runat="server" CssClass="submitButton"
  Text="<%$ Resources:,  ButtonFindResource1.Text %>" />
```

Explicit localization requires that you write markup for every control property you want to attach to a resource. Therefore, if you want to externalize another property as a resource, you must both add the resource to the resource file and add the markup to your page, whereas with implicit localization, you simply define the resource by using the appropriate naming convention (Key.Property).

Creating Language-Specific Local Resources

You typically create culture-specific and language-specific resource files by first creating a default resource file. You can use this default file as a base. You copy and paste it to create a new resource file for the target language or culture and name the file accordingly. You then need to modify the resource values for the new language or culture. To copy the default resource file, follow these steps:

1. In Solution Explorer, right-click your default resource file and select Copy.

2. Right-click the App_LocalResources folder, and then select Paste.

3. Right-click the new resource file, and then select Rename. Type a new name for the resource file that includes the language and culture code before the file extension. For example, you might name the file CustomerLookup.aspx.fr.resx to create a French-language version of the page ("fr" is the abbreviation for French).

4. Double-click the new resource file to open it in Visual Studio. Visual Studio displays a table containing values and comments for each resource. Update the values for the new culture, and then save the resource file.

You repeat these steps to create resource files for every language and culture that you want to support. Recall that if you want to create a culture-specific file (in addition to a language-specific one), you do so by separating culture and language with a hyphen, as in "es-mx" for Spanish language, Mexican culture.

Testing Resource Files for Other Cultures

ASP.NET automatically determines the user's preferred culture based on information provided by the web browser. When the request is sent to the page, ASP.NET sets the Page.UICulture property based on the request. You can use this property in your code. ASP.NET uses the same property to select an appropriate resource file.

A web browser's language preferences are set during installation. However, they can be modified by users. You can also modify them to help test your site. To test other cultures by using Windows Internet Explorer, update the preferred language by following these steps:

1. Open Internet Explorer. From the Tools menu, select Internet Options to launch the Internet Options dialog box.

2. On the General tab, click Languages in the Appearance group. This opens the Language Preference dialog box.

3. In the Language Preference dialog box, click Add.

4. In the Add Language dialog box, under Language, select the language you want to test, and then click OK.

5. Figure 6-3 shows the English (Belize) (en-BZ) setting added to the language preferences. From here, you select the language you want to test, and then click Move Up to move that language to the top of the list. Finally, click OK twice to close the open dialog boxes.

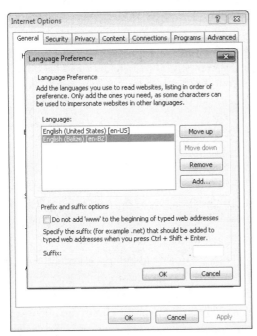

FIGURE 6-3 Redefining your preferred language in Internet Explorer to test your website localization.

You can now visit the webpage of your site and view the selected culture's resource file. When you are done testing, remember to reset your browser to your actual preferred language and culture.

Using Global Resources

A global resource is one that is defined to be read from any page or code that is in the website. Global resources are not page-specific resources like local resources. Rather, global resources are designed for when you need to access a single resource from multiple webpages in your site. In this way, you can define the resource once and share its value across pages.

Global resources are still .resx files. You still create a default file and a version for each language and culture you intend to support. The file naming scheme remains the same as for local resource files. However, global resource files are stored in the App_GlobalResources folder at the root of an application. ASP.NET also generates an object that allows you to easily access your global resources through code. In markup, you must use a global resource explicitly (global resources are not used implicitly).

Creating Global Resources

To create a global resource, you start by creating a resource file and storing it in the App_GlobalResources folder. This file should externalize all the resources you intend to share across pages. You can then explicitly map individual control properties across pages to the resource of choice. You can also use the resource in code. Finally, you can create separate versions of the global resource file for each language and culture you intend to support. ASP.NET will automatically associate the right version of the global resource file based on the user's defined language and culture setting (just as with local resources).

To create a global resource file, follow these steps:

1. In Solution Explorer, right-click the root of your website. Select Add ASP.NET Folder, and then select App_GlobalResources. This will add a folder of the same name to the root of your site.

2. Next, right-click the App_GlobalResources folder, and then select Add New Item.

3. In the Add New Item dialog box, select Resource File. In the Name text box, type any file name with a .resx extension. For example, you could name your global resource file SharedLocalizedText.resx. Click Add to add the resource file to your site.

4. Open the new resource file in Visual Studio. Visual Studio displays a table-like format for adding and editing resources. From here you can add strings, images, icons, audio, files, and other resources (see the Note on the next page). Remember, this is your default resource file (based on the naming convention). Therefore, you add items here that are meant to be in the default language and culture (when no language-specific resource file version is found).

5. After you have defined your default resource file, you copy and paste it to create resource files for different languages. You name these files the same way you would local resource files. For example, you might name a French global resource file SharedLocalizedText.fr.resx. You then open each language-specific version and edit it to provide the resource translation.

> **NOTE** **CREATING NON-STRING RESOURCES**
>
> You do not store non-string resources such as images as resources. Rather, you store the name of the file and its path that the item represents. The resource XML stores information that will link you to the actual file. You can then map this information to a control property such as an Image control's ImageUrl property.

Attaching Control Properties to Global Resources

After you have defined a global resource file, you can explicitly associate control properties (such as Label.Text) from different pages to the global resource. In this way, you can share the resource file across pages. ASP.NET will automatically display the correct text from your resource file based on the user's defined culture. Therefore, if you have a Label that displays a greeting message on every page, you only need to define the message once for each culture (rather than defining it in separate resource files for each webpage).

In design mode, you can associate a control's property value with a global resource by using the Expressions property. To do so, follow these steps:

1. Open your page in Design view in Visual Studio. View the Properties pane for one of the controls.

2. Select the Expressions property (in the Data category). Click the ellipsis (...) button next to the property to launch the control's Expressions dialog box.

3. From the Bindable Properties list, select a property that you want to bind to a resource.

4. From the Expression type list, select Resources.

5. In the Expression Properties list, set ClassKey to the name of your global resource file (without the extension). Under that, set ResourceKey to the name of the resource within the resource file. Figure 6-4 shows an example.

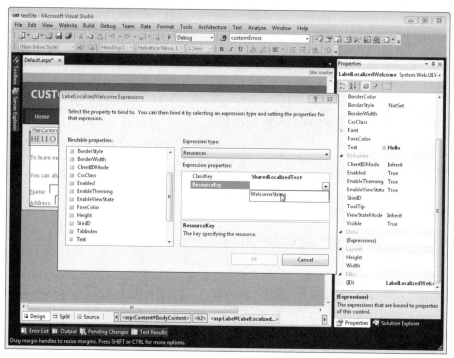

FIGURE 6-4 Using expressions to bind controls to global resources.

6. Click OK to close the dialog box.

After a resource is set, Visual Studio displays the default resource value for the control in design view. Of course, this will be changed to display the language-specific resource when a user visits the webpage.

Within the page markup, Visual Studio updates the control's Text property to explicitly bind to the resource. For example, if you are binding a Label control's Text property to a resource named WelcomeString in the SharedLocalizedText resource file(s), the markup looks as follows.

```
<asp:Label ID="LocalizeWelcome"
  Text="<%$ Resources:SharedLocalizedText, WelcomeString %>" runat="server"></asp:Label>
```

EXAM TIP

You should be sure to know how to use the explicit <%$ Resources:*ResourceFile*, *ResourceID* %> format for the exam.

Accessing Resource Values Programmatically

ASP.NET creates an object that allows you to access global resource values programmatically by using the Resources.*ResourceFilename.Resource* syntax . This is a strongly typed class of the Resources.Resource object for each global resource file. The class is created based on the file name (minus the language and culture extensions).

Each resource in the file is a member of the class. For example, if you add a value named WelcomeString to the resource file, SharedLocalizedText, you can assign the value to a Label control's Text property inside your page's code-behind by using the following syntax.

Sample of Visual Basic Code

```
LabelLocalizedWelcome.Text = Resources.SharedLocalizedText.WelcomeString
```

Sample of C# Code

```
LabelLocalizedWelcome.Text = Resources.SharedLocalizedText.WelcomeString;
```

The preceding example assumes that you are accessing global resources programmatically and that those resources are available at design time. However, your resource files might not be available at design time, or you might want to access local resources programmatically. For these purposes, ASP.NET provides the GetLocalResourceObject and GetGlobalResourceObject methods. Each of these methods looks for a resource file, reads it, and provides the right resource.

To use the GetLocalResourceObject method, simply provide the name of the resource. To use GetGlobalResourceObject, provide both the resource file name (without the extension) and the resource name. For example, the following code uses these methods to get resources for two different controls.

Sample of Visual Basic Code

```
Button1.Text = GetLocalResourceObject("Button1.Text").ToString()
Image1.ImageUrl = CType(GetGlobalResourceObject("WebResourcesGlobal", "LogoUrl"), String)
```

Sample of C# Code

```
Button1.Text = GetLocalResourceObject("Button1.Text").ToString();
Image1.ImageUrl = (String)GetGlobalResourceObject("WebResourcesGlobal", "LogoUrl");
```

 Quick Check

1. In which folder should you store global resource files?

2. In which folder should you store local resource files?

Quick Check Answers

1. Global resources should be stored in the App_GlobalResources folder.

2. Store local resources in the App_LocalResources folder.

HTML Layout Best Practices

Globalization can be as simple as replacing text with text from another language and reformatting numbers and symbols. However, some languages, such as Arabic languages, require different layouts because text flows from right to left. To allow webpages to be used by the widest variety of cultures, follow these guidelines:

- **Avoid using absolute positioning and sizes for controls**   Rather than specifying control locations in pixels, allow the web browser to position your controls automatically. You can do this by simply not specifying a size or location. The easiest way to determine whether any controls have absolute positions is to view the source for a webpage. For example, the following illustrates a control that uses absolute positioning (which should be avoided).

```
<div id = idLabel style = "position: absolute; left: 0.98em; top: 1.21em;
   width: 4.8em; height: 1.21em;">
```

- **Use the entire width and height of forms**   Although many websites specify the number of pixels for the width of a form or table column, this can cause formatting problems for languages that use more letters or a different text layout. Instead of indicating a specific width, use 100 percent of the width of the web browser, as the following sample demonstrates.

```
<table width=100%>
```

- **Use a separate table cell for each control**   This allows text to wrap independently and ensures correct alignment for cultures in which text layout flows from right to left.

- **Avoid enabling the NoWrap property in tables**   Setting HtmlTableCell.NoWrap to true disables word wrapping. Although word wrapping might work well in your native language, other languages can require more space and might not display correctly.

- **Avoid specifying the Align property in tables**   Setting a left or right alignment in a cell can override layout in cultures that use right-to-left text.

- **Decouple check boxes and radio buttons from their text**   Putting the text that describes a radio button or check box in a separate table cell allows that text to wrap to accommodate larger text when translated.

In summary, the less explicitly you configure layout, the better your page can be localized, because you leave layout decisions to the rendering engine and the client's browser.

Setting the Culture

Often, web browsers are configured with the user's language preferences. However, many times a user's web browser is not configured correctly. For example, an American tourist at an Internet café in Mexico might use a web browser that has been configured for Spanish.

Of course, it is likely that the American would prefer to read your site in English. For this reason, you should use the browser's setting as the default but allow users to override that default setting in your application. This is often done by providing a setting value of the home page that includes text in multiple languages describing how to change the language setting. When a user changes the setting, you execute code to use this new setting (which is stored in a cookie, session variable, or similar element).

In an ASP.NET webpage, you use two different Page properties to set language and culture:

- **Culture** This object dictates the results of culture-dependent functions, such as the date, number, and currency formatting. You can only define the Culture object with specific cultures that define both language and regional formatting requirements, such as es-MX or fr-FR. You cannot define the Culture object with neutral cultures that define only a language, such as es or fr.

- **UICulture** This property dictates which global or local resources are to be loaded for the page. You can define UICulture with either neutral or specific cultures.

You define the Culture and UICulture properties by overriding the page's InitializeCulture method. From this method, define the Culture and UICulture properties, and then call the page's base InitializeCulture method. The following code sample demonstrates this, assuming that DropDownList1 contains a list of cultures.

Sample of Visual Basic Code

```vb
Protected Overloads Overrides Sub InitializeCulture()
    If Not (Request.Form("DropDownList1") Is Nothing) Then
        'define the language
        UICulture = Request.Form("DropDownList1")
        'define the formatting (requires a specific culture)
        Culture = Request.Form("DropDownList1")
    End If
    MyBase.InitializeCulture()
End Sub
```

Sample of C# Code

```csharp
protected override void InitializeCulture()
{
    if (Request.Form["DropDownList1"] != null)
    {
        //define the language
        UICulture = Request.Form["DropDownList1"];

        //define the formatting (requires a specific culture)
        Culture = Request.Form["DropDownList1"];
    }
    base.InitializeCulture();
}
```

Normally, you should provide users with a list of cultures and languages for which you have configured resources. For example, if you have configured resources for English, Spanish, and French, you should only allow users to choose from those three options. However, you can also retrieve an array of all available cultures by calling the System. Globalization.CultureInfo.GetCultures method. Pass this method a CultureTypes enumeration that specifies which subset of available cultures you want to list. The most useful CultureTypes values are the following:

- **AllCultures**   This represents all cultures included with the .NET Framework, including both neutral and specific cultures. If you use AllCultures in your code, be sure to verify that a selected culture is a specific culture before assigning it to the Culture object.

- **NeutralCultures**   Neutral cultures provide only a language and not regional formatting definitions.

- **SpecificCultures**   Specific cultures provide both language and regional formatting definitions.

Setting Culture Declaratively at the Page or Site Level

You can also declaratively set the culture for a website or webpage. To define the culture for an entire website, add a *<globalization>* section to the Web.config file, and then set the UICulture and Culture attributes, as the following sample demonstrates.

```
<globalization uiculture="es" culture="es-MX" />
```

To declare a culture for a webpage, define the UICulture and Culture attributes of the @ Page directive, as shown here.

```
<%@ Page uiculture="es" culture="es-MX" %>
```

> **NOTE   LOCALIZING CLIENT SCRIPT**
>
> This lesson discussed localization as a server-based model. All localization is done on the server, and the page is returned appropriately. However, you might need to use localization when working with Asynchronous JavaScript and XML (AJAX) and client script. ASP.NET supports this in a similar manner as discussed. For more information, search MSDN for "Localizing Resources for Component Libraries Overview."

PRACTICE   **Creating a Webpage That Supports Multiple Cultures**

In this practice, you create a site that uses resource files for different languages.

EXERCISE Creating a Webpage for Both English and Spanish

In this exercise, you create a webpage that displays language-specific text based on the user's browser preference, while allowing users to overwrite the default setting.

1. Open Visual Studio. Create a new file-based website (File | New | Web Site) called **GlobalSite**.

    By default, Visual Studio will create your site to use master pages. This example will not use master pages (see the note later in this step for more information).

2. Delete the Default.aspx page. Add a new page to your site (right-click the site and select Add New Item). Make sure that the Select Master Page check box is not selected in the Add New Item dialog box. Name your page **Default.aspx**.

NOTE **MASTER PAGES AND INITIALIZECULTURE**

Master pages in ASP.NET do not include the InitializeCulture event. Therefore, you cannot simply override this method in the master page and be done with setting your localization for your site. Instead, you must override this event in every page of your site that uses the master page. This typically involves creating a base page (that inherits from Page) for each of your webpages so that you only have to write this code once.

In addition, the InitializeCulture event fires very early in the page life cycle. When master pages are used, you do not have access to the form's controls by their actual ID property. ASP.NET has yet to convert them from its version to your naming standard. Therefore, you have to reference controls by their ASP.NET name, such as Request.Form["ctl00$MainContent$DropDownListLang"], instead of Request.Form["DropDownListLang"].

Of course, there are other possible implementations that developers have come up with (some involving the Application_BeginRequest event, for instance). All of this has to do with how the page life cycle and master pages work (and not globalization). Therefore, this practice is constrained to a single webpage with no master page.

3. Open the Default.aspx form. Add a Label and a DropDownList control to the page. Name the controls **LabelWelcome** and **DropDownListLang**, respectively.

4. You will use the Label control to display a culture-specific greeting to the user. The DropDownList control allows a user to choose a specific language. Set the DropDown-List.AutoPostBack property to true. Your markup should look similar to the example on the following page.

```
<div>
    <h1>
        <asp:Label ID="LabelWelcome" runat="server"
            Text="Welcome" meta:resourcekey="LabelWelcomeResource1"></asp:Label>
    </h1>
    <br />
    <asp:DropDownList ID="DropDownListLang" runat="server"
        AutoPostBack="true">
    </asp:DropDownList>
</div>
```

5. Make sure Default.aspx is open in Design view in Visual Studio. From the Tools menu, select Generate Local Resource. This will create the App_LocalResources folder and the Default.aspx.resx file. It will also set the Culture and UICulture directives for the page to Auto and set the meta:ResourceKey attribute. The Generate Local Resource command is not available in Visual Web Developer 2010 Express.

6. In Solution Explorer, double-click Default.aspx.resx. For the LabelWelcomeResource1.Text value, type **Hello**. For the PageResource1.Title value, type **English** (replace existing text). Close and save the Default.aspx.resx file.

7. In Solution Explorer, right-click Default.aspx.resx, and then click Copy. Right-click App_LocalResources and click Paste. Next, rename the new resource file Default.aspx.es.resx.

8. Double-click Default.aspx.es.resx. For the LabelWelcomeResource1.Text value, type **Hola**. For the PageResource1.Title value, type **Español**. Then close and save the Default.aspx.es.resx file.

9. Run your page in a web browser. Notice that the Label control displays "Hello" even though you never directly set the LabelWelcome.Text property to this value. (You can return to the markup on the page to see that the meta:resourcekey attribute of the control was set by Visual Studio.) Also notice that the page title (shown in the Internet Explorer title bar) displays "English".

10. In Internet Explorer, follow these steps:
    a. From the Tools menu, select Internet Options.
    b. In the Internet Options dialog box, click the Languages button (at the bottom).
    c. In the Language Preference dialog box, click Add.
    d. In the Add Language dialog box, under Language, select Spanish (Mexico) [es-mx]. Click OK.
    e. Back in the Language Preference dialog box, select Spanish from the Language list and then click Move Up to make it your preferred language.
    f. Click OK twice to return to Internet Explorer.Refresh the webpage, and verify that the page displays the Spanish resources you provided.

11. Return to Visual Studio and open the code-behind file for Default.aspx. Add the System.Globalization namespace to the page (with an Imports or using statement) to allow the CultureInfo object to be used.

12. Add a Page_Load event handler to the code (or use the existing one). Write code to populate the DropDownListLang control with a list of cultures. The following code sample illustrates this.

Sample of Visual Basic Code

```vb
For Each ci As CultureInfo In CultureInfo.GetCultures_
  (CultureTypes.NeutralCultures)
    DropDownListLang.Items.Add(New ListItem(ci.NativeName, ci.Name))
Next
```

Sample of C# Code

```csharp
foreach (CultureInfo ci in CultureInfo.GetCultures(CultureTypes.
  NeutralCultures))
{
    DropDownListLang.Items.Add(new ListItem(ci.NativeName, ci.Name));
}
```

> **NOTE NEUTRAL VS. SPECIFIC CULTURES**
>
> This code sample uses CultureTypes.NeutralCultures to get a list of cultures that provide just language information (for example, en instead of en-us). You can use CultureTypes.SpecificCultures instead if you want the user to pick both language and culture. You can use neutral cultures to define the UICulture object, but you can only use specific cultures to define the Culture object.

13. Now create a method that overrides the InitializeCulture method for the page. This method should include code that sets the page's culture based on the item selected from the DropDownListLang control. Because you are defining only language, use the UICulture object, rather than the Culture object. Call the base InitializeCulture event after you have defined UICulture. The following code sample demonstrates this.

Sample of Visual Basic Code

```vb
Protected Overloads Overrides Sub InitializeCulture()
    If Not (Request.Form("DropDownListLang") Is Nothing) Then
        UICulture = Request.Form("DropDownListLang")
    End If
    MyBase.InitializeCulture()
End Sub
```

Sample of C# Code

```csharp
protected override void InitializeCulture()
{
    if (Request.Form["DropDownListLang"] != null)
    {
        UICulture = Request.Form["DropDownListLang"];
    }
    base.InitializeCulture();
}
```

14. Run the page in a web browser. From the drop-down list, select English, as shown in Figure 6-5.

FIGURE 6-5 Selecting a new language and posting back to the page to fire the InitializeCulture event.

15. The page should reload and display the English greeting. Select Español, and notice that the page changes back to Spanish.

   The drop-down list and your implementation of InitializeCulture allow ASP.NET to automatically select the browser's preferred language, yet still giving users the option of overriding the default choice.

16. Repeat step 10 to reconfigure Internet Explorer to your normal language settings.

Lesson Summary

- Local resource files allow you to provide translations for controls on a single webpage. Local resource files are named by using the format *<PageName>.[languageId]*.resx.

- Global resources provide translations for phrases that can be assigned to any control in the web application. They should be placed in the App_GlobalResources folder at the root of the application.

- To make your page as easy to globalize as possible, follow these best practices:
  - Avoid using absolute positioning and sizes for controls.
  - Use the entire width and height of forms.
  - Size elements relative to the overall size of the form.
  - Use a separate table cell for each control.
  - Avoid enabling the NoWrap property in tables.
  - Avoid specifying the Align property in tables.

- To programmatically set the language, set the UICulture object to the neutral or specific culture abbreviation. To programmatically set the regional formatting preferences, set the Culture object to the specific culture abbreviation.

Lesson Review

You can use the following questions to test your knowledge of the information in Lesson 1, "Configuring Globalization and Localization." The questions are also available on the companion CD in a practice test, if you prefer to review them in electronic form.

> **NOTE ANSWERS**
>
> Answers to these questions and explanations of why each answer choice is correct or incorrect are located in the "Answers" section at the end of the book.

1. You need to create a webpage that is available in both the default language of English and for users whose browsers identify them as German. Which of the following resource files should you create? (Choose all that apply.)

   A. App_LocalResources/Page.aspx.resx.de

   B. App_LocalResources/Page.aspx.resx

   C. App_LocalResources/Page.aspx.de.resx

   D. App_LocalResources/Page.aspx.en.resx

2. What must you do to enable users to select their own language preferences (outside of browser and machine settings)? (Choose all that apply.)

A. Set the Page.Culture property.

B. Set the Page.UICulture property.

C. Override the Page.InitializeCulture method.

D. Override the Page.ReadStringResource method.

3. What markup would you write to explicitly attach the local resource, SubmitButtonText, found inside the application's collection of MyLocalResources.aspx.*<language>*.resx files, to the Text property of a button control?

A. `<asp:Button ID="Button1" runat="server" Text="<%$ Resources:, SubmitButtonText %>" />`

B. `<asp:Button ID="Button1" runat="server" Text="<%$ Resources:MyLocalResources, SubmitButtonText %>" />`

C. `<asp:Button ID="Button1" runat="server" Text="<%$ SubmitButtonText, Resources:%>" />`.

D. `<asp:Button ID="Button1" runat="server" Text="<%$ SubmitButtonText, Resources:MyLocalResources %>" />`

4. You add a global resource with the name Login to the resource file named Resource.resx. How can you access that global resource programmatically?

A. Resources.Resource.Login

B. Resources.Resource("Login")

C. Resources("Login")

D. Resources.Login

Lesson 2: Configuring Accessibility

Whether you are creating a public website for millions to use or a small intranet web application, you should recognize the need to make it usable for those who need large text and nontraditional input devices. For example, many users do not use a conventional mouse, instead using an equivalent such as a foot switch, wand, eye or head tracking device, or even speech recognition software. Others use screen readers that speak text on websites aloud rather than displaying it on a monitor, or perhaps they use high-contrast display settings. This lesson provides best practices for making your web application more accessible to these users and their devices.

Public Accessibility Guidelines

Many people are working to make technology accessible to the widest audience possible. One of the most prominent groups is the World Wide Web Consortium (W3C), a web standards organization. Through the Web Accessibility Initiative (WAI), W3C has created the Web Content Accessibility Guidelines (WCAG).

MORE INFO WCAG

WCAG is very thorough; this book only attempts to cover the key points as they relate to ASP.NET development. For more information about WCAG, go to the Web Accessibility Initiative at *http://www.w3.org/WAI*.

The United States government has also created accessibility standards in Section 508 of the Rehabilitation Act. Depending on the organization for which you are developing a web application, you might be required to conform your application to these standards. The Section 508 guidelines are conceptually similar to the WCAG guidelines.

MORE INFO SECTION 508 GUIDELINES

For more information about Section 508 guidelines, visit http://www.section508.gov.

How ASP.NET Controls Support Accessibility

ASP.NET controls are designed to be accessible by default. For example, login controls such as Login, ChangePassword, PasswordRecovery, and CreateUserWizard use text boxes with associated labels that identify these controls on a page and thus help users who use screen readers or do not use a mouse for input. These controls also use input controls with tab index settings, to make data entry without a mouse easier.

Another way in which some ASP.NET controls support accessibility is by allowing users to skip link text. Screen readers typically read the text of links from the top to the bottom of a page while allowing users to choose a specific link. ASP.NET controls that include navigation links provide the SkipLinkText property, which is enabled by default and allows screen readers to skip past the link text (instead of reading a URL back to the user). The CreateUserWizard, Menu, SiteMapPath, TreeView, and Wizard controls each support skipping links. These links are not visible to users viewing the page with a traditional web browser. For example, the following HTML source code (which has been slightly simplified) is generated and rendered to the browser by default when you use a Menu control on a webpage.

```
<a href="#Menu1_SkipLink">
    <img alt="Skip Navigation Links"
    src="/WebResource.axd?d=_9Q2Lm" width="0" height="0" />
</a>
... menu links ...
<a id="Menu1_SkipLink"></a>
```

As the HTML demonstrates, a zero-pixel image file with the alternative text "Skip Navigation Links" links to a location on the page immediately after the menu. Whereas traditional browsers do not display the zero-pixel image, screen readers read the alternative text and allow users to skip past the menu. The simplest way to follow this best practice is to use one of the ASP.NET controls that provides the SkipLinkText property. However, if you implement custom controls with navigation links, you can provide similar functionality.

Although ASP.NET controls are designed to be as accessible as possible, you, as the developer, must take advantage of these features by providing text descriptions for some controls. The next sections provide more detailed information.

Improving Visual Accessibility

Many users have tools that supplement or replace a traditional monitor, including screen readers and magnifiers. High-contrast display settings are also often used to enhance visibility. To make your application as accessible as possible for users of these tools and techniques, follow these guidelines:

- **Describe every image by using the AlternateText property to provide alternative text.** This is useful for users who have images disabled in browsers or otherwise cannot see the pictures. Screen readers, which use speech synthesis to verbally read text on a webpage, can read alternative text descriptions. You can also set the Image.DescriptionUrl property to specify an HTML page that further describes an image, but you should only configure it if you want to provide a longer description than is possible with AlternateText. If an image is not important (such as an image that forms a border), set the GenerateEmptyAlternateText property to True to cause screen readers to ignore it.

- **Use solid colors for background, and use contrasting colors for text.** All users appreciate easy-to-read text, especially users who might not be able to perceive low-contrast text. Therefore, you should avoid text that is a similar shade to the background color.

- **Create a flexible page layout that scales correctly when text size is increased.** Internet Explorer and other browsers support the ability to increase text size, which makes text easier to read. This is useful for both users who have specialized accessibility settings and those with high-resolution displays.

- **Set the Table.Caption property to a description of the table.** Screen readers can read the Table.Caption property to describe the purpose of the data contained in a table to users. This allows the user to quickly determine whether he or she wants to hear the contents of the table or skip past it. ASP.NET controls that render tables (and support the Caption property) include Table, Calendar, DetailsView, FormView, and GridView.

- **Provide a way to identify column headers.** You can create table headers by using the TableHeaderRow class and setting the TableSection property to the TableHeader enumeration of the TableRowSection class. This causes the table to render a <thead> element. When you create cells with the TableCell control, you can set each AssociatedHeaderCellID property for the cell to the ID of a table header cell. This causes the cell to render a headers attribute that associates the cell with the corresponding column heading, simplifying table navigation for users with screen readers. The Calendar, DetailsView, FormView, and GridView ASP.NET server controls render HTML tables with these features.

- **Avoid defining specific font sizes.** Use heading tags (such as <H1> or <H3>) instead of font sizes to support the user's formatting options. Heading tags are available on the Visual Studio Formatting toolbar.

- **Avoid requiring client scripts.** Assistive technologies often cannot render client scripts, so you should use client script only for nonessential effects, such as mouse rollovers. For example, validator controls use client scripts to determine whether input meets specified requirements, and then to dynamically display error messages. However, screen readers and other assistive technologies might not render this correctly. Therefore, you should set the EnableClientScript property to false to improve accessibility. WCAG standards do not allow controls that require client scripts, so if you must comply with these standards, you should also avoid using the LinkButton, ImageButton, and Calendar controls.

> **NOTE   WCAG STANDARDS AND CLIENT SCRIPTS**
>
> In practice, your users might not have problems with the client scripts included with ASP.NET server controls. These client scripts have been developed to comply with WCAG accessibility guidelines. However, total WCAG compliance does require you to avoid insisting on client script support.

If you cannot meet accessibility goals, consider providing alternative text-only webpages. You can use global resources to allow both accessible and nonaccessible versions of a webpage to share the same text content.

Improving the Accessibility of Forms That Require User Input

Many users prefer not to use a mouse or have difficulty using pointing devices. For these users, it's critical that you make your web application usable by keyboard alone. Although providing keyboard shortcuts is common in Windows Forms applications, it's less common in web applications.

To make your application as accessible as possible from a keyboard, follow these guidelines:

- **Set the DefaultFocus property for a form to place the cursor in the logical location where data entry normally begins.**   DefaultFocus defines the placement of the cursor when the user opens a webpage. Typically, you set the default focus to the topmost editable field on a page.

- **Define the tab order in a logical way so that the user can complete forms without using a mouse.**   Ideally, the user should be able to complete one text box and then press the Tab key to jump to the next text box.

- **Specify default buttons for forms and Panel controls by setting the DefaultButton property.**   Default buttons can be accessed simply by pressing Enter. Not only does this make user input simpler for a user who doesn't use a mouse, but it can speed data entry for all users.

- **Provide useful link text.**   Screen readers read hyperlinked text aloud to enable users to choose links. Therefore, hyperlinked text should describe the link. Avoid adding hyperlinks to text such as "Click here," because users with a screen reader will not be able to distinguish it from other links. Instead, provide the name of the link destination with the hyperlink, as in "Instructions for contacting Contoso headquarters."

- **Define access keys for button controls by setting the AccessKey property.**   You can use access keys for web controls just like you would for a Windows Forms application. When you set the AccessKey property for a control, the user can hold down the Alt key and press the specified letter to immediately move the cursor to that control. The standard method of indicating a shortcut key is to underline a letter in the control. The next guideline describes how to provide shortcut keys for TextBox controls.

- **Use Label controls to define access keys for text boxes.**   TextBox controls do not have descriptions that can be easily read by screen readers. Therefore, you should associate a descriptive Label control with a TextBox control and use the Label control to define the TextBox control's shortcut key. To associate the Label with another control, define both the AccessKey and AssociatedControlID properties. Also, underline the access key in the label's text by using the underline HTML element (<u>). Users can then access the specified TextBox control by selecting Alt+<AccessKey>.

The following source code demonstrates a Label control and an associated TextBox control.

```
<asp:Label
  AccessKey="N"
  AssociatedControlID="TextBox1"
  ID="Label1"
  runat="server"
  Text="<u>N</u>ame:">
</asp:Label>
 
<asp:TextBox ID="TextBox1" runat="server" />
```

■ **Use the Panel control to create subdivisions in a form, and define the Panel.GroupingText property with a description of the controls in that panel.** ASP.NET uses the GroupingText property to create <fieldset> and <legend> HTML elements, which can make forms easier for users to navigate. For example, you might define separate Panel controls to collect a user's shipping, billing, and credit card information on a checkout page. The following HTML demonstrates how ASP.NET renders the Panel.GroupingText property as a <legend> element.

```
<form  method="post" action="Default.aspx" id="form1">
<div id="Panel1" style="height:50px;width:125px;">
  <fieldset>
    <legend>
      Shipping Information
    </legend>
    <input name="TextBox2" type="text" id="TextBox2" />
  </fieldset>
</div>
<div id="Panel2" style="height:50px;width:125px;">
  <fieldset>
    <legend>
      Billing Information
    </legend>
    <input name="TextBox1" type="text" id="TextBox1" />
  </fieldset>
</div>
</form>
```

■ **Specify meaningful error messages in the Text and ErrorMessage properties of validator controls.** Although the default asterisk (*) is sufficient to identify input controls that need to be completed for some users, it is not useful to users with screen readers. Instead, provide descriptive error messages, such as "You must provide your email address."

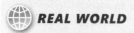
REAL WORLD

Mike Snell

If you have ever spent time writing accessible web applications, you have probably noticed that your efforts have proved worthwhile for all users of your site. Of course, this includes those users who do not use traditional monitors, keyboards, or other input devices. However, I am surprised by how much the experience is also improved for users who use standard equipment. These users benefit from descriptive text, quick access keys, scaling fonts, and more. Accessibility not only helps people, it is also good design.

 Quick Check

1. What can you do to make a webpage more useful to users who use special displays or screen readers to make text more readable?

2. What can you do to make a webpage more useful to a user who does not use a mouse?

Quick Check Answers

1. First, avoid specifying font sizes or using colors that might be difficult to read. Second, provide descriptions for images, tables, and forms that screen readers can use.

2. Provide access keys for all controls that require user input, and underline the access keys in associated labels. Define a logical tab order that allows the user to progress through a form by using the Tab key. Additionally, specify default buttons for forms and Panel controls.

Testing Accessibility

Visual Studio can test webpages or entire web applications for compliance with WCAG and Section 508 standards. The sections that follow describe how to use Visual Studio to automatically test your work.

Checking the Accessibility of a Single Page

To use Visual Studio to test the accessibility of a webpage, follow these steps:

1. In Visual Studio, open the page you want to check.

2. From the View menu, select Error List to display the Error List window.

3. From the Tools menu, select Check Accessibility. The Accessibility Validation dialog box appears, as shown in Figure 6-6.

FIGURE 6-6 Using the Accessibility Validation dialog box in Visual Studio to check the accessibility of a webpage.

4. Select the check boxes for the type and level of accessibility checking that you want to perform, and then click Validate. The results of the check are displayed in the Error List pane.

Automatically Checking the Accessibility of a Web Application

You can use Visual Studio to automatically test the accessibility of an entire web application as you are building it. To do so, follow these steps:

1. In Solution Explorer, right-click your website and select Property Pages.

2. Click the Accessibility node. Figure 6-7 shows an example.

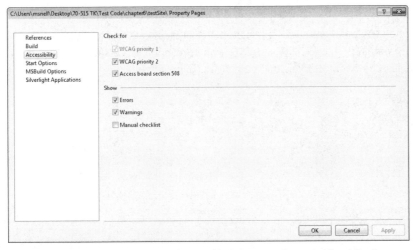

FIGURE 6-7 The Accessibility options in a project's Property Pages in Visual Studio.

3. Select the check boxes for the type and level of accessibility checking that you want to perform, and then click Apply.

4. Next, select the Build node of the Property Pages dialog box.

5. In the Accessibility Validation group, select one or both of the following check boxes, depending on whether you want to check individual pages, the entire website, or both when building the website:

   - Include Accessibility Validation When Building Page
   - Include Accessibility Validation When Building Web

Figure 6-8 shows an example.

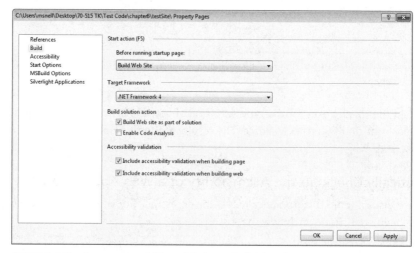

FIGURE 6-8 Turning on accessibility validation at build time for a website.

6. Click OK to close the Property Pages dialog box.

Now, when you build your web application, Visual Studio automatically generates a list of accessibility warnings. Accessibility warnings won't prevent a successful build. You will have to manually view the Error List to examine the accessibility issues. Figure 6-9 shows an example.

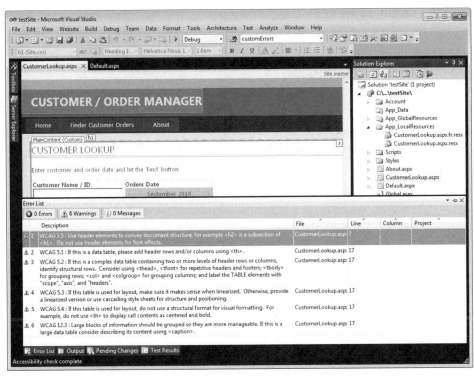

FIGURE 6-9 The accessibility validation warnings generated at build time for a sample website.

Improving the Accessibility of a Webpage

In this practice, you improve the accessibility of an ASP.NET web application.

> **ON THE COMPANION MEDIA**
>
> If you encounter a problem completing an exercise, you can find the completed projects in the samples installed from this book's companion CD. For more information about the project files and other content on the CD, see "Using the Companion Media" in this book's Introduction.

EXERCISE   Making an Accessible Checkout Page

In this exercise, you update an existing (simplified) e-commerce checkout page to make it more accessible by following accessibility best practices.

1. Navigate to the source code samples installed from the companion CD for this book. Open the website inside the Lesson2-Exercise1-Partial-CS-VB folder. The website folder is called AccessibilitySite.

2. Run the application and view the Default.aspx page in a browser. Make note of the nonaccessible aspects of the page, including the following:

   - Lack of panels to divide the form

   - Noncontrasting colors

   - Lack of alternative text for images

   - No tab order specified

   - Labels not associated with text boxes

   - No default focus

   - No default button configured

   Figure 6-10 shows an example of this page in a browser.

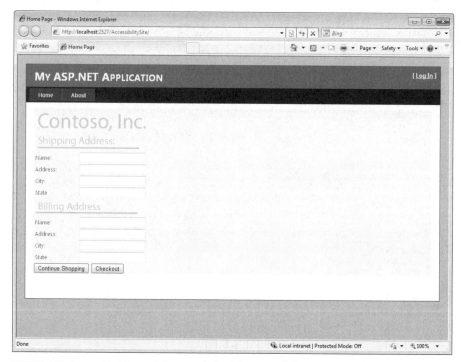

FIGURE 6-10 A page that has not been optimized for accessibility.

3. To begin fixing these problems, in Visual Studio first add two Panel controls to the page: one for the shipping address and the other for the billing address. Next, move the shipping address and billing address images and tables into their respective panels.

4. Set the GroupingText property for the new Panel controls to **Shipping Address** and **Billing Address** respectively. Remove the shipping address and billing address images from the form.

   The Panel controls help with accessibility by enabling users to easily navigate to different parts of a form, and the GroupingText property replaces the shipping and billing address images (which screen readers cannot read).

5. Using the image editor of your choice, replace the Contoso-Logo.gif file with a logo that has colors with more contrast. The existing foreground and background colors are too similar and are not easily readable.

   You might also want to remove the background color altogether from the outer <div> tag.

NOTE **COMPLYING WITH LOGO REQUIREMENTS**

Many organizations have very strict logo requirements that specify the colors that must be used when displaying the logo. However, most organizations also have a high-contrast version of their logo. For more information, contact the public relations group within your organization.

---

6. Provide alternative text for the logo by setting the Image1.AlternateText property to **Contoso, Inc. logo**.

7. Specify a tab order for the text boxes by setting the TextBox.TabIndex property for each text box. Set the text box at the top of the page to **1**, and number the rest sequentially as you work down the page. Also, set the TabIndex properties for the two buttons at the bottom of the page.

8. Replace the text that is currently labeling the text boxes with Label controls. For each Label control, define a unique AccessKey property and underline that letter in the label. Also, define the AssociatedControlID property to associate each label with the correct TextBox control.

9. Configure a default button and default focus. Typically this is done through attributes of the <form> tag. However, you do not have access to these tags when using master pages. Therefore, you must write code to set these values. Add the following code to your page's load event.

Sample of Visual Basic Code
```
Protected Sub Page_Load(ByVal sender As Object, _
                        ByVal e As System.EventArgs) Handles Me.Load
  Me.Form.DefaultFocus = TextBox1.ClientID
  Me.Form.DefaultButton = Button2.UniqueID
End Sub
```

```csharp
protected void Page_Load(object sender, EventArgs e)
{
    this.Form.DefaultFocus = TextBox1.ClientID;
    this.Form.DefaultButton = Button2.UniqueID;
}
```

10. Run the application in a web browser. Use the shortcut keys to navigate between fields (Alt+<AccessKey>). View the alternative text for the logo by pointing to the logo.

11. Return to Visual Studio. From the Tools menu, select Check Accessibility. Examine the errors that are displayed in the Error List pane to see accessibility issues. Accessibility testing is not available in Visual Studio Web Developer 2010 Express.

Lesson Summary

- Two of the most prominent accessibility standards are W3C's WCAG standards and the United States government's Section 508 standards.

- ASP.NET controls support accessibility whenever possible. For example, controls that provide multiple navigation links give users with screen readers the opportunity to skip the links.

- To make webpages as visually accessible as possible, follow these guidelines:

  - Provide good alternative (alt) text for all graphics.

  - Write useful link text.

  - Use tables and their alternatives correctly.

  - Avoid requiring client scripts.

- To make webpages accessible for users with different input tools, design good keyboard navigation by providing keyboard shortcuts, default buttons, and logical tab orders.

- Visual Studio can test your webpage or an entire web application for WCAG and Section 508 compliance.

Lesson Review

You can use the following questions to test your knowledge of the information in Lesson 2, "Configuring Accessibility." The questions are also available on the companion CD as a practice test, if you prefer to review them in electronic form.

> **NOTE ANSWERS**
>
> Answers to these questions and explanations of why each answer choice is correct or incorrect are located in the "Answers" section at the end of the book.

1. Which Image properties can you define to enable screen readers to describe a picture on a webpage? (Choose all that apply.)

   A. AccessKey

   B. AlternateText

   C. DescriptionUrl

   D. ToolTip

2. Which of the following are accessibility features provided by ASP.NET? (Choose all that apply.)

   A. Controls provide properties that enable you to provide hidden descriptions that are available to screen readers.

   B. Controls are displayed in high contrast by default.

   C. Controls that include a list of links at the top provide hidden links to skip over the links.

   D. Controls display text in large font sizes by default.

3. For which of the following guidelines does ASP.NET provide automated testing? (Choose all that apply.)

   A. WCAG Priority 1

   B. WCAG Priority 2

   C. ADA

   D. Access Board Section 508

Case Scenarios

In the following case scenarios, you apply what you've learned in this chapter. If you have difficulty completing this work, review the material in this chapter before beginning the next chapter. You can find answers to these questions in the "Answers" section at the end of this book.

Case Scenario 1: Upgrading an Application for Multiple Languages

You are an application developer for Contoso, Inc., which manufactures shelving and display units that are used by retail outlets. Traditionally, Contoso's sales staff has been focused entirely within the United States. Typically, a sales representative develops a relationship with a retail chain, and then provides access to the Contoso web application for new orders and support. You are responsible for developing that web application.

Contoso has decided to expand globally. First the company plans to expand into Canada, and later into Mexico. The sales staff is struggling, however, because Contoso's identity is too focused around the English-speaking United States. Sales staff members in Canada complain that although in some parts of Canada people prefer to speak French, the website is English only. Similarly, Mexican sales staff members have requested a Spanish website with regional settings that are aligned with those commonly used in Mexico.

Answer the following questions for your manager.

1. How can we provide a French version of our website?

2. How can translators provide updated text for the website?

3. How can users choose between the French and English versions of our website?

4. How can we distinguish between Mexican regional requirements and those of other Spanish-speaking countries, such as Spain?

Case Scenario 2: Making a Web Application Accessible

You are an application developer working for Humongous Insurance. Recently, management has begun an initiative to make all facilities and other resources usable with alternative input and display devices, using the United States government's Rehabilitation Act, Section 508, as a guideline. Your intranet web application is included within the scope of this initiative.

Answer the following questions for your manager.

1. How can we determine whether any aspects of your web application are not compliant with Section 508?

2. What does it mean for an application to be accessible?

3. Will the updated web application be awkward to use with a traditional keyboard, mouse, and monitor if we make it accessible?

4. What types of things do you need to do to make your web application compliant with Section 508?

Suggested Practices

To successfully master the exam objective presented in this chapter, complete the following tasks.

Implement Globalization

For this task, you should complete Practices 1, 2, and 3 for a better understanding of how to provide web applications for multiple languages and cultures. If you want an understanding of the real-world complexity of providing web application translations, complete Practice 4 as well.

- **Practice 1**   Update the web application you created in Lesson 1 to also display French and German languages.

- **Practice 2**   Update the web application you created in Lesson 1 to display a list of specific cultures, and add resources for multiple specific cultures.

- **Practice 3**   Configure Internet Explorer to use a different preferred language. Then visit your favorite websites to see which ones provide alternative languages. Make note of which elements of the page have changed.

- **Practice 4**   Create an application to enable translators who are not developers to create local and global resource files. Then use the tool to provide an alternative language version of the last web application you created.

Implement Accessibility

For this task, you should complete Practice 1 to understand the accessibility tools in Windows 7. Practices 2 gives you an idea of how screen readers work. Practice 3 will give you an understanding of how to best develop accessible web applications.

- **Practice 1**   Experiment with the Windows 7 accessibility tools. To use these accessibility tools, click Start, click Control Panel, click Ease Of Access, and then click Ease Of Access Center.

- **Practice 2**   Experiment with the screen reader simulation at *http://www.webaim.org /simulations/screenreader.php* to experience how screen readers can be used to interact with webpages.

- **Practice 3**   Using the last production web application you created, use the Check Accessibility tool to identify any accessibility problems. Then address as many of the accessibility problems as possible.

Take a Practice Test

The practice tests on this book's companion CD offer many options. For example, you can test yourself on just the lesson review questions in this chapter, or you can test yourself on all the 70-515 certification exam objectives. You can set up the test so it closely simulates the experience of taking a certification exam, or you can set it up in study mode so you can look at the correct answers and explanations after you answer each question.

> **MORE INFO**   **PRACTICE TESTS**
>
> For details about all the practice test options available, see the "How to Use the Practice Tests" section in this book's Introduction.

Creating Custom Web Controls

Microsoft ASP.NET provides you with a basis on which to build new controls, create new controls by combining existing controls, and extend the controls that ship with the Microsoft .NET Framework. As you work in your business domain, there are many times when you need to create and share common functionality across pages. Often this functionality is specific to the needs of your application. For example, imagine that you are coding a human resources application that enables users to edit employee data. In this case, you might encapsulate the employee editing feature as a control and expose it on multiple webpages (perhaps once to the employee and again to an administrator). Your new control might rely on existing controls such as TextBox, Button, and Label controls. Using this approach to create a control allows you to share this common functionality across webpages and centralize your support to a single location.

With ASP.NET, you can create two levels of controls: user controls and web server controls. *User controls* group existing controls together to provide encapsulated functionality inside a single site. *Web server controls* are just like the ASP.NET controls that ship with the .NET Framework. They take advantage of design-time support in the Integrated Development Environment (IDE) and can be used across sites. This chapter covers how to create and use these two primary types of custom web controls.

Exam objectives in this chapter:

- Developing and Using Web Forms Controls
    - Implement user controls.
    - Implement server controls.

Lessons in this chapter:

Before You Begin

To complete the lessons in this chapter, you should be familiar with developing applications with Microsoft Visual Studio by using Microsoft Visual Basic or Microsoft Visual C#. In addition, you should be comfortable with all of the following:

- The Visual Studio 2010 IDE
- Using Hypertext Markup Language (HTML) and client-side scripting
- Creating ASP.NET websites and forms
- Adding web server controls to a webpage
- Working with Microsoft ADO.NET, XML, and Microsoft Language-Integrated Query (LINQ)

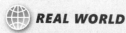 **REAL WORLD**

Mike Snell

Custom web controls offer development teams many advantages. However, I have seen a lot of teams that ignore custom web controls, don't know how to create them, or simply don't see the benefits. The benefits are significant: code can be reused; there is less code to support; there is a single source for updates; developers can quickly compose pages made up of multiple bits of functionality; and more.

These benefits are hard to ignore. I therefore recommend that teams start by at least creating user controls for almost everything. User controls are as easy to create as a webpage (often becoming even easier as the developed functionality is further encapsulated) and provide most of the big benefits of custom web controls. Think user control first and you will start to see these benefits in your code base.

As you develop your site, you will undoubtedly discover those bits of functionality that would be useful to both your site and to other sites you plan to build (or sites that others in your organization will build). In this case, you should first determine whether this functionality is specific to your business domain. If it is not, you might want to seek out controls that already offer this functionality. You can typically download very good controls for a reasonable price. If the functionality is specific to your domain and used across sites, you should seek sponsorship from management for turning that functionality into a custom web server control. You will be glad you did every time someone adds that control to a page.

Lesson 1: Creating User Controls

A user control is a file you create that contains a set of other ASP.NET controls and code grouped together to provide common functionality. The user control can then be used on different pages within a website.

User controls in ASP.NET are created as ASCX files. An ASCX file is similar to the webpage's ASPX file and can have its own code-behind page. To enable reuse, you must include the ASCX and code-behind files in each project that requires the user control. For this reason, user controls are typically reserved for reuse within a particular site. If you need the control to be reusable between sites, you should consider abstracting the functionality as a web server control. (See Lesson 2, "Creating Web Server Controls," in this chapter.)

In this lesson, you learn how to create a standard user control and use it on a webpage. You then explore how to create a user control that defines different templates for layout.

After this lesson, you will be able to:

- Create a user control.
- Add a user control to a webpage.
- Handle events within the user control code-declaration block or code-behind file.
- Create and use a templated user control.

Estimated lesson time: 40 minutes

Creating User Controls

User controls provide an easy way to combine several controls into a single unit of functionality that can be dragged onto multiple webpages in the same site. Pages within a site often contain common functionality that uses similar sets of controls. In these cases, encapsulating this functionality allows for reuse and helps define a consistent user interface (UI). As an example, imagine a site that needs to prompt users for address information during the checkout process. The site might request both billing and shipping information. You might encapsulate several ASP.NET controls to allow for the input of name, address, city, state or province, and postal code into a single user control. This user control can be reused whenever address input is required.

The user controls that you create inherit from the UserControl class. This class inherits from the TemplateControl class. The full class hierarchy is shown in Figure 7-1.

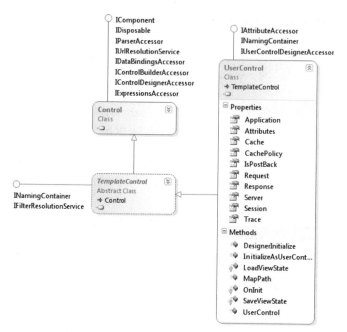

FIGURE 7-1 The UserControl class is the base class for creating user controls.

User controls are created by using a procedure similar to building a standard webpage. You create a user control in Visual Studio from the Add New Item dialog box. From there, you select Web User Control. This adds a file with the .ascx extension to your application. The user control has both a Design view and a Source view, similar to that of an ASPX page. However, a quick glance at the markup reveals the @ Control directive instead of the @Page directive of an ASPX page. The following markup shows an example.

Sample of Visual Basic Code

```
<%@ Control Language="VB"
  AutoEventWireup="false"
  CodeFile="MyWebUserControl.ascx.vb"
  Inherits="MyWebUserControl" %>
```

Sample of C# Code

```
<%@ Control Language="C#"
  AutoEventWireup="true"
  CodeFile=" MyWebUserControl.ascx.cs"
  Inherits=" MyWebUserControl" %>
```

You drag controls onto a user control just as you would onto a page. For example, if you were developing the Address control discussed previously, you might add text, TextBox controls, Button controls, and style and layout information to the user control. Of course, the resulting user control needs to be added to a webpage for it to work. However, the design experience when building a user control is very similar to that of building a page. Figure 7-2 shows a custom Address user control in the Visual Studio designer.

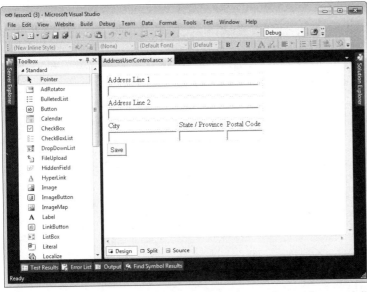

FIGURE 7-2 User control design uses either Design view or Source view, much like webpage design.

> **NOTE** **SEPARATE YOUR CONTROLS FROM THEIR DESIGN**
>
> Generally, it is wise to refrain from putting much style information beyond layout inside a user control. This allows a user control to take on the styles and themes defined by the pages and site to which it is added.

Defining User Control Events

User controls can have their own encapsulated events. These include life cycle events such as Init and Load. These events are called in sync with the events on the page. For example, before the page's Init event is called, the Init event for each control on the page is called. Processing then returns to the page for the Load event. First, the page's OnLoad event is called. Next, the OnLoad event is called for each control on the page. Finally, the page's Load event is called; then, each control on the page gets its Load event fired. This model allows you to develop user controls in a manner similar to developing a webpage.

User controls can also cause a postback for the webpage to which they belong. When a user control causes a postback, its events are raised accordingly along with the events of the page. The event handlers for a user control, however, are typically encapsulated in the particular user control. This ensures that the code for these events can be maintained independent of the pages that use the user controls.

Consider the Address user control example. This control has a Save button. You might want to trigger an event that saves the address information for the user and the address type (billing or shipping, for instance) when the user clicks this button. To do so, you add a button click event handler to the user control and put your code there. When the user control is added to a page and the page is executed, a click of the Save button executes the code on the user control. The following code shows a simple example of the Address user control's Save button click event calling out to a custom class called UserProfile.

Sample of Visual Basic Code

```vb
Protected Sub ButtonSave_Click(ByVal sender As Object, _
  ByVal e As System.EventArgs) Handles ButtonSave.Click

  'to do: validate user input

  'save new address for user
  UserProfile.AddNewAddress(Me.UserId, Me.AddressType, _
    TextBoxAddress1.Text, TextBoxAddress2.Text, _
    TextBoxCity.Text, TextBoxState.Text, TextBoxPostalCode.Text)

End Sub
```

Sample of C# Code

```csharp
protected void ButtonSave_Click(object sender, EventArgs e)
{
  //to do: validate user input

  //save new address for user
  UserProfile.AddNewAddress(this.UserId, this.AddressType,
    TextBoxAddress1.Text, TextBoxAddress2.Text,
    TextBoxCity.Text, TextBoxState.Text, TextBoxPostalCode.Text);
}
```

Notice that in the preceding code, the calls to the AddNewAddress method also include access to properties on the user control (UserId and AddressType). The properties were added to the user control definition and are discussed In the upcoming section entitled "Defining Properties in User Controls."

Passing Events Up to the Page

Often you do not know the actual implementation of a particular control's event at design time. In such cases, you can add the control, such as a Button control, to your user control and allow the developer who uses the user control to implement the event handler for the Button control's click event. You can do so by defining an event on your user control and passing this event to the webpage when the Button control's click event fires.

As an example, let's look again at the Address user control's Save button. You might need to define an event that is passed to the page when this button is clicked. This event would most likely pass the values from the user control's subcontrols back to the page (unless they are exposed as properties, as discussed in the next section). Therefore, you would modify the Address user control to expose an event and raise that event in response to a Save button click.

The following code block steps you through sample code for this example. First, you should define the event arguments class, which should inherit from EventArgs. The class will be used by the event to pass the address information from the user control to the page. You then add properties that align with your scenario to the class.

Sample of Visual Basic Code

```vb
Public Class AddressEventArgs
  Inherits EventArgs

  Public Sub New(ByVal addressLine1 As String, _
    ByVal addressLine2 As String, ByVal city As String, _
    ByVal state As String, ByVal postalCode As String)

    Me._addressLine1 = addressLine1
    Me._addressLine2 = addressLine2
    Me._city = city
    Me._state = state
    Me._postalCode = postalCode
  End Sub

  Private _addressLine1 As String
  Public ReadOnly Property AddressLine1() As String
    Get
      Return _addressLine1
    End Get
  End Property

  Private _addressLine2 As String
  Public ReadOnly Property AddressLine2() As String
    Get
      Return _addressLine2
    End Get
  End Property

  Private _city As String
  Public ReadOnly Property City() As String
    Get
      Return _city
    End Get
  End Property

  Private _state As String
  Public ReadOnly Property State() As String
    Get
      Return _state
    End Get
  End Property

  Private _postalCode As String
  Public ReadOnly Property PostalCode() As String
    Get
      Return _postalCode
    End Get
  End Property

End Class
```

Sample of C# Code

```csharp
public class AddressEventArgs : EventArgs
{
  public AddressEventArgs(string addressLine1, string addressLine2,
    string city, string state, string postalCode)
  {
    this.AddressLine1 = addressLine1;
    this.AddressLine2 = addressLine2;
    this.City = city;
    this.State = state;
    this.PostalCode = postalCode;
  }

  public string AddressLine1 { get; private set; }
  public string AddressLine2 { get; private set; }
  public string City { get; private set; }
  public string State { get; private set; }
  public string PostalCode { get; private set; }
}
```

The next step is to add code that declares an event to the user control's class. You then add code that handles the Button click event. Inside the click event, you raise your event back to the consuming page. The page that uses your user control can then trap the event and respond accordingly. The following shows an example of both the event declaration and the Button click event.

Sample of Visual Basic Code

```vbnet
Public Event SaveButtonClick(ByVal sender As Object, ByVal e As AddressEventArgs)

Protected Sub ButtonSave_Click(ByVal sender As Object, _
  ByVal e As System.EventArgs) Handles ButtonSave.Click

  Dim addArgs As New AddressEventArgs(TextBoxAddress1.Text, _
    TextBoxAddress2.Text, TextBoxCity.Text, _
    TextBoxState.Text, TextBoxPostalCode.Text)

  RaiseEvent SaveButtonClick(Me, addArgs)

End Sub
```

Sample of C# Code

```csharp
public event EventHandler<AddressEventArgs> SaveButtonClick;

protected void ButtonSave_Click(object sender, EventArgs e)
{
  if (SaveButtonClick != null)
  {
    SaveButtonClick(this, new AddressEventArgs(TextBoxAddress1.Text,
      TextBoxAddress2.Text, TextBoxCity.Text, TextBoxState.Text,
      TextBoxPostalCode.Text));
  }
}
```

The last step is to consume the event on the page to which the user control was added. You will see how to add a user control to a page in the upcoming section "Adding a User Control to a Page." After you have added the user control to the page, you must write code to trap the event raised by the user control. In Visual Basic, you can add a handler for the user control's exposed event in the code editor simply by using the Handles keyword. (You can generate this event by using the drop-down menus at the top of the Visual Basic code window.) In C#, you wire up a handler by using the += syntax inside the Page_Init method. Inside your handler, you use AddressEventArgs as required (in this scenario, to save the address information to the user's profile). The following is an example. Note that the example assumes that a UserProfile class exists and that two properties were added to the user control (UserId and AddressType). You will learn how to add properties to a user control in the next section.

Sample of Visual Basic Code

```
Protected Sub AddressUserControl1_SaveButtonClick(ByVal sender As Object, _
   ByVal e As AddressEventArgs) Handles AddressUserControl1.SaveButtonClick

  UserProfile.AddNewAddress(AddressUserControl1.UserId, _
    AddressUserControl1.AddressType, e.AddressLine1, e.AddressLine2, _
    e.City, e.State, e.PostalCode)

End Sub
```

Sample of C# Code

```
protected void Page_Init(object sender, EventArgs e)
{
    AddressUserControl1.SaveButtonClick += this.AddressUserControl1_SaveButtonClick;
}

private void AddressUserControl1_SaveButtonClick(object sender, AddressEventArgs e)
{
    UserProfile.AddNewAddress(AddressUserControl1.UserId,
        AddressUserControl1.AddressType, e.AddressLine1, e.AddressLine2,
        e.City, e.State, e.PostalCode);
}
```

Defining Properties in User Controls

The user controls you create often need configuration data. You can define this configuration data by using properties on the user control itself. Properties added to user controls can then be configured in the markup for the page that uses the control and on the Properties pane in the design editor. When developers use the user control, they can set the properties declaratively through markup. These properties are also available through IntelliSense.

Properties that will be configured by developers when using a user control can be set at design time or at run time and are available on postback. This is the same as with other controls in ASP.NET. Properties that are set through code must be reset on postback to avoid being lost. Again, this is the same as with other ASP.NET controls.

You define a user control property as you would any other class-level property in the .NET Framework. For example, to add the UserId and AddressType properties to the Address user control, you would add code as follows to the user control's class.

Sample of Visual Basic Code

```
Public Property UserId() As Integer
Public Property AddressType() As UserProfile.AddressType
```

Sample of C# Code

```
public int UserId { get; set; }
public UserProfile.AddressType AddressType { get; set; }
```

As you saw previously, you can set these properties on the page to which you add the user control. In "Adding a User Control to a Page" later in this section, you will learn how to add a user control to a page and set its properties.

Accessing Control Values

Often you have to write code that works with the values of controls contained inside a user control. Controls contained within a user control are declared as protected members of the control. This means that they are not directly accessible outside the user control class. Therefore, to gain access to a control, you can return a reference to it through a property setting. However, this exposes the entire control. A more common scenario is to define at least a property that allows a user to set and get the values of a control. This allows you to contain the user control but provide access to the enclosed controls.

As an example, suppose that the Address user control needs to allow users to preset values of the controls contained by the user control. In this case, you can expose the TextBox.Text properties as properties of the user control. The following code sample shows one of the user control's TextBox.Text properties (TextBoxAddress1) exposed as a value from the user control. You could repeat this code for the other controls inside the Address user control if you needed direct access to these control values.

Sample of Visual Basic Code

```
Public Property AddressLine1() As String
  Get
    Return TextBoxAddress1.Text
  End Get
  Set(ByVal value As String)
    TextBoxAddress1.Text = value
  End Set
End Property
```

Sample of C# Code

```
public string AddressLine1
{
  get { return TextBoxAddress1.Text; }
  set { TextBoxAddress1.Text = value; }
}
```

Adding a User Control to a Page

You can add a user control to a webpage by simply dragging it from Solution Explorer to a webpage in Design view. When you add the user control to a page, you can see the control's visual makeup in Design view. If you switch to Source view, you can see the markup information that Visual Studio added to your page. The following shows sample markup of the Address user control when it is added to a webpage.

```
<%@ Page Language="VB" AutoEventWireup="false"
  CodeFile="UserProfileUpdate.aspx.vb" Inherits="UserProfileUpdate" %>

<%@ Register src="AddressUserControl.ascx" tagname="AddressUserControl"
  tagprefix="uc1" %>

<!DOCTYPE html PUBLIC "-//W3C//DTD XHTML 1.0 Transitional//EN"
  "http://www.w3.org/TR/xhtml1/DTD/xhtml1-transitional.dtd">

<html xmlns="http://www.w3.org/1999/xhtml">
<head runat="server">
    <title></title>
</head>
<body>
    <form id="form1" runat="server">
    <div>
        <uc1:AddressUserControl ID="AddressUserControl1" runat="server"
      AddressType="Home" />
    </div>
    </form>
</body>
</html>
```

Notice the @ Register directive at the top of the page. You must include this directive to register the user control on the page. The TagPrefix attribute is a namespace identifier for the control. Your markup uses this prefix to define the control. The default TagPrefix is uc1 (as in User Control 1). Of course, you can change this value. The TagName attribute is the name of the control. The Src attribute is the location of the user control file. The actual instance definition for the control is nested within the <form> tag. Notice that the ID is automatically created as AddressUserControl1. Also, notice that the AddressType custom property is defined as an attribute of the control. The other property, UserId, is meant to indicate a unique ID of the user whose address values are being modified. Therefore, this property would most likely be set in code (from a query string value, session state, a cookie, or something similar).

Dynamically Loading User Controls

Like other server controls, user controls can be loaded dynamically. Loading controls dynamically can be useful in situations in which you want to add a variable number of instances of a control to a page.

To dynamically load a user control, you use the LoadControl method of the Page class. This method takes the name and path to a file that contains the user control's definition. The method also returns a reference to the control class it creates. You can set this to a variable by casting the returned object to a strong type. For this to work, the control must already be registered with the page.

For example, suppose that you need to add multiple instances of the Address user control discussed previously to a new page at run time, and that the number of instances you need to add is based on the number of stored addresses for the user. The following code shows an example of how you would dynamically load the control.

Sample of Visual Basic Code

```
Dim addressControl As AddressUc = _
    CType(LoadControl("AddressUserControl.ascx"), AddressUc)

form1.Controls.Add(addressControl)
```

Sample of C# Code

```
AddressUc addressControl =
    (AddressUc)LoadControl("AddressUserControl.ascx");

form1.Controls.Add(addressControl);
```

Notice the second line of code. After the control has been loaded, it needs to be added to the Form object for display and use.

Creating a Templated User Control

A templated user control provides separation of control data from the presentation of that data. A templated user control does not provide a default UI layout. Instead, this layout is provided by the developer who uses the user control on his or her page. This provides increased flexibility in terms of layout while keeping the encapsulation and reuse benefits of a user control.

There are several steps for creating a templated user control:

1. Start by adding a user control file to your web application.

2. Add an ASP.NET PlaceHolder control to the user control's markup. This defines a placeholder for the templated layout. You will expose this placeholder as a property of your user control. Developers who use your control will then define their markup layout code inside this template.

3. Create a class file in your site to serve as a naming container for your control. A *naming container* is simply a control container that allows you to search for a contained child control by using FindControl, which you've used with both Page and MasterPage in previous chapters. This is important to know because in addition to containing controls, your templated, UserControl-based class file will need to contain a reference to the data with which your user control works. This data will be bound to the child controls when a developer creates his or her own layout template based on your control.

The naming container-based class you'll create inherits from Control and implements the INamingContainer interface, just as is done with UserControl itself. The class should also contain public properties for any data elements it is meant to contain.

4. In your user control's code-behind file, implement a property of type ITemplate. This property will serve as the template for users of your control (and exposes the placeholder created in step 2). The name you give this property will be the name of the template tag in any consuming page's markup.

    Apply the TemplateContainerAttribute attribute to the ITemplate property; this marks the property as a template. To this attribute, pass the type of the naming container class for binding data (created in step 3) as an argument of the constructor. This serves to allow binding between the container and the template definition markup when the user control is added to a page.

    In this step you also apply the PersistenceModeAttribute attribute to the ITemplate property. You pass the enumeration value of PersistenceMode.InnerProperty into the attribute's constructor.

5. Add code to the Page_Init method of the user control. Here you test for the ITemplate property. If the ITemplate property is set, you create an instance of the naming container class and create an instance of the template in the naming container. You then add the naming container instance to the Controls collection of the PlaceHolder server control.

6. You might also need to pass data from your user control to the naming container. This allows users to set properties of your user control, and store and use them in the container. For these situations, you must define this data in your user control as properties that a developer who is using your user control can set. You then must pass a reference to this data to the naming container. This ensures that the naming container is updated when the property values change on the user control.

As an example, suppose you want to implement the Address control discussed previously as a templated user control so that developers can define their own layout when using your control. To get started, you create a web User Control and add a PlaceHolder control to its markup, as shown in the following.

The Address User Control Markup
Sample of Visual Basic Code

```
<%@ Control Language="VB" AutoEventWireup="false"
  CodeFile="AddressUcTemplated.ascx.vb" Inherits="AddressUcTemplated" %>

<asp:PlaceHolder runat="server"
  ID="PlaceHolderAddressTemplate">
</asp:PlaceHolder>
```

Sample of C# Code

```
<%@ Control Language="C#" AutoEventWireup="true"
  CodeFile="AddressUcTemplated.ascx.cs" Inherits="AddressUcTemplated" %>

<asp:PlaceHolder runat="server"
  ID="PlaceHolderAddressTemplate">
</asp:PlaceHolder>
```

You then add code to the code-behind file for the user control. This includes the ITemplate property and the Page_Init code. The ITemplate property is used to define the layout area for users of the user control. The Page_Init code is where you instantiate the naming container you created and connect it to the layout template.

In addition, the code-behind file should contain any properties you want the user to be able to access from the user control. In our example, we would probably define an Address property that exposes a custom Address class (not shown). This class contains the address properties discussed previously. The following shows an example of the code-behind file for the Address user control.

The Address User Control's Code-Behind File
Sample of Visual Basic Code

```vb
Partial Class AddressUcTemplated
    Inherits System.Web.UI.UserControl

  Public Sub Page_Init(ByVal sender As Object, _
        ByVal e As EventArgs) Handles Me.Init

    'clear the controls from the placeholder
    PlaceHolderAddressTemplate.Controls.Clear()

    If LayoutTemplate Is Nothing Then
      PlaceHolderAddressTemplate.Controls.Add( _
        New LiteralControl("No template defined."))
    Else

      Dim container As New AddressUcContainer(Me.Address)

      Me.LayoutTemplate.InstantiateIn(container)

      'add the controls to the placeholder
      PlaceHolderAddressTemplate.Controls.Add(container)
    End If

  End Sub

  Private _layout As ITemplate
  <PersistenceMode(PersistenceMode.InnerProperty)> _
  <TemplateContainer(GetType(AddressUcContainer))> _
  Public Property LayoutTemplate() As ITemplate
    Get
      Return _layout
    End Get
    Set(ByVal value As ITemplate)
      _layout = value
    End Set
  End Property
```

```
  Private _address As New Address()
  Public Property Address() As Address
    Get
      Return _address
    End Get
    Set(ByVal value As Address)
      _address = value
    End Set
  End Property

End Class
```

Sample of C# Code
```csharp
public partial class AddressUcTemplated :
  System.Web.UI.UserControl
{
    protected void Page_Init(object sender, EventArgs e)
    {
      //clear the controls from the placeholder
      PlaceHolderAddressTemplate.Controls.Clear();

      if (LayoutTemplate == null)
      {
        PlaceHolderAddressTemplate.Controls.Add(
          new LiteralControl("No template defined."));
      }
      else
      {
        AddressUcContainer container = new
          AddressUcContainer(this.Address);
        this.LayoutTemplate.InstantiateIn(container);
        //add the controls to the placeholder
        PlaceHolderAddressTemplate.Controls.Add(container);
      }
    }

    [PersistenceMode(PersistenceMode.InnerProperty)]
    [TemplateContainer(typeof(AddressUcContainer))]
    public ITemplate LayoutTemplate { get; set; }
    private Address_address = new Address();
    public Address Address
{

    get { return_address }
    set { _address = value; }
}
```

The final step is to define the naming container. Note that the preceding code actually used the naming container (AddressUcContainer) as if it were already defined. Recall that the naming container must inherit from Control and implement the INamingContainer interface. Property values passed from the user control to the naming container should be passed in the constructor. If you need to be able to set properties of the user control and have those property values reflected in the naming container, you must set the properties as an object reference. The following code shows an example of exposing the Address class through the naming container (this assumes a using or imports statement for System.Web.UI).

The Naming Container Class
Sample of Visual Basic Code

```vb
Public Class AddressUcContainer
  Inherits Control
  Implements INamingContainer

  Public Sub New(ByVal address As Address)
    Me.Address = address
  End Sub

  Private _address As Address
  Public Property Address() As Address
    Get
      Return _address
    End Get
    Set(ByVal value As Address)
      _address = value
    End Set
  End Property

End Class
```

Sample of C# Code

```csharp
public class AddressUcContainer : Control, INamingContainer
{
  public AddressUcContainer(Address address)
  {
    this.Address = address;
  }

  public Address Address { get; set; }
}
```

Using a Templated User Control

Like any user control, a templated user control must be used within the same site or project and can be added to a webpage by dragging it from Solution Explorer onto the page. Recall that this registers the control with the page as follows.

```
<%@ Register src="AddressUcTemplated.ascx" tagname="AddressUcTemplated"
  tagprefix="uc1" %>
```

You then define the template for the user control's layout. In the Address user control example, this means nesting layout and code within the <LayoutTemplate> tag that was defined with the ITemplate property. Inside the template, you can reference data by calling the Container object. This object is an instance of the naming container class created as part of the templated user control process. The following markup shows the definition of the user control on a page.

```
<uc1:AddressUcTemplated ID="AddressUcTemplated1"
  runat="server" AddressType="Home">
  <LayoutTemplate>
      <h1>Edit Home Address</h1>
      <table>
        <tr>
          <td>Address Line 1:</td>
          <td>
            <asp:TextBox ID="TextBoxAddress" runat="server"
              Text="<%#Container.Address.AddressLine1%>"></asp:TextBox>
          </td>
        </tr>
        <tr>
          <td>Address Line 2:</td>
          <td>
            <asp:TextBox ID="TextBoxAddressLine2" runat="server"
              Text="<%#Container.Address.AddressLine2%>"></asp:TextBox>
          </td>
        </tr>
        <tr>
          <td>City:</td>
          <td>
            <asp:TextBox ID="TextBoxCity" runat="server"
              Text="<%#Container.Address.City%>"></asp:TextBox>
          </td>
        </tr>
        <tr>
          <td>State:</td>
          <td>
            <asp:TextBox ID="TextBoxState" runat="server"
              Text="<%#Container.Address.State%>"></asp:TextBox>
          </td>
        </tr>
        <tr>
          <td>Postal Code:</td>
          <td>
            <asp:TextBox ID="TextBoxPostalCode" runat="server"
              Text="<%#Container.Address.PostalCode%>"></asp:TextBox>
          </td>
        </tr>
        <tr>
          <td></td>
          <td>
            <asp:Button ID="ButtonSave" runat="server" Text="Save"
              OnClick="ButtonSave_Click"/>
          </td>
        </tr>
      </table>
  </LayoutTemplate>
</uc1:AddressUcTemplated>
```

You must also add code to the consuming page's code-behind file. This code should call the Page.DataBind method to ensure that the container is bound to the templated layout. The following code shows an example.

Sample of Visual Basic Code

```vb
Protected Sub Page_Load(ByVal sender As Object, _
  ByVal e As System.EventArgs) Handles Me.Load

    'simulate getting a user and loading his or her profile
    AddressUcTemplated1.Address.AddressLine1 = "1234 Some St."
    AddressUcTemplated1.Address.City = "Pontiac"
    AddressUcTemplated1.Address.State = "MI"
    AddressUcTemplated1.Address.PostalCode = "48340"

    'bind data to controls
    Page.DataBind()

End Sub
```

Sample of C# Code

```csharp
protected void Page_Load(object sender, EventArgs e)
{
  //simulate getting a user and loading his or her profile
  AddressUcTemplated1.Address.AddressLine1 = "1234 Some St.";
  AddressUcTemplated1.Address.City = "Ann Arbor";
  AddressUcTemplated1.Address.State = "MI";
  AddressUcTemplated1.Address.PostalCode = "48888";

  //bind data to controls
  Page.DataBind();
}
```

Note that the templated user control does not display in the Visual Studio Design view. You need to create a custom web control for that to work (see Lesson 2). However, when you run the webpage, it displays as designed. Figure 7-3 shows an example of the AddressUcTemplated user control running in a browser.

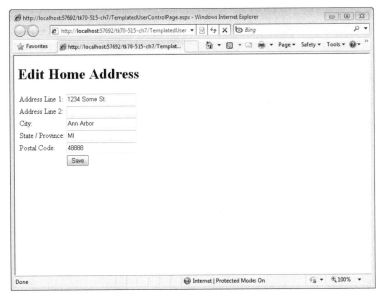

FIGURE 7-3 The templated Address user control.

 Quick Check

1. Without writing much code, what is the easiest way to group several TextBox and Label controls that offer shared functionality so that they can be dragged onto a webpage as a unit?

2. What type of control can be used to provide data that is to be rendered but that allows the webpage designer to specify the layout of the data?

Quick Check Answers

1. Create a web user control.

2. A templated user control can be used.

In this practice, you create a version of the Address user control discussed in the text.

> **ON THE COMPANION MEDIA**
>
> If you encounter a problem completing an exercise, you can find the completed projects in the samples installed from this book's companion CD. For more information about the project files and other content on the CD, see "Using the Companion Media" in this book's Introduction.

EXERCISE 1 Creating the Website and the User Control

In this exercise, you create a new website, add a web user control, and define the user control's functionality.

1. Open Visual Studio and create a new website by using your preferred programming language (File | New | Web Site). Name the website **UserControlLab**.

2. Add a web user control to the site: right-click the website in Solution Explorer and choose Add New Item. In the Add New Item dialog box, select Web User Control. Name the user control **AddressUserControl.ascx**.

3. Open the user control and add input elements to the markup for address, city, state/province, and postal code. Your control markup should look similar to the following.

```
<%@ Control Language="C#" AutoEventWireup="true"
    CodeFile="AddressUserControl.ascx.cs" Inherits="AddressUserControl" %>

<div>
  Address
  <br />
  <asp:TextBox ID="TextBoxAddress" runat="server" Width="325px"
    Height="80px" TextMode="MultiLine"></asp:TextBox>
  <div style="width: 450px">
    <div style="float: left; margin-right: 3px">
      City
      <br />
      <asp:TextBox ID="TextBoxCity" runat="server" Width="150"></asp:TextBox>
    </div>
    <div style="float: left; margin-right: 3px">
      State / Province
      <br />
      <asp:TextBox ID="TextBoxStateProv" runat="server" Width="80"></asp:TextBox>
    </div>
    <div style="float: left">
      Postal Code
      <br />
      <asp:TextBox ID="TextBoxPostalCode" runat="server" Width="70"></asp:TextBox>
    </div>
  </div>
  <asp:Button ID="ButtonSave" runat="server" Text="Save"
    onclick="ButtonSave_Click" />
</div>
```

4. Open the code-behind file and add properties to expose the Text property of the user control's TextBox controls. Your code should look similar to the following.

Sample of Visual Basic Code

```vb
Partial Class AddressUserControl
  Inherits System.Web.UI.UserControl

  Public Property Address() As String
    Get
      Return TextBoxAddress.Text
    End Get
    Set(ByVal value As String)
      TextBoxAddress.Text = value
    End Set
  End Property

  Public Property City() As String
    Get
      Return TextBoxCity.Text
    End Get
    Set(ByVal value As String)
      TextBoxCity.Text = value
    End Set
  End Property

    Public Property StateProvince() As String
        Get
            Return TextBoxStateProv.Text
        End Get
        Set(ByVal value As String)
            TextBoxStateProv.Text = value
        End Set
    End Property

    Public Property PostalCode() As String
        Get
            Return TextBoxPostalCode.Text
        End Get
        Set(ByVal value As String)
            TextBoxPostalCode.Text = value
        End Set
    End Property
End Class
```

```
Sample of C# Code
public partial class AddressUserControl : System.Web.UI.UserControl
{
  public string Address
  {
    get { return TextBoxAddress.Text; }
    set { TextBoxAddress.Text = value; }
  }
  public string City
  {
    get { return TextBoxCity.Text; }
    set { TextBoxCity.Text = value; }
  }
  public string StateProvince
  {
    get { return TextBoxStateProv.Text; }
      set { TextBoxStateProv.Text = value; }
  }
  public string PostalCode
  {
    get { return TextBoxPostalCode.Text; }
      set { TextBoxPostalCode.Text = value; }
  }
}
```

5. Next, you will define the event handler for the Save button. This event will raise an event to the host of the user control. Given that the user control already exposes properties for reading its values, the event will not pass them as an argument; it will simply raise a generic event. Add the event declaration to the user control's code-behind class file. This code should read as follows.

```
Sample of Visual Basic Code
Public Event SaveButtonClick(ByVal sender As Object, ByVal e As EventArgs)
```

```
Sample of C# Code
public event EventHandler SaveButtonClick;
```

6. Finally, add code to the button's click event that raises this event. The following is an example.

```
Sample of Visual Basic Code
Protected Sub ButtonSave_Click(ByVal sender As Object, _
  ByVal e As System.EventArgs) Handles ButtonSave.Click

  RaiseEvent SaveButtonClick(Me, New EventArgs())

End Sub
```

Sample of C# Code

```csharp
protected void ButtonSave_Click(object sender, EventArgs e)
{
  if (SaveButtonClick != null)
  {
    SaveButtonClick(this, new EventArgs());
  }
}
```

7. Compile your code and make sure there are no errors.

EXERCISE 2 Hosting the User Control on a Webpage

In this exercise, you consume the user control created in the previous exercise.

1. Continue editing the project you created in the previous exercise. Alternatively, you can copy the completed Lesson 1, Exercise 1 project from the CD to your hard drive and begin from there.

2. Open the Default.aspx page in Design view. Delete the content inside the MainContent control. While still in Design view, drag AddressUserControl.ascx to the page from Solution Explorer. Figure 7-4 shows an example of the page in Design view.

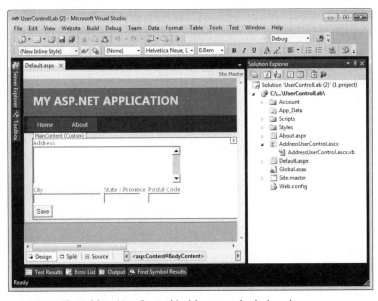

FIGURE 7-4 The AddressUserControl inside a page in design view.

3. Change to Source view for the page. Start typing inside the control's tag. Notice that you can initialize the control's custom properties through markup and that IntelliSense is fully aware of these properties and even offers them to you as it would any other standard ASP.NET property. These properties are also available in the Properties window in Design view.

4. In this step, you add an event handler to trap the event fired by the user control when a user clicks the Save button. Start by opening the code-behind file for the Default.aspx page.

   ■ In Visual Basic, use the drop-down control at the top left of the code editor to select the user control (AddressControl1). Then use the drop-down list on the right to select the SaveButtonClick event handler. This should generate your event handler stub as follows.

```
Protected Sub AddressUserControl1_SaveButtonClick(ByVal sender As Object, _
    ByVal e As System.EventArgs) Handles AddressUserControl1.SaveButtonClick

End Sub
```

   ■ In C#, you need to first add a method to the page. This method should have the same signature as the event exposed by the user control. You then need to associate the event from the user control to the newly defined method. You can do this inside the page's Init method. The following code shows an example.

```
protected void AddressUserControl1_SaveButtonClick(object sender, EventArgs e)
{
}

protected void Page_Init(object sender, EventArgs e)
{
    AddressUserControl1.SaveButtonClick +=
  this.AddressUserControl1_SaveButtonClick;
}
```

5. You now need to add code to the intercepted event. For this example, this code will simply take the user's input and write it out to the debug window. The following shows an example.

```
Sample of Visual Basic Code
Protected Sub AddressUserControl1_SaveButtonClick(ByVal sender As Object, _
    ByVal e As System.EventArgs) Handles AddressUserControl1.SaveButtonClick

    System.Diagnostics.Debug.WriteLine("Address: " & _
        AddressUserControl1.Address & _
        " City: " & AddressUserControl1.City & _
        " State or Province: " & AddressUserControl1.StateProvince & _
        " Postal Code: " & AddressUserControl1.PostalCode)

End Sub
```

Sample of C# Code

```
protected void AddressUserControl1_SaveButtonClick(object sender, EventArgs e)
{
    System.Diagnostics.Debug.WriteLine("Address: " +
        AddressUserControl1.Address +
        " City: " + AddressUserControl1.City +
        " State or Province: " + AddressUserControl1.StateProvince +
        " Postal Code: " + AddressUserControl1.PostalCode);

}
```

6. Finally, run the application in debug mode to view the results. (You might be prompted to enable debugging for the site. Click OK to enable debugging.) Enter address information in the user control. Click the Save button. Return to Visual Studio and view the Output window (View | Output) to see the results of the trapped Save button's event.

Lesson Summary

- User controls enable web developers to easily combine ASP.NET controls into a single control for encapsulating common functionality.

- A user control cannot be compiled to its own dynamic-link library (DLL) and shared. It can only be shared within a single website (with the exception of copy and paste, of course).

- A user control follows the same life cycle events as a page. The user control's events are called in sync with the corresponding page events (such as Init and Load).

- You can expose properties, events, and methods in a user control.

- You add a control to a webpage by using the @ Register directive and indicating the source ASCX file for the user control.

- You can dynamically load a user control at run time by using the LoadControl method of the Page class.

- You can create templated user controls, which allow the webpage designer to specify the formatting of data that the user control provides. A templated user control requires a Placeholder control and a class that implements the INamingContainer interface.

Lesson Review

You can use the following questions to test your knowledge of the information in Lesson 1, "Creating User Controls." The questions are also available on the companion CD in a practice test, if you prefer to review them in electronic form.

1. You want to create a user control that will encapsulate basic data entry functionality and that will be reused across a site. What steps should you take? (Choose all that apply.)

   A. Create an ASPX file and use the @ Register directive at the top of the page to indicate that the markup in the file is a user control.

   B. Create a code-behind file for your user control that contains a class that inherits from System.Web.UI.UserControl.

   C. Create a code-behind file for your user control that contains a class that inherits from System.Web.UI.Page.

   D. Create an ASCX file and use the @ Control directive at the top of the page to indicate that the markup in the file is a user control.

2. You want to consume a user control on a page. However, you do not know the number of instances you want to create. This information will be available at run time. Therefore, you want to dynamically create these controls. Which actions should you take? (Choose all that apply.)

   A. Add the controls by using the Controls.Add method of the page instance.

   B. Add the controls by using the Controls.Add method of the form instance.

   C. Call the form's LoadControl method for each control you want to add to the page.

   D. Call the page's LoadControl method for each control you want to add to the page.

3. You want to create a user control to display data, but you are concerned that you don't know how the webpage designers want to format the data. Also, some of the page designers mention that the format of the data might be different, depending on the webpage. How can you best create a user control to solve this problem?

   A. Create a separate user control for each webpage and get each webpage designer to tell you the format to implement in each user control.

   B. Create a separate user control for each variation of the format after the webpage designers give you the desired formatting options.

   C. Create a templated user control that exposes the data to the webpage designers so they can specify their desired format.

   D. Create a user control that simply renders the data and let the webpage designers specify the style properties for the user control.

4. You have two TextBox controls inside your user control. You want to allow a developer using the user control to initialize, read, and modify the Text property of these controls. What step should you take?

    A. Add a constructor to the user control. The constructor should take parameters for each of the TextBox.Text properties. It will then set these parameter values appropriately.

    B. Create properties on the user control that allow users to get and set the Text property of each TextBox control.

    C. You don't need to do anything. Controls added to a user control, by default, expose their default property.

    D. Add code to the Init method of the user control. This code should raise an event. The page that hosts the control can then use this event to set the TextBox.Text properties accordingly.

Lesson 2: Creating Custom Web Server Controls

Lesson 1 showed you how to encapsulate functionality into a user control that can be shared within the boundaries of a single website. There are many times, however, when you write functionality that can be useful to multiple websites. The functionality could be a specialized calendar control, a corporate user lookup control, a specialized data validation control, or something similar. In these situations, you can encapsulate the functionality into a web server control that can be deployed as a DLL file and used across multiple websites.

Custom web server controls are easier for developers to use than mere user controls. You can define a full design-time experience for the consumers of your control. This experience includes Toolbox and designer functionality. Of course, this support means that developers will treat the control as an encapsulated entity, no different than any built-in control provided by ASP.NET. Therefore, you typically end up writing more code when creating a web server control (as compared to a simple user control). This lesson explores the creation of web server controls for ASP.NET developers.

> **After this lesson, you will be able to:**
> - Create a custom web server control.
> - Add custom web server controls to a webpage.
> - Add Toolbox support for a custom web server control.
> - Create a custom designer for a custom web server control.
> - Consume a custom web server control in a website.
>
> **Estimated lesson time: 60 minutes**

REAL WORLD
Mike Snell

I n my experience, I have seen very few instances of development teams that create custom web server controls. I attribute this to the ease of creating user controls versus the perceived difficulty of building and supporting custom web server controls. My advice, however, is to create custom web server controls where they make sense: as reusable controls across websites. After creating the first control, I think you will find custom web server controls easy enough to create and worth the effort.

Creating a Custom Web Server Control

A *custom web control* is a control that you write that inherits either from the WebControl class or from an existing web server control. Each custom web control contains the code necessary to render the control (or inherits it from another control). The control can be compiled into a separate DLL file that can be shared among applications and can optionally be installed in the global assembly cache (GAC).

There are two common approaches to creating a custom web server control. The first approach is to create a web server control that inherits directly from WebControl. The WebControl class provides a base set of functionality. With this functionality, you can handle styles by using UI-related properties such as BackColor, ForeColor, Font, Height, and Width. However, this leaves you with a lot of work to finish developing the control. The second approach is to inherit from an existing web server control that already provides the core features you need for your control. This can give you a jump start and allow you to focus on what makes your control different. This is the more common scenario. This section explores both approaches.

Regardless of the approach, you should carefully consider how the control will be reused. If the custom web server control is targeted to multiple websites, you should place the new custom web server control class into a class library project to create a DLL file that can be shared. If the custom web server control is only meant for the current website, you can add the custom web server control's class file to the website (or create a user control instead).

EXAM TIP
Be sure to know the difference between user controls and web server controls. You should have a solid understanding of both applicable usage and how to create both types of controls.

Inheriting from an Existing ASP.NET Web Server Control

A common scenario is to create a custom web server control by inheriting from an existing ASP.NET web server control and adding additional functionality. This method ensures that you get the base functionality from the inherited control. You then extend this functionality with your custom code.

As an example, suppose you want to create a control that includes both a label and a TextBox control. You might call this control LabeledTextBox. This custom control will include text that labels the TextBox (such as "User Name" or "Address"). This text should be set by developers when they use your control. You might also want to allow them to set the width of this text to help with alignment.

To create this control, you can start by adding a class file to your website (do this only if you do not intend to share the control across sites), create a class library project and set a reference to System.Web, or create an ASP.NET Server Control project (the preferred method).

You then define a class that inherits from TextBox. You must also set a reference to the System.Web namespace inside your class library. You then create properties that allow developers to set the label text and the width of the label prompt. Because the control inherits from TextBox, it will also expose the properties of the TextBox control by default.

The final step is to render the display of your custom web server control. For this you must override the Render method of the TextBox control. The Render method will use an HtmlTextWriter to write your display information (the TextBox prompt) and the base rendering of the TextBox control. The following code shows an example of the complete, custom LabeledTextBox web control.

Sample of Visual Basic Code

```vb
Public Class LabeledTextBox
    Inherits TextBox

    Public Property PromptText() As String
    Public Property PromptWidth() As Integer

    Protected Overrides Sub Render(ByVal output As HtmlTextWriter)

        output.Write( _
            "<span style=""display;inline-block;width:{0}px"">{1} </span>", _
          PromptWidth, PromptText)

        MyBase.Render(output)

    End Sub

End Class
```

```csharp
public class LabeledTextBox : TextBox
{
    public string PromptText { get; set; }
    public int PromptWidth { get; set; }

    protected override void Render(HtmlTextWriter output)
    {
        output.Write(
            @"<span style=""display:inline-block;width:{0}px"">{1} </span>",
            PromptWidth, PromptText);

        base.Render(output);
    }
}
```

Note that this control does not, at present, provide much design-time support. However, the control can still be used as a server control on a webpage. If the control is to be externalized into its own project, you must build it and set a reference to it from a website. The control should then show up by default in the Toolbox (if you created an ASP.NET Server Control project). You can then add your control to a webpage or create it inside code (as you would any other control). The following code shows how to create two instances of the control inside a webpage's the Page_Init event. (Note that this code assumes the use of a master page.)

Sample of Visual Basic Code

```vbnet
Protected Sub Page_Init(ByVal sender As Object, ByVal e As System.EventArgs) _
    Handles Me.Init

    Dim content As ContentPlaceHolder = _
        CType(Me.Master.FindControl("MainContent"), ContentPlaceHolder)

    Dim width As Integer = 150
    Dim prompt1 As New MyUserControls.LabeledTextbox()

    prompt1.PromptText = "Enter Name:"
    prompt1.PromptWidth = width

    content.Controls.Add(prompt1)

    Dim br As New LiteralControl("<br />")
    content.Controls.Add(br)

    Dim prompt2 As New MyUserControls.LabeledTextbox()
    prompt2.PromptText = "Enter Address:"
    prompt2.PromptWidth = width
    content.Controls.Add(prompt2)

End Sub
```

Sample of C# Code

```csharp
protected void Page_Init(object sender, EventArgs e)
{
    ContentPlaceHolder content =
        (ContentPlaceHolder)this.Master.FindControl("MainContent");
    int width = 150;
    MyUserControls.LabeledTextBox prompt1 = new
        MyUserControls.LabeledTextBox();

    prompt1.PromptText = "Enter Name:";
    prompt1.PromptWidth = width;
    content.Controls.Add(prompt1);

    LiteralControl br = new LiteralControl("<br />");
    content.Controls.Add(br);

    MyUserControls.LabeledTextBox prompt2 = new
      MyUserControls.LabeledTextBox();
    prompt2.PromptText = "Enter Address:";
    prompt2.PromptWidth = width;
    content.Controls.Add(prompt2);
}
```

Figure 7-5 shows the rendered webpage.

FIGURE 7-5 The LabeledTextBox control rendered on a webpage.

Support for ViewState in Custom Control Properties

You might have noticed in the previous example that the two custom properties (PromptText and PromptWidth) do not provide ViewState support. This might not be a problem if you expect the users of your control to set this value in markup and not change it. However, if these properties need to be manipulated inside code, you might want to provide ViewState support to ensure a consistent developer experience similar to that of other ASP.NET controls. This will ensure that the properties set inside server code are not suddenly switched back to markup values after a postback.

You can add ViewState support for your properties by expanding Set and Get. The Set method simply adds the value to the ViewState. The Get method looks for the value in the ViewState and, if the value is found, returns it. The following shows example code for adding ViewState support for the PromptText property in the prior example.

Sample of Visual Basic Code

```vb
Private _promptText As String
Public Property PromptText() As String
    Get
        Dim s As String = CStr(ViewState("PromptText"))
        If s Is Nothing Then
            Return String.Empty
        Else
            Return s
        End If
    End Get

    Set(ByVal Value As String)
        ViewState("PromptText") = Value
    End Set
End Property
```

Sample of C# Code

```csharp
public string PromptText
{
    get
    {
        String s = (String)ViewState["PromptText"];
        return ((s == null) ? String.Empty : s);
    }

    set
    {
        ViewState["PromptText"] = value;
    }
}
```

Inheriting Directly from the WebControl Class

Another approach to creating a custom web control is to create a control that inherits directly from the WebControl class. This approach is preferable when there is no existing control that provides enough default behavior similar to the control you want to implement. When inheriting from the WebControl class, you typically override the Render method to provide the HTML output you want for your control. However, you might also use one of the other Render methods shown in Table 7-1.

TABLE 7-1 Rendering Methods of the WebControl Class

METHOD	DESCRIPTION
Render	You can use the Render method when you want to control all output of your control's HTML to the client. By default, the Render method will first call RenderBeginTag, then RenderContents, and finally RenderEndTag. If you override this method, you control whether or not these other methods are called.
RenderContents	You use this method to ensure that the HTML for your control is rendered between the appropriate begin and end HTML tags. When Render is called on your control (manually or automatically by ASP.NET), it will call three methods in a sequence: RenderBeginTag, RenderContent, and RenderEndTag. Any custom code you add to these methods through overriding will be executed.
RenderBeginTag and RenderEndTag	These methods are used to render HTML both at the beginning of a control listing and at the end. You override these methods when creating custom controls that display multiple controls between opening and closing tags.
RenderChildren	If your custom control has child controls inside its ControlCollection, you can call this method to ensure that each is rendered as part of the HTML output.

As an example, suppose you want to create a custom control that allows a user to display a logo and an associated company name for the logo. For this, you might create two properties: LogoUrl and CompanyName. You would then add code to render the output. In the following example, the RenderBeginTag and RenderContents methods are used to display the HTML for the control. Note that RenderEndTag is not required, because it is automatically called and will render an end tag based on the supplied begin tag.

Sample of Visual Basic Code

```vb
Public Class LogoControlVb
    Inherits WebControl

    Public Property LogoPath As String
    Public Property CompanyName As String

    Public Overrides Sub RenderBeginTag(ByVal writer As System.Web.UI.HtmlTextWriter)
        writer.RenderBeginTag("div")
    End Sub

    Protected Overrides Sub RenderContents(ByVal output As HtmlTextWriter)
        output.Write("<img src=""{0}"" alt=""Logo"" /><br />", LogoPath)
        output.Write(CompanyName + "<br />")
    End Sub
End Class
```

Sample of C# Code

```csharp
public class LogoControl : WebControl
{
    public string LogoPath { get; set; }
    public string CompanyName { get; set; }

    public override void RenderBeginTag(HtmlTextWriter writer)
    {
        writer.RenderBeginTag("div");
    }

    protected override void RenderContents(HtmlTextWriter output)
    {
        output.Write(@"<img src=""{0}"" alt=""Logo"" /><br />", LogoPath);
        output.Write(CompanyName + "<br />");
    }
}
```

Figure 7-6 shows the control being used inside an ASPX page. Notice that the LogoPath and CompanyName properties are defined in the markup. These are then being used inside the RenderContents method. LogoPath is used to assign an <img/> tag's src attribute set to the logo's path. CompanyName is used to set text on the line that follows the image.

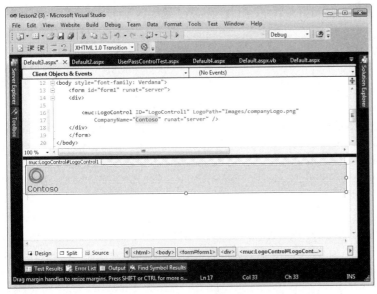

FIGURE 7-6 The LogoControl inside the Visual Studio page designer.

When this control is rendered, a <div/> tag is sent to the browser from the call to RenderBeginTag. The RenderContent method sends an <img/> tag and company name within the <div/> tag. The following shows the markup as sent to a browser.

```
<html xmlns="http://www.w3.org/1999/xhtml">
<head><title></title></head>
<body style="font-family: Verdana">
<form method="post" action="Default3.aspx" id="form1">

    <div class="aspNetHidden">
        <input type="hidden" name="__VIEWSTATE" id="__VIEWSTATE"
    value="/wEPDwUKMTEzOTYwMzMxMGRk+C8ZqFrvNTacdRCm30XWc6KmAgUUjwIAf5zk3FGVKvc=" />
    </div>

    <div>
        <div>
            <img src="Images/companyLogo.png" /><br />Contoso<br />
        </div>
    </div>

</form>
</body>
</html>
```

Adding Toolbox Support for a Custom Web Server Control

Developers are used to working with controls that originate from the Visual Studio Toolbox and provide design-time, declarative markup support. As a web server control developer, you should strongly consider providing this functionality to your users (other developers).

The primary requirement that allows a custom web control to be added to the Toolbox is that the web control be placed into a separate DLL file. This typically means that the control must be created in a stand-alone ASP.NET Server Control project. To accomplish this, you can either set a project-based reference to the control (if it is in the same solution as your website) or you can right-click the Toolbox and select Choose Items. The latter option will let you browse to the user control's DLL file to add the control or controls that are contained in the file to the Toolbox.

To demonstrate, suppose that the custom server controls in the examples earlier in this lesson are in their own class library, MyUserControls.dll. You can set a reference to this DLL file to add the DLL to the Bin folder of your website. You can then use the Choose Toolbox Items dialog box to select any controls within the library and add them to the Toolbox. After they have been added, you can drag these controls from the Toolbox to a webpage to set their properties declaratively.

Figure 7-7 shows an example. Notice that the controls are defined in their own grouping at the top of the Toolbox. When you drag a control to the page, the control will automatically be registered; this markup is shown at the top of the page. The bottom of the page shows the control defined declaratively (including custom properties). Finally, notice on the right side of the figure that the control's DLL file is placed inside the Bin folder for the website.

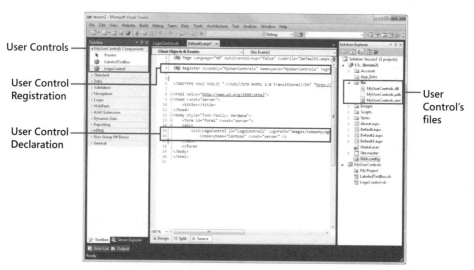

FIGURE 7-7 Externalizing controls as separate DLL files to allow for Toolbox support in Visual Studio.

Defining a Custom Icon for Your Control

As shown earlier in Figure 7-7, the example control uses a default icon. You can add your own custom icon by using an attribute called ToolboxBitmap, which is contained in the System.Drawing namespace. You apply this attribute to your server control class. The attribute uses a custom bitmap that is 16 × 16 pixels in size to set a custom image in the Toolbox.

The attribute allows you to specify a path to the icon as an absolute path with a drive letter specified. It also allows you to reference an embedded bitmap in your control's assembly. Clearly the second option is more practical, because it allows you to deploy your control as a single file, and you do not need to worry about where an image file might be on a user's drive.

To embed your image, you first add it to your project. You then select the file in Solution Explorer and view the Properties window. From the Properties window, you set the Build Action property to Embedded Resource. This tells the compiler to embed the image as part of the DLL file. After that, all you need to do is reference the embedded image by using the ToolboxBitmap attribute class.

As an example, suppose you want to create a custom icon for the LabeledTextBox web server control shown previously in Figure 7-5. You should first use the Import directive (in Visual Basic) or the using directive (in C#) to qualify use of the System.Drawing namespace to your class. You then add a 16 × 16 bitmap to the root of your project and set its Build Action to Embedded Resource. Finally, you set the ToolBoxBitmap class to point to the embedded resource, as shown in the following code.

Sample of Visual Basic Code

```
<ToolboxBitmap(GetType(LabeledTextBox), _
    "LabeledTbControlIcon.bmp")> _
Public Class LabeledTextBox
    Inherits TextBox
...
```

Sample of C# Code

```
[ToolboxBitmap(typeof(LabeledTextBox),
    "LabeledTbControlIcon.bmp")]
public class LabeledTextBox : TextBox
{
...
```

Figure 7-8 shows the results in the Toolbox. You can see that the web server control, LabeledTextBox, has a custom icon.

FIGURE 7-8 Custom icons for web server controls can be defined by using the ToolboxBitmap attribute.

Providing a Default Property for Your Custom Web Server Control

You can specify a default property of your control to be focused in the Properties window when the user selects the property in the Visual Studio designer. This is useful if your control has a key property to which you want to draw the developer's attention.

You indicate this property for your control by using the DefaultProperty attribute class in the System.ComponentModel namespace. Note that this should not be confused with a default property in Visual Basic or C# that takes a parameter and is often used for the Item property of a collection class. Rather, it simply signifies the property to be focused when the user selects your control in the designer.

You apply this attribute at the class level, and simply pass the name of one of your properties to this attribute. The following code shows an example of setting the PromptText property as the default for the LabeledTextBox control.

Sample of Visual Basic Code

```
<DefaultProperty("PromptText")> _
Public Class LabeledTextBox
  Inherits TextBox
```

Sample of C# Code

```
[DefaultProperty("PromptText")]
public class LabeledTextBox : TextBox
```

Figure 7-9 shows the resulting design-time experience for a developer. Notice that the custom web server control is selected and its PromptText property is focused in the Properties pane.

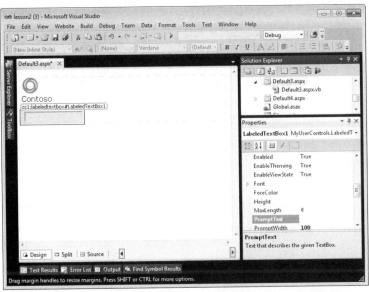

FIGURE 7-9 The DefaultProperty attribute class is used to indicate a property of your control to be high-lighted in the Properties window when a user selects the control in the designer.

Defining Attributes for Your Control Properties

There are several attribute classes you can apply to the properties of your control to change how those properties are managed by Visual Studio. Table 7-2 lists some of these key attribute classes.

TABLE 7-2 Attributes Typically Applied to Control Properties

ATTRIBUTE	DESCRIPTION
Bindable	You use the Bindable property to indicate whether a control's property should be bound to data. If you set this value to Bindable(true), the property will be displayed in the DataBindings section of the property grid in Visual Studio. By default, properties are assumed to be Bindable(false).
Category	You use the Category attribute to indicate the category (or group) in which the property should be displayed in the Properties window grid when a developer changes the Properties view to Categorized. By default, your properties will show up in the Misc category. For example, you can set Category("Appearance") to indicate that your property should be shown in the Appearance category in the Properties window grid.

(continued)

ATTRIBUTE	DESCRIPTION
Description	You use the Description attribute to provide a brief description of your property's usage. This description is shown at the bottom of the Properties pane in Visual Studio when the property is selected.
DefaultValue	You use the DefaultValue attribute to set a default value for your property.
Localizable	You use the Localizable attribute to indicate whether your property should (or can) be localized. Setting Localizable(true) indicates that the property should be serialized as a localized resource.

The following code shows an example of applying some of these properties to the PromptText property of the LabledTextBox control.

Sample of Visual Basic Code

```
<Bindable(True), _
Category("Appearance"), _
Description("Text that describes the purpose of the TextBox."), _
Localizable(True)> _
Public Property PromptText() As String
```

Sample of C# Code

```
[Bindable(true),
Category("Appearance"),
Description("Text that describes the purpose of the TextBox."),
Localizable(true)]
public string PromptText { get; set; }
```

This code indicates that the property can be bound to data and can be localized. It also indicates that the property should be displayed in the Appearance category of the Properties window and provides a description when the user selects the property in the Properties window. Figure 7-10 shows the newly decorated property inside the Properties window.

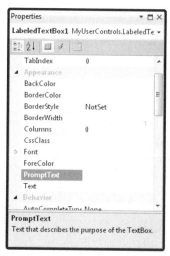

FIGURE 7-10 The PromptText property shown in its category and with its description.

Controlling the Markup Generated for Your Custom Web Server Control

You can further change the way your custom server control behaves when it is dropped onto the webpage by setting the ToolboxData attribute in your control class. This attribute is used to change the markup that is generated by Visual Studio. A common scenario is to set default values for properties on the control inside the generated markup.

The following code shows an implementation of the ToolboxData attribute for the LabeledTextBox control.

Sample of Visual Basic Code

```
<ToolboxData( _
    "<{0}:LabeledTextBox runat=""server"" PromptText="""" PromptWidth=""100""  />")> _
Public Class LabeledTextBox
Inherits TextBox
```

Sample of C# Code

```
[ToolboxData(
    @"<{0}:LabeledTextBox runat=""server"" PromptText="""" PromptWidth=""100"" />")]
public class LabeledTextBox : TextBox
```

In this example, the {0} placeholder contains the namespace prefix as defined by the webpage designer. Notice that the PromptText and PromptWidth attributes are inserted automatically. PromptWidth is assigned the default value of 100. When the control is added to a page, the following markup is generated.

```
<cc1:LabeledTextBox ID="LabeledTextBox1" runat="server" PromptText="" PromptWidth="100">
</cc1:LabeledTextBox>
```

You can also provide the namespace prefix that is assigned to your control by the webpage designer by assigning the TagPrefixAttribute of the System.Web.UI namespace to the assembly that contains your custom control. (Visual Studio will assign a default value such as "uc1" if you do not.) To do so, you add the following attribute declaration to the AssemblyInfo class file in your control (you might have to create this class file for Visual Basic projects). The following code shows the namespace prefix being changed to "muc" (my user controls) from cc1 for the controls in the MyUserControls project.

Sample of Visual Basic Code

```
Imports System.Web.UI
<Assembly: TagPrefix("MyUserControls", "muc")>
```

Sample of C# Code

```
using System.Web.UI;
[assembly: TagPrefix("MyUserControls", "muc")]
```

With the previous change to the LabeledTextBox control, the @ Register directive will change as follows when a user drags the control onto a page.

```
<%@ Register Assembly="MyUserControls" Namespace="MyUserControls" TagPrefix="muc" %>
```

The control will also change to use the new prefix, as displayed here.

```
<muc:LabeledTextBox ID="LabeledTextBox1" runat="server" PromptText="" PromptWidth="100">
</muc:LabeledTextBox>
```

Creating a Custom Designer for a Custom Web Server Control

Controls added from the Toolbox already have design-time support; that is, you can see them in the Design view of the page and work with their properties in the Properties window. However, you might want to alter the default rendering of the control in design mode. In addition, some controls might not be visible because they contain code that must be run to populate specific properties. In these cases, you can specify a custom designer for your control.

To do so, you start by adding a reference to the System.Design.dll assembly in your custom server control. You then create a new class in your user control that inherits from the ControlDesigner class. This class will override the GetDesignTimeHtml method of the ControlDesigner class to render separate design-time HTML that can be set based on the property settings of the control instance. You then apply the Designer attribute to your control. To this, you pass an instance of your ControlDesigner class.

For example, suppose you want to customize the design-time view of the LabelTextBox control. You might set the control to display a reminder to users when they have not yet set the PromptText property. To get started, you add a new class to your control and make sure it inherits from ControlDesigner and overrides the GetDesignTimeHtml method. This override should get an instance of the control and check it to see whether the PromptText value has been set. If not, it should display an alternate view. The following code shows an example. (This code requires a project reference to System.Design.)

Sample of Visual Basic Code

```vbnet
Imports System.Web.UI.Design
Imports System.ComponentModel

Public Class LabeledTextBoxDesigner
    Inherits ControlDesigner

    Private _labeledTextBoxControl As LabeledTextBox

    Public Overrides Function GetDesignTimeHtml() As String

        _labeledTextBoxControl = CType(Component, LabeledTextBox)
        If (_labeledTextBoxControl.PromptText.Length = 0) Then
            Return "<div style='color: Gray'>[Define PromptText]</div>"
        Else
            Return MyBase.GetDesignTimeHtml()
        End If

    End Function

End Class
```

Sample of C# Code

```csharp
using System.Web.UI.Design;
using System.ComponentModel;

namespace MyUserControlsCs
{
    class LabeledTextBoxDesigner : ControlDesigner
    {
        private LabeledTextBox _labeledTextBoxControl;

        public override string GetDesignTimeHtml()
        {
            if (_labeledTextBoxControl.PromptText.Trim().Length == 0)
                return "<div style='color: Gray'>[Define PromptText]</div>";
            else
                return base.GetDesignTimeHtml();
        }

        public override void Initialize(IComponent component)
        {
            _labeledTextBoxControl = (LabeledTextBox)component;
            base.Initialize(component);
            return;
        }
    }
}
```

After the class is created, you can assign the DesignerAttribute to the user control class, as shown in the following code.

Sample of Visual Basic Code

```vbnet
<Designer("MyUserControls.LabeledTextBoxDesigner, MyUserControls")> _
Public Class LabeledTextBox
  Inherits TextBox
```

Sample of C# Code

```csharp
[Designer("MyUserControls.LabeledTextBoxDesigner, MyUserControls")]
public class LabeledTextBox : TextBox
```

Now when the control is dragged onto a webpage, the designer code executes and determines the layout (custom or base). If the PromptText property is not set, the control is displayed as shown in Figure 7-11. When the property is set, the control displays as before.

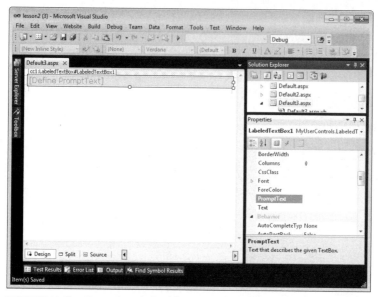

FIGURE 7-11 Creating a class derived from ControlDesigner creates a custom designer for custom web server controls.

Creating a Composite Control

A composite control is a custom web control that contains other web server controls. This sounds a lot like a user control. However, a composite control doesn't provide an ASCX file or a designer that lets you drag controls on it at design time. Instead, a composite control is a custom web server control that inherits from the CompositeControl class. You then add constituent controls to this control. The composite control handles events raised by its child controls.

A composite control is rendered as a tree of constituent controls, each having its own life cycle. Together, these constituent controls form a new control. Because each of the child controls handles its own ViewState and postback data, you don't need to write extra code to deal with this.

To create a composite control, you start by creating a class that inherits from the CompositeControl class and overrides the CreateChildControls method. The CreateChildControls method contains the code to instantiate the child controls and set their properties.

If you want to be able to assign styles to the composite control, you should create an instance of the Panel class to provide a container that can have attributes assigned to it. In this case, you add the container to the Controls collection of your composite control, and then add your controls to the Panel control.

As an example, suppose you want to create a composite control that includes controls for prompting a user for a user name and password. You might also include a submit button with a click event that can be subscribed to. You start by defining a class that inherits from

CompositeControl. The following code shows the implementation of this control.

Sample of Visual Basic Code

```vb
Imports System.Web.UI
Imports System.Web.UI.WebControls

Public Class UserPasswordControl
    Inherits CompositeControl

    Public Event Submitted As System.EventHandler

    Public Property UserName() As String
        Get
            Dim txt As TextBox
            txt = CType(Me.FindControl("UserName"), TextBox)
            Return txt.Text
        End Get
        Set(ByVal Value As String)
            Dim txt As TextBox
            txt = CType(Me.FindControl("UserName"), TextBox)
            txt.Text = Value
        End Set
    End Property

    Public Property Password() As String
        Get
            Dim txt As TextBox
            txt = CType(Me.FindControl("Password"), TextBox)
            Return txt.Text
        End Get
        Set(ByVal Value As String)
            Dim txt As TextBox
            txt = CType(Me.FindControl("Password"), TextBox)
            txt.Text = Value
        End Set
    End Property

    Protected Overrides Sub CreateChildControls()
        Dim pnl As New Panel()
        Dim txtUserName As New TextBox()
        Dim txtPassword As New TextBox()
        Dim btnSubmit As New Button()
        AddHandler btnSubmit.Click, AddressOf btnSubmit_Click

        'start control buildup
        Controls.Add(pnl)
        'add user name row
        pnl.Controls.Add(New LiteralControl("<table><tr><td>"))
        pnl.Controls.Add(New LiteralControl("User Name:"))
        pnl.Controls.Add(New LiteralControl("</td><td>"))
        pnl.Controls.Add(txtUserName)
        pnl.Controls.Add(New LiteralControl("</td></tr>"))
```

```
                    'add password row
                    pnl.Controls.Add(New LiteralControl("<tr><td>"))
                    pnl.Controls.Add(New LiteralControl("Password:"))
                    pnl.Controls.Add(New LiteralControl("</td><td>"))
                    pnl.Controls.Add(txtPassword)
                    pnl.Controls.Add(New LiteralControl("</td></tr>"))
                    'add submit button row
                    pnl.Controls.Add(New LiteralControl( _
                      "<tr><td colspan=""2"" align=""center"" >"))
                    pnl.Controls.Add(btnSubmit)
                    pnl.Controls.Add(New LiteralControl("</td></tr></table>"))

                    'set up control properties
                    pnl.Style.Add("background-color", "silver")
                    pnl.Style.Add("width", "275px")
                    txtUserName.ID = "UserName"
                    txtUserName.Style.Add("width", "170px")
                    txtPassword.ID = "Password"
                    txtPassword.TextMode = TextBoxMode.Password
                    txtPassword.Style.Add("width", "170px")
                    btnSubmit.Text = "Submit"

            End Sub

            Public Sub btnSubmit_Click(ByVal sender As Object, ByVal e As EventArgs)
                RaiseEvent Submitted(Me, e)
            End Sub

    End Class
```

Sample of C# Code

```
using System;
using System.ComponentModel;
using System.Web.UI;
using System.Web.UI.WebControls;
using System.Drawing;

public class UserPasswordControl : CompositeControl
{

  public event System.EventHandler Submitted;

  public string UserName
  {
    get
    {
      TextBox txt = (TextBox)FindControl("UserName");
      return txt.Text;
    }
    set
    {
      TextBox txt = (TextBox)FindControl("UserName");
      txt.Text = value;
    }
  }
}
```

```csharp
public string Password
{
  get
  {
    TextBox pwd = (TextBox)FindControl("Password");
    return pwd.Text;
  }
  set
  {
    TextBox pwd = (TextBox)FindControl("Password");
    pwd.Text = value;
  }
}

protected override void CreateChildControls()
{
  Panel pnl = new Panel();
  TextBox txtUserName = new TextBox();
  TextBox txtPassword = new TextBox();
  Button btnSubmit = new Button();
  btnSubmit.Click += new EventHandler(btnSubmit_Click);

  //start control buildup
  Controls.Add(pnl);
  //add user name row
  pnl.Controls.Add(new LiteralControl("<table><tr><td>"));
  pnl.Controls.Add(new LiteralControl("User Name:"));
  pnl.Controls.Add(new LiteralControl("</td><td>"));
  pnl.Controls.Add(txtUserName);
  pnl.Controls.Add(new LiteralControl("</td></tr>"));
  //add password row
  pnl.Controls.Add(new LiteralControl("<tr><td>"));
  pnl.Controls.Add(new LiteralControl("Password:"));
  pnl.Controls.Add(new LiteralControl("</td><td>"));
  pnl.Controls.Add(txtPassword);
  pnl.Controls.Add(new LiteralControl("</td></tr>"));
  //add submit button row
  pnl.Controls.Add(new LiteralControl(
    @"<tr><td colspan=""2"" align=""center"" >"));
  pnl.Controls.Add(btnSubmit);
  pnl.Controls.Add(new LiteralControl("</td></tr></table>"));

  //set up control properties
  pnl.Style.Add("background-color", "silver");
  pnl.Style.Add("width", "275px");
  txtUserName.ID = "UserName";
  txtUserName.Style.Add("width", "170px");
  txtPassword.ID = "Password";
  txtPassword.TextMode = TextBoxMode.Password;
  txtPassword.Style.Add("width", "170px");
  btnSubmit.Text = "Submit";
}

void btnSubmit_Click(object sender, EventArgs e)
{
  if (Submitted != null) Submitted(this, e);
}
}
```

In this code, the UserName and Password properties are exposed to give users of the control access to this data. Notice that these properties use the FindControl method to expose the properties of the constituent controls. An event called Submitted is also created so that users of the control can receive notification when the Submit button's Click event fires. The CreateChildControls method performs the work to instantiate the child controls for this composite control.

This control can be tested by adding it to a webpage. You use the same techniques described for the other custom web controls to do so. In the following markup, you can see the control added to a page. Notice that the control's Submitted event is bound to a handler in the code-behind for the page.

```
<%@ Page Title="" Language="VB" MasterPageFile="~/Site.master"
    AutoEventWireup="false" CodeFile="UserPassControlTest.aspx.vb"
    Inherits="UserPassControlTest" %>

<%@ Register Assembly="MyUserControls" Namespace="MyUserControls"
    TagPrefix="muc" %>

<asp:Content ID="Content1" ContentPlaceHolderID="HeadContent" Runat="Server">
</asp:Content>

<asp:Content ID="Content2" ContentPlaceHolderID="MainContent" Runat="Server">

    <muc:UserPasswordControl ID="UserPasswordControl1" runat="server"
        OnSubmitted="UserPasswordControl1_Submitted" />

</asp:Content>
```

When this test webpage is run, the UserPasswordControl is displayed. After typing a user name and password, you can click the Submit button to execute the event handler in the code-behind page. Figure 7-12 shows the control running in a browser.

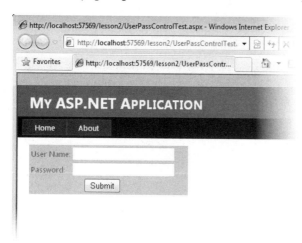

FIGURE 7-12 A composite custom web server control created by using the CompositeControl class.

Quick Check

1. You want to create a new, custom web server control that does not rely on any existing ASP.NET control. From what class should you inherit?

2. You want to create a control that can be distributed as a DLL. The control contains several TextBox, Label, and Button controls, and you want to be able to add the control to the Toolbox. What is the best choice of control to create?

3. You want to create a new, custom control that extends from the CheckBox control. From which class should you inherit?

Quick Check Answers

1. Inherit from the WebControl class.

2. Create a composite control.

3. You should inherit directly from the CheckBox class.

Creating a Templated Custom Web Server Control

A templated custom web control provides separation of control data from its presentation. This means that a templated control does not provide a default UI. For example, if you know that you need to display product data, but you don't know how the developer who intends to use your control wants to format the product data, you could create a templated control called ProductControl that allows the page designer to supply the format for the product data as a template.

A templated control must provide a naming container and a class with properties and methods that are accessible to the host page. The template contains the UI for the templated web server control and is supplied by the page developer at design time. The templates can contain controls and markup. You can create a templated control by following these steps:

1. Create a ClassLibrary (DLL) project for your templated control.

2. Add a reference to the System.Web.dll library.

3. Add a container class to your project. The class should have public properties for the data that you want to be able to access via the Container object in your template.

4. In the container class file, add an Imports directive (a using directive in C#) for the System.Web.UI namespace.

5. Code your container class to inherit from the System.Web.UI.Control class and implement the INamingContainer interface.

6. Add a class to the project for your templated control.

7. In the class file, add an Imports directive (a using directive in C#) for the System.Web.UI namespace.

8. Code your templated control to inherit from the System.Web.UI.Control class and implement the INamingContainer interface.

9. Add the ParseChildren(true) attribute to the class. This attribute provides direction to the page parser to indicate that the nested content contained within the server control is parsed as a control and not used to set properties of the templated control.

10. Create one or more properties in the templated control class with the data type of ITemplate. These properties will be used by the page developer to define the actual layout of the control. These properties must have the TemplateContainer attribute set to the data type of the container, which might be the templated control. Alternatively, you can create a subcontainer if you have repeating items to display in the template. Also, these properties must have the PersistenceMode attribute set to PersistenceMode.InnerProperty, which allows page designers to add inner HTML elements to the HTML source of the templated control.

11. Add the properties you want to the template container so that they will be accessible by the template.

12. The DataBind method must be overridden to call the EnsureChildControls method on the base Control class.

13. The CreateChildControls method must be overridden to provide the code to instantiate the template by using the InstantiateIn method of the ITemplate interface. Code should also be provided for a default implementation if no template is provided.

As you can see, many of the steps to create a templated custom web server control are similar to those for creating a templated user control (see Lesson 1). The primary differences are in how you actually create the custom web server control versus creating a user control.

Registering Your Controls in Web.config

Each time you add a custom control (or even a user control) to a webpage, Visual Studio generates the @ Register directive to ensure that the control is registered for the page. However, you can register controls globally to your site by using the Web.config file. This allows you to use them on pages much as you would any other ASP.NET control (without the @ Register directive).

The following code shows the Web.config markup required to register a custom control as a DLL (MyUserControls) and a user control stored in an ASCX file (AddressControl.ascx). Adding this code to the Web.config file eliminates the need to call @ Register on pages that use these controls.

```
<system.web>
    <pages>
        <controls>
            <add assembly="MyUserControls"
                    namespace="MyUserControls"
                    tagPrefix="muc" />
            <add src="~/Controls/AddressUserControl.ascx"
                    tagName="AddressUserControl"
                    tagPrefix="uc1" />
        </controls>
    </pages>
</system.web>
```

PRACTICE **Working with Custom Web Server Controls**

In this practice, you create a custom web server control called StateListControl that displays a list of states in the United States. Of course, you can repurpose this control to display a static list of almost anything.

> **ON THE COMPANION MEDIA**
>
> If you encounter a problem completing an exercise, you can find the completed projects in the samples installed from this book's companion CD. For more information about the project files and other content on the CD, see "Using the Companion Media" in this book's Introduction.

EXERCISE 1 **Creating the Visual Studio Projects and Defining the Custom Web Server Control**

In this exercise, you create the projects used by this practice. You also write the code for the custom server control.

1. Open Visual Studio and create a new website called **CustomControlLab** by using your preferred programming language. This website will serve to host the custom control on a page.

2. Add an ASP.NET Server Control project to your solution. Name this project **MyCustomControls**.

3. Rename ServerControl1 to **StateListControl** by right-clicking the file in Solution Explorer and choosing Rename. When asked if you would like to rename the class and reference, select Yes.

4. Open the StateListControl class file. Delete the Text property and the RenderContents method.

5. Change the StateListControl class to inherit from DropDownList. Also, remove the DefaultProperty attribute from the class declaration and change the ToolboxData attribute to use the text StateListControl for the tags instead of ServerControl1. Also, add the ID property to the generated markup for the control.

6. Add code to the constructor of the StateListControl class to create a ListItem for each state. Add the ListItems to the Items collection of the DropDownList. The ListItem for each state displays the full name of the state, but the posted value is the two-character state abbreviation. The following is an example.

Sample of Visual Basic Code
```vb
Imports System.Web.UI
Imports System.Web.UI.WebControls

<ToolboxData(
"<{0}:StateListControl ID=""StateListControl1""
  runat=""server""></{0}:StateListControl>")> _
  Public Class StateListControl
    Inherits DropDownList

    Public Sub New()
        Me.Items.Add(New ListItem("Alabama", "AL"))
        Me.Items.Add(New ListItem("Alaska", "AK"))
        Me.Items.Add(New ListItem("Arizona", "AZ"))
        Me.Items.Add(New ListItem("Arkansas", "AR"))
        Me.Items.Add(New ListItem("California", "CA"))
        'and more ...
    End Sub

End Class
```

Sample of C# Code
```csharp
using System.Web.UI;
using System.Web.UI.WebControls;

namespace MyCustomControls
{
    [ToolboxData(
  @"<{0}:StateListControl ID=""StateListControl1""
  runat=""server""></{0}:StateListControl>")]
    public class StateListControl : DropDownList
    {
        public StateListControl()
        {
            this.Items.Add(new ListItem("Alabama", "AL"));
            this.Items.Add(new ListItem("Alaska", "AK"));
            this.Items.Add(new ListItem("Arizona", "AZ"));
            this.Items.Add(new ListItem("Arkansas", "AR"));
            this.Items.Add(new ListItem("California", "CA"));
            //and more ...
        }
    }
}
```

7. Build the MyCustomControls project. Also, note that you do not need to expose the Items property or manage its ViewState. That is taken care of already by the base class (DropDownList). Users can add and remove items from the default list of states that the control exposes. You will see that in the next exercise.

EXERCISE 2 Adding the Custom Web Server Control to a Webpage

In this exercise, you add the StateListControl created in the prior exercise to a webpage.

1. Continue editing the project you created in the previous exercise. Alternatively, you can open the completed Lesson 2, Exercise 1 project from the sample files installed from the CD and begin from there.

2. Inside the website, add the StateListControl to the Toolbox. You can do this one of two ways. One way is to add a reference to MyCustomControls by right-clicking the website, selecting Add Reference, choosing the Projects tab, and selecting MyCustomControls. Alternatively, you could right-click the Toolbox and select Choose Items. You would then browse and locate the MyCustomControls.dll assembly. Whichever approach you use, the StateListControl should be displayed in the Toolbox when you have a webpage open in the designer.

   Note that if you chose the Add Reference option, you might have to rebuild the solution to get the control to show in the Toolbox. You might also have to switch the page from Source view to Design view.

3. Open the Default.aspx page. Delete the contents already inside the BodyContent content control.

4. Drag a StateListControl from the Toolbox onto the page. This will register the control with the page and add it to the markup.

5. Add a Button control and a Label control to the page to demonstrate adding to the StateListControl, handling postback, and displaying the user's selection. Your markup inside the BodyContent for the page should look as follows:

```
<asp:Content ID="BodyContent" runat="server" ContentPlaceHolderID="MainContent">

    <ccl:StateListControl ID="StatListControl1" runat="server">
    </ccl:StateListControl>
    <br />
    <asp:Button ID="ButtonSubmit" runat="server" Text="Submit" />
    <br />
    <asp:Label ID="LabelSelected" runat="server" Text=""></asp:Label>

</asp:Content>
```

6. Switch to Design view for the page, and double-click the Submit button. This should take you to the code-behind file for the page and generate an event handler for the button's click event. Add code to this event to render the selected text and value of the StateListControl to the LabelSelected control.

7. Add a Page_Load event to the page (in C# it should already be there). Add code to this event to add an item to the StateListControl if the request is not a postback.

The following shows what your code-behind file should look like.

Sample of Visual Basic Code
```vb
Partial Class _Default
    Inherits System.Web.UI.Page

    Protected Sub Page_Load(ByVal sender As Object, _
        ByVal e As System.EventArgs) Handles Me.Load

        If Not IsPostBack Then
            StateListControl1.Items.Add(New ListItem("Michigan", "MI"))
        End If

    End Sub

    Protected Sub ButtonSubmit_Click(ByVal sender As Object, _
        ByVal e As System.EventArgs) Handles ButtonSubmit.Click

        LabelSelected.Text = StateListControl1.SelectedItem.Text & ", " _
            & StateListControl1.SelectedItem.Value

    End Sub

End Class
```

Sample of C# Code
```csharp
public partial class _Default : System.Web.UI.Page
{
    protected void Page_Load(object sender, EventArgs e)
    {
        if (!IsPostBack)
        {
            StateListControl1.Items.Add(new ListItem("Michigan", "MI"));
        }
    }
    protected void ButtonSubmit_Click(object sender, EventArgs e)
    {
        LabelSelected.Text = StateListControl1.SelectedItem.Text + ", "
            + StateListControl1.SelectedItem.Value;
    }
}
```

8. Make sure the website is set as the startup project. (Right-click the project in Solution Explorer and choose Set As StartUp Project.) Run the website. You should be able to test the control in a browser. Figure 7-13 shows an example.

FIGURE 7-13 The StateListControl running in a browser.

Lesson Summary

- You can build a custom web control by inheriting from the WebControl class or through inheriting directly from an existing ASP.NET control's class, if you want to extend the features of that control.

- You can create a composite web control when you need to base your control on multiple ASP.NET controls. You do so by inheriting from the CompositeControl class.

- You can add Toolbox support to your custom control to control the icon, the generated markup, and the display of the control in the designer.

- You can control how Visual Studio manages the properties of your control by using the Category, Bindable, Description, DefaultValue, and Localizable attribute classes.

- You can create a templated custom web server control to allow users to define the layout of the control at design time.

- You can register your controls for your entire website inside the Web.config file.

Lesson Review

You can use the following questions to test your knowledge of the information in Lesson 2, "Creating Custom Web Server Controls." The questions are also available on the companion CD in a practice test, if you prefer to review them in electronic form.

> **NOTE ANSWERS**
>
> **Answers to these questions and explanations of why each answer choice is correct or incorrect are located in the "Answers" section at the end of the book.**

1. You are creating a custom web server control that extends the features of the ASP.NET Button control. Which steps should you take? (Choose all that apply.)

   A. Ensure that your control inherits from the WebControl class and exposes the base Button control as a property of the class.

   B. Ensure that your control inherits directly from the Button control.

   C. Override the Render method of your control and be sure to call base.Render (C#) or MyBase.Render (Visual Basic).

   D. Override the RenderChildren method of your control and be sure to call base.RenderChildren (C#) or MyBase.RenderChildren (Visual Basic).

2. You want to define a custom image to be displayed in the Toolbox for your custom web server control. Which actions do you take? (Choose all that apply.)

   A. Set a reference to the System.Design namespace.

   B. Set a reference to the System.Drawing namespace.

   C. Add the ToolboxData attribute to the class.

   D. Add the ToolboxBitmap attribute to the class.

3. You are going to create a custom web server control that inherits directly from the WebControl class. Which method do you need to override to get your control to display in the browser window?

   A. OnInit

   B. Finalize

   C. ToString

   D. Render

4. You are creating a composite control. You create a class that inherits from the CompositeControl class. What method must be overridden so you can provide code to instantiate the child controls and set their properties?

   A. CreateChildControls

   B. DataBindChildren

   C. CreateControlStyle

   D. BuildProfileTree

Case Scenarios

In the following case scenarios, you apply what you've learned in this chapter. If you have difficulty completing this work, review the material in this chapter before beginning the next chapter. You can find answers to these questions in the "Answers" section at the end of this book.

Case Scenario 1: Sharing Controls Between Applications

You are a developer working for the Contoso corporation. You have reviewed the requirements for a new website and realize that on multiple pages a user has to review, update, and enter the same group of information. You propose grouping this functionality into a control for easier use. When you do, an architect on the team indicates that the same functionally is actually required by other websites in the corporation. You both agree that you should standardize the layout and behavior of collecting this data.

Answer the following questions related to how you will develop the control.

1. What type of control should you create?

2. Based on your answer to question 1, why have you excluded other types of controls?

Case Scenario 2: Providing Layout Flexibility

You are a web developer at Contoso Ltd., a pharmaceutical company. As you are working on an existing website, you notice that there are several areas in which customer information is displayed throughout the site. After additional investigation, you notice that the customer information needs to be rendered uniquely in many of the areas in which it is defined. You want to provide a common control that can be used within this site to display this customer information.

Answer the following questions related to how you will develop the control.

1. Should you create a custom web server control or a user control?

2. How should you lay out the control?

3. From what class should your control inherit?

Suggested Practices

To successfully master the exam objectives presented in this chapter, complete the following tasks.

Create a New User Control

For this task, you should complete both practices.

- **Practice 1**   Consider a common feature of some of the sites you've developed. Take that feature and create a user control. The user control should contain other ASP.NET controls and expose them as properties. Practice adding the user control to several webpages, and write code to access the properties of the user control.

- **Practice 2**   Add one or more custom events to the user control. Subscribe to these events from the hosting page.

Create a New Custom Web Server Control

For this task, you should complete Practice 1 to get an overview of creating controls that inherit from WebControl. Practices 2 and 3 extend Practice 1 and help you develop additional skills.

- **Practice 1**   Consider a feature that is common across different sites you've developed; try to think of a feature that does not involve a specific, existing control. Use this feature to develop a new custom web server control that inherits from the WebControl class.

- **Practice 2**   Create a custom bitmap for the control you created in Practice 1. Add the file to your project. Embed the bitmap as a resource to the project, and apply it to the class. Compile the application and use it on a webpage. Be sure to add the control to the Toolbox.

- **Practice 3**   Return to your control. Add a custom designer layout to be displayed when the control is in a certain state.

Create a New Composite Web Server Control

For this task, you should complete both practices.

- **Practice 1**   Create a class library project that contains a new class that inherits from the System.Web.UI.CompositeControl class. Implement code to add constituent controls to your composite control and add properties to the composite control. Compile and add the custom web control to the ToolBox.

- **Practice 2**   Practice adding the composite control to several webpages, and write code to access the composite control properties.

Create a New Templated Control

For this task, you should complete both practices.

- **Practice 1**   Return to the LabeledTextbox control created earlier in this chapter. Convert this control to a custom web server control with a layout that is based on templates.

- **Practice 2**   Practice adding the templated control to several webpages and defining different layouts.

Take a Practice Test

The practice tests on this book's companion CD offer many options. For example, you can test yourself on just the lesson review questions in this chapter, or you can test yourself on all the 70-515 certification exam objectives. You can set up the test so it closely simulates the experience of taking a certification exam, or you can set it up in study mode so you can look at the correct answers and explanations after you answer each question.

> **MORE INFO**   **PRACTICE TESTS**
>
> For details about all the practice test options available, see the "How to Use the Practice Tests" section in this book's Introduction.

CHAPTER 8

Debugging and Deploying

A large part of the development process involves removing bugs and resolving other issues in your application. Microsoft Visual Studio and Microsoft ASP.NET provide several tools to support these tasks. These tools allow you to set breakpoints in code, step through your code by using the Integrated Development Environment (IDE), view variable values in watch windows and DataTips, execute code in the command window, and more. These debugging tools work for all the applications you create with Visual Studio, not just websites. Websites do, however, present their own set of challenges. A website runs in a distributed environment in which the network, database, and client are all running on separate processes. This can make it difficult just to get debugging set up and to get the right troubleshooting information from your application and its environment.

After you've developed and tested your application, it's time to deploy it to a production environment. In most real-world scenarios, deployment involves moving an application from a staged area, where users have reviewed and tested its functionality, to one or more production servers. The deployment process can be automated with tools and scripts, managed and governed by IT departments, or deployed directly by developers through Visual Studio. The method you will use to build, verify, and deploy your application really depends on your scenarios, the type of application, and the environment.

This chapter explores how you debug, monitor, troubleshoot, and deploy websites. The first lesson covers setting up debugging, creating custom error pages, debugging on a remote server, and debugging client script. The second lesson is about troubleshooting and monitoring a running ASP.NET site. The third lesson explores those tools and features of Visual Studio that make deploying websites easier.

Exam objectives in this chapter:

- Configuring and Extending a Web Application
  - Debug a Web application.
  - Deploy a Web application.

Lessons in this chapter:

Before You Begin

To complete the lessons in this chapter, you should be familiar with developing applications with Visual Studio by using Microsoft Visual Basic or Microsoft Visual C#. In addition, you should be comfortable with all of the following:

- The Visual Studio 2010 IDE
- Debugging Windows applications
- Using Hypertext Markup Language (HTML) and client-side scripting
- Creating ASP.NET websites and forms

 **REAL WORLD**

Tony Northrup

If you're like me and you hate debugging, give this chapter extra attention. After you learn how to use the ASP.NET and Visual Studio 2010 debugging tools, you'll be able to diagnose and fix bugs faster than ever.

I prefer to debug an ASP.NET website the same way I debug a traditional Windows application. I run the website on my local computer, and I make use of breakpoints, watch lists, and DataTips to examine the inner workings of the website. Those technologies are all discussed in the first lesson. I only resort to tracing, as discussed in the second lesson, when a website is running on a remote server and I can't set up a remote debugger.

For more complex problems, I make use of troubleshooting tools that I don't describe in this book. Microsoft Network Monitor (or any sniffer) allows you to see the communications sent between browsers and web servers. For troubleshooting communications between the web server and the database, I use the Microsoft SQL Server Profiler. For troubleshooting performance issues, I use Page Speed (available at *http://code.google.com/speed/page-speed/*) when I can reproduce the problem locally, and WebPagetest (available at *http://webpagetest.org*) when I need to analyze requests sent across the Internet.

Lesson 1: Debugging Websites

Debugging websites is more complex than debugging Windows applications because web requests are very short-lived, the client and server are typically running on different computers, and client browsers have widely varying capabilities. In addition, the state that the application uses is also distributed among database, web server, cache, session, cookie, and so on. Fortunately, Visual Studio and ASP.NET have several tools that allow you to get debugging information from your site during development.

This lesson covers the setup and configuration of the ASP.NET debugging features. Coverage includes remote debugging and client-side script debugging.

> *NOTE* **SCOPE OF CHAPTER CONTENT**
>
> This lesson covers the configuration and setup of debugging with ASP.NET and Visual Studio. It does not cover the basics of using the Visual Studio debugger, such as how to set break-points and how to view variables in watch windows. Rather, it focuses on managing the debugging of an ASP.NET website.

> **After this lesson, you will be able to:**
>   - Configure a website for debugging with Visual Studio.
>   - Set up remote debugging between a development machine and a server.
>   - Redirect users to a default error page or custom error pages based on Hypertext Transfer Protocol (HTTP) status codes.
>   - Debug client-side script.
>
> **Estimated lesson time: 30 minutes**

Configuring ASP.NET for Debugging

You can debug an ASP.NET application by using the standard features of the Visual Studio debugger, such as breakpoints, watch windows, code step-through, and error information. To do so, you must first configure ASP.NET for debugging. There are two areas where you set this information: the project's property page and the Web.config file.

Activating the ASP.NET Debugger

The first step is to configure the ASP.NET debugger settings in your project's Property Pages dialog box, including those that determine whether or not to allow Visual Studio to run the debugger. When installed, Visual Studio enables ASP.NET debugging and establishes default debugger settings. However, if you need to set or modify this setting, you can do so by following these steps:

1. Right-click the website in Solution Explorer and then click Property Pages. This will open the Property Pages dialog box for the website, as shown in Figure 8-1.

2. Select Start Options from the left side of the dialog box.

3. In the Debuggers section, at the bottom of the dialog box, select (or clear) the ASP.NET check box to enable (or disable) the ASP.NET debugger for Visual Studio.

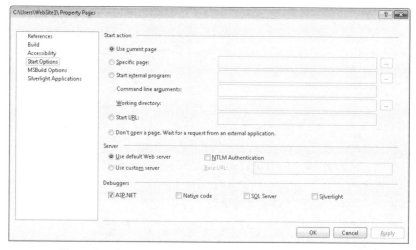

FIGURE 8-1 The project Property Pages dialog box for an ASP.NET website.

Configuring Debugging

Assuming that you allow Visual Studio to run the ASP.NET debugger, the second step is to enable debugging either for your entire site or on a page-by-page basis. Even though ASP.NET debugging in general might be enabled from a Visual Studio perspective, individual sites can disable debugging for security reasons. By default, websites that Visual Studio creates individually disable the debugger for just this reason. Enabling debugging for your site will add debug symbols into the compiled code. Visual Studio uses these symbols to provide debugging support. However, this can slow the performance of your website. In addition, turning on debugging will transmit error information to the web browser when you run the page outside of Visual Studio. This can present a security risk, because error information provides potential attackers with a lot of information about how your site works. For these reasons, you should only turn debugging on during development.

You enable debugging for your entire site by editing a setting in the Web.config file. In Web.config, you set the debug attribute of the compilation element to true. If you use Visual Studio to start debugging, Visual Studio will prompt you to automatically enable this setting. The following markup shows an example that includes the nesting level of the compilation element.

```
<configuration>
  <system.web>
    <compilation debug="true" targetFramework="4.0"/>
  <system.web>
</configuration>
```

You might not always want to turn on debugging for your entire site. In these cases, you can switch debugging on and off at the individual page level. This will ensure that only the designated pages will be compiled with the debug symbols. The rest of the site will be compiled without debugging. To enable page-level debugging, set the Debug attribute of the @ Page directive (found at the top of the markup for an ASPX page). The following shows an example.

```
<%@ Page Debug="true" ... %>
```

After you have debugging enabled, you can use the many features of the Visual Studio debugger. When you run your application, Visual Studio automatically attaches to the running ASP.NET web server process (unless you are developing remotely, which is discussed later in this lesson). You can then set breakpoints in your code, step through line by line, and view variable values in the watch window. In addition, if debugging is enabled, you can get error information sent to the browser window even when you are not running your application through Visual Studio.

New Debugging Features in Visual Studio 2010

This book assumes that you have some familiarity with the Visual Studio development environment and does not explain the details of setting breakpoints and monitoring values. It is assumed that you know that you can set a breakpoint to pause a running webpage at a specific line and then examine the values of different variables.

In Visual Studio 2010, you can export and import a set of breakpoints by using the Debug window. First, display the window by clicking the Debug menu, selecting Windows, and then selecting Breakpoints. On the Breakpoints toolbar, click the Export button to save the current set of breakpoints to a file. Later, use the Import button to read them back in. This allows you to quickly set up debugging for a recurring problem.

While debugging, you can point to a variable to view its current value in a DataTip. With Visual Studio 2010, you can click the pushpin icon on the DataTip, as shown in Figure 8-2. The value will then always appear in the debugger, and you can add comments that you can view later. After you stop debugging, Visual Studio displays a pushpin icon in the left margin. Point to the pushpin to view the DataTip's value from the last debugging session. You can import and export pinned DataTips by using the Debug menu.

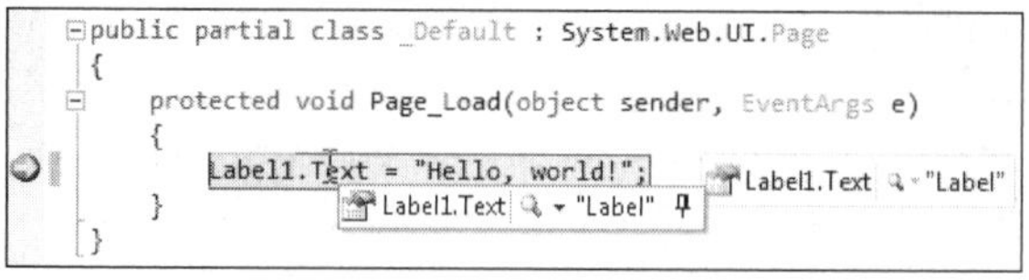

```
public partial class _Default : System.Web.UI.Page
{
    protected void Page_Load(object sender, EventArgs e)
    {
        Label1.Text = "Hello, world!";        Label1.Text  - "Label"
    }                    Label1.Text    - "Label"  ╫
}
```

FIGURE 8-2 Pinning a value in Visual Studio 2010.

There are many other useful debugging improvements. For detailed information, see
"VS 2010 Debugger Improvements" at *http://weblogs.asp.net/scottgu/archive/2010/04/21
/vs-2010-debugger-improvements-breakpoints-datatips-import-export.aspx.*

Defining Custom Error Pages

In your production environment, it is likely that you do not want to show users the default
ASP.NET error page if your site breaks. This holds true for the default Internet Information
Services (IIS) error pages as well. Rather, you most likely want users to see a page that tells
them how to contact support to resolve the problem. You can also configure your site to
display a generic error page if users encounter an unhandled error. You can set this page
at the site level. You can also set individual pages for specific error types.

Configuring a Custom Site-Level Error Page

You configure custom errors inside the Web.config file by using the <customErrors> element
nested inside <system.web>. This element has the mode and defaultRedirect attributes. The
mode attribute can be set to on to turn custom errors on, off to turn them off, or RemoteOnly
to turn custom errors on for remote clients only. With RemoteOnly, if the user (typically an
administrator) is on the server, he or she will not get the custom error, but instead will get
the real error message.

The defaultRedirect attribute is used to indicate the path to a default error page. This
page will be displayed when an unhandled exception occurs on the site. The only time
this will not happen is when a specific custom error page is added to the <error> child
elements of <customErrors> (as discussed in the next section). The following example
shows markup for a custom error definition inside Web.config.

```
<configuration>
  <system.web>
    <customErrors defaultRedirect="SiteErrorPage.aspx" mode="RemoteOnly">
    </customErrors>
  <system.web>
</configuration>
```

Notice that in this markup, the page is set to an ASPX page. You can set this to an HTM
page, an ASPX page, or another resource to which the web server can redirect.

On redirection, the server passes the path of the page that caused the error. This path is provided as part of the query string by using the named parameter aspxErrorPath; you can use this information to track errors on your site. For example, the following shows the browser's URL when the SiteErrorPage.aspx page is displayed based on an error thrown on Default.aspx:

Configuring Error-Specific Error Pages

It is also possible to define specific pages for various HTTP status codes. This allows you to provide more specific information to users when a configured status code is returned. For example, if users do not have access to a requested page or resource, their request results in an HTTP 403 return code. This status code indicates that they are denied access to the resource. You can then write a custom page that explains the process for requesting access to the page. Use the <error> element to redirect to that custom page. The following markup shows an example.

```
<configuration>
  <system.web>
    <customErrors defaultRedirect="SiteErrorPage.aspx" mode="RemoteOnly">
      <error statusCode="403" redirect="RestrictedAccess.aspx" />
    </customErrors>
  <system.web>
</configuration>
```

There are many HTTP status codes. Errors fall in the range from 400 to 600. Codes with numbers 400 to 499 are reserved for request errors and codes 500 to 599 are set aside for server errors. Table 8-1 lists some common HTTP status codes for errors. For a complete list, see *http://www.w3.org/Protocols/rfc2616/rfc2616-sec10.html#sec10*.

TABLE 8-1 Common HTTP Status Codes

CODE	DESCRIPTION
400	The request is not understood (unintelligible).
403	The user does not have access to the requested resource.
404	The file is not found at the requested URL.
405	The request method is not supported.
406	The requested Multipurpose Internet Mail Extensions (MIME) type is not accepted.
408	The request has timed out.
500	An internal server error has occurred.
503	The capacity of the server has been reached.

MORE INFO   **IIS 7 HTTP STATUS CODES**

The HTTP status codes in IIS 7 have been extended to provide some additional information—they now include decimal point values. For example, the 403 code indicating that access is forbidden includes 403.1 to 403.19, to provide details on why access was forbidden. For more information, see "The HTTP status codes in IIS 7.0" (which also applies to IIS 7.5) in the MSDN Knowledge Base at *http://support.microsoft.com/kb/943891*.

Debugging Remotely

In most scenarios, you debug a website by running it locally on your development machine. This puts the client browser, the development environment (Visual Studio), and the web server on a single machine. In this case, Visual Studio automatically connects to the running site's process and allows you to debug your website. However, there might be occasions when you need to debug an issue against a remote server—when an error appears after a website has been deployed to the production environment, for example. In these scenarios, you will need to enable remote debugging.

Some of the details of enabling remote debugging are specific to the environment. There are slight modifications to the process depending on your domain, credentials, and the operating systems in use by the developer and the server. However, the process of enabling remote debugging is made easier with the Visual Studio Remote Debugging Monitor (msvsmon.exe). You run this tool on the server you intend to debug. The tool can be found inside your 32-bit development environment installation folder (for example, Program Files\Microsoft Visual Studio 10.0\Common7\IDE\Remote Debugger\). If you have installed a 64-bit version of Visual Studio, it will be installed within the Program Files (x86) folder. You can copy the file to a file share or over to the server. You can also install the tool from the Visual Studio DVD set.

When you run the tool, it first determines whether Windows Firewall is configured to allow remote debugging, and prompts you to open the remote debugging port if necessary. You can find a detailed walkthrough of manual configuration of the firewall in the MSDN documentation (see "How to: Manually Configure the Windows Vista Firewall for Remote Debugging," at *http://msdn.microsoft.com/library/bb385831.aspx*). When it is running, the remote debugger (as shown in Figure 8-3) displays debugging events.

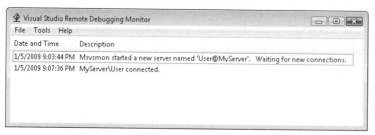

FIGURE 8-3 The Remote Debugging Monitor user interface.

You can use the Remote Debugging Monitor tool to set remote debugging security options on the server. To do so, from the Tools menu, select Options. This opens the Options dialog box, as shown in Figure 8-4. Here you set the server name to a user and a server. Each instance of the remote debugger running on a server has a unique server name. You typically run an instance of the remote debugger for each developer who is doing remote debugging on the server. The Options dialog box also allows you to set the user authentication mode and permissions. Typically this is set to Windows Authentication. You then give the appropriate user in the Active Directory repository access rights to remotely debug.

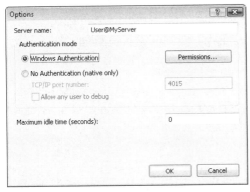

FIGURE 8-4 The Options dialog box for the Remote Debugging Monitor.

You begin a remote debugging session by opening Visual Studio and a solution that includes the code you intend to debug. You can then attach to the server that is running the Remote Debugging Monitor application by selecting Attach To Process from the Debug menu. This opens the Attach To Process dialog box shown in Figure 8-5.

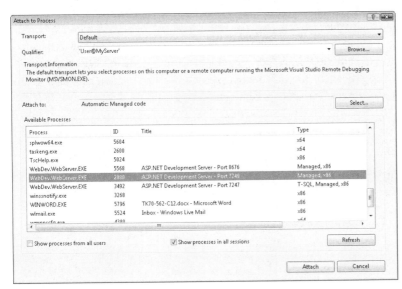

FIGURE 8-5 The Attach To Process dialog box in Visual Studio.

In this dialog box, you set the qualifier to the name of the server running the Remote Debugging Monitor. Recall that this is the server name you set in the Options dialog box for the Remote Debugging Monitor and typically is defined as *User@Server*. You will then see a list of running processes on the server. Select the ASP.NET web server process, and click Attach to start remote debugging. You can then access the server through a browser to cause a breakpoint to fire or an error to occur. Doing so will send you into debug mode in Visual Studio.

EXAM TIP

For the exam, and for real life, know how to configure ASP.NET debugging for a remote Web server running IIS. Be sure you understand the permissions you need and how to attach to a remote process.

For information on debugging an ASP.NET application running on a Server Core installation of Windows Server 2008 R2, see "How to Get Started with ASP.NET Applications on Server Core" at *http://code.msdn.microsoft.com/R2CoreASPNET*.

Debugging Client-Side Script

Visual Studio also allows you to debug client script running in a browser. This is useful if you write a lot of JavaScript and need to walk through the code line by line and use the other features of the debugging toolset.

To get started, you need to enable script debugging support in the browser. To do so, open Windows Internet Explorer and select Tools | Internet Options. Click the Advanced tab of the Internet Options dialog box, as shown in Figure 8-6. Find the Browsing node in the Settings tree and clear the Disable Script Debugging (Internet Explorer) check box.

You can then begin debugging client script. You can get started by setting a breakpoint in your client script and running the site through Visual Studio. You can also manually attach to code running in a browser. You do this by first opening the source code in Visual Studio and then using the Attach To Process dialog box discussed in the previous section to attach to the browser's process. Any error will give you the option to debug.

NOTE DEBUGGING AJAX

For more information on debugging client script that uses the Microsoft Asynchronous JavaScript and XML (AJAX) Library, see "Tracing AJAX Applications" in Lesson 2 of this chapter.

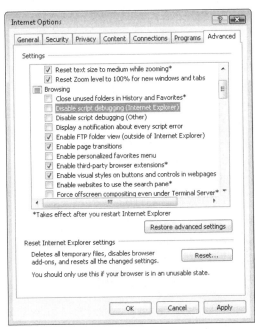

FIGURE 8-6 Using the Internet Options dialog box to enable script debugging for Internet Explorer.

 **Quick Check**

1. In which dialog box do you enable the ASP.NET debugger for a project?

2. What is the name of the element in the Web.config file that you use to define the debug attribute to turn on debugging for your site?

Quick Check Answers

1. You can enable the ASP.NET debugger from your project's Property Pages dialog box.

2. You can turn on debugging by using the debug attribute of the compilation element.

In this practice, you configure a website to support debugging and custom error pages. You also set up Internet Explorer to support script debugging.

> **ON THE COMPANION MEDIA**
>
> If you encounter a problem completing an exercise, you can find the completed projects in the samples installed from this book's companion CD. For more information about the project files and other content on the CD, see "Using the Companion Media" in this book's Introduction.

EXERCISE 1 Configuring a Website for Debugging

In this exercise, you create a website and configure it for debugging.

1. Open Visual Studio. Create a new, file-based website.

2. Open the Web.config file and navigate to the compilation node. Change the default <compilation debug /> setting from false to true.

3. Create a new web form named **Default2.aspx** without a master page. Inside the Page.Load event handler (which you will need to add if you are using Visual Basic), throw an exception. The following code shows an example.

    Sample of Visual Basic Code
    ```
    Protected Sub Page_Load(ByVal sender As Object, _
        ByVal e As System.EventArgs) Handles Me.Load

        Throw New ApplicationException("Example exception.")

    End Sub
    ```

    Sample of C# Code
    ```
    protected void Page_Load(object sender, EventArgs e)
    {
        throw new ApplicationException("Example exception.");
    }
    ```

4. Run the Default2.aspx page in a browser by right-clicking the page in Solution Explorer and choosing View In Browser. This displays the debugging error information, as shown in the example in Figure 8-7.

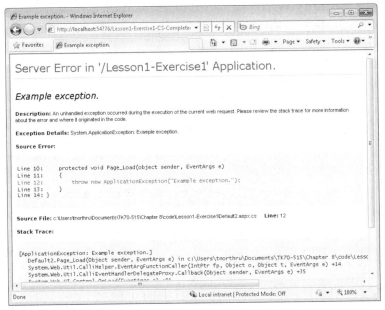

FIGURE 8-7 The ASP.NET debugging error information in a web browser.

EXERCISE 2   Adding a Custom Error Page

In this exercise, you create a custom error page and configure your site to redirect to it for a specific HTTP status code.

1. Open the project you created in the previous exercise. Alternatively, you can open the completed Lesson 1, Exercise 1 project in the samples installed from the CD.

2. Add a new web form to the site. Name this form **ResourceNotFound.aspx**. Add text to the body of this page to display a custom error message to users when they try to access a resource that is not on the web server. You can use the aspxerrorpath query string parameter to display the path of the requested resource in the message.

3. Open the Web.config file again. Add the customErrors section and turn on custom errors. Add an error element for HTTP status code 404 (resource not found). The following markup shows an example.

```
<customErrors mode="On">
  <error statusCode="404" redirect="ResourceNotFound.aspx" />
</customErrors>
```

4. View Default.aspx in a browser again. Notice that the debugging error message is no longer shown. This is because the on setting in the customErrors node indicates that the site should only display custom errors. Next, change the URL in your browser to request fakepage.aspx (which should not exist in your site). This will redirect the browser to the ResourceNotFound.aspx page.

EXERCISE 3   Enabling Script Debugging

In this exercise, you enable client script debugging for a website.

1. Open the project you created in the previous exercise. Alternatively, you can open the completed Lesson 1, Exercise 2 project in the samples installed from the CD.

2. Add a new web form to your site. Name the page **ScriptDebug.aspx**.

3. Add a JavaScript function to the markup. This can be a simple script, as follows.

```
<script language="javascript" type="text/jscript">
  function buttonClick() {
    alert('Button clicked.');
  }
</script>
```

4. Add an HTML button to the page. Set the OnClick event to call the JavaScript function, as follows.

```
<input id="Button1" type="button" value="button" onclick="buttonClick()" />
```

5. Open Internet Explorer and select Tools | Internet Options. Click the Advanced tab and clear the Disable Script Debugging (Internet Explorer) check box. If Internet Explorer is not currently your default browser, configure it as the default to allow client script debugging from Visual Studio. To make it the default browser, click the Make Default button on the Programs tab. Click OK.

6. Return to Visual Studio. Set a breakpoint on the buttonClick function in the markup. You can do so by clicking the margin area in the code editor (on the left side).

7. Run the application from Visual Studio by choosing Start Debugging from the Debug menu (or by simply pressing F5). Navigate to the ScriptDebug.aspx page. Click the button to break into the script debugger.

Lesson Summary

- You turn on debugging for your website in the Web.config file by setting the debug attribute of the compilation element to true. You can also turn on debugging at the individual page level by using the Debug attribute of the @ Page directive.

- You can set a custom error page for your entire site by setting the defaultRedirect attribute of the customErrors element. You can also map specific pages to HTTP status codes by using the errors child element.

- The Remote Debugging Monitor (msvsmon.exe) allows you to configure debugging on a remote server. After it is configured, you need to attach to your site's ASP.NET process from Visual Studio.

- You can set an option in Internet Explorer to allow you to debug client script from Visual Studio. This allows you to use the debugging features of Visual Studio with client-side JavaScript.

Lesson Review

You can use the following questions to test your knowledge of the information in Lesson 1, "Debugging Websites." The questions are also available on the companion CD as a practice test, if you prefer to review them in electronic form.

> **NOTE   ANSWERS**
>
> Answers to these questions and explanations of why each answer choice is correct or incorrect are located in the "Answers" section at the end of the book.

1. You are debugging an application on a test server. You have an issue on a particular page and need to get the error details. You do not want to turn on debugging for the entire site. What actions should you take? (Choose all that apply.)

    A. In the Web.config file, set the debug attribute of the compilation element to true.

    B. In the Web.config file, set the debug attribute of the compilation element to false.

    C. On the page that throws the error, set the debug attribute of the @ Page directive to true.

    D. On the page that throws the error, set the debug attribute of the @ Page directive to false.

2. You are deploying your application to a production environment. You want to redirect users to a default error page if they encounter any unhandled exceptions or HTTP errors within the site. You also want to indicate the user's requested resource on the error page to help with support calls. What actions should you take? (Choose all that apply.)

    A. Set the redirect attribute of the error element to an error page within your site.

    B. Set the defaultRedirect attribute of the customErrors element to an error page within your site.

    C. Use the statusCode query string parameter to retrieve the requested resource to display on the error page.

    D. Use the aspxerrorpath query string parameter to retrieve the requested resource to display on the error page.

3. You are investigating an error that only occurs when the application is deployed to the development or test server. You need to debug this error remotely. What actions should you take? (Choose all that apply.)

   A. Run the Remote Debugging Monitor (Msvsmon.exe) on the development computer that is doing the debugging. Use the tool to define connection rights to the server you want to debug.

   B. Run the Remote Debugging Monitor (Msvsmon.exe) on the server you want to debug. Use the tool to define connection rights for the developer doing the debugging.

   C. In Visual Studio, use the Attach To Process dialog box to attach to the ASP.NET process on the server you want to debug.

   D. In Visual Studio, use the Attach To Process dialog box to attach to the browser process that is running the application you want to debug.

Lesson 2: Troubleshooting Websites

Not all issues can be found by using Visual Studio. Therefore, ASP.NET provides tools with which you can trace and monitor your code as it executes in a test or production environment. These facilities of ASP.NET can be used to troubleshoot and diagnose problems that might otherwise prove impossible to recreate. In addition, these features allow you to examine statistics and usage on your website.

This lesson first covers enabling and configuring tracing in ASP.NET. It then explores how you can monitor a running website.

After this lesson, you will be able to:

- Enable and configure ASP.NET tracing.
- Understand the data that is available through ASP.NET tracing.
- Work with monitoring tools to evaluate a running ASP.NET site.

Estimated lesson time: 20 minutes

Implementing Tracing

Tracing is the process of emitting data about a running application. In ASP.NET, this data is logged to a trace log file that you can access through a web browser. The data provides important information about your site, such as who accessed the site, what the results were, what the HTTP data looked like, and much more. You can also inject your own tracing calls into your code. This data will be emitted alongside the ASP.NET data.

You enable tracing through the Web.config file. You can edit this file manually, or you can use the ASP.NET Web Site Administration Tool (WSAT) to provide an administrator-friendly interface to enable and configure tracing.

Enabling Tracing by Using the WSAT

The following steps show how to enable and configure the trace facility by using the WSAT:

1. Open the WSAT by selecting Website | ASP.NET Configuration from the Visual Studio menu.

2. On the home page, click the Application tab of the WSAT. This will bring up settings for your application.

3. On the Application tab, click Configure Debugging And Tracing (in the lower-right corner). This will display the configuration options for debugging and tracing, as shown in Figure 8-8.

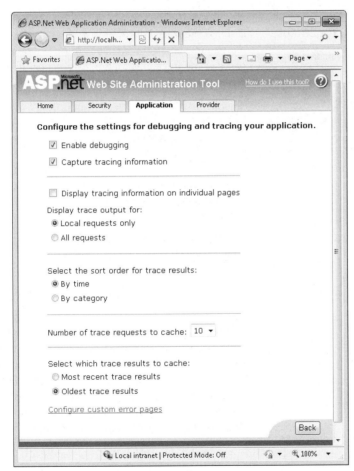

FIGURE 8-8 The debugging and tracing options in the WSAT.

4. Select the Capture Tracing Information check box. This enables the tracing features to be changed as necessary.

As you can see from Figure 8-8, there are many options you can configure with respect to tracing. These options also map to Web.config settings (because that is what the WSAT administers). Table 8-2 describes each of the options, from the perspective of both the WSAT and Web.config.

TABLE 8-2 ASP.NET Trace Settings

WSAT SETTING	WEB.CONFIG SETTING	DESCRIPTION
Capture Tracing Information	enabled	Enables tracing for your application. When this is set to true, the other trace options are also made available.
Display Tracing Information On Individual Pages	pageOutput	Displays the trace information directly on the webpage that is being traced. Depending on the page content, the trace information displays either at the bottom of the webpage or behind the regular webpage content.
Display Trace Output For	localOnly	Designates whether you intend to display tracing just for local requests or for all requests. When set to Local Requests Only, the trace facility operates only with requests from the computer on which the web server is running. The All Requests setting enables tracing for all requests from any computer to the website.
Select The Sort Order For Trace Results	traceMode	Enables sorting of the trace output either by time or by category.
Number Of Trace Requests To Cache	requestLimit	Sets the number of records to hold in the cache (or trace log).
Select Which Trace Results To Cache	mostRecent	Designates whether to store the most recent trace result or the oldest trace results. When set to Most Recent Trace Results, the cache continues to update, holding only the latest results. When set to Oldest Trace Results, as soon as the number of requests has been met, the cache no longer updates until after the website is restarted or the log is cleared.

Enabling Tracing by Using the Web.config File

You can enable tracing manually by editing the Web.config file of an ASP.NET site. You do so by editing attributes (as listed in Table 8-2 in the previous section) of the <trace> element. This element is nested under <configuration><system.web>. The following markup shows an example.

```
<configuration>
  <system.web>
    <trace enabled="true"
      requestLimit="100"
      pageOutput="false"
      traceMode="SortByTime"
      localOnly="false"
      mostRecent="true" />
  <system.web>
</configuration>
```

In the preceding markup, tracing is enabled (enabled="true") for all requests to the server (localOnly="false"). The trace log will cache the most recent 100 requests (requestLimit="100" and mostRecent="true"). The trace log will be sorted by time (traceMode="SortByTime"). The data will only be viewable through the trace log and not on each individual page (pageOutput="false").

Enabling Tracing at the Page Level

You can also enable tracing for specific pages only. This is useful if you do not want to turn on tracing at the site level, but instead enable it only on a page that you are troubleshooting. You enable tracing at the page level by setting the trace attribute of the @ Page directive to true. This attribute is found at the top of the page's markup. The following shows an example.

```
<@Page trace="true" ... />
```

Viewing Trace Data

After ASP.NET trace data has been configured and turned on, you can view the data on each webpage (Trace="true") or view the trace output by navigating to the Trace.axd page on the current website (*http://server/application/trace.axd*). When viewed on the same page, the trace information is appended to the bottom of the page (for pages that use flow layout). Figure 8-9 shows an example.

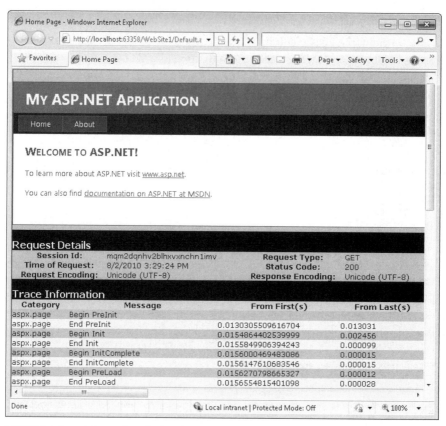

FIGURE 8-9 Trace information displayed on an ASP.NET page.

To view your entire log, you navigate to the Trace.axd page for your site. This page will show a log event if pageOutput is set to true. The first page of the log is a summary page. This page contains a list of trace results that are in the cache. Figure 8-10 shows an example.

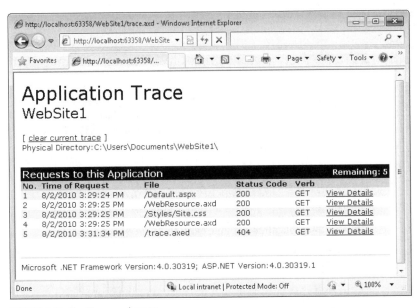

FIGURE 8-10 The Trace.axd page.

You can click one of the cached results to view the details of the trace record for a single page request. These details are similar to the information that is shown on each webpage (as shown previously, in Figure 8-9).

SECURITY ALERT

If you opt to display the trace information on individual pages, the trace information can be displayed on any browser that makes a request. This is a potential security threat, because sensitive information such as server variables will be displayed. Be sure to disable page tracing on production web servers.

The trace result page is separated into sections, as described in Table 8-3. The information in these sections can be very useful when you are trying to identify performance issues and resource usage.

TABLE 8-3 Trace Result Sections

TRACE RESULT SECTION	DESCRIPTION
Request Details	Provides general details about the page request.
Trace Information	Displays performance information related to the webpage's life-cycle events. The From First(s) column displays the running time from when the page request started. The From Last(s) column shows the time elapsed since the previous event.
Control Tree	Displays information about each control on the webpage, such as the size of the rendered controls.
Session State	Displays all session variables and their values.
Application State	Displays all application variables and their states.
Request Cookies Collection	Displays the list of cookies that are passed to the server as part of the request.
Response Cookies Collection	Displays the list of cookies that are passed to the browser as part of the response.
Headers Collection	Displays the list of HTTP headers that are sent to the web server as part of the request.
Form Collection	Displays the list of values that are posted back to the web server.
QueryString Collection	Displays the list of values that are included in the query string.
Server Variables	Displays all server variables.

Emitting Custom Trace Data

You can use the Trace class in the System.Diagnostics namespace to add your own trace messages to the data that is displayed by ASP.NET tracing. This class is exposed as a member of the Page object. This allows you to call Page.Trace (or just Trace). You use the Write method of this object to write a message to the trace log. When doing so, you can provide a category and the message.

The following shows an example of writing to the trace log. Here a message is added to the log when the page is loaded and when a user clicks the button on the page. The category of the message is set to Custom Category. This category allows you to find your message easily. Custom messages are embedded in the Trace Information section of the trace details.

Sample of Visual Basic Code
```vb
Protected Sub Page_Load(ByVal sender As Object, _
  ByVal e As System.EventArgs) Handles Me.Load

  Trace.Write("Custom Category", "Page_Load called")

End Sub

Protected Sub Button1_Click(ByVal sender As Object, _
  ByVal e As System.EventArgs) Handles Button1.Click

  Trace.Write("Custom Category", "Button1_Click called")

End Sub
```

Sample of C# Code
```csharp
protected void Page_Load(object sender, EventArgs e)
{
  Trace.Write("Custom Category", "Page_Load called");
}

protected void Button1_Click(object sender, EventArgs e)
{
  Trace.Write("Custom Category", "Button1_Click called");
}
```

Tracing AJAX Applications

Debugging an AJAX application presents its own issues. You do not have a server process on which to rely. Instead, you have to try to debug the code as it executes in the browser. In the previous section, you saw how to do this. However, AJAX-enabled applications tend to have a lot of client code, so they might present more issues when they are being debugged. For this reason, the Microsoft AJAX Library provides the Sys.Debug client-side namespace.

The tracing you enable on the server is not fired for AJAX partial-page requests. Therefore, you will see nothing in the Trace.axd log for these types of requests. Instead, you must use the features of Sys.Debug to write out trace messages. The Debug class includes the assert, trace, clearTrace, traceDump, and fail methods. These methods can be used to display and manage messages to a trace log based on your needs.

As an example, suppose you write out a message by using Sys.Debug.trace. Of course, your page must include the Microsoft AJAX Library JavaScript file. You make this happen by adding a ScriptManager control to your page. (See Chapter 9, "Working with Client-Side Scripting, AJAX, and jQuery," for more details on working with AJAX.) The following markup shows part of an ASPX page that includes a ScriptManager control and a JavaScript function named button1_onclick. When this function is fired (when the user clicks button1), the trace method is called.

```
<html xmlns="http://www.w3.org/1999/xhtml">
<head id="Head1" runat="server">
  <title>AJAX Trace Example</title>

  <script language="javascript" type="text/javascript">
    function button1_onclick() {
      Sys.Debug.trace("Button1 clicked");
    }
  </script>

</head>
<body>
  <form id="form1" runat="server">
    <div>

    <asp:ScriptManager ID="ScriptManager1" runat="server">
    </asp:ScriptManager>

    <input id="Button1" type="button" value="button"
      onclick="button1_onclick()" />

  </div>
  </form>
</body>
</html>
```

 REAL WORLD

Tony Northrup

Visual Studio 2010 is definitely the best tool for writing and debugging ASP.NET code. When it comes to debugging complex problems in client-side JavaScript, however, you can do better. Visual Studio almost always gives you broad errors that make it difficult to isolate the real problem, and it often highlights code within a library, rather than in your JavaScript.

The most efficient tool I've found for debugging JavaScript is the free Firebug plug-in for the Firefox browser. It provides excellent warnings about inconsistencies in your code (such as a missing quote or bracket), and it gives genuinely useful feedback about problems.

You can view the trace messages displayed by the Microsoft AJAX Library in the Visual Studio Output window. This works if you are using Internet Explorer and Visual Studio, and if you are debugging on the same machine on which the website is running. However, you can also create a TextArea control on the page that includes your JavaScript. If you set the TextArea control's ID to TraceConsole. this tells the Microsoft AJAX Library to display its trace messages to this TextArea for you to view. If the browser you are using for debugging has a debugging console (as the Apple Safari and Opera browsers do), that console can also be used to view the trace messages. Figure 8-11 shows the result of the preceding markup as displayed to the Visual Studio Output window (at the bottom of the screen).

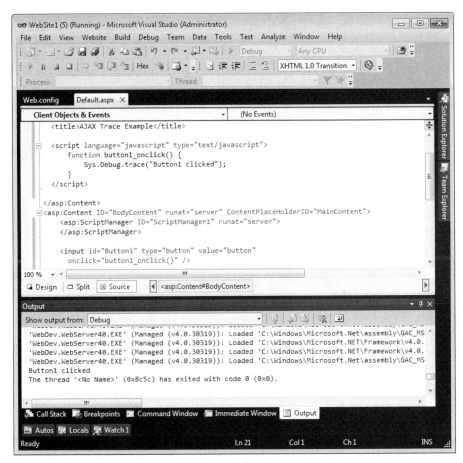

FIGURE 8-11 The Sys.Debug.trace message in the Output window.

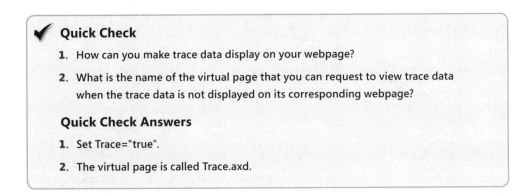

✔ **Quick Check**

1. How can you make trace data display on your webpage?

2. What is the name of the virtual page that you can request to view trace data when the trace data is not displayed on its corresponding webpage?

Quick Check Answers

1. Set Trace="true".

2. The virtual page is called Trace.axd.

Monitoring a Running Web Application

Tracing provides diagnostic information about a page. This can be very useful for trouble-shooting problems with pages in a test environment. However, you often need information about the overall health of your application. You should be able to monitor the application and be notified of various events such as error conditions, security issues, and request failures. You can do so by using the features of ASP.NET health monitoring.

ASP.NET health monitoring provides a set of classes in the System.Web.Management namespace for tracking the health of your application. You can use these classes to create your own events and your own custom event listeners (and viewers). You can also use the default features exposed by these classes to monitor most aspects of any running website. This section focuses on the latter option.

The Health Monitoring Classes

The health monitoring system works by raising and logging ASP.NET events based on your configuration. You enable these events based on what you want to monitor with respect to your application's performance and health. The monitoring occurs in a deployed environment. You can use the features of health monitoring to receive email messages about important activities, log information to the event log, and log information to SQL Server.

The first step in health monitoring is to determine which events to listen for. These events are defined as classes. The classes are based on a class hierarchy that defines the data that is logged with the event. For example, a web health monitoring event class might contain information about the process that is executing your code, the HTTP request, the HTTP response, and error conditions.

You can also use the base web event classes in the System.Web.Management namespace to write your own web events for health monitoring purposes. Table 8-4 lists the key web event classes and their basic use.

TABLE 8-4 The Web Event Classes in ASP.NET

CLASS NAME	DESCRIPTION
WebBaseEvent	The base class for creating your own web events
WebManagement-Event	The base class for creating web events that contain application process information
WebHeartbeatEvent	Serves as a periodic event that raises information about your application at set intervals
WebRequestEvent	The base class that contains web request information
WebApplication-LifetimeEvent	Raised when a significant application event occurs, such as application start or shutdown
WebBaseErrorEvent	The base class for creating error-based events
WebErrorEvent	Used to provide information about an error when it occurs in your application

CLASS NAME	DESCRIPTION
WebRequestErrorEvent	Contains request data for request errors
WebAuditEvent	The base class for creating audit (security) events
WebSuccessAuditEvent	Raised when a successful security operation occurs for your application
WebAuthentication-SuccessAuditEvent	Used to provide information when a successful user authentication occurs on the site
WebFailureAuditEvent	Raised when a failed security operation occurs
WebAuthentication-FailureAuditEvent	Used to provide information when a failed attempt at user authentication occurs on the site
WebViewStateFailure-AuditEvent	Raised when the view state fails to load (typically as a result of tampering)

When you know which events to listen for, the second step is to enable a listener (or log). The ASP.NET health monitoring system defines a set of providers (or listeners) that are used to collect the web event information. These listeners consume the web health events and typically log the event details. You can use the default listeners or write your own by extending the existing WebEventProvider class. The default providers include EventLogWebEventProvider, WmiWebEventProvider, and SqlWebEventProvider. You configure web events and web providers in ASP.NET configuration files, which are discussed next.

Configuring Health Monitoring

To configure health monitoring, you turn on web events and connect them to listeners in the Web.config file. You do so by configuring the <healthMonitoring> element of the <system.web> section of the Web.config file. The <healthMonitoring> element contains the enabled attribute, which you set to true to enable health monitoring. It also contains the heartbeatInterval attribute, which you can set to the number of seconds to wait between raising the WebHeartbeatEvent events. The individual events themselves also contain the minInterval attribute, which works in a similar fashion.

The process of configuring a web event and provider is as follows:

1. Add an eventMappings child element to healthMonitoring. You use the add element to add the web event class you want to use.

2. Add a providers child element to healthMonitoring. This indicates your health monitoring listener(s).

3. Finally, add a rules element to healthMonitoring. You use the add child element of rules to indicate an association between a registered web event and a registered listener.

Fortunately, you do not need to register the default web events and providers. These are already registered for you by the overall configuration file on your server. Therefore, you need only add rules to your Web.config file to turn these events on. As an example, the following configuration turns on the heartbeat and application lifetime events. These events are written to the EventLogProvider.

```
<configuration>
  <system.web>
    <healthMonitoring enabled="true" heartbeatInterval="1">

      <rules>
        <add name="Heart Beat"
          eventName="Heartbeats"
          provider="EventLogProvider"
          profile="Default"/>
        <add name="App Lifetime"
          eventName="Application Lifetime Events"
          provider="EventLogProvider"
          profile="Default"
          minInstances="1" minInterval=""
          maxLimit="Infinite"/>
      </rules>

    </healthMonitoring>
  <system.web>
<configuration>
```

Notice that this configuration requires you to know the configured name of the event class and the provider. You can look up these names in your root configuration file. You can also find them on MSDN in the "healthMonitoring Element (ASP.NET Settings Schema)" article. The default configuration markup is listed there.

Figure 8-12 shows a logged event in Event Viewer. Notice that this event fired when the application unexpectedly shut down. This was the result of the firing of the application lifetime event (WebApplicationLifetimeEvent).

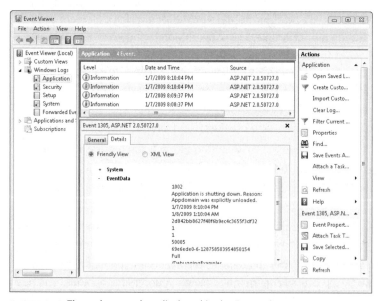

FIGURE 8-12 The web event data displayed in the Event Viewer.

In this practice, you create a basic website and enable ASP.NET tracing. You then execute the site and view the trace details both at the page level and by using the ASP.NET trace listener.

> **ON THE COMPANION MEDIA**
>
> If you encounter a problem completing an exercise, you can find the completed projects in the samples installed from this book's companion CD. For more information about the project files and other content on the CD, see "Using the Companion Media" in this book's Introduction.

EXERCISE Enabling ASP.NET Tracing

In this exercise, you work with ASP.NET tracing to view details about a running page in your site.

1. Open Visual Studio. Create a new, file-based website called **TracingCode**.
2. Open the WSAT from the Visual Studio menu by selecting Website | ASP.NET Configuration.
3. Click the Application tab to display the application settings. Click Configure Debugging And Tracing.
4. Select the Capture Tracing Information check box. This enables tracing for your site. Make the following additional changes on this page:
   - Ensure that the Display Tracing Information On Individual Pages check box is cleared.
   - Set the Display Trace Output For option to Local Requests Only.
   - Set the Select The Sort Order For Trace Results option to By Time.
   - Set Number Of Trace Requests To Cache to 50.
   - Set the Select Which Trace Results To Cache option to Most Recent Trace Results.
   - Close the WSAT when finished.
5. Open the Web.config file. Navigate to the trace element. The trace element should look as follows (notice that the defaults are not listed; only the items that had to be overridden must be specified).

   ```
   <trace
     enabled="true"
     mostRecent="true"
     requestLimit="50" />
   ```

6. Run the website. Refresh the webpage a few times to write more results to the trace log.
7. In the Address bar of the browser, change the URL to access Trace.axd for the site. This will bring up the trace log. You should see an entry for each time you requested the page. Click one of the View Details links to open a record. Notice that the Trace Information section contains the timings for the events in the webpage life cycle. Close the web browser.
8. Open Default.aspx in Visual Studio. Add the Trace="true" attribute to the @ Page directive at the top of the page. Run the site again; notice that the page now includes the trace information written out. Close the web browser.

9. Open the code-behind file for Default.aspx in Visual Studio. Add an event handler for the Page_Load event, the handler for which will already exist in the code-behind file if you are using C#. In the event handler, use Page.Trace to write out a tracing message. Your code should look as follows.

Sample of Visual Basic Code

```
Protected Sub Page_Load(ByVal sender As Object, _
  ByVal e As System.EventArgs) Handles Me.Load

  Trace.Write("Custom Category", "Page.Load called")

End Sub
```

Sample of C# Code

```
protected void Page_Load(object sender, EventArgs e)
{
  Trace.Write("Custom Category", "Page.Load called");
}
```

10. Run the application again. Notice your custom tracing message in the Trace Information section of the page's trace output.

Lesson Summary

- You can use ASP.NET tracing to troubleshoot and diagnose problems with a page in your website. It displays information about the request, the response, and the environment.

- You can use the trace method to display custom trace messages to the trace log.

- An AJAX-enabled page can use the client-side Sys.Debug.trace method to render tracing information to a webpage (by using a TextArea control), to the Visual Studio Output window, or to a browser's debug console.

- ASP.NET provides health monitoring tools (which you'll find in the System.Web. Management namespace) to enable you to monitor a running website. You can configure web events with listeners by using rule child elements of the <healthMonitoring> element inside Web.config.

Lesson Review

You can use the following questions to test your knowledge of the information in Lesson 2, "Troubleshooting Websites." The questions are also available on the companion CD as a practice test, if you prefer to review them in electronic form.

> **NOTE ANSWERS**
>
> Answers to these questions and explanations of why each answer choice is correct or incorrect are located in the "Answers" section at the end of the book.

1. You want to identify which event in the webpage life cycle takes the longest time to execute. How can you accomplish this?

   A. Turn on ASP.NET tracing and run the website. After that, review the trace results.

   B. To each of the life-cycle events, add a line of code that will print the current time.

   C. In the Web.config file, add the monitorTimings attribute and set it to true.

   D. In the website properties, turn on the performance monitor and run the website. After that, open the performance monitor to see the timings.

2. You want to run a trace continuously to enable you to quickly look at the 10 most recent traces from anyone using your website, but you are concerned about filling your hard drive with excessive data. Which of the following settings will accomplish your objective?

   A.
   ```
   <trace
       enabled="false"
       requestLimit="10"
       pageOutput="false"
       traceMode="SortByTime"
       localOnly="true"
       mostRecent="true"
   />
   ```

   B.
   ```
   <trace
       enabled="true"
       requestLimit="10"
       pageOutput="true"
       traceMode="SortByTime"
       localOnly="true"
       mostRecent="true"
   />
   ```

   C.
   ```
   <trace
       enabled="true"
       requestLimit="10"
       pageOutput="false"
       traceMode="SortByTime"
       localOnly="true"
       mostRecent="false"
   />
   ```

   D.
   ```
   <trace
       enabled="true"
       requestLimit="10"
       pageOutput="false"
       traceMode="SortByTime"
       localOnly="false"
       mostRecent="true"
   />
   ```

3. You are interested in examining the data that is posted to the web server. What trace result section can you use to see this information?

   A. The Control Tree section

   B. The Headers Collection section

   C. The Form Collection section

   D. The Server Variables section

4. You want to configure ASP.NET health monitoring to log information every time a user fails to log on to the server. Which web event class should you use?

   A. WebRequestEvent

   B. WebAuditEvent

   C. WebApplicationLifetimeEvent

   D. WebAuthenticationFailureAuditEvent

Lesson 3: Deploying Websites

With Windows applications, you have no choice but to consider deployment; typically, the client needs to be installed on every user's computer. With websites, deployment tends to be an afterthought, because users already have their web browsers installed.

However, developers often need to deploy code to staging and production servers on a regular basis, which can be tedious. In addition, many websites are deployed to multiple web servers simultaneously to provide high availability and performance. Finally, many web developers must release their applications commercially; this means that other people need to be able to deploy them in environments that the developer knows nothing about.

For each of these scenarios, the developer must create a plan to deploy the application and any updates that need to be released in the future. This lesson describes the different techniques available for deploying websites: manually copying files, publishing web applications, creating a Web Deployment Project, creating a Web Setup Project, using the Copy Web tool, and publishing websites.

After this lesson, you will be able to:

- Create a Web Setup Project and use the resulting files to deploy your application.
- Update and deploy websites in environments with multiple developers and servers by using the Copy Web tool.
- Precompile websites by using the Publish Web Site tool.

Estimated lesson time: 60 minutes

Publishing Web Applications

Depending on the scenario, a Microsoft .NET Framework website can be extremely easy to deploy. Websites, by default, are entirely file based. This means that the source code is usually deployed to the server. The server then compiles that code when pages are requested. In this scenario, you can deploy a website to a web server by simply copying the files to the correct directory on the server.

Even if you are deploying a new version of your site, in most cases you can simply overwrite the old files with the new ones. In addition, if you are creating a website that works on a single server and is file based, there is often no real need to run any type of setup process, edit the registry, or add items to the start menu. Configuration settings are defined with the Web.config file, and application code is contained entirely within the website folder structure. This means that you can deploy the entire website by using the simple xcopy shell command; no special deployment software is required.

This simplicity provides a great deal of flexibility in other scenarios, too. If your website is to be deployed to an array of web servers (in which multiple web servers host the same website for scalability and availability), you can use any file-synchronization tool to copy the files between the servers. This allows you to deploy to a master server and have the deployment synchronized across the web farm.

If your website has a database, requires special web server configuration, or needs different configuration settings in a release environment, simply copying files will be insufficient. In these cases, publishing a website typically involves:

- Configuring an application in IIS.
- Copying website files to the web server.
- Setting up a database.
- Configuring the website with the production database connection.
- Modifying other configuration settings, such as disabling detailed error messages.

Visual Studio 2010 includes a new Publish Web dialog box that allows you to configure each of these settings once, and then publish a website to one or more web servers with a single click. This section describes this tool in more detail.

Web.config Transformations

Applications that have different debugging, staging, and release environments typically have different application settings as well. For example, during debugging, an application might use a local file system database. However, in the production environment, the application might connect to a central database running Microsoft SQL Server.

Web.config transformations allow you to create separate Web.config files for different release types. Therefore, you can create debugging, staging, and release versions of the Web.config file with settings specific to each release type. To simplify management, you only need to specify settings that must be added, changed, or removed from the base Web.config file.

By default, Visual Studio adds Web.config transformations for the Debug and Release configurations for new ASP.NET Web Application projects. You can view and edit the transformations from Solution Explorer by expanding the Web.Config node and then double-clicking either Web.Debug.Config or Web.Release.Config. If you add more configurations (such as a staging configuration), you can add an associated transformation by right-clicking Web.config in Solution Explorer and then clicking Add Config Transformations.

The sections that follow describe the syntax for adding, replacing, and removing settings. For detailed information about more complex transformations, read "Web.config Transformation Syntax for Web Application Project Deployment" at *http://msdn.microsoft.com/en-us/library/dd465326.aspx.*

ADDING A SETTING

Web.config transformations contain only those settings that should be different from the standard Web.config file. To add a new setting to a Web.config file that is generated when publishing a web application, simply add the setting to the Web.config transformation file. For example, defining the following Web.Release.Config file will add the connection string to the Web.config file when you publish the web application by using the Release setting:

```
<configuration>
  <connectionStrings>
    <add name="MyDatabase" xdt:Transform="Insert"
        connectionString="data source=.\SQLEXPRESS;Integrated
          Security=SSPI;AttachDBFilename=|DataDirectory|\mydb.mdf;User Instance=true"
          providerName="System.Data.SqlClient" />
  </connectionStrings>
</configuration>
```

REPLACING A SETTING

If you need to define different settings for the same value in your base Web.config file and in a Web.config transformation, add the element to the Web.config transformation and specify the xdt:Transform="Replace" property. Any settings defined within the element will replace those in the base Web.config file when your web application is published.

For example, to replace the settings for custom errors so that the release version of your web application does not display detailed error information to remote users, you could add the following code to the Web.Release.Config file. Notice the xdt:Transform property in bold.

```
<configuration>
  <system.web>
      <customErrors defaultRedirect="GenericError.htm"
        mode="RemoteOnly" xdt:Transform="Replace">
        <error statusCode="500" redirect="InternalError.htm"/>
      </customErrors>
  </system.web>
</configuration>
```

You can use the xdt:Locator property to selectively replace settings when a property matches a specified value. Set the value of xdt:Locator to a conditional method call. For example, to verify that one of the properties you specify must match the property in the base Web.config file, use the Match method. The following example would replace an <add> connection string element only if the name property matched exactly.

```
<configuration>
    <connectionStrings>
      <add name="MyDB"
        connectionString="Data Source=ReleaseSQLServer;
          Initial Catalog=MyReleaseDB;Integrated Security=True"
        xdt:Transform="SetAttributes" xdt:Locator="Match(name)"/>
    </connectionStrings>
</configuration>
```

If you were to remove the xdt:Locator property, the Web.config transformation would replace all connection strings.

REMOVING A SETTING

You can remove an attribute by using the RemoveAttributes() method and specifying the name of the attribute to remove as the parameter. For example, to remove the <debug> attribute from the <compilation> section, you would add the following code to your Web.Release.Config file:

```
<configuration>
  <system.web>
    <compilation xdt:Transform="RemoveAttributes(debug)" />
  </system.web>
</configuration>
```

Configuring Deployment

You can deploy databases along with your web application. To configure the database to be deployed, right-click the project in Solution Explorer and then click Package/Publish Settings. Then click Package/Publish SQL. The Package/Publish SQL tab appears, as shown in Figure 8-13.

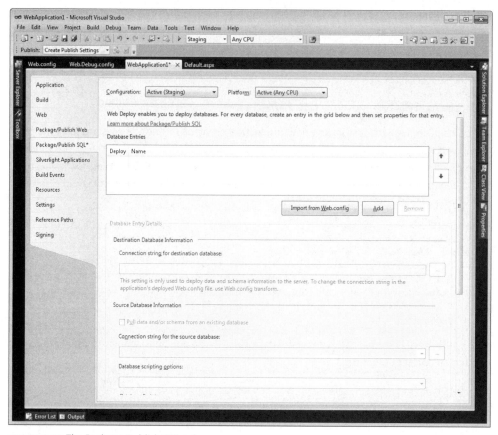

FIGURE 8-13 The Package/Publish SQL tab.

From this tab, click Import From Web.config to automatically configure any databases you have added to the <connectionStrings> section. For databases not in the Web.config file, click the Add button to configure a database to be deployed, and then type a connection string or click the ellipses to connect to the database.

If the database does not yet exist on the server to which you are deploying your web application, select the Pull Data And/Or Schema From An Existing Database check box to have Visual Studio create a database schema and optionally populate the database with data. Then configure the connection string for the source database from which Visual Studio will create the new database. Click the Database Scripting Options list to select whether to deploy the schema, the data, or both. Finally, you can add SQL scripts to perform additional, custom database configuration.

After you have configured the database, you can configure additional deployment settings by selecting the Package/Publish Web tab (as shown in Figure 8-14).

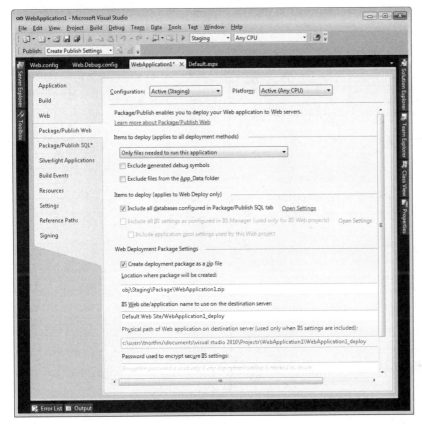

FIGURE 8-14 The Package/Publish Web tab.

If you configured databases for deployment, select the Include All Databases Configured In Package/Publish SQL Tab check box. If your application requires settings configured in IIS manager (but not defined in Web.config), select the Include All IIS Settings As Configured In IIS Manager check box. This setting also enables you to specify the Physical Path Of Web Application On Destination Server check box. The remaining settings define whether Visual Studio will create a .zip file containing all of your project files and where it will be stored.

Publishing a Website

After you have configured the publishing settings, you can publish a web application by right-clicking the project in Solution Explorer and then clicking Publish. Visual Studio displays the Publish Web dialog box, as shown in Figure 8-15.

FIGURE 8-15 The Publish Web dialog box.

You can use the Publish Web dialog box to define the publication settings and save them as a publish profile by defining the profile name. The individual settings are:

- **Publish Method**   This is the communications protocol that Visual Studio will use to connect to the web server. Web Deploy uses HTTPS (HTTP Secure), FTP uses unencrypted File Transfer Protocol (FTP) communications, FPSE uses encrypted FTP communications, and File System uses standard network file sharing. Any of the settings allows you to deploy files. If you choose Web Deploy, you can publish IIS web server settings, database schema and data, database scripts, security settings, and more.

- **Service URL**   This is the URL of the remote server's web service, which the web server's systems administrator will provide for you. If the hosting provider supports the Windows Management Service, the path will include MsDeploy.axd.

- **Site/Application**   This is the name of the IIS website, which can include a virtual directory.

- **Mark As IIS Application On Destination**   Select this check box if your website is the root of an IIS website or if the virtual directory should act as a separate application from the parent folder.
- **Leave Extra Files On Destination**   Clear this check box to delete existing files in the web server virtual directory.
- **Credentials**   This allows you to provide credentials to connect to the web server.

After you have defined the settings, click the Save button to save the profile. Click Publish to deploy the web application to the remote server.

After saving profile settings, you can publish the website by using the Web One-Click Publish toolbar; simply select the profile and then click the Publish Web button on the toolbar.

Deployment Packages

If you will not be deploying the website directly, you can package it (along with the database and settings) into a .zip file that a systems administrator can install. After configuring publishing for the project, right-click the project in Solution Explorer and then click Build Deployment Package. Visual Studio generates several files in the folder you specified in the Location Where Package Will Be Created box in the Package/Publish Web dialog box:

- *<Application>*.zip   Your web application's files, database, and settings.
- *<Application>*.deploy.cmd   The script that the IIS systems administrator will run, with administrative credentials, on the web server. The web server must have Web Deploy (MSDeploy.exe) installed. For more information about Web Deploy, go to *http://go.microsoft.com/?linkid=9278654*.
- *<Application>*.deploy-readme.txt   The traditional "readme" file that administrators refer to before installing. You can edit this just like any text file to provide customized instructions.
- *<Application>*.SourceManifest.xml   Contains settings to be added to the IIS manifest. You or the administrator can edit this prior to deployment.
- *<Application>*.SetParameters.xml   Contains IIS parameters to be added during installation. You or the administrator can edit this prior to deployment.

You must provide all of the files to the administrator, who must keep them in the same folder. You cannot deploy the .zip file alone.

Web Deployment Projects

After the release of Visual Studio 2010, Microsoft released the Web Deployment Projects tool to extend Visual Studio 2010 by adding a user interface to manage build configurations, merging, and using pre-build and post-build tasks. Web Deployment Projects work with both ASP.NET web applications and websites.

Web Deployment Projects provide several capabilities not provided by other deployment technologies:

- The ability to precompile websites.
- The ability to merge all files into a single assembly, merge folders into individual assemblies, or create separate assemblies for each page and control. If you merge content into assemblies, users with access to the web server will not be able to directly access your source code.
- Strong naming and delayed signing of assemblies.

As with publishing websites, Web Deployment Projects allow you to change the Web.config file for the release environment and create IIS virtual directories.

To download the Web Deployment Projects tool, search the Microsoft Download Center for "Web Deployment Projects RTW" or go to *http://www.microsoft.com/downloads/en/details.aspx?FamilyID=89f2c4f5-5d3a-49b6-bcad-f776c6edfa63*. After you have the tool installed, you can add a Web Deployment Project to a website or web application by clicking the solution in Solution Explorer and then clicking Add Web Deployment Project. Then double-click the Web Deployment Project to edit its properties, as shown in Figure 8-16.

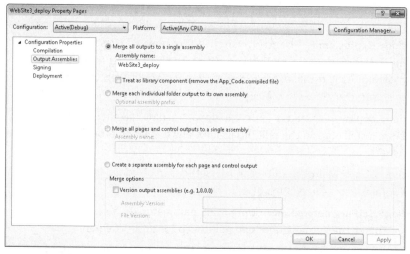

FIGURE 8-16 Web Deployment Project properties.

After configuring the Web Deployment Project, right-click it in Solution Explorer and then click Build to generate the assembly or assemblies.

EXAM TIP

For the real world, know that you need to use Web Deployment Projects when you do not want to store the source code on the web server or when management requires signed assemblies. Because it is an add-on for Visual Studio 2010, you probably will not see any questions about it on the exam, however.

Web Setup Projects

Publishing websites gives you a great deal of control over the website configuration while still providing a high level of automation. However, it requires administrators to have specially configured the web server to allow you to publish the website. Even if you create a package for the administrators to perform the installation, administrators will not be able to easily take advantage of a software distribution infrastructure that requires Microsoft Windows Installer (MSI) packages. Finally, Visual Studio does not precompile published websites.

The sections that follow describe how to create a Web Setup Project, which provides the highest level of flexibility for deploying a website. Although Web Setup Projects are more complex for the developer, they allow you to generate an MSI package, precompile a website, and perform virtually any setup task that your application might require. This section describes how to configure deployment properties, how to configure deployment conditions, and how to deploy websites that meet the requirements of the aforementioned scenarios.

Creating a Web Setup Project

Web Setup Projects are very similar to the standard setup projects used for Windows Forms applications; however, Web Setup Projects provide specialized capabilities that are required by websites. To add a Web Setup Project to a website, follow these steps:

1. Open your website in Visual Studio.

2. From the File menu (or by right-clicking your solution in Solution Explorer), select Add, and then select New Project to launch the Add New Project dialog box.

3. Under Installed Templates, expand Other Project Types, expand Setup And Deployment, and then select Visual Studio Installer. From the list of available templates, select Web Setup Project. In the Name text box, type a name for your project. An example of the Add New Project dialog box is shown in Figure 8-17.

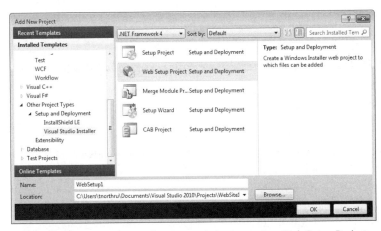

FIGURE 8-17 Adding a new project to a website to create a Web Setup Project.

4. After you have created a new Web Setup Project, Visual Studio adds the project to your solution and displays the File System editor. The typical next step is to create a project output group by right-clicking the Web Application Folder, selecting Add, and then selecting Project Output. In the Add Project Output Group dialog box, you select the project to deploy, the Content Files option, and the configuration (which is Active by default). This ensures that your setup project will deploy the contents of the selected project.

After you have created a Web Setup Project, you can add more folders, files, assemblies, and configuration settings that are not part of your project output to the Web Setup Project. This might be necessary if, for example, you have a separate folder containing images that you have not added to your website project, or if you need to define registry values.

Building a Web Setup Project

Web Setup Projects are not automatically built when you build or run your website. You must manually select the Web Setup Project in Solution Explorer and choose Build. You can do so by right-clicking the project or by using the Build menu.

When you build the setup project, Visual Studio validates your code in the website. It then builds an MSI file and packages each element of your site in the MSI. You can follow the build process in Visual Studio in the Output window (View | Output). The script in the Output windows shows you each step and where the MSI file is generated. By default, the file is placed in the folder that contains your solution file. Figure 8-18 shows an example of a process as shown in the Output window.

FIGURE 8-18 An MSI build in the Output window of Visual Studio.

Many websites do not require custom configuration. In these cases, you can simply build your MSI file and be ready to deploy. However, more complex scenarios include dependencies (such as particular operating system versions or service packs), custom registry entries, or administrator configuration. Web Setup Projects allow you to deploy websites that meet these requirements. The sections that follow help you with each of these specific scenarios.

Creating Launch Conditions

A launch condition is used to define the server requirements for your application installation. For example, you can check for specific versions of Windows or verify that specific service packs are present before you allow an installation. The web setup template includes the IIS launch condition. This searches for the presence of the correct version of IIS and displays an error message to users if this version is not present, as shown in Figure 8-19.

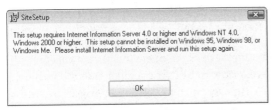

FIGURE 8-19 The Launch Conditions error message.

To create and manage launch conditions, you use the Launch Conditions editor in Visual Studio. You can access this tool by selecting your project in Visual Studio and then clicking the View menu. You will see an Editor submenu that contains several setup editors, including those for Registry, File System, File Types, User Interface, Custom Actions, and Launch Conditions.

Selecting the Launch Conditions submenu opens the Launch Conditions editor, as shown in Figure 8-20. Notice that you right-click the Launch Conditions folder to add a new condition (this is discussed more fully in the next section).

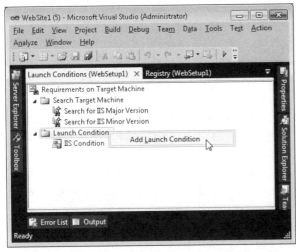

FIGURE 8-20 Using the Launch Conditions editor to configure requirements for a target computer.

There are two main branches of the Launch Conditions editor: Search Target Machine and Launch Conditions. Each is described here:

- **Search Target Machine**   This branch allows you to define the criteria to search for prior to installation. By default, this node contains nodes for searching for major and minor versions of IIS. You can add file, registry, and Windows Installer search conditions. Typically, you pair a search condition that determines whether a change is necessary with a launch condition that performs the change.

- **Launch Conditions**   This branch allows you to create new launch conditions that define conditions that must be met prior to installation. These conditions can be based on search conditions or other criteria (such as the operating system version). A launch condition can provide a useful message to the user if a requirement is missing. It can then automatically retrieve a webpage. By default, Web Setup Projects include conditions for ensuring the presence of the correct version of IIS (later than version 7, for example).

Typically, you must add an item to each of these two nodes to require a single component as part of your installation. For example, if you want to verify that a specific DLL is present, you must create a search condition under Search Target Machine and store the result of the search in a property. You then create a launch condition that uses the search condition's property. If the required condition is not met (if the file is missing), you specify an error message to be displayed to the user. You can also choose to add a URL that directs the user to the required component for download.

ADDING A SIMPLE SEARCH CONDITION

You can add both search and launch conditions manually by right-clicking the appropriate folder and choosing an item to add. This allows you to create both search and launch conditions at a granular level and decide how to connect them.

To add a basic search condition, start by right-clicking the Search Target Machine node in the Launch Conditions editor. You will have three search condition types to choose from: Add File Search, Add Registry Search, and Add Windows Installer Search. Each is a different search type. Depending on your selection, different property values must be set. The following provides an overview of each search type's options.

- **File Search**   This search type allows you to define a search for a file. You set FileName to the name of the file you are searching for, Folder to the name of the folder in which to search, and Property to a variable name to be used for tracking the results of the search.

- **Registry Search**   This search type allows you to specify a registry search. You set the Root property to a place to start looking in the registry, RegKey to a registry key to search for, and the Value property to a value you expect to be set for the specified key. You store the results of your search in the Property property as a variable name that can be used in a related launch condition.

- **Windows Installer Search**   This search type allows you to search for a registered component. You set the ComponentId property to the globally unique identifier (GUID) of the component for which you are searching. You set the Property property to a variable that indicates the results of your search.

You can also rename your search and launch conditions to something that makes sense to your specific scenario.

ADDING A SIMPLE LAUNCH CONDITION

You can manually add a launch condition that must be met before your website can be installed. To do so, you right-click the Launch Conditions folder, and then select Add Launch Condition.

With the new launch condition selected, you access the Properties window to configure your launch condition. You can set the Condition property to match the Property value of a search condition or to specify a different condition entirely. To allow the user to download software to resolve the launch condition, provide a URL in the InstallUrl property. In the Message property, type a message to be displayed to the person installing your website if a condition is not met.

You can configure launch conditions to require specific operating system versions, specific service pack levels, and other criteria by setting the Condition property to an environment variable or keyword and using both an operand and a value. Table 8-5 lists some common launch conditions.

TABLE 8-5 Windows Installer Launch Conditions

CONDITION	DESCRIPTION
VersionNT	The version number for operating systems based on Windows NT, including Windows 2000, Windows XP, and Windows Server 2003
Version9X	The version number for early Windows consumer operating systems, including Windows 95, Windows 98, and Windows Millennium Edition
ServicePackLevel	The version number of the operating system service pack
WindowsBuild	The build number of the operating system
SystemLanguageID	The default language identifier for the system
AdminUser	The tool that determines whether the user has administrative privileges
PhysicalMemory	The size of the installed RAM in megabytes
IISMAJORVERSION	The major version of IIS, if installed
IISMINORVERSION	The minor version of IIS, if installed

To evaluate environment variables, preface the variable name with a % symbol, as this example illustrates.

```
%HOMEDRIVE = "C:" (verify that the home drive is C)
```

To simply check a property for a specific value, you can use the = operator, as the following example shows.

```
IISVERSION = "#6" (check for IIS 6.0)
VersionNT = 500 (check for Windows 2000)
```

You can also check for ranges.

```
IISVERSION >= "#7" (check for IIS 4.0 or later)
Version9X <= 490 (check for Windows Me or earlier)
```

You can also check for multiple conditions by using Boolean operators: Not, And (which returns true if both values are true), Or (which returns true if either value is true), Xor (which returns true if exactly one value is true), Eqv (which returns true if both values are the same), and Imp (which returns true if the left term is false or the right term is true). The following example demonstrates a Boolean operator.

```
WindowsBuild=2600 AND ServicePackLevel=1 (check for Windows XP with Service Pack 1)
```

CREATING PREGROUPED LAUNCH CONDITIONS

You can also create pregrouped search and launch condition sets for common scenarios. Doing so simply creates both a search and a launch condition, with both items preconfigured to work together. You simply need to adjust their properties according to your needs. To create a grouped launch condition, you right-click the root node in the Launch Conditions editor (Requirements On Target Machine) and select one of the following:

- Add File Launch Condition
- Add Registry Launch Condition
- Add Windows Installer Launch Condition
- Add .NET Framework Launch Condition
- Add Internet Information Services Launch Condition

As an example, adding file-based conditions (such as DLL conditions) is a common practice. The following steps walk through the creation of a file-based, pregrouped launch condition:

1. In the Launch Conditions editor, right-click the Requirements On Target Machine root node. Select Add File Launch Condition to get started.

   The Launch Conditions editor adds a search condition (Search For File1) to the Search Target Machine node and a launch condition (Condition1) to the Launch Conditions node. The new search condition's Property property value has a default name of FILEEXISTS1. This value links it to the Condition property of the launch condition.

2. You can rename both the new search condition and the new launch condition so that the names indicate the file you are searching for.

   Figure 8-21 shows an example of both conditions added to the Launch Conditions editor. Notice that the Search For File1 condition is selected and its Properties window is displayed. Notice that the Property property is set to FILEEXISTS1.

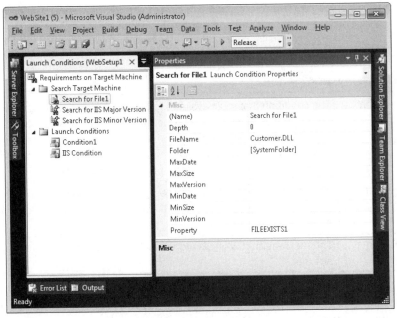

FIGURE 8-21 The file search criterion and related condition.

3. In Figure 8-21, notice that there are several search condition properties in the Properties window. For a file search, you typically configure these properties as described in Table 8-6.

TABLE 8-6 File Search Condition Properties

PROPERTY	DESCRIPTION
FileName	The name of the file to look for. Just specify the file name with its extension, not the folder.
Folder	The folder in which to search for the file. Here you can select a special folder such as [CommonFilesFolder] or [WindowsFolder]. You can also hardcode a direct path to the file. You can search subfolders by specifying the Depth field.
Depth	The number of nested folders within the specified folder to search.
MinDate, MaxDate	The minimum and maximum last modified date of the file.
MinSize, MaxSize	The minimum and maximum size of the file.
MinVersion, MaxVersion	The minimum and maximum version of the file.
Property	The name of the property that stores the results of this search. You specify this property name in the corresponding launch condition.

4. Next, you select the new launch condition and view its Properties window. The properties are typically configured as described in Table 8-7.

TABLE 8-7 Launch Condition Properties

PROPERTY	DESCRIPTION
Condition	The condition that must evaluate to true for installation to continue. By default, this is the name of a property assigned to a search condition, and if the search finds the required file or other object, the launch condition is fulfilled. You can specify more complex conditions to check for operating system version, service pack levels, and other criteria.
InstallUrl	The URL to be retrieved by the setup project if the launch condition is not met. The user can access this resource to install the required component. This is an optional setting.
Message	The message that is displayed to the user if the launch condition is not met.

In this example, the setup project would look for the dependent file as configured in the search condition. The launch condition would then execute and throw an error if the file is not found.

Writing to the Registry as Part of Deployment

Storing information in the registry used to be the preferred way to store application settings. With the .NET Framework, the best practice for configuring .NET Framework applications is to store settings in configuration files. However, there might still be times when you need to add registry entries during setup (although such situations are rare). For example, you might need to configure an aspect of the operating system or another application.

To configure a Web Setup Project to add a registry entry during setup, follow these steps:

1. In Solution Explorer, select your setup project.

2. From the View menu, select Editor, and then select Registry. The Registry editor opens.

3. The core folders of the registry are shown by default. To add a registry setting in a nested key, you need to add each nested key to the editor. For example, to add a setting to HKEY_LOCAL_MACHINE\SOFTWARE\Microsoft\ASP.NET\, you need to add the SOFTWARE, Microsoft, and ASP.NET keys to the HKEY_LOCAL_MACHINE hive in the Registry Settings editor.

4. Right-click the key to which you want to add a setting, select New, and then select String Value, Environment String Value, Binary Value, or DWORD Value. Type the name of the value, and then press Enter.

5. To define the value, select the registry value, view the Properties window, and set the Value property. To make the installation of the value conditional, define the Condition property.

Figure 8-22 shows an example of the Registry editor in Visual Studio.

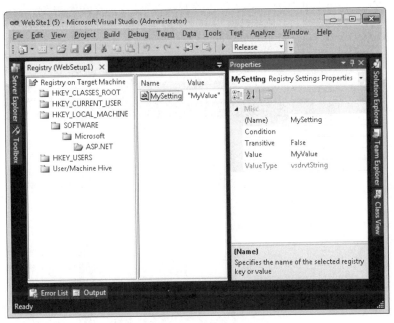

FIGURE 8-22 Adding a registry entry to the deployment process.

By default, registry keys are not removed when an application is uninstalled. To automatically remove a registry key during uninstallation, select the key and view the Properties window. Then set the DeleteAtUninstall property to true.

Adding a Custom Setup Page

Administrators responsible for deploying and managing your websites can customize settings by editing your Web.config file. To enable simpler configuration at setup time, you can add custom setup wizard pages. With these pages, you can prompt users to custom-configure information and then provide that information as parameters for custom actions. When combined, custom setup wizard pages and custom actions enable you to perform the following types of tasks at setup time:

- **Display a license agreement** The Web Setup Project template provides a dialog box template for requiring the user to accept a license agreement.
- **Modify settings in the Web.config file** You can use user input to modify configuration settings without requiring administrators to know how to configure an Extensible Markup Language (XML) file.
- **Perform custom configuration** You can use a custom configuration to prompt the user for information that will be stored in the registry or in another unusual location.
- **Activate or register your application** You can prompt the user for a product key or registration information. Prompts can specify either required or optional responses.

To add a custom setup wizard page to your Web Setup Project, you use the User Interface editor (View | Editor | User Interface). The User Interface editor displays the different setup phases for both standard and administrative installations of your application. Figure 8-23 shows the default view of the User Interface editor.

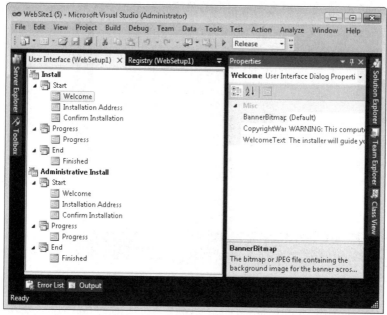

FIGURE 8-23 Using the User Interface editor to add pages to a setup wizard.

To add a custom setup page, you right-click the setup phase to which you want to add, and then select Add Dialog. Normally you add dialog boxes to the Start phase under the Install node. The Add Dialog window, shown in Figure 8-24, shows you the dialog boxes that can be added to the selected installation setup.

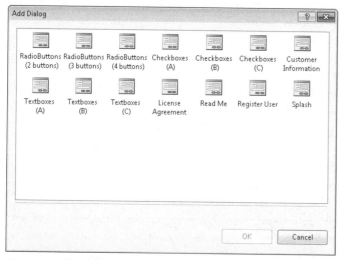

FIGURE 8-24 The Add Dialog setup pages.

The Administrative Install node is more restrictive. There you can add only a splash page, a license agreement page, or a readme page.

Each dialog box template allows you to collect a different type of information during setup. You can customize these dialog boxes only by hiding some controls and displaying different labels.

You customize these controls through the Properties window. There you can configure all aspects of a dialog box; Visual Studio does not provide a designer. To control the information for which a dialog box prompts the user, edit the labels and property names for the dialog box. For the text box and radio button types of dialog boxes, you can configure the label for each field (for example, Edit1Label or Button1Label), the name in which the value is to be stored (for example, Edit1Property or ButtonProperty), and the default value (for example, Edit1Value or DefaultValue). The License Agreement template allows you to specify a license agreement file, and the Splash template allows you to display a bitmap file.

You can also control the order in which your dialog boxes are shown to a user during setup. To do so, right-click a dialog box node in the editor, and then click Move Up or Move Down. You can delete a step in the process by right-clicking the step and then selecting Delete.

When you run the Web Setup Project, your custom dialog boxes appear as setup wizard pages. If you configured pages to collect custom information from users, you can reference that data in custom actions, as described in the next section.

Adding Custom Actions to Your Deployment

Web Setup Projects provide a great deal of flexibility and can meet most setup requirements. If you have more demanding requirements, such as submitting registration information to a web service or validating a product key, you can add custom actions to your setup project. Custom actions can run in any of the four phases of setup:

- **Install** This phase performs the bulk of the work done during setup by adding the files and creating the configuration settings that are required to run your application.
- **Commit** After the Install phase is complete and all of the changes that are required to run your application have been made, the Commit phase finalizes these changes. After the Commit phase is complete, setup cannot be rolled back, and the application must be uninstalled with Add Or Remove Programs if removal is required.
- **Rollback** The Rollback phase runs only if setup fails or is cancelled. In such a case, the Rollback phase occurs instead of the Commit phase and removes any new files or settings.
- **Uninstall** This phase removes files and settings from the computer when the application is removed with Add Or Remove Programs. Often, uninstall routines leave settings and databases in place so that they can be restored if the application is later reinstalled.

You add a custom action to your setup project through the Custom Actions editor. You can access this editor by first selecting your setup project in Solution Explorer and then selecting View | Editor | Custom Actions.

The Custom Actions editor displays the four setup phases. You can right-click the phase to which you want to add a custom action. You then select Add Custom Action. Doing so launches the Select Item In Project dialog box. From here you can choose to add a custom .exe or script file that will execute at the appropriate phase of deployment. If you add more than one custom action to a single phase, you can rearrange the custom actions by right-clicking an action and then clicking Move Up or Move Down.

Deploying Web Applications by Using a Web Setup Project

After you configure your Web Setup Project and build it with Visual Studio, you are ready to deploy it to an application server. To do so, you need to use the files generated as part of the build process. There are typically two generated to the target build directory for Web Setup Projects: an .exe file and an MSI file. These files are described in more detail here:

- **Setup.exe** This is an executable file that installs the files and settings you added to your Web Setup Project. When the file is being run, the setup wizard guides the user through the installation process and prompts for any required configuration settings, such as the website, virtual directory, and application pool (or process). Figure 8-25 shows an example.

FIGURE 8-25 Web Setup Projects use a setup wizard to install a website.

- **<WebSetupProjectName>.msi** This is the Windows Installer file that contains any files you added to your Web Setup Project. The user can install this file by double-clicking it and launching the setup wizard. This is equivalent to running the Setup.exe file. Alternatively, network administrators can distribute the MSI file by using Active Directory software distribution.

Although most users are probably more familiar with using Setup.exe to install an application, the Windows Installer file is smaller, far more versatile, and familiar to most systems administrators.

Deploying Web Applications by Using the Copy Web Tool

Web Setup Projects are useful if you are providing a website to many users or to an administrative team. However, if you are responsible for updating the website, it might be impractical to log on to the web server, copy over an installation, and run the Windows Installer package each time you make an update to the site. This is especially true if you frequently deploy to a development or test server.

For some development scenarios, you might be able to edit the website directly on the web server. However, changes you make are immediately implemented on that server. Of course, this includes any bugs that might be lurking in the new code.

There are many scenarios in which you simply need to copy changes between two servers. These might be changes from your development environment up to staging, or even from staging to production, in some limited scenarios. In these cases, you can use the Copy Web tool to publish changes between any two web servers.

The Copy Web tool can copy individual files or an entire website. You can select a source and a remote site and move files between them. You can also use the tool to synchronize files. This involves copying only changed files and detecting possible versioning conflicts in which the same file on both the source and the remote site have been separately edited. The Copy Web tool, however, does not merge changes within a single file; it only does complete file copies.

You launch the Copy Web tool from Visual Studio. To do so, you typically open the website you intend to use as the source (from which to copy). You can then right-click the site in Solution Explorer and choose Copy Web Site. This launches the Copy Web tool, as shown in Figure 8-26.

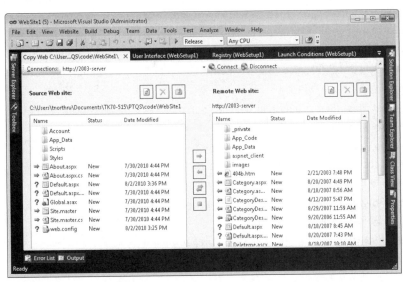

FIGURE 8-26 Using the Copy Web tool to synchronize two websites.

The Copy Web tool displays two panes: Source Web Site and Remote Web Site. The source website is the site from which you want to copy. The remote website is the copy-to site or destination. To set up a remote website, you must create a connection by clicking Connect at the top of the tool. This launches the Open Web Site dialog box, which allows you to find a website. There are four options for navigating to a remote website:

- **File system**   This option provides a destination website on a local hard drive or a shared folder. A network drive connected to a shared folder on the remote web server is the fastest way to transfer a website to a server on your intranet. You must have previously configured the website on the server and shared the website folder. This technique transfers your source code across the network in clear text unless you have network-layer encryption, such as that provided by Internet Protocol security (IPsec).

- **Local IIS**   This provides a destination website running within IIS on your local computer. You can use this interface to create a new website on your local server.

- **FTP site**   This provides a destination remote website for which the server is configured to run an FTP server and allow uploads and downloads to the website folder. You must have previously configured the website on the server and shared the website folder. This technique transfers your user credentials and your source code across the network in clear text, and therefore is not recommended.

- **Remote site**   This provides an interface with which you can transfer files to and from a remote website by using HTTP, if you have configured the web server to allow this type of update. You can use this interface to create a new website on your server. To prevent your source code from being sent across the network in clear text, configure the website with a Secure Sockets Layer (SSL) certificate and select the Connect Using Secure Sockets Layer check box in the Open Web Site dialog box.

Visual Studio will save configured connections for future use. After the connection has been established, you can copy or synchronize files between the source and the remote website in several different ways:

- **Copy individual files**   Select files in either the source or the remote website, and then click the directional Copy Selected Files buttons.

- **Copy the entire site**   Right-click the Source Web Site pane, and then select Copy Site To Remote. To copy the Remote Web Site to the source website, right-click the Remote Web Site pane, and then select Copy Site To Source.

- **Synchronize individual files**   Select files in either the source or the remote website, and then click Synchronize Selected Files.

- **Synchronize the entire site**   Right-click the Source Web Site pane, and then select Synchronize Site.

When you are copying or synchronizing files, versioning conflicts might arise if another developer modifies the remote copy of a file that you edited. Visual Studio doesn't have the capability to merge or analyze these changes. Therefore, the Copy Web tool simply notifies you of the conflict and lets you choose whether to overwrite the remote file with your local file, overwrite your local file, or not overwrite either file. Unless you know exactly what changed on a file, you should never overwrite it. Instead, you should analyze the file, determine what changed, and attempt to manually merge the changes. Otherwise, you might overwrite a coworker's development effort.

Precompiling and Publishing ASP.NET Websites

Projects created with the ASP.NET Web Site template are compiled by the web server the first time a user requests a page from a new or updated website. Compiling doesn't usually take long (often less than a second or two), but the first few webpage requests are delayed while the website is compiled. To avoid this delay, you can precompile your website before you publish it to a server.

> **NOTE PRECOMPILING WEB APPLICATIONS**
>
> This section applies to ASP.NET websites, but not to ASP.NET web applications. Visual Studio always precompiles code files contained within projects created with the ASP.NET Web Application template.

To precompile and publish a website, follow these steps:

1. Open the website you want to precompile and publish. Next, right-click your website in Solution Explorer and select Publish Web Site. Alternatively, you can select the Build menu and then choose Publish Web Site.

2. In the Publish Web Site dialog box, specify a location to which to publish. If you click the ellipsis button (...), you can browse the file system, local IIS, an FTP site, or a remote site, exactly as you would if you were using the Copy Web tool.

3. In the Publish Web Site dialog box, select your options:

    - **Allow This Precompiled Site To Be Updatable**   This check box, when selected, specifies that the content of ASPX pages are not compiled into an assembly; instead, the markup is left as is, allowing you to change HTML and client-side functionality after precompiling the website. Selecting this check box is equivalent to adding the -u option to the aspnet_compiler.exe command.

    - **Use Fixed Naming And Single Page Assemblies**   This option specifies that batch builds are turned off during precompilation to generate assemblies with fixed names. Themes and skin files continue to be compiled to a single assembly. This option is not available for in-place compilation.

- **Emit Debug Information**   Select this check box if you might need to debug the site after you publish it.

- **Enable Strong Naming On Precompiled Assemblies**   This check box, when selected, specifies that the generated assemblies are strongly named by using a key file or key container to encode the assemblies and to ensure that they have not been tampered with. After you select this check box, you can do the following:

  - Specify the location of a key file to use to sign the assemblies. If you use a key file, you can select Delay Signing, which signs the assembly in two stages: first with the public key file, and then with a private key file that is specified later during a call to the aspnet_compiler.exe command.

  - Specify the location of a key container from the system's cryptographic service provider (CSP) to use to name the assemblies.

  - Specify whether to mark the assembly with the AllowPartiallyTrustedCallers property, which allows strongly named assemblies to be called by partially trusted code. If you do not specify this declaration, only fully trusted code can use such assemblies.

4. Click OK to compile and publish the website.

Publishing a website can be an easy way to move a website from a development server to a staging or production server.

Installing ASP.NET 4 on IIS

The .NET Framework 4 was released after Windows 7 and Windows Server 2008 R2 were released. Therefore, as of the time of this writing, no operating system has built-in support to run ASP.NET 4 applications. Before you can run an ASP.NET 4 application on a server, you will need to install the .NET Framework 4. Naturally, Visual Studio 2010 installs the .NET Framework 4 automatically, so your development computer will run your websites correctly with no additional software.

Microsoft released an optional Windows Update package to install the .NET Framework 4 on computers with Windows XP, Windows Vista, Windows 7, Windows Server 2003, Windows Server 2008, and Windows Server 2008 R2 operating systems. Therefore, systems administrators might have already installed the necessary components. If not, have the systems administrators install the update.

After the .NET Framework 4 is installed, you need to configure IIS to run ASP.NET 4 applications by using the aspnet_regiis.exe command-line tool. The tool is located in the .NET Framework directory, which is typically %windir%\Microsoft.NET\Framework\v4.0.30319 \aspnet_regiis.exe (for 32-bit systems) or %windir%\Microsoft.NET\Framework64\v4.0.30319 (for 64-bit systems).

Usually you will only need to use the following options:

- **-i** This installs ASP.NET 4 and updates both the IIS Classic mode and IIS Integrated mode handlers and script mappings. When you use this option, aspnet_regiis.exe updates the standard DefaultAppPool and Classic .NETAppPool application pools to use the .NET Framework 4 version of the Common Language Runtime. This will not usually cause compatibility problems. However, because it changes the configuration of all existing ASP.NET websites, you should thoroughly test your applications with the newer version of the CLR prior to using this option. This option also interrupts running applications, causing active users to be logged out (when you are using forms-based logons) and ViewState to be lost. For those reasons, avoid using this option on production servers.

- **-ir** Like -i, this installs ASP.NET 4. This option does not change the existing application pools, however, reducing potential application compatibility problems.

- **-iru** This performs a -i installation if ASP.NET is not currently registered. If ASP.NET is currently registered, this performs a -ir installation.

- **-enable** This enables the ASP.NET Internet Server Application Programming Interface (ISAPI) extension for IIS 6.0 or IIS 7.0 in Classic mode.

- **-s** *path* This option updates scriptmaps and application-pool assignments for the specified path and all subdirectories to ASP.NET 4. If the server is running IIS 6.0, aspnet_regiis.exe updates the scriptmaps. If the server is running IIS 7.0, aspnet_regiis.exe maps the application to a new ASP.NET 4 application pool. Specify the metabase path, which might resemble W3SVC/1/ROOT/*myapp* or W3SVC/1634748923. To find the path for IIS 6.0, search the metabase.xml file in the %windir%\system32\inetsrv\ folder for the name of your website.

- **-sn** *path* This updates scriptmaps and application-pool assignments for the specified path to ASP.NET 4. Unlike –s, -sn does not apply to subdirectories.

- **-lv** This option displays the installation path of all versions of ASP.NET.

For a description of all available options, see "ASP.NET IIS Registration Tool" at *http://msdn.microsoft.com/en-us/library/k6h9cz8h.aspx*.

 Quick Check

1. What launch condition does a Web Setup Project include by default?
2. What are the four phases of a Web Setup Project deployment?

Quick Check Answers

1. By default, a Web Setup Project checks for an IIS version later than 4.0.
2. Install, Commit, Rollback, and Uninstall are the four phases of Web Setup Project deployment.

In this practice, you deploy applications by using two techniques: a Web Setup Project and the Copy Web tool.

> **ON THE COMPANION MEDIA**
>
> If you encounter a problem completing an exercise, you can find the completed projects in the samples installed from this book's companion CD. For more information about the project files and other content on the CD, see "Using the Companion Media" in this book's Introduction.

EXERCISE Creating a Web Setup Project

In this exercise, you create a new ASP.NET website and a related Web Setup Project.

1. Open Visual Studio and create a new website by using the language of your preference. This site will serve as the basis for your setup project.

2. Add some simple pages to the site. This will give you something to set up and deploy. These pages could include order.aspx, product.aspx, customer.aspx, and vendor.aspx.

3. Add a Web Setup Project to your solution. To do so, from the File menu, select Add, and then select New Project. Under Project Types, expand Other Project Types, expand Setup And Deployment, and then select Visual Studio Installer. Under Templates (on the right side), select Web Setup Project. Name the project **MyWebSetup**, and click OK.

   You should see a new project in Visual Studio Solution Explorer. You should also see the File System editor for the setup project.

4. Next, you need to connect the setup project to your website. Within the left pane of the editor, right-click Web Application Folder, select Add, and then select Project Output. In the Add Project Output Group dialog box, select Content Files, and click OK.

   If you were to build and install your project at this point, it would copy the site pages and code-behind files to the location specified by a user during setup.

5. In the File System editor, expand the Web Application Folder. Notice that there is a Bin directory. This is where you would embed any DLL files that might need to be included by your solution. You would embed these files by right-clicking Bin and selecting Add to add a file. For this practice, there are no dependent DLL files, so you can skip this.

6. Next, add a folder and a file that should be included with the build. To do so, right-click the Web Application Folder in the File System editor. Select Add, and then select Web Folder. Name the folder **Images**.

7. Right-click the Images folder, select Add, and then select File. Navigate to the Pictures folder on your computer. Select a few sample pictures, and click Open.

8. Now add a launch condition. From the View menu, select Editor, and then select Launch Conditions. In the Launch Conditions editor, right-click Requirements On Target Machine, and then select Add File Launch Condition. Rename the new search condition (currently named Search For File1) to **Search for Browscap**. Select the new search condition and view the Properties window.

   ■ Set the FileName property to **Nothing.ini**. (This file doesn't exist, but you'll fix the error later.)

   ■ Set the Folder property to [WindowsFolder] and set the Depth property to **4**. This tells setup to search the system folder and all subfolders four levels deep for a file named Nothing.ini. Note that the Property value is set to FILEEXISTS1.

9. Rename the new launch condition (currently named Condition1) to **Browscap Condition**. Select the new launch condition and view the Properties window.

   ■ Set the InstallUrl property to **http://blogs.iis.net/dmnelson/archive/2009/05/14/ updating-browscap-ini-for-internet-explorer-8.aspx**, which contains information about the Browscap.ini file. In the real world, you would provide a link with instructions on how to fulfill the requirement.

   ■ Set the Message property to **You must have a Browscap.ini file to complete installation. Would you like more information?**. Notice that the Condition property is already set to FILEEXISTS1, which corresponds to the search condition Property value.

10. Build the Web Setup Project. Right-click your setup project in Solution Explorer and then select Build. In the Output window, make note of the folder containing the output files. Open the output folder in Windows Explorer and examine the files that are present. You should see both an MSI and a setup.exe file.

11. Open the folder that contains the MSI file. Double-click the MSI file to launch setup. After a few seconds, you should see an error message indicating that the Browscap.ini file does not exist, as shown in Figure 8-27.

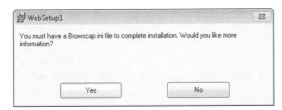

FIGURE 8-27 The MSI file error message.

Recall that we added this condition in step 9. We also set the FileName property of the search condition to Nothing.ini in step 8, which is why this error is being thrown.

12. Click Yes. You will be taken to the InstallUrl set as part of the condition.

13. Return to Visual Studio. Open the Launch Conditions editor for the Web Setup Project.

14. Select Search For Browscap under Search Target Machine. View the Properties window. Change the FileName property to look for the file **Browscap.ini**.

15. Rebuild the Web Setup Project (right-click and select Rebuild).

16. Return to the directory in which the MSI file exists. Rerun the MSI file. This time, the computer should meet the setup requirements because the Browscap.ini file exists in the Windows folder.

> **NOTE   INSTALLATION ISSUES**
>
> Depending on your environment, you might run into additional issues. If, for example, you are running Windows Vista and IIS 7.0, you need an IIS 6-compatible metabase for the IIS condition to validate. You can tweak the condition or add the IIS 6 metabase to IIS 7.0 from Control Panel (classic view) | Programs And Features | Turn Windows Feature On Or Off | Internet Information Services | Web Management Tools | IIS 6 Management Compatibility. Another issue is security in Windows Vista and Windows 7. You might have to run the Setup.exe file (and not the MSI file) by right-clicking Setup.exe and selecting Run As Administrator.

17. On the Select Installation Address page, notice that you have the opportunity to select the website, virtual directory, and application pool. Choose a unique virtual directory name and make note of it. Click Next.

18. Finish walking through the installation steps.

19. Open the Internet Information Services console (Control Panel | Administrative Tools | Internet Information Services [IIS] Manager). Find the virtual directory in which you installed the website. Verify that the pages, code-behind files, and images exist.

As you can see, deploying a website can be as easy as installing a Windows Forms application. Although this process takes you through a manual installation of a Windows Installer package, you can also deploy the MSI file in an automated manner.

Lesson Summary

- Web Setup Projects allow you to create executable Setup.exe files and Windows Installer packages (MSI files) that administrators can use to easily deploy your applications to a web server.

- The Copy Web tool can synchronize a website between a remote server and your local computer. This is useful if you want to do deployment and testing on your local computer and then upload the website to a remote web server. The Copy Web tool can also be useful in environments with multiple developers because it detects versioning conflicts.

- Precompiling a website removes the delay that occurs when ASP.NET compiles an application after the first user request. To precompile a website, use the Publish Web Site tool.

Lesson Review

You can use the following questions to test your knowledge of the information in Lesson 1, "Deploying Websites." The questions are also available on the companion CD in a practice test, if you prefer to review them in electronic form.

> **NOTE ANSWERS**
>
> Answers to these questions and explanations of why each answer choice is correct or incorrect are located in the "Answers" section at the end of the book.

1. You need to add a registry entry to make your application function. In which phase of the Web Setup Project should you add the registry entry?

   A. Install

   B. Commit

   C. Rollback

   D. Uninstall

2. You need to make a change to an operating system–related registry entry to make your application function. You want to ensure that you remove this change if setup is cancelled or the application is removed from the computer. In which phases should you undo your registry modification? (Choose all that apply.)

   A. Install

   B. Commit

   C. Rollback

   D. Uninstall

3. Which of the following deployment tools enables multiple developers to work on a site simultaneously while detecting potential versioning conflicts?

   A. A setup project

   B. A Web Setup Project

   C. The Copy Web tool

   D. The Publish Web Site tool

4. Which of the following deployment tools has the potential to improve responsiveness of the website to end users?

   A. A setup project

   B. A Web Setup Project

   C. The Copy Web tool

   D. The Publish Web Site tool

Case Scenarios

In the following case scenarios, you apply what you've learned in this chapter. If you have difficulty completing this work, review the material in this chapter before beginning the next chapter. You can find answers to these questions in the "Answers" section at the end of this book.

Case Scenario 1: Debugging

You are an application developer for Fabrikam, Inc., a financial services company. You have been told that users are receiving errors on certain pages in the site. You need to turn off the detailed errors in production and direct users to a default error page. However, administrators executing code directly on the server should still be able to see the errors.

You also need to debug these errors. You cannot reproduce them on your machine. Therefore, you need to debug them against the staging server.

Answer the following questions based on the scenario just defined.

1. How will you disable transmitting error detail to users of the site?
2. How will you implement a default error page for users?
3. How will you ensure that errors are still available for administrators to view?
4. How can you debug against the staging environment?
5. How can you apply these settings when you publish the web application in the future, while keeping the current settings for use in your development environment?

Case Scenario 2: Troubleshooting

You are an application developer for Fabrikam, Inc., a financial services company. The configuration changes you made to your application in the previous scenario have been very successful. However, you still have one persistent issue that you cannot seem to solve in development or staging. Therefore, you want to turn tracing on for the specific page and view the results by accessing the page from the server. In addition, your manager has asked you to begin monitoring key events in the system to verify the application's health.

Answer the following questions based on the scenario just defined.

1. How should you configure tracing for the issue?
2. How should you enable health monitoring for your application?

Case Scenario 3: Deploying a Website

You are a developer for Contoso, Ltd, a video streaming company. You are the sole developer of the company's external website, which allows customers to rent and view videos online. The reliability of the application is critical, so the quality assurance team must test any changes you make on a staging server before you make changes to the production web server.

You frequently work from your home. Unfortunately, Contoso's virtual private network (VPN) is unreliable, so you must do your development on your laptop computer. You can only access the staging and production web servers from the internal network or the VPN, but that's not a problem because you don't need to make updates to those servers very frequently. Additionally, your Internet connection is a low-bandwidth cellular link, so you need to avoid sending large updates across the connection.

Answer the following questions.

1. Which tool would you use to update the staging server?

2. Which tool should the quality assurance people use to update the production server?

Suggested Practices

To successfully master the exam objectives presented in this chapter, complete the following tasks.

Debug a Website

For this task, you should complete the first practice to gain experience working with remote debugging. Practice 2 helps with client script debugging.

- **Practice 1**   Find some ASP.NET code that matches code deployed on a development server. Deploy the remote debugging tool to the development server. Run the remote debugging tool from the server. Use Visual Studio to open the code, attach to the running server process, and step into code based on a request.

- **Practice 2**   Find (or write) some code that contains client-side JavaScript. You can find appropriate code on this book's CD (in the samples for Chapters 7 and 8. Open the code in Visual Studio. Run the webpage in a browser. Configure Internet Explorer to allow script debugging. Use Visual Studio to connect to the browser's process and step into the client-side code.

Troubleshoot a Website

For this task, you should complete the first item for practice with tracing. The second practice should help with health monitoring.

- **Practice 1** Turn on tracing for one of your existing websites. Be sure to do so only in a test environment. Review the trace data about your pages. Look carefully and determine whether there are unexpected results.

- **Practice 2** Turn on health monitoring for one of your existing websites. Again, be sure to do so only in a test environment. Review the data logged over a few days and assess the results.

Publish a Web Application

For this task, complete at least Practices 1 and 2. If you want experience publishing to a public hosting provider, complete Practice 3 as well.

- **Practice 1** Complete the one-click publishing walkthroughs listed at *http://msdn.microsoft.com/en-us/library/dd394698.aspx.*

- **Practice 2** Configure an IIS Web server to support one-click publishing. For detailed instructions, read "Configuring MSDeploy in IIS 7" at *http://william.jerla.me/post/2010/03/20/Configuring-MSDeploy-in-IIS-7.aspx.*

- **Practice 3** Publish a database-driven web application to a public hosting provider that supports one-click publishing. Although none of them are free, Microsoft provides a list of hosting providers at *http://www.asp.net/find-a-hoster.*

Use a Web Setup Project

For this task, you should complete at least Practices 1 and 2 to get a solid understanding of how to use Web Setup Projects. If you want a better understanding of how applications are distributed in enterprises and you have sufficient lab equipment, complete Practice 3 as well.

- **Practice 1** Create a Web Setup Project that prompts the user to provide database connection information, and then stores the connection information as part of a connection string in the Web.config file.

- **Practice 2** Using the most recent real-world application you created or one of the applications you created for an exercise in this book, create a Web Setup Project. Deploy the Web Setup Project to different operating systems, including Windows 2000, Windows XP, Windows Server 2003, and Windows Server 2008. Verify that the deployed application works on all platforms. If it does not work, modify your Web Setup Project to make it work properly. Make note of how the Web Setup Project handles computers that lack the .NET Framework 4.

- **Practice 3** Create a Web Setup Project and generate a Windows Installer file. If you have sufficient lab equipment, use Active Directory software distribution to distribute the website automatically to multiple servers.

Use the Copy Web Tool

For this task, you should complete both practices to gain experience with using the Copy Web tool.

- **Practice 1**   Use the Copy Web tool to create a local copy of your most recent real-world website. With your computer disconnected from the network, make an update to the website. Then use the Copy Web tool to update that single file on the remote web server.

- **Practice 2**   Using a local copy of a website, make an update to different files on both your local copy and the remote website. Then use the Copy Web tool to synchronize the local and remote websites.

Precompile and Publish a Web Application

For this task, you should complete the practice to gain an understanding of the performance benefits that can be realized by precompiling an application.

- Enable tracing in a website. Then modify the Web.config file and save it to force the application to restart. Open a page several times, and then view the Trace.axd file to determine how long the first and subsequent requests took. Next, use the Publish Web Site tool to precompile the application. Open a page several times, and then view the Trace.axd file to determine how long the first and subsequent requests took with the precompiled application.

Take a Practice Test

The practice tests on this book's companion CD offer many options. For example, you can test yourself on just the lesson review questions in this chapter, or you can test yourself on all the 70-515 certification exam objectives. You can set up the test so it closely simulates the experience of taking a certification exam, or you can set it up in study mode so you can look at the correct answers and explanations after you answer each question.

> **MORE INFO**   **PRACTICE TESTS**
>
> For details about all the practice test options available, see the "How to Use the Practice Tests" section in this book's Introduction.

CHAPTER 9

Working with Client-Side Scripting, AJAX, and jQuery

R ich Internet applications (RIAs) are becoming the norm on the web. Users expect a high degree of interactivity when working with modern websites—the same interactivity that was once only expected of applications running on the desktop. This includes functionality such as modal dialog boxes and pop-up windows, partial screen (or page) updates, controls that dynamically collapse or resize on a page, application progress indicators, and much more.

Microsoft ASP.NET includes tools for building web applications that provide this level of richness. These tools include controls for handling client-based interactivity, an extensive library for working with client-side JavaScript, a programming model for creating your own JavaScript–enabled controls, and newly added support for the jQuery library. This chapter covers these scenarios and shows you how to enrich your users' experiences with your websites.

Exam objectives in this chapter:

- Implementing Client-Side Scripting and AJAX

    - Implement ASP.NET AJAX.

    - Add dynamic features to a page by using JavaScript.

    - Handle JavaScript events.

    - Alter a page dynamically by manipulating the DOM.

    - Implement AJAX by using jQuery.

Lessons in this chapter:

Before You Begin

To complete the lessons in this chapter, you should be familiar with developing applications with Microsoft Visual Studio 2010 by using Microsoft Visual Basic or Microsoft Visual C#. In addition, you should be comfortable with all of the following:

- The Visual Studio 2010 Integrated Development Environment (IDE)
- Using Hypertext Markup Language (HTML) and client-side scripting
- Creating ASP.NET websites and forms
- Adding web server controls to a webpage

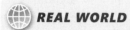 **REAL WORLD**

Mike Snell

I am fortunate enough to have been around when building web applications first took off. The early applications we built were nothing more than hyperlinked HTML and some images. Soon we added server-side script and database connectivity to enable more meaningful scenarios.

The power of having a server-based, near-zero–deployment, ubiquitous, cross-platform application environment has been (and still is) the driving force that pushes us to build web applications. There has always been, however, a major gap in the richness of the user interface (UI) between a desktop application accessing the web and a web browser. We've seen many attempts to close this gap, including Java, Microsoft ActiveX, ActiveX Documents, Dynamic Hypertext Markup Language (DHTML), and others.

It remains to be seen whether this gap will ever really be closed. However, Asynchronous JavaScript and XML (AJAX) and jQuery both provide a nice compromise between a rich client and a web-only application. These technologies extend what is capable on the client without breaking the paradigm of a web application. AJAX is rooted in the web and, like its counterparts HTML and DHTML, it is standards driven, cross platform, and ubiquitous. This makes it a great choice for adding client interactivity to applications that must remain true to the concept of a website.

Lesson 1: Creating AJAX-Enabled Web Forms

Much of what makes Web 2.0 applications so appealing to users is provided by AJAX. This technology enables increased user interactivity when an application running in a browser is used, because the application requires fewer page refreshes. The result is a better user experience on the web.

AJAX is a platform-independent technology that works with web applications running in Windows Internet Explorer, Firefox, Safari, and other browsers. It is an ECMAScript-compliant technology. (ECMAScript is the foundational language from which JavaScript and JScript are derived—see *http://en.wikipedia.org/wiki/ECMAScript*.) This makes AJAX a logical choice for providing a richer UI for browser-based, cross-platform web applications.

You can add AJAX to any web application. Like other web standards such as HTML, it is not specific to ASP.NET. However, ASP.NET does provide many tools that make building AJAX-enabled webpages easier. These include controls to manage partial-page updates, a code library that enables object-oriented development on the client with JavaScript, the ability to call web services from client code, the ability to create your own AJAX-enabled controls, and more.

This lesson covers building interactive web forms by using the AJAX controls built into ASP.NET 4. The JavaScript object library and building AJAX-enabled controls are covered in Lesson 2 of this chapter.

After this lesson, you will be able to:

- Understand and use the AJAX Extensions controls built into ASP.NET.
- Create a web form that performs partial-page updates to the server (without a full-page refresh).
- Display the progress of a request that is being processed on the server.
- Periodically update portions of a webpage based on a time interval.

Estimated lesson time: 40 minutes

Introducing ASP.NET AJAX

ASP.NET includes many components that help to enable AJAX features for developers. These components have a common goal: to improve the user's experience by providing developers with the ability to create more responsive web applications. The tools are many and varied, and choosing the appropriate approach depends on your specific needs. The following are the ASP.NET components related to AJAX capabilities:

- **Microsoft AJAX Library** The Microsoft AJAX Library is a set of JavaScript files that make programming client-side JavaScript easier. It provides an object-oriented model that supports AJAX technology when ASP.NET is being used. The library includes support for classes, namespaces, event handling, data types, and more. It also has support for error handling, debugging, and globalization.

  The library combines JavaScript features and DHTML. Like JavaScript, it works across browsers and across platforms. This library is used by ASP.NET and the AJAX Control Toolkit. You can also use this library to extend your own controls with AJAX behaviors.

- **ASP.NET AJAX server controls** ASP.NET ships with a set of AJAX server controls that can be embedded in your webpages to enable partial-page updates, communicate with a server process to indicate progress, and periodically update portions of a page.

- **jQuery** jQuery is a code library that makes it easier to write client-side scripts and AJAX applications. It is actually an open source library (see *http://jquery.com/*). ASP.NET includes the scripts for jQuery and jQuery IntelliSense support within the Visual Studio IDE. Lesson 3 of this chapter covers implementing jQuery in ASP.NET.

- **AJAX Control Toolkit** The AJAX Control Toolkit is a set of community-created and supported controls that show off the power of AJAX. You can use these controls in your webpages to enable many client-side features typically found only in applications running on the desktop, controls such as masked edit boxes, slider controls, filtered text boxes, modal pop-up windows, and much more.

> **NOTE** **THE AJAX CONTROL TOOLKIT**
>
> The AJAX Control Toolkit is an extension of Visual Studio and ASP.NET. It is therefore not covered in this book or on the exam. There is a new version that works with ASP.NET 4. You can learn more by going to *http://www.asp.net/ajax/*.

- **Client-side web service support** ASP.NET and AJAX provide support for calling web services asynchronously from the client by using JavaScript Object Notation (JSON) serialization and XML. This functionality is covered in Chapter 10, "Writing and Working with HTTP Modules and Web Services."

- **ASP.NET standard controls** The controls that ship with ASP.NET also make use of JavaScript on the client. It is easy to forget about this because you are not required to write any JavaScript to get this interactivity. Examples of ASP.NET controls that use JavaScript include the validation controls, the Web Part controls, the menu control, the TreeView control, and the Calendar control.

Uses and Benefits of ASP.NET AJAX

The features built into ASP.NET AJAX allow you to provide users with a richer experience than that of a standard, all-server-side web application. The following lists some of the key usage scenarios and related benefits of building web applications with ASP.NET AJAX:

- **Partial-page updates**   This feature allows you to define an area of a webpage to post back and update independently from the rest of the page. Only the updated content will be refreshed when the request completes. This ensures that the user stays within his or her current context. It also gives users the feeling that they are interacting with the application (and not a server).

- **Client-side processing**   This interactivity provides immediate feedback and responsiveness to users. With client script, you can enable functionality such as collapsible areas of a page, tabs on a webpage, data sorting on the client, and much more.

- **Desktop-like UI**   With AJAX, you can provide users with controls such as modal dialog boxes, progress indicators, masked edit boxes, tooltips, and more. This helps make the user experience between web and rich desktop applications much more similar.

- **Progress indication**   This allows you to track the progress of a server-side process and continuously update the user. This gives users the feeling that they are in control and assures them that the application is still processing (as with a desktop application).

- **Improved performance and higher scale**   You can achieve increased performance and scale by processing portions of a page on just the client. You then take advantage of the user's machine, which takes the load off the server. This results in real and perceived performance and scalability increases.

- **Web service calls from the client**   This allows you to call back to the server directly from client script running in a browser and then show the results to the user (often by using partial-page updates).

- **Cross-browser, cross-platform support**   JavaScript, AJAX, and jQuery are all supported on multiple browsers and multiple platforms. This allows you to write interactive applications that run in more client environments than the average desktop application.

The AJAX Server Controls

The controls that ship with ASP.NET are meant to provide two basic AJAX features: partial-page updates and server-to-client progress updates. You work with these controls much as you do with other ASP.NET controls. You can drag them onto your page from the Toolbox, manipulate their properties, and code against them. Figure 9-1 shows a model of the AJAX Extensions controls in ASP.NET.

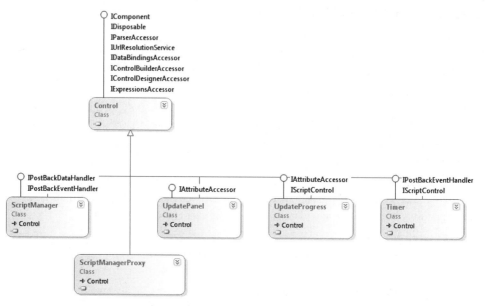

FIGURE 9-1 The AJAX Extensions controls in ASP.NET provide partial-page update and server progress updates.

Each of these controls inherits from the System.Web.UI.Control class. This ensures that they work in a similar manner as other ASP.NET web controls. The sections that follow cover each of these controls in detail.

The ScriptManager and ScriptManagerProxy Controls

Each page you write that uses ASP.NET AJAX requires one (and only one) instance of a ScriptManager control. The ScriptManager control is responsible for pushing the Microsoft AJAX Library down to the client when your page is requested. It also manages partial-page updates, progress indicators, and more.

You add the ScriptManager control to your page source. It does not have a visual representation. It is simply a control used to manage AJAX processing. The basic page markup for a ScriptManager control in Source view looks as follows.

```
<asp:ScriptManager ID="ScriptManager1" runat="server">
</asp:ScriptManager>
```

By default, the ScriptManager control's EnablePartialRendering property is set to true. This indicates that the page supports partial-page updates. You can use this property to turn this feature off if needed.

The ScriptManager control is also used to register custom scripts with the Microsoft AJAX Library. In this way, if you write a script, it can be registered and managed with the Microsoft AJAX Library. This is covered in Lesson 2 of this chapter. Similarly, you can use the ScriptManager control to register web service method calls from the client. This is covered in Chapter 10.

USING AJAX WITH MASTER PAGES AND USER CONTROLS

You will often need to support AJAX in a user control you write or directly in the master page of a site. This presents an issue, because a page can contain only a single ScriptManager control. Having one inside your user control and another inside the page that consumes the user control, for example, would be a problem. To overcome this issue, you can use the ScriptManagerProxy control.

The ScriptManagerProxy control can be used either by child pages that use a master page that already defines a ScriptManager control or by user and custom controls that you write. You use it much the same way you would a ScriptManager control. You can register scripts that are specific to the child page or control that you are writing. ASP.NET takes care of the rest.

The UpdatePanel Control

The UpdatePanel control allows you to define areas of a page that should post back to the server independent of the rest of the page. This allows the client to work more independently. Rather than the entire page being requested and thus refreshed on return, with partial-page updates, you can post portions of a page to the server and receive updates to only those portions. In this way, the user does not see a full-screen refresh and does not lose context where he or she is on the page.

It is important to note that partial-page updates give the *illusion* of running on the client side. However, they do not actually run on the client side. Rather, they are smaller, asynchronous postbacks to the server. The ScriptManager control manages the communication between this call and its return message.

The UpdatePanel control is a container for other controls. The controls you put inside the UpdatePanel control that cause a postback to the server will be managed as partial-page updates.

As an example, consider a GridView control that allows users to page through data. By default, each time the user selects another page of data, the entire webpage is refreshed and redisplayed. If you embed the GridView control inside an UpdatePanel, you can still process the data paging on the server. However, you now eliminate the full-page updates on the client. The following shows the markup of an UpdatePanel that includes a GridView control.

```
<asp:UpdatePanel ID="UpdatePanel1" runat="server">
    <ContentTemplate>
        <asp:GridView ID="GridView1" runat="server" AutoGenerateColumns="False"
            DataKeyNames="SupplierID" DataSourceID="SqlDataSourceNwd" Width="600"
            AllowPaging="True">
        <Columns>
            <asp:BoundField DataField="SupplierID" HeaderText="ID"
                InsertVisible="False" ReadOnly="True" SortExpression="SupplierID" />
            <asp:BoundField DataField="CompanyName" HeaderText="Company"
                SortExpression="CompanyName" />
            <asp:BoundField DataField="City" HeaderText="City"
                SortExpression="City" />
            <asp:BoundField DataField="Phone" HeaderText="Phone"
                SortExpression="Phone" />
            <asp:BoundField DataField="ContactName" HeaderText="Contact"
                SortExpression="ContactName" />
        </Columns>
```

```
    </asp:GridView>
    <asp:SqlDataSource ID="SqlDataSourceNwd" runat="server"
        ConnectionString="<%$ ConnectionStrings:NwdConnectionString %>"
        SelectCommand="SELECT [SupplierID], [CompanyName], [City], [Phone],
[ContactName] FROM [Suppliers]">
    </asp:SqlDataSource>
    </ContentTemplate>
</asp:UpdatePanel>
```

CONTROLLING PARTIAL-PAGE UPDATES

You can combine multiple UpdatePanel controls on the same page. Each can update portions of the page independently or in a coordinated fashion. You might also have controls that cause standard postbacks on the same page as those that cause asynchronous postbacks. In each of these cases, you need to be able to control how and when the page elements update. The UpdatePanel exposes the UpdateMode and ChildrenAsTriggers properties for controlling when a postback should occur to trigger an update of content contained in an UpdatePanel.

The first property, UpdateMode, has two possible settings: Always and Conditional. The Always value is used to indicate that the content of an UpdatePanel should be updated on every postback that originates from the page. This includes other asynchronous updates that are the result of another UpdatePanel on the page as well as those that are simply standard postbacks on the page.

The Conditional value of the UpdatePanel.UpdateMode property is more complex. It indicates that an update to the UpdatePanel is conditional on something else on the page. For example, consider the case of nested UpdatePanels. If you set the nested UpdatePanel control's UpdateMode property to Conditional, it will only be updated when the parent UpdatePanel causes a postback.

Another way to trigger an update to an UpdatePanel with an UpdateMode set to Conditional is to explicitly call its Update method from server-side code. This might be done as the result of another asynchronous update on the page.

If you set the UpdateMode to the Conditional value, by default nested UpdatePanel controls will not cause an update to their parent. You can change this behavior by setting the outer UpdatePanel control's ChildrenAsTriggers property to true. When you do so, any updates triggered by the nested UpdatePanel will also trigger an update to the parent UpdatePanel.

You can also explicitly define the controls that you want to use to trigger an update to an UpdatePanel. These controls can be inside or outside the UpdatePanel, and the update will be triggered for both Conditional mode and Always mode. When you add a trigger to an UpdatePanel, when a user triggers a postback from the trigger control, the UpdatePanel content will also post back and be refreshed.

As an example, consider the GridView control discussed previously. This control is inside an UpdatePanel, as shown in Figure 9-2. It updates itself when a user pages through the data. Now, notice that the page also supports a search function. The search is triggered by a button named ButtonSearch (also displayed in Figure 9-2).

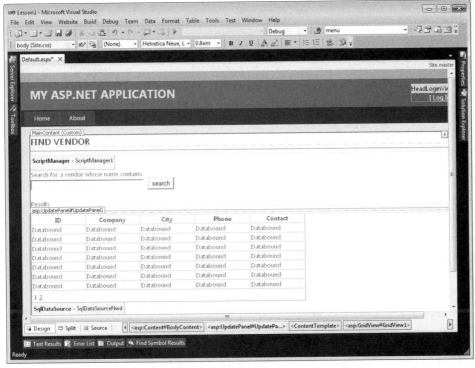

FIGURE 9-2 An ASPX page with a search button and a GridView control.

You might want the search to also result in a partial-page update to GridView. To make this happen, you can add a trigger to the UpdatePanel that contains the GridView control. A trigger can be defined directly in markup (or through the Property window in Design view or in your code). The following markup shows an example.

```
<asp:UpdatePanel ID="UpdatePanel1" runat="server">
  <Triggers>
    <asp:AsyncPostBackTrigger ControlID="ButtonSearch" EventName="Click" />
  </Triggers>
  <ContentTemplate>

    ... Grid View markup ...

  </ContentTemplate>
</asp:UpdatePanel>
```

Notice that the trigger is of type AsyncPostBackTrigger. It contains both the ID of the control that causes the postback and the name of the trigger control's event that causes the postback. You can add more than one trigger to the UpdatePanel as well. In this example, clicking the search button will update the GridView as a partial-page update.

PARTIAL-PAGE UPDATES AND ERROR HANDLING

You can handle errors that occur during a partial-page update by writing a handler for the AsyncPostBackError event of the ScriptManager control. This event is raised on the server when an asynchronous postback throws an error. You can also set the AsyncPostBackErrrorMessage of the ScriptManager control to an error message to be displayed to the user when a partial-page update error occurs.

The UpdateProgress Control

The UpdateProgress control is used to provide information in the form of graphics or text that is displayed to the user during a partial-page update. For example, you might display an animated GIF image that shows that the system is processing while the user waits for the partial-page update to complete.

You can add an UpdateProgress control to an UpdatePanel control by nesting it inside the UpdatePanel control's ContentTemplate tag. This effectively associates the UpdateProgress control with the UpdatePanel. You then define the information you want to display to the user inside the ProgressTemplate tag of the UpdateProgress control. Content inside this element can be an image, text, or similar HTML content. The content will be rendered to the browser as a hidden <div> tag that will be shown when the partial-page update is executed. The following markup shows an example.

```
<asp:UpdatePanel ID="UpdatePanel1" runat="server">
  <ContentTemplate>
    <asp:GridView ID="GridView1" runat="server">
    </asp:GridView>
    <asp:UpdateProgress ID="UpdateProgress1" runat="server">
      <ProgressTemplate>
        <div style="font-size: large">Processing ...</div>
      </ProgressTemplate>
    </asp:UpdateProgress>
  </ContentTemplate>
</asp:UpdatePanel>
```

The UpdateProgress control can also be associated directly with an UpdatePanel control through the AssociatedUpdatePanelId property. You set this property to the ID value of the UpdatePanel control to which you want to associate.

If you do not set the AssociatedUpdatePanelId property of the UpdateProgress control, any UpdatePanel that causes an asynchronous postback will trigger the UpdateProgress control. In this way, you can use a single UpdateProgress control for multiple UpdatePanels on a single webpage.

By default, the UpdateProgress control is displayed a half-second after the partial-page update starts. You can set the DisplayAfter property to the number of milliseconds to wait before displaying the UpdateProgress content. This can prevent the control from showing for very quick operations and show it only for longer operations.

The Timer Control

The ASP.NET Timer control is an AJAX control that can be used to update portions of a page on a periodic, timed basis. This is useful if you need to update an image such as an advertisement on a webpage or perhaps a value such as a stock ticker or a news ticker. The Timer control can also be used to simply run code on the server on a periodic basis.

You can add a Timer control directly to an UpdatePanel control. The Timer will then automatically trigger a partial-page update of the UpdatePanel based on a time defined by the Timer control's Interval property (in milliseconds). The following shows an example of a Timer control embedded in an UpdatePanel.

```
<asp:UpdatePanel ID="UpdatePanel1" runat="server">
  <ContentTemplate>
    <asp:Image ID="Image1" runat="server"
      ImageUrl="~/images/contoso.png" />
    <asp:Timer ID="Timer1" runat="server"
      Interval="5000" ontick="Timer1_Tick">
    </asp:Timer>
  </ContentTemplate>
</asp:UpdatePanel>
```

In this example, the Timer is set to fire every five seconds. When it does, the Timer control's Tick event is raised on the server and the content of the UpdatePanel is refreshed. In this case, the Tick event simply cycles images to be displayed to the user. When you use a Timer with an UpdatePanel, the Timer starts again after the page has completed its postback to the server.

A Timer can also be used outside of an UpdatePanel control. As with UpdatePanel, the Timer control requires the ScriptManager control. In this way, you can use the Timer control to update more than one UpdatePanel on the page or the entire page itself. To associate a Timer control that is outside an UpdatePanel to an UpdatePanel on the page, you use a trigger, as discussed earlier.

Note that in the scenario in which the trigger is outside an UpdatePanel, the timed interval resets as soon as it fires. It does not wait for the postback to complete. This can provide more exact timing of intervals. However, if a postback is still processing when the Timer fires, the first postback is canceled.

PRACTICE Building an AJAX-Enabled Webpage

In this practice, you create a webpage and enable partial-page updates. You also add support for notifying the user when the application connects to the server. Finally, you add a Timer control to periodically update a second portion of your page.

> **ON THE COMPANION MEDIA**
>
> If you encounter a problem completing an exercise, you can find the completed projects in the samples installed from this book's companion CD. For more information about the project files and other content on the CD, see "Using the Companion Media" in this book's Introduction.

EXERCISE 1 Enabling Partial-Page Updates

In this exercise, you create a new ASP.NET website and define support for partial-page updates.

1. Open Visual Studio and create a new ASP.NET website named **AjaxExample** in either C# or Visual Basic.

2. Add the northwnd.mdf database file to the App_Data folder of the site. The database file can be found in the sample files installed from the CD inside the App_Data folder for this exercise. This database file is a Microsoft SQL Server Express database that contains a copy of the Northwind sample database.

3. Open Default.aspx in Source view. Delete the contents inside the BodyContent control.

4. Add a ScriptManager control to the body of the page from the AJAX Extensions tab of the Toolbox.

5. Add text to the page to serve as a title followed by a horizontal line. Your markup inside the BodyContent control might look as follows.

```
<asp:Content ID="BodyContent" runat="server" ContentPlaceHolderID="MainContent">

    <asp:ScriptManager ID="ScriptManager1" runat="server">
    </asp:ScriptManager>

    <h2>Suppliers</h2>
    <hr />

</asp:Content>
```

6. Add an AJAX UpdatePanel control to the page from the AJAX Extensions tab of the Toolbox.

7. Switch to Design view and add a GridView control inside the UpdatePanel. Design view provides UI support for binding the GridView to the database table, which you will do in the next step.

8. Bind the GridView to the vendors stored in the Suppliers table in the northwnd.mdf database. To start, click the smart tag in the upper-right section of the GridView control to open the GridView Tasks window. From here, click the ChooseDataSource list and select New Data Source. This opens the Data Source Configuration Wizard.

   a. In the first step of the wizard, select Database and enter the ID for the data source as **SqlDataSourceNwd**. Click OK to open the Choose Your Data Connection page.

   b. Next, select northwnd.mdf from the Connection list and click Next. (If the northwind.mdf option does not appear in the Connection list, select New Connection and create a connection to the northwnd.mdf file.)

   c. On the next page, choose to save the connection string and name it **NwdConnectionString**. Click Next to continue.

   d. Next, configure the SQL statement to access the Suppliers table. Select the following fields: SupplierID, CompanyName, ContactName, City, and Phone. Sort the query by the CompanyName field (click ORDER BY and select CompanyName in the Sort By list). Click Next to continue, and then close the wizard by clicking Finish.

9. Again, open the GridView Tasks window by using the smart tag. Select the Enable Paging check box.

10. Run the application and view the Default.aspx page in a browser. Click the data page numbers to move between data pages. Notice that only the grid is being updated and not the entire page; this is because the UpdatePanel control wraps requests for data and replaces the markup for the grid rather than refreshing the entire page.

11. Next, add a section at the top of the form (outside of the UpdatePanel) that allows the user to enter a new contact and have it added to the database. Your markup code might look as follows.

```
<div style="margin: 20px 0px 20px 40px">
    Company<br />
    <asp:TextBox ID="TextBoxCompany" runat="server" Width="200"></asp:TextBox>
    <br />
    Contact Name<br />
    <asp:TextBox ID="TextBoxContact" runat="server" Width="200"></asp:TextBox>
    <br />
    City<br />
    <asp:TextBox ID="TextBoxCity" runat="server" Width="200"></asp:TextBox>
    <br />
    Phone<br />
    <asp:TextBox ID="TextBoxPhone" runat="server" Width="200"></asp:TextBox>
    <br />
    <asp:Button ID="ButtonSave" runat="server" Text="add"
        style="margin-top: 15px" onclick="ButtonSave_Click" />
</div>
```

12. Next, define an InsertQuery for the SqlDataSource control. You do so by selecting the SqlDataSource control from the Default.aspx page in Design view. Then click the ellipsis button next to the InsertQuery property in the Properties pane. This will launch the Command And Parameter Editor.

a. First, add parameters for company, contact, city, and phone. Set the source for each of these parameters to a Control, and select the ControlID of the corresponding TextBox. This will bind the TextBox controls to an insert query.

b. Next, use the Query Builder button to define an insert query for the Suppliers table. Your markup for the SqlDataSource control should look similar to the following.

```
<asp:SqlDataSource ID="SqlDataSourceNwd" runat="server"
    ConnectionString="<%$ ConnectionStrings:NwdConnectionString %>"
    SelectCommand="SELECT [SupplierID], [CompanyName], [ContactName], [City],
[Phone] FROM [Suppliers] ORDER BY [CompanyName]"
    InsertCommand="INSERT INTO Suppliers(CompanyName, ContactName, City, Phone)
VALUES (@company, @contact, @city, @phone)">
    <InsertParameters>
        <asp:ControlParameter ControlID="TextBoxCompany" Name="company"
            PropertyName="Text" />
        <asp:ControlParameter ControlID="TextBoxContact" Name="contact"
            PropertyName="Text" />
        <asp:ControlParameter ControlID="TextBoxCity" Name="city"
            PropertyName="Text" />
        <asp:ControlParameter ControlID="TextBoxPhone" Name="phone"
            PropertyName="Text" />
    </InsertParameters>
</asp:SqlDataSource>
```

13. Next, add a Click event to the ButtonSave button defined in step 11 (onclick="ButtonSave_ Click"). This Click event will execute the insert query defined in step 12 and result in a new row being added to the Suppliers table in the database. At the end of this event, rebind the GridView control. The following code shows an example.

```
Sample of Visual Basic Code
Protected Sub ButtonSave_Click(ByVal sender As Object, _
    ByVal e As System.EventArgs)

    SqlDataSourceNwd.Insert()
    GridView1.DataBind()

End Sub
```

```
Sample of C# Code
protected void ButtonSave_Click(object sender, EventArgs e)
{
    SqlDataSourceNwd.Insert();
    GridView1.DataBind();
}
```

Note that this code is very basic. It does not validate the data entered by the user and is therefore prone to error. It is simply an example.

14. Run the application and enter a row in the table. Notice that the entire page refreshes. Add behavior to the page so that the Add button triggers a partial-page update to the GridView control. To do so, add a trigger to the UpdatePanel control and connect the trigger to the ButtonEnter control. The following markup shows an example.

```
<asp:UpdatePanel ID="UpdatePanelVendors" runat="server">
  <Triggers>
    <asp:AsyncPostBackTrigger ControlID="ButtonSave" EventName="Click" />
  </Triggers>
  <ContentTemplate>
    <asp:GridView ...
```

15. Run the application again and notice that now only GridView updates when a new row is added.

EXERCISE 2 Adding a Progress Indicator

In this exercise, you add functionality that provides a notice to the user when the page is being partially updated on the server.

1. Continue editing the project you created in the previous exercise. Alternatively, you can open the completed Lesson 1, Exercise 1 project in the sample files installed from the CD.

2. Open Default.aspx in Source view. Add an UpdateProgress control to the UpdatePanel. Add the control to the bottom of the panel just inside the ContentTemplate element.

3. Add text inside the ProgressTemplate elements of the UpdateProgress control to notify the user that processing is happening on the server. The following shows a sample markup.

```
<asp:UpdateProgress ID="UpdateProgress1" runat="server">
    <ProgressTemplate>
        <div style="margin-top: 20px; font-size: larger; color: Green">
            Processing, please wait ...
        </div>
    </ProgressTemplate>
</asp:UpdateProgress>
```

4. The processing happens pretty fast. Therefore, add a line of code to the end of the ButtonSave_Click event to pause the server-side processing. You can simply put the thread to sleep for a few seconds. The following code shows an example.

Sample of Visual Basic code
```
System.Threading.Thread.Sleep(2000)
```

Sample of C# code
```
System.Threading.Thread.Sleep(2000);
```

5. Run the application and notice that the notification is shown to the user when you enter a new record in the GridView control.

6. You might have noticed that when you add a new record, the TextBox controls do not clear because the full page is not being updated. To fix this, add another UpdatePanel control to your page and nest the TextBox controls and the ButtonSave inside it. Inside the ButtonSave_Click event, set the Text property of each TextBox control to "".

EXERCISE 3 Using the Timer Control

In this exercise, you add functionality that uses the Timer control. You will add an area on the page that displays a series of graphics files by using a timed interval.

1. Continue editing the project you created in the previous exercise. Alternatively, you can open the completed Lesson 1, Exercise 2 project in the sample files installed from the CD.

2. Open the Default.aspx page in Source view.

3. Add an UpdatePanel control to the right of the supplier data entry form. (You can do so by creating a table with two columns.) This control will work like a rotating advertisement. It will periodically update and show a new image from the server.

4. Inside the UpdatePanel control's ContentTemplate element, add a label with the text **Advertisement**. Under this text, add an image control. You can add a couple of your own images to your project (or copy some from the sample files installed from the CD).

5. Under the image control (and still inside the ContentTemplate element), add a Timer control from the AJAX Extensions tab of the Toolbox. Set the Timer control's Interval attribute to 4,000 milliseconds (4 seconds).

6. Add an event handler for the Timer control's Tick event. Inside this event, add code to cycle between images (a simple if statement should suffice).

7. Run the application and wait until the Timer event fires. Your application should look similar to the one shown in Figure 9-3.

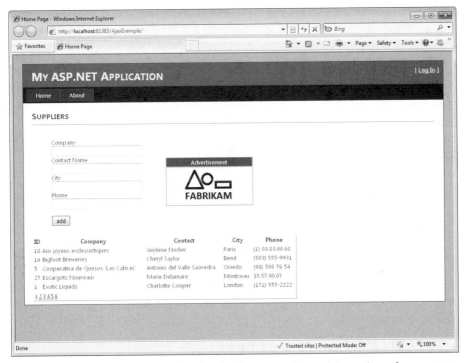

FIGURE 9-3 Using an UpdatePanel control and a Timer control to update portions of a page on a periodic basis.

Lesson Summary

- AJAX is a platform-independent, ECMAScript-compliant technology for communicating between code running on the client and code running on the server.

- ASP.NET includes both a set of server controls for working with AJAX and a set of client-side JavaScript files called the Microsoft AJAX Library.

- The ScriptManager control is required on all pages that work with the AJAX Extensions for ASP.NET. It manages the JavaScript files sent to the client and the communication between the server and the client.

- The ScriptManagerProxy control is used on pages that work with a master page that already defines a ScriptManager control or with user controls that will be used on pages that include a ScriptManager control.

- The UpdatePanel control allows you to define an area within your page that can post back to the server and receive updates independent of the rest of the page.

- The UpdateProgress control is used to provide notice to the user that the page has initiated a callback to the server.

- The Timer control is used to periodically send a partial-page request (by using an UpdatePanel control) to the server at timed intervals.

Lesson Review

You can use the following questions to test your knowledge of the information in Lesson 1, "Creating AJAX-Enabled Web Forms." The questions are also available on the companion CD as a practice test, if you prefer to review them in electronic form.

> **NOTE ANSWERS**
>
> Answers to these questions and explanations of why each answer choice is correct or incorrect are located in the "Answers" section at the end of the book.

1. You are working on a long data-entry webpage. In the middle of the page, you need to reach out to the server to get information based on a user's entry for a related field. However, you do not want the user to lose his or her focus or context within the page. Therefore, you decide to implement this feature by using the ASP.NET AJAX controls. Which of these controls must you add to the page to enable this scenario? (Choose all that apply.)

   A. UpdatePanel

   B. AsyncPostBackTrigger

   C. ScriptManager

   D. ScriptManagerProxy

2. You need to write a control that will be used across multiple pages. This control should contain updated sales figures. The control should update itself at various intervals if a containing page is left open. Which controls should you use to enable this scenario? (Choose all that apply.)

   A. UpdatePanel

   B. Timer

   C. ScriptManager

   D. ScriptManagerProxy

3. You have an UpdatePanel control defined on a page. You need to indicate that a specified Button control outside of the UpdatePanel should cause the UpdatePanel to execute an update. What steps should you take?

   A. Set the AsyncPostBackTrigger attribute of the UpdatePanel to the ID of the Button control.

   B. Set the AsyncPostBackTrigger attribute of the Button control to the ID of the UpdatePanel.

   C. Add a Trigger control to the AsyncPostBackTriggers section of the UpdatePanel. Set the ControlID attribute of the Trigger control to the ID of the Button control.

   D. Add an AsyncPostBackTrigger control to the Triggers section of the UpdatePanel. Set the ControlID attribute of the AsyncPostBackTrigger control to the ID of the Button control.

4. You are creating a page that contains an UpdatePanel control for partial-page updates. You want to notify the user that the update is processing only if the update takes longer than five seconds. Which actions should you take?

   A. Add a second UpdatePanel to the page. Set it to trigger based on the first UpdatePanel. Set the contents of this UpdatePanel to read "Processing, please wait."

   B. Add an UpdateProgress control to the UpdatePanel. Set its DisplayAfter attribute to 5,000. Set its ProgressTemplate contents to read "Processing, please wait."

   C. Add a ProgressBar control to the page. Write code on the server to call back to the client asynchronously to update the ProgressBar control after five seconds.

   D. Create a hidden <div> tag on your page that contains the text "Processing, please wait." Set the <div> tag's ID to match that of the UpdatePanel. Set the UpdatePanel control's Interval property to 5,000.

Lesson 2: Creating Client Scripts with the Microsoft AJAX Library

It is important to note that JavaScript is not new. It is also not really Java. It is a C-based scripting language invented by Netscape to add client scripting capabilities to a browser. It is now supported as part of every major browser on the market. The actual language is controlled and managed by a standards body, the European Computer Manufacturers Association (ECMA). Because it is widely deployed and offers developers the ability to write code on the client, it has become increasingly popular. This has been especially true in recent years as features for communicating between the client script and server code via JSON and XML have become prevalent and controls were created to take advantage of these features.

However, the JavaScript language still lacks basic object-oriented concepts found in modern programming languages. It also lacks a standard framework for developers to program against. The Microsoft AJAX Library was written (in JavaScript) to provide these constructs. This library, combined with the AJAX server controls, and the support for Visual Studio IntelliSense for JavaScript makes building AJAX-enabled applications more approachable.

This lesson covers the basics of client scripting with JavaScript. It then introduces the Microsoft AJAX Library and shows how you can use this library to add client-side functionality to your server controls.

> **After this lesson, you will be able to:**
> - Add client-side script blocks to your page and call them from client-side events.
> - Use the ClientScriptManager class to add script to a page dynamically at run time.
> - Register your client script with a page by using the ScriptManager class.
> - Understand the capabilities and use of the Microsoft AJAX Library.
> - Add AJAX support for client components and server controls.
>
> **Estimated lesson time: 40 minutes**

Creating Your Own Client Scripts

Scripts that execute on the client have been around a lot longer than AJAX. Client scripts add a client-side, dynamic nature to a web UI. It is AJAX programming, however, that has pushed a resurgence in JavaScript on the client. You will work with the Microsoft AJAX Library in a later section in this lesson. First, however, you learn the ways in which you can define client script on your ASP.NET webpage. There are three basic approaches to doing so:

- Define a script block on your webpage. This script block might define client-side code or an include attribute that references a JavaScript (.js) file.
- Use the ClientScriptManager class to dynamically add JavaScript to a page at run time based on server-side processing.
- Use the ScriptManager server control to register JavaScript with your webpage.

These methods represent a more traditional approach to working with client-side script. Each is covered in the following sections.

Adding Script Blocks to an ASP.NET Webpage

You can add client script to a webpage through a script block that includes code or through an include attribute that references a JavaScript (.js) file. Adding JavaScript to a webpage has been done for a long time. This is the traditional method of working with JavaScript on a webpage. It enables client-side functionality, but it does not necessarily take advantage of the features built into the Microsoft AJAX Library. The JavaScript elements are not created dynamically in this case, and they do not require the advanced features provided by the Microsoft AJAX Library. However, this method can be useful when you need basic JavaScript functionality for your page.

As an example, suppose you want to provide client-side functionality that hides an area of a webpage when the user toggles an open/close button. This provides the user with control over what is shown on his or her UI. To enable this scenario, you must first lay out the webpage.

In this example, the webpage might contain a titled area that includes a button for opening and closing an area on the page. This title area should always be shown so that the user can reopen the area if required. Next, you need to define an area of the page that contains content to be shown or hidden. Both of these areas can be defined by <div> tags. The following markup shows an example inside a content area of a child page that uses a master page.

```
<asp:Content ID="BodyContent" runat="server" ContentPlaceHolderID="MainContent">

    <div>
        <div style="width: 200px; background-color: Blue; color: White;
            border-style: solid; border-width: thin; border-color: Blue; height: 30px">

            <div style="float: left; vertical-align: middle; margin-top: 3px">
                Element Title
            </div>
            <div style="float: right; vertical-align: middle">
                <input id="ButtonCollapse" type="button" value="Close"
                    onclick="Collapse()" />
            </div>

        </div>

        <div id="DivCollapse" style="width: 200px; height: 200px;
            border-style: solid; border-width: thin; border-color: Blue">
            <div style="margin-top: 10px; text-align: center;">
                Content area ...
            </div>
        </div>

    </div>

</asp:Content>
```

In the preceding markup, the onclick event of the input button is set to call the Collapse method. This is a JavaScript method that will collapse (hide) the content <div> tag (called DivCollapse). The next step is to write this function. You can do so inside the head section of the ASPX markup for a standard ASPX page. If you use a child page based on a master page, you should add this block to the HeadContent content tag. The following code shows this latter option (a <script/> block and a function inside the HeadContent area).

```
<asp:Content ID="HeaderContent" runat="server" ContentPlaceHolderID="HeadContent">
    <script language="javascript" type="text/javascript">

        function Collapse() {
            if (DivCollapse.style.display == "") {
                DivCollapse.style.display = "none";
                document.forms[0].ButtonCollapse.value = "Open";
            }
            else {
                DivCollapse.style.display = "";
```

```
                    document.forms[0].ButtonCollapse.value = "Close";
                }
            }

        </script>
    </asp:Content>
```

When you run the code, the two areas defined by the <div> tags are shown along with the toggle button. Clicking this button executes the JavaScript on the client. Figure 9-4 shows an example of what the page looks like in the browser.

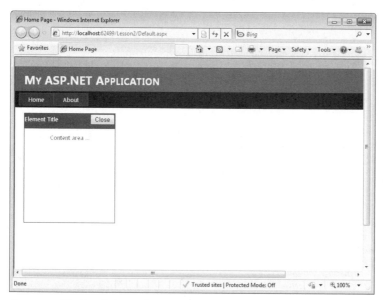

FIGURE 9-4 The JavaScript and HTML in the browser window.

> **NOTE   A BASIC EXAMPLE**
>
> This is a basic example. This type of functionality is also provided by the AJAX Control Toolkit and Web Parts in ASP.NET.

In this example, the JavaScript code is embedded directly in the page. If your JavaScript code is to be reused across multiple pages, you might want to externalize it into separate .js files. This allows both reuse and caching. The JavaScript files will be cached by browsers and thus the performance of your page will be improved. You provide this functionality by first creating the .js file and then placing your code inside it. You then reference the file inside a <script/> tag in the <head/> area of your page. The following code shows an example.

```
<script type="text/javascript" src="SiteScripts.js"></script>
```

The preceding example does not use many ASP.NET controls. Instead, it uses the standard HTML <Input/> tag to define a button. This tag's onClick event will simply execute a JavaScript method. However, for an ASP.NET Button control, the onClick attribute is used to declaratively connect an ASP.NET Button control to its server-side event. Therefore, to connect an ASP.NET Button control to a client-side JavaScript method, you can use the onClientClick attribute. In fact, you can set both the onClick and onClientClick attributes to respond to both a server-side and a client-side event for the same control. (Note that returning false from onClientClick negates the postback, but using onClientClick is preferred for client-side–only event processing.)

The following code shows an example of how you might replace the Input tag in the previous example with an ASP.NET Button control.

```
<asp:button id=" ButtonCollapse" runat="server" text="Close"
  onClientClick="Collapse();" />
```

It is also important to note that you can reference ASP.NET controls inside your client-side script. You reference them based on their rendering as HTML. The ASP.NET controls have the ClientId property for referencing the control inside client script or CSS rules. This property's value is generated based on how you set the ClientIDMode attribute. For example, to guarantee the ClientID value is always set to the value of the ID property, you can set ClientIDMode to Static. By default, the ClientIDMode is set to Predictable which means the ClientID value is generated by concatenating the ClientID of the parent container with the ID value of the control.

Adding Script Dynamically to an ASP.NET Page

Sometimes you might need to generate your JavaScript and add it to your page at run time. This could be because your controls are created at run time or because information that is added to the page determines the JavaScript that should be defined for the page. In either case, you can use the ClientScriptManager class to register JavaScript dynamically.

An instance of the ClientScriptManager class is exposed through the Page object's ClientScript property. You use this property to add JavaScript to the page at run time, to determine whether a script has already been registered, and for other related tasks. To add a script, you define it inside a string or point to its file. You then call the Page.ClientScript.RegisterClientScriptBlock method. This method takes a type (typically the instance of the page or control), a key that uniquely identifies the script (to help avoid collisions), the script itself, and a Boolean value indicating whether you need the registration to generate script tags.

As an example, suppose you have a TextBox that allows the user to enter a password. Suppose you also want to give the user the ability to check the password's strength as it is typed. You might leave this feature turned off by default but allow users to turn it on. When they do so, you need to dynamically register a client script with the page from your code. The following code shows the markup for this example page.

```
<asp:Content ID="Content2" ContentPlaceHolderID="MainContent" Runat="Server">

    <div>
        Enter Password<br />
        <asp:TextBox ID="TextBoxPassword" runat="server" Width="250"></asp:TextBox>
          <span id="passwordStrength"></span>
        <br />
        <asp:CheckBox ID="CheckBoxPassStrengthOn" runat="server"
            Text="Turn on password strength checking" AutoPostBack="true"
            oncheckedchanged="CheckBoxPassStrengthOn_CheckedChanged" />
    </div>

</asp:Content>
```

Notice that this markup is inside an <asp:Content/> tag, indicating that this page uses a master page. In the case of master pages, your control IDs are reset by ASP.NET to include the ContentPlaceholderID content area, followed by an underscore and the control name. Therefore, to use JavaScript to reference the TextBoxPassword control in this example, you would use the MainContent_TextBoxPassword as the ID.

This markup also includes a CheckBox control that is set to automatically post back when the user selects the check box (AutoPostBack="true"). Therefore, you need to handle its CheckedChanged event in your code. Here you can check to see if the check box is selected and if so, register client script to verify the password. The following code listing shows an example.

Sample of Visual Basic Code

```vb
Partial Class PasswordCheckTestVb
    Inherits System.Web.UI.Page

    Protected Sub CheckBoxPassStrengthOn_CheckedChanged(ByVal sender As Object, _
        ByVal e As System.EventArgs) Handles CheckBoxPassStrengthOn.CheckedChanged

        If CheckBoxPassStrengthOn.Checked Then

            Dim passFunc As New StringBuilder()
            passFunc.Append("function CheckPassword() {")
            passFunc.Append("var passLen = document.forms[0].MainContent_
TextBoxPassword.value.length;")
            passFunc.Append(" if (passLen < 4) {")
            passFunc.Append(" document.getElementById(""passwordStrength"").")
            passFunc.Append("innerText = ""weak"";")
            passFunc.Append(" document.getElementById(""passwordStrength"").")
            passFunc.Append("style.color = ""red"";}")
            passFunc.Append(" else if (passLen < 6) {")
            passFunc.Append(" document.getElementById(""passwordStrength"").")
            passFunc.Append("innerText = ""medium"";")
            passFunc.Append(" document.getElementById(""passwordStrength"").")
            passFunc.Append("style.color = ""blue"";}")
            passFunc.Append(" else if (passLen > 9) {")
            passFunc.Append(" document.getElementById(""passwordStrength"").")
            passFunc.Append("innerText = ""strong"";")
            passFunc.Append(" document.getElementById(""passwordStrength"").")
            passFunc.Append("style.color = ""green"";}}")

            'register the script
            Page.ClientScript.RegisterClientScriptBlock(Me.GetType(), _
              "CheckPasswordScript", passFunc.ToString(), True)

            'add an event to the text box to call the script
            TextBoxPassword.Attributes.Add("onkeyup", "CheckPassword()")

        Else
            'remove the event from the text box
            TextBoxPassword.Attributes.Remove("onkeyup")
        End If

    End Sub

End Class
```

Sample of C# Code

```csharp
public partial class PasswordCheckTest : System.Web.UI.Page
{
    protected void CheckBoxPassStrengthOn_CheckedChanged(object sender, EventArgs e)
    {
        if (CheckBoxPassStrengthOn.Checked)
        {

            System.Text.StringBuilder passFunc = new System.Text.StringBuilder();
            passFunc.Append("function CheckPassword() {");
            passFunc.Append(
                @"var passLen = document.forms[0].MainContent_
TextBoxPassword.value.length;");
            passFunc.Append(@" if (passLen < 4) {");
            passFunc.Append(@" document.getElementById(""passwordStrength"").");
            passFunc.Append(@"innerText = ""weak"";");
            passFunc.Append(@" document.getElementById(""passwordStrength"").");
            passFunc.Append(@"style.color = ""red"";}");
            passFunc.Append(@" else if (passLen < 6) {");
            passFunc.Append(@" document.getElementById(""passwordStrength"").");
            passFunc.Append(@"innerText = ""medium"";");
            passFunc.Append(@" document.getElementById(""passwordStrength"").");
            passFunc.Append(@"style.color = ""blue"";}");
            passFunc.Append(@" else if (passLen > 9) {");
            passFunc.Append(@" document.getElementById(""passwordStrength"").");
            passFunc.Append(@"innerText = ""strong"";");
            passFunc.Append(@" document.getElementById(""passwordStrength"").");
            passFunc.Append(@"style.color = ""green"";}}");

            //register the script
            Page.ClientScript.RegisterClientScriptBlock(this.GetType(),
              "CheckPasswordScript", passFunc.ToString(), true);

            //add an event to the text box to call the script
            TextBoxPassword.Attributes.Add("onkeyup", "CheckPassword()");
        }
        else
        {
            //remove the event from the text box
            TextBoxPassword.Attributes.Remove("onkeyup");
        }
    }
}
```

When you run the page, users have no indication of their password strength. However, if they select the check box, the page posts to the server and a client script is added to the page as a response to the postback. Users can now verify their password strength, as shown in Figure 9-5. Also, notice in the preceding code listing that the event handler is removed from the TextBox control if the check box is not selected. This is necessary to avoid encountering an error as the script is removed after a postback (unless it is added back in).

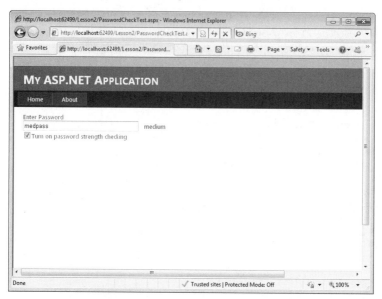

FIGURE 9-5 Dynamically adding JavaScript to a page by using RegisterClientScriptBlock.

You can also register client scripts to be executed only when the page is submitted. This allows the application to know when the user has caused a page submission. The page can then use your script code to validate the submission and cancel it if necessary. To register a client script to be executed only on page submission, you use the RegisterOnSubmitStatement method of the ClientScriptManager. This method works in a fashion similar to the operation of RegisterClientScriptBlock. It takes a type, a key, and the script as parameters.

Registering Client Scripts with the ScriptManager Control

The ScriptManager control, as discussed in the previous lesson, is used by the ASP.NET AJAX Extensions server controls. It automatically registers the appropriate script files defined by the Microsoft AJAX Library. If you are using a ScriptManager control, you can also use this library in your scripts. (This is discussed in greater detail later in the lesson.)

In addition, you can use the ScriptManager control to register your own scripts with the page. You can do so declaratively or programmatically. To add a script to the ScriptManager declaratively, you use the <Scripts> collection element of the ScriptManager control. The following markup shows an example.

```
<asp:ScriptManager ID="ScriptManager1" runat="server">
  <Scripts>
    <asp:ScriptReference Name="AppScripts.js" />
  </Scripts>
</asp:ScriptManager>
```

Note that if your JavaScript file is embedded in an assembly, you can add the Assembly attribute to the ScriptReference tag and point to the DLL file. This is useful when you do not have full source code files or are working with precompiled objects.

You can also register scripts from your server code. You do so by creating an instance of the ScriptReference class. You then add this instance to the Scripts collection of the ScriptManager control, as the following code illustrates.

Sample of Visual Basic Code

```
Dim sr As New ScriptReference("AppScripts.js")
ScriptManager1.Scripts.Add(sr)
```

Sample of C# Code

```
ScriptReference sr = new ScriptReference("AppScripts.js");
ScriptManager1.Scripts.Add(sr);
```

If you are using a ScriptManager control on your page already, you can use it to register client scripts. If you are not using AJAX features associated with a ScriptManager control, you are better off using the ClientScriptManager object (exposed through Page.ClientScript) mentioned earlier, because it does not have the overhead of the ScriptManager server control.

> **IMPORTANT SCRIPT REGISTRATION**
>
> Only scripts registered with the ScriptManager are available for use in partial-page update scenarios. If you need your script in these scenarios, you must register it with the ScriptManager class.

 Quick Check

1. In JavaScript, how do you reference an ASP.NET control added to a standard ASPX webpage? How do you reference the same control added to a child ASPX page that uses a master page?

2. Where should you place client script you intend to use across multiple pages of a site?

3. What property and method of the Page object do you use to register client script dynamically from code?

Quick Check Answers

1. In JavaScript, you can reference the ASP.NET control added to a standard ASPX page by using its ID. If the control is added to a master page, you must use the ContentPlaceHolderID_ControlId naming convention.

2. You should place shared script code in a .js file. This allows you to easily share the code between pages. It also allows browsers to cache this code.

3. Page.ClientScript.RegisterClientScriptBlock is used to dynamically register client script from code.

Creating Your Own Client Callbacks

In the previous lesson, you learned how to implement partial-page updates by using the UpdatePanel control and other features of the Microsoft ASP.NET AJAX-oriented controls. These controls make it easy to create a client callback (a call to the server followed by a call back to the client from the server). There may be times, however, when you need more control over how you call to the server from the client and vice versa. In these cases, you need to write your own asynchronous client callbacks.

Creating a page with its own client callback code follows a standard set of steps. First, you must define the server-side code. To do so:

1. Implement the System.Web.UI.ICallbackEventHandler for your ASP.NET page. This server-side interface is used to set up both the receive call from the client (RaiseCallbackEvent) and the method that returns processing to the client (GetCallbackResults).

2. Implement the RaiseCallbackEvent method for the ICallbackEventHandler interface. This method is called by the client. You can use it to receive parameter values from the client.

3. Implement the GetCallbackResult method for the ICallbackEventHandler interface. This function is used to return the results of any server-side processing. The results are sent as a string back to the client code.

After the server-side code is written, the next task is to create the client-side code. This also follows a standard set of steps:

4. Add a client script function that will be called by the server as the result of the server processing. You can use this function to process any results coming back from the server. This function's name should be the same as the name you registered with the GetCallbackEventReference inside your server-side code when the page is loaded. This ensures that the callback gets called after server-side processing.

5. Create another JavaScript function that calls the server from the client. This function is typically created in your server-side code when the page is loaded. Doing so allows you to register the client-side function by using the RegisterClientScriptBlock method of the ClientScriptManager control. This function is then used by one or more controls on your page to initiate the client-side call to the server.

6. The final JavaScript function that is inserted into the rendered page is actually generated for you by ASP.NET. This is the function that actually does the calling between the client and server. This function is generated when you use the GetCallbackEventReference method of the ClientScriptManager control in your server-side code.

As an example, suppose you have a webpage that contains a DropDownList control. Imagine that you want to call the server when the user selects an item from the DropDownList, but you do not want to do a full-page post. Rather, you want to initiate an asynchronous client callback. You can then do some processing on the server and return the results to the client. The client page can then be updated without causing a refresh.

Let's see how to implement this example. First, you would need to implement the ICallbackEventHandler interface for the code-behind page. This code might look as follows.

Sample of Visual Basic Code
```
Partial Class _Default
  Inherits System.Web.UI.Page
  Implements System.Web.UI.ICallbackEventHandler
```

Sample of C# Code
```
public partial class Default :
  System.Web.UI.Page, System.Web.UI.ICallbackEventHandler
```

Next, you would implement the RaiseCallbackEvent. This event is called by the client during a callback. It receives any event arguments from the client as a string. For this example, these event arguments represent the selected choice in the DropDownList. Suppose you want to store these event arguments in a class-level variable. Your code should look as follows.

Sample of Visual Basic Code
```
Dim _callbackArgs As String

Public Sub RaiseCallbackEvent(ByVal eventArgument As String) _
    Implements System.Web.UI.ICallbackEventHandler.RaiseCallbackEvent

    _callbackArgs = eventArgument

End Sub
```

Sample of C# Code
```
string _callbackArgs;

public void RaiseCallbackEvent(string eventArgument)
{
    _callbackArgs = eventArgument;
}
```

You also would have to implement the GetCallbackResult method. This method returns a result back to the client following the server-side processing. In our example, we simply return the user's selected item from the DropDownList. In a real-world scenario, you might do some processing, calling the database, and so forth. The code for this method looks as follows.

Sample of Visual Basic Code
```
Public Function GetCallbackResult() As String _
    Implements System.Web.UI.ICallbackEventHandler.GetCallbackResult

    Return _callbackArgs

End Function
```

Sample of C# Code
```
public string GetCallbackResult()
{
    return _callbackArgs;
}
```

The next step is to add code to the page load event that registers the various client scripts. First, you register the client script that will be called by the server following the server-side processing. In this example, this script is called ClientCallbackFunction. This function is defined in the markup for the page. Next, you create a JavaScript function that is used to call the server-side code. In the example, this function is called MyServerCall. It is referenced in the page markup to make the server-side call. You register this function with the ClientScriptManager by using the RegisterClientScriptBlock method, as shown here.

Sample of Visual Basic Code

```
Protected Sub Page_Load(ByVal sender As Object, _
    ByVal e As System.EventArgs) Handles Me.Load

    'register the name of the client-side function that will
    ' be called by the server
    Dim callbackRef As String = Page.ClientScript.GetCallbackEventReference( _
      Me, "args", "ClientCallbackFunction", "")

    'define a function used by the client to call the server
    Dim callbackScript As String = String.Format( _
        "function MyServerCall (args) {{{0};}}", callbackRef)

    'register the client function with the page
    Page.ClientScript.RegisterClientScriptBlock(Me.GetType(), _
        "MyServerCall", callbackScript, True)

End Sub
```

Sample of C# Code

```
protected void Page_Load(object sender, EventArgs e)
{
    //register the name of the client-side function that will
    // be called by the server
    string callbackRef = Page.ClientScript.GetCallbackEventReference(
      this, "args", "ClientCallbackFunction", "");

    //define a function used by the client to call the server
        string callbackScript = String.Format(
            "function MyServerCall(args) {{{0};}}", callbackRef);

    //register the client function with the page
    Page.ClientScript.RegisterClientScriptBlock(this.GetType(),
        "MyServerCall", callbackScript, true);
}
```

The last step in this example is to write the page markup. Here you define a client script that receives the callback from the server. Recall that this script is named ClientCallbackFunction and takes a string (args) as a parameter. In this example, this function writes out the args value to a Label control. You also must initiate the call to the server from the client. For this, recall that you need to call the MyServerCall method. In the example, this method is called as a result of the OnChange event for the DropDownList control. The example passes the selected item as a parameter. These page markup items look as follows.

```
<script type="text/javascript">
function ClientCallbackFunction(args)
{
    LabelMessage.innerText = args;
}
</script>

<asp:DropDownList ID="DropDownListChoice" runat="server"
    OnChange="MyServerCall(DropDownListChoice.value)">

    <asp:ListItem>Choice 1</asp:ListItem>
    <asp:ListItem>Choice 2</asp:ListItem>
    <asp:ListItem>Choice 3</asp:ListItem>
</asp:DropDownList>
<br /><br />
<asp:Label ID="LabelMessage" runat="server"></asp:Label>
```

When the page is run, a user selects a choice from the drop-down list. This calls the MyServerCall client-side method, which initiates a call to the server. The RaiseCallbackEvent method is then called on the server; this accepts the event arguments (the user's choice). The server processes the request and calls the GetCallbackResult method. The results are then passed back to the client. When back on the client, the ClientCallbackFunction JavaScript method is executed, and the result (the user's choice) is shown to the user.

Working with the Microsoft AJAX Library

As you have seen, you can create your own JavaScript and embed it in an ASP.NET page. However, JavaScript can be challenging to program with, especially if you are used to developing in an object-oriented world with a strong type system, a framework, and error handling and debugging support. The Microsoft AJAX Library helps solve these issues by bringing support for these items in the form of a wrapper library for the JavaScript language.

This section provides an overview of the Microsoft AJAX Library. It then covers how you can leverage this library to create AJAX-enabled server controls, client components, and behaviors that can be attached to client controls.

Features of the Microsoft AJAX Library

The Microsoft AJAX Library is actually written in JavaScript. It is a set of files that are sent to the browser to provide a base of capabilities on which you can build. ScriptManager automatically injects these scripts into the page markup. ScriptManager first determines which files are required, and if they are, it manages their inclusion in the markup. Microsoft AJAX Library support is not available unless you include a ScriptManager on your page or explicitly including these files.

The Microsoft AJAX Library is meant to make your JavaScript more robust, easier to write, and more reusable. The following are the core features and benefits of the library:

- **Object-oriented support**   The library allows you to define namespaces; build classes that contain fields, properties, and methods; create event handlers; implement inheritance and interfaces; use data types and enumerations; and support reflection.

- **Base classes**   The library includes a Global namespace that provides extensions to the JavaScript base types, including String, Number, Date, Boolean, Array, and Object. It also adds the Type class to the language for registering namespaces, classes, and more.

- **A framework (or set of namespaces)**   The Microsoft AJAX Library includes a root namespace called Sys that contains classes and other namespaces that make programming AJAX applications easier. Think of the Sys namespace as a client-side equivalent to System in the Microsoft .NET Framework (although obviously not as rich). Other namespaces include Sys.Net, Sys.Services, Sys.UI, Sys.WebForms, and Sys.Serialization.

- **Browser compatibility**   JavaScript is a standards-driven language. However, there are multiple quirks to the implementations of that language across browsers, just as there are for HTML. The Microsoft AJAX Library takes these into account and has built-in support for browser compatibility with Internet Explorer, Firefox, and Safari.

- **Debugging and error handling**   The Microsoft AJAX Library includes debugging extensions to make debugging easier. In fact, there are two versions of the library: a release version and a debug version. In addition, the library includes an extended Error object that provides more error information. It also includes tracing support with Sys.Debug.trace.

- **Globalization support**   The Microsoft AJAX Library supports building global, localized client scripts for working across languages and cultures. Your single JavaScript code base can then provide localized UI support without posting back to the server. This is achieved through number and data format methods that work with the language and culture settings in the browser.

Next you will learn more about the contents of the Sys namespaces, how to code against the library, and how to work with client events. Following this, you will read about how you can use this information to add client-side capabilities to the page.

The Microsoft AJAX Library Namespaces

The Microsoft AJAX Library is about two things: extending the JavaScript language and providing a base framework for common AJAX tasks. There are many types, controls, enumerations, and members found in the library. The following provides an overview of how the library's namespaces are organized:

- **Global** The Global namespace represents an extension of JavaScript itself. It extends many of the core elements and capabilities of the language. For example, the Number, String, Date, Array, and other types are given new functionality by the Microsoft AJAX Library. In addition, the Global namespace adds the Type class to JavaScript. The Type class is used to register object-oriented items in JavaScript like namespaces, classes, interfaces, and enumerations. The following line of JavaScript code shows an example of using the Type class to register a namespace.

```
Type.registerNamespace("MyCompany.MyApplication");
```

- **Sys** The Sys namespace is the root namespace of the AJAX Library. The Global namespace extends JavaScript, whereas the Sys namespace contains a framework for AJAX programming with JavaScript. There are several core classes in the Sys namespace. They include the Application class, which is a run-time version of the library used for connecting to client-side events.

  The Component class is also in the Sys namespace. It is used for registering and creating instances of the components you create for use with the library. You use it by calling the Component.create method (also accessed via the shortcut $create). The Component class also serves as the base class for the Control and Behavior classes discussed later in this section.

  The Sys namespace includes other notable classes such as StringBuilder for concatenating strings; Debug for debug and tracing support; EventArgs, which is used as a base class for passing parameters to events; and more.

- **Sys.Net** The Sys.Net namespace contains classes focused on the communication between the browser and the server. The classes in this namespace provide the basis for doing partial-page updates and calling web services from the browser. Classes in this namespace include the Sys.Net.WebRequest class, which is covered in Chapter 10 in the web services discussion.

- **Sys.Serialization** The Sys.Serialization namespace is also used to communicate between client and server. It contains a single class: JavaScriptSerializer. This class is used to serialize and deserialize data to be passed from browser and server in web service calls.

- **Sys.Services** The Sys.Services namespace contains classes for working with the AJAX authentication and profile services from script.

- **Sys.UI** The Sys.UI namespace contains the classes used to add AJAX features to the UI. It includes the Behavior, Control, and DomElement classes , and more. You use these classes when building your own AJAX UI features. These classes are covered in later sections in this lesson.

- **Sys.WebForms** The Sys.WebForms namespace encapsulates the classes for partial-page updates. These classes are used by the UpdatePanel control. You can also use these to create your own partial-page scenarios. The PageRequestManager class is found here; it can be used to customize asynchronous postbacks.

This number of namespaces can seem a little daunting at first. As in any library, however, there are some features you will end up using a lot and others you won't usually need. We cannot cover every class and method here. You will see, however, that much of the action takes place in the Sys.UI namespace; this is where you interact to write AJAX UI elements.

> **MORE INFO MICROSOFT AJAX LIBRARY REFERENCE**
>
> If you get stuck with a specific class or method in the framework or in one of the following examples, you can look up the item in the complete library reference. This can be found on MSDN—see the "Microsoft Ajax Library Client Reference" at *http://msdn.microsoft.com /en-us/library/bb397536.aspx*.

Object-Oriented AJAX Development

JavaScript has support for many basic features such as simple classes, data types, and operators. However, it is missing key object-oriented features. These include support for namespaces, inheritance, interfaces, fields, properties, enumerations, events, reflection, and more. The Microsoft AJAX Library extends the language by providing support for these items.

A natural question to ask is why you need this type of support for JavaScript. The answer is that in many cases you do not. However, if you are building your own controls or need to enable very specific programming on the client, this library will help you. The best way to use the library is to define your requirements; create a JavaScript class definition in a .js file that will provide methods, properties, and other items you need to meet those requirements; and then register that file with your page. You can then create an instance of your class and work with it on the page. This includes associating the class items with the actions on controls.

This section covers the "create-a-class" step. You will read about how to connect to this class on your page in the sections that follow and in the practice.

NAMESPACES

The Microsoft AJAX Library adds the ability to work with namespaces to JavaScript. A namespace is a way to encapsulate code into a library for easier classification and reference. It also helps manage name collisions, because two classes cannot have the same name in a single namespace. In addition, namespaces that you create and register with the library are then available in IntelliSense in Visual Studio, making development a little easier.

The library provides an important class called Type. The Type class represents a typing system for JavaScript. It is the key class that enables you to have namespaces, classes, enumerations, and things like that. The class sits inside the Global namespace.

You use the registerNamespace method of the Type class to define a namespace. This is typically done at the top of your class file. You then use the namespace you define here throughout your class definition to add classes, enumerations, and so forth. The following line of code shows an example.

```
Type.registerNamespace("Contoso.Utilities");
```

In this example, the Contoso.Utilities namespace is being defined. Consider this a company-wide utility namespace that might include helper classes for a development team.

CLASSES (CONSTRUCTORS, FIELDS, PROPERTIES, AND METHODS)

The Microsoft AJAX Library also allows you to define class definitions. The syntax for creating a class with the library is Namespace.ClassName. You assign the class name to a function that also serves as your constructor. This function can also take parameters.

For example, suppose you want to add a class to the Contoso.Utilities namespace defined earlier. The requirements for this class are to provide validation features (on the client) related to the process of a user changing his or her password. You might name this class ChangePasswordValidator. The following code shows a definition of this class.

```
//define class name (as function), create constructor, and
//    set class-level field values
Contoso.Utilities.ChangePasswordValidator =
    function(requirePasswordsNotMatch, requireNumber)
{
    Contoso.Utilities.ChangePasswordValidator.initializeBase(this);
    this.RequirePasswordsNotMatch = requirePasswordsNotMatch;
    this.RequireNumber = requireNumber;
    this._passwordRuleViolations = new Array();
}
```

Notice that the class is set to a function. This function serves as the constructor for the class. When a developer uses the new keyword to create an instance of your class, he or she will be shown this constructor by IntelliSense and have to provide the two parameters defined by the function. These parameters are specific to the password scenario and facilitate how the password rules will process. The parameters are set to field-level items on the class inside the constructor. This is shown by the following call.

```
this.<FieldName> = <parameter>
```

The following is an example.

```
this.RequireNumber = requireNumber;
```

Also notice the call to initializeBase. This ensures that the base class from which your class derives gets its constructor called, too. You typically derive your classes from Sys.Component or one of its derivates. However, you do not have to. You derive from Sys.Component, Sys.UI.Behavior, or Sys.UI.Control if you intend to use the class as part of an AJAX control (more on this later).

After you define the class and its constructor, the next step is to define the fields, properties, methods, and other items that make up the actual class. You do so by defining a prototype for the class. You set the prototype definition to include fields, methods, and methods that act as properties.

For example, to define a prototype for the ChangePasswordValidator class, you make a call to the JavaScript prototype property and set it equal to a class definition (enclosed in braces). To define fields for the class, you simply declare variables at the class level and set their data type. Fields are essentially name-value pairs in which the name is an element of the prototype (or class definition) and the value is set by the user of the class. The following code shows the start of a class definition that also defines two Boolean fields.

```
//define class contents (fields, properties, methods)
Contoso.Utilities.ChangePasswordValidator.prototype =
{

    //declare fields
    RequirePasswordsNotMatch: Boolean,
    RequireNumber: Boolean,
    ...

}
```

The next step is to add properties to the class definition just started. By default, JavaScript does not really support properties. Instead, you can define methods that act as properties by declaring two functions. One function returns the value of an internal member and the other function receives a value to be assigned to this internal member. The convention for naming properties in the Microsoft AJAX Library is to use set_propertyName and get_propertyName for the setter and getter, respectively. The internal variables are defined with leading under-scores (_), as in _privateMember. This indicates to the library that these items should remain private to the class (even if JavaScript does not actually support private fields).

As an example, consider the class discussed earlier for a user who is changing his or her password. You might want to define write-only properties for the current password and the new password. You can do so by simply implementing a set_ function (and not a get_). This is shown in the following code example, along with a property to return all password violations that occur during validation.

```
//properties
set_currentPassword: function(value)
{
    this._currentPassword = value;
},

set_changeToPassword: function(value)
{
    this._changeToPassword = value;
},

get_passwordRuleViolations: function()
{
    return this._passwordRuleViolations;
},
```

You add methods to a class prototype in much the same way that you add a function. The following code shows two example functions. The first, CheckPasswordStrength, takes a string and returns an enumeration value, Contoso.Utilities.PasswordStrength (more on this in a moment). The second function definition, AllowPasswordChange, can be called to determine whether a user's changed password meets the criteria for a change. If not, rules are added to an Array, and the false value is returned by the function. These rules (or password error conditions) can then be accessed through the property defined previously.

```
//methods
CheckPasswordStrength: function(password)
{
    var strPass = new String(password.toString());
    if (strPass.length < 4)
    {
        return Contoso.Utilities.PasswordStrength.Weak;
    }
    else if (strPass.Length < 7)
    {
        return Contoso.Utilities.PasswordStrength.Medium;
    }
    else
    {
        return Contoso.Utilities.PasswordStrength.Strong;
    }
},

AllowPasswordChange: function()
{

    var pass1 = new String(this._currentPassword);
    var pass2 = new String(this._changeToPassword);

    //use new, extended Array type
    var ruleViolations = new Array();

    //min length rule
    if (pass2.length < 5)
    {
        Array.add(ruleViolations, 'Password too short.');
    }

    //check if passwords match
    if (this.RequirePasswordsNotMatch)
    {
        if (pass1 == pass2)
        {
            Array.add(ruleViolations, 'Passwords cannot match.');
        }
    }
```

```
        //contains numbers
        if (this.RequireNumber)
        {
            if (pass2.match(/\d+/) == null)
            {
                Array.add(ruleViolations, 'Password must include a number.');
            }
        }

        //reset rule violations property
        this._passwordRuleViolations = ruleViolations;

        //determine if change allowed
        if (ruleViolations.length > 0)
        {
            return false;
        }
        else
        {
            return true;
        }
    }
}
```

As with a namespace, you must also register a class with the Microsoft AJAX Library for it to be available with the ScriptManager at run time and through IntelliSense at design time. You register a class by calling the registerClass extension method of your object. This method has three parameters: typeName, baseType, and interfaceTypes. TypeName is the full name of the class you intend to register. BaseType is the class on which the new class builds. This is how inheritance is supported by the library. If your class should stand alone, you can pass null into this parameter. If your class is meant to be an AJAX control or a behavior, you pass in Sys.UI.Control or Sys.UI.Behavior, respectively. Finally, the interfaceTypes parameter indicates the interfaces that the class must implement. You can define your own interfaces with the library. You can also implement one or more framework interfaces. This parameter is an array, so you can pass multiple interfaces into it. The following code shows an example of the registerClass method.

```
//register code as an actual class
Contoso.Utilities.ChangePasswordValidator.registerClass(
    'Contoso.Utilities.ChangePasswordValidator', null, Sys.IDisposable);
```

ENUMERATIONS

The Microsoft AJAX Library provides support for enumerations. These enumerations are simply named integer values. Like enumerations in other languages (C# and Visual Basic included), enumerations provide a more readable and maintainable coding style.

You define an enumeration the same way you define a class, by using the prototype property. You then define fields for the class and set their initial value. Finally, you call the registerEnum method of the Type class (which is used to extend the JavaScript library). The following is an example of an enumeration created to define a password's strength.

```
//create and register an enumeration
Contoso.Utilities.PasswordStrength = function(){};
Contoso.Utilities.PasswordStrength.prototype =
{
    Weak: 1,
    Medium: 2,
    Strong: 3
}
Contoso.Utilities.PasswordStrength.registerEnum(
    "Contoso.Utilities.PasswordStrength");
```

INHERITANCE

Support for inheritance is also available with the Microsoft AJAX Library. This allows a JavaScript class to inherit the properties and methods of a base class. Of course, the inheriting class can also override those properties and methods. This is similar to inheritance in other object-oriented languages.

You implement inheritance through the registerClass method discussed earlier by setting the baseType property during registration. This enables single inheritance (similar to how the .NET Framework works). If you want to override a function, you simply redefine it by using the same name in the new class.

INTERFACES

You can also define and implement interfaces with the Microsoft AJAX Library. These interfaces are again similar to those in the .NET Framework; they represent contracts that the class must implement. You can also implement multiple interfaces in a class.

You indicate that a class should implement an interface by using the registerClass method. This was shown earlier and is repeated in the following code. The third parameter of this method represents the interfaceTypes that the class implements. You can pass a single interface (as shown here with Sys.IDisposable) or multiple interfaces.

```
Contoso.Utilities.ChangePasswordValidator.registerClass(
    'Contoso.Utilities.ChangePasswordValidator', null, Sys.IDisposable);
```

The library also allows you to define and implement your own interfaces. To create an interface, you define it as you would a class. However, you do not add implementation to the interface, you just include method stubs. You then call the registerInterface method of the Type class. This registers your interface for use with the library. The following code shows an example of defining and registering an interface with the library.

```
//declare an interface
Contoso.Utilities.IValidationLogic = function() {}
Contoso.Utilities.IValidationLogic.prototype =
{
    get_isValid: function(){},
    get_validationRules: function() {},
    validate: function(){}
}
Contoso.Utilities.IValidationLogic.registerInterface(
    "Contoso.Utilities.IValidationLogic");
```

Using Custom Classes

Classes you create with the Microsoft AJAX Library can be used directly within your ASPX pages. To do so, you must first register the class with the ScriptManager. This tells the ScriptManager you have a class that is built with the library in mind. It also ensures that you get IntelliSense in the IDE for your namespaces, classes, methods, and so on. The following page script shows an example of how you would add the script that was defined in the previous section to the page.

```
<asp:ScriptManager ID="ScriptManager1" runat="server">
    <Scripts>
        <asp:ScriptReference path="ContosoUtilities.js" />
    </Scripts>
</asp:ScriptManager>
```

After the custom classes have been defined, you can use the class library as required in page-level script. For example, you can create a new instance of the ChangePasswordValidator control created earlier by using the new keyword and passing in the appropriate parameters to the constructor. The following code shows an example of creating an instance of the class and uses the enumeration, calling properties, and calling methods.

```
<script language="javascript" type="text/javascript">

    //call constructor
    var validator =
        new Contoso.Utilities.ChangePasswordValidator(true, true, true);

    //check the password strength
    strength = validator.CheckPasswordStrength("password");
    switch (strength)
    {
        case Contoso.Utilities.PasswordStrength.Weak:
            alert("Weak");
            break;
        case Contoso.Utilities.PasswordStrength.Medium:
            alert("Medium");
            break;
        case Contoso.Utilities.PasswordStrength.Strong:
            alert("Strong");
            break;
    }
```

```
    //set properties
    validator.set_currentPassword("password");
    validator.set_changeToPassword("pas2");

    //call methods
    if (validator.AllowPasswordChange())
    {
        alert("Password may be changed");
    }
    else
    {
        var violations = validator.get_passwordRuleViolations();

        alert("Rule violations: " + violations.length);
        for (i = 0; i < violations.length; i++)
        {
            alert("Rule violation " + i + " = " + violations[i]);
        }
    }

</script>
```

AJAX Client-Side Life Cycle Events

The Microsoft AJAX Library also includes a client-based event life cycle. You can use this life cycle to intercept events when the page runs, and load your code as required. Think of this as similar to how you work with code-behind files. For example, in a code-behind file you might write code in the Page_Load event. Similarly, in the code you write to run in the browser, you can implement the Sys.Application.load event.

Fortunately, the life cycle of your client code is very similar to that of your server code. This includes events for init, load, unload, and disposing. In this way, the Application client object works in a similar way as the Page object in your server code. To take advantage of this event model you must, of course, use a ScriptManager control on your page. You register an event in script by using the add_event syntax. The following code shows how you would register code with the Sys.Application.Load event.

```
Sys.Application.add_load(PageLoad);
function PageLoad(sender)
{
    //page-load code goes here
}
```

The library also allows you to unregister (or remove) events. You do so in a similar manner, by using the remove_<event name> syntax. The following shows an example.

```
Sys.Application.remove_load(PageLoad);
```

You can follow this similar model to trap other events in the library. For example, another important class with events that you might want to work with is the PageRequestManager class of the Sys.WebForms namespace. This class is used for partial-page updates and asynchronous postbacks. It includes the following events:

- **initializeRequest** Raised before the asynchronous postback starts
- **beginRequest** Raised as the asynchronous postback is sent to the server
- **pageLoading** Raised when the asynchronous postback response first comes back from the server
- **pageLoaded** Raised after the content has been loaded from the results of the asynchronous postback
- **endRequest** Raised when the asynchronous postback has been completed

As you might have guessed, the UpdatePanel control relies heavily on these events. You can also use these events to cancel asynchronous postbacks, provide custom information or animation to the user when these events are fired, or simply run your code at specific times within the request.

Building Client Capabilities with AJAX

Thus far, you've seen how to program against the Microsoft AJAX Library. You can use the skills you've learned to create client-side controls that are built on the Microsoft AJAX Library and thus are managed by it. It is important to remember that these are not server controls. Rather, they are controls that implement AJAX features on the client.

There are three types of client objects you can create with the Microsoft AJAX Library: *component*, *control*, and *behavior* objects. The following provides a brief description of each:

- **Sys.Component** This object provides a base class for creating reusable AJAX components. Classes that derive from Sys.Component do not generate UI elements. Instead, they work as common controls that provide functionality across pages. For example, the Timer control in the Microsoft AJAX Library implements Sys.Component.
- **Sys.UI.Control** This object provides a base class for creating reusable, AJAX-enabled client controls. These controls are typically related to a single Document Object Model (DOM) element (such as an input box or button). They provide additional functionality to the DOM element with which they are meant to work.
- **Sys.UI.Behavior** This object represents a base class for creating behaviors that can be added to one or more DOM elements at design time. A behavior is not associated with a single DOM element. Rather, it can extend the DOM elements to which it is applied. For example, you might create a behavior that opens a new window when the cursor points to the element. You could then apply this behavior to a button, input box, hyperlink, or other element.

Every control you create to work with the Microsoft AJAX Library will derive from one of these objects as its base. The sections that follow provide additional details on the three types of client objects you can create with the Microsoft AJAX Library.

Creating an AJAX Client Component

An AJAX client component is a class you create that derives from the Sys.Component class. You derive from this class when you want to create a class that gets managed by the Microsoft AJAX Library but does not work directly with the UI. This is similar to the class that was created in the previous section. However, in this case, you inherit the Sys.Component base class. This ensures that the library knows how to manage the lifetime of your object from initialize through disposal.

As an example (and building on the password example), consider a class that you write as a component that provides methods for verifying the strength of a password on the client. You would create this class the same way classes were created in the previous section. However, for the client component you have a couple of additional items to consider.

First, when you define the class constructor, you should make sure to initialize the base constructor in the base class. The following code shows an example.

```
Type.registerNamespace("AjaxEnabled");

//create constructor
AjaxEnabled.PasswordStrengthComponent = function() {
    AjaxEnabled.PasswordStrengthComponent.initializeBase(this);
}
```

Next, you might consider overriding the base class's methods. When you do, you should also make sure to call the methods of the base class you are overriding. You can do so by calling the callBaseMethod method (of the Type class). As an example, if you override the initialize method of the base class, you should write the following code to call its base init method.

```
initialize: function() {
    AjaxEnabled.PasswordStrengthComponent.callBaseMethod(this, 'initialize');
    //add custom initialization here
}
```

Finally, when you register the actual component, you must indicate that you are inheriting from the Sys.Component base class. The following shows an example of the registerClass method indicating inheritance of the Component class.

```
//register class as a Sys.Component
AjaxEnabled.PasswordStrengthComponent.registerClass(
    'AjaxEnabled.PasswordStrengthComponent', Sys.Component);
```

> **NOTE   ADDING A REFERENCE TO THE MICROSOFT AJAX LIBRARY**
>
> When working with JavaScript files in the code editor, you can add a reference to the Microsoft AJAX Library. This will ensure that your coding includes IntelliSense for the library. This is similar to the using statement in C# and the Imports statement in Visual Basic. You embed this reference in a comment at the top of your .js file. The following shows an example.
>
> ```
> /// <reference path="MicrosoftAjax.js"/>
> ```

Using the client component is the same as using any other Microsoft AJAX Library class. You first register it with the ScriptManager. You can then create an instance of it in your page and work with it as you would any other AJAX class (as discussed earlier). The first practice at the end of this lesson walks you through creating this component and working with it on an ASPX page.

Creating an AJAX Client Control

An AJAX client control is a control that you create that is meant to provide additional, client-side functionality to a DOM element (such as a button or an input box). A client control is meant to work as a single, encapsulated control much the same way as the ASP.NET server controls or the custom controls you might write. It is possible, however, to attach an AJAX client control to an existing DOM element or server control without creating a custom control. The more robust scenario is to create a custom server control that embeds the AJAX client control to provide additional features. This section explores both of these options.

AJAX client controls extend the functionality of a DOM element. Therefore, you must provide a means to indicate the DOM element that the AJAX control is meant to extend. This can be done in the constructor. For example, consider a password strength control that works with a text box to turn the text box different colors as the user types. These colors are based on the strength of the password after each keystroke. To start this control, you might define the following constructor.

```
//define the namespace
Type.registerNamespace('AjaxEnabled');

//create constructor
AjaxEnabled.PassTextBox = function(element) {
    AjaxEnabled.PassTextBox.initializeBase(this, [element]);

    this._weakCssClass = null;
    this._mediumCssClass = null;
    this._strongCssClass = null;

}
```

Notice that the constructor takes the element parameter. This represents the DOM element that the control is meant to extend. The first line of the constructor calls the initialize method of the base class (Sys.UI.Control) and passes an instance of this class and a reference to the element being extended by this class.

The next step is to define the class itself. This is the same as creating AJAX classes, which we discussed previously. However, most client controls you write will intercept events fired from the DOM element that they are intended to extend. They can also raise their own events to be used by the client. To enable this functionality, you need to override the initialize method of the Sys.UI.Control base class. The following code shows an example of this function inside the class's prototype.

```
//initialize the UI control
initialize: function() {
    AjaxEnabled.PassTextBox.callBaseMethod(this, 'initialize');

    this._onKeyupHandler = Function.createDelegate(this, this._onKeyup);
    $addHandlers(this.get_element(), {'keyup' : this._onKeyup}, this);
},
```

Notice the first line in the code just given. Here you indicate that the initialize method should also call the base class's initialize method. The next line creates a delegate to the method onKeyup that you define in your class. You then register this method as a handler for the element. The $addHandlers method does this. The first parameter is the DOM element for which you want to intercept events. You can call the get_element method to return the element associated with the class (from the constructor). The next parameter to the $addHandlers call is an array of the events you want to intercept. Each event is referenced by name, followed by the name of the method in your class you want to have called when the event fires. In the final parameter, you pass an instance of the running class.

In addition to the initialize event, you will also want to override dispose to clean things up. For example, you might want to remove the event handlers you added during initialize. Of course, here, too, you will want to make sure to call the base class's dispose method. The following shows an example of doing both of these things.

```
dispose: function() {
    $clearHandlers(this.get_element());
    AjaxEnabled.PassTextBox.callBaseMethod(this, 'dispose');
},
```

The next step is to define code for the events you intend to intercept. You do so by creating a function (with the same name as the event you indicated in the createDelegate and $addHandlers calls) that takes a single parameter as the event argument. Inside the event, you have access to the DOM element that the control extends through the call, this.get_element(). The following code shows an example of the intercepted keystroke event to be called when a user types in a text box.

```
//define keystroke event
_onKeyup : function(e) {

    //get password text
    var pass = this.get_element().value;
    var strength = this.returnPasswordStrength(pass);

    switch (strength) {
        case "Weak":
            this.get_element().className = this._weakCssClass;
            break;
        case "Medium":
            this.get_element().className = this._mediumCssClass;
            break;
        case "Strong":
            this.get_element().className = this._strongCssClass;
            break;
    }
},
```

The next step is to finish the class definition by creating your properties and methods. For this example, these items are covered in Practice 2 of this lesson.

Finally, you register the class with the Microsoft AJAX Library. When doing so, you indicate that the class inherits Sys.UI.Control. The following code shows an example.

```
//register class as a Sys.Control
AjaxEnabled.PassTextBox.registerClass('AjaxEnabled.PassTextBox', Sys.UI.Control);
```

When it is complete (see Practice 2 later in this lesson for a complete class listing), you can use the class on a page. You have two options for doing so: registering the class on the page through JavaScript, or creating a custom control to encapsulate this client control. The following sections look at both options.

USING AN AJAX CLIENT CONTROL ON A PAGE

You can use the client control with existing ASP.NET controls and DOM elements by directly accessing it on your page. To do so, you must first add a ScriptManager control to your page. Inside it, you reference the script that contains your client control. The following code shows an example of this for the password strength control discussed earlier.

```
<asp:ScriptManager ID="ScriptManager1" runat="server">
    <Scripts>
        <asp:ScriptReference Path="PasswordStrength.js" />
    </Scripts>
</asp:ScriptManager>
```

You also need to add the DOM element you intend to extend to the page. This is as straightforward as adding a control to the page. The password strength example is meant to work with a text box. Therefore, you can add either an <input /> box or an <asp:TextBox /> control to the page. The following shows an example of the latter.

```
<asp:TextBox ID="TextBoxPass" runat="server" TextMode="Password"></asp:TextBox>
```

The final step is to create an instance of the client control and connect it to the DOM element. You will typically perform such actions inside the application init method of the Microsoft AJAX Library. Therefore, you must create an override for this method. Inside the override, you use the $create method (a shortcut to Sys.Component.create) to both create an instance of your AJAX client control and connect that instance with the DOM element. The $create method has five parameters, as follows:

- **type** This parameter indicates the class instance you intend to create.
- **properties** This parameter is used to indicate properties and property values of the class instance that should be set when the item is created.
- **events** This parameter is used to indicate the events you intend to register from the client code to the client control.
- **references** This parameter indicates references to other components.
- **element** This parameter is used to indicate the DOM element to which your client control should be attached.

The following code shows a call to the $create method for the password strength control. Complete Practice 2 of this lesson to see the control in action.

```
<script language="javascript" type="text/javascript">

    var app = Sys.Application;
    app.add_init(appInit);

    function appInit(sender, args) {

        $create(AjaxEnabled.PassTextBox,
            {weakCssClass : 'weak', mediumCssClass : 'medium',
                strongCssClass : 'strong'},
            null, null, $get('TextBoxPass'));

    }

</script>
```

ENCAPSULATING AN AJAX CLIENT CONTROL INTO A CUSTOM SERVER CONTROL

A more robust solution for creating AJAX-enabled controls is to embed your client-side functionality into a custom control. Custom controls are covered in depth in Chapter 7, "Creating Custom Web Controls." You might want to make sure you have read that chapter if you need a quick overview of custom controls.

To create a custom control that embeds your client script, you must define a server-side class and use it to write the custom control. This class can be part of your website in the App_Code directory or can be embedded in its own assembly. The latter option allows you to isolate the control from the website and even use it across websites. The former option is great for dynamically compiling your control and deploying it on the code files associated with it (and not the DLL of a component).

The class itself must inherit from a control. This can be either an existing control you intend to extend or a base control (such as System.Web.UI.Control). The control must also implement the IScriptControl interface . This interface is used to implement methods to embed your JavaScript in the control. The following code example shows the password strength example control inheriting from TextBox and implementing the IScriptControl interface.

Sample of Visual Basic Code

```
Namespace AjaxEnabled

    Public Class PassTextBox
        Inherits TextBox
        Implements IScriptControl
        ...
```

Sample of C# Code

```
namespace AjaxEnabled
{
    public class PassTextBoxCs : TextBox, IScriptControl
    {
        ...
```

The next step is to create a class-level variable to represent the ScriptManager that works with the control. You can declare this variable and then override the OnPreRender event of the control to set its value. You do so by calling the ScriptManager.GetCurrent static method and passing in the page containing the control. The following shows an example.

Sample of Visual Basic Code

```vb
Private _sMgr As ScriptManager
Protected Overrides Sub OnPreRender(ByVal e As EventArgs)
    If Not Me.DesignMode Then

        'test for the existence of a ScriptManager
        _sMgr = ScriptManager.GetCurrent(Page)

        If _sMgr Is Nothing Then _
            Throw New HttpException( _
            "A ScriptManager control must exist on the page.")

        _sMgr.RegisterScriptControl(Me)
    End If

    MyBase.OnPreRender(e)
End Sub
```

Sample of C# Code

```csharp
private ScriptManager sMgr;
protected override void OnPreRender(EventArgs e)
{
    if (!this.DesignMode)
    {
        //test for the existence of a ScriptManager
        sMgr = ScriptManager.GetCurrent(Page);

        if (sMgr == null)
            throw new HttpException(
                "A ScriptManager control must exist on the page.");

        sMgr.RegisterScriptControl(this);
    }

    base.OnPreRender(e);
}
```

Next, you define the properties of the control that users will set. In the password example, there are properties defined for the three style class names that should be set on the text box for each of the password strengths (weak, medium, and strong). You can add fields or properties to the server control to represent these items. You then create a GetScriptDescriptors method to map these properties or fields to properties of the control. The following shows an example.

Sample of Visual Basic Code

```vb
Public WeakCssClass As String
Public MediumCssClass As String
Public StrongCssClass As String

Protected Overridable Function GetScriptDescriptors() _
    As IEnumerable(Of ScriptDescriptor)

    Dim descriptor As ScriptControlDescriptor = _
        New ScriptControlDescriptor("AjaxEnabled.PassTextBox", Me.ClientID)

    descriptor.AddProperty("weakCssClass", Me.WeakCssClass)
    descriptor.AddProperty("mediumCssClass", Me.MediumCssClass)
    descriptor.AddProperty("strongCssClass", Me.StrongCssClass)

    Return New ScriptDescriptor() {descriptor}

End Function
```

Sample of C# Code

```csharp
public string WeakCssClass;
public string MediumCssClass;
public string StrongCssClass;

protected virtual IEnumerable<ScriptDescriptor> GetScriptDescriptors()
{
    ScriptControlDescriptor descriptor =
        new ScriptControlDescriptor("AjaxEnabled.PassTextBox", this.ClientID);

    descriptor.AddProperty("weakCssClass", this.WeakCssClass);
    descriptor.AddProperty("mediumCssClass", this.MediumCssClass);
    descriptor.AddProperty("strongCssClass", this.StrongCssClass);

    return new ScriptDescriptor[] { descriptor };
}
```

You must also register the actual JavaScript code to be used by your control. You do so by writing a GetScriptReferences method. This method references the .js file that you intend to use to extend your custom control. There are two ways to implement this method, one for controls in the App_Code directory of the website and another for controls you create as stand-alone assemblies. The following code shows an example of the former, a custom control created in the website's App_Code directory and referencing a JavaScript file in the same website.

Sample of Visual Basic Code

```vb
Protected Overridable Function GetScriptReferences() _
    As IEnumerable(Of ScriptReference)

    Dim reference As ScriptReference = New ScriptReference()
    reference.Path = ResolveClientUrl("PasswordStrength.js")

    Return New ScriptReference() {reference}

End Function
```

Sample of C# Code

```csharp
protected virtual IEnumerable<ScriptReference> GetScriptReferences()
{
    ScriptReference reference = new ScriptReference();
    reference.Path = ResolveClientUrl("PasswordStrength.js");

    return new ScriptReference[] { reference };
}
```

The latter method, embedding the control in its own assembly, is covered in Practice 3 at the end of this lesson.

To use the custom control, you register it with the page and then define its tag. For example, to use the password strength custom control created inside the App_Code directory, you add the following directive to the top of your webpage source.

```
<%@ Register Namespace="AjaxEnabled" TagPrefix="AjaxEnabled" %>
```

You then add a ScriptManager to your page. You can then define the control's markup as you would any other server control. The following shows the control in the example. Notice that the three properties of the control that manage the style of the text box are being set declaratively to style class names defined elsewhere on the page.

```
<asp:ScriptManager ID="ScriptManager1" runat="server">
</asp:ScriptManager>

<AjaxEnabled:PassTextBox ID="textbox1" runat="server"
    TextMode="Password" WeakCssClass="weak" MediumCssClass="medium"
    StrongCssClass="strong"></AjaxEnabled:PassTextBox>
```

Creating an AJAX Behavior for Client Controls

Fortunately, an AJAX behavior client control works in much the same way an AJAX client control does. The biggest distinction is that behaviors are meant to be more general and are created to extend one or more controls (and not to be embedded as a stand-alone UI control). Behaviors are meant to be applied to DOM elements at design time and thus extend the behavior of the controls to which it is applied.

For the most part, you write a behavior control as you would a client control, by writing a JavaScript file that provides extensions to a control. However, you inherit from Sys.UI.Behavior instead of Sys.UI.Control.

ENCAPSULATING THE AJAX BEHAVIOR AS AN EXTENDER CONTROL

The difference between client and behavior controls, although slight, is in how you use the control. Rather than being a custom control based on a single web control (as discussed in the previous section), a custom behavior control inherits from the ExtenderControl class. In addition, when you define the class, you add the TargetControlType attribute to the class definition. This allows users of the control to set the control they want to have extended during design time. The following shows a basic class definition of a custom extender control.

Sample of Visual Basic Code

```
<TargetControlType(GetType(Control))> _
Public Class MyExtender
    Inherits ExtenderControl

End Class
```

Sample of C# Code

```
[TargetControlType(typeof(Control))]
public class MyExtender : ExtenderControl
{

}
```

From there, you use the same methods to build out the rest of the control as discussed for an AJAX custom server control previously. This includes a call to GetScriptReferences to set a reference to the AJAX behavior class used by the custom control.

USING THE AJAX BEHAVIOR

The AJAX behavior is encapsulated in a custom control that inherits from the ExtenderControl class. You therefore use the control as you would any other custom control (as discussed previously). You first register the control on the page by using the @ Register directive. You then define an instance of the control in your markup. Because it is an extender control, however, you must also define the control it extends by setting the control's TargetControlId property to the ID of another control on the page. This indicates the control to which you want to provide additional behavior. The following provides an example of what the markup looks like.

```
<asp:Button ID="Button1" runat="server" Text="Button" />

<ajaxEnabled: MyExtender runat="server"
    ID=" MyExtender1" TargetControlID="Button1"
    PropertyCssClass="MyCssClassName"/>
```

PRACTICE 1 Creating and Using an AJAX Component

In this practice, you create an AJAX client component. This component does not have a UI. Rather, it is meant to be used to provide additional functionality to the pages that use it. In the second exercise, you register and use the component on a page.

> **ON THE COMPANION MEDIA**
>
> If you encounter a problem completing an exercise, you can find the completed projects in the samples installed from this book's companion CD. For more information about the project files and other content on the CD, see "Using the Companion Media" in this book's Introduction.

EXERCISE 1   Creating the AJAX Component

In this exercise, you create a new ASP.NET website and add a client component inside a JavaScript file. The client component defines a method for determining a password's strength.

1. Open Visual Studio and create a new ASP.NET website named **AjaxEnabled** in either C# or Visual Basic.

2. Add a new JavaScript file to the site. Right-click the Scripts folder in the website and select Add New Item. In the Add New Item dialog box, select Jscript File. Name the file **PasswordStrengthComponent.js**.

3. Open the newly created JavaScript file. At the top of the file, add code to reference the MicrosoftAjax.js library and to register a new namespace. The following shows an example.

```
/// <reference name="MicrosoftAjax.js"/>

Type.registerNamespace("AjaxEnabled");
```

4. Next, define the constructor for your JavaScript class as a function. This is a simple AJAX component, so not much happens here. The following shows an example:

```
//create constructor
AjaxEnabled.PasswordStrengthComponent = function() {
    AjaxEnabled.PasswordStrengthComponent.initializeBase(this);
}
```

5. The next step is to define the inside of the class. You do so by creating its prototype. Inside the prototype, declare a function called returnPasswordStrength that takes a password, checks its value, and returns its strength. The following shows an example class definition that also includes the dispose method.

```
//define class
AjaxEnabled.PasswordStrengthComponent.prototype = {
    initialize: function () {
        //add custom initialization here
        AjaxEnabled.PasswordStrengthComponent.callBaseMethod(this, 'initialize');
    },

    returnPasswordStrength: function (password) {
        var strPass = new String(password.toString());
        if (strPass.length < 5) {
            return "Weak";
        }
        else {
            if (strPass.length < 8) {
                return "Medium";
            }
            else {
                return "Strong";
            }
        }
    },
```

```
    dispose: function () {
        //add custom dispose actions here
        AjaxEnabled.PasswordStrengthComponent.callBaseMethod(this, 'dispose');
    }
}
```

6. Finally, add code to the class to register it with the Microsoft AJAX Library by calling the registerClass method of the component. Be sure to indicate that the class inherits the Sys.Component class from the library. The following code shows an example.

```
//register class as a Sys.Component
AjaxEnabled.PasswordStrengthComponent.registerClass(
    'AjaxEnabled.PasswordStrengthComponent', Sys.Component);
```

7. Save the file. You have completed the creation of the component. In the next exercise, you will use this component on a webpage.

EXERCISE 2   Calling the AJAX Component from a Webpage

In this exercise, you add the AJAX component created in the previous exercise to a webpage.

1. Continue editing the project you created in the previous exercise. Alternatively, you can open the completed Lesson 2, Practice 1, Exercise 1 project in the sample files installed from the CD.

2. Open the Default.aspx page in Source view. Remove the markup inside the BodyContent tags.

3. Add a ScriptManager control from the Toolbox to the page. Inside the ScriptManager control, set a reference to the PasswordStrengthComponent.js file created previously. The following shows an example.

```
<asp:Content ID="BodyContent" runat="server" ContentPlaceHolderID="MainContent">
    <asp:ScriptManager ID="ScriptManager1" runat="server">
        <Scripts>
            <asp:ScriptReference Path="Scripts/PasswordStrengthComponent.js" />
        </Scripts>
    </asp:ScriptManager>
</asp:Content>
```

4. Next, add controls to the page (under the ScriptManager markup) that represents a user logon form. This includes a text box control used for entering a password. Your UI controls might look as shown on the next page.

```
<div style="font-size: large; font-weight: bold">User Logon</div>
<hr />
<br />
<br />
User Name:
<br />
<asp:TextBox ID="TextBoxUserName" runat="server" Width="200"></asp:TextBox>
<br />
Password:
<br />
<asp:TextBox ID="TextBoxPassword" runat="server"
    TextMode="Password" Width="200"></asp:TextBox>
<asp:Label ID="LabelStrength" runat="server" Text=""></asp:Label>
<br />
<input id="ButtonSubmit" type="button" value="Log On" />
```

5. The next step is to add JavaScript to your page to work with your client component. In this example, you create an event that fires as the user presses a key inside the Password text box. Each time, you grab the contents of the text box and verify the data by using the custom library that you wrote. You write the results out to the screen by using a label control that you define on the page (LabelStrength, defined in the previous step). The following code is placed inside the HeaderContent tags on the page.

```
<asp:Content ID="HeaderContent" runat="server" ContentPlaceHolderID="HeadContent">
    <script language="javascript" type="text/javascript">

        function _OnKeypress() {
            var checker = new AjaxEnabled.PasswordStrengthComponent();
            var pass =
                document.getElementById("MainContent_TextBoxPassword").value;
            var strength = checker.returnPasswordStrength(pass);
            document.getElementById(
                "MainContent_LabelStrength").innerText = strength;
        }

    </script>
</asp:Content>
```

6. The last step is to make sure that this event is registered for the Password text box. You can do so by adding the onkeyup="_OnKeypress()" attribute to the TextBoxPassword control defined previously.

7. Finally, run your page. Enter values in the Password text box and notice how the labels change as you type. Figure 9-6 shows an example of the page in action.

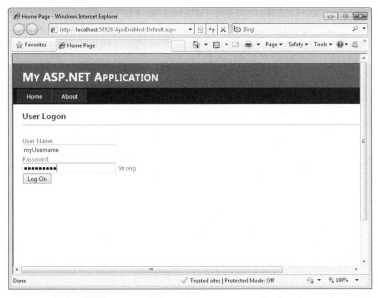

FIGURE 9-6 The AJAX password client component running in a browser.

Creating and Using an AJAX Client Control

In this practice, you create an AJAX client control that works with a text box DOM element to show users their password strength. In Exercise 2, you add this control to a webpage and wire it to a text box. This same control is used in Practice 3, in which you wrap the control as a custom server control.

> **ON THE COMPANION MEDIA**
>
> If you encounter a problem completing an exercise, you can find the completed projects in the samples installed from this book's companion CD. For more information about the project files and other content on the CD, see "Using the Companion Media" in this book's Introduction.

EXERCISE 1 Creating an AJAX Client Control

In this exercise, you create a JavaScript file for checking password strength.

1. Open Visual Studio and create a new ASP.NET website named **AjaxEnabled** (if you have a conflict with the website you created in Practice 1, place this project in a different folder) in either C# or Visual Basic.

2. Add a new JavaScript file to the root of the site. Right-click the website and select Add New Item. In the Add New Item dialog box, select Jscript File. Name the file **PassTextBox.js**.

3. Open the newly created JavaScript file. At the top of the file, add code to reference the MicrosoftAjax.js library and to register a new namespace. The following shows an example.

```
/// <reference name="MicrosoftAjax.js"/>

Type.registerNamespace("AjaxEnabled");
```

4. Next, define the constructor for your JavaScript class as a function. In this case, the constructor takes the element parameter. This is meant to represent the DOM element that the control extends. Use this element to initialize the base class of System.UI.Control. This control will set the style of a text box based on the strength of the password. Therefore, it exposes three properties, one for each password strength. Inside the constructor, initialize the private fields used to represent these properties.

The following shows an example of the constructor.

```
//create constructor
AjaxEnabled.PassTextBox = function (element) {
    AjaxEnabled.PassTextBox.initializeBase(this, [element]);

    this._weakCssClass = null;
    this._mediumCssClass = null;
    this._strongCssClass = null;
}
```

5. The next step is to define the inside of the class by creating its prototype. The prototype of this class will include both an initialize and a dispose method. It will also include event code called onKeyup that handles the text box keyup event. Finally, the code includes several properties for managing the setting and getting of the password style classes. The following shows an example of the prototype definition. Note: Most of this code was covered in the lesson. Refer back to the text if you have trouble following the code.

```
//define class
AjaxEnabled.PassTextBox.prototype = {

    //initialize the UI control
    initialize: function() {
    AjaxEnabled.PassTextBox.callBaseMethod(this, 'initialize');

     this._onKeyupHandler = Function.createDelegate(this, this._onKeyup);
     $addHandlers(this.get_element(), {'keyup' : this._onKeyup}, this);
     },

     dispose: function() {
     $clearHandlers(this.get_element());
     AjaxEnabled.PassTextBox.callBaseMethod(this, 'dispose');
     },

     //define keystroke event
     _onKeyup : function(e) {

      //get password text
```

```
            var pass = this.get_element().value;
            var strength = this.returnPasswordStrength(pass);

            switch (strength) {
                case "Weak":
                        this.get_element().className = this._weakCssClass;
                        break;
                case "Medium":
                        this.get_element().className = this._mediumCssClass;
                        break;
                case "Strong":
                        this.get_element().className = this._strongCssClass;
                        break;
            }
        },

        //define properties
        get_weakCssClass: function() {
            return this._weakCssClass;
        },
        set_weakCssClass: function(value) {
            this._weakCssClass = value;
        },
        get_mediumCssClass: function() {
            return this._mediumCssClass;
        },
        set_mediumCssClass: function(value) {
            this._mediumCssClass = value;
        },
        get_strongCssClass: function() {
            return this._strongCssClass;
        },
        set_strongCssClass: function(value) {
            this._strongCssClass = value;
        },

        returnPasswordStrength: function(password) {
            var strPass = new String(password.toString());
            if (strPass.length < 5)
            {
                return "Weak";
            }
            else
            {
                if (strPass.length < 8)
                {
                 return "Medium";
                }
                else
                 {
                 return "Strong";
                }
            }
        }
}
```

6. Finally, add code to the class to register it with the Microsoft AJAX Library by calling the registerClass method of the component. Be sure to indicate that the class inherits the Sys.UI.Control class from the library. The following code shows an example.

```
//register class as a Sys.UI.Control
AjaxEnabled.PassTextBox.registerClass('AjaxEnabled.PassTextBox',
    Sys.UI.Control);
```

7. Save the file. You have completed creating the AJAX UI portion of the control. In the next exercise, you will use this control on a webpage. In Practice 3, you will wrap this script into a custom server control.

EXERCISE 2   Using the AJAX Client Control on a Webpage

In this exercise, you add the AJAX UI control created in the previous exercise to a webpage and connect it to a text box control.

1. Continue editing the project you created in the previous exercise. Alternatively, you can open the completed Lesson 2, Practice 2, Exercise 1 project in the sample files installed from the CD.

2. Open the Default.aspx page in Source view. Remove the content inside the BodyContent area of the page.

3. Add a ScriptManager control from the Toolbox to the page. Inside the ScriptManager control, set a reference to the PassTextBox.js file created previously. The following shows an example.

```
<asp:Content ID="BodyContent" runat="server" ContentPlaceHolderID="MainContent">
    <asp:ScriptManager ID="ScriptManager1" runat="server">
        <Scripts>
            <asp:ScriptReference Path="PassTextBox.js" />
        </Scripts>
    </asp:ScriptManager>

</asp:Content>
```

4. Next, add controls under the ScriptManager control that represents a user logon form. This includes a text box control used for entering a password. Your UI controls might look as follows.

```
<div style="font-size: large; font-weight: bold">User Logon</div>
<hr />
<br />
User Name:
<br />
<asp:TextBox ID="TextBoxUserName" runat="server" Width="200"></asp:TextBox>
<br />
```

```
Password:
<br />
<asp:TextBox ID="TextBoxPassword" runat="server"
    TextMode="Password" Width="200"></asp:TextBox>
<asp:Label ID="LabelStrength" runat="server" Text=""></asp:Label>
<br />
<input id="ButtonSubmit" type="button" value="Log On" />
```

5. In addition, add style class definitions to the page for each of the password strengths. These will change the look of the text box based on the strength of the password. The following shows an example added to the HeaderContent section of the page source.

```
<asp:Content ID="HeaderContent" runat="server"
    ContentPlaceHolderID="HeadContent">

    <style type="text/css">
      .weak
      {
        border: thin solid #FF0000;
      }
      .medium
      {
        border: thin solid #FFFF00;
      }
      .strong
      {
        border: medium solid #008000;
      }
    </style>

</asp:Content>
```

6. The next step is to define JavaScript on the page to create an instance of the AJAX UI control and connect it to the TextBoxPassword control. You can do so in the Microsoft AJAX Library's application initialize event. When you create an instance of the control, you will want to pass in property definition settings and a reference to the text box. The following code should be added to the page under the ScriptManager control markup.

```
<script language="javascript" type="text/javascript">

    var app = Sys.Application;
    app.add_init(appInit);

    function appInit(sender, args) {

        $create(AjaxEnabled.PassTextBox,
            { weakCssClass: 'weak', mediumCssClass: 'medium',
                strongCssClass: 'strong' }, null, null,
            $get('MainContent_TextBoxPassword'));
    }

</script>
```

7. Finally, run your page. Enter values in the Password text box and notice how the style of the text box changes as you type. Figure 9-7 shows an example of the page in action. When the user enters a strong password, the text box border turns thicker and green.

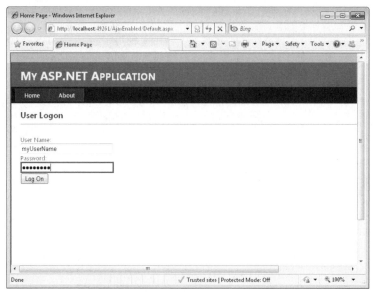

FIGURE 9-7 The AJAX password client UI control running in a browser.

In this practice, you encapsulate the AJAX UI control created in the previous example as a custom control. You then register and use it on the page.

> **ON THE COMPANION MEDIA**
>
> If you encounter a problem completing an exercise, you can find the completed projects in the samples installed from this book's companion CD. For more information about the project files and other content on the CD, see "Using the Companion Media" in this book's Introduction.

EXERCISE 1 Embedding an AJAX Client Control as a Custom Control

In this exercise, you create a custom control that encapsulates the AJAX client control created in the previous practice.

Note that this practice uses the JavaScript file (PassTextBox.js) created in Practice 2.

1. Open Visual Studio and create a new ASP.NET Web site named **AjaxEnabled** (if you have a conflict, place the project in a separate folder) in either C# or Visual Basic.

2. Add a new class library to the solution: right-click the solution and choose Add New Project | Select Windows | Class Library. Name this class library **PassTextBox**.

3. Add references to the project: right-click the PassTextBox project and select Add Reference. On the .NET tab of the Add Reference dialog box, select the following references: System.Drawing, System.Web, and System.Web.Extensions. Close the dialog box.

4. Open the class file in the code editor. Set the root/default namespace of the class to **AjaxEnabled**. You can do so from the project Properties dialog box for the class library. Also, set the assembly name to **AjaxEnabled**. This is done through the project Properties dialog box.

5. Name the class **PassTextBox** (you should also change the filename). Indicate that the class inherits from the TextBox control and implements the IScriptControl.

6. Add using statements (or, in Visual Basic, Imports) for System.Web.UI.WebControls, System.Web.UI, and System.Web.

7. Next, add a private variable to track a ScriptManager control at the class level. Also, add three fields to the control for managing the password text box style properties based on password strength. The top portion of your control should now look as follows.

```
Sample of Visual Basic Code
Public Class PassTextBox
    Inherits TextBox
    Implements IScriptControl

    Private _sMgr As ScriptManager

    Public WeakCssClass As String
    Public MediumCssClass As String
    Public StrongCssClass As String
...
```

```
Sample of C# Code
public class PassTextBox : TextBox, IScriptControl
{

    private ScriptManager sMgr;

    public string WeakCssClass;
    public string MediumCssClass;
    public string StrongCssClass;
```

8. Next, add a method called GetScriptDescriptors. This method is meant to define the properties and events that work with the client control. Here you add three property descriptors, one for each password strength style. The following code shows an example.

Sample of Visual Basic Code

```vb
Protected Overridable Function GetScriptDescriptors() _
    As IEnumerable(Of ScriptDescriptor)

    Dim descriptor As ScriptControlDescriptor = _
        New ScriptControlDescriptor("AjaxEnabled.PassTextBox", Me.ClientID)

    descriptor.AddProperty("weakCssClass", Me.WeakCssClass)
    descriptor.AddProperty("mediumCssClass", Me.MediumCssClass)
    descriptor.AddProperty("strongCssClass", Me.StrongCssClass)

    Return New ScriptDescriptor() {descriptor}

End Function
```

Sample of C# Code

```csharp
protected virtual IEnumerable<ScriptDescriptor> GetScriptDescriptors()
{
    ScriptControlDescriptor descriptor =
        new ScriptControlDescriptor("AjaxEnabled.PassTextBox", this.ClientID);

    descriptor.AddProperty("weakCssClass", this.WeakCssClass);
    descriptor.AddProperty("mediumCssClass", this.MediumCssClass);
    descriptor.AddProperty("strongCssClass", this.StrongCssClass);

    return new ScriptDescriptor[] { descriptor };
}
```

9. Now add a method called GetScriptReference. This method is meant to get a reference to the JavaScript that is used by this custom control. In this case, the JavaScript will be embedded in the same assembly. Therefore, add the following code.

Sample of Visual Basic Code

```vb
Protected Overridable Function GetScriptReferences() _
    As IEnumerable(Of ScriptReference)

    Dim reference As ScriptReference = New ScriptReference()

    reference.Assembly = "AjaxEnabled"
    reference.Name = "AjaxEnabled.PassTextBox.js"

    Return New ScriptReference() {reference}

End Function
```

Sample of C# Code

```csharp
protected virtual IEnumerable<ScriptReference> GetScriptReferences()
{
    ScriptReference reference = new ScriptReference();
    reference.Assembly = "AjaxEnabled";
    reference.Name = "AjaxEnabled.PassTextBox.js";

    return new ScriptReference[] { reference };
}
```

10. You now need to fill out the rest of this class. This code is straightforward and common to all controls of this nature. The rest of the members of the class are as follows.

Sample of Visual Basic Code

```vbnet
Protected Overrides Sub OnPreRender(ByVal e As EventArgs)
    If Not Me.DesignMode Then

        'test for the existence of a ScriptManager
        _sMgr = ScriptManager.GetCurrent(Page)

        If _sMgr Is Nothing Then _
            Throw New HttpException( _
            "A ScriptManager control must exist on the page.")

        _sMgr.RegisterScriptControl(Me)
    End If

    MyBase.OnPreRender(e)
End Sub

Protected Overrides Sub Render(ByVal writer As HtmlTextWriter)
    If Not Me.DesignMode Then _
        _sMgr.RegisterScriptDescriptors(Me)
    MyBase.Render(writer)
End Sub
Function IScriptControlGetScriptReferences() _
  As IEnumerable(Of ScriptReference) _
  Implements IScriptControl.GetScriptReferences

    Return GetScriptReferences()

End Function

Function IScriptControlGetScriptDescriptors() _
  As IEnumerable(Of ScriptDescriptor) _
  Implements IScriptControl.GetScriptDescriptors

    Return GetScriptDescriptors()

End Function
```

```
protected override void OnPreRender(EventArgs e)
{
    if (!this.DesignMode)
    {
        //test for the existence of a ScriptManager
        sMgr = ScriptManager.GetCurrent(Page);

        if (sMgr == null)
            throw new HttpException(
                "A ScriptManager control must exist on the page.");

        sMgr.RegisterScriptControl(this);
    }

    base.OnPreRender(e);
}

protected override void Render(HtmlTextWriter writer)
{
    if (!this.DesignMode)
        sMgr.RegisterScriptDescriptors(this);

    base.Render(writer);
}

IEnumerable<ScriptReference> IScriptControl.GetScriptReferences()
{
    return GetScriptReferences();
}

IEnumerable<ScriptDescriptor> IScriptControl.GetScriptDescriptors()
{
    return GetScriptDescriptors();
}
```

11. The next step is to embed your JavaScript file as a resource to this class.

   a. Copy the PassTextBox.js file created in the earlier practice to your PassTextBox class library project (or get it from the sample files installed from the CD).

   b. In Solution Explorer, view properties for the PassTextBox.js file. In the Properties window, set the Build Action property to Embedded Resource.

   c. Open the project's AssemblyInfo file. You might have to click the Show All Files toolbar button from Solution Explorer. In Visual Basic, you can then find this file under the My Project folder. In C#, it is under a folder called Properties. Open this file and add the following Web resource assembly definition.

   Sample of Visual Basic Code
   ```
   <Assembly: System.Web.UI.WebResource("AjaxEnabled.PassTextBox.js", "text/
   javascript")>
   ```

Sample of C# Code

```
[assembly: System.Web.UI.WebResource("AjaxEnabled.PassTextBox.js", "text/
javascript")]
```

12. Finally, build the project. You should now have a custom server control based on the TextBox class that also uses an embedded AJAX UI control targeted to work with the Microsoft AJAX Library. In the next exercise, you will practice how to use this control.

EXERCISE 2   Using the Custom AJAX Control on a Webpage

In this exercise, you add the custom AJAX control created in the previous exercise to a webpage.

1. Continue editing the project you created in the previous exercise. Alternatively, you can open the completed Lesson 2, Practice 3, Exercise 1 project in the sample files installed from the CD.

2. Open the website project.

3. Add a project reference to the PassTextBox control. Because both your website and your custom control are in the same solution, you can add a project reference from the website to the text box control by right-clicking the website project and choosing Add Reference. Select the Projects tab in the Add Reference dialog box and select the PassTextBox project. (If your projects are not in the same solution, you must copy the DLL files from the previous exercise to the Bin directory of the website.)

4. Open the Default.aspx page in Source view. Remove the content inside the BodyContent tags.

5. Add a ScriptManager control from the Toolbox to the BodyContent area of the page.

6. At the top of the page, under the @ Page directive, add an @ Register directive to register the custom control. This directive should point to the assembly that contains the custom control created previously.

   If you are following along closely, the name of this assembly is AjaxEnabled. If you went fast and perhaps missed step 4 in Exercise 1 of this practice, your assembly might be named PassTextBox. You can check the Bin directory of the site to be sure.

   ```
   <%@ Register Assembly="AjaxEnabled" Namespace="AjaxEnabled"
     TagPrefix="ajaxEnabled" %>
   ```

7. Next, add controls to the page that represents a user logon form. These controls should be similar to those found at the end of the previous practice. Note: Be sure to include the style definitions set there as well. However, in this case, you do not define a password text box and connect it to the AJAX UI control. Instead, you define an instance of the already-embedded custom control as follows.

   ```
   <ajaxEnabled:PassTextBox ID="textbox1" runat="server" width="200"
     TextMode="Password" WeakCssClass="weak" MediumCssClass="medium"
     StrongCssClass="strong"></ajaxEnabled:PassTextBox>
   ```

8. Finally, run your page. Enter values in the Password text box and notice how the style of the text box changes as you type.

> **NOTE POTENTIAL NAMESPACE CONFLICT**
>
> If you are using C#, you might get an error due to a namespace conflict. The assembly name of the website and the assembly name of the control are set to the same value, AjaxEnabled. You can overcome this by changing the website's assembly name and namespace. To do so, right-click the website and choose Properties. Here you can set the values for these two items to AjaxEnabled2.

Lesson Summary

- You can define client script for a page by using the <script/> tag. You can write JavaScript inside this tag or you can use it to point to a .js file.
- The ClientScriptManager class is used to register client script dynamically from server-side code. An instance of this class is accessible from the Page.ClientScript property.
- The ScriptManager control can also be used to register your own custom client scripts. This is useful if you are already using this control for partial-page updates or to access the Microsoft AJAX Library.
- The Microsoft AJAX Library provides object-oriented support for building JavaScript code that extends the features of the client's browser. This includes a set of base classes and a framework (Sys).
- There are typically three types of objects you create for use with the Microsoft AJAX Library: components, controls, and behaviors. A component is a class that has no UI. A control is typically a single control that provides AJAX capabilities. A behavior provides extended capabilities that can be attached to a control at design time.
- You can wrap an AJAX client control into a custom server control. To do so, you implement the IScriptControl interface.

Lesson Review

You can use the following questions to test your knowledge of the information in Lesson 2, "Creating Client Scripts with the Microsoft AJAX Library." The questions are also available on the companion CD as a practice test if you prefer to review them in electronic form.

> **NOTE ANSWERS**
>
> Answers to these questions and explanations of why each answer choice is correct or incorrect are located in the "Answers" section at the end of the book.

1. Which of the following lines of JavaScript registers a new class to be used as an extension to a DOM element?

   A. `MyNamespace.MyClass.registerClass('MyNamespace.MyClass ', Sys.UI.Control);`

   B. `MyNamespace.MyClass.registerClass('MyNamespace.MyClass ', null, Sys.IDis-`
   `posable);`

   C. `MyNamespace.MyClass.registerClass('MyNamespace.MyClass ', null);`

   D. `MyNamespace.MyClass.registerClass('MyNamespace.MyClass ', Sys.UI.Behavior);`

2. You are creating an AJAX component that does an asynchronous postback to the server for partial-page updates. You need your code to be notified when the partial-page response first comes back from the server. Which event should you intercept?

   A. endRequest

   B. pageLoading

   C. pageLoaded

   D. beginRequest

3. You write a JavaScript class that uses the Microsoft AJAX Library. You intend to use the class on a webpage. Which of the following actions should you take?

   A. Add the following markup to the <head /> section of the ASPX page.

   `<script src="ContosoUtilities.js" type="text/javascript"></script>`

   B. Add a ScriptManager control to your page. It automatically finds your .js files in your solution. You can then work with them by using IntelliSense.

   C. Add a ScriptManager control to your page. Add a reference nested inside the ScriptManager control that points to your JavaScript file.

   D. Use the ScriptReference class in your code-behind file and set its path to the path of your .js file.

4. You want to create a custom control that works as an AJAX client behavior. What action(s) should you take? (Choose all that apply.)

   A. Create a custom server-side class that inherits from a valid System.Web.UI.Control.

   B. Create a custom server-side class that inherits from ExtenderControl.

   C. Create a custom server-side class that implements the interface IScriptControl.

   D. Create a custom server-side class that is decorated with the attribute TargetControlType.

Lesson 3: Implementing jQuery

Programming in the browser has been problematic for years. Different browsers support the JavaScript language in different ways. Writing code to run on the client often meant rewriting it for various browsers or supporting only one or two browsers. Fortunately, jQuery solves this problem.

jQuery is an open source library that simplifies the way JavaScript is written. It works across all modern browsers and is lightweight. You can use it for a variety of client-side programming tasks, such as selecting items inside your page, manipulating those items, changing styles, doing animations and effects, handling user events on the client side, and calling web services by using AJAX. There are also several plug-ins available for jQuery that provide rich controls that execute inside a browser window.

Visual Studio 2010 and ASP.NET 4 now fully support jQuery for client-side development. The jQuery library is installed by default when you create a new ASP.NET website.

This lesson covers the core aspects related to jQuery development. It includes an introduction and a tutorial on building your first jQuery page. It then covers the many uses for jQuery, including selecting and traversing the DOM, working with DOM elements, responding to user events inside the client, doing animations and effects, and implementing AJAX behavior by using jQuery.

> **After this lesson, you will be able to:**
> - Select, filter, find, and traverse page items by using jQuery.
> - Add, remove, and modify page elements by using jQuery.
> - Add effects and animations to your page by using jQuery.
> - Handle control events with jQuery.
> - Demonstrate AJAX capabilities by calling a web service and client script from jQuery.
>
> **Estimated lesson time: 40 minutes**

 REAL WORLD

Mike Snell

Developers are using the jQuery library. The simplicity, power, and speed of the library are all contributing to its rapid adoption. I have had the opportunity to speak with a wide audience of web developers, and the majority are taking advantage of this library. Microsoft's inclusion of the default templates in ASP.NET will result in an even wider adoption (and better user experiences).

Introducing the jQuery Library

jQuery is simply a file of JavaScript code that allows you to more easily write JavaScript code that runs in many different browsers. This code can do many things; it can work with UI styles, handle user events, animate parts of your page, call back to the server via AJAX, and more.

The jQuery library has a core set of features on which you can build. In fact, there are many extensions and plug-ins available for jQuery that help with menus, UI controls, page layout, navigation, and much more. In this lesson, however, you will focus on the core aspects of the library. The following list outlines the essential functionality that jQuery provides. We will go over each of these areas in greater details in later sections.

- **Core**   The core of the jQuery library allows you to identify code that can execute only after a document has fully loaded, create DOM elements dynamically, iterate selected elements, create extensions to jQuery itself, and more.

- **Selecting**   jQuery's power is in its ability to quickly select items in the DOM. You can easily return a single item from your page's DOM or many items that match a pattern without having to write much code. You use the jQuery selectors to find specific HTML tags or to find form elements by ID, cascading style sheet class name, attribute or attribute value, and more.

- **Filtering and Traversing**   You can create filters to select only those DOM elements that meet your filter criteria. You can also traverse through your selection and act upon the selected items (by changing their style or adding an event, for example). Some important filter and traverse functions are first, last, odd, visible, match, selected, contains, enabled, find, next, prev, parent, and siblings.

- **Manipulation**   After you have selected an item (or multiple items), you can also use jQuery to manipulate the item. This might be as simple as evaluating the HTML contents or setting the text contents of the selected item. You can also use functions such as append, insert, replaceWith, wrap, and remove (among others) to add, modify, or remove content from the selected DOM item.

- **Cascading style sheets**   jQuery also provides functions for working with cascading style sheets. This includes finding and setting styles, positioning items, setting height and width, and more.

- **Events**   The jQuery library allows you to attach client code to user events in the browser. This decouples your event code from the actual markup. You can handle almost any user input event, including hover, toggle, click, dblclick, keydown, keyup, focus, mousedown, mouseenter, mouseleave, scroll, resize, and more.

- **Animation and Effects**   jQuery provides functions for adding effects to and animating the items on your page. Functions include show, hide, fadeIn, fadeOut, fadeTo, slideDown, slideUp, animate, and more.

- **AJAX**   The jQuery library supports AJAX calls from the browser to the server. It allows you to call a web service or client script on the server and return the results to the page without refreshing the entire page.

- **Utilities**   There are several utility functions inside the jQuery language for working with browser compatibility, arrays, strings, and more.

> **NOTE   THE JQUERY LIBRARY WEBSITE**
>
> You can find more information about jQuery from the official jQuery library website. This site provides updates to the library, tutorials, full documentation, and plug-ins. All of this can be found at *http://www.jquery.com/*.

Adding the jQuery Library to a Webpage

A new ASP.NET 4 website will include the jQuery files inside the Scripts directory by default. Note that if you are working with an existing site that does not include jQuery, you can easily copy the files into your site. The jQuery language is contained in a single file, jquery-*<version>*.min.js, in which *version* is the current version (1.4.1 at the time of this writing).

Notice in Figure 9-8 that there are actually three jQuery files inside the Scripts directory. The jquery-1.4.1-vsdoc.js file is used by Visual Studio to provide IntelliSense in the text editor for jQuery code. Visual Studio simply looks for this file based on the naming convention and will provide the appropriate IntelliSense. The jquery-1.4.1.js file is the debug version of jQuery. This is a version of the code that is readable. You will want to reference this file in your code when you are debugging your client scripts. The jquery-1.4.1.min.js file is the "minified" version of the jQuery language. You use this file for production applications because it is a smaller client download and executes faster.

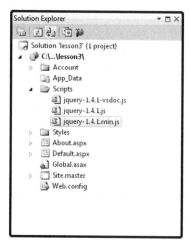

FIGURE 9-8 The production version of jQuery is a single file, jquery-1.4.1.min.js.

The first step to using the jQuery language is to reference it on your page. You can do so with a simple <script/> block added to the top of the page. The following line of code shows an example of referencing the debug version of the jQuery language on a webpage.

```
<script src="Scripts/jquery-1.4.1.js" type="text/javascript"></script>
```

You can also reference the library by using the ScriptManager control. You would add a script reference just as you would to any other .js file. You typically use the ScriptManager when you intend to mix Microsoft AJAX Library code with jQuery.

> **NOTE** **HOSTING THE JQUERY LANGUAGE FILES**
>
> The jQuery language files are actually hosted by several content delivery networks (or CDNs). This ensures faster downloads and caching of the jQuery language. Microsoft provides a CDN host of jQuery at *http://ajax.microsoft.com/ajax/jquery/jquery-1.4.2.min.js*. You can use this URL to reference the jQuery language in your production applications.

Writing Your First jQuery Script

There are many basic jQuery blocks of code that do approximately the same three things: ensure that the entire document has been loaded by the browser, select one or more elements from the DOM, and manipulate that element in some way (by changing the style, adding event code, adding items to the page, and so on). Of course, this does not represent the full capability of jQuery, just some of the most basic (and frequently used) functionality.

As an example, suppose you want to add a simple fade-in effect to the title of your page. You would first reference the jQuery script file. You would then write code to execute a function when the full document has been loaded by the browser. Inside this function, you would write code to find the title and then animate it. Finally, you would write markup for the actual title on the page. The following code illustrates this example with a page that derives from a master page.

```
<%@ Page Title="Home Page" Language="C#" MasterPageFile="~/Site.master"
    AutoEventWireup="true" CodeFile="Default.aspx.cs" Inherits="_Default" %>

<asp:Content ID="HeaderContent" runat="server" ContentPlaceHolderID="HeadContent">
    <script src="Scripts/jquery-1.4.1.js" type="text/javascript"></script>
</asp:Content>

<asp:Content ID="BodyContent" runat="server" ContentPlaceHolderID="MainContent">

    <script type="text/javascript">
        $(document).ready(function () {
            $("h2").fadeIn("slow");
        });
    </script>

    <h2  style="display: none">
        Page Title
    </h2>

</asp:Content>
```

There are few things to notice about this code and markup. First, notice that the script reference to the jQuery library is added to the HeaderContent content area because this code uses a master page. Next, notice that the title of the page is contained in an <h2> tag. This tag also has its display style set to none when the page loads (because you plan to fade it in).

Now take a look at the jQuery code. Notice the use of the dollar sign ($); this is equivalent to calling the core jQuery() function. This function is used to select items in your webpage and to respond to jQuery life cycle events. The code, $(document).ready(), is actually selecting the entire document and then indicating what to do when the ready event fires. The ready event is a jQuery client-side event that triggers when the full DOM has been loaded by the browser (like an ASP.NET Page_Load event on the server). You then pass an anonymous function to be executed when this event fires. Note that you could write a function and then pass its name. However, anonymous functions make the code easier to write and to read.

Finally, the line that reads, $("h2").fadeIn("slow");, uses the jQuery selector function $() to find all instances of the tag <h2>. You then indicate that for all found items, you want to call the jQuery fadeIn function and fade these items in slowly.

You should now have a good overview of just how the jQuery language can be used on a webpage in ASP.NET. In the next few sections, you will explore searching the DOM, handling client-side events, adding effects, and making AJAX calls with jQuery in more detail.

Selecting and Traversing the DOM

Much of jQuery is about finding items on your page and then doing something with (or to) them. The jQuery functions that find items on your page are called selectors. The base function in jQuery is jQuery() or $() and works as the base selector function. There are three primary ways to pass string arguments to this function:

- **Select by element**   Finds all elements with a specified tag name and returns an array of those elements. You simply pass the name of the tag to the selector function, as in $("h2").

- **Select by ID**   Allows you to select a single element by its ID. You use the pound (#) character to indicate that you are searching by ID. For example, the element, <span id="someId"> can be searched for by using the function call $("#someId").

- **Select by cascading style sheet**   Allows you to find all tags with a specific cascading style sheet class name. You use a period (.) to indicate the class name. For example, to find all elements with the cascading style sheet class name of userInputStyle (as in <div class="userInputStyle">), you would use the $(".userInputStyle") selector.

Advanced Selectors

The jQuery selectors are very flexible. You can combine the three selection types just listed to get specific with your searches. For example, to select all <span> tags with the cascading style sheet style of sectionHeading, you would write $("span.sectionHeading").

There are also several keywords you can use within the selection string to refine your selection, such as :first, :last, :even, :odd, :not, :first-child, and :last-child. You use these keywords appended to your selection parameter with a colon as in $("span:first") to find the first <span/> tag in the page.

jQuery also lets you search the DOM for elements with specific attributes. You do so by using square brackets, as in $("a[href*=MyDomain]"). This code finds all anchor (<a/>) tags in the page that have the text "MyDomain" as part of the href attribute. The *= indicates a find all search. Table 9-1 describes the available search characters

TABLE 9-1 jQuery Search Characters

SEARCH CHARACTER	DESCRIPTION	EXAMPLE
* (asterisk)	Searches for the search term in all text in the string	$("a[href*=MyDomain]")
^ (caret)	Searches for the search term at the beginning of the string	$("a[href^=Folder/]")
$ (dollar sign)	Searches for the search term at the end of the string	$("a[href$=.com]")
! (exclamation point)	Searches for elements whose attributes do not match the search string	$("a[href!=http://www.MyDomain.com]")

You can see that jQuery is a powerful DOM search tool. There are many ways in which to find a group of elements on your page. Table 9-2 shows some examples and provides a description of each. Of course, you can modify these examples to create even more scenarios.

TABLE 9-2 jQuery Selector Examples

JQUERY SELECTOR EXAMPLE	DESCRIPTION
$("h2:first")	Used to find the first instance of the <h2> element. Similar syntax can be used for last, odd, and even.
$("div:first-child")	Used to select all first child elements inside <div> tags on the page. Similar syntax can be used with last-child.
$("#div1:nth-child(4)")	Used to select the fourth child element inside the tag whose ID is div1.
$("span:not(.sectionHead)")	Used to select all <span/> tags that do not have the sectionHead cascading style sheet class.
$(":enabled")	Returns all enabled elements on the page. The same syntax can also be used for disabled.

(continued)

JQUERY SELECTOR EXAMPLE	DESCRIPTION
$(":checked")	Returns all checkbox elements on the page that are checked. Similar syntax can be used for selected items in a list.
$("div:hidden")	Returns all hidden <div/> tags on the page. Similar syntax can be used for visible.
$(":contains(.docx)")	Used to find all elements on the page that contain the text .docx.
$("#div1 #div2")	Finds any <div/> tags with the ID of div2 nested inside another <div/> tag with the ID of div1.
$(":button")	Used to find all elements of type button. You can use similar syntax with input, text, password, radio, submit, checkbox, and image.

EXAM TIP

Be sure you know the basics of the jQuery syntax for the exam. You will have to be able to read and understand this code, which is different from standard JavaScript or .NET Framework code.

Traversing Your Selection

The result returned by a jQuery selector is a set of elements that match the selection criteria. Even if you only get a single element back in your selection, jQuery gives you a set of elements. This allows you to work with a single item or a collection of items by using the same syntax.

You call functions on the returned set to work with the returned elements. These functions might actually manipulate the elements, bind client-side events to an element, change a style, or add an effect. You can also traverse the collection by walking through it, filtering it, and selecting specific items inside it. These functions are referred to as *traversing and filtering functions* in jQuery.

As an example, suppose you want to traverse the items of a returned selection set and execute code against each item. In this case, you can use the .each() function. It works much like the For...Each statement in the .NET Framework languages. The following sample code demonstrates this. This code finds all <h2/> tags on a page and appends a sequential section ID to the title text. Notice that you pass an anonymous function to the .each() function. This function is executed once for each element in the set.

```
<script type="text/javascript">
    $(document).ready(function () {
        $("h2").each(function (index) {
            this.innerHTML = "Section " + index;
        });
    });
</script>
```

jQuery provides several functions, such as .each(), that can be used for filtering and traversing sets of found elements. Table 9-3 lists many common examples you are likely to encounter and provides a description of each.

TABLE 9-3 Query Traversing and Filtering Functions

JQUERY TRAVERSING / FILTERING EXAMPLE	DESCRIPTION
$("span").get(0) $("span")[0]	The .get() function allows you to select a single item inside a result set. Both lines of code search the DOM for all <span/> tags and return the first item inside the set of found items.
var items = $("h2").size();	The .size function allows you to determine the number of elements in the result set. This code returns the number of found items and sets the value to a variable.
$("h2").add("span").css("color", "green");	The .add() function allows you to add things to found items. This code finds all <h2/> elements and adds a <span/> tag with the cascading style sheet color style set to green. You can use the .add() function to add selected elements, HTML fragments, another element, and more.
$("h2").eq(1).css("color", "green");	The .eq() function allows you to cut down the size of your result set to a single item from the returned set. This code selects the second <h2/> item and turns it green. (Note that the index is zero based.)

(continued)

JQUERY TRAVERSING / FILTERING EXAMPLE	DESCRIPTION
$("#div1").children()	The .children() function allows you to select all child elements for a specified result set.
	This code finds the <div/> element with the ID of div1 and then selects all of its first-level children.
	There are overloads to the .children() function that allow you to add a selector to further refine your results.
	Remember, the original selector might return a set of objects. Calling .children() is actually calling .children() for each item in the set.
$("#div1").find("h2")	The .find() function is similar to a sub-search in that it allows you to search through your result set.
	This code first finds everything inside a <div/> tag with the ID of div1 and then selects only those elements that are defined as <h2/>.

$("h2").filter(function(index) {
  return $("b", this).length == 1;
}).css("color", "green");
	The .filter() function works like find() (see previous entry). However, it also contains an overload that allows you to pass a function to the function that can be used to evaluate each item in the result set and determine whether the item should be filtered out.

	This code finds all <h2/> elements and then iterates over them by using a filter function. Inside the filter function, it looks for a <b/> tag inside each element (this). If the tag is found (.length == 1), that item is returned as part of the results and its color is set to green.
$("h2").slice(2)	The .slice() function allows you to cut the results based on a start and optional end position in the zero-bound array.
	This code finds all <h2/> elements and reduces the set to the third element through the end.

JQUERY TRAVERSING / FILTERING EXAMPLE	DESCRIPTION
$("h2").next()	The .next() function returns the element immediately following the selected element. This code finds each <h2/> element on the page and returns the element that immediately follows each found item. Note that the .prev() function works the same way but returns the element immediately before the selected element.
$("#div1").nextUntil("p")	The nextUntil() function finds all elements returned from a previous search until it finds a specific element that tells it to stop. This code finds the <div/> tag with the ID of div1 and then gets all elements following the <div/> tag's end tag until it comes across a <p/> tag.

Manipulating Your Selection

jQuery allows you to quickly narrow your selection to the elements on which you want to focus and traverse the selection. The next step is usually to manipulate those elements in some way. There are many manipulation functions; some allow you to change an attribute, others allow you to impact the cascading style sheet, and others allow you to modify the entire set of selected elements in some way. Table 9-4 provides some examples and a description of each.

TABLE 9-4 jQuery Manipulation Functions

JQUERY MANIPULATION EXAMPLE	DESCRIPTION
$("h2").append(" : <a href='default.aspx'> home</a>");	You use the .append() function to insert HTML at the end of a found element. jQuery will append your HTML as the last child item of the found element. This code finds <h2/> elements and then appends a hyperlink at the end of the <h2/> content.
$("#div1").detach();	The .detach() function removes the found elements from the DOM. This sample code finds the <div/> tag with the div1 ID and removes it and its contents. Note that .detach() is similar to .remove(). detach() keeps the removed items around in case you intend to reinsert them somewhere else. The .remove() method removes the items altogether.

(continued)

JQUERY MANIPULATION EXAMPLE	DESCRIPTION
$(document).height();	You use the .height() function when you need the pixel value of the height of something (typically to calculate layout spacing). This code finds the height of the entire document. jQuery includes similar functions for .width(), .innerHeight(), .innerWidth(), .outerHeight(), and .outerWidth().
$("#div1").after($("#div2"));	The .after() method allows you to insert content after a found item (or set of items). You can also use it to insert one found item after another (as in the example). This code finds the <div/> tag with the ID of div2 and inserts it after the found <div/> tag with the ID of div1. jQuery includes similar functions called .before(), .insertAfter(), and .insertBefore().
$("h2").replaceWith ("<h1>Page Title</h1>");	The .replaceWith() method removes content from the DOM and replaces it with something else. This sample code finds all <h2/> tags on the page and removes them. It then puts the provided content in place of these tags. Note that it replaces the entire group of tags with just a single instance of the provided content.
$("h2").wrapInner("<span class='pageTitle' />");	The .wrapInner() function wraps HTML content around the content of selected elements. In this example, the <span/> tag is wrapped around the content contained between any found <h2/> tags. jQuery provides similar functions called .wrap(), .wrapAll(), and .unwrap().

Handling Client-Side Events

The jQuery language allows you to bind scripts to client-side events such as button clicks, mouse movement, and keyboard interaction. These scripts can be written in separate .js files or within the page. They are then bound to events by using the jQuery .bind() method. There is no need to add markup to the page to do this binding. This ensures a clean separation between your markup and your client-side code.

As an example, suppose you are creating a page that searches for employees based on their ID. This page might include a text box and a search button, as in the following markup (which uses a master page).

```
<asp:Content ID="Content2" ContentPlaceHolderID="MainContent" Runat="Server">
    <h2>Employee Search</h2>
    <hr />
    Enter Employee ID
    <br />
    <asp:TextBox ID="TextBoxEmpId" runat="server"></asp:TextBox> 
    <span id="msgValidEmpId" style="color: Red">*</span>
    <br />
    <input type="button" id="ButtonSearch" runat="server" value="Search" />
</asp:Content>
```

You may want to bind code to the click event of the input button. The event code might then validate the user's input and, if it is valid, contact the server for search data. You could add the following jQuery code to your page to set up this binding.

```
<script type="text/javascript">
    $(document).ready(function () {
        $("#MainContent_ButtonSearch").click(validateEmpId);
    });
</script>
```

Note that this code uses the .click() method to define a binding to the validateEmpId JavaScript function. The .click() method is a shortcut. You could also call .bind("click", "validateEmpId").

The code inside validateEmpId might also use jQuery to find the user's input, validate it, and then set an appropriate message on the page. Of course, if the ID is valid, you would also want to reach out to the server for the search results; you will look at this in "Implementing AJAX with jQuery," later in this lesson. The following shows a version of the validateEmpId client-script.

```
function validateEmpId() {
    var empId = $("#MainContent_TextBoxEmpId").val();
    if (empId.length < 8 || empId.length > 10) {
        $("#msgValidEmpId").text("* Invalid Employee ID");
    }
    else {
        $("#msgValidEmpId").text("*");
        /// call back to server ...
    }
}
```

Figure 9-9 shows the page running in a browser. Notice the message displayed next to the text box. This is displayed after the search button click.

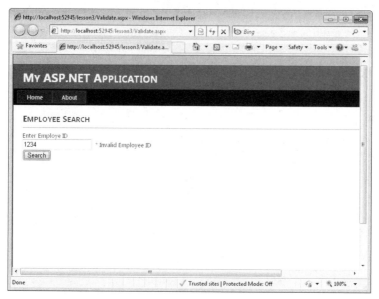

FIGURE 9-9 The jQuery event bound to a button on the page.

The jQuery library provides many events to which you can bind. These include events related to input tags (such as button), page-level actions, and user input events. You can trap these events and respond accordingly to make your page more interactive. All element events can be bound by using the .bind("event", handler) syntax. jQuery also provides short-cut methods based on event names (such as click). You use these shortcut methods to directly bind to an event without the use of the .bind() method. These all work in a similar manner: you indicate the event name as the method name and pass a function pointer to it. Table 9-5 lists some event methods you can use to bind to found elements.

TABLE 9-5 jQuery Client-Side Event Shortcut Methods

JQUERY EVENT METHOD	DESCRIPTION
.blur()	Bind to this event to execute code when an element loses focuses.
.click(), .dblclick()	Bind to these events to execute code when a user clicks or double-clicks on a specified element.
.error()	Bind to this event to trap element errors such as a broken link or a missing image.
.focus(), .focusin(), .focusout()	Bind to the .focus() event to execute code when an element receives focus. The .focusin() event will be triggered for child elements when a parent element receives focus. The .focusout() event triggers when focus is lost by an element or its parent.

JQUERY EVENT METHOD	DESCRIPTION
.hover()	Bind to this event to execute code when the mouse pointer is within the context of a specified element.
.keydown(), .keyup(), .keypress()	Bind to these events to trap user keyboard input associated with the bound element.
.mousedown(), .mouseup(), .mouseenter(), .mouseleave(), .mouseout(), .mouseover(), .mousemove()	The mouse events (along with .hover()) are used to trap events related to the user's mouse pointer and a specified page element.
.load(), .unload()	These methods are triggered when a specified element is loaded or unloaded on the page.
.resize()	Bind to this event to trap when the browser changes sizes.
.scroll()	Use this event to execute code when a user scrolls a specified element (such as a text box or select list).
.select()	This event is triggered when a user selects data or other child elements contained within a parent element.
.unbind()	Use this event to unbind code from an element's event.

Adding Effects and Animations to a Page

The jQuery library provides methods for adding client-side effects to your elements such as show, hide, fade in, and more. These effects and animations are easy to use. You simply find your elements by using a jQuery search and then call the effect you want. You can also combine effects in a queue-like manner through method chaining. This is as simple as adding one method call after another, as in the following.

```
.fadeIn().fadeOut().fadeIn()
```

As an example, suppose you want to add an effect to a page's title in order to highlight it for the user. The following code finds the first <h2/> element on the page, waits one second after the page has been loaded, and then slides the title text into view in a downward motion.

```
$(document).ready(function () {
    $("h2:first").delay(1000).slideDown();
});
```

jQuery provides several methods for managing similar effects and element animations. Table 9-6 provides a list of many of these methods and a description of each.

TABLE 9-6 jQuery Animation and Effects Methods

JQUERY ANIMATION / EFFECT EXAMPLE	DESCRIPTION
.delay()	Used to delay the call of the subsequent method in a method chain. You pass the number of milliseconds you want to delay to the method.
.fadeIn(), .fadeOut(), .fadeTo()	Allow you to fade an element into view (as long as it is set to have no display in the markup), out of view, or to another element, as in .fadeTo().
jQuery.fx.off	Set to true to turn off all jQuery effects for the page.
.show(), .hide()	Allow you to show or hide one or more selected elements. This method shows or hides an element by fading it into or out of view, providing a rudimentary form of animation.
.slideDown(), .slideUp(), .slideToggle()	Allow you to animate the showing of an item, fading it into view in a sliding motion. Note that .slideToggle() allows you to fade an element into and out of view (and toggle the current shown or hidden state).
.toggle()	Allows you to bind two functions to alternating click events. This way, one set of code executes the first time a user clicks an element and another set of code executes the second time they click the same element (and alternating thereafter).
.stop()	Used to stop any effect or animation that is running for the selected elements.

Implementing AJAX with jQuery

As you saw in Lesson 1, you can use AJAX to call back to the server from the client, get a response, and then update only a portion of the page without doing a refresh. This makes for a better, more interactive user experience. However, Lesson 1 relied on the ASP.NET AJAX Extensions controls to handle the details of setting up the client-to-server calls and the page update.

The jQuery library provides similar AJAX functionality but does so by calling web services you define. You can call a stand-alone web service from jQuery and then use the results to update a portion of the page (without causing a refresh). Alternatively, you can write your code to call back to just the page itself and execute a method in the same way. You will take a look at both of these options.

Calling a Web Service with $.ajax()

The jQuery.ajax() method enables you to call a web service and then update your page with the results. This method performs an asynchronous HTTP request, passes data to the request, and gets the results. You can use this method for a variety of tasks, including loading and executing a .js file, posting data to a web form, getting the HTML of a page, and sending and receiving XML data. The typical use, however, is posting to web services for partial page updates.

This method takes several name-value pairs as a parameter, called *settings*. The settings include the URL of your request, the content-type, the HTTP method (GET or POST), and the user name and password of the request. In fact, there are more than 20 settings with which you can work.

Let's look at an example of using jQuery to call a typical ASP.NET web service (ASMX file). Note that web services are covered in detail in the Chapter 10. In this simple example, the web service takes an employeeId as a parameter and returns a name as a result. The first step is to set up the web service. The following code shows an example.

Sample of Visual Basic Code

```vb
<System.Web.Script.Services.ScriptService()> _
Public Class EmployeeServiceVb
    Inherits System.Web.Services.WebService

    <WebMethod()> _
    Public Function GetEmployee(ByVal employeeId As String) As String
        'simulate employee name lookup
        Return "Jane Developer"
    End Function
End Class
```

Sample of C# Code

```csharp
[System.Web.Script.Services.ScriptService]
public class EmployeeService : System.Web.Services.WebService
{
    [WebMethod]
    public string GetEmployee(string employeeId)
    {
        //simulate employee name lookup
        return "Jane Developer";
    }
}
```

Notice the ScriptService attribute in the code. You adorn your code with this attribute to indicate that the service can be called from client-side script such as jQuery.

The next step is to make the AJAX call from a webpage. Assume that you have a form (based on a master page) that allows a user to enter an employee ID and then click a search button with the ButtonSearch ID to trigger the client-side JavaScript. You would then write the jQuery code shown on the following page.

```
<script type="text/javascript">
    $(document).ready(function () {
        $("#MainContent_ButtonSearch").click(function () {

            var empId = $("#MainContent_TextBoxEmpId").val();

            $.ajax({
                type: "POST",
                dataType: "json",
                contentType: "application/json",
                url: "EmployeeService.asmx/GetEmployee",
                data: "{'employeeId': '" + empId + "'}",
                success: function (data) {
                    alert("Employee name: " + data.d);
                },
                error: function () {
                    alert("Error calling the web service.");
                }
            });
        });
    });
</script>
```

Let's walk through this code. Note that the code is bound to the button click event when the page loads. Next, the user's input is assigned to a variable, empId. Then the call to $.ajax() is made. Notice that the settings are passed as name-value pairs separated by a colon. There is no set order to these pairs. The following list describes each setting:

- **type**   This is the HTTP request type, which in this case is POST.

- **contentType**   This indicates the request's Multipurpose Internet Mail Extensions (MIME) type. Here it is set to a JSON message format. The JSON message type is a lightweight standard that does not contain the overhead of XML. It is typically used by client-side AJAX.

- **dataType**   This parameter indicates the MIME type of data you want to have returned from the request; this too is set to JSON.

- **url**   This is the URL pointing to the web service. Notice that you append the service method name to the end of the URL.

- **data**   If the web service takes parameters, you pass these through to the data setting. This too is a set of name-value pairs contained in braces. In this case, the web method takes the employeeId parameter to which you pass the user input.

- **success**   Here you indicate a function to be called if the AJAX call is successful. The results of the call are passed to a parameter you provide (data). Recall that the results are in JSON format and thus can be translated into an object. You reference the results through data.d. In this case, the results are simply a string. If your results are a complex data type, you would reference the return values as data.d.PropertyName. (See the practice at the end of the chapter for an example.)

- **error**   This parameter allows you to define a function to be called if the AJAX call results in an error.

In this example, the results of the call are displayed to the user in a client-side alert. You will create a more robust example in this lesson's practice. First, however, let's look at making the same call back to the page (and not to a web service).

Calling Back to the Webpage with $.ajax()

If your page is self-contained, you might not want to expose a set of web services. In this case, ASP.NET allows you to add your web methods directly to your page and thus not have to create separate web services. The jQuery.Ajax method can then call the page directly to execute this code.

Let's look that the prior example again, but this time contain it to a single page. The first step, as before, is to write the web method. This time, you write the web method inside the page itself. Note that you can do so either as part of the code-behind file or within the page by using a <script runat="server"> tag. The following shows the web method used earlier, this time inside a page.

Sample of Visual Basic Code

```vb
<script runat="server">
    < System.Web.Services.WebMethod()> _
    Public Function GetEmployee(ByVal employeeId As String) As String
        'simulate employee name lookup
        Return "Jane Developer"
    End Function
</script>
```

Sample of C# Code

```csharp
<script runat="server">
    [System.Web.Services.WebMethod]
    public static string GetEmployee(string employeeId)
    {
        //simulate employee lookup
        return "Jane Developer";
    }
</script>
```

Notice that, in this case, you do not need to use the ScriptService attribute. ASP.NET assumes that code marked as a WebMethod inside a page is meant to be called from AJAX.

The $.ajax() call to this code is the same as before, with one exception: the URL. You would change the URL to point to the ASPX page instead of the service. In this case, that setting would look as follows.

```
url: "EmployeeLookupWebForm.aspx/GetEmployee",
```

Everything else about the page works in the same way. This technique simply provides encapsulation of the page and its code.

Additional AJAX Methods in the jQuery Library

The jQuery library exposes some additional jQuery methods that allow you to work with AJAX. These methods act as shorthand methods to the .ajax() method. They allow you to submit an HTTP POST or GET directly to a page, get JSON encoded data from the server, or get a JavaScript file for execution. Table 9-7 lists many of these shorthand methods and provides a brief description of each.

TABLE 9-7 jQuery AJAX Methods

JQUERY AJAX METHOD	DESCRIPTION

$.getJSON()	This is a shorthand version of $.ajax(). However, in this case, the dataType setting is automatically set to a JSON message and the request type is HTTP GET.
	
	For example, suppose you have the following JSON formatted message saved as a text file called States.txt.
	
	`{`
	`"state": ["Alabama", "Alaska", "Arkansas"]`
	`}`
	
	You could use .getJSON() to retrieve the data in this file and display the results, as in the following.
	
	`$.getJSON("States.txt",`
	`    function(data) {`
	`        alert("First states: " + data.`
	`            state[1]);`
	`    });`

$.get()	This is a shorthand version of $.ajax(). In this case, the request type is automatically set to HTTP GET. You can pass the URL and message dataType settings as parameters.
	
	As an example, the following jQuery code returns the full contents of the DataList.txt file.
	
	`$.get("DataList.txt", null, function (html) {`
	`    alert(html);`
	`}, "text");`
	
	Note that the last parameter is the dataType setting—in this case, "text". This tells jQuery how to parse your results. If this were a structured message type, you would want to use a parser such as HTML, XML, script, or JSON.

JQUERY AJAX METHOD	DESCRIPTION
$.post()	This is a shorthand version of $.ajax(). In this case, the request type is automatically set to HTTP POST. You can pass the URL, data to be sent to the page, and the dataType structure of the return message as parameters.
	You typically use this when you need to post data to the page and return the results. The following example posts the empId value to the EmpDetails.aspx page and returns the HTML results.

	<pre>$.post("EmpDetails.aspx",
	    { "empId": "AB123" }, function (data) {
	        alert(data);
	    }, "html");</pre>

	Note that in this case, the EmpDetails.aspx page is expecting a form value for empId in a post, as in Request.Form["empId"].
$.getScript()	This is a shorthand version of $.ajax(). In this case, the dataType is automatically set to script. You pass the URL to the script file. jQuery will get the script and load it. You can then call the methods in the loaded script.
	The following example loads a .js file called UpdateContents.js that includes a function called GetContent. After the file is loaded, the function is called.

	<pre>$.getScript('jquery/UpdateContents.js',
	function() {
	    GetContent();
	});</pre>

✔ **Quick Check**

1. Which jQuery library file should you deploy with your production applications?

2. How can you ensure that the browser has loaded the full content of the DOM prior to executing any jQuery code?

3. How would you use jQuery to select the <div id="employeeDetails"> element?

4. How would you pass parameters to a jQuery AJAX call?

Quick Check Answers

1. You should use the jquery-1.4.1.min.js file, which has been minified and thus optimized for download and performance.

2. You can use the $(document).ready() event to execute code only after the DOM has been loaded.

3. You would use the jQuery method and pass the ID as a parameter prepended with the pound (#) symbol, as in $("#employeeDetails").

4. You pass parameters to a jQuery call by enclosing them in braces and separating them as name-value pairs with a colon, as in the following:

```
data: "{'myParameter': 'paramValue'}",
```

PRACTICE Creating a jQuery Webpage that Works with AJAX

In this practice, you use the jQuery skills for selectors, animation, and AJAX that you learned in the lesson. You create a webpage to look up an employee and display the results back to the page.

ON THE COMPANION MEDIA

If you encounter a problem completing an exercise, you can find the completed projects in the samples installed from this book's companion CD. For more information about the project files and other content on the CD, see "Using the Companion Media" in this book's Introduction.

EXERCISE 1 Building the Webpage and Writing the Web Service

In this exercise, you create the website, lay out the webpage, and define an ASMX service to be called from jQuery.

1. Open Visual Studio and create a new website called **jQueryExample**. Notice the jQuery scripts installed in the Scripts folder.

2. Open Default.aspx and remove the markup inside the MainContent content control.

3. Add markup to allow a user to enter an employee ID and click a search button. Also, add markup to show the results of the lookup. These results should be enclosed in a <div/> tag with a style set for no display. The following markup shows an example.

```
<asp:Content ID="BodyContent" runat="server" ContentPlaceHolderID="MainContent">

    <h2>Employee Lookup</h2>
    <hr />
    Enter Employee ID
    <br />
    <asp:TextBox ID="TextBoxEmpId" runat="server"></asp:TextBox> 
    <br />
    <input type="button" id="ButtonSearch" runat="server" value="Search" />

    <div id="empDetails" style="display: none; margin-top: 40px">
        <h2>Employee Details</h2>
        <hr />
        <b>ID:</b> <span id="textId"></span><br />
        <b>Name:</b> <span id="textName"></span><br />
        <b>Title:</b> <span id="textTitle"></span><br />
        <b>Department:</b> <span id="textDepartment"></span><br />
    </div>

</asp:Content>
```

4. Add a web service to your website. You can do so by right-clicking the project in Solution Explorer and choosing Add New Item. Select Web Service from the Add New Item dialog box. Name your service **EmployeeService.asmx**.

5. Inside the web service code (App_Code/EmployeeService.cs or App_Code /EmployeeService.vb), add a class to represent an Employee. This class can be added to the bottom of the file (or as a separate file altogether). Make sure that this class has a default constructor. Create a separate constructor to return an instance based on employee ID. The following code shows an example.

```
Sample of Visual Basic Code
<Serializable()> _
Public Class Employee

    Public Sub New(ByVal empId As String)
        'simulate looking up an employee
        Me.ID = empId
        Me.FullName = "Joe Developer"
        Me.Title = "ASP.NET Sr. Developer"
        Me.Department = "Application Development"
    End Sub

    Public Sub New()

    End Sub
```

```
    Public Property FullName() As String
    Public Property ID As String
    Public Property Title As String
    Public Property Department As String

End Class
```

Sample of C# Code
```
[Serializable]
public class Employee
{
    public Employee(string empId)
    {
        //simulate looking up an employee
        this.ID = empId;
        this.FullName = "Joe Developer";
        this.Title = "ASP.NET Sr. Developer";
        this.Department = "Application Development";
    }

    public Employee()
    {
    }

    public string FullName { get; set; }
    public string ID { get; set; }
    public string Title { get; set; }
    public string Department { get; set; }
}
```

6. Next, uncomment the line related to the ScriptService attribute at the top of the web service class.

7. You can remove the constructor and the HelloWorld web methods from the code. Then create a web service to return an Employee object based on an ID. The following code shows an example.

Sample of Visual Basic Code
```
<WebService(Namespace:="http://tempuri.org/")> _
<WebServiceBinding(ConformsTo:=WsiProfiles.BasicProfile1_1)> _
<System.Web.Script.Services.ScriptService()> _
Public Class EmployeeService
    Inherits System.Web.Services.WebService

    <WebMethod()> _
    Public Function GetEmployeeById(ByVal employeeId As String) As Employee
        'simulate employee name lookup
        Return New Employee(employeeId)
    End Function

End Class
```

Sample of C# Code

```csharp
[WebService(Namespace = "http://tempuri.org/")]
[WebServiceBinding(ConformsTo = WsiProfiles.BasicProfile1_1)]
[System.Web.Script.Services.ScriptService]
public class EmployeeService : System.Web.Services.WebService {

    [WebMethod]
    public Employee GetEmployeeById(string employeeId)
    {
        //simulate employee name lookup
        return new Employee(employeeId);
    }

}
```

8. Build your solution and verify that there are no errors.

EXERCISE 2   Writing the jQuery Code to Animate the Page and Call the Web Service

In this exercise, you add jQuery selectors, animation, and an AJAX call to the website created in the previous exercise.

1. Continue editing the project you created in the previous exercise. Alternatively, you can open the completed Lesson 3, Exercise 1 project in the sample files installed from the CD.

2. Open the Default.aspx page in Source view. Add a reference to the jQuery library to the HeadContent content control. Note that you might want to use the debug version if you plan to walk through any jQuery code. The following shows an example.

```
<asp:Content ID="HeaderContent" runat="server" ContentPlaceHolderID="HeadContent"
    <script src="Scripts/jquery-1.4.1.js" type="text/javascript"></script>
</asp:Content>
```

3. Add a <script/> tag to the MainContent area of the page. Inside this script, you will write jQuery code to be bound to the ButtonSearch control when the page loads. The following shows an example.

```
<script type="text/javascript">
    $(document).ready(function () {
        $("#MainContent_ButtonSearch").click(function () {


    });
</script>
```

4. Add jQuery code to the button click function (shown previously) to hide the employee details <div/> tag (in case it is shown from a previous lookup), get the user's input (employee ID), make the .ajax() call to the web service, display the results, and show the employee details with animation. The following is a full listing of the jQuery JavaScript for the page.

```
<script type="text/javascript">

    $(document).ready(function () {
        $("#MainContent_ButtonSearch").click(function () {

            /// hide employee details (if shown)
            $("#empDetails").hide("slow");

            var empId = $("#MainContent_TextBoxEmpId").val();

            $.ajax({
                type: "POST",
                dataType: "json",
                contentType: "application/json",
                url: "EmployeeService.asmx/GetEmployeeById",
                data: "{'employeeId': '" + empId.toString() + "'}",
                success: function (data) {
                    $("#textId").html(data.d.ID);
                    $("#textName").html(data.d.FullName);
                    $("#textTitle").html(data.d.Title);
                    $("#textDepartment").html(data.d.Department);

                    /// show employee details
                    $("#empDetails").show("slow");
                },
                error: function () {
                    alert("Error calling the web service.");
                }
            });
        });
    });

</script>
```

5. Save and run the page. Notice how each lookup of an employee animates the display to the user. This is because the .show() and .hide() methods were included. Figure 9-10 shows an example of what you should see.

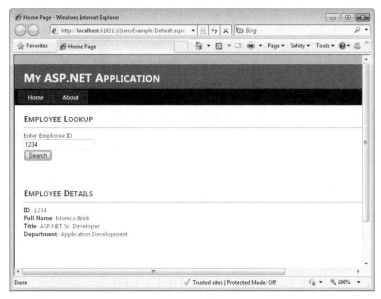

FIGURE 9-10 The Employee Lookup page running jQuery and AJAX in a browser.

Lesson Summary

- You can use jQuery to select elements on the page, filter your selection, and then manipulate the results.

- You can select elements by using a tag name, as in $("h2"); an id, as in $("#tagId"); and cascading style sheet style, as in $(".styleClassName").

- jQuery will select all found elements and return them as a group. You can use the .each() method to traverse the collection, much as you would with For...Each.

- You use the .bind() method in jQuery to bind elements to client-side event code. Events can be keyboard input, mouse clicks, page events, and more.

- The $.ajax() method takes a group of settings as name-value pairs to call back to a web service or webpage asynchronously as part of a partial-page update.

- You can use the $.ajax() shorthand methods $.getJSON(), $.get(), $.post(), and $.getScript() to execute specific versions of an AJAX request.

Lesson Review

You can use the following questions to test your knowledge of the information in Lesson 3, "Implementing jQuery." The questions are also available on the companion CD as a practice test, if you prefer to review them in electronic form.

> **NOTE ANSWERS**
>
> Answers to these questions and explanations of why each answer choice is correct or incorrect are located in the "Answers" section at the end of the book.

1. You need to write jQuery code to select the first heading (h2) tag on the page and then slowly fade the item into view. Which line(s) of code would accomplish this task? (Choose all that apply.)

   A. `$("#h21").fadeIn(500);`

   B. `$("h2:first").fadeIn("slow");`

   C. `$(".h2:first").fadeIn(500);`

   D. `$("h2:first").fadeIn(500);`

2. You want to execute a function after the DOM has loaded. This function should bind an event code to be run when the user presses a key on the keyboard inside a text box control with the textBox1 ID. Which steps should you take? (Choose all that apply.)

   A. Bind to the keyPress event by using the following code.

   ```
   $("#textBox1").bind("keyPress", ())
   ```

   B. Add your event binding code to the $(document).ready() event at the top of your script.

   C. Add your event binding code to the $(document).load() event at the top of your script.

   D. Bind to the keyPress event by using the following code.

   ```
   $("#textBox1").add("keyPress", ()).
   ```

3. You want to use the .ajax() method to call a web method named GetCityCodes. This web method is contained on the same webpage as the jQuery code and UI markup. This method should be called by using JSON. The web method takes the state parameter. Which of the following calls would you use?

   A.
   ```
   $.ajax({
       type: "POST",
       dataType: "json",
       contentType: "application/json",
       url: "CityLookup.aspx/GetCityCodes",
       data: "{'state': '" + state + "'}",
       success: function (data) {
           alert(data.d);
       },
   ```

B. `$.ajax({`

    `type: "POST",`

    `dataType: "json",`

    `contentType: "application/json",`

    `url: "CityLookup.asmx/GetCityCodes",`

    `data: "{'state': '" + state + "'}",`

    `success: function (data) {`

        `alert(state.d);`

    `},`

C. `$.ajax({`

    `type: "POST",`

    `dataType: "json",`

    `contentType: "application/json",`

    `url: "CityLookup.aspx/GetCityCodes/" + state,`

    `success: function (data) {`

        `alert(data.d);`

    `},`

D. `$.ajax({`

    `type: "POST",`

    `dataType: "json",`

    `contentType: "application/json",`

    `url: "CityLookup.asmx/GetCityCodes",`

    `data: "state:" + state,`

    `success: function (data) {`

        `alert(data.d);`

    `},`

4. You want to use an HTTP GET to retrieve a basic text file from the server by using AJAX and jQuery. Which of the following jQuery methods would you use?

   A. `$.post()`

   B. `$.getScript()`

   C. `$getJSON()`

   D. `$.get()`

Case Scenarios

In the following case scenarios, you apply what you've learned about AJAX in ASP.NET and jQuery. If you have difficulty completing this work, review the material in this chapter before beginning the next chapter. You can find answers to these questions in the "Answers" section at the end of this book.

Case Scenario 1: Using the ASP.NET AJAX Extensions

You are an application developer for Contoso, Ltd, a pharmaceuticals company. You have recently converted your internal data analysis application over to an ASP.NET website. This has provided users with additional access to the application and has allowed for easier deployment. However, users are trying to get used to having to search and page through data rather than having a more direct connection to it.

One complaint has been lodged about a particularly feature-rich page. This page contains multiple data grids and several user actions. The page can take 5 to 10 seconds to fully load. However, when they are in the page, users typically work on the same page for many minutes.

In addition, the page contains a grid of data near the bottom. This grid is searchable and can show only 25 records at a time. Each search or request for an additional page of data requires a refresh of the page. Users complain that they then lose the context of the page and have to scroll back down to the area in which they were working (in addition to waiting another 5 to 10 seconds for the page to load).

You have been asked to take a look at these issues and come up with a plan.

1. What ASP.NET AJAX control could you use to stop the page from fully refreshing when users search for new data in the grid?

2. You decide to use ASP.NET AJAX to help solve some of these issues. What control *must* you add to the page?

3. When the page executes an asynchronous postback, you want to notify the user as to the progress of the postback. What ASP.NET control can you use to do so?

Case Scenario 2: Using the Microsoft AJAX Library

You are a developer at Fabrikam, Inc. The new product that you put in the field will be web based. You know that users need a highly interactive client, so you decide to implement ASP.NET AJAX. You have identified and plan to write the following components for the site:

- A clock that shows how long any page on the site has been open in the browser window
- The ability to highlight the control that has the current focus on the page
- Logic that can be used by the client to validate data including part numbers, vendor codes, and more

Thinking about the solution you intend to write, answer the following questions.

1. Using the Microsoft AJAX Library, how would you implement each of these in terms of component, control, or behavior?

2. Which of these features would you wrap as a custom server control and what class would you use to implement it?

Case Scenario 3: Using jQuery

You are a developer working for Adventure Works, a sporting goods retailer. You have been asked to write a webpage that allows a user to work interactively to learn more about selected bicycle models. You have decided on a design with a selected group of users. When a user clicks on a section of the bicycle, the page should load details of the selected bike component (wheels, seat, brakes, cranks, handlebars, and so on). These details can be retrieved from a product catalog web service exposed as ASMX. When you display the details, you want to animate them onto the web form without performing a full page refresh.

Answer the following questions about how you will develop the solution.

1. You decide to implement the bike photo in an Image control. How can you use jQuery to bind to the click event for the control? How do you ensure that the DOM has been loaded prior to binding? How can you tell where the user has clicked on the bike?

2. How would you call the web service to process an asynchronous update to the page without causing a refresh? What attribute would need to be applied to the web service?

3. What jQuery methods would you use to animate the display of the bicycle data to the user?

Suggested Practices

To help you successfully master the exam objectives presented in this chapter, complete the following tasks.

Add Partial-Page Update Support to a Page

For this task, you should complete Practice 1 to gain experience with partial-page updates. Practice 2 shows you how you can leverage the Timer control. Practice 3 demonstrates the UpdateProgress control.

- **Practice 1**   Find a page in your current website that uses a data grid to display data. Put this data grid into an UpdatePanel to enable partial-page updates when paging through the data.

- **Practice 2**   Create a webpage that allows a user to cycle through a series of pictures. Use the Timer control to automatically update the graphic on display at periodic intervals.

- **Practice 3**   Find a page in your current application that takes a long time to load and provides a lot of user interaction. Add partial-page update to this page. When the page updates, use the UpdateProgress control to notify the user.

Create Client Code by Using the Microsoft AJAX Library

For this task, you should complete Practice 1 to learn the basics of building a control with the Microsoft AJAX Library. Practice 2 will give you insight into building a client behavior control.

- **Practice 1**   Create an AJAX client control that extends an ASP.NET button with a confirmation alert window. Wrap the control as a custom server control by using the IScriptControl interface.

- **Practice 2**   Create an AJAX client behavior control that highlights a control as it receives focus. Wrap the control as a custom server control by using the ExtenderControl class.

Write Interactive Client Code with jQuery

For this task, you should complete Practice 1 to practice the basics of using jQuery on a webpage. Practice 2 will give you experience calling services with jQuery.

- **Practice 1**   Add the jQuery library to an existing website with which you work. Encapsulate an area inside a <div/> tag. Use jQuery to select this area and animate its display to the user (slide it down or fade it in).

- **Practice 2**   Find an existing webpage inside the site you are currently creating that posts back to the page and then updates the user (or create a new page). Take the postback and related method of the page and mark it as a web method (do not create a new web service). Then use jQuery to call this same method as a partial-page update.

Take a Practice Test

The practice tests on this book's companion CD offer many options. For example, you can test yourself on just the lesson review questions in this chapter, or you can test yourself on all the 70-515 certification exam objectives. You can set up the test so it closely simulates the experience of taking a certification exam, or you can set it up in study mode so you can look at the correct answers and explanations after you answer each question.

> **MORE INFO**   **PRACTICE TESTS**
>
> For details about all the practice test options available, see the "How to Use the Practice Tests" section in this book's Introduction.

CHAPTER 10

Writing and Working with HTTP Modules and Web Services

Web services are a versatile tool; they enable you to perform system integration, execute business process workflow across boundaries, provide for business logic reuse, and much more. There are two primary ways to create services in Microsoft ASP.NET. You can create web services based on the classic ASP.NET XML web service (ASMX) model. This is a familiar ASP.NET programming experience for developers of services that are meant to be exclusively bound to Hypertext Transfer Protocol (HTTP) and hosted by Internet Information Services (IIS) and ASP.NET. You can also use Windows Communication Foundation (WCF) to create web services. This model allows developers to write services that can be configured to work with a variety of hosts, protocols, and clients. Of course, this includes hosting in IIS and communicating through HTTP.

This chapter first covers creating HTTP handlers and modules, which includes responding to requests for specific file types such as PDF (Portable Document Format), XPS (XML Paper Specification), and similar types. It also includes creating modules that are called for specific application events across all requests to the server. Though they are not exactly web services, both HTTP handlers and modules are meant to respond to specialized HTTP requests. The chapter then moves on to cover programming actual web services. This includes Extensible Markup Language (XML) web services and those based on WCF (including WCF data services).

Exam objectives in this chapter:

- Configuring and Extending a Web Application
    - Create and configure HttpHandlers and HttpModules.
    - Reference and configure ASMX and WCF services.
- Displaying and Manipulating Data
    - Create and consume a data service.

Lessons in this chapter:

Before You Begin

To complete the lessons in this chapter, you should be familiar with developing applications with Microsoft Visual Studio 2010 by using Microsoft Visual Basic or Microsoft Visual C#. In addition, you should be comfortable with all of the following:

- The Visual Studio 2010 Integrated Development Environment (IDE)
- Using Hypertext Markup Language (HTML) and client-side scripting
- Creating ASP.NET websites and forms
- Adding web server controls to a webpage
- Using AJAX on a webpage

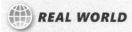

REAL WORLD
Mike Snell

Most websites do not require you to write your own custom HTTP handlers. Rather, these are reserved for very special cases, such as when you are writing a specialized application, a custom processing framework, or a file processor of some kind. That said, most developers I know just can't stand not knowing how their code is processed and executed. Understanding HTTP handlers (and modules) is key to unlocking how HTTP requests are linked to your ASP.NET pages.

Lesson 1: Creating HTTP Handlers and HTTP Modules

Some web development tasks require you to write code to handle the actual HTTP request sent to the server. You might need to write a specialized image server, a file processor, or a process to handle a custom level of security. This type of code is written as either an HTTP handler or an HTTP module.

An *HTTP handler* is an endpoint on the server that responds to requests for different resources. A familiar HTTP handler is the ASP.NET page handler that is called when an ASPX page is requested from the server. You can write similar custom handlers to be called when a resource with a specific file extension is requested of the server. An example of this is the ASP.NET tracing infrastructure, which is built by using a handler that accepts resource requests for Trace.axd files.

An *HTTP module* is code that gets called for every request or response routed to your application. This code is registered with the server and can subscribe to events within the request-and-response pipeline. You can write HTTP modules to manage custom security levels, do custom logging, or execute similar tasks.

This lesson describes how you can write your own HTTP handlers and HTTP modules to work with ASP.NET and IIS.

After this lesson, you will be able to:

- Create a custom HTTP handler to respond to requests for nonstandard file types.
- Enable asynchronous communication inside a webpage.
- Create a custom HTTP module as part of the ASP.NET page life cycle.

Estimated lesson time: 30 minutes

Creating a Custom HTTP Handler

An HTTP handler is code that executes when an HTTP request for a specific resource is made to the server. For example, when a user requests an ASPX page from IIS, the ASP.NET page handler is executed. When an ASMX file is accessed, the ASP.NET service handler is called. You can create your own custom HTTP handlers, register them with IIS, and receive notice when a specific request has been made. This allows you to interact with the request and write your own custom output to the browser.

You create a custom, synchronous HTTP handler by implementing the IHttpHandler interface. This interface requires you to implement the IsReusable property to indicate whether your handler can be reused. If IsReusable is set to true, your handler will be put into a pool to help increase performance across requests.

The IHttpHandler interface also requires you to implement the ProcessRequest method. This method is called by ASP.NET when your handler executes. You write code in this to produce a response for the HTTP request. Note that an HTTP handler exists inside ASP.NET. Therefore, it has access to the application context, including the session state, application state, and identity of the user making the request.

After you have created your custom HTTP handler, you register it with IIS. You can do so explicitly by using the IIS configuration tools. This mapping is based on file extension. You first map your custom file extension to ASP.NET and then map the extension to your custom handler from within your ASP.NET application. ASP.NET also allows you to use the .ashx extension to automatically register a custom HTTP handler. In this case, you create a page with the .ashx extension and use the @ WebHandler directive to point to your custom HTTP handler code. This will automatically register your HTTP handler with IIS and ASP.NET.

As an example, consider the processing of image requests in ASP.NET. Each image in an HTML page requires a separate browser request and a separate response from the web server. By default, IIS does not pass requests for images to ASP.NET. Instead, IIS simply reads the image file from the file system and sends it directly to the web browser as static content.

But suppose you want to handle requests for images in your ASP.NET code instead of just passing them back by IIS. You might want to do this so you can dynamically generate a chart displaying performance information over a period of time or dynamically create thumbnails in a photo album application. In these circumstances, you can either periodically generate the images in advance or you can create a custom HTTP handler to receive the image requests, process them, and render a response. It is the latter option on which this example focuses. The following outlines how you can configure ASP.NET (and your custom HTTP handler code) to receive requests for images:

1. Write code to act as the HTTP handler for a specific file type (in this case, JPG).

2. Configure IIS to pass requests for the required image types to ASP.NET, and configure your ASP.NET application to pass the request to your custom HTTP handler.

Creating the Handler

Remember, to create the HTTP handler, you implement the IHttpHandler interface. The output you want to render should be put inside the ProcessRequest method. The following code demonstrates a simple HTTP handler. You add this code as a class file to your website's App_Code directory. You will get a chance to work with this example in the practice for this lesson.

Sample of Visual Basic Code

```vb
Public Class ImageHandler
    Implements IHttpHandler

    Public ReadOnly Property IsReusable As Boolean _
        Implements System.Web.IHttpHandler.IsReusable
        Get
            Return False
        End Get
    End Property

    Public Sub ProcessRequest(ByVal context As System.Web.HttpContext) _
        Implements System.Web.IHttpHandler.ProcessRequest

        'set the MIME type
        context.Response.ContentType = "image/jpeg"

        Dim Request As HttpRequest = context.Request
        Dim Response As HttpResponse = context.Response

        If Request.RawUrl.ToLower.Contains("jellyfish.jpg") Then
            Response.TransmitFile(Request.PhysicalApplicationPath & _
                "/images/Jellyfish.jpg")
        ElseIf Request.RawUrl.ToLower.Contains("koala.jpg") Then
            Response.TransmitFile(Request.PhysicalApplicationPath & _
                "/images/Koala.jpg")
        Else
            Response.Write("File not found")
        End If

    End Sub

End Class
```

Sample of C# Code

```csharp
public class ImageHandler : IHttpHandler
{
    public bool IsReusable
    {
        get { return false; }
    }

    public void ProcessRequest(HttpContext context)
    {
        //set the MIME type
        context.Response.ContentType = "image/jpeg";

        HttpRequest Request = context.Request;
        HttpResponse Response = context.Response;

        if(Request.RawUrl.ToLower().Contains("jellyfish.jpg"))
        {
            Response.TransmitFile(Request.PhysicalApplicationPath +
                "/images/Jellyfish.jpg");
        }
        else if (Request.RawUrl.ToLower().Contains("koala.jpg"))
        {
            Response.TransmitFile(Request.PhysicalApplicationPath +
                "/images/Koala.jpg");
        }
        else
        {
            Response.Write("File not found");
        }
    }
}
```

Registering the Handler by Using Web.config

There are two ways to register the handler with IIS and ASP.NET: you can either configure IIS to send the request to ASP.NET and your application, or you can add configuration code to your Web.config file to register the custom handler when your application is deployed. Let's look at the second option first.

You can register your custom handler by using the Web.config file. This registration differs between IIS 6.0 and IIS 7.0. In IIS 6.0, you create an <add> element in the <configuration> <system.Web><httpHandlers> section of your Web.config file for each file extension you want to register with your handler. The following markup demonstrates how to point requests sent to your application for files of type JPG to your custom class, ImageHandler.

```xml
<configuration>
  <system.Web>
    <httpHandlers>
      <add verb="*" path="*.jpg" type="ImageHandler"/>
    </httpHandlers>
  </system.Web>
</configuration>
```

In IIS 7.0, you write similar configuration code. However, you place it inside the <configuration><system.WebServer><handlers> section of your Web.config file, as the following markup illustrates.

```
<configuration>
    <system.WebServer>
        <handlers>
            <add verb="*" path="*.jpg" type="ImageHandler"
                name="ImageHandler"/>
        </handlers>
    </system.WebServer>
</configuration>
```

In either case, any requests sent by IIS to ASP.NET for files ending in .jpg will be forwarded to the ImageHandler class. For this to work properly, either the ImageHandler assembly must be available in the application's Bin folder or the source code must be in the App_Code folder.

Configuring IIS to Forward Requests to ASP.NET

For performance reasons, IIS passes only requests for specific file types to ASP.NET. For example, IIS passes requests for files with the .aspx, .axd, .ascx, and .asmx extensions to the Aspnet_Isapi.dll file that performs the ASP.NET processing. For all other file types, including HTML, JPG, and GIF, ASP.NET simply passes the file from the file system directly to the client browser.

You have seen how you can use the Web.config file to change this. You can also use the IIS 7.0 administration tools to configure an IIS application mapping from the image file extension to the Aspnet_Isapi.dll file. The process of configuring this information also differs between IIS 6.0 and IIS 7.0. The following steps outline the process for configuring with IIS 7.0:

1. Open the IIS Manager.

2. Expand the nodes until you get to your site or to the default website. Select the node for your application.

3. Double-click the Handler Mappings icon in the center pane of the IIS Manager. Note that if you have used the Web.config method of registration, you should see that registration in the Handler Mappings list.

4. In the Actions pane (on the right side), select Add Managed Handler.

5. In the Add Managed Handler dialog box, shown in Figure 10-1, set Request Path to the file name or extension you want to map; in this case, .jpg. The Type list allows you to choose the class name of the HTTP handler. The Name field is simply for entering a descriptive name.

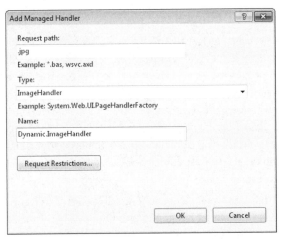

FIGURE 10-1 Configuring an application mapping to process image requests in IIS 7.0.

After you have configured the application extension mapping, all requests for that file type are forwarded to ASP.NET and to your handler. To enable normal image processing in most areas of your website, create a separate virtual directory just for dynamically generated images.

Creating Automatically Registered Handlers by Using the .ashx Extension

By default, ASP.NET reserves the .ashx file extension for custom HTTP handlers. This means that you can write a page with the .ashx file extension that points to your custom HTTP handler and not be concerned with registration. The request will be routed to ASP.NET, and ASP.NET will route the request to your HTTP handler.

For example, suppose you rewrote the HTTP handler that processes image requests so that it is based on the query string instead of the file name. You could do so simply by changing the evaluation inside the If statements to something like the following.

```
Request.QueryString.ToString().ToLower().Contains("jellyfish")
```

You can then add a file to your site with the .ashx extension, as in MyImageHandler.ashx. You add only one line of markup to this file. This line uses the @ WebHandler directive to point to your custom HTTP handler, as in the following.

```
<%@ WebHandler Language="C#" Class="ImageHandlerQs" %>
```

You can then deploy and call this handler without additional configuration. You would call this handler by using the query string, as in the following.

```
http://localhost:56560/lesson1/MyImageHandler.ashx?jellyfish
```

Asynchronous Handlers and Pages

Asynchronous programming allows a request to execute on a non-ASP.NET thread, allowing ASP.NET to continue to process incoming requests and making your site more responsive, especially when serving long-running requests. An asynchronous handler returns the request processing thread to ASP.NET and enables it to perform additional actions while the asynchronous task executes. In most web applications, the user cannot interact with the page until page rendering is complete (this applies to partial page updates as well). Therefore, most asynchronous programming in web applications is done to improve the efficiency of long-running webpages by performing multiple actions simultaneously and freeing the ASP.NET threads to respond to additional requests.

For example, consider a webpage that must query a network resource (such as a web service). Because IIS and ASP.NET can only render a limited number of pages simultaneously, the ASP.NET thread pool can become completely consumed, creating a performance bottleneck. When the thread pool has been consumed, your server waits for pages to finish rendering before beginning to process other pages. Even though the server might have available processor cycles, requests are queued. If your application executes these calls asynchronously, the server can begin rendering more pages simultaneously, improving efficiency and increasing scale.

> **NOTE   IMPROVING PERFORMANCE WITH THREAD POOLING**
>
> Thread pooling can be tricky. When implementing asynchronous handlers and webpages, use a performance testing tool to verify performance under a heavy load. Sometimes the overhead introduced by asynchronous programming can offset the benefits. Whether performance improves depends on many aspects of the application and web server configuration. One sure way to get performance gains is to create a new thread. There is only one Common Language Runtime (CLR) thread pool per AppDomain, so you must be sure to not just consume the same threads ASP.NET would be using. Instead, create your own.

Creating an Asynchronous HTTP Handler

An asynchronous HTTP handler differs from a synchronous one in that when it is executed, ASP.NET will put the handler code on a separate thread, one obtained from the CLR. The thread that would normally run a synchronous handler is then placed back into the thread pool to handle additional user requests. This reduces the chance that the limited set of ASP.NET threads will block processing, and thus can improve overall performance.

You create an asynchronous handler much like you would a synchronous handler. You use a similar interface called IHttpAsyncHandler and then override the IsReusable property and the BeginProcessRequest method. You write code inside this method to initiate an asynchronous call. You also provide a callback method that gets called when the asynchronous operation completes. Finally, you write code inside the EndProcessRequest method to deal with any cleanup when the process completes.

Consider the image handler created in the previous example. We can rewrite that example to demonstrate asynchronous processing. You start by implementing the IHttpAsyncHandler interface. Remember, you write your code inside the BeginProcessRequest method. You must also include code for IsReusable, EndProcessRequest, and ProcessRequest. You can make the latter simply throw an exception if your handler is called in a synchronous way.

Inside BeginProcessRequest, you create an instance of a class that implements the IAsyncResult interface. This custom class is where you put your code that is to be run on a separate thread. In the example code shown next, that is done inside the StartAsync method. Notice the call to ThreadPool.QueueUserWorkItem. This passes the name of the method (StartAsyncOperation) you want to run on a separate thread. When a thread becomes available, this method will execute. When it is finished, the method running on the separate thread invokes the callback delegate, which is of type AsyncCallback.

Sample of Visual Basic Code

```vb
Imports Microsoft.VisualBasic
Imports System.Threading

Public Class AsynchImageHandler
    Implements IHttpAsyncHandler

    Public ReadOnly Property IsReusable As Boolean _
        Implements System.Web.IHttpHandler.IsReusable
        Get
            Return False
        End Get
    End Property

    Public Function BeginProcessRequest(ByVal context As System.Web.HttpContext, _
        ByVal cb As System.AsyncCallback, ByVal extraData As Object) _
        As System.IAsyncResult _
        Implements System.Web.IHttpAsyncHandler.BeginProcessRequest

        context.Response.Write("<p>BeginProcessRequest starting ...</p>")

        Dim imageOperation As New ImageAsynchOperation(cb, context, extraData)
        imageOperation.StartAsync()

        context.Response.Write("<p>BeginProcessRequest queued ...</p>")

        Return imageOperation

    End Function
```

```vb
Public Sub EndProcessRequest(ByVal result As System.IAsyncResult) _
    Implements System.Web.IHttpAsyncHandler.EndProcessRequest

        'process any cleanup code here

    End Sub

    Public Sub ProcessRequest(ByVal context As System.Web.HttpContext) _
        Implements System.Web.IHttpHandler.ProcessRequest

        Throw New InvalidOperationException()

    End Sub

End Class

Class ImageAsynchOperation
    Implements IAsyncResult

    Private _completed As Boolean
    Private _state As [Object]
    Private _callback As AsyncCallback
    Private _context As HttpContext

    Public Sub New(ByVal callback As AsyncCallback, _
        ByVal context As HttpContext, _
        ByVal state As [Object])

        _callback = callback
        _context = context
        _state = state
        _completed = False

    End Sub

    ReadOnly Property IsCompleted() As Boolean _
            Implements IAsyncResult.IsCompleted
        Get
            Return _completed
        End Get
    End Property

    ReadOnly Property AsyncWaitHandle() As WaitHandle _
            Implements IAsyncResult.AsyncWaitHandle
        Get
            Return Nothing
        End Get
    End Property
```

```
    ReadOnly Property AsyncState() As [Object] _
            Implements IAsyncResult.AsyncState
        Get
            Return _state
        End Get
    End Property

    ReadOnly Property CompletedSynchronously() As Boolean _
            Implements IAsyncResult.CompletedSynchronously
        Get
            Return False
        End Get
    End Property

    Public Sub StartAsync()

        ThreadPool.QueueUserWorkItem(New _
            WaitCallback(AddressOf StartAsyncOperation), Nothing)

    End Sub

    Private Sub StartAsyncOperation(ByVal workItemState As [Object])

        Dim Request As HttpRequest = _context.Request
        Dim Response As HttpResponse = _context.Response

        If Request.RawUrl.ToLower.Contains("jellyfish") Then
            Response.Write("<p>JellyFish</p>")
        ElseIf Request.RawUrl.ToLower.Contains("koala") Then
            Response.Write("<p>Koala</p>")
        Else
            Response.Write("<p>Not found.</p>")
        End If

        Response.Write("<p>Asynch operation completed.</p>")

        _completed = True
        _callback(Me)

    End Sub

End Class
```

Sample of C# Code

```csharp
using System;
using System.Web;
using System.Threading;

public class AsynchImageHandler : IHttpAsyncHandler
{
    public bool IsReusable
    {
        get { return false; }
    }

    public AsynchImageHandler()
    {
    }

    public IAsyncResult BeginProcessRequest(HttpContext context,
        AsyncCallback cb, object extraData)
    {
        context.Response.Write("<p>BeginProcessRequest starting ...</p>");

        ImageAsynchOperation imageOperation =
            new ImageAsynchOperation(cb, context, extraData);
        imageOperation.StartAsync();

        context.Response.Write("<p>BeginProcessRequest queued ...</p>");

        return imageOperation;
    }

    public void EndProcessRequest(IAsyncResult result)
    {
        //process any cleanup code here
    }

    public void ProcessRequest(HttpContext context)
    {
        throw new InvalidOperationException();
    }
}

class ImageAsynchOperation : IAsyncResult
{
    private bool _completed;
    private object _state;
    private AsyncCallback _callback;
    private HttpContext _context;

    public ImageAsynchOperation(AsyncCallback callback,
        HttpContext context, object state)
    {
        _callback = callback;
        _context = context;
        _state = state;
        _completed = false;
    }
```

```
        public bool IsCompleted
        {
            get { return _completed; }
        }

        public System.Threading.WaitHandle AsyncWaitHandle
        {
            get { return null; }
        }

        public object AsyncState
        {
            get { return _state; }
        }

        public bool CompletedSynchronously
        {
            get { return false; }
        }

        public void StartAsync()
        {
            ThreadPool.QueueUserWorkItem(new WaitCallback(StartAsyncOperation), null);

        }

        public void StartAsyncOperation(object workItemState)
        {

            HttpRequest Request = _context.Request;
            HttpResponse Response = _context.Response;

            if (Request.RawUrl.ToLower().Contains("jellyfish"))
            {
                Response.Write("<p>JellyFish</p>");
            }
            else if (Request.RawUrl.ToLower().Contains("koala"))
            {
                Response.Write("<p>Koala</p>");
            }
            else
            {
                Response.Write("<p>Not found.</p>");
            }

            Response.Write("<p>Asynch operation completed.</p>");

            _completed = true;
            _callback(this);
        }
}
```

The final step is to register your HTTP handler in the Web.config file. This process is the same as discussed previously (in the "Registering the Handler by Using Web.config" section). In this example, the handler will respond to files with *.asynchJpg extensions. Figure 10-2 shows the code running in a browser. Notice the order in which the messages are written out to the browser. This illustrates the different threads and the callback.

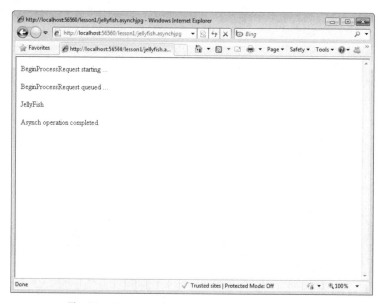

FIGURE 10-2 The IHttpAsyncHandler prevents thread blocking in your code.

Creating an Asynchronous Webpage

You can follow the asynchronous HTTP handler model to create an asynchronous webpage. This is a webpage that works with the IHttpAsynchHandler interface (instead of a registered handler for a specified file extension).

For example, assume you were writing the asynchronous HTTP handler in the previous example as a webpage. This webpage would still use the same ImageAsynchOperation class that implements IAsynchResult as defined above. However, it would use this class not in a handler, but on a webpage. The following steps walk you through the basic process of implementing this example inside a standard ASPX page.

1. Add the Async="true" attribute to the @ Page directive inside your markup. This indicates that the page implements the IHttpAsynchHandler interface. The following shows an example.

   Sample of Visual Basic Code
   ```
   <%@ Page Language="VB" Async="true" AutoEventWireup="false" %>
   ```

Sample of C# Code

```
<%@ Page Language="C#" Async="true" AutoEventWireup="true" %>
```

2. Inside your page's code-behind file, create methods that get called to start and end your asynchronous operation typically named BeginProcessRequest and EndProcessRequest. The following shows an example. Notice that you no longer need to get a context object; the webpage provides this.

Sample of Visual Basic Code

```
Public Function BeginProcessRequest(ByVal sender As Object, _
    ByVal e As EventArgs, ByVal cb As System.AsyncCallback, _
    ByVal extraData As Object) As System.IAsyncResult

    Response.Write("<p>BeginProcessRequest starting ...</p>")

    Dim imageOperation As New ImageAsynchOperation(cb, Me.Context, extraData)
    imageOperation.StartAsync()

    Response.Write("<p>BeginProcessRequest queued ...</p>")

    Return imageOperation

End Function

Public Sub EndProcessRequest(ByVal result As System.IAsyncResult)
    'process any cleanup code here

End Sub
```

Sample of C# Code

```
protected IAsyncResult BeginProcessRequest(object sender,
    EventArgs e, AsyncCallback cb, object extraData)
{
    Response.Write("<p>BeginProcessRequest starting ...</p>");

    ImageAsynchOperation imageOperation =
        new ImageAsynchOperation(cb, this.Context, extraData);
    imageOperation.StartAsync();

    Response.Write("<p>BeginProcessRequest queued ...</p>");

    return imageOperation;
}

protected void EndProcessRequest(IAsyncResult result)
{
    //process any cleanup code here
}
```

3. Call the AddOnPreRenderCompleteAsync method inside the Page_Load event to declare the event handlers you just created. The following code demonstrates.

Sample of Visual Basic Code
```
Protected Sub Page_Load(ByVal sender As Object, _
    ByVal e As System.EventArgs) Handles Me.Load

    AddOnPreRenderCompleteAsync(AddressOf BeginProcessRequest, _
        AddressOf EndProcessRequest)

End Sub
```

Sample of C# Code
```
protected void Page_Load(object sender, EventArgs e)
{
    AddOnPreRenderCompleteAsync(
        new BeginEventHandler(BeginProcessRequest),
        new EndEventHandler(EndProcessRequest));
}
```

That is all that is required to create a webpage that acts as an asynchronous HTTP handler. There is no registration required in Web.config or with IIS; you can just run the page.

Creating a Custom HTTP Module

When you write your own HTTP module, the module's code is executed every time a page is requested from the server or a response is sent back to a requestor. This might be to implement a specific security model, to do extra logging, to rewrite a request, or to perform some similar function. In this way, HTTP modules are like the old Internet Server API (ISAPI) filters; however, all ASP.NET modules are managed (or, in other words, executed) within the CLR. ASP.NET itself uses HTTP modules for things such as session state and caching.

You create an HTTP module by writing code that implements the IHttpModule interface. This code can be created as a separate assembly and shared across multiple web applications. You can also just write a class file and place it in your App_Code directory.

ASP.NET creates an instance of the HttpApplication class when your application starts. This class finds any registered HTTP modules and creates an instance of each. You register an HTTP module by using the Web.config file (similar to registering an HTTP handler). When each module is created, its Init method is called. You override the IHttpModule.Init method to indicate the application events to which you want to subscribe. These are typically application life cycle events such as BeginRequest, AuthenticateRequest, ProcessRequest, and others. Your code is then called when these events fire for each request.

EXAM TIP

Be sure to understand the differences between HTTP Handlers and HTTP Modules when preparing to take the exam. It can be easy to get them confused with each other.

As an example, suppose you want to write an HTTP module to log all page requests to the application event log on a particular server. You would do so by creating a class that implements the IHttpModule interface. You would then override the Init method and provide code for the appropriate application events. The following code shows an example. Notice that you have full access to the ASP.NET context inside your HTTP module.

Sample of Visual Basic Code

```vb
Imports Microsoft.VisualBasic
Imports System.Diagnostics
Imports System.Web

Public Class LoggingModule
    Implements IHttpModule

    Public ReadOnly Property ModuleName() As String
        Get
            Return "LoggingModule"
        End Get
    End Property

    Public Sub Dispose() Implements _
        IHttpModule.Dispose

    End Sub

    Public Sub Init(ByVal context As System.Web.HttpApplication) _
        Implements IHttpModule.Init

        AddHandler context.BeginRequest, _
            AddressOf Me.Application_BeginRequest
        AddHandler context.EndRequest, _
            AddressOf Me.Application_EndRequest

    End Sub
```

```vb
Private Sub Application_BeginRequest(ByVal source As Object, _
    ByVal e As EventArgs)

    Dim application As HttpApplication = CType(source, HttpApplication)
    Dim context As HttpContext = application.Context

    If VirtualPathUtility.GetExtension( _
        context.Request.FilePath) = ".aspx" Then

        Dim eLog As EventLog = New EventLog()
        eLog.Source = "Application"
        eLog.WriteEntry("Begin .aspx request :: " & _
            DateTime.Now.ToLongDateString() & " :: " & _
            context.Server.MachineName, _
            EventLogEntryType.Information)
    End If


End Sub

Private Sub Application_EndRequest(ByVal source As Object, _
    ByVal e As EventArgs)
    Dim application As HttpApplication = CType(source, HttpApplication)
    Dim context As HttpContext = application.Context

    If VirtualPathUtility.GetExtension( _
        context.Request.FilePath) = ".aspx" Then

        Dim eLog As EventLog = New EventLog()
        eLog.Source = "Application"
        eLog.WriteEntry("End .aspx request :: " & _
            DateTime.Now.ToLongDateString() & " :: " & _
            context.Server.MachineName, _
            EventLogEntryType.Information)
    End If

End Sub

End Class
```

Sample of C# Code

```csharp
using System;
using System.Web;
using System.Diagnostics;

public class LoggingModule: IHttpModule
{
    public LoggingModule()
    {
    }
```

```
public String ModuleName
{
    get { return "LoggingModule"; }
}

public void Dispose() { }

public void Init(HttpApplication context)
{
    context.BeginRequest +=
        (new EventHandler(this.Application_BeginRequest));
    context.EndRequest +=
        (new EventHandler(this.Application_EndRequest));
}

private void Application_BeginRequest(Object source, EventArgs e)
{
    HttpApplication application = (HttpApplication)source;
    HttpContext context = application.Context;

    if (VirtualPathUtility.GetExtension(
        context.Request.FilePath) == ".aspx")
    {
        EventLog eLog = new EventLog();
        eLog.Source = "Application";
        eLog.WriteEntry("Begin .aspx request :: " +
            DateTime.Now.ToLongDateString() + " :: " +
            context.Server.MachineName,
            EventLogEntryType.Information);
    }
}

private void Application_EndRequest(Object source, EventArgs e)
{
    HttpApplication application = (HttpApplication)source;
    HttpContext context = application.Context;

    if (VirtualPathUtility.GetExtension(
        context.Request.FilePath) == ".aspx")
    {
        EventLog eLog = new EventLog();
        eLog.Source = "Application";
        eLog.WriteEntry("End .aspx request :: " +
            DateTime.Now.ToLongDateString() + " :: " +
            context.Server.MachineName,
            EventLogEntryType.Information);
    }
}
}
```

You then must register your HTTP module inside the Web.config file (or through the IIS management console). If you are running in IIS 6.0 (or IIS 7.0 in classic mode) you would register the module in the Web.config file, inside the <system.Web> element, as shown on the following page.

```
<httpModules>
    <add name="LoggingModule" type="LoggingModule" />
</httpModules>
```

If you are running IIS 7.0 in integrated mode, then you register the HTTP module under the <system.WebServer> element as follows:

```
<modules>
    <add name="LoggingModule" type="LoggingModule" />
</modules>
```

> **NOTE   HTTP MODULES AND GLOBAL.ASAX EVENTS**
>
> Like an HTTP module, the Global.asax file can also be used to register code to be called for application events. You do this by adding code to events such as Application_BeginRequest, Application_EndRequest, Application_LogRequest, and others. This code will run just like an HTTP module and does not need additional registration. You typically create an HTTP module if you intend to encapsulate complex code or want to share code across websites. If your needs are simpler, the Global.asax might be a better choice. For more information on working with the Global.asax file, see Chapter 3, "Handling Events and Managing State."

 Quick Check

1. When you are writing an HTTP handler, which method of the IHttpHandler interface should you implement to produce a response for a specific HTTP request?

2. You are running IIS 7.0 in integrated mode. You want to register an HTTP handler or module by using the Web.config file. To which configuration element do you add your handler or module?

3. How do you create an asynchronous HTTP handler?

4. In what method would you register your application events when creating an HTTP module by using the IHttpModule interface?

Quick Check Answers

1. You should implement the ProcessRequest method. This method will be called by ASP.NET for your registered HTTP handler.

2. You add the configuration information to the <system.WebServer> element when using IIS 7.0 in integrated mode.

3. You would implement the IHttpAsyncHandler interface, which would include the BeginProcessRequest and EndProcessRequest methods.

4. You would implement the IHttpModule.Init method and use it to register your code to application events.

In this practice, you create a custom HTTP handler to dynamically return images based on a request for files of type JPG.

> ### ON THE COMPANION MEDIA
>
> If you encounter a problem completing an exercise, you can find the completed projects in the samples installed from this book's companion CD. For more information about the project files and other content on the CD, see "Using the Companion Media" in this book's Introduction.

EXERCISE   Creating a Custom Image Handler

In this exercise, you create an ASP.NET website and a custom HTTP handler to return images based on user requests.

1. Open Visual Studio and create a new website called **JpegHandler**.

2. Right-click your website in Solution Explorer and choose Add ASP.NET Folder and then App_Code.

3. Add a new class file to the App_Code directory. Name the class **JpegHandler**.

4. Edit the automatically generated class declaration so that it implements the IHttpHandler interface, as the following shows.

Sample of Visual Basic Code

```
'Public Class JpegHandler
    Implements IHttpHandler

End Class
```

Sample of C# Code

```
public class JpegHandler : IHttpHandler
```

5. Use Visual Studio to automatically generate the required IHttpHandler members IsReusable and ProcessRequest. You can do so by pointing to the IHttpHandler interface declaration and using the smart tag.

6. Implement the IsReusable property by returning false.

Sample of Visual Basic Code

```
Public ReadOnly Property IsReusable As Boolean _
    Implements System.Web.IHttpHandler.IsReusable
    Get
        Return False
    End Get
End Property
```

```
Sample of C# Code
public bool IsReusable
{
    get { return false; }
}
```

7. Add a folder called Images to your website. From the sample images folder on your machine, add the Koala.jpg and Jellyfish.jpg images. Alternatively, you can copy them from the CD for this book.

8. Implement the ProcessRequest method. Inside this method, check the requested URL. If one of the images is requested, transmit the file as part of the response. You could use this simple example to reroute user requests for images to other locations, to a database, or to dynamically generated images. The following code shows an example.

```
Sample of Visual Basic Code
Public Sub ProcessRequest(ByVal context As System.Web.HttpContext) _
    Implements System.Web.IHttpHandler.ProcessRequest

    'set the MIME type
    context.Response.ContentType = "image/jpeg"

    Dim Request As HttpRequest = context.Request
    Dim Response As HttpResponse = context.Response

    If Request.RawUrl.ToLower.Contains("jellyfish.jpg") Then
        Response.TransmitFile(Request.PhysicalApplicationPath & _
            "/Images/Jellyfish.jpg")
    ElseIf Request.RawUrl.ToLower.Contains("koala.jpg") Then
        Response.TransmitFile(Request.PhysicalApplicationPath & _
            "/Images/Koala.jpg")
    Else
        Response.Write("File not found")
    End If

End Sub
```

```
Sample of C# Code
public void ProcessRequest(HttpContext context)
{
    //set the MIME type
    context.Response.ContentType = "image/jpeg";

    HttpRequest Request = context.Request;
    HttpResponse Response = context.Response;

    if(Request.RawUrl.ToLower().Contains("jellyfish.jpg"))
    {
        Response.TransmitFile(Request.PhysicalApplicationPath +
            "/Images/Jellyfish.jpg");
    }
```

```
        else if (Request.RawUrl.ToLower().Contains("koala.jpg"))
        {
            Response.TransmitFile(Request.PhysicalApplicationPath +
                "/Images/Koala.jpg");
        }
        else
        {
            Response.Write("File not found");
        }
    }
```

> **NOTE** **DEFINING THE MIME TYPE**
>
> This code sample sets the context.Response.ContentType property to "image/jpeg". You should use this property to define the correct Multipurpose Internet Mail Extensions (MIME) type so that the browser knows how to handle the file you send it. Otherwise, the browser might try to display it as text.

9. Open the Web.config file. Add an <httpHandler> element to the <system.Web> element. The following markup demonstrates this.

```
<httpHandlers>
    <add verb="*" path="*.jpg" type="JpegHandler"/>
</httpHandlers>
```

10. Run your application. Edit the URL in the browser to point to either Koala.jpg or Jellyfish.jpg and notice the results. Try another file name and notice that your JpegHandler indicates that the file is not found.

Lesson Summary

- By default, ASP.NET handles a limited number of file types, including ASPX, ASCX, and AXD. You can configure ASP.NET to handle any file type, which is useful if you need to dynamically generate normally static files, such as images. To configure ASP.NET to receive requests for other types, you create a custom HttpHandler class and add the type to the Web.config file in the <httpHandlers> section.

- You can use the .ashx file extension to create a basic, page-based HTTP handler.

- You can create asynchronous HTTP handlers by implementing the IHttpAsyncHandler. Typically these handlers are meant to perform multiple actions simultaneously to help improve application performance.

- Asynchronous webpages can improve performance in scenarios in which the thread pool might be limiting performance. To enable asynchronous pages, first add the Async="true" attribute to the @ Page directive. Then create events to start and end your asynchronous code.

- You can create a custom HTTP module to respond to application events for every request made to your website. You do so by implementing the IHttpModule interface and registering your events inside its Init method.

Lesson Review

You can use the following questions to test your knowledge of the information in Lesson 1, "Creating HTTP Handlers and HTTP Modules." The questions are also available on the companion CD in a practice test, if you prefer to review them in electronic form.

> **NOTE ANSWERS**
>
> Answers to these questions and explanations of why each answer choice is correct or incorrect are located in the "Answers" section at the end of the book.

1. You need to have ASP.NET dynamically generate Microsoft Word documents when a web browser requests a file ending in a .docx extension. How can you do this?

   A. Implement the IPartitionResolver interface.

   B. Implement the IHttpModule interface.

   C. Implement the IHttpHandler interface.

   D. Implement the IHttpHandlerFactory interface.

2. You are writing a custom HTTP handler to be hosted in IIS 7.0 integrated mode. You intend to register the handler by using the Web.config file. What should you do? (Choose all that apply.)

   A. Define an <add/> element inside the <httpHandlers/> element.

   B. Define an <add/> element inside the <handlers/> element.

   C. Add a <httpHandlers/> element to the <system.Web/> element.

   D. Add a <handlers/> element to the <system.WebServer/> element.

3. You want to create custom code that will be run for each request made to a website. What steps should you take? (Choose all that apply.)

   A. Create a class file that implements the IHttpHandler interface.

   B. Implement the Init method to connect your code to specific application events.

   C. Implement the ProcessRequest method to wire up your code to specific application events.

   D. Create a class file that implements the IHttpModule interface.

Lesson 2: Creating and Consuming XML Web Services

Web services have become the common programming model for implementing interoperability between systems that would otherwise have no connectivity. Before web services were conceived, connecting applications in meaningful ways was a challenge. This challenge was exacerbated by the need to cross application domains, servers, networks, data structures, security boundaries, and so on. However, with the increasing predominance of the Internet, web services have become a common model for accessing data, performing distributed transactions, and exposing business process workflow.

The Microsoft .NET Framework programmer has many options for creating and consuming web services. These include the use of jQuery and the Microsoft AJAX Library (both of which were discussed in Chapter 9, "Working with Client-Side Scripting, AJAX, and jQuery"). They also include the ASMX model and WCF; it is on these models that this lesson and the next focus. This lesson starts by covering the basics of building an XML web service on the ASMX model, including defining web service projects and the web services themselves. You will then see how to consume these services with ASP.NET.

After this lesson, you will be able to:

- Understand how ASP.NET uses Internet standards to allow you to build XML web services.
- Create XML web services.
- Consume XML web services inside an ASP.NET page.
- Call an XML web service from client-side script.

Estimated lesson time: 45 minutes

 REAL WORLD

Mike Snell

I have been lucky to observe web services move from an idea to a real solution for real business problems. Whereas developers in the past faced a very difficult integration challenge, now they can simply declare that "we will expose it as a web service." I have seen projects that expose billing data, customer data, reporting information, business workflow, course information, schedules, and much more. In addition, software vendors have added services as part of their base offering. It used to be commonplace to provide an application programming interface (API) with your application. Now applications typically include a base set of services that the application uses and that you can use to extend the application. Some great examples of applications that provide these services include Microsoft Office SharePoint Server and Visual Studio Team Foundation Server. Fortunately, web services is one technology that has really lived up to its original promise.

Creating an ASP.NET Web Service

The Internet and its supported standards for HTTP and XML make web services possible. However, having to program directly against HTTP, XML, and SOAP is a challenging (and time-consuming) proposition. Luckily, ASP.NET provides a model for building and consuming XML web services. With it, you can define a web service as an ASMX file and related code-behind class. ASP.NET will then wrap this code as a web service object and expose your service endpoint as the URL to your ASMX file. ASP.NET will take care of deserializing SOAP requests, executing your .NET Framework code, and serializing your response to be sent back to the requesting client as a SOAP message.

ASP.NET Web Service Templates

An XML web service in ASP.NET is defined in an ASMX file. This file can be added directly to an existing website. This is useful if you want your website to expose web services in addition to webpages. Of course, you can also create an empty website project and use it for only ASMX web service files.

A web service website works like any other ASP.NET website. It includes the standard ASP.NET folders, a Web.config file, and related elements. It is important to note that a web service is hosted within ASP.NET and by IIS; therefore, it has access to features such as session state, security model, configuration, and so on.

Like a webpage, web services are exposed through URLs. This means that you access a web service by using your domain name followed by a page name, as in *http://MyDomain /MyService.asmx*. The resource for an XML web service is accessed through the ASMX file. This file is nothing more than a simple text file that is used as a pointer to the code for your web service.

You add an ASMX file to your site for each web service you want to expose. You can do so by using the Add New Item dialog box and selecting the Web Service template. When you do, Visual Studio creates an ASMX file and puts a related class file inside the App_Code directory. As an example, suppose you want to write an XML web service that exposes methods related to working with the author data in Microsoft's sample database, Pubs. You might start by creating an ASMX file called Authors.asmx. This file would contain an @ WebService directive that points to the actual code for the web service. The following shows an example of the markup you would see in the ASMX file.

Sample of Visual Basic Code

```
<%@ WebService Language="VB" CodeBehind="~/App_Code/Authors.vb" Class="Authors" %>
```

Sample of C# Code

```
<%@ WebService Language="C#" CodeBehind="~/App_Code/Authors.cs" Class="Authors" %>
```

This markup is similar to what you would see for a webpage. However, there is no additional markup included inside a web service. Instead, the web service is defined entirely in code, which in this case would be the Authors.cs file. Think of the web service class file as an object that only exposes methods. Therefore, each web service can expose multiple methods. We will look at writing the actual web services next.

The Web.Services Namespace

An ASP.NET XML web service class file inherits from the System.Web.Services.WebService class. This class provides a wrapper for your web service code. In this way, you are free to write web methods in pretty much the same way you would write any other method. The WebService class and ASP.NET take care of the rest. Figure 10-3 shows the objects used by most ASP.NET XML web services.

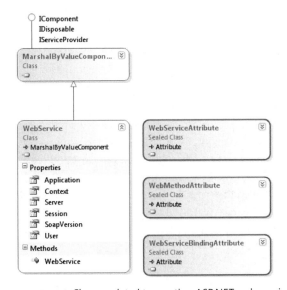

FIGURE 10-3 Classes related to creating ASP.NET web services.

Each of these classes controls how your web service works and how ASP.NET and the compiler view your web service code. You can inherit from the WebService class to get access to standard ASP.NET features. The attribute classes allow you to mark parts of your code as related to XML web services. Items marked for use as web services are identified by ASP.NET. It then knows how to deserialize requests for your service, call your service, and serialize the response. It also handles working with SOAP, XML, Web Services Description Language (WSDL), and the related web service standards. You will see how each of these classes is used for creating web services in the upcoming sections.

NOTE WEB SERVICE DESIGN CONSIDERATIONS

When you write a class that contains a web service, it is important to remember that this class's methods will be invoked across a network and into other application domains. You send XML web service method invocations as messages by using HTTP. These messages must be packaged (serialized) and unpackaged (deserialized) for transport in both directions. These types of method invocations, although powerful, can be expensive in terms of processing time. Therefore, you will want to make the most of these invocations. For this reason, you should define each of your methods to do a large amount of work and then return the results. You do not want web services that maintain state on the server and require a lot of smaller calls to access and set class data. These calls should be saved for working with in-process objects only.

The WebService Class

The WebService class represents a base class for creating XML web services in ASP.NET. This class is similar to the Page class for webpages. It provides access to ASP.NET objects such as Application and Session.

It is important to note that this class is optional: you do not need to inherit from this class to create XML web services. Instead, you use this class as a base class only when you want to access and use the features of an ASP.NET application. You might, for example, need to use session state between service calls. You could do so easily by first inheriting from this class and then accessing the session object as if you were coding an ASP.NET webpage. If, however, you simply want to expose methods over HTTP and don't need to access the features of ASP.NET, your web service need not inherit from this class (or any other class).

The following code shows the start of the Authors example web service. Here, the Authors class inherits directly from the WebService base class.

Sample of Visual Basic Code
```
Public Class Authors
  Inherits System.Web.Services.WebService
```

Sample of C# Code
```
public class Authors : System.Web.Services.WebService
```

The WebServiceAttribute Class

The WebServiceAttribute class can be used to provide information about your web service. This information is used by client applications that want to reference the web service. You use this attribute to decorate your class with this information.

The WebServiceAttribute class can be used to provide both a namespace and a description of your web service. This is done through parameters passed to the attribute class. The description parameter is simply text you write to identify the high-level intent of your web service. The namespace parameter sets the namespace of your web service. This should be a domain name under your control and where your web service is hosted. Visual Studio uses the *http://tempuri.org* namespace as a placeholder until you define your actual namespace.

As an example, suppose again that you are creating a web service centered on exposing author information from the pubs database. You would define your class inside the Authors.cs file as discussed previously. You could then add the WebService attribute to the class, as shown in the following code.

Sample of Visual Basic Code

```
< WebService(Description:="Services related to published authors", _
    Namespace:="http://mydomain.com/")> _
Public Class Authors
```

Sample of C# Code

```
[WebService(Description = "Services related to published authors",
    Namespace = "http://mydomain.com/")]
public class Authors : WebService
```

The WebMethodAttribute Class

Your web service exposes web methods. Each of these methods provides some sort of functionality encapsulated by the web service. Your class can identify these methods through the use of the WebMethod attribute. You apply this attribute to any public method in your web service class you want to expose as part of your service.

You can assign the WebMethod attribute to a class without setting any of the parameters of the WebMethod class. This simply identifies your method as a web service method. However, the WebMethod attribute class also has several constructors that can be used for various groups of parameter values. The parameters include the following:

- **enableSessionState** This parameter is used to indicate whether the method should be able to work with session state. You set this value to false to disable the use of session state for the specified web method.

- **transactionOption** This parameter is used to indicate whether your web method supports transactions. The parameter is of the type System.EnterpriseServices. TransactionOption. Web services are stateless HTTP calls. Therefore, you can only use an XML web service as the root of a transaction. This means that the TransactionOptions that indicate a root transaction are equivalent (Required, RequiresNew). All other transaction options indicate no transaction support for the service (Disabled, NotSupported, Supported).

- **cacheDuration** This parameter is used to define the number of seconds for which the response should be cached by the server. This is useful if your service has a high volume of access and the data is relatively static. In this case, you can cache results between calls to increase performance.

- **bufferResponse** This parameter is used to indicate whether the web service response should be buffered back to the client.

Consider the author example. Suppose you have a public method called GetAuthorTitles that returns a list of titles based on the ID of a specified author. Because this data only changes when an author publishes a new book, it is also a good candidate for caching. The following shows the WebMethod attribute applied to this method. Here, the cacheDuration parameter is set to five minutes (300 seconds).

Sample of Visual Basic Code

```
<WebMethod(CacheDuration:=300)> _
Public Function GetAuthorTitles(ByVal authorId As String) As DataTable
  ...
End Function
```

Sample of C# Code

```
[WebMethod(CacheDuration=300)]
public DataTable GetAuthorTitles(string authorId)
{
  ...
}
```

Web Services and Data Types

Notice that the previous example method, GetAuthorTitles, returns a DataTable object. This return type is possible because the DataTable object supports serialization; it can serialize itself into XML. As long as the calling client is also based on the .NET Framework, the client application can deserialize the XML data stream back into a strongly typed DataTable. In this case, ASP.NET does the serialization for you without you having to really think about it.

To provide for wider interoperability, however, you probably will need to provide instances of your own classes as return values of your functions or as parameters. You can do so by creating the object inside the web service application. In this case, the compiler will take care of making the objects you expose serializable. These objects simply need a default constructor that does not accept parameters. You can also use the Serializable attribute class to tag classes outside your web service. This ensures that any public members of the class can be serialized by ASP.NET.

Consuming an ASP.NET Web Service

You can consume an ASP.NET web service in any application capable of making an HTTP call. This means that any .NET Framework applications can call web services, including console applications, applications based on the Windows operating system, and ASP.NET applications themselves. This section focuses on calling an XML web service from another ASP.NET website.

Referencing a Web Service

ASP.NET provides a simple client model for consuming web services. A proxy object is generated for you when you reference a web service. You can then program against this proxy object as if you were calling in-process code. The proxy object takes care of serialization, SOAP messaging, and the related processes.

To get started, you need to have access to a published web service. This web service can be published on a server or can be another project in your solution. Either way, as long as it is a valid web service, you will be able to set a reference to it (and generate a proxy object to call it).

The first step is to create a web reference from your website to the service. You do this by right-clicking your project file and choosing Add Web Reference. This opens the Add Web Reference dialog box. In this dialog box, you define the URL of your service, select the service (ASMX file), and set a name for the reference. This name will be used by the generated proxy class to define the namespace for accessing your service. Figure 10-4 shows an example of connecting to the Authors.asmx service.

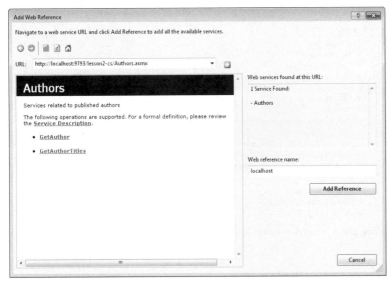

FIGURE 10-4 Using the Add Web Reference dialog box to generate a proxy for calling a web service.

After you have established the reference (by clicking the Add Reference button, as shown in Figure 10-4), Visual Studio and ASP.NET generate a Proxy class for working with the service. This allows you to write code using the service as if the service was just another class local to your application. This proxy class does all the work of communicating to and from the web service, serializing and deserializing data, and more.

As an example, the Authors.asmx file has two web methods: GetAuthor and GetAuthorTitles. The first returns an instance of the Author class as defined by the service. The second returns a DataTable. To work with the Author class (of which the web application originally knows nothing before the reference is set), Visual Studio generates this type from the WSDL of the web service and puts a version of it inside the proxy's namespace. Figure 10-5 shows an example of the contents inside the generated proxy namespace for the Author.asmx web service reference.

FIGURE 10-5 The web service client proxy generated for the Authors service.

Calling a Web Service

You call the web service through this generated proxy class. This is as simple as writing code to call a method. For example, the following code shows how you would call the GetAuthor method from the Authors.asmx web service discussed previously.

Sample of Visual Basic Code

```vb
Dim authSrv As New AuthorsSrv.Authors()
Dim auth As AuthorsSrv.Author = authSrv.GetAuthor("AuthorId")

Label1.Text = auth.FirstName
Label2.Text = auth.LastName
```

Sample of C# Code

```csharp
AuthorsSrv.Authors authSrv = new AuthorsSrv.Authors();
AuthorsSrv.Author auth = authSrv.GetAuthor("AuthorId");

Label1.Text = auth.FirstName;
Label2.Text = auth.LastName;
```

Note that in the preceding example code, only the call to GetAuthor actually invokes the web service. The object creation and property gets are simply calls to the proxy object and are thus in-process calls.

You can also bind to the web service call. Remember, the web service is exposed through a local proxy object. Therefore, you can use object data binding to bind to the web service (via the proxy). As an example, recall the GetAuthorTitles web service. This service is accessed via a proxy object method of the same name. You can set this method as the SelectMethod of an object data source, as shown in the following code. You can then bind the results to a GridView control.

```
<asp:ObjectDataSource runat="server"
  ID="ObjectDataSourceAuthors"
  TypeName="AuthorsSrv.Authors">
  SelectMethod="GetAuthorTitles"
  <SelectParameters>
    <asp:QueryStringParameter
      Name="authorId"
      QueryStringField="auId"
      Type="String" />
  </SelectParameters>
</asp:ObjectDataSource>

<asp:GridView ID="GridView1" runat="server"
  DataSourceID="ObjectDataSourceAuthors">
</asp:GridView>
```

Calling a Web Service from Client Script by Using AJAX

You can use the AJAX functionality built into ASP.NET to call a web service directly from client-side JavaScript. This is useful if you want to initiate an operation on the server from the user's browser. When the results are returned, the user's browser can then be updated. Of course, this all takes place asynchronously and without a browser refresh. Refer back to Chapter 9 if you need a quick review. Also, recall that you saw a partial example in the practice for Lesson 3 of that chapter (creating a web service and calling it from jQuery).

There are several steps required to set up your web service to enable it to support AJAX client requests. First, your client-side page and your XML web service (ASMX file) must be in the same domain. From there, you should be sure to perform all of the following steps:

- Mark your web service class with the ScriptServiceAttribute class. This indicates that the web methods inside the web service can be called from client script.

- Add a ScriptManager control to your client page. The ScriptManager control is required for all AJAX-enabled pages. However, inside it you need to set a ServiceReference. This reference should point to the XML web service (ASMX file). Doing so will tell ASP.NET to generate a JavaScript client proxy to your web service.

- Add a JavaScript method to your page. You can add code inside this method to call your web service through the client-side proxy generated by ASP.NET. Your web method can be referenced through the class name of the web service and the method name of the web method. Of course, you can also opt to pass parameters to the web service.

- Optionally, you can add another JavaScript method to your client page to serve as the callback handler. This method will be called by the JavaScript proxy and receive the results of the web service call. You can use this method to update the page the user is viewing.

As an example, suppose you want to call the Authors web service from AJAX. To begin, you would mark the web service with the ScriptService attribute. The following shows an example.

Sample of Visual Basic Code

```
<System.Web.Script.Services.ScriptService()> _
<WebService(Description:="Services related to published authors", _
    Namespace:="http://mydomain.com/")> _
Public Class Authors
  Inherits WebService
```

Sample of C# Code

```
[System.Web.Script.Services.ScriptService]
[WebService(Description = "Services related to published authors",
    Namespace = "http://mydomain.com/")]
public class Authors : WebService
```

Remember, the web service exposes two methods: GetAuthor and GetAuthorTitles. You can review the practice for this lesson to see more on these methods.

You now need to create a client webpage to call the service. Remember, this webpage must be in the same domain as the web service. Inside the webpage markup, you add a ScriptManager control. This control should be set to reference the actual web service (ASMX file). The following shows an example of this markup.

```
<asp:ScriptManager ID="ScriptManager1" runat="server">
    <Services>
        <asp:ServiceReference Path="Authors.asmx" />
    </Services>
</asp:ScriptManager>
```

The next step would be to add JavaScript functionality to call the web service, passing the user's input. In addition, you need to write a simple callback function that takes the results and displays them to the user. The following code demonstrates this. The user input is inside the TextBoxAuthId, and the results are shown by using LabelResults. Both of these controls are inside a content control of a child page that uses a master page. Therefore, they are referenced as MainContent_ControlName in the JavaScript.

```
<script type="text/javascript">
    function GetAuthor() {
        var val = document.getElementById("MainContent_TextBoxAuthId");
        Authors.GetAuthor(val.value, FinishCallback);
    }
```

```
        function FinishCallback(result) {
            var results = document.getElementById("MainContent_LabelResults");
            results.innerHTML = result.FirstName + " " + result.LastName;
        }
</script>
```

Finally, you need to add the remaining markup to the page. This simply consists of the user input information. The following shows an example of the full MainContent content area control (the ScriptManager markup is repeated for clarity).

```
<asp:Content ID="BodyContent" runat="server" ContentPlaceHolderID="MainContent">
    <asp:ScriptManager ID="ScriptManager1" runat="server">
        <Services>
            <asp:ServiceReference Path="Authors.asmx" />
        </Services>
    </asp:ScriptManager>
    <h2>
        Get Author Page
    </h2>
    <asp:TextBox ID="TextBoxAuthId" runat="server"></asp:TextBox>
    <br />
    <input id="Button1" type="button" value="Get" onclick="GetAuthor()" />
    <hr />
    <asp:Label ID="LabelResults" runat="server" Text=""></asp:Label>
</asp:Content>
```

Notice that in this markup, the GetAuthor JavaScript method defined earlier is called when the user clicks the Get button. This triggers the web service. The results are returned to the FinishCallback JavaScript method and then displayed in the Label control. Figure 10-6 shows the call in action.

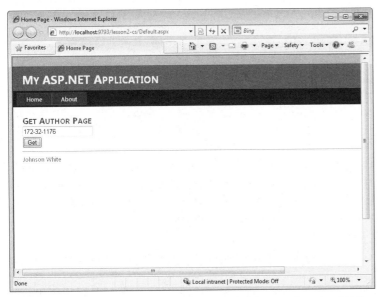

FIGURE 10-6 You can call a web service from the web browser by using AJAX.

Authentication and XML Web Services

You will often need to authenticate callers to your XML web services hosted by ASP.NET. To do so, you can use one of the standard ASP.NET security methods to authenticate and authorize users. This is similar to securing any ASP.NET resources, such as webpages, directories, or other files. Alternatively, you can use Web Services Enhancements (WSE) 3.0 to build secure XML web services.

> **NOTE** **WSE 3.0**
>
> WSE was written as an add-on product to the .NET Framework and provides developers with an easy solution for securing web services. It is based on standards and hence will usually work across platforms. If you need to create secure XML web services, WSE 3.0 is a preferred solution. For more details, go to *http://msdn.microsoft.com/en-us/library /ms977317.aspx*.

ASP.NET Security

There several ways in which you can use the authentication and authorization methods of ASP.NET to secure your XML web services. Fortunately, these techniques are not much different from those used to secure other ASP.NET resources, because the web service works much like a webpage. Both web services and webpages have a URL that points to a file. You can therefore lock down this file as you would any ASP.NET resource.

Configuring and setting up ASP.NET security is similar for both web services and ASP.NET pages and is covered in Chapter 13, "Implementing User Profiles, Authentication, and Authorization."

> **NOTE** **SEE MSDN FOR MORE DETAILS**
>
> You can also review the "How to: Configure an XML Web Service for Windows Authentication" section on MSDN for additional information. See *http://msdn.microsoft.com/en-us/library /bfazk0tb.aspx*.

Passing Credentials

To pass basic authentication credentials from your web server to a web service, you first create a NetworkCredentials class. This class contains the user name, password, and domain information. You can then create a CredentialCache object to which you add the NetworkCredentials instance. You then set the web service's generated client proxy's Credentials property to the newly created CredentialCache object.

If you are using Windows Integrated Security between the web server and the web service, you set the Credentials property of the web service proxy class to System.Net.CredentialCache. DefaultCredentials. The web server running your webpage will then pass credentials to the web service.

Quick Check

1. What type of file would you use to create an XML web service?

2. What is the name of the attribute class you would apply to your web service?

3. How can you identify a method as exposed as part of a web service?

Quick Check Answers

1. You would add a new ASMX file to a website to create an XML web service.

2. You would use the WebServiceAttribute class to mark a class as an XML web service.

3. You would use the WebMethodAttribute class to tag a method as a web method.

PRACTICE Creating and Consuming ASP.NET Web Services

In this practice, you create a web service that works with information in the Pubs database. You then create a web client interface to call that web service.

ON THE COMPANION MEDIA

If you encounter a problem completing an exercise, you can find the completed projects in the samples installed from this book's companion CD. For more information about the project files and other content on the CD, see "Using the Companion Media" in this book's Introduction.

NOTE

This practice uses standard ADO.NET programming to connect to data. You will see how you can use LINQ to SQL and the Entity Framework in later chapters. You will also see how you can replace your SQL queries with Language-Integrated Query (LINQ) queries.

EXERCISE 1 Creating an ASP.NET XML Web Service

In this exercise, you create the XML web service website and define the web service.

1. Open Visual Studio and create a new ASP.NET website by using either C# or Visual Basic. Name the project **PubsServices**.

2. Add the pubs.mdf file to the App_Data directory of the web service application. The database file is provided in the samples installed from this book's companion CD.

3. Add a new service file called **Authors.asmx** to your site by right-clicking the project and choosing Add New Item. Select the Web Service template from the Add New Item dialog box.

4. The class file for Authors.asmx should open in the code editor. If it does not, open it from the App_Code directory.

5. Delete the HelloWorld web method in the service file template. There is no need to inherit from the WebService class, because this service does not use the features of ASP.NET. Therefore, remove this inheritance from the class definition.

6. Edit the WebServiceAttribute class and set a default namespace. Your class definition should look similar to the following.

Sample of Visual Basic Code
```
<WebService(Namespace:="http://mydomain.org/")> _
<WebServiceBinding(ConformsTo:=WsiProfiles.BasicProfile1_1)> _
Public Class Authors
    Inherits System.Web.Services.WebService

End Class
```

Sample of C# Code
```
[WebService(Namespace = "http://mydomain.com/")]
[WebServiceBinding(ConformsTo = WsiProfiles.BasicProfile1_1)]
public class Authors {

    public Authors () {
    }


}
```

7. Open the Web.config file. Find the <connectionStrings /> element. Add markup to define a connection to the pubs.mdf database.

   The following shows an example.
```
<connectionStrings>
    <add name="PubsConnectionString" connectionString="Data Source=.\
    SQLEXPRESS;AttachDbFilename=|DataDirectory|\pubs.mdf;
    Integrated Security=True;User Instance=True"
    providerName="System.Data.SqlClient"/>
</connectionStrings>
```

8. Return to the Authors.cs class file. Add using (Imports in Visual Basic) statements to the class file for System.Data.SqlClient, System.Configuration, and System.Text.

9. Add a private variable at the class level to store the connection string to the Pubs database. Name this variable _cnnString, as shown in the following code.

Sample of Visual Basic Code
```
Private _cnnString As String = _
    ConfigurationManager.ConnectionStrings("PubsConnectionString").ToString
```

Sample of C# Code
```
private string _cnnString =
    ConfigurationManager.ConnectionStrings["PubsConnectionString"].ToString();
```

10. Add a method to the class to return all titles for a specified author based on the authorId. These titles can be returned as a DataTable instance. Name this method GetAuthorTitles.

11. Tag the GetAuthorTitles method with the WebMethodAttribute class. Set the CacheDuration to 300 seconds. Your method should look as follows.

Sample of Visual Basic Code

```vb
<WebMethod(CacheDuration:=300)> _
Public Function GetAuthorTitles(ByVal authorId As String) As DataTable

    Dim sql As StringBuilder = New StringBuilder()
    sql.Append("SELECT titles.title, titles.type, titles.price, ")
    sql.Append("titles.pubdate FROM titleauthor INNER JOIN titles ON ")
    sql.Append("titleauthor.title_id = titles.title_id ")
    If authorId <> "0" Then sql.Append("WHERE (titleauthor.au_id = @AuthorId) ")

    Dim cnn As New SqlConnection(_cnnString)
    Dim cmd As New SqlCommand(sql.ToString(), cnn)
    cmd.Parameters.Add("AuthorId", SqlDbType.VarChar, 11).Value = authorId

    Dim adp As New SqlDataAdapter(cmd)
    Dim ds As New DataSet()

    adp.Fill(ds)

    Return ds.Tables(0)

End Function
```

Sample of C# Code

```csharp
[WebMethod(CacheDuration = 300)]
public DataTable GetAuthorTitles(string authorId)
{
    StringBuilder sql = new StringBuilder();
    sql.Append("SELECT titles.title, titles.type, titles.price, ");
    sql.Append("titles.pubdate FROM titleauthor INNER JOIN titles ON ");
    sql.Append("titleauthor.title_id = titles.title_id ");
    if (authorId != "0")
        sql.Append("WHERE (titleauthor.au_id = @AuthorId) ");

    SqlConnection cnn = new SqlConnection(_cnnString);
    SqlCommand cmd = new SqlCommand(sql.ToString(), cnn);
    cmd.Parameters.Add("AuthorId", SqlDbType.VarChar, 11).Value = authorId;

    SqlDataAdapter adp = new SqlDataAdapter(cmd);
    DataSet ds = new DataSet();

    adp.Fill(ds);

    return ds.Tables[0];
}
```

12. Compile your application and make sure there are no errors. Right-click the Authors.asmx file and choose Set As Start Page. Run your application and use the host generated by ASP.NET to test your application. You can select an author ID from the Pubs database for testing, or you can pass the value zero (0) to return all titles. You should see the results in XML.

EXERCISE 2   Consuming an ASP.NET Web Service

In this exercise, you create a client for accessing an ASP.NET web service.

1. Continue editing the solution you created in the previous exercise. Alternatively, you can open the completed Lesson 2, Exercise 1 project in the samples installed from the CD.

2. Add a new website to the solution: Right-click the solution and choose Add | New Web Site. Select the ASP.NET Web Site template. Name the website **PubsClient**. Right-click the website and choose Set As StartUp Project.

3. Add a web reference to the web service created in Exercise 1. Start by right-clicking the PubsClient website and then choose Add Web Reference. In the Add Web Reference dialog box, select the Web Services In This Solution link. This should display the Authors service. Click the Authors service. On the right side of the dialog box, change the web reference name to **PubsService**. Finish by clicking Add Reference.

> **NOTE   VIEWING THE GENERATED PROXY CLASS**
>
> If you want to see the generated proxy class, you should change your project type from website to web application. When you do so, your code is compiled as DLL files and the generated code is exposed. For websites, Visual Studio generates code and compiles it on demand.

4. Open the Default.aspx page in the PubsClient website. Delete the content from the MainContent area.

5. From the Toolbox under the Data tab, add an ObjectDataSource control to the page. Configure it to use the web service proxy class. Set the authorId parameter to contained in the auId query string value.

6. Add a GridView control to the page and set its DataSourceId property to the object data source. Your markup inside the MainContent area should look as follows.

```
<asp:Content ID="BodyContent" runat="server" ContentPlaceHolderID="MainContent">

    <asp:ObjectDataSource runat="server"
      ID="ObjectDataSourceAuthors"
      TypeName="PubsService.Authors"
      SelectMethod="GetAuthorTitles">
      <SelectParameters>
        <asp:QueryStringParameter
          Name="authorId"
          QueryStringField="auId"
          Type="String"
          DefaultValue="0" />
      </SelectParameters>
    </asp:ObjectDataSource>

    <asp:GridView ID="GridView1" runat="server"
        DataSourceID="ObjectDataSourceAuthors">
    </asp:GridView>

</asp:Content>
```

7. Run the application to see the results. Notice that by default, zero (0) is passed to the web service so that all titles are displayed. Manipulate the query string to show only a specific author ID (you can get an ID from the database table).

Lesson Summary

- You create an XML web service in ASP.NET by defining an ASMX file. You use the WebServiceAttribute attribute class to mark a class as a web service. You use the WebMethod attribute class to define the methods in that class that should be exposed as web services. You can also inherit from WebService if you intend to use the features of ASP.NET (such as session) inside your service.

- You can consume an XML web service in an ASP.NET website by setting a web reference to it. This generates a proxy class. You can program against the proxy as if the web service were actually running on the same server. The proxy class handles the rest.

- You can call a web service from the client by using ASP.NET AJAX extensions. You first must mark the web service with the ScriptServiceAttribute. You then use the ScriptManager class to reference a web service that is in the same domain as the webpage. A JavaScript client proxy is then generated. You can use this proxy to call your web service. ASP.NET AJAX takes care of the rest.

- You secure a web service in ASP.NET as you would any other ASP.NET resource. You can also define custom web service security through custom SOAP headers.

Lesson Review

You can use the following questions to test your knowledge of the information in Lesson 2, "Creating and Consuming XML Web Services." The questions are also available on the companion CD as a practice test, if you prefer to review them in electronic form.

> **NOTE ANSWERS**
>
> Answers to these questions and explanations of why each answer choice is correct or incorrect are located in the "Answers" section at the end of the book.

1. You want to create a new web service that will expose multiple methods that are meant to work with user-specific data via a transaction. You decide to use ASP.NET session state to manage the user's context on the server between web service requests. How should you define your web service?

   A. Define a class that inherits from WebServiceAttribute.

   B. Define a class that inherits from WebService.

   C. Define a class that inherits from WebMethodAttribute.

   D. Do not inherit from a base class. Hosting the web service in ASP.NET is sufficient.

2. You want to consume an existing web service from your ASP.NET website. What actions should you take? (Choose all that apply.)

   A. Use the Add Reference dialog box to set a reference to the WSDL file that contains the web service.

   B. Use the Add Web Reference dialog box to point to the URL of the web service.

   C. Write a method in your website that has the same function signature as your web service. Do not implement this method. Instead, mark it with the WebMethod attribute.

   D. Call a proxy class that represents your web service.

3. You need to secure your web service. The service will be accessed over the Internet by multiple systems of different types. Authentication information should be secured. You want to trust only those clients who have been verified as trusted. What type of security should you consider?

   A. Windows Basic

   B. Windows Digest

   C. Client certificates

   D. Custom SOAP headers

4. You want to create a web service and call it from client-side script. What actions should you take? (Choose all that apply.)

   A. Add the ScriptService attribute to the web service class.

   B. Write client-side JavaScript to call your service through a proxy object.

   C. Add a ScriptManager class to your webpage. Set the ServiceReference to point to the ASMX web service.

   D. Make sure that your webpage and service are in the same domain.

Lesson 3: Creating and Consuming WCF Services

In the previous lesson, you learned about creating XML web services with ASP.NET. This is a very useful, straightforward way to create web services that you intend to host in IIS and call over HTTP. However, the service model can be extended beyond HTTP. For example, you might want to write a service that is accessed inside the firewall over Transmission Control Protocol (TCP) instead of HTTP. Working over TCP within your own application often results in better performance than you would attain with services implemented by using HTTP. In earlier versions of the .NET Framework, this meant that you wrote the service by using Remoting. However, if the same service code needed to be called over both HTTP and TCP, you had to write and host it twice. This is one of the many problems that WCF solves.

WCF is a unifying programming model. It defines a single approach to writing services and thereby unify technologies such as web services (ASMX), .NET Remoting, Microsoft Message Queue (MSMQ), Enterprise Services (COM+), and Web Services Enhancements (WSE). It does not replace these technologies on an individual basis. Instead, it provides a single programming model that you can use to take advantage of all of these technologies at once. With WCF, you can create a single service that can be exposed as HTTP, TCP, named pipes, and so on. You also have multiple hosting options.

This lesson covers the basics of WCF to give you a solid footing when working with this technology. This lesson is not all-encompassing on WCF. Rather, it focuses on those areas inside WCF that are specific to ASP.NET development: writing, hosting, and calling WCF services with ASP.NET websites.

> **After this lesson, you will be able to:**
> - Understand the architecture of WCF.
> - Create a WCF service in ASP.NET and host it.
> - Call a WCF service from an ASP.NET webpage.
> - Create and consume a WCF Data Service.
>
> **Estimated lesson time: 45 minutes**

Introducing WCF

Before you build your first Windows Communication Foundation (WCF) service application, it is important for you to get an overview of how the technology works. WCF enables message-based communication to and from endpoints. You write your service and then attach, or configure, the endpoints. A service can have one or more endpoints attached to it. Each WCF endpoint defines a location to which messages are sent and received. This location includes an address, a binding, and a contract. This address, binding, and contract concept is often referred to as the ABCs of WCF. The following list describes each of these in detail:

- **A is for address**   The endpoint's address is a Uniform Resource Identifier (URI) that defines the location of the service. Each endpoint of a service must have a unique address. Therefore, if you have a service that exposes more than one end-point (or transport protocol), you will uniquely identify the address based on the endpoint's transport protocol. This might mean changing a port number, defining the address as HTTPS, or taking a similar action.

- **B is for binding**   The binding defines how the service communicates, via such proto-cols as HTTP, TCP, MSMQ, Binary HTTP, and so on. The protocol used is referred to as the binding's *transport*. You can add multiple bindings to a single service. Bindings can include other information, too, such as encoding and security. Each binding must, at a minimum, define a transport.

- **C is for contract**   The contract represents the public definition, or interface, of the service. It defines things such as the namespace of the service, how messages should be sent, callbacks, and related contract items. There are multiple contract types in WCF, including service contracts, operation contracts, message contracts, fault contracts (for error handling), and data contracts. These contracts work together to indicate to the client code that is consuming the WCF service how it should define communication messages.

After you have defined your WCF service and configured at least one endpoint, you must host it. There are a few options for this, which are discussed later in this section. However, the host that this lesson focuses on is IIS and ASP.NET. To call the service, a client generates a compatible endpoint. This endpoint indicates where the service is, how communication should work, and the format of that communication. At run time, clients typically initiate requests to a hosted service. Like a web service, the WCF service processes the request and returns results—all by using the defined endpoint information.

The good news is that there are multiple tools and plentiful configuration support options for creating WCF services. Again, it is still important to understand how this works. As an additional overview, the following section presents the layers of the WCF architecture.

The Layers of the WCF Architecture

A WCF application has multiple layers that work together to provide a wide range of functionality and options for building a service-oriented application (SOA). For the most part, these layers are behind the scenes, and the configuration of services is done for you or through configuration tools that make it easy. Figure 10-7 shows an overview of the core layers of the WCF architecture.

Contract Layer
Service, operation, data, message, policy and binding

Runtime Layer
Transactions, concurrency, dispatch, parameter filtering, throttling, error, metadata, instance, message inspection

Messaging Layer
HTTP, TCP, named pipes, MSMQ, transaction flow, WS security, WS reliable messaging, encoding (text, binary, etc.)

Hosting Layer
IIS, Windows Activation Service (WAS), Windows Service, EXE, COM+ (Enterprise Services)

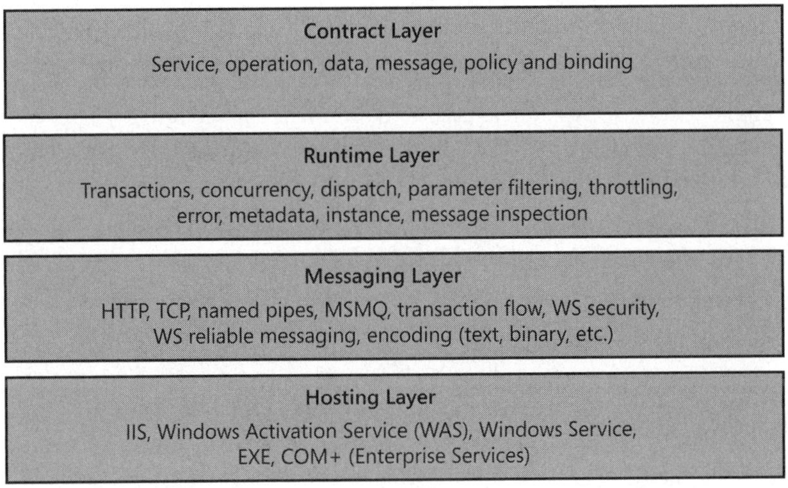

FIGURE 10-7 The layers of the WCF architecture.

It is important to understand these layers and the many options they provide to you for service development. The following list provides an overview of each layer.

- **Contract layer**   The contract layer defines the contract your service exposes to end clients. This includes the message that the service supports for calling operations, receiving results, and managing errors. In addition, the contract includes the endpoint information for policy and binding. For example, the contract might indicate that the service requires HTTP with a binary encoding.

- **Runtime layer**   The service runtime layer controls how your service is executed and how the message body is processed. You can configure this layer to support trans-actions, handle concurrency, and emit error information. For example, you can use throttling to indicate the number of messages your service can process; you can use the instance functionality to indicate how many instances of your service should be created to manage requests.

- **Messaging layer**   The messaging layer represents the WCF channel stack in terms of transport and protocol. Transport channels work to convert messages to work across HTTP, named pipes, TCP, and related protocols. Protocol channels work to process messages for aspects such as reliability and security.

- **Hosting layer**   The hosting layer defines the host, or executable file, that runs the service in process. Services can be self-hosted (that is, they can run in an executable file) or they can be hosted by IIS, Windows Activation Service (WAS), a Windows Service, or COM+. Choosing a host for your service depends on a number of factors such as client access, scalability, reliability, and the need for other services of the host (such as ASP.NET). In most enterprise application cases, you will want to use an existing host for your service rather than writing your own.

You can see that there are many options for creating, configuring, and hosting a wide array of services. Again, this chapter covers building, hosting, and calling WCF services with respect to ASP.NET (HTTP transport and IIS hosting).

Creating a WCF Service with ASP.NET

Creating and consuming WCF services follows a standard set of programming tasks. You follow these steps every time you want to create and consume a new WCF service:

1. Define the service contract.

2. Implement (or write) the service contract.

3. Configure a service endpoint or endpoints.

4. Host the service in an application.

5. Reference and call the service from a client application.

As you can see, a WCF service application starts with the contract. This contract indicates the features and functionality your service will offer to calling clients. In WCF programming, you create this contract by first defining an interface and decorating that interface with attributes. Figure 10-8 shows an overview of the key WCF attribute classes used most commonly.

FIGURE 10-8 The basic attribute classes used by WCF services.

The ServiceContract and OperationContract WCF attribute classes are found in the System.ServiceModel namespace, and the DataContract and DataMember classes are found in the System.Runtime.Serialization namespace. These classes are used to define the details of the contract that your service will have with calling clients. For example, you can indicate whether your service contract is a one-way, request-reply, or duplex contract. These attributes also define your service operations and the data that defines these operations. The following list provides a description for each of these classes.

- **ServiceContract** The ServiceContract attribute class is used to indicate that an interface (or class) is a WCF service. The ServiceContract attribute class has parameters for setting things such as whether the service requires a session (SessionMode), the namespace, the name of the contract, the return contract on a two-way contract (CallbackContract), and more.

- **OperationContract** The OperationContract attribute class is used to mark methods inside an interface (or class) as service operations. Methods marked with OperationContract represent those exposed by the service to clients. You can use the parameters of the OperationContract attribute class to define settings such as whether the contract does not return a reply (IsOneWay), the message-level security (ProtectionLevel), or whether the method supports asynchronous calls (AsyncPattern).

- **DataContract** The DataContract attribute class is used to mark types (classes, enumerations, or structures) that you write as participating in WCF serialization via the DataContractSerializer. Marking your classes with this attribute ensures that they can be sent efficiently to and from disparate clients.

- **DataMember** The DataMember attribute class is used to mark individual fields and properties that you want to serialize. You use this class in conjunction with the DataContract class.

The WCF Service Templates

Visual Studio and ASP.NET define the WCF Service Application project template. This template defines a web project that hosts the WCF service. This project template contains a reference to System.ServiceModel, which contains the WCF classes. Creating a new instance of this project template will also generate a default service (Service1.svc) and a related contract interface file (IService1.vb or IService1.cs).

The contract file is simply a code file that defines an interface to be used to define the interface for your service. You decorate the members of this interface with the service attribute classes. These include the service (ServiceContract), the operations (OperationContract), and the data members (DataContract for the class and DataMember for any class members).

The SVC file is a webpage that provides a URL for the service and its related code-behind file. The webpage uses the @ ServiceHost directive to indicate that the page is a service. The code-behind file implements the interface defined by the aforementioned contract.

Finally, a WCF service application is automatically configured to be hosted in IIS and expose a standard HTTP endpoint. This information can be found inside the <system.servicemodel> section of the Web.config file.

As you can see, the WCF service application in ASP.NET takes care of many of the common steps for creating a WCF service. In fact, steps 1, 3, and 4, as discussed previously, are taken care of by default. That leaves step 2, implementing the service, and step 5, calling the service from a client application.

Note that you can also add a WCF service to an existing ASP.NET website. You can do so from the Add New Item dialog box. This will create the SVC file and add both a related interface file and a class file to the App_Code directory. It will also update the Web.config file to expose the web service from your website.

Implementing the WCF Service

To implement the service, you start by defining the contract via the interface. For example, suppose you want to create a service that exposes methods that work with the Shippers table in the Northwind database. You might start by creating a Shipper class and marking it as a DataContract, marking its members as DataMembers. This allows you to pass the Shipper class in and out of the service. The following code shows an example.

Sample of Visual Basic Code

```
<DataContract()> _
Public Class Shipper

  Private _shipperId As Integer

  <DataMember()> _
  Public Property ShipperId() As Integer
    'implement property (see practice)
  End Property

  'implement remaining properties (see practice)

End Class
```

Sample of C# Code

```
[DataContract]
public class Shipper
{
  [DataMember]
  public int ShipperId { get; set; }

  //implement remaining properties (see practice)
}
```

The next step is to define the methods of your interface. You mark those with the OperationContract attribute and mark the interface with the ServiceContract attribute. For example, suppose that the shipping service exposes operations for retrieving a single shipper and saving a single shipper. In this case, your interface should look as follows.

Sample of Visual Basic Code
```
<ServiceContract()> _
Public Interface IShipperService

  <OperationContract()> _
  Function GetShipper(ByVal shipperId As Integer) As Shipper

  <OperationContract()> _
  Sub SaveShipper(ByVal shipper As Shipper)

End Interface
```

Sample of C# Code
```
[ServiceContract]
public interface IShipperService
{
  [OperationContract]
  Shipper GetShipper(int shipperId);

  [OperationContract]
  Shipper SaveShipper(Shipper shipper);
}
```

This interface will be used by WCF to expose a service. Of course, the service will be configured based on the information inside the Web.config file. You still need to implement the service interface, which you do inside the code-behind file for the SVC file. For example, if you were to implement the interface contract defined previously for working with the Shipper data, you would do so as shown in the following code.

Sample of Visual Basic Code
```
Public Class ShipperService
  Implements IShipperService

  Public Function GetShipper(ByVal shipperId As Integer) As Shipper _
    Implements IShipperService.GetShipper

    'code to get the shipper from the database and return it (see practice)

  End Function

  Public Function SaveShipper(ByVal shipper As Shipper) As Shipper _
    Implements IShipperService.SaveShipper

    'code to save the shipper to the database (see practice)

  End Sub

End Class
```

Sample of C# Code
```csharp
public class ShipperService : IShipperService
{
  public Shipper GetShipper(int shipperId)
  {
    //code to get the shipper from the database and return it (see practice)
  }

  public Shipper SaveShipper(Shipper shipper)
  {
    //code to save the shipper to the database (see practice)
  }
}
```

Consuming a WCF Service in an ASP.NET Page

After exporting your service methods, you can add a reference from a client to the service. In this case, we assume that the client is another ASP.NET website. However, it could easily be a Windows application or another application on a different platform.

Recall that the WCF service created previously has a contract defined via the IShipperService interface. The contract is implemented inside the ShipperService.svc file. An endpoint is configured via the default HTTP endpoint set up inside the Web.config file. The service is hosted by IIS and ASP.NET (or your local web server).

To create the client, you need to generate a proxy class for calling the WCF service. This can be done by using Visual Studio. You right-click your client website and select Add Service Reference. This opens the Add Service Reference dialog box, as shown in Figure 10-9.

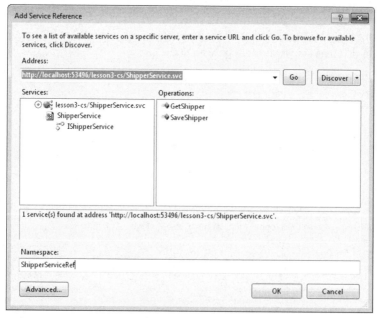

FIGURE 10-9 The Add Service Reference dialog box for generating a WCF service client proxy.

This dialog box allows you to define an address for your service. Again, this is based on the endpoint that your service exposes. In this example, a connection is being made to the ShipperService.svc file created in the previous section. Notice that the contract is shown via the service's interface.

Also, notice in Figure 10-9 that a namespace was provided. The namespace defines the name for the proxy class that is generated by Visual Studio. This proxy class is a WCF service client that allows you to program against the service without having to deal with the intricacies of WCF. This is similar to how you worked with XML web services in the previous lesson.

You can view the contents of the service reference by selecting its source file in Solution Explorer. Figure 10-10 shows the many files of this service reference.

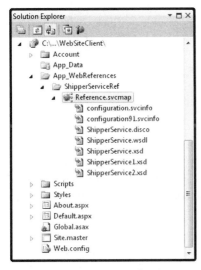

FIGURE 10-10 The service reference expanded inside of Solution Explorer.

The Reference.cs (or Reference.vb) file contains the actual proxy class (which is not shown for a website, only for web application projects). The other files are used by this proxy class when working with the service. This proxy class communicates with the web service. In fact, it contains classes and methods that look just like those of the service, because of the service contract. Figure 10-11 shows an overview of the types found inside Reference.cs (or Reference.vb). Notice that you can call the ShipperServiceClient code and even pass a local type called Shipper that contains the same properties defined by the service contract.

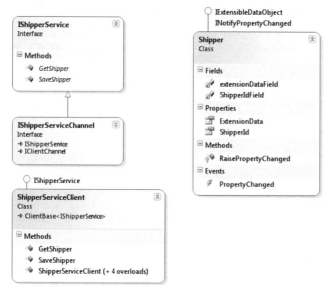

FIGURE 10-11 The generated service client proxy types.

Your client code must also define binding and endpoint information. The Add Service Reference task generates the appropriate endpoint information automatically when you add the service reference. This information can be found inside the Web.config file of the service client website. It is nested under the <system.serviceModel> element. The following shows an example.

```
<system.webServer>
    <modules runAllManagedModulesForAllRequests="true"/>
</system.webServer>
<system.serviceModel>
<bindings>
    <basicHttpBinding>
    <binding name="BasicHttpBinding_IShipperService" closeTimeout="00:01:00"
        openTimeout="00:01:00" receiveTimeout="00:10:00" sendTimeout="00:01:00"
        allowCookies="false" bypassProxyOnLocal="false"
        hostNameComparisonMode="StrongWildcard"
        maxBufferSize="65536" maxBufferPoolSize="524288" maxReceivedMessageSize="65536"
        messageEncoding="Text" textEncoding="utf-8" transferMode="Buffered"
        useDefaultWebProxy="true">
        <readerQuotas maxDepth="32" maxStringContentLength="8192" maxArrayLength="16384"

        maxBytesPerRead="4096" maxNameTableCharCount="16384" />
        <security mode="None">
        <transport clientCredentialType="None" proxyCredentialType="None"
            realm="" />
        <message clientCredentialType="UserName" algorithmSuite="Default" />
        </security>
    </binding>
    </basicHttpBinding>
</bindings>
```

```
<client>
    <endpoint address="http://localhost:53496/lesson3-cs/ShipperService.svc"
    binding="basicHttpBinding" bindingConfiguration="BasicHttpBinding_IShipperService"
    contract="ShipperServiceRef.IShipperService"
    name="BasicHttpBinding_IShipperService" />
</client>
</system.serviceModel>
```

All that remains is to write a webpage that works with the proxy class to call the service. You will look at an example of doing just that in the practice for this lesson.

Calling a WCF Service from Client Script by Using AJAX (REST and JSON)

WCF allows you to create and work with many different types of services. Remember, it is a technology used to define service endpoints that have an address, binding, and contract. This level of flexibility built into the framework allows it to support various message types and communication protocols.

One such service type is based on representational state transfer (REST) and JavaScript Object Notation (JSON). Services based on these concepts have become very popular as AJAX programming has become more prevalent. Programming with AJAX becomes easier with a simple service (REST) based on a simple message format (JSON). WCF and the .NET Framework have built-in support for both.

A REST service is a web service you create that responds to basic HTTP requests such as GET, POST, PUT, and DELETE. Clients can therefore call a REST service the same way they would call a web page. This includes a simple GET using a URL and a query string and a POST request. The server then responds with text, as it would for any HTTP request. This way, a REST service does not require knowledge of the XML schema used to call the service. Instead, it simply sends the request and processes the text-based response (usually JSON formatted data).

> *NOTE* **SECURING A REST-BASED SERVICE**
>
> REST-based services do not use SOAP. Many service-based security models are based on SOAP. Therefore, if the security of the data being passed is a concern, you should use HTTPS between the client and server for all RESTful services.

The response of a REST service is typically in the form of JSON data. JSON is a message data format that evolved from the heavy use of AJAX. The message format is not based on XML. Instead, it is simple, lightweight, and text based. A JSON message can be processed easily by the JavaScript engine that exists inside nearly all web browsers. This makes it ideal when you are calling services from JavaScript. In fact, a JSON message can be parsed by using the JavaScript eval function, because basically it is syntactically formatted JavaScript.

The following is an example of a JSON-formatted message.

```
{
  "productName": "Computer Monitor",
  "price": "229.00",
  "specifications": {
    "size": 22,
    "type": "LCD",
    "colors": ["black", "red", "white"]
  }
}
```

Writing a WCF Service Based on REST and JSON

Creating a WCF service based on REST and JSON is somewhat simplified in ASP.NET. This is due in part to the AJAX support built into ASP.NET. Because of this, there is a WCF template that you can use to quickly create a service that takes advantage of the REST calling mechanism and the JSON data format.

This AJAX-WCF item template is called the AJAX-Enabled WCF Service template. It can be found in the Add New Item dialog box for a website project. The template defines a class that can be used to create a WCF service for use with AJAX.

As an example, suppose you were creating a service to calculate a product's full price based on the item ID and the postal code to which you are shipping the item. The following code shows an example of an AJAX-enabled WCF service that simulates such a method.

Sample of Visual Basic Code

```vb
<ServiceContract(Namespace:="PricingServices")> _
<AspNetCompatibilityRequirements( _
    RequirementsMode:=AspNetCompatibilityRequirementsMode.Allowed)> _
Public Class PricingService

    <OperationContract()> _
    <WebInvoke()> _
    Public Function CalculatePrice(ByVal itemId As String, _
        ByVal shipToPostalCode As String) As Double

        Dim price As Double

        'simulate product price lookup based on item ID
        price = 45

        'simulate calculation of sales tax based on shipping postal code
        price = price * 1.06

        'simulate calculation of shipping based on shipping postal code
        price = price * 1.1

        Return price

    End Function

End Class
```

Sample of C# Code

```csharp
namespace PricingServices
{
    [ServiceContract(Namespace = "PricingServices")]
    [AspNetCompatibilityRequirements(RequirementsMode =
        AspNetCompatibilityRequirementsMode.Allowed)]
    public class PricingService
    {
        [OperationContract]
        [WebInvoke]
        public double CalculatePrice(string itemId, string shipToPostalCode)
        {
            double price;

            //simulate product price lookup based on item ID
            price = 45;

            //simulate calculation of sales tax based on shipping postal code
            price = price * 1.06;

            //simulate calculation of shipping based on shipping postal code
            price = price * 1.1;

            return price;
        }
    }
}
```

Notice that the service method is marked with the WebInvoke attribute. This indicates that the method can be called by an HTTP request. Methods marked with WebInvoke are called by using HTTP POST. This can be important if you are sending data to the server to be written or if you do not want your request to be cached by a browser or the server. If, however, your service typically returns data that is somewhat static, you might mark the method with the WebGet attribute. This indicates an HTTP GET request is supported and the results can be cached. This is the only reason to use the WebGet attribute. The ASP.NET AJAX ScriptManager control can work with both HTTP GET and POST services.

Visual Studio also updates the site's Web.config file when the AJAX-enabled WCF service is added to the project. The following shows an example. Notice the <enableWebScript> element. This indicates that the endpoint is a RESTful service that uses the JSON data format and can therefore be consumed by AJAX. Also notice that the binding is set to webHttpBinding, indicating again that this service is called via HTTP (and not SOAP).

```xml
<system.serviceModel>
    <services>
        <service name="PricingService">
            <endpoint address=""
                behaviorConfiguration="PricingServiceAspNetAjaxBehavior"
                binding="webHttpBinding" contract="PricingService" />
        </service>
    </services>
```

```
        <behaviors>
            <endpointBehaviors>
                <behavior name="PricingServiceAspNetAjaxBehavior">
                    <enableWebScript />
                </behavior>
            </endpointBehaviors>
            <serviceBehaviors>
                <behavior name="">
                    <serviceMetadata httpGetEnabled="true" />
                    <serviceDebug includeExceptionDetailInFaults="false" />
                </behavior>
            </serviceBehaviors>
        </behaviors>
        <serviceHostingEnvironment aspNetCompatibilityEnabled="true"
            multipleSiteBindingsEnabled="true" />
</system.serviceModel>
```

As you can see, ASP.NET simplifies the creation of WCF services based on REST and JSON. You can also use the features of WCF and the .NET Framework to define REST services and JSON-based messages outside of ASP.NET. In fact, the .NET Framework supports serialization between .NET Framework types and JSON data structures.

Calling a JSON-Based WCF Service from AJAX

The AJAX support in ASP.NET also makes calling a REST-based service from AJAX a relatively straightforward process. The ScriptManager control allows you to set a service reference to the specified RESTful WCF service. It then defines a JavaScript proxy class for you to call. This proxy class manages the call from the AJAX-enabled page to the WCF service.

For example, to call the service defined previously, you start by adding a ScriptManager control to your page. You then define a ServiceReference to the actual service. The following markup shows an example.

```
<asp:ScriptManager ID="ScriptManager1" runat="server">
    <Services>
        <asp:ServiceReference Path="PricingService.svc" />
    </Services>
</asp:ScriptManager>
```

You can then define a script block on your page to call the proxy class that is generated based on this service reference. In the example, the service takes a product ID and a postal code. The following JavaScript assumes that these values are entered by a user in a couple of text box controls. The code also responds when the user clicks a button on the page.

```
<script language="javascript" type="text/javascript">
    function ButtonCalculate_onclick() {
        var service = new PricingServices.PricingService();
        service.CalculatePrice(document.forms[0].MainContent_TextBoxProduct.value,
            document.forms[0].MainContent_TextBoxPostCode.value,
                onSuccess, onFail, null);
    }
```

```
        function onSuccess(result){
            LabelPrice.innerText = result;
        }

        function onFail(result){
            alert(result);
        }
</script>
```

Notice that the call to the CalculatePrice method goes through a proxy that defines some additional parameters. This allows you to pass in a JavaScript method name to be called by the ScriptManager after the service is called. You can define a method both for success and for failure. In this case, a successful call writes the results to a Label control.

The following code shows the markup for the page's controls, to complete the example.

```
<div>
    Product:<br />
    <asp:TextBox ID="TextBoxProduct" runat="server"></asp:TextBox>
    <br />
    Ship to (postal code):<br />
    <asp:TextBox ID="TextBoxPostCode" runat="server"></asp:TextBox>
    <br />

    <input name="ButtonCalculate" type="button" value="Get Price"
        onclick="ButtonCalculate_onclick()" />

    <br />
    <asp:Label ID="LabelPrice" runat="server"></asp:Label>
</div>
```

> **NOTE   COMPLEX TYPES AND AJAX**
>
> There are times when you will want to pass complex types between the server and a JavaScript function. Fortunately, the ScriptManager control already supports this. It converts your complex type into a JSON message structure. After the call completes, you can access the individual values of the complex type by using the *result.member* syntax, where *result* is the name of your complex type and *member* is a property name of the complex type.

Creating WCF Data Services

WCF Data Services allow you to expose and work with data by using the Open Data Protocol (OData). Data is exposed over REST-based services to allow for standard HTTP GET and POST requests. The data can be accessed based on a URL and standard query string formats for accessing tables and filtering data. These formats allow access from any client that can receive XML or JSON message notations.

There is a standard set of steps to follow when creating OData services with ASP.NET. These steps include the following:

1. Define a data model that uses an Entity Data Model (EDM) by using the ADO.NET Entity Data Model template. For more information on EDM, see Chapter 12, "Working with Data Source Controls and Data-Bound Controls."

2. Create a data service by using the WCF Data Service template.

3. Add code to the data service to enable access to the EDM.

4. Create a client application to access the exposed data service.

5. Add a service reference to the client application to call the data service. This will generate a WCF proxy for calling the service.

6. Write code to work with the exposed data. You can query the data by using LINQ (see Chapter 11, "Connecting to and Querying Data with LINQ"), bind the data to controls (see Chapter 12), and use the proxy class to save any changes.

Let's look at an example. Suppose you want to expose portions of the Northwind sample database using WCF Data Services. You would start by creating an ADO.NET Entity Data Model based on the Northwind database. Assume that this model is called NwdModel.edmx.

Next, you would create the WCF Data Services-based service by using Visual Studio's Add New Item dialog box. You could call this file NwdDataService.svc. Like other WCF services in ASP.NET, this service includes an SVC file that is used as a URI for the services. The file contains the @ ServiceHost directive, which points to the actual service class and indicates that this service is a data service. The following shows sample markup.

```
<%@ ServiceHost Language="C#" Factory="System.Data.Services.DataServiceHostFactory"
    Service="NwdDataService" %>
```

The actual service class is inside the App_Code directory for the website. This class inherits from System.Data.Services.DataService. This is a generic class. Here you indicate the Entity Data Model you intend your service to expose—in this case, northwndModel.NwdEntities. The following code shows an example.

Sample of Visual Basic Code

```
Public Class NwdDataService
    Inherits DataService(Of northwndModel.northwndEntities)
```

Sample of C# Code

```
public class NwdDataService : DataService<northwndModel.NwdEntities>
{
```

You then add rules to the data service inside the InitializeService method to indicate which entities in your model are visible and can be updated. The following code indicates that the customer table is exposed as a data service. This also provides for the ability to write and to read the entire table. This code is called once to initialize the service.

Sample of Visual Basic Code

```
Public Shared Sub InitializeService(ByVal config As DataServiceConfiguration)

    config.DataServiceBehavior.MaxProtocolVersion = DataServiceProtocolVersion.V2

    config.SetEntitySetAccessRule("Customers", EntitySetRights.AllRead _
        Or EntitySetRights.AllWrite)
End Sub
```

Sample of C# Code

```
public static void InitializeService(DataServiceConfiguration config)
{
    config.DataServiceBehavior.MaxProtocolVersion = DataServiceProtocolVersion.V2;

    config.SetEntitySetAccessRule("Customers", EntitySetRights.AllRead
        | EntitySetRights.AllWrite );
}
```

The service itself is now complete. In fact, it can be accessed by using the OData querystring syntax. For example, the following request returns a single customer based on ID.

```
http://localhost:53908/WcfDataSrv-cs/NwdDataService.svc/Customers('ALFKI')
```

> **NOTE ODATA URI CONVENTIONS**
>
> The OData specification provides several ways in which you can access and filter data by using the query string. For more details, review the specification at *http://www.odata.org /developers/protocols/uri-conventions*.

The results of this REST call are shown in Figure 10-12. Note that you must turn off the feed reader view in Windows Internet Explorer to see the actual XML (Tools | Internet Options | Content | Feeds And Web Slices Settings).

FIGURE 10-12 Calling a WCF data service by using basic REST protocol and OData syntax.

The final step is to write a client application and add a service reference to the WCF Data Service. This will generate a WCF Data Services client proxy that will allow you to work with the data directly. Your client application could be a Windows application, a console application, Microsoft Silverlight, ASP.NET, or any other client capable of calling a service. In this example, we will create an ASP.NET website client.

After the client has been created, you right-click the project and choose Add Service Reference as you would for any WCF service. You give the service a namespace to be used for the proxy, which in this case will be NwdEntitiesSrv. You can then use this reference, along with the WCF Data Services client libraries, to work with the WCF Data Services. As an example, the following code instantiates a reference to the service, gets all customers back from the service, and binds the results to a GridView control.

Sample of Visual Basic Code

```vb
Dim svcUri As Uri = New Uri("http://localhost:53908/WcfDataSrv/NwdDataService.svc")

Dim nwd As NwdEntitiesSrv.northwndEntities =
    New NwdEntitiesSrv.northwndEntities(svcUri)

Dim q As DataServiceQuery(Of NwdEntitiesSrv.Customer) = nwd.Customers

Me.GridViewCustomers.DataSource = q
Me.GridViewCustomers.DataBind()
```

Sample of C# Code

```csharp
Uri svcUri = new Uri("http://localhost:53908/WcfDataSrv/NwdDataService.svc");
NwdEntitiesSrv.NwdEntities nwd =
    new NwdEntitiesSrv.NwdEntities(svcUri);

DataServiceQuery<NwdEntitiesSrv.Customer> q = nwd.Customers;

this.GridViewCustomers.DataSource = q;
this.GridViewCustomers.DataBind();
```

This is simply an overview of the WCF Data Services client library (System.Data.Services.Client). This library can do many things. For more information, see "Using a Data Service in a Client Application" (*http://msdn.microsoft.com/en-us/library/dd728282.aspx*).

 Quick Check

1. How do you mark a class or interface as a WCF service?

2. How do you mark methods in an interface or class so that they are exposed as part of the class's service contract?

3. Which attribute do you add to a WCF service to indicate that it can be called by an HTTP request that uses REST?

4. From what class should your WCF Data Services derive?

Quick Check Answers

1. You use the ServiceContractAttribute class to tag an interface or class as a WCF service.

2. You use the OperationContractAttribute class to tag a method as a service method.

3. You mark the service with either the WebInvokeAttribute or WebGetAttribute class.

4. You should derive from the DataService class found in the System.Data.Services namespace.

PRACTICE   Creating and Consuming a WCF Service

In this practice, you create a WCF service that works with information in the Northwind database. You then create a webpage to call that WCF service.

ON THE COMPANION MEDIA

If you encounter a problem completing an exercise, you can find the completed projects in the samples installed from this book's companion CD. For more information about the project files and other content on the CD, see "Using the Companion Media" in this book's Introduction.

EXERCISE 1   Creating a WCF Service Application

In this exercise, you create the WCF Service application project and define the WCF service.

1. Open Visual Studio and create a new website by using either C# or Visual Basic. Name the site **NorthwindServices**.

2. Copy the Northwind database (Northwnd.mdf) into the App_Data directory of your project. You can find the file in the samples installed from the CD.

3. Add a new WCF service to the application: right-click the project and choose Add | New Item. Select the WCF Service template. Name the service **ShipperService.svc**.

    Notice that three files are created: an interface file named IShipperService, a class file named ShipperService, and a ShipperService.svc file. The former two files should be in the App_Code directory; the latter should be in the root of the site.

4. Open the Web.config file. Navigate to the <connectionStrings> node. Add a connection string for the Northwind database. This connection string should read as follows (formatted here to fit on the printed page).

```
<connectionStrings>
  <add name="NwConnectionString" connectionString="Data Source=.\SQLEXPRESS;
    AttachDbFilename=|DataDirectory|\northwnd.mdf;Integrated Security=True;
    User Instance=True" providerName="System.Data.SqlClient"/>
</connectionStrings>
```

5. Open IShipperService.vb (or IShipperService.cs). Define a data contract class at the bottom of the file to represent a Shipper object. Remember to use the DataContract and DataMember attributes. Your code should read as follows.

```
Sample of Visual Basic Code
<DataContract()> _
Public Class Shipper

    <DataMember()> _
    Public Property ShipperId() As Integer

    <DataMember()> _
    Public Property CompanyName As String

    <DataMember()> _
    Public Property Phone As String

End Class
```

```
Sample of C# Code
[DataContract]
public class Shipper
{
    [DataMember]
    public int ShipperId { get; set; }

    [DataMember]
    public string CompanyName { get; set; }

    [DataMember]
    public string Phone { get; set; }
}
```

6. Add a using (Imports in Visual Basic) statement for System.Runtime.Serialization (it may already be present in your C# file).

7. Next, define the interface for the Shipper class. Create one method for returning a Shipper instance and another for accepting a Shipper instance for updating. Remember to use the ServiceContract and OperationContract attributes. Your code should look as follows.

```
Sample of Visual Basic Code
<ServiceContract()> _
Public Interface IShipperService

    <OperationContract()> _
    Function GetShipper(ByVal shipperId As Integer) As Shipper

    <OperationContract()> _
    Sub SaveShipper(ByVal shipper As Shipper)

End Interface
```

```
Sample of C# Code
[ServiceContract]
public interface IShipperService
{
    [OperationContract]
    Shipper GetShipper(int shipperId);

    [OperationContract]
    void SaveShipper(Shipper shipper);
}
```

8. Open the ShipperService.cs (or ShipperService.vb) code. Add using (Imports in Visual Basic) statements for System.Data, System.Data.SqlClient, and System.Configuration.

9. Add code to the top of the interface implementation source file to get the connection string from the database.

10. Implement the GetShipper method by calling the database to retrieve a record from the Shipper table. Copy this data into a Shipper instance and return it as a result of the function.

11. Implement the SaveShipper method by updating a shipping record with data inside a Shipper instance. Your code for the service implementation should read as follows.

Sample of Visual Basic Code

```vb
Public Class ShipperService
  Implements IShipperService

  Private _cnnString As String = _
     ConfigurationManager.ConnectionStrings("NwConnectionString").ToString

  Public Function GetShipper(ByVal shipperId As Integer) As Shipper _
    Implements IShipperService.GetShipper

    Dim sql As New StringBuilder()
    sql.Append("SELECT shipperId, companyName, phone ")
    sql.Append("FROM shippers WHERE (shipperId = @ShipperId) ")

    Dim cnn As New SqlConnection(_cnnString)
    Dim cmd As New SqlCommand(sql.ToString(), cnn)
    cmd.Parameters.Add("ShipperId", SqlDbType.Int, 0).Value = shipperId

    Dim adp As New SqlDataAdapter(cmd)
    Dim ds As New DataSet()

    adp.Fill(ds)

    Dim s As New Shipper()
    s.ShipperId = shipperId
    s.CompanyName = ds.Tables(0).Rows(0)("companyName").ToString()
    s.Phone = ds.Tables(0).Rows(0)("phone").ToString()

    Return s

  End Function

  Public Sub SaveShipper(ByVal shipper As Shipper) _
    Implements IShipperService.SaveShipper

    Dim sql As New StringBuilder()
    sql.Append("UPDATE Shippers SET phone=@Phone, ")
    sql.Append("companyName=@CompanyName WHERE shipperId = @ShipperId ")

    Dim cnn As New SqlConnection(_cnnString)
    Dim cmd As New SqlCommand(sql.ToString(), cnn)
    cmd.Parameters.Add("Phone", SqlDbType.NVarChar, 24).Value = shipper.Phone
    cmd.Parameters.Add("CompanyName", SqlDbType.NVarChar, 40).Value = _
      shipper.CompanyName
    cmd.Parameters.Add("ShipperId", SqlDbType.Int, 0).Value = shipper.ShipperId
    cnn.Open()
    cmd.ExecuteNonQuery()
    cnn.Close()

  End Sub

End Class
```

Sample of C# Code

```csharp
public class ShipperService : IShipperService
{
    private string _cnnString =
        ConfigurationManager.ConnectionStrings["NwConnectionString"].ToString();

    public Shipper GetShipper(int shipperId)
    {
        StringBuilder sql = new StringBuilder();
        sql.Append("SELECT shipperId, companyName, phone ");
        sql.Append("FROM shippers WHERE (shipperId = @ShipperId) ");
        SqlConnection cnn = new SqlConnection(_cnnString);

        SqlCommand cmd = new SqlCommand(sql.ToString(), cnn);
        cmd.Parameters.Add("ShipperId", SqlDbType.Int, 0).Value = shipperId;

        SqlDataAdapter adp = new SqlDataAdapter(cmd);
        DataSet ds = new DataSet();

        adp.Fill(ds);

        Shipper s = new Shipper();
        s.ShipperId = shipperId;
        s.CompanyName = ds.Tables[0].Rows[0]["companyName"].ToString();
        s.Phone = ds.Tables[0].Rows[0]["phone"].ToString();

        return s;
    }

    public void SaveShipper(Shipper shipper)
    {
        StringBuilder sql = new StringBuilder();
        sql.Append("UPDATE Shippers set phone=@Phone, ");
        sql.Append("companyName=@CompanyName WHERE shipperId = @ShipperId ");

        SqlConnection cnn = new SqlConnection(_cnnString);
        SqlCommand cmd = new SqlCommand(sql.ToString(), cnn);
        cmd.Parameters.Add("Phone", SqlDbType.NVarChar, 24).Value =
            shipper.Phone;
        cmd.Parameters.Add("CompanyName", SqlDbType.NVarChar, 40).Value =
            shipper.CompanyName;
        cmd.Parameters.Add("ShipperId", SqlDbType.Int, 0).Value =
            shipper.ShipperId;

        cnn.Open();
        cmd.ExecuteNonQuery();
        cnn.Close();
    }
}
```

12. Right-click your ShipperService.svc file and choose Set As Start Page. Compile and run your service application. Doing so should launch the service in a web browser. Here you will see details on how your WCF service should be called.

13. Click the link at the top of the webpage to see the WSDL for your WCF service. Click the back button to return to the page. Copy the line that starts with svcutil.exe.

14. Generate a test client for your WCF service by using Svcutil.exe. Start by opening a Visual Studio command prompt (Start | All Programs | Microsoft Visual Studio 2010 | Visual Studio Tools). Use commands to navigate to a directory to which you want to generate the test client. Paste the command copied from the top of the webpage into the command window, and press Enter. Exit the command prompt.

15. Navigate to the files you generated. Open these files and examine them. There should be a configuration file that defines an endpoint for communicating with the service. There should also be a code file that shows how to call the WCF service. This is the proxy class you can use to write an actual client. These are also the same files that get generated when you set a service reference to a WCF service.

EXERCISE 2   Consuming a WCF Service

In this exercise, you create a web client for accessing the WCF service created in the previous exercise.

1. Continue editing the solution you created in the previous exercise. Alternatively, you can open the completed Lesson 3, Exercise 1 solution in the samples installed from the CD.

2. Add a new website to the solution: right-click the solution and choose Add | New Web Site. Select ASP.NET Web Site. Name the website **ShipperClient**. Right-click the website and choose Set As StartUp Project.

3. Right-click the newly added website and choose Add Service Reference. Click Discover in the Add Service Reference dialog box. Select the ShipperService. Set the namespace to **NwServices**. Click OK to close the dialog box.

4. Open the Default.aspx page of the ShipperClient site. Add controls to the page to allow the user to select a shipper based on ID, display the details of that shipper, edit the shipper details, and save the details back to the WCF service. Your form layout should be similar to that shown in Figure 10-13.

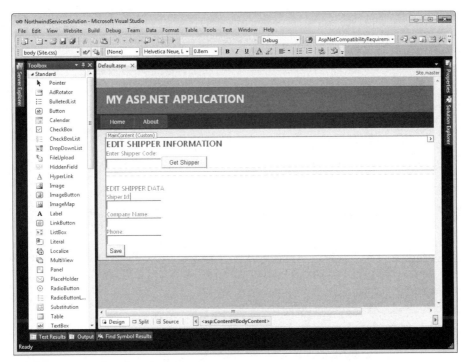

FIGURE 10-13 The client form layout.

5. Add code to the Get Shipper button's click event to call the WCF service and put the
results into the Shipper Data form. Your code should look as follows.

Sample of Visual Basic Code

```vb
Protected Sub ButtonGet_Click(ByVal sender As Object, _
  ByVal e As System.EventArgs) Handles ButtonGetShipper.Click

    'todo: add validation & error handling
    Dim shipperId As Integer = Integer.Parse(TextBoxShipperCode.Text)

    Dim nwShipper As New NwServices.ShipperServiceClient()

    Dim shipper As NwServices.Shipper
    shipper = nwShipper.GetShipper(shipperId)

    TextBoxShipperId.Text = shipper.ShipperId.ToString()
    TextBoxCompany.Text = shipper.CompanyName
    TextBoxPhone.Text = shipper.Phone

End Sub
```

Sample of C# Code

```csharp
protected void ButtonGet_Click(object sender, EventArgs e)
{
  //todo: add validation & error handling
  int shipperId = int.Parse(TextBoxShipperCode.Text);

  NwServices.ShipperServiceClient nwShipper =
    new NwServices.ShipperServiceClient();

  NwServices.Shipper shipper = new NwServices.Shipper();
  shipper = nwShipper.GetShipper(shipperId);

  TextBoxShipperId.Text = shipper.ShipperId.ToString();
  TextBoxCompany.Text = shipper.CompanyName;
  TextBoxPhone.Text = shipper.Phone;
}
```

6. Add code to the Save button's click event to call the WCF service with the values from the various TextBox controls. Your code should look as follows.

Sample of Visual Basic Code

```vb
Protected Sub ButtonSave_Click(ByVal sender As Object, _
  ByVal e As System.EventArgs) Handles ButtonSave.Click

  'todo: add validation & error handling
  Dim shipper As New NwServices.Shipper()
  shipper.ShipperId = Integer.Parse(TextBoxShipperId.Text)
  shipper.CompanyName = TextBoxCompany.Text
  shipper.Phone = TextBoxPhone.Text

  Dim nwShipper As New NwServices.ShipperServiceClient()
  nwShipper.SaveShipper(shipper)

End Sub
```

Sample of C# Code

```csharp
protected void ButtonSave_Click(object sender, EventArgs e)
{
  //todo: add validation & error handling
  NwServices.Shipper shipper = new NwServices.Shipper();
  shipper.ShipperId = int.Parse(TextBoxShipperId.Text);
  shipper.CompanyName = TextBoxCompany.Text;
  shipper.Phone = TextBoxPhone.Text;

  NwServices.ShipperServiceClient nwShipper = new NwServices.ShipperServiceClient();
  nwShipper.SaveShipper(shipper);
}
```

7. Run the application. Enter a Shipper ID (**1**, **2**, or **3**). Edit the data and save it back to the database.

Lesson Summary

- WCF is a unifying programming model for creating service-oriented applications. With WCF, you can create services that work with HTTP, TCP, MSMQ, and named pipes.

- ASP.NET and IIS allow you to host WCF services that you want to expose as HTTP. You can use this model to write services that take advantage of ASP.NET features such as session state and security.

- You write a WCF service by first defining a contract (typically as an interface). The contract uses the ServiceContract and OperationContract attribute classes to define the service and its methods, respectively.

- You can write WCF services that can be called from AJAX by using the REST protocol and JSON message format. You do so by decorating your service with the WebInvokeAttribute class.

- You can create WCF Data Services to be used with the Open Data Protocol (OData). You do so by inheriting from the DataServices class and using the DataServiceConfiguration class to indicate which items of your data model you intend to expose.

Lesson Review

You can use the following questions to test your knowledge of the information in Lesson 3, "Creating and Consuming WCF Services." The questions are also available on the companion CD as a practice test, if you prefer to review them in electronic form.

> **NOTE** **ANSWERS**
>
> Answers to these questions and explanations of why each answer choice is correct or incorrect are located in the "Answers" section at the end of the book.

1. You want to write a WCF service application. You intend to host the service in IIS and use ASP.NET to build the service. What type of project should you create?

   A. A WCF Service library

   B. A WCF service application

   C. An ASP.NET Web Service application

   D. A Windows Service application

2. You define your own custom type to be used with your WCF service. This type represents a product at your company. It contains several public properties. You want to expose this type so that it can be serialized and defined by an XML Schema Definition (XSD) schema. What actions should you take? (Choose all that apply.)

   A. Mark your product class with the DataContract attribute.

   B. Mark your product class with the ServiceContract attribute.

   C. Mark the public members of your product class with the OperationContract attribute.

   D. Mark the public members of your product class with the DataMember attribute.

3. You want to expose a portion of your data model as a service by using OData. Which actions should you take? (Choose all that apply.)

   A. Create a service class that inherits from DataService.

   B. Create a service class that inherits from DataContract.

   C. Indicate what the service should expose inside the InitializeService method.

   D. Indicate what the service should expose inside the Init method.

4. You want to write a client to work with a WCF Data Service. Which actions should you take? (Choose all that apply.)

   A. Set a web reference to the data service.

   B. Set a service reference to the data service.

   C. Create an instance of the data service proxy and pass a URI object to point to the data service.

   D. Use the classes in System.Data.Services.Client to write code to access the data exposed by the service.

Case Scenarios

In the following case scenarios, you apply what you've learned in this chapter. If you have difficulty completing this work, review the material in this chapter before beginning the next chapter. You can find answers to these questions in the "Answers" section at the end of this book.

Case Scenario 1: Working with HTTP Requests

You are a web developer working for Contoso, Ltd, a financial services company. You have been asked to create a feature that returns a custom-generated financial document based on a request made for a report. Requests are made to the reports by using the format report.xps. The data is time sensitive, so it needs to be generated dynamically upon request and then returned to the user as an XPS document.

This feature needs to be secured by a custom security model implemented in code. In fact, all requests to the site that hosts the feature should be authenticated based on this model and logged to a custom event log.

Thinking about how you will build this feature, answer the following questions:

1. How would you intercept requests for all XPS documents, execute the code to dynamically create the report, and return the results to the user?

2. What would you do to implement the custom security and logging feature for all requests to the site?

Case Scenario 2: Selecting a Service Model

You are a web developer for Fabrikam Inc., a specialty retail company. You have been asked to write a set of services that allow your partners to view your product catalog and inventory. This information updates daily and is shared across partners.

You and your partners work exclusively over the web and have no special communication infrastructure outside of the Internet.

You should also expose services that allow these partners to process a user through the shopping experience: cart, checkout, shipping, order history, and so on. You need to be able to track users through the process without committing their details to the transaction system until they submit their order.

Thinking about how you will build these services, answer the following questions:

1. What type of service programming model should you implement?

2. Where should you host your service application?

3. How might you manage access to common data such as catalog and product information?

4. How might you handle user information through the checkout process?

Suggested Practices

To help you successfully master the exam objectives presented in this chapter, complete the following tasks.

Work with XML HTTP Handlers and Modules

For this task, you should complete Practice 1 for additional experience in configuring HTTP handlers for IIS 6.0 and IIS 7.0. Complete Practice 2 to gain more experience in handling application events with an HTTP module.

- **Practice 1** Create a custom HTTP handler for managing requests for a custom file type of your choosing. Configure this handler as if using IIS 6.0. Publish the site to IIS 7.0 running in integrated mode. Reconfigure the handler to work with IIS 7.0. You should do this both in the Web.config file and from the management console (for practice).

- **Practice 2** Create a basic HTTP module that logs events. You can follow the text in the chapter to create this. When your module is working, re-create the same functionality by using the Global.asax file.

Work with XML Web Services

For this task, you should complete Practices 1 and 2 to practice basic skills for working with XML web services. Complete Practice 3 to get experience with ASP.NET security. Complete Practice 4 for more work with AJAX.

- **Practice 1** Return to the practice code created in Lesson 1. Extend the Authors.asmx service by adding support for returning a single author as a serialized, custom class that you write. Also, add support for receiving an instance of this class through a service and updating the database.

- **Practice 2** Use the code created in Practice 1 to add client support for working with the custom object returned from the service. Notice how Visual Studio generates a version of the Author class as part of the Proxy reference class.

- **Practice 3** Add security to the web service defined in the practice for Lesson 1. Set the service to use Windows Integrated Security. Change the calling client to pass credentials to the service by using the NetworkCredentials class.

- **Practice 4** Use the example code in Lesson 1 for calling a web service by using AJAX to create your own web service and client-side call.

Work with WCF Services

For this task, you should complete Practice 1. Complete Practice 2 for more work with AJAX.

- **Practice 1** Return to the practice code for Lesson 3. Add another WCF service for returning all shippers in a single call to be displayed in a list. Change the WCF client code to show all shippers, and change the search feature to work against the list of shippers returned by the WCF services.

- **Practice 2** Call a WCF service from client script by using ASP.NET AJAX. Follow the pattern discussed in Lesson 1, and apply it to WCF.

Take a Practice Test

The practice tests on this book's companion CD offer many options. For example, you can test yourself on just the lesson review questions in this chapter, or you can test yourself on all the 70-515 certification exam objectives. You can set up the test so it closely simulates the experience of taking a certification exam, or you can set it up in study mode so you can look at the correct answers and explanations after you answer each question.

> *MORE INFO* **PRACTICE TESTS**
>
> For details about all the practice test options available, see the "How to Use the Practice Tests" section in this book's Introduction.

CHAPTER 11

Connecting to and Querying Data with LINQ

Microsoft Language-Integrated Query (LINQ) is both a language feature and an extension to the Microsoft .NET Framework. It was introduced with the .NET Framework version 3.5 to help bridge the gap between programming objects and working with data. LINQ turns data access and queries into language constructs in Microsoft Visual Basic and Microsoft Visual C#. This provides a consistent model for working with data no matter where that data comes from. It also allows you to write .NET Framework code (in lieu of SQL syntax). This means that you can use compile-time syntax checking against your data, static typing, and IntelliSense in the code editor. All of these features make programming data retrieval functionality easier and more consistent, regardless of the origin of the data.

This chapter starts by introducing the core language concepts of programming with LINQ and discusses how to write queries and transform data by using LINQ to Objects and LINQ to XML. Lesson 2 focuses in on the connection between LINQ and Microsoft ADO.NET, covering LINQ to SQL, LINQ to DataSet, and LINQ to Entities.

Exam objective in this chapter:

- Displaying and Manipulating Data
    - Query and manipulate data by using LINQ.

Lessons in this chapter:

Before You Begin

To complete the lessons in this chapter, you should be familiar with developing applications with Microsoft Visual Studio 2010 by using Visual Basic or C#. In addition, you should be comfortable with all of the following:

- The Visual Studio 2010 Integrated Development Environment (IDE)
- Using Hypertext Markup Language (HTML) and client-side scripting
- Creating ASP.NET websites and forms
- Adding web server controls to a webpage
- Understanding how generic types work in C# or Visual Basic
- Understanding the concepts behind ADO.NET, including DataTable, DataRow, and System.Data.SqlClient

 REAL WORLD

Mike Snell

've been writing webpages against databases since the first version of ASP and Microsoft Visual InterDev. This means that I've witnessed the evolution of DBO to ADO to ADO.NET and beyond. Things have certainly come a long way since the ADO Recordset object. There was always a disconnect between the wonderful world of object-oriented programming and having to code against a relational database. Colleagues and I have discussed over the years the possibility that we would someday all be using an object-oriented database. Although these technologies have existed for some time, there is just too much existing code and knowledge surrounding the use of relational databases (and they work very well). Fortunately, the current evolution has brought us the Microsoft ADO.NET Entity Framework and LINQ to Entities. This finally makes writing database code almost an afterthought compared to working with previous technologies. For many scenarios, application developers can focus on the business domain and let the database persistence work just happen.

Lesson 1: Getting Started with LINQ

This lesson helps you get started in programming with LINQ. The lesson begins by introducing the LINQ concepts and programming style. It then covers querying data with LINQ and finishes with using LINQ to transform data into different formats, including XML and JavaScript Object Notation (JSON).

> **After this lesson, you will be able to:**
> - Understand the concepts of programming with LINQ.
> - Use LINQ to query data sources by filtering, grouping, joining, and ordering data.
> - Transform data you access with LINQ into other formats, including XML and JSON.
>
> **Estimated lesson time: 30 minutes**

Introducing LINQ

LINQ changes the way you access and query data. Before LINQ was created, most queries were expressed as text that was executed against a database. This SQL text was often specific to the underlying technology of the database being queried. LINQ elevates the process of querying for data to actual language constructs and keywords. This has two primary advantages: First, it provides type checking of your query code at compile time; this means that you are likely to encounter fewer errors, you can use IntelliSense, and it will be easier to write code. Second, it provides a consistent model for querying against all database technologies and all data, including lists, XML, arrays, database tables, and more.

LINQ and IEnumerable

LINQ queries introduce several contracts and keywords to Visual Basic and C#. These are discussed in detail in the next section. These keywords allow you to write queries against anything that supports the base interface, IEnumerable or IEnumerable<T>. In the .NET Framework, this means nearly all collections of data, including DataSet, List<T>, Array, and many more. For example, assuming that you have a list of Employee objects named employees, the following LINQ query code would return all employees working in the IT department from that list.

Sample of Visual Basic Code

```
Dim empQuery As IEnumerable(Of Employee) = From emp In employees
                                Where emp.Department = "IT Department"
                                Select emp
```

Sample of C# Code

```
IEnumerable<Employee> empQuery = from emp in employees
                    where emp.Department == "IT Department"
                    select emp;
```

Notice that the LINQ query is actually saved to a typed variable, in this case IEnumerable<Employee>. You can save your query to what are called *queryable types*. The common ones are IEnumerable<T> and IQueryable<T>. These allow the query to actually automatically examine ("iterate over") each piece of data when executed. You can skip using this typed syntax and simply use the var keyword in C# or no type value in Visual Basic to declare your query variable. The following shows an example.

Sample of Visual Basic Code

```
Dim empQuery = From emp In employees
               Where (emp.Department = "IT Department")
               Select emp
```

Sample of C# Code

```
var empQuery = from emp in employees
               where emp.Department == "IT Department"
               select emp;
```

In this case, the compiler will infer the IEnumerable<Employee> type by looking at the actual data source. However, this shortcut can make your code difficult to read. There are times, however, when you will need to use the var keyword (or no type declaration in Visual Basic): when you are assigning a query result to a new, anonymous type that you are creating. You can't strongly type the result set when the type itself is anonymous and not created until run time.

Note too that when the LINQ query is assigned to a variable it is only saved to the variable; the query does not actually execute until it is iterated over. This means that you have to do something with the data before LINQ will expend the processing required to actually execute the query. One way to iterate over the query is with a simple For...Each statement. The following shows an example.

Sample of Visual Basic Code

```
For Each emp As Employee In empQuery
    Response.Write(emp.Department)
Next
```

Sample of C# Code

```
foreach (var emp in empQuery)
{
    Console.WriteLine(emp.Department);
}
```

Of course, there are other ways to force your query to run. You can use the Count, Max, Average, or First methods to return an aggregate value. This will ensure that the query runs immediately. The following code shows an example.

Sample of Visual Basic Code

```
Dim cnt as Integer = empQuery.Count()
```

Sample of C# Code

```
int cnt = empQuery.Count();
```

You might also call ToList<T> or ToArray<T> to execute the query and cache the results in a list object or an array. The following code shows an example.

Sample of Visual Basic Code

```vb
Dim empQuery As List(Of Employee) = (From emp In employees
                                     Where (emp.Department = "IT Department")
                                     Select emp).ToList()
```

Sample of C# Code

```csharp
List<Employee> empQuery = (from emp in employees
                           where emp.Department == "IT Department"
                           select emp).ToList();
```

Introducing LINQ Data Providers

The LINQ language extensions allow you to query data in a consistent manner. You will see more on this in the next section. However, LINQ also includes additions to the .NET Framework itself for working with specific types of data such as relational databases, XML, and objects. These additions allow you to connect to this data, query against it, and insert, update, and delete items within the data all by using strongly typed objects. The following lists the core data types LINQ supports in the .NET Framework:

- **LINQ to SQL**   This addition allows you to connect to a SQL database and query data. You can create an object model to represent your database. You can then use LINQ to insert, update, and delete records as well as query this strongly typed object model.

- **LINQ to DataSet**   This addition allows you to query against an in-memory, ADO.NET DataSet object. You can use the power of LINQ along with the ubiquity of DataSet objects to simplify working with cached data.

- **LINQ to Entities**   This addition allows you to write queries against data modeled by using the Entity Framework (EF). The EF is a conceptual model of a database that typically involves an object-to-database mapping layer. LINQ to Entities allows you to query against this object layer by using the power of LINQ.

- **LINQ to XML**   This addition provides a LINQ-based interface for working with XML data structures. You can use LINQ to XML to create XML, load an XML file, query XML data, manipulate the XML, and transform the XML into another shape.

- **LINQ to Objects**   This is the base level of LINQ programming. With LINQ to Objects, you are not writing queries by using an intermediate LINQ provider (such as LINQ to SQL or LINQ to XML). Instead, LINQ to Objects is simply the term for querying directly against any collection that implements the IEnumerable or IEnumerable<T> interface. Possible collections of this kind include List<T>, Array, Dictionary<TKey, TValue>, or even a string array.

Most of the data types LINQ supports are covered in detail throughout the rest of this chapter. The next section covers some of the basics of writing queries against LINQ to Objects, whereas Lesson 2 focuses on LINQ to DataSet, LINQ to SQL, and LINQ to Entities.

Querying Data with LINQ

You saw in the previous section that querying data in LINQ uses some basic keywords such as From, Where, and Select. You use these keywords (along with others) to write LINQ queries against a data source. Of course, the first step is to actually define a data source against which you can query. Recall that this might be any object that implements the IEnumerable interface (or a derivative of that interface). After you have your data source, you then can define a strongly typed query against that data. The final step is to execute that query and return the results. The following sections focus on the core concepts of writing LINQ queries against a data source.

EXAM TIP

The LINQ language constructs can seem odd at first. They do not look like traditional .NET Framework code, and they do not quite follow standard SQL syntax. Be sure you know how to read LINQ for the exam.

Defining a Data Source

You must have a data source defined before you can write a query against it. LINQ can query nearly all collections of data in the .NET Framework. This means that your data source could be an XML document loaded into an object, an entity model defined with either the Entity Framework or a LINQ to SQL model, or simply an array of values.

The following sections provide a few examples of defining different types of data sources and writing basic LINQ queries against them.

DATA IN AN ARRAY

You can write LINQ queries against the .NET Framework arrays. The following example shows an array of strings. You can then see the LINQ query that is written against this array. Notice that the range variable (emp) used in the From clause gets automatically defined as a string because the array includes string values. You can iterate over the underlying collection defined by the LINQ query by using an iterative technique such as For...Each.

Sample of Visual Basic Code

```
Dim employees As String() = {"Michael", "Hank", "Benjamin", "Gail"}

    Dim empQuery = From emp In employees
                   Where emp.Length > 5
                   Select emp
```

Sample of C# Code

```
string[] employees = {"Michael", "Hank", "Benjamin", "Gail"};

var empQuery = from emp in employees
               where emp.Length > 5
               select emp;
```

LIST DATA

You can use LINQ to query against data stored in a collection class, such as the List<T> class (among many others). The following code creates a new List<Employee> collection. The Employee class is simply a custom class that was written to hold a few properties. The code then defines a simple LINQ query against the class. You can then iterate over the collection defined by the query.

Sample of Visual Basic Code

```vb
Dim employees As List(Of Employee) = New List(Of Employee) From
    {New Employee With {.First = "Michael",
                        .ID = 111,
                        .Department = "IT Department",
                        .City = "Pittsburgh"},
    New Employee With {.First = "Hank",
                        .ID = 112,
                        .Department = "IT Department",
                        .City = "Redmond"},
    New Employee With {.First = "Benjamin",
                        .ID = 113,
                        .Department = "Human Resources",
                        .City = "Chicago"},
    New Employee With {.First = "Gail",
                        .ID = 113,
                        .Department = "Marketing",
                        .City = "Ann Arbor"}
    }

Dim empQuery As IEnumerable(Of Employee) = From emp In employees
                                           Where emp.First.Length > 5
                                           Select emp
```

Sample of C# Code

```csharp
List<Employee> employees = new List<Employee>()
{
    new Employee {First="Michael",
        ID=111,
        Department="IT Department",
        City="Pittsburgh"},
    new Employee {First="Hank",
        ID=112,
        Department="IT Department",
        City="Redmond"},
    new Employee {First="Benjamin",
        ID=113,
        Department="Human Resources",
        City="Chicago"},
    new Employee {First="Gail",
        ID=114,
        Department="Marketing",
        City="Ann Arbor"},
};

IEnumerable<Employee> empQuery = from emp in employees
                                where emp.First.Length > 5
                                select emp;
```

XML DATA

You can use LINQ to query XML data sources too. In this case, you actually use the language features of LINQ to write your queries. However, to work with the data, you use LINQ to XML (defined in System.Xml.Linq). This namespace makes working with XML data easier and exposes your XML so that LINQ can query the XML data. For example, the following code uses the XElement class to load an XML file that can easily be queried by LINQ.

Sample of Visual Basic Code

```vb
Dim empXml As XElement = XElement.Load("c:\code\employees.xml")
```

Sample of C# Code

```csharp
XElement empXml = XElement.Load(@"c:\code\employees.xml");
```

You can also use the XElement class to actually create XML on the fly. The following code shows just that. Notice that the Visual Basic code uses the Visual Basic XML literals feature to create the XML in code. The C# example relies on the XElement constructors for creating the XML. Notice also the LINQ query against the XML. This is a query of a collection of XElement objects. To access actual items within the XML, you use the Descendants or Element properties.

Sample of Visual Basic Code

```vb
Dim empXml As XElement = New XElement(
    <Employees>
        <Employee>
            <ID>111</ID>
            <FirstName>Michael</FirstName>
            <Department>IT Department</Department>
            <City>Pittsburgh</City>
        </Employee>
        <Employee>
            <ID>112</ID>
            <FirstName>Hank</FirstName>
            <Department>IT Department</Department>
            <City>Redmond</City>
        </Employee>
        <Employee>
            <ID>113</ID>
            <FirstName>Benjamin</FirstName>
            <Department>Human Resources</Department>
            <City>Chicago</City>
        </Employee>
        <Employee>
            <ID>114</ID>
            <FirstName>Gail</FirstName>
            <Department>Marketing</Department>
            <City>Ann Arbor</City>
        </Employee>
    </Employees>)

Dim empQuery As IEnumerable(Of XElement) =
    From emp In empXml.Descendants("Employee")
    Where emp.Element("FirstName").Value.Length > 5
    Select emp
```

Sample of C# Code

```csharp
XElement empXml = new XElement("Employees",
    new XElement("Employee",
        new XElement("ID", "111"),
        new XElement("FirstName", "Michael"),
        new XElement("Department", "IT Department"),
        new XElement("City", "Pittsburgh")
        ),
    new XElement("Employee",
        new XElement("ID", "112"),
        new XElement("FirstName", "Hank"),
        new XElement("Department", "IT Department"),
        new XElement("City", "Redmond")
        ),
    new XElement("Employee",
        new XElement("ID", "113"),
        new XElement("FirstName", "Benjamin"),
        new XElement("Department", "Human Resources"),
        new XElement("City", "Chicago")
        ),
    new XElement("Employee",
        new XElement("ID", "114"),
        new XElement("FirstName", "Gail"),
        new XElement("Department", "Marketing"),
        new XElement("City", "Ann Arbor")
        )
);

IEnumerable<XElement> empQuery =
    from emp in empXml.Descendants("Employee")
    where emp.Element("FirstName").Value.Length > 5
    select emp;
```

DATABASE DATA

You will learn a lot about querying database data with XML in the next lesson. However, the code in this section provides a basic demonstration of using LINQ to SQL (found in the System.Data.Linq namespace).

The first step is to create an object model that maps to your data structures. Visual Studio provides tools for this, but you can also use code. The System.Data.Linq.Mapping namespace provides attribute classes for defining objects that map your data structures. For example, the following Employee class is marked to map to the employee table in the pubs sample database. Notice that two columns are mapped to two properties (emp_id to EmployeeId and fname to FirstName) by using the Column attribute.

Sample of Visual Basic Code

```vb
<Table(Name:="employee")> _
Public Class Employee

    Private _empID As String

    <Column(IsPrimaryKey:=True, Storage:="_empID", Name:="emp_id")> _
    Public Property EmployeeId() As String
```

```vb
        Get
            Return _empId
        End Get
        Set(ByVal value As String)
            _empId = value
        End Set
    End Property


    Private _firstName As String

    <Column(Storage:="_firstName", Name:="fname")> _
    Public Property FirstName() As String
        Get
            Return _firstName
        End Get
        Set(ByVal value As String)
            _firstName = value
        End Set
    End Property

End Class
```

Sample of C# Code
```csharp
[Table(Name = "employee")]
public class Employee
{
    private string _empID;
    [Column(IsPrimaryKey = true, Storage = "_empID", Name = "emp_id")]
    public string EmployeeId
    {
        get
        {
            return this._empID;
        }
        set
        {
            this._empID = value;
        }
    }

    private string _firstName;
    [Column(Storage = "_firstName", Name = "fname")]
    public string FirstName
    {
        get
        {
            return this._firstName;
        }
        set
        {
            this._firstName = value;
        }
    }
}
```

The next step is to define a connection to the database. If you are using a file-based database, you can simply point to the file. If you are using a server, you would use a connection string. In either case, your connection is defined as a DataContext object. The following code shows an example.

Sample of Visual Basic Code

```
Dim pubs As DataContext = New DataContext("c:\code\pubs.mdf")
```

Sample of C# Code

```
DataContext pubs = new DataContext(@"c:\code\pubs.mdf");
```

You can now set a reference to a table in the database by using the Table<T> object. You can then run a LINQ query against this table and store the results in a list of Employee objects. LINQ to SQL will take care of the mapping for you. The following code shows an example.

Sample of Visual Basic Code

```
Dim Employees As Table(Of Employee) = pubs.GetTable(Of Employee)()

Dim empQuery As IEnumerable(Of Employee) =
    From emp In Employees
    Where emp.FirstName.Length > 5
    Select emp
```

Sample of C# Code

```
Table<Employee> Employees = pubs.GetTable<Employee>();

IEnumerable<Employee> empQuery = from emp in Employees
                                 where emp.FirstName.Length > 5
                                 select emp;
```

Of course, you can iterate over the results as you would with any other IEnumerable list of objects. You can also use LINQ to SQL to insert, update, and delete rows in your database.

Selecting

As you have seen, you use the From keyword to indicate a range variable and a data source for your LINQ query. The range variable is like the variable in a For...Each loop. The compiler infers this type, so you need not declare it. In the following example, the From keyword is used with the emp range variable against a data source, employees.

Sample of Visual Basic Code

```
Dim empQuery As IEnumerable(Of Employee) =
          From emp In employees
          Select emp
```

Sample of C# Code

```
IEnumerable<Employee> empQuery =
    from emp in employees
    select emp;
```

Notice also the use of the Select keyword. This indicates what should be selected as the result of the query. In this example, this is the entire Employee object. In the example that follows, however, the Select keyword indicates that you want to return only the employee's first name. This will create a list of string objects (and not Employee).

Sample of Visual Basic Code

```
Dim empQuery As IEnumerable(Of String) =
        From emp In employees
        Select emp.First
```

Sample of C# Code

```
IEnumerable<string> empQuery =
    from emp in employees
    select emp.First;
```

This type of selection, one that changes the results, is called a *projection* in LINQ. You will see more of this in the upcoming "Transforming Data with LINQ" section.

Filtering

You can use the Where keyword in LINQ to filter your result sets. You pass one or more Boolean expressions to this clause, and those elements whose evaluations result in true are returned as part of the query. LINQ also supports multiple Where clauses in a single query. You can combine Boolean expressions in your Where clause with And (&& in C#) and Or (|| in C#). For example, the following code returns all employees that work in the IT department and live in Redmond.

Sample of Visual Basic Code

```
Dim empQuery As IEnumerable(Of Employee) =
    From emp In employees
    Where emp.Department = "IT Department" And
        emp.City = "Redmond"
    Select emp
```

Sample of C# Code

```
IEnumerable<Employee> empQuery =
    from emp in employees
    where emp.Department == "IT Department" &&
        emp.City == "Redmond"
    select emp;
```

Ordering

You can use the Order By keyword to indicate a sort order for the selected elements. Items will be sorted by their default comparer. In the following example, the type being sorted is a string. Therefore, items will be sorted from A to Z. You can add the Descending keyword to reverse the sort order.

Sample of Visual Basic Code

```vb
Dim empQuery As IEnumerable(Of Employee) =
    From emp In employees
    Order By emp.Department
    Select emp
```

Sample of C# Code

```csharp
IEnumerable<Employee> empQuery =
    from emp in employees
    orderby emp.Department
    select emp;
```

Grouping

The Group keyword allows you to group returned results into separate lists. When you use the Group keyword, you actually return a list of lists. For example, if you were to group the employee list in the examples by department, you would get an object with three items, one for each department (IT Department, Marketing, and Human Resources). Each item in this list would contain a key. The key would be based on the unique group name (in this case, the department). The item would also contain a list of Employee objects in the group.

Visual Basic and C# handle grouping differently. In C#, items are created as actual typed lists of lists. The following code shows an example. Notice that the query indicates a list (IEnumerable) of lists (IGrouping). Each IGrouping list contains a key and a list of Employee objects in the group. Notice too that you can iterate over the two lists by using a nested For...Each loop.

Sample of C# Code

```csharp
IEnumerable<IGrouping<string, Employee>> empQuery =
    from emp in employees
    group emp by emp.Department;

foreach (IGrouping<string, Employee> group in empQuery)
{
    Response.Write(group.Key);

    foreach (Employee e in group)
    {
        Response.Write(e.First);
    }
}
```

Visual Basic has the same concept. However, it creates anonymous types based on your grouping. For example, in the following code, an anonymous type is created to hold each group. This type is given the department property based on the Group By department statement in the query. This same anonymous type also includes the EmployeeGroup property, which is based on the Into EmployeeGroup = Group statement. You can see that this makes it slightly easier to iterate over these nested lists.

```
Dim empQuery =
    From emp In employees
    Group By department = emp.Department
    Into EmployeeGroup = Group

For Each group In empQuery
    Response.Write(group.department)

    For Each e As Employee In group.EmployeeGroup
        Response.Write(e.First)
    Next
Next
```

Joining

You can use the Join keyword to join data from two or more data sources. This data can be joined in the query and then returned as a new object. All joins created with the Join keyword are equivalent to INNER JOINs in SQL. The join combines the two data sources based on matching keys. For example, the following code joins both the employees list and the timesheets list based on the employee ID. A new, anonymous type is created that has the EmployeeId, EmployeeName, and VacationHours properties . Note that the results will be a row for each joined item. This means that if one employee has three timesheets there will be three rows in the results for that employee.

Sample of Visual Basic Code

```
Dim empQuery = From emp In employees
    Join ts In timesheets On emp.ID Equals ts.EmployeeId
    Select EmployeeId = emp.ID,
        EmployeeName = (emp.First & " " & emp.Last),
        VacationHours = ts.HoursVacation
```

Sample of C# Code

```
var empQuery = from emp in employees
    join ts in timesheets on emp.ID equals ts.EmployeeId
    select new { EmployeeId=emp.ID,
        EmployeeName=emp.First + " " + emp.Last,
        VacationHours = ts.HoursVacation};
```

You can also group your joins into objects. In the following example, the timesheet object is placed in the tms variable. This variable is then added to the anonymous type. This results in a list of employees, each of which contains a property called VacationHours that contains a list of timesheets. In Visual Basic this is accomplished via the Group Join keyword, along with Into. In C#, all that is required is into. Notice too how you iterate over the results in a nested For...Each loop.

```vb
Dim empQuery = From emp In employees
               Group Join ts In timesheets On
               emp.ID Equals ts.EmployeeId
               Into tms = Group
               Select EmployeeId = emp.ID,
                   EmployeeName = (emp.First & " " & emp.Last),
                   VacationHours = tms

For Each emp In empQuery
    Console.WriteLine(emp.EmployeeName)
    For Each t As Timesheet In emp.VacationHours
        Console.WriteLine(t.HoursVacation.ToString())
    Next
```

Sample of C# Code

```csharp
var empQuery = from emp in employees
    join ts in timesheets on emp.ID equals ts.EmployeeId into tms
    select new { EmployeeId=emp.ID,
        EmployeeName=emp.First + " " + emp.Last,
        VacationHours = tms};

foreach (var emp in empQuery)
{
    Response.Write(emp.EmployeeName);
    foreach (Timesheet t in emp.VacationHours)
    {
        Response.Write(t.HoursVacation.ToString());
    }
}
```

Transforming Data with LINQ

You can use the features of LINQ to get data from a source such as a database or object and produce output in another format such as XML, JSON, or a new type altogether. This section highlights many of these possibilities.

Mapping to Another Type or to an Anonymous Object

LINQ allows you to use the Select keyword to push your results to an instance of a strongly typed object or even a new, anonymous type. In the following example, a query is executed against a list of strongly typed Employee objects. The results are a list of strongly typed User objects; this is accomplished through the Select New User code statement.

```
Dim users As IEnumerable(Of User) = From emp In employees
                                    Where emp.ID <> 0
                                    Select New User With
                                           {.EmployeeId = emp.ID,
                                            .Name = emp.First & " " & emp.Last}
```

Sample of C# Code

```
IEnumerable<User> users = from emp in employees
                          where emp.ID != 0
                          select new User
                          {
                              Name = emp.First + " " + emp.Last,
                              EmployeeId = emp.ID
                          };
```

Note that you can use the same syntax to create an anonymous type as your result. To do so, you simply use Select new and do not specify a type. You also need to allow the compiler to determine your type at run time. This means using var (or an undefined type in Visual Basic). The following code shows an example.

Sample of Visual Basic Code

```
Dim users = From emp In employees
        Where emp.ID <> 0
        Select New With
            {.EmployeeId = emp.ID,
             .Name = emp.First & " " & emp.Last}
```

Sample of C# Code

```
var users = from emp in employees
    where emp.ID != 0
    select new
    {
        Name = emp.First + " " + emp.Last,
        EmployeeId = emp.ID
    };
```

Merging Multiple Data Sources

You saw in an earlier section that you could use the join and group join operations to join data and produce new results. LINQ also lets you merge two similar datasets by using the Concat method from the list object. The result is a new object made up of both data sources.

The following code example queries the employees list for all employees living in Redmond. It then queries the consultants list for consultants living in Redmond. It merges the result into a list of names.

```vb
Dim employeesAndConsul = (From emp In employees
    Where emp.City = "Redmond"
    Select (emp.First + " " + emp.Last)).Concat(
        From cn In consultants
        Where cn.Location = "Redmond"
        Select cn.Name)
```

Sample of C# Code

```csharp
var employeesAndConsul = (from emp in employees
    where emp.City == "Redmond"
    select emp.First + " " + emp.Last).Concat(
        from cn in consultants
        where cn.Location == "Redmond"
        select cn.Name);
```

Performing Operations on Results

You can perform mathematical and string operations on your result sets. In fact, you have already seen examples of concatenating two values to produce a new field. The following code shows another example. Here, a new field in an anonymous type is created by using String.Format and concatenation. Another new field is created by adding the values from two fields together.

Sample of Visual Basic Code

```vb
Dim users = From emp In employees
    Select New With
        {.Employee = String.Format("Employee ({0}), {1}",
        emp.ID, emp.First & " " & emp.Last),
        .RemainingHoursOff = emp.RemainingVacation + emp.RemainingPersonalTime}
```

Sample of C# Code

```csharp
var users = from emp in employees
    select new
    {
        Employee = string.Format("Employee ({0}), {1}",
        emp.ID, emp.First + " " + emp.Last),
        RemainingHoursOff = emp.RemainingVacation + emp.RemainingPersonalTime
    };
```

Transforming Results into XML

You can use LINQ to XML (System.Xml.Linq) to transform data from a LINQ query into an XML structure. You do so by using the XElement class and the LINQ Select keyword to create new elements nested inside one another like an XML tree. As an example, the following code takes the employee list data and coverts it into an XML tree with the root node of <Employees> and child nodes of <Employee>.

```
Dim empXml = New _
    XElement("Employees", From emp In employees
    Select New _
        XElement("Employee",
            New XElement("Id", emp.ID),
            New XElement("Name", emp.First & " " & emp.Last),
            New XElement("Department", emp.Department)
        )
    )
```

Sample of C# Code

```
var empXml = new
    XElement("Employees", from emp in employees
    select new
        XElement("Employee",
            new XElement("Id", emp.ID),
            new XElement("Name", emp.First + " " + emp.Last),
            new XElement("Department", emp.Department)
        )
    );
```

Transforming Results into JSON

Given the increased use of JQuery and AJAX, you might need to transform your LINQ query results into JSON format for working with these client-side libraries. You could do so by writing a custom class that can parse a list of objects into a JSON message. You might also download one of the LINQ to JSON libraries available from third parties on the Internet. However, the .NET Framework does provide a serializer for creating JSON messages from IEnumerable lists.

This serializer can be found in the System.Runtime.Serialization.Json namespace. The actual class name of the serializer is DataContractJsonSerializer. It can be used to serialize types and lists of types that are marked as DataContract. You can also use this object to take a JSON message and deserialize it back to objects.

As an example, the following code creates a LINQ query and then uses the DataContractJsonSerializer class to write the query results to a MemoryStream. The results are formatted in JSON and then sent to the screen.

Sample of Visual Basic Code

```
Dim empJson As IEnumerable(Of Employee) =
    From emp In employees
    Where emp.Department = "IT Department"
    Select emp

Dim ser As DataContractJsonSerializer = _
    New DataContractJsonSerializer(GetType(IEnumerable(Of Employee)))
```

```
Dim ms As MemoryStream = New MemoryStream()

ser.WriteObject(ms, empJson)

Dim json As String = System.Text.Encoding.Default.GetString(ms.ToArray())
ms.Close()

Response.Write(json)
```

Sample of C# Code

```csharp
IEnumerable<Employee> empJson = from emp in employees
                                where emp.Department == "IT Department"
                                select emp;

DataContractJsonSerializer ser =
    new DataContractJsonSerializer(typeof(IEnumerable<Employee>));

MemoryStream ms = new MemoryStream();

ser.WriteObject(ms, empJson);

string json = Encoding.Default.GetString(ms.ToArray());
ms.Close();

Response.Write(json);
```

The following shows an example of the message displayed in JSON format. Each employee that belongs to the IT department (see the query) is displayed.

```
[{"City":"Pittsburgh","Department":"IT Department","First":"Michael","ID":111,
"Last":null},{"City":"Redmond","Department":"IT Department","First":"Hank","ID":112,
"Last":null}]
```

PRACTICE Working with LINQ

In this practice, you create a website and define some XML data. You then use LINQ to XML and standard LINQ language features to work with this data.

> **ON THE COMPANION MEDIA**
>
> If you encounter a problem completing an exercise, you can find the completed projects in the samples installed from this book's companion CD. For more information about the project files and other content on the CD, see "Using the Companion Media" in this book's Introduction.

EXERCISE Creating the ASP.NET Website and Working with LINQ

In this exercise, you create the website, define the XML file, and write LINQ queries to work with the XML.

1. Open Visual Studio and create a new ASP.NET website called **LinqExample** by using either C# or Visual Basic.

2. Add the employees.xml file to the App_Data directory of your solution. You can get this file from the CD for this book. This file contains several Employee elements. Each Employee element contains the ID, FirstName, LastName, Department, and Location child elements.

3. Add a new class file called Employee to the solution. Visual Studio will ask to create the App_Code directory and add it to the solution for you; click Yes. This class represents an employee object and will be used when the XML is turned into a collection of strongly typed objects. The following code shows an example.

```vb
Sample of Visual Basic Code
Public Class Employee

    Public Property Id As String
    Public Property FirstName As String
    Public Property LastName As String
    Public Property Department As String
    Public Property Location As String

End Class
```

```csharp
Sample of C# Code
public class Employee
{
    public string Id { get; set; }
    public string FirstName { get; set; }
    public string LastName { get; set; }
    public string Department { get; set; }
    public string Location { get; set; }
}
```

4. Add a new class file called EmployeeServices to the solution. This class will expose methods that use LINQ to work with the XML file.

5. Add a using (Imports in Visual Basic) statement at the top of the file for System.Xml.Linq.

6. Add a class-level variable that reads the XML file.

The following shows an example of what your class should look like. Note that you could read the XML file's location from the Web.config file. This sample hard-codes the path to the XML file; you will most likely need to edit this.

Sample of Visual Basic Code
```vbnet
Imports Microsoft.VisualBasic
Imports System.Xml.Linq

Public Class EmployeeServices

    Dim _empXml As XElement = XElement.Load( _
    "C:\Code\Lesson1-Exercise1-Completed-CS\LinqExample\App_Data\employees.xml")
...
```

Sample of C# Code
```csharp
using System;
using System.Collections.Generic;
using System.Linq;
using System.Xml.Linq;

public class EmployeeServices
{

    XElement _empXml = XElement.Load(
    @"C:\Code\Lesson1-Exercise1-Completed-CS\LinqExample\App_Data\employees.xml");
...
```

7. Add a method called GetDepartments to the EmployeeServices class. Write a LINQ query to return just the distinct departments from the XML file. You can do so by using Group By and then selecting only the first elements in the result. The following shows an example.

Sample of Visual Basic Code
```vbnet
Public Function GetDepartments() As List(Of String)

    'query the XML and group by department
    '  select only the departments in the group
    Dim deptQuery =
        From emp In _empXml.Descendants("Employee")
        Group emp By emp.Element("Department").Value
        Into empGroup = Group
        Select empGroup.First().Element("Department").Value

    Return deptQuery.ToList()

End Function
```

```
public List<string> GetDepartments()
{
    //query the XML and group by department
    //  select only the departments in the group
    var deptQuery =
        from emp in _empXml.Descendants("Employee")
        group emp by emp.Element("Department").Value
            into empGroup
            select empGroup.First().Element("Department").Value;


    return deptQuery.ToList();

}
```

8. Add another method to EmployeeServices. Name this method GetEmployeeByDept. This method takes a department name as a parameter. It will then query the employee.xml file and return departments with a matching name. The query will transform the data into a list of Employee objects. The following code shows an example.

Sample of Visual Basic Code

```
Public Function GetEmployeesByDept(ByVal department As String) _
    As List(Of Employee)

    'query the XML list by department and return a list of
    '  Employee(objects)
    Dim empQuery As IEnumerable(Of Employee) =
        From emp In _empXml.Descendants("Employee")
        Where emp.Element("Department").Value = department
        Select New Employee With {
            .Id = emp.Element("ID").Value,
            .Department = emp.Element("Department").Value,
            .FirstName = emp.Element("FirstName").Value,
            .LastName = emp.Element("LastName").Value,
            .Location = emp.Element("Location").Value
        }

    Return empQuery.ToList()

End Function
```

Sample of C# Code

```
public List<Employee> GetEmployeesByDept(string department)
{

    //query the XML list by department and return a list of Employee objects
    IEnumerable<Employee> empQuery =
        from emp in _empXml.Descendants("Employee")
        where emp.Element("Department").Value == department
        select new Employee
```

```
            {
                Id = emp.Element("ID").Value,
                Department = emp.Element("Department").Value,
                FirstName = emp.Element("FirstName").Value,
                LastName = emp.Element("LastName").Value,
                Location = emp.Element("Location").Value
            };

        return empQuery.ToList();

}
```

9. Open the Default.aspx page. Add a DropDownList, Button, GridView, and ObjectDataSource control to the page.

10. Configure the ObjectDataSource to point to the EmployeeServices.GetDepartments method. (See Chapter 12, "Working with Data Source Controls and Data-Bound Controls" for more information on ObjectDataSource.)

11. Configure the DropDownList to use the ObjectDataSource.

    Your markup inside the MainContent placeholder should look similar to the following.

```
<asp:Content ID="BodyContent" runat="server" ContentPlaceHolderID="MainContent">
    <h2>View Employees by Department</h2>

    Select a Department<br />
    <asp:DropDownList ID="DropDownListDepts" runat="server"
        DataSourceID="ObjectDataSourceDepts">
    </asp:DropDownList>
    <asp:Button ID="ButtonUpdate" runat="server" Text="Update"
        onclick="ButtonUpdate_Click" />
    <hr />

    <asp:GridView ID="GridViewEmployees" runat="server" CellPadding="4"
        ForeColor="#333333" GridLines="None">
        <AlternatingRowStyle BackColor="White" ForeColor="#284775" />
        <EditRowStyle BackColor="#999999" />
        <FooterStyle BackColor="#5D7B9D" Font-Bold="True" ForeColor="White" />
        <HeaderStyle BackColor="#5D7B9D" Font-Bold="True" ForeColor="White" />
        <PagerStyle BackColor="#284775" ForeColor="White" HorizontalAlign="Center" />
        <RowStyle BackColor="#F7F6F3" ForeColor="#333333" />
    </asp:GridView>

    <asp:ObjectDataSource ID="ObjectDataSourceDepts" runat="server"
        SelectMethod="GetDepartments"
        TypeName="EmployeeServices"></asp:ObjectDataSource>

</asp:Content>
```

12. Add a click event to the Button control. Inside the code for the click event, call the EmployeeServices.GetEmployeesByDept method and pass the selected method from the DropDownList. Update the data in the GridView control with the results. This code should look similar to the following.

Sample of Visual Basic Code

```vb
Protected Sub ButtonUpdate_Click(ByVal sender As Object, _
    ByVal e As System.EventArgs) Handles ButtonUpdate.Click

    Dim empSrv As EmployeeServices = New EmployeeServices()
    GridViewEmployees.DataSource =
        empSrv.GetEmployeesByDept(DropDownListDepts.SelectedItem.Text)
    GridViewEmployees.DataBind()

End Sub
```

Sample of C# Code

```csharp
protected void ButtonUpdate_Click(object sender, EventArgs e)
{
    EmployeeServices empSrv = new EmployeeServices();
    GridViewEmployees.DataSource =
        empSrv.GetEmployeesByDept(DropDownListDepts.SelectedItem.Text);
    GridViewEmployees.DataBind();
}
```

13. Run your application. Select a department and click the Update button. Your results should look similar to those in Figure 11-1.

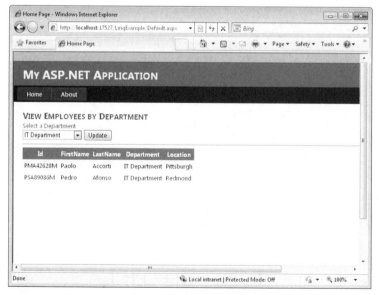

FIGURE 11-1 The LINQ queries being used on a webpage.

Lesson Summary

- You can write LINQ queries against any objects that support IEnumerable. These include most collection classes in the .NET Framework.

- A LINQ query only executes when it is acted upon, as when For...Each is used or ToList is called.

- There are several specialized providers that allow LINQ to work with specific data sources. These include LINQ to SQL, LINQ to DataSet, LINQ to Entities, and LINQ to XML. The use of standard LINQ to work with collection classes is referred to as LINQ to Objects.

- LINQ queries are written with the LINQ language extension, which includes keywords such as From, Select, Where, Group By, Join, Order By, Into, Concat, and others.

- You can use LINQ to transform data from one format into another. This allows you to create new types, new anonymous types, XML files, and even JSON-formatted output.

Lesson Review

You can use the following questions to test your knowledge of the information in Lesson 1, "Getting Started with LINQ." The questions are also available on the companion CD in a practice test, if you prefer to review them in electronic form.

> **NOTE ANSWERS**
>
> Answers to these questions and explanations of why each answer choice is correct or incorrect are located in the "Answers" section at the end of the book.

1. Against which of the following classes can you write a LINQ query? (Choose all that apply).

    A. DataSet

    B. List<T>

    C. Array

    D. Dictionary<TKey, TValue)

2. You need to write a LINQ query to retrieve a list of state hospitals. The results should be sorted and grouped first by county. For each county, the hospitals should be sorted by city. Which of the following LINQ queries would you write? (Choose all that apply.)

    A.

    Visual Basic Code

    ```
    Dim hsQ = From hspt In hospitals
            Order By hspt.County, hspt.City
            Group hspt By hspt.County Into hsptGroup = Group
    ```

    C# Code

    ```
    var hsQ = from hspt in hospitals
            orderby hspt.County, hspt.City
            group hspt by hspt.County;
    ```

B.

Visual Basic Code

```
Dim hsQ = From hspt In hospitals
        Order By hspt.County
        Group hspt By hspt.County Into hsptGroup = Group
        Order By hsptGroup.Last.City
```

C# Code

```
var hsQ = from hspt in hospitals
            orderby hspt.County
            group hspt by hspt.County into hsptGroup
            orderby hsptGroup.Last().City
            select hsptGroup;
```

C.

Visual Basic Code

```
Dim hsQ = From hspt In hospitals
        Order By hspt.County, hspt.City
        Group hspt By hspt.County Into hsptGroup = Group
        Order By hsptGroup.First.County
```

C# Code

```
var hsQ = from hspt in hospitals
            orderby hspt.County
            group hspt by hspt.County into hsptGroup
            orderby hsptGroup.Key
            select hsptGroup;
```

D.

Visual Basic Code

```
Dim hsQ = From hspt In hospitals
            Order By hspt.City
            Group hspt By hspt.County Into hsptGroup = Group
            Order By hsptGroup.First.County
```

C# Code

```
var hsQ = from hspt in hospitals
            orderby hspt.City
            group hspt by hspt.County into hsptGroup
            orderby hsptGroup.First().County
            select hsptGroup;
```

3. You want to merge the results from two separate LINQ queries into a single result set. How would you accomplish this?

A. Use the ToList method.

B. Use the DataContractJsonSerializer class.

C. Use the XElement class.

D. Use the Concat method.

Lesson 2: LINQ and ADO.NET

Business developers write applications that typically work with data. This has traditionally involved writing different layers of code: database code (such as Transact-SQL) for querying data, ADO.NET code for connecting to a database and executing statements, and additional object code for working with the data. Some developers have also written application tiers whose role is to translate the database code into objects. This makes the database easier to code against but can require the writing and maintenance of a lot of time-consuming, often repetitive code.

The LINQ language features and ADO.NET LINQ technologies were created to simplify writing all of this code. First, you can use LINQ to write strongly typed queries (rather than SQL scripts) against your data structures. Secondly, you can use technologies such as LINQ to SQL and LINQ to Entities to generate strongly typed objects that match your database schema. This lesson explores how you can use these technologies in your applications.

> **After this lesson, you will be able to:**
> - Load data into a DataSet object and use LINQ to DataSet to query that data.
> - Define a database schema by using LINQ to SQL and work with that data (query, insert, update, and delete) by using LINQ to SQL.
> - Create an entity model by using the Entity Framework and work with data in that model by using LINQ to Entities.
>
> **Estimated lesson time: 40 minutes**

 REAL WORLD

Mike Snell

I have noticed a rapid adoption of LINQ to SQL and the Entity Framework by developers. These technologies really do add big productivity gains when working with data. It seems that in the long term, the technologies are also a hit. Nearly all of the developers I speak with would not want to go back to writing all the basic database code; they already see that as an "old" or "legacy" way of coding against data.

LINQ to DataSet

The DataSet and DataTable objects allow you to store a lot of data in memory and even share that data between requests (through caching). However, these objects have limited data query functionality. That is, you cannot query a DataSet the same way you would query a database. LINQ to DataSet changes this. It allows you to use the standard query features of LINQ to query data stored in a DataSet.

A DataSet is a memory-based relational representation of data and is the primary disconnected data object used in many ASP.NET applications. A DataSet contains a collection of DataTable and DataRelation objects, as shown in Figure 11-2 (which was built with the DataSet designer in Visual Studio).

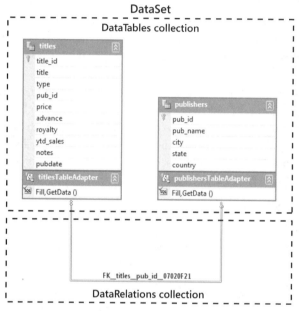

FIGURE 11-2 The DataSet object contains a collection of DataTable and DataRelation objects.

The DataTable objects contain the data in the DataSet. The table schema is defined as a collection of DataColumn objects. The data itself is stored in a collection of DataRow objects.

The DataRelation objects define relationships between DataTable objects in the DataSet. These relationships are defined through DataColumn objects. Relationships are similar to foreign-key constraints in a database. These relationships are enforced in the DataSet.

The DataSet class also provides methods for cloning the DataSet schema, copying the DataSet, merging with other DataSet objects, and retrieving changes from the DataSet.

Defining the DataSet Schema

Before you work with actual data, you need to define the schema—the layout or structure of the data. You can do so automatically when you load a DataSet from a database (see the next section, "Populating the DataSet"). You can also define the schema programmatically or by providing an XML schema definition. The following code demonstrates the creation of a simple DataSet object in code. This DataSet contains a DataTable for companies and a DataTable for employees. The two DataTable objects are joined by using a DataRelation named Company_Employee.

Sample of Visual Basic Code

```vb
Private Function GetDataSet() As DataSet

    Dim companyData As New DataSet("CompanyList")

    Dim company As DataTable = companyData.Tables.Add("company")
    company.Columns.Add("Id", GetType(Guid))
    company.Columns.Add("CompanyName", GetType(String))
    company.PrimaryKey = New DataColumn() {company.Columns("Id")}

    Dim employee As DataTable = companyData.Tables.Add("employee")
    employee.Columns.Add("Id", GetType(Guid))
    employee.Columns.Add("companyId", GetType(Guid))
    employee.Columns.Add("LastName", GetType(String))
    employee.Columns.Add("FirstName", GetType(String))
    employee.Columns.Add("Salary", GetType(Decimal))
    employee.PrimaryKey = New DataColumn() {employee.Columns("Id")}

    companyData.Relations.Add( _
        "Company_Employee", _
        company.Columns("Id"), _
        employee.Columns("CompanyId"))

    Return companyData

End Function
```

Sample of C# Code

```csharp
private DataSet GetDataSet()
{
    DataSet companyData = new DataSet("CompanyList");

    DataTable company = companyData.Tables.Add("company");
    company.Columns.Add("Id", typeof(Guid));
    company.Columns.Add("CompanyName", typeof(string));
    company.PrimaryKey = new DataColumn[] { company.Columns["Id"] };

    DataTable employee = companyData.Tables.Add("employee");
    employee.Columns.Add("Id", typeof(Guid));
    employee.Columns.Add("companyId", typeof(Guid));
    employee.Columns.Add("LastName", typeof(string));
    employee.Columns.Add("FirstName", typeof(string));
    employee.Columns.Add("Salary", typeof(decimal));
    employee.PrimaryKey = new DataColumn[] { employee.Columns["Id"] };

    companyData.Relations.Add(
        "Company_Employee",
        company.Columns["Id"],
        employee.Columns["CompanyId"]);

    return companyData;
}
```

Populating the DataSet

There are several ways to actually get data into the DataTable objects of a DataSet. Recall that you first must define the schema. You can then write code to add rows. Alternatively, you can use a DataAdapter to fill a DataTable from an existing data source (such as a Microsoft SQL Server database). This section examines both of these options.

ADDING DATA PROGRAMMATICALLY

The following code sample shows how to add rows to existing DataTable objects. These objects were defined in the previous example. This code uses the DataTable.Rows.Add method. This method allows you to define a new DataRow object and add it to the Rows collections. The code populates the Id columns by creating a new globally unique identifier (GUID). After a company is created and added to the company DataTable, the employee names for that company are created and added.

Sample of Visual Basic Code

```vb
Dim company As DataTable = companyData.Tables("Company")
Dim employee As DataTable = companyData.Tables("Employee")

Dim coId, empId As Guid
coId = Guid.NewGuid()
company.Rows.Add(coId, "Northwind Traders")
empId = Guid.NewGuid()
employee.Rows.Add(empId, coId, "JoeLast", "JoeFirst", 40.00)
empId = Guid.NewGuid()
employee.Rows.Add(empId, coId, "MaryLast", "MaryFirst", 70.00)
empId = Guid.NewGuid()
employee.Rows.Add(empId, coId, "SamLast", "SamFirst", 12.00)

coId = Guid.NewGuid()
company.Rows.Add(coId, "Contoso")
empId = Guid.NewGuid()
employee.Rows.Add(empId, coId, "SueLast", "SueFirst", 20.00)
empId = Guid.NewGuid()
employee.Rows.Add(empId, coId, "TomLast", "TomFirst", 68.00)
empId = Guid.NewGuid()
employee.Rows.Add(empId, coId, "MikeLast", "MikeFirst", 18.99)
```

Sample of C# Code

```csharp
DataTable company = companyData.Tables["Company"];
DataTable employee = companyData.Tables["Employee"];

Guid coId, empId;
coId = Guid.NewGuid();
company.Rows.Add(coId, "Northwind Traders");
empId = Guid.NewGuid();
employee.Rows.Add(empId, coId, "JoeLast", "JoeFirst", 40.00);
empId = Guid.NewGuid();
employee.Rows.Add(empId, coId, "MaryLast", "MaryFirst", 70.00);
empId = Guid.NewGuid();
employee.Rows.Add(empId, coId, "SamLast", "SamFirst", 12.00);
```

```
coId = Guid.NewGuid();
company.Rows.Add(coId, "Contoso");
empId = Guid.NewGuid();
employee.Rows.Add(empId, coId, "SueLast", "SueFirst", 20.00);
empId = Guid.NewGuid();
employee.Rows.Add(empId, coId, "TomLast", "TomFirst", 68.00);
empId = Guid.NewGuid();
employee.Rows.Add(empId, coId, "MikeLast", "MikeFirst", 18.99);
```

USING THE DATAADAPTER

The DbDataAdapter object is used to retrieve and update data between a DataTable and a data store (such as a SQL Server database). The DbDataAdapter is derived from the DataAdapter class and is the base class of the provider-specific DbDataAdapter classes. Provider-specific versions of DbDataAdapter are created for each type of provider, such as SQL Server, Oracle, and XML.

The DbDataAdapter class has the SelectCommand property that you use to define how data is to be retrieved. The SelectCommand must contain a valid DbCommand object, which must have a valid connection. You can also use DbDataAdapter to update changes to the data source. You'll learn more about this in the next section.

The DataAdapter.Fill method moves data from the data store to the DataTable object that you pass into this method. The Fill method has several overloads, some of which accept only a DataSet as a parameter. When a DataSet is passed to the Fill method, a new DataTable object is created in the DataSet if a source DataTable object is not specified.

The following code uses the System.Configuration.ConfigurationManager to read the connection string from a Web.config file. It then uses System.Data.Common.DbConnection to represent a database connection. It also uses System.Data.SqlClient to work directly with a SQL Server database. Finally, it shows how you can use the DataAdapter.Fill method to load a DataTable directly from a SQL Server database.

Sample of Visual Basic Code

```
Dim pubs As ConnectionStringSettings
pubs = ConfigurationManager.ConnectionStrings("PubsData")

Dim connection As DbConnection = New SqlConnection()
connection.ConnectionString = pubs.ConnectionString

Dim cmd As SqlCommand = CType(connection.CreateCommand(), SqlCommand)
cmd.CommandType = CommandType.Text
cmd.CommandText = "SELECT pub_id, pub_name FROM publishers"

Dim pubsDataSet As New DataSet("Pubs")
Dim da As New SqlDataAdapter(cmd)
da.Fill(pubsDataSet, "publishers")
```

Sample of C# Code

```
ConnectionStringSettings pubs =
    ConfigurationManager.ConnectionStrings["PubsData"];
DbConnection connection = new SqlConnection(pubs.ConnectionString);
```

```
SqlCommand cmd = (SqlCommand)connection.CreateCommand();
cmd.CommandType = CommandType.Text;
cmd.CommandText = "SELECT pub_id, pub_name FROM Publishers";

SqlDataAdapter da = new SqlDataAdapter(cmd);
DataSet pubsDataSet = new DataSet("Pubs");
da.Fill(pubsDataSet, "publishers");
```

Saving Changes to the Database

The DataAdapter.Update method retrieves the changes from a DataTable object and executes the appropriate InsertCommand, UpdateCommand, or DeleteCommand to send each change to the data store on a row-by-row basis. The Update method retrieves the DataRow objects that have been changed by looking at the RowState property of each row. If the RowState is anything but Unchanged, the Update method sends the change to the database.

For the Update method to work, all four commands (select, insert, update, and delete) must be assigned to the DbDataAdapter. Normally this means creating individual DbCommand objects for each command. You can easily create the commands by using the DbDataAdapter configuration wizard, which starts when a DbDataAdapter is dropped onto a webpage. The wizard can generate stored procedures for all four commands.

Another way to populate the DbDataAdapter object's commands is to use the DbCommandBuilder object. This object creates the InsertCommand, UpdateCommand, and DeleteCommand as long as a valid SelectCommand exists.

SAVING CHANGES TO THE DATABASE IN BATCHES

One way to increase update performance is to send the changes to the database server in batches instead of sending changes on a row-by-row basis. You can do this by assigning a value to the DbDataAdapter object's UpdateBatchSize property. This property defaults to 1, which causes each change to be sent to the server on a row-by-row basis. Setting the value to 0 instructs the DbDataAdapter object to create the largest possible batch size for changes, or you can set the value to the number of changes you want to send to the server in each batch. Setting the UpdateBatchSize to a number greater than the number of changes that need to be sent is equivalent to setting it to 0.

You can confirm that the changes are being sent to the database server in batches by adding a RowUpdated event to the DbDataAdapter object. The event handler method exposes the number of rows affected in the last batch. When the UpdateBatchSize is set to 1, the RecordsAffected property is always 1. In the following code, the Publishers table contains eight rows. The pubsDataSet is filled, and then the pub_name field is modified on all eight rows. Before the Update method is executed, the UpdateBatchSize is changed to 3. When the Update method is executed, the changes are sent to the database as a batch of three changes, another batch of three changes, and, finally, a batch of two changes. This code contains a RowUpdated event handler to collect batch information, which is displayed after the Update method is executed.

```vb
Public WithEvents da As New SqlDataAdapter()
Public sb As New System.Text.StringBuilder()

Private Sub rowUpdated(ByVal sender As Object, _
    ByVal e As SqlRowUpdatedEventArgs) Handles da.RowUpdated
    sb.Append("Rows: " & e.RecordsAffected.ToString() & vbCrLf)
End Sub

Protected Sub ButtonUpdate_Click(ByVal sender As Object, _
    ByVal e As System.EventArgs) Handles ButtonUpdate.Click

    Dim pubs As ConnectionStringSettings
    pubs = ConfigurationManager.ConnectionStrings("PubsData")
    Dim connection As DbConnection = New SqlConnection()
    connection.ConnectionString = pubs.ConnectionString
    Dim cmd As SqlCommand = _
        CType(connection.CreateCommand(), SqlCommand)
    cmd.CommandType = CommandType.Text
    cmd.CommandText = "SELECT * FROM publishers"
    Dim pubsDataSet As New DataSet("Pubs")
    da.SelectCommand = cmd
    Dim bldr As New SqlCommandBuilder(da)
    da.Fill(pubsDataSet, "publishers")

    'Modify data here
    For Each dr As DataRow In pubsDataSet.Tables("publishers").Rows
     dr("pub_name") = "Updated Toys " _
        + DateTime.Now.Minute.ToString() _
        + DateTime.Now.Second.ToString()
    Next
    da.UpdateBatchSize = 3
    da.Update(pubsDataSet, "publishers")

    Dim lbl As Label = GetLabel(275, 20)
    lbl.Text = sb.ToString()

End Sub
```

Sample of C# Code

```csharp
public SqlDataAdapter da = new SqlDataAdapter();
public System.Text.StringBuilder sb = new System.Text.StringBuilder();

private void rowUpdated(object sender, SqlRowUpdatedEventArgs e)
{
    sb.Append("Rows: " + e.RecordsAffected.ToString() + "\r\n");
}
```

```
protected void ButtonUpdate_Click(object sender, EventArgs e)
{
    //event subscription is normally placed in constructor but is here
    //to encapsulate the sample
    da.RowUpdated += new SqlRowUpdatedEventHandler(rowUpdated);
    ConnectionStringSettings pubs =
        ConfigurationManager.ConnectionStrings["PubsData"];
    DbConnection connection = new SqlConnection(pubs.ConnectionString);
    SqlCommand cmd = (SqlCommand)connection.CreateCommand();
    cmd.CommandType = CommandType.Text;
    cmd.CommandText = "SELECT * FROM Publishers";
    da.SelectCommand = cmd;
    DataSet pubsDataSet = new DataSet("Pubs");
    SqlCommandBuilder bldr = new SqlCommandBuilder(da);
    da.Fill(pubsDataSet, "publishers");
    //Modify data here
    foreach (DataRow dr in pubsDataSet.Tables["publishers"].Rows)
    {
        dr["pub_name"] = "Updated Toys "
            + DateTime.Now.Minute.ToString()
            + DateTime.Now.Second.ToString();
    }
    da.UpdateBatchSize = 3;
    da.Update(pubsDataSet, "publishers");

    //if event subscription is in the constructor, no need to
    //remove it here. . ..
    da.RowUpdated -= new SqlRowUpdatedEventHandler(rowUpdated);

    Label lbl = GetLabel(275, 20);
    lbl.Text = sb.ToString();
}
```

Creating Typed DataSets

A typed DataSet is a DataSet that is based on strongly typed objects that exist at design time (and are typically auto-generated by Visual Studio). Typed DataSets allow you to program against the actual table and field schemas for your database instead of relying on strings. For example, if you have a DataSet called salesData that includes a company table, you can access this table as follows.

Sample of Visual Basic Code

```
Dim companyTable as DataTable = salesData.Tables("Company")
```

Sample of C# Code

```
DataTable companyTable = salesData.Tables["Company"];
```

However, if you misspell the name of the table, an exception is thrown at run time. This can be problematic. The same is true for fields in the table. Each is typically accessed through a string value. In addition, each field is only type-checked at run time. You can overcome all of these issues at compile time by creating a typed DataSet.

A typed DataSet inherits from the DataSet object. You define a property for each of the tables in the DataSet. You do the same for each field in the table. For example, a typed DataSet class might contain a property called Company that represents the Company table and has its schema as properties. You can access this table as shown in the following code. In this example, a compile-time error is generated if Company is not spelled correctly.

Sample of Visual Basic Code

```
Dim companyTable as DataTable = vendorData.Company
```

Sample of C# Code

```
DataTable companyTable = vendorData.Company;
```

You can provide an XML Schema Definition (XSD) file to generate a typed DataSet class. You can also use the DataSet Editor to graphically create and modify an XSD file, which, in turn, can be used to generate the typed DataSet class. Figure 11-3 shows the DataSet Editor working with the pubs database. You can drag tables from the database onto the design surface. Visual Studio then generates the appropriate typed DataSet class for you to work with.

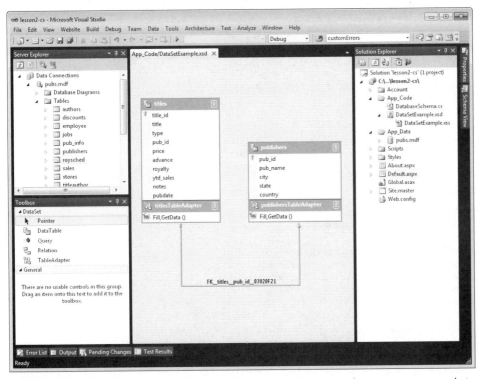

FIGURE 11-3 The DataSet template contains an XML schema definition and generates source code to create a typed DataSet.

Code is written differently against typed DataSets. With typed DataSets, you can write against strongly typed objects. As you will see in an upcoming section, this also changes the way you write your LINQ queries.

Querying with LINQ to DataSet

The DataSet object already exposes DataTable objects as IEnumerable collections of data. Therefore, writing LINQ queries against a DataSet or DataTable are not much different than writing against other collections of data. As an example, imagine that you have a large DataTable that contains employee records. Assume that you have to write a LINQ query against it. You first define your query variable of a type that implements the IEnumerable(T) interface. This ensures that the query can execute and iterate over the data. You then define this variable by using the From <element> In <collection> LINQ syntax. You can then define a Where clause, Order By clause, and more. The following code shows an example of defining a query against a single database table (employee) stored in a DataSet object.

Sample of Visual Basic Code

```
Dim employees As DataTable = _
    MyDataProvider.GetEmployeeData()

Dim query As EnumerableRowCollection(Of DataRow) = _
    From employee In employees.AsEnumerable() _
    Where employee.Field(Of Decimal)("salary") > 20 _
    Order By employee.Field(Of Decimal)("salary") _
    Select employee

For Each emp As DataRow In query
    Response.Write(emp.Field(Of String)("LastName") & ": ")
    Response.Write(emp.Field(Of Decimal)("salary") & "<br />")
Next
```

Sample of C# Code

```
DataTable employees =
    MyDataProvider.GetEmployeeData();

EnumerableRowCollection<DataRow> query =
    from employee in employees.AsEnumerable()
    where employee.Field<Decimal>("salary") > 20
    orderby employee.Field<Decimal>("salary")
    select employee;

foreach (DataRow emp in query)
{
    Response.Write(emp.Field<String>("LastName") + ": ");
    Response.Write(emp.Field<Decimal>("salary") + "<br />");
}
```

The query in the example is a *deferred query* (like all LINQ queries). It does not actually execute until it is iterated over with For...Each, ToList, or a similar method that forces the query to execute.

Notice the call to AsEnumerable. This returns an IEnumerable list for the query to work with. Next, notice that table fields are referenced by their data type and name. This is because the query is going against a generic DataSet rather than a strongly typed DataSet.

You can use LINQ to DataSet to perform many different queries against your data, including adding calculated fields to the data based on data groupings. As an example, suppose you want to calculate the average salary in the employee DataSet. You can group the DataSet as a single group (and thus return a single row). You then use the Select New construct to define new fields. You can then use the group definition to calculate the average of a specified field. The following code shows an example.

Sample of Visual Basic Code

```
Dim queryAvg = _
    From employee In employees.AsEnumerable() _
    Group employee By empId = "" Into g = Group _
    Select New With _
    { _
        .AvgSalary = g.Average(Function(employee) _
            employee.Field(Of Decimal)("Salary")) _
    }

For Each emp In queryAvg
    Response.Write(emp.AvgSalary & "<br />")
Next
```

Sample of C# Code

```
var queryAvg =
    from employee in employees.AsEnumerable()
    group employee by "" into g
    select new
    {
        AvgSalary = g.Average(employee =>
            employee.Field<Decimal>("Salary"))
    };

foreach (var emp in queryAvg)
{
    Response.Write(emp.AvgSalary.ToString() + "<br />");
}
```

LINQ provides an easier way to get at this same data. You can use the methods of the enumerator to get at counts, maximum values, averages, and more. This type of query is also called a *singleton query*, because it returns a single value. The following code uses a lambda expression to pass the salary field from the employee table into the Average function.

```
Dim avgSalary As Decimal = _
    employees.AsEnumerable.Average(Function(employee) _
    employee.Field(Of Decimal)("Salary"))

Response.Write(avgSalary.ToString())
```

Sample of C# Code

```
Decimal avgSalary =
    employees.AsEnumerable().Average(
    employee => employee.Field<Decimal>("Salary"));

Response.Write(avgSalary.ToString());
```

Querying with Typed DataSet Objects

Recall that a typed DataSet inherits from the DataSet class, so it functionally is a DataSet that contains multiple DataTable objects. However, these DataTable objects are exposed as strongly typed objects, collections, and fields. This makes the LINQ queries you write strongly typed too. You do not need to use the Field method. Instead, you can query directly against the Tablename.Fieldname construct.

As an example, suppose you created the typed DataSet shown back in Figure 11-3. You can load this typed DataSet by passing it to a DataAdapter instance. You can then use LINQ to DataSet to write a strongly typed LINQ query against the cached results. The following code shows just that. The results are then bound to a GridView control.

Sample of Visual Basic Code

```
Dim pubsCnn As ConnectionStringSettings = _
    ConfigurationManager.ConnectionStrings("PubsData")

Dim pubs As PubsDataSet = New PubsDataSet()

Dim adp As SqlDataAdapter = New SqlDataAdapter(
    "select * from publishers;", pubsCnn.ConnectionString)

adp.Fill(pubs, "publishers")

Dim pubsQuery As IEnumerable(Of DataRow) =
    From p In pubs.publishers
    Where p.country = "USA"
    Select p

GridView1.DataSource = pubsQuery
GridView1.DataBind()
```

Sample of C# Code

```
ConnectionStringSettings pubsCnn =
    ConfigurationManager.ConnectionStrings["PubsData"];
```

```
PubsDataSet pubs = new PubsDataSet();

SqlDataAdapter adp = new SqlDataAdapter(
    "select * from publishers;", pubsCnn.ConnectionString);

adp.Fill(pubs, "publishers");

IEnumerable<DataRow> pubsQuery = from p in pubs.publishers
                where p.country == "USA"
                select p;

GridView1.DataSource = pubsQuery;
GridView1.DataBind();
```

Cross-Table LINQ to DataSet Queries

You can use the LINQ join feature discussed in Lesson 1 to join two different DataSet objects in a single query and produce a new result set. The following code shows an example.

First, the DataSet is loaded with two tables from the pubs database (publishers and titles). Note that this code is not shown but simply uses a DataAdapter to fill two different tables in the same DataSet.

Next, both DataTable objects are set to variables. These variables are used in the LINQ query in the join clause. Notice that the tables are simply joined on the pub_id field. The results of the query are then pushed into a new anonymous type. Finally, the query is bound to a GridView control for display to a user.

Sample of Visual Basic Code

```
Dim dbSchema As DatabaseSchema = New DatabaseSchema()

Dim pubs As DataSet = dbSchema.GetPubsData()

Dim publishers As DataTable = pubs.Tables("publishers")
Dim titles As DataTable = pubs.Tables("titles")

Dim pubQuery =
    From title In titles.AsEnumerable()
    Join pub In publishers.AsEnumerable()
    On title.Field(Of String)("pub_id") Equals
        pub.Field(Of String)("pub_id")
    Where title.Field(Of Decimal)("price") < 10
    Order By title.Field(Of String)("title")
    Select New With
    {
        .Publisher = pub.Field(Of String)("pub_name"),
        .Title = title.Field(Of String)("title"),
        .Price = title.Field(Of Decimal)("price")
    }

GridView1.DataSource = pubQuery
GridView1.DataBind()
```

```csharp
DatabaseSchema dbSchema = new DatabaseSchema();

DataSet pubs = dbSchema.GetPubsData();

DataTable publishers = pubs.Tables["publishers"];
DataTable titles = pubs.Tables["titles"];

var pubQuery =
    from title in titles.AsEnumerable()
    join pub in publishers.AsEnumerable()
    on title.Field<string>("pub_id") equals
        pub.Field<string>("pub_id")
    where title.Field<decimal>("price") < 10
    orderby title.Field<string>("title")
    select new
    {
        Publisher = pub.Field<string>("pub_name"),
        Title = title.Field<string>("title"),
        Price = title.Field<decimal>("price")
    };

GridView1.DataSource = pubQuery;
GridView1.DataBind();
```

Comparing Data in DataSet Objects

You can use LINQ features to compare data contained in one or more DataTables. These features include the following operators:

- **Distinct**   Used to return distinct DataRows in a collection
- **Union**   Joins two like DataTable objects together
- **Intersect**   Returns a collection of DataRow objects that appear in both DataTable objects
- **Except**   Returns those DataRow objects that are different between two DataTable objects

You use the DataRowComparer when using these operators. This ensures that DataRows are compared against one another for equal values across columns.

In the following example, a DataSet is created from the titles table in the pubs database. A LINQ query then runs to get all price values for books that have sold more than 1000 copies. The Distinct method is then used to show a list of distinct prices across this list of books.

Sample of Visual Basic Code

```vbnet
Dim dbSchema As DatabaseSchema = New DatabaseSchema()

Dim titlesDs As DataSet = dbSchema.GetTitles()
Dim titleQuery = From title In titlesDs.Tables("titles")
                 Where title.Field(Of Integer)("ytd_sales") > 1000
                 Order By title.Field(Of Decimal)("price")
                 Select title.Field(Of Decimal)("price")

Dim prices = titleQuery.Distinct()

GridView1.DataSource = prices
GridView1.DataBind()
```

Sample of C# Code

```csharp
DatabaseSchema dbSchema = new DatabaseSchema();

DataSet titlesDs = dbSchema.GetTitles();
var titleQuery = from title in titlesDs.Tables["titles"].AsEnumerable()
                 where title.Field<int>("ytd_sales") > 1000
                 orderby title.Field<decimal>("price")
                 select title.Field<decimal>("price");

var prices = titleQuery.Distinct();

GridView1.DataSource = prices;
GridView1.DataBind();
```

As another example, the following code executes two queries against the titles DataSet. The first query returns all titles that were written with an advance of $5,000 or more. The second query returns all titles with year-to-date sales greater than $3,000. These queries are each converted into separate DataTable objects by using the CopyToDataTable method. Finally, the Intersect method is called to return all titles that match between the two DataSet objects.

Sample of Visual Basic Code

```vbnet
Dim dbSchema As DatabaseSchema = New DatabaseSchema()

Dim titlesDs As DataSet = dbSchema.GetTitles()

Dim titleAdvQuery = From title In titlesDs.Tables("titles")
                    Where title.Field(Of Decimal)("advance") > 5000
                    Select title

Dim titleSalesQuery = From title In titlesDs.Tables("titles")
                      Where title.Field(Of Integer)("ytd_sales") > 3000
                      Select title

Dim dtAdvance As DataTable = titleAdvQuery.CopyToDataTable()
Dim dtSales As DataTable = titleSalesQuery.CopyToDataTable()

Dim advanceSales As IEnumerable(Of DataRow) = _
    dtAdvance.AsEnumerable().Intersect( _
    dtSales.AsEnumerable(), DataRowComparer.Default)

GridView1.DataSource = advanceSales.CopyToDataTable()
GridView1.DataBind()
```

Sample of C# Code

```csharp
DatabaseSchema dbSchema = new DatabaseSchema();

DataSet titlesDs = dbSchema.GetTitles();

var titleAdvQuery = from title in titlesDs.Tables["titles"].AsEnumerable()
                    where title.Field<decimal>("advance") > 5000
                    select title;
```

```
var titleSalesQuery = from title in titlesDs.Tables["titles"].AsEnumerable()
                      where title.Field<int>("ytd_sales") > 3000
                      select title;

DataTable dtAdvance = titleAdvQuery.CopyToDataTable();
DataTable dtSales = titleSalesQuery.CopyToDataTable();

IEnumerable<DataRow> advanceSales = dtAdvance.AsEnumerable().Intersect(
    dtSales.AsEnumerable(), DataRowComparer.Default);

GridView1.DataSource = advanceSales.CopyToDataTable();
GridView1.DataBind();
```

LINQ to SQL

LINQ to SQL is a technology in ADO.NET built to work directly with a SQL Server database to enable LINQ-style programming against it. With LINQ to SQL, you build an object-relational (O/R) map that connects .NET classes to database elements. This O/R map can be built in several ways (which will be discussed later in this section). After the map is built, you can program against your database as if you were writing code against objects (because you are). This greatly simplifies and accelerates database development. Instead of writing SQL script and code that is not strongly typed, you are able to write .NET, object-oriented code to work with your database.

> **NOTE   LINQ TO SQL VS. LINQ TO ENTITIES**
>
> Microsoft has released the Entity Framework, which provides similar features as LINQ to SQL but is not so directly tied to SQL Server. If you are writing a new application, you might want to consider the Entity Framework as an alternative to LINQ to SQL. The Entity Framework is covered in the next section.

To enable LINQ to SQL programming, you must follow a few basic steps before you can get started writing LINQ code against your database. The following is an overview:

1. Add a reference to the System.Data.Linq namespace to your project. This namespace contains the DataContext object, which is the core object that connects the database to the O/R map.

2. Create an O/R map that connects objects to data tables, columns, and more. There are multiple ways to create an O/R map in the .NET Framework. We look at three of them in the next section.

3. Connect to your database by using the LINQ to SQL DataContext object. Again, this object represents the pipeline between the database and your objects.

4. Use the features of LINQ and LINQ to SQL to work with your database. For instance, you can write queries by using strongly typed objects. In addition, you can use the features of LINQ to SQL to insert, update, and delete data.

It is important to note that LINQ to SQL is part of ADO.NET. Therefore, you can use it with other ADO.NET components, such as transactions. This allows you to build LINQ to SQL items but still take advantage of any existing objects you've written against ADO.NET. In addition, LINQ to SQL allows you to use your existing database code, including stored procedures.

Mapping Objects to Relational Data

To program against objects that represent your database, you have to create them. The good news is that the Visual Studio tools provide two automated code generators that help you create the O/R map objects. In addition, you can manually code your own O/R map for full control over the mapping for specific scenarios. This section shows how to use all three options.

MAPPING WITH THE VISUAL STUDIO DESIGNER TOOL

The easiest way to build your O/R map is by using the Visual Studio LINQ to SQL designer. This provides a design surface on which you can build your classes. To get started, you add a LINQ to SQL Classes file to your project. You can do so through the Add New Item dialog box.

The LINQ to SQL Classes file is of type DBML, which stands for database markup language. The file contains XML that defines the metadata of your database. Behind this XML file, you will find a layout file for use by the designer, and a code file (.vb or .cs). The code file contains the actual objects against which you write your database code.

You build your map by dragging database entities from Visual Studio's Server Explorer onto the design surface. Visual Studio does the rest by generating the code that relates these entities. The designer also understands foreign key relationships in the database. It implements these same relationships in the class model. In addition, you can drag stored procedures from the database into a method window to generate code that allows these stored procedures to act as .NET methods.

As an example, suppose you are working with the pubs database and want to generate an O/R map for the author and title database tables. You can do so by opening the DBML file in the designer, opening the database in Server Explorer, and then dragging tables from Server Explorer onto the design surface. Figure 11-4 shows an example. Notice the byroyalty stored procedure (in the upper right) added to the method window of the DBML design surface.

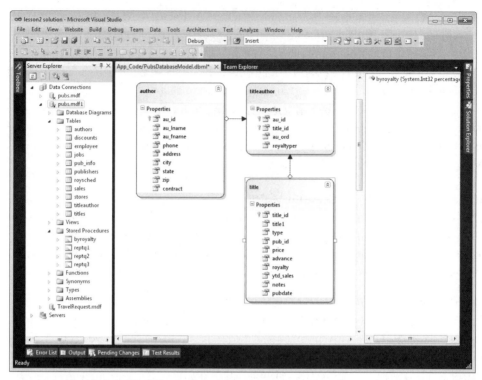

FIGURE 11-4 The LINQ to SQL O/R mapping tool.

What is generated by this designer is XML that represents the metadata of the database (including the stored procedure) and code that allows a developer to work with the database by using objects. For example, the top portion of the XML for the pubs DBML file table looks as follows. Notice that the DBML includes its connection string information. (Only the author table is shown.)

```xml
<?xml version="1.0" encoding="utf-8"?>
<Database Name="pubs" Class="PubsDatabaseModelDataContext"
        xmlns="http://schemas.microsoft.com/linqtosql/dbml/2007">
   <Connection Mode="WebSettings"
              ConnectionString="Data Source=.\SQLEXPRESS;AttachDbFilename=
|DataDirectory|\pubs.mdf;Integrated Security=True;User Instance=True"
              SettingsObjectName="System.Configuration.ConfigurationManager.
ConnectionStrings"
              SettingsPropertyName="PubsData" Provider="System.Data.SqlClient" />
   <Table Name="dbo.authors" Member="authors">
      <Type Name="author">
         <Column Name="au_id" Type="System.String" DbType="VarChar(11) NOT NULL"
                IsPrimaryKey="true" CanBeNull="false" />
         <Column Name="au_lname" Type="System.String" DbType="VarChar(40) NOT NULL"
                CanBeNull="false" />
         <Column Name="au_fname" Type="System.String" DbType="VarChar(20) NOT NULL"
                CanBeNull="false" />
```

```
            <Column Name="phone" Type="System.String" DbType="Char(12) NOT NULL"
                CanBeNull="false" />
            <Column Name="address" Type="System.String" DbType="VarChar(40)"
                CanBeNull="true" />
            <Column Name="city" Type="System.String" DbType="VarChar(20)"
                CanBeNull="true" />
            <Column Name="state" Type="System.String" DbType="Char(2)"
                CanBeNull="true" />
            <Column Name="zip" Type="System.String" DbType="Char(5)"
                CanBeNull="true" />
            <Column Name="contract" Type="System.Boolean" DbType="Bit NOT NULL"
                CanBeNull="false" />
            <Association Name="author_titleauthor" Member="titleauthors" ThisKey="au_id"
                    OtherKey="au_id" Type="titleauthor" />
        </Type>
    </Table>
```

The code generated by the tool is generated in either Visual Basic or C#, depending on your preference. The code defines an object for each table and properties within the object for each field of the table. This code is very readable and easy to understand. You can examine it in the code-behind file for your DBML model. You will see an example of writing some of this code yourself in an upcoming section.

MAPPING WITH THE COMMAND-LINE TOOL

You can use the SqlMetal.exe command-line tool to generate both DBML files and O/R code for a database. This tool is very useful for large databases, for which it might not be practical to drag objects onto a designer. The files it generates, however, are the same: a DBML file and a code file (.vb or .cs).

There are many options available from this tool, but there are a few key ones. First, you can simply point to a database (MDF) file as the basis of the generation. If you are using a SQL Server database server, you can instead define the /server, /database, /user, and /password options to set connection information. Alternatively, you can use /conn to define a connection string. Another option is /language for setting the language of the file you want to generate (the options are vb or cs).

You typically first generate a DBML file. You can indicate the type of file through the /dbml option or the /code option. To do so, launch a Visual Studio command prompt (Start | All Programs | Microsoft Visual Studio 2010 | Visual Studio Tools). You might then want to change the directory to the location where you want your DBML file to be generated. The following command line shows an example of generating a DBML file. (For C#, change the language parameter to cs.)

```
sqlmetal "C:\Code\pubs.mdf" /language:vb /dbml:Pubs.dbml
```

To create the code, you simply indicate the /code option as follows.

```
sqlmetal "C:\Code\pubs.mdf" /language:vb /code:Pubs.vb
```

You can then add these files to the App_Code directory of your project. You work with them in the same way as with any other DBML file.

MAPPING OBJECTS TO ENTITIES IN THE CODE EDITOR

The third option for connecting classes to database objects is to write the code yourself. This can provide granular control, but it can also be a lot of work. It is recommended that you use an automated tool, but this section demonstrates how you can define your own O/R map.

To get started, you first create a class file. At the top of the class file, you should define an Imports statement (a using statement in C#) to include the following namespaces.

Sample of Visual Basic Code

```
Imports System.Data.Linq
Imports System.Data.Linq.Mapping
```

Sample of C# Code

```
using System.Data.Linq;
using System.Data.Linq.Mapping;
```

The next step is to link your class to a table in the database through the Table attribute. The following code shows an example.

Sample of Visual Basic Code

```
<Table(Name:="Authors")> _
Public Class Author
```

Sample of C# Code

```
 [Table(Name="Authors")]
public class Author
{
```

The next step is to create properties on the object, with the Column attribute applied to each, that map the database table columns to the specified property. This class lets you set the name of the database field (if it is different from the name of the property), the variable you intend to use to store the field's value, the data type, whether the item is a primary key, and more. The following code shows an example of two properties mapped to columns in the authors table of the pubs database.

Sample of Visual Basic Code

```
Private _authorId As String
<Column(IsPrimaryKey:=True, Storage:="_authorId", name:="au_id")> _
Public Property Id() As String
  Get
    Return _authorId
  End Get
  Set(ByVal value As String)
    _authorId = value
  End Set
End Property

Private _lastName As String
<Column(Storage:="_lastName", name:="au_lname")> _
Public Property LastName() As String
  Get
    Return _lastName
```

```
    End Get
    Set(ByVal value As String)
      _lastName = value
    End Set
 End Property
```

Sample of C# Code

```csharp
private string _authorId;
[Column(IsPrimaryKey=true, Storage="_authorId", Name="au_id")]
public string Id
{
  get
  {
    return _authorId;
  }
  set
  {
    _authorId = value;
  }
}

private string _lastName;
[Column(Storage = "_lastName", Name = "au_lname")]
public string LastName
{
  get
  {
    return _lastName;
  }
  set
  {
    _lastName = value;
  }
}
```

The final step is to create a class that exposes your tables. You do so by inheriting from the DataContext object. This object acts as the go-between for your database and your objects. You then expose your database and its tables as properties of this class. You can define the class to automatically get a connection to the database when it is created. Alternatively, you can pass a database connection string to it. The following example shows how to provide the connection string to the constructor of the class.

Sample of Visual Basic Code

```vbnet
Public Class PubsDb
  Inherits DataContext

  Public Authors As Table(Of Author)
  Public Titles As Table(Of Title)

  Public Sub New(ByVal connection As String)
    MyBase.New(connection)
  End Sub

End Class
```

Sample of C# Code

```csharp
public class PubsDb: DataContext
{
  public Table<Author> Authors;
  public Table<Title> Titles;

  public PubsDb(string connection) : base(connection)
  {
  }
}
```

When your code is complete, you can use your custom O/R map class as you would one that was generated from a code generator. If you add other (nonmapped) properties, fields, and methods, they are ignored at run time. In this way, you control the logic you intend to put in your classes when you write your O/R map.

Querying Data with LINQ to SQL

You query data with LINQ to SQL much like you write any LINQ query. The big difference is the simplified way in which you connect to the actual data and the fact that you can write your queries by using the O/R mapped objects.

If you are using an auto-generated DBML file, the file will inherit from DataContext and will already be set up to get a connection to the database. You simply need to create an instance of this file and write your query. As an example, the following code shows how to define a query against the authors table and then bind the results to a GridView.

Sample of Visual Basic Code

```vb
Dim pubs As PubsDatabaseModelDataContext = _
    New PubsDatabaseModelDataContext()

Dim authQuery = From auth In pubs.authors
                Where auth.state = "CA"
                Order By auth.au_lname
                Select auth

GridView1.DataSource = authQuery
GridView1.DataBind()
```

Sample of C# Code

```csharp
PubsDatabaseModelDataContext pubs =
    new PubsDatabaseModelDataContext();


var authQuery = from auth in pubs.authors
                where auth.state == "CA"
                orderby auth.au_lname
                select auth;

GridView1.DataSource = authQuery;
GridView1.DataBind();
```

Notice in this example that you are using the strong types for tables, collections, and fields. This makes the programming easier, faster, and more readable because types are checked at compile time.

Inserting, Updating, and Deleting with LINQ to SQL

LINQ to SQL makes inserting, updating, and deleting data in your database a very simple process. It creates the connections between your O/R map and your database. You simply need to make a modification to object instances and then save the changes. You work with your object model to add a new instance to a collection, modify an object, or remove an object from the collection. When your change is complete, you call the SubmitChanges method of the DataContext object to write the results back to the database.

For example, if you want to add a new author to the pubs database, you start by creating a new author object. You then add it to the Authors table by using the InsertOnSubmit method. When you are ready to submit all changes, you call SubmitChanges. The following code shows this example.

Sample of Visual Basic Code

```
Dim pubs As PubsDatabaseModelDataContext = _
    New PubsDatabaseModelDataContext()

Dim auth As New author
auth.au_id = "000-00-0001"
auth.au_fname = "Monica"
auth.au_lname = "Brink"
auth.address = "555 Some St."
auth.state = "WA"
auth.city = "Redmond"
auth.contract = False
auth.phone = "555-1212"
auth.zip = "12345"

pubs.authors.InsertOnSubmit(auth)
pubs.SubmitChanges()
```

Sample of C# Code

```
PubsDatabaseModelDataContext pubs =
    new PubsDatabaseModelDataContext();

author auth = new author();
auth.au_id = "000-00-0001";
auth.au_fname = "Monica";
auth.au_lname = "Brink";
auth.address = "555 Some St.";
auth.state = "WA";
auth.city = "Redmond";
auth.contract = false;
auth.phone = "555-1212";
auth.zip = "12345";

pubs.authors.InsertOnSubmit(auth);
pubs.SubmitChanges();
```

Deleting data works much the same way. You call the DeleteOnSubmit method instead. You pass the instance you want to delete to this method. You then call SubmitChanges.

To update data, you first retrieve the data by using a query (or by using the GetTable method of the DataContext object). You then update the data and call SubmitChanges to save your changes to the database.

LINQ to Entities

LINQ to Entities works in a manner that is similar to that of LINQ to SQL. You define a model to represent your application domain. You then create a map between this model and your actual data source. You can then load data into the model and query against it by using LINQ. However, LINQ to Entities uses the ADO.NET Entity Framework as a basis for the models. These models can be created for any data source (not just for SQL Server).

The ADO.NET Entity Framework allows you to create a conceptual model of your application domain. This ensures that you write application code against the conceptual domain objects rather than directly against a relational database. This allows your model and database to evolve independently. If changes need to be made to either, you only need to change the mappings. In this way, you can even change your storage schemas without having to change your actual application code. You would just change the mapping.

Creating an Entity Model

You create an Entity Framework model by using the ADO.NET Entity Data Model template from the Add New Item dialog box in Visual Studio. This file is an EDMX file. Like a LINQ to SQL DBML file, this file has an XML representation of the schema (which can be edited in the designer). It also includes a code-behind class file that contains the actual entity objects in your model as well as the database connectivity and the table and column mappings.

When you add a new ADO.NET Entity Data Model to your website, Visual Studio walks you through the Entity Data Model Wizard. Here you can choose to create your model from scratch or generate it from an existing database structure. You can also select the connection to an actual database. Finally, you select the items you want to include in your model. Figure 11-5 shows an example. Notice that you can also pluralize or singularize object names to make sure individual objects are singular and collections of those objects have plural names.

When you have finished using the wizard to associate your entities with their data source counterparts, Visual Studio generates the EDMX file. Again, this includes a definition of the current database structure, an object structure, and a mapping between these two structures. Figure 11-6 shows an example of the pubs database generated as an Entity Framework model.

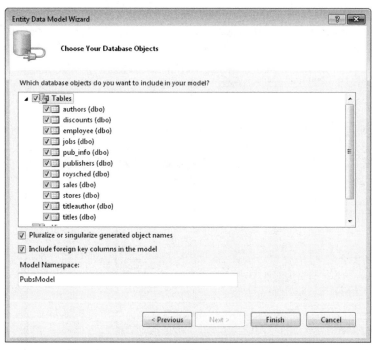

FIGURE 11-5 Using the Entity Data Model Wizard to create an Entity Framework model of an existing data source.

FIGURE 11-6 The Entity Data Model as laid out in Visual Studio.

You can use the Visual Studio tools to edit this model and the related mapping. For example, by default, the object model is generated as a 1:1 mapping with the database. The object model includes the name of classes and properties. Figure 11-7 shows the Author class selected with the mapping editor open. Notice that the class has been renamed along with all the properties of the class. However, the map is still defined to connect this object and these properties to their counterparts in the database.

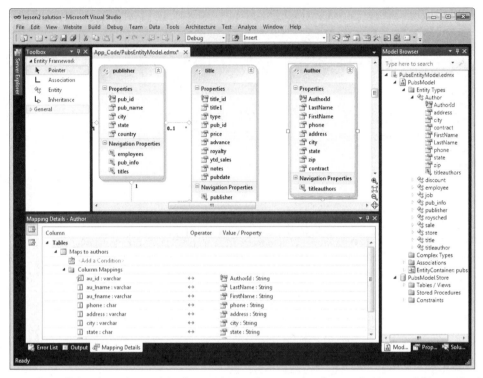

FIGURE 11-7 Using the entity model editor to change the structure of an application model but maintain the mapping back to the database.

These tools allow you to do several additional things, such as generate a database from the model, validate the model mapping against a data source, map to stored procedures, and update the database portion of the model from an actual database. Notice the Model Browser in Figure 11-7 (on the right side). You can clearly see here that the model (top) is independent of the database information (bottom).

Writing LINQ to Entities Queries

You can use what you've learned thus far to write LINQ to Entities queries. You simply create a new instance of your entity model, and then you can write queries against the data it represents.

An entity model inherits from System.Data.Objects.ObjectContext. This context object provides access to your application model and provides functionality to map that model to the data source. The following code shows a basic example of creating a new instance of an entity model and then writing a query against the Authors collection. Note that the ObjectContext is wrapped in a using statement. This is not required but is good practice, to make sure that the context is properly disposed when the data retrieval is finished.

Sample of Visual Basic Code

```
Using pubs As New PubsModel.pubsEntities()

    Dim authQuery = From a In pubs.Authors
                    Where a.State = "CA"
                    Order By a.LastName
                    Select a

    GridView1.DataSource = authQuery
    GridView1.DataBind()

End Using
```

Sample of C# Code

```
using (PubsModel.pubsEntities pubs = new PubsModel.pubsEntities())
{
    var authQuery = from a in pubs.Authors
                    where a.state == "CA"
                    orderby a.LastName
                    select a;

    GridView1.DataSource = authQuery;
    GridView1.DataBind();
}
```

Of course, you can write more complex queries with LINQ to Entities (as you can with all LINQ data sources). You can also take advantage of the entity model relationships between objects. You will see an example of this in the upcoming practice.

1. When writing a LINQ query against a standard DataSet, how do you access the DataTable and the column or columns you want to query against?

2. What are three ways to create an O/R map by using LINQ to SQL?

3. From what class does a LINQ to Entities model inherit?

Quick Check Answers

1. Because a standard DataSet is not strongly typed, you must use the DataSet.Tables and DataTable.Field properties to access the table and its columns in a LINQ query. You pass the names (as string values) to these methods.

2. You can use the LINQ to SQL Classes template to create a DBML file and drag tables onto the design surface. You can also use the command-line tool, SqlMetal. Finally, you can code your entities manually as class files that use the System.Data.Linq.Mapping attributes to identify tables and columns.

3. An entity model inherits from the System.Data.Objects.ObjectContext class. This class provides the mapping from an application model to a data source.

PRACTICE **Working with LINQ to Entities**

In this practice, you create a website and define an entity model. You then use LINQ to Entities to work with this data on a webpage.

> **ON THE COMPANION MEDIA**
>
> If you encounter a problem completing an exercise, you can find the completed projects in the samples installed from this book's companion CD. For more information about the project files and other content on the CD, see "Using the Companion Media" in this book's Introduction.

EXERCISE 1 Creating the ASP.NET Website and Entity Model

In this exercise, you create the website, define the XML file, and write LINQ queries to work with the XML.

1. Open Visual Studio and create a new ASP.NET website called **LinqEntityModelExample** by using either C# or Visual Basic.

2. Add the pubs.mdf file to the App_Data directory of your solution. You can get this file from the CD for this book.

3. Add a new ADO.NET Entity Data Model to your solution. You can do so by right-clicking the website and choosing Add New Item. Name this model **PubsEntityModel.edmx**.

Allow Visual Studio to create the App_Code directory and add the file into that directory for you. This will launch the Entity Data Model Wizard.

a. On the first page, select Generate From Database and click the Next button.

b. On the second page, select pubs.mdf as the database. Allow the wizard to save your connection string in the Web.config file as PubsEntities. Click Next.

c. On the third page, expand the Tables collection. Select publishers and titles. You can select other tables; however, this example only uses these two tables. Make sure that the check boxes are selected. Set the model namespace to PubsEntityModel. Click Finish to complete the wizard.

4. The entity designer should now be open in Visual Studio. One at a time, right-click each entity name in the model and rename it to capitalize both class names. Next, do the same for each property to rename these properties with capital letters and, optionally, more descriptive names. (Figure 11-8 provides suggested names.)

5. Open the Model Browser by right-clicking the design surface and choosing Model Browser. Expand the EntityContainer.PubsEntities folder. Expand Entity Sets. Right-click each item (Publishers1 and Title1) in turn and choose Properties. Use the Name property to eliminate the numeral 1 from each name.

Figure 11-8 shows an example of what your model should look like.

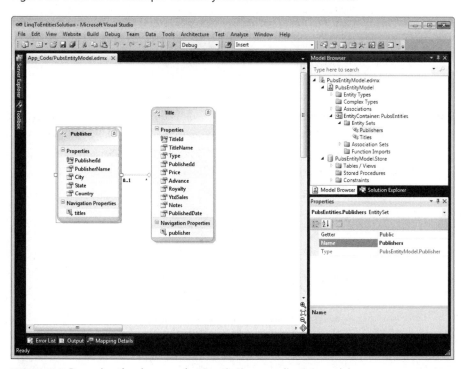

FIGURE 11-8 Renaming the classes and properties in an application model.

6. Note that this will not impact the table mapping. To verify, right-click an entity and choose Table Mapping to review.

7. You now have an entity model with which to work. You can examine the code for this model by opening the code-behind file for the model from Solution Explorer. You can also look at the EDMX markup by right-clicking the file and choosing Open With. From there you can select the Xml (Text) Editor.

EXERCISE 2 Writing the LINQ Queries and Connecting to a Webpage

In this exercise, you write queries against the entity model created previously and bind the results to controls on a webpage.

1. Continue editing the solution you created in the previous exercise. Alternatively, you can open the completed Lesson 2, Exercise 1 project in the samples installed from the CD.

2. Open the Default.aspx page. Lay out a form to include DropDownList, Button, and GridView controls. Your markup inside the MainContent content placeholder should look similar to the following.

```
<asp:Content ID="BodyContent" runat="server" ContentPlaceHolderID="MainContent">
    <h2>View Publisher Titles</h2>
    Select a publisher from the list:<br />
    <asp:DropDownList ID="DropDownListPublishers" runat="server">
    </asp:DropDownList>
    <asp:Button ID="ButtonShowTitles" runat="server" Text="Show Titles"
        onclick="ButtonShowTitles_Click" />
    <hr />
    <asp:GridView ID="GridViewTitles" runat="server">
    </asp:GridView>
</asp:Content>
```

3. Open the code-behind file for the Default.aspx page. Define a Page_Load event that populates the DropDownList control with publishers from the entity model. You should only call this code if the page is a get request (not a postback). Your code should look similar to the following.

```
Sample of Visual Basic Code
Protected Sub Page_Load(ByVal sender As Object, _
    ByVal e As System.EventArgs) Handles Me.Load

    If Not IsPostBack Then

        Dim pubs As PubsEntityModel.PubsEntities = _
            New PubsEntityModel.PubsEntities()

        Dim pubQuery = From p In pubs.Publishers
                        Order By p.PublisherName
                        Select p
```

```
        DropDownListPublishers.DataTextField = "PublisherName"
        DropDownListPublishers.DataValueField = "PublisherId"
        DropDownListPublishers.DataSource = pubQuery
        DropDownListPublishers.DataBind()

    End If

End Sub
```

Sample of C# Code
```
protected void Page_Load(object sender, EventArgs e)
{
    if (!IsPostBack)
    {
        PubsEntityModel.PubsEntities pubs = new PubsEntityModel.PubsEntities();

        var pubQuery = from p in pubs.Publishers
                       orderby p.PublisherName
                       select p;

        DropDownListPublishers.DataTextField = "PublisherName";
        DropDownListPublishers.DataValueField = "PublisherId";
        DropDownListPublishers.DataSource = pubQuery;
        DropDownListPublishers.DataBind();
    }
}
```

4. Add a click event for the Button control. Add code to this control to select titles based on the selected publisher. Bind the results to the GridView control. Your code should look as follows.

Sample of Visual Basic Code
```
Protected Sub ButtonShowTitles_Click(ByVal sender As Object, _
    ByVal e As System.EventArgs) Handles ButtonShowTitles.Click


    Using pubs As New PubsEntityModel.PubsEntities()

        Dim titleQuery = From t In pubs.Titles
                         Where t.PublisherId =
                             DropDownListPublishers.SelectedValue
                         Order By t.TitleName
                         Select t

        GridViewTitles.DataSource = titleQuery
        GridViewTitles.DataBind()

    End Using
End Sub
```

```
protected void ButtonShowTitles_Click(object sender, EventArgs e)
{
    using (PubsEntityModel.PubsEntities pubs = new
  PubsEntityModel.PubsEntities())
    {
        var titleQuery = from t in pubs.Titles
                         where t.PublisherId ==
                             DropDownListPublishers.SelectedValue
                         orderby t.TitleName
                         select t;

        GridViewTitles.DataSource = titleQuery;
        GridViewTitles.DataBind();

    }
}
```

5. Run the application and view the results.

Lesson Summary

- You can use LINQ to DataSet to write queries against in-memory representations of data tables. You use the DataAdapter object to fill a DataSet with data. You can then use the DataTable.Tables method and DataTable.Field method to reference the table and column you want to use in your query. You can also fill a strongly typed DataSet object and thus write queries against strongly typed object collections instead of just DataRow collections.

- LINQ to SQL allows you to define an O/R map as a DBML file that creates objects to represent your database tables. You can then write LINQ queries against these objects as well as insert, update, and delete data in the database.

- You can create an Entity Data Model (EDMX file) to work with LINQ to Entities. This model includes an application model, a database schema, and a map to keep the two in sync. You can then write LINQ queries against the application model objects without concerning yourself with the ADO.NET code.

Lesson Review

You can use the following questions to test your knowledge of the information in Lesson 2, "LINQ and ADO.NET." The questions are also available on the companion CD in a practice test, if you prefer to review them in electronic form.

> **NOTE   ANSWERS**
>
> Answers to these questions and explanations of why each answer choice is correct or incorrect are located in the "Answers" section at the end of the book.

1. You need to write a where clause in a LINQ query against a strongly typed DataSet of universities (from u in universities). The where clause should select all universities with more than 10,000 enrolled students. Which where clause would you write?

   A. `where u.Field("EnrolledStudents") > 10000`

   B. `where u.EnrolledStudents > 10000`

   C. **C#:** `where u["EnrolledStudents"] > 10000`
   Visual Basic: `where u("EnrolledStudents") > 10000`

   D. `where university.Fields.EnrolledStudents > 10000`

2. Which of the following objects represents a LINQ to SQL O/R map?

   A. DataSet

   B. XElement

   C. ObjectContext

   D. DataContext

3. You are using an Entity Data Model object. Which of the following lines of code will initialize this object and connect to the associated database? (Choose all that apply.)

   A. `MyModel.myEntities model = new MyModel.myEntitites()`

   B. `MyModel.myEntities model = new MyModel.myEntitites(cnnString)`

   C. `PubsModel.pubsEntities pubs = new PubsModel.pubsEntities(`
   `    new System.Data.EntityClient.EntityConnection(cnnString))`

   D. `MyModel.myEntities model = new MyModel.myEntitites(`
   `    new DataContext(cnnString))`

Case Scenarios

In the following case scenarios, you apply what you've learned in this chapter. If you have difficulty completing this work, review the material in this chapter before beginning the next chapter. You can find answers to these questions in the "Answers" section at the end of this book.

Case Scenario 1: Writing LINQ Queries

You are a developer working for the School of Fine Art. You have been asked to write a new application for working with high school transcripts of incoming freshman. Many of these transcripts are available from a central high school reporting XML web service. Others have been sent to the university as XML files to be placed into a standard directory using a standard format.

You have been asked to write a few reports that use this data. One report classifies incoming freshman according to their high school grade point average. Another report identifies new students based on high school size.

Thinking about how you will write these queries, answer the following questions:

1. What will you use to combine the results of both data sources?

2. How will you write your queries?

Case Scenario 2: Working with LINQ and ADO.NET

You are a developer working for Contoso, Ltd., a propane supplier. The company includes multiple subsidiaries that came about by acquisition. Each subsidiary has similar data. However, each database technology and schema is different. You have been asked to write a new application that each subsidiary will install to run its business. However, too much is tied to each subsidiary's database schema. Therefore, the individual databases will not be re-written.

Thinking about how you will write this application, answer the following question.

- What data access technology should you use?

Suggested Practices

To successfully master the exam objective presented in this chapter, complete the following tasks.

Write LINQ Queries

For this task, you should complete at least Practice 1 for a better understanding of writing LINQ queries. You can complete Practice 2 to gain more advanced experience.

- **Practice 1**   Create a set of custom objects as class files. Create list instances of these custom objects. Use these lists to practice writing basic LINQ queries, including joins and groups. Display your results to a webpage.

- **Practice 2**   Return to the practice for Lesson 1. Modify the code to expose the XML data as a web service formatted as JSON. Implement the button click event as a JQuery request that calls this new service without refreshing the page.

Work with LINQ and ADO.NET

You should complete Practice 1 to gain experience writing queries against LINQ to DataSets. Practice 2 will give you experience with LINQ to SQL. Complete Practice 3 to gain experience with LINQ to Entities.

- **Practice 1**   Add the Northwind database to a website project. Create and fill DataSet objects with data from the database. Write LINQ queries against this data, including transformations, joins, and groups.

- **Practice 2**   Add the Northwind database to a website project. Create a LINQ to SQL Classes DBML file for the database. Write LINQ queries against this data, including transformations, joins, and groups.

- **Practice 3**   Add the Northwind database to a website project. Create an ADO.NET Entity Data Model EDMX file by using the database. Modify the application schema to be different than the database schema. Write LINQ queries against this data, including transformations, joins, and groups.

Take a Practice Test

The practice tests on this book's companion CD offer many options. For example, you can test yourself on just the lesson review questions in this chapter, or you can test yourself on all the 70-515 certification exam objectives. You can set up the test so it closely simulates the experience of taking a certification exam, or you can set it up in study mode so you can look at the correct answers and explanations after you answer each question.

> **MORE INFO** **PRACTICE TESTS**
>
> For details about all the practice test options available, see the "How to Use the Practice Tests" section in this book's Introduction.

CHAPTER 12

Working with Data Source Controls and Data-Bound Controls

Microsoft ASP.NET provides several server controls that build on top of the features of Microsoft ADO.NET, LINQ to SQL, and LINQ to Entities. These controls simplify the development of data-driven websites. They make it easier to build webpages that access, display, manipulate, and save data. Using these controls can provide development efficiency when you are building business applications that rely heavily on data.

This chapter first presents the ASP.NET data source controls. You use these controls to configure access to data that you intend to use on a webpage. A data source can be a relational database, data stored inside of in-memory objects (such as a DataSet or an Entity Data Model), XML-based data, or data you retrieve via Microsoft Language-Integrated Query (LINQ). The second lesson in this chapter demonstrates how you can bind to data to allow users to interact with it. The lesson covers using web server controls such as GridView, Repeater, DetailsView, and many more. The last lesson presents the new Dynamic Data features of ASP.NET that allow you to easily create websites for working with the create, read, update, and delete (CRUD) operations of an entire data model that exists as either a DataContext (such as LINQ to SQL) or an ObjectContext (such as LINQ to Entities).

Exam objectives in this chapter:

- Displaying and Manipulating Data
    - Implement DataSource controls.
    - Implement data-bound controls.
    - Create and configure a Dynamic Data project.

Lessons in this chapter:

Before You Begin

To complete the lessons in this chapter, you should be familiar with developing applications with Microsoft Visual Studio 2010 by using Microsoft Visual Basic or Microsoft Visual C#. In addition, you should be comfortable with all of the following:

- The Visual Studio 2010 Integrated Development Environment (IDE)
- Using Hypertext Markup Language (HTML) and client-side scripting
- Creating ASP.NET websites and forms
- Adding web server controls to a webpage
- Understanding how generic types work in C# or Visual Basic
- Understanding how to use ADO.NET to connect to and work with data
- Writing LINQ queries and working with LINQ data–specific providers

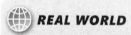 **REAL WORLD**

Mike Snell

Not all applications require developers to write custom, abstracted data layers and reusable frameworks. I've seen many simple business applications that suffered from over-engineering. Many of these smaller applications can take advantage of the simple data-binding techniques built into the Visual Studio ASP.NET tools. These applications can be created quickly, typically do not require much testing, and allow developers to focus on solving business problems rather than building frameworks and reusable objects that might never realize the goal of reusability. In fact, ASP.NET and ADO.NET can now generate a data layer for you by using LINQ to Entities.

Applications that can benefit from this approach often have a common profile: they typically have compressed schedules, are meant to be websites from beginning to end, and might fill a somewhat temporary need. When optimizing for these considerations, you might find that building data-bound applications by using the server controls in ASP.NET is fast, easy, and economical.

Lesson 1: Connecting to Data with Data Source Controls

Data source controls are server controls that you can drag onto your page at design time. A data source control does not have a direct visual component (you use data-bound controls for actual data display, as discussed in the next lesson). Instead, they allow you to declaratively define access to data found in objects, XML, and databases. This lesson examines how you can use data source controls to make connecting to and working with data in an ASP.NET webpage a fast and straightforward development process.

After this lesson, you will be able to:

- Use the data source controls (LinqDataSource, ObjectDataSource, SqlDataSource, AccessDataSource, XmlDataSource, SiteMapDataSource, and EntityDataSource) to select data and bind it to a data-bound control.
- Pass parameter values to data source controls to allow data filtering.
- Enable data sorting with data source controls.
- Modify data and save the changes to a data store by using data source controls.

Estimated lesson time: 40 minutes

Understanding the Data Source Controls

The data source controls in ASP.NET manage the tasks of selecting, updating, inserting, and deleting data on a webpage. They do so in combination with data-bound controls. The data-bound controls provide the user interface (UI) elements that allow a user to interact with the data by triggering events that call the data source controls.

There are multiple data source controls in ASP.NET. Each is meant to provide specialized access to a certain type of data, such as direct access to a database, objects, XML, or LINQ-based queries. These controls can be found in the System.Web.UI.WebControls namespace. Figure 12-1 shows an overview of the data source controls in ASP.NET.

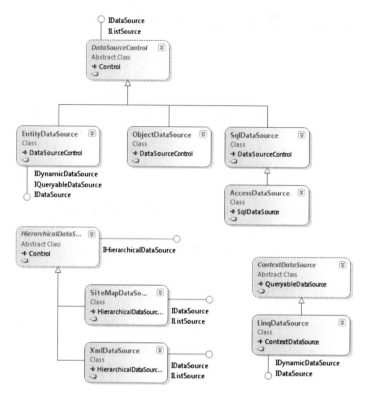

FIGURE 12-1 The DataSource web control classes.

Each data source control is used in a similar manner. You can drag the control onto your webpage from the Toolbox in Visual Studio. You can then use the Configure Data Source Wizard to connect to your data and generate markup for the data source control. Connecting to data with markup (instead of code) is referred to as *declarative data binding*, because you are declaring your data access rather than writing ADO.NET code. Figure 12-2 shows the step for selecting data in this wizard.

This wizard creates the declarative markup used to define the data source connection information. This markup can contain connection information, data manipulation statements (such as SQL), and more. The following shows an example of the SqlDataSource control's markup for connecting to the Products table in the Northwind database.

```
<asp:SqlDataSource ID="SqlDataSource1" runat="server"
    ConnectionString="<%$ ConnectionStrings:NorthwindCnnString %>"
    SelectCommand="SELECT * FROM [Alphabetical list of products]">
</asp:SqlDataSource>
```

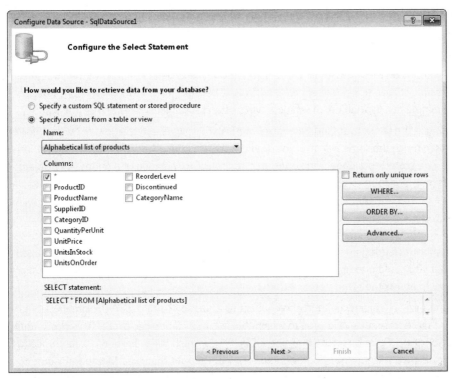

FIGURE 12-2 The Configure Data Source Wizard in Visual Studio allows you to select the data to be exposed by your data source control.

EXAM TIP

The wizard-based UI is a great tool for defining many of your data source declarations. However, it is important that you know the markup syntax for working with these controls. This will help with both programming against the controls and taking the exam. Therefore, the rest of this lesson focuses on the markup (and not the wizard-based UI).

Each data source control is specialized for the type of data with which it is meant to work. The following sections provide an overview of what makes each of these controls unique. The discussion includes some of the common uses of data source controls, such as binding, filtering, sorting, and modifying data.

Using Objects as Data Sources with ObjectDataSource

Many web applications work with a middle tier, or business layer, for retrieving and working with application data. This middle tier encapsulates database code inside classes. Web developers can then call methods on these classes to select, insert, modify, and delete data. With this structure, developers do not have to write direct ADO.NET code, because the code is written by whoever wrote the middle tier. In addition, this middle tier is often reusable across different applications.

You can use the ObjectDataSource control in ASP.NET to connect to and work with middle-tier objects in much the same way that you would work with the other data source objects. This control can be added to a page and configured to create an instance of a middle-tier object and call its methods to retrieve, insert, update, and delete data. The ObjectDataSource control is responsible for the execution lifetime of the object. It creates it and disposes of it. Therefore, the business layer code should be written in a stateless manner. Alternatively, if the business layer uses static methods (or shared methods, in Visual Basic), the ObjectDataSource can use these methods without creating an instance of the actual business object. In this case, however, keep in mind that you could end up with performance issues related to thread contention as multiple requests try to access the same static method.

You configure an ObjectDataSource to connect to a class by setting its TypeName attribute to a string that represents a valid type to which the web application has access. This class might be inside your App_Code directory or inside a DLL file to which the website has a reference (it should not be in your webpage's code-behind file). You then set the SelectMethod attribute to a valid method name on the class. The ObjectDataSource control will then call this method when the data is requested.

As an example, imagine that you need to write an interface to allow a user to manage the shipper table inside the Northwind database. You might have a business object that can return all the shippers in the database and that looks as follows.

Sample of Visual Basic Code

```vb
Public Class Shipper

    Private Shared _cnnString As String = _
            ConfigurationManager.ConnectionStrings("NorthwindConnectionString").ToString

    Public Shared Function GetAllShippers() As DataTable
        Dim adp As New SqlDataAdapter( _
            "SELECT * FROM shippers", _cnnString)

        Dim ds As New DataSet("shippers")
        adp.Fill(ds, "shippers")

        Return ds.Tables("shippers")
    End Function

End Class
```

Sample of C# Code

```csharp
public class Shipper
{
    private static string _cnnString =
        ConfigurationManager.ConnectionStrings["NorthwindConnectionString"].ToString();

    public static DataTable GetAllShippers()
    {
        SqlDataAdapter adp = new SqlDataAdapter(
            "SELECT * FROM shippers", _cnnString);

        DataSet ds = new DataSet("shippers");
        adp.Fill(ds, "shippers");

        return ds.Tables["shippers"];
    }
}
```

The Shipper class just listed returns a DataTable as a result of a call to GetAllShippers. You can configure an ObjectDataSource control to provide this data to a webpage by setting the TypeName and SelectMethod attributes as in the following code.

```
<asp:ObjectDataSource
  ID="ObjectDataSource1"
  runat="server"
  TypeName="Shipper"
  SelectMethod="GetAllShippers">
</asp:ObjectDataSource>
```

You can then use this data source control to bind to a web control (more on this in the next lesson). For example, the following markup binds the ObjectDataSource to a DetailsView control to display the information to the user.

```
<asp:DetailsView
  ID="DetailsView1"
  runat="server"
  DataSourceID="ObjectDataSource1"
  AllowPaging="true">
</asp:DetailsView>
```

Figure 12-3 shows an example of the output.

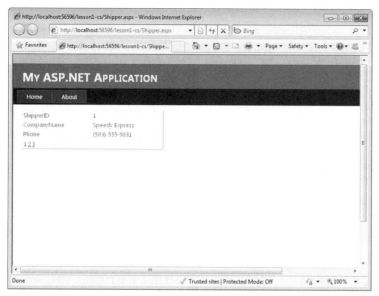

FIGURE 12-3 An ObjectDataSource bound to a DetailsView control.

Notice that the Shipper.GetAllShippers method returns a DataTable. An ObjectDataSource class can work with any data that implements any of the following interfaces: IEnumerable, IListSource, IDataSource, or IHierarchicalDatasource. This means that as long as your business object class returns data as a DataTable, a DataSet, or some form of a collection, you can be sure that this data can be used with an ObjectDataSource control.

Passing Parameters

The business objects with which you work will undoubtedly define methods that take parameter values. These parameters might define a filter on the data or indicate values to be used when inserting or updating data. Fortunately, you can use the ObjectDataSource to map various page-level elements to parameters to be passed to your objects.

There are multiple sets of parameters you can define for an ObjectDataSource. These sets include Select, Insert, Update, Delete, and Filter parameters. These parameters work in conjunction with the method of the same name. For example, the <SelectParameters> set works with the method defined by the SelectMethod attribute.

The source of a parameter's value can come from multiple places in your page or site, including Cookie, Control, Session, QueryString, Form, or Profile objects. These options make defining and mapping a data source an easier task. You can also define the source value in code.

As an example, suppose that you have a business object name Customer. Assume that this object contains the GetCustomersByCity method, which takes a city value as string. The method then returns a list of customers for the specified city parameter. Now suppose that you need to create a data source control to map to this class. The ObjectDataSource should pass the value for the city to the method from the query string. In this case, you would create a SelectParameters set that includes a QueryStringParameter definition. The QueryStringParameter definition would map between the name of the query string parameter and the name of the method's parameter. The following code shows an example.

```
<asp:ObjectDataSource
    ID="ObjectDataSource1"
    runat="server"
    TypeName="Customer"
    SelectMethod="GetCustomersByCity">
    <SelectParameters>
        <asp:QueryStringParameter
            Name="city"
            QueryStringField="city"
            Type="String" />
    </SelectParameters>
</asp:ObjectDataSource>
```

You might then attach this data source to a GridView or similar control. You can then call the page by passing in the appropriate query string value, as follows.

```
http://localhost:5652/DataSourceSamples/Customers.aspx?city=London
```

You can use this same technique to pass multiple parameters of various types and from various sources. You can also use this same technique to pass parameters meant to handle inserting, updating, and deleting, as discussed in the next section.

Inserting, Updating, and Deleting

You can also use an ObjectDataSource control to define how data should be inserted, updated, and deleted. The InsertMethod, UpdateMethod, and DeleteMethod attributes can be mapped directly to the methods of an object that are to be called when these activities are invoked. You then use parameter definitions to map values to these method calls.

As an example, recall the Shipper class discussed previously. Now suppose that additional methods have been added to this object. These method signatures might look as follows.

Sample of Visual Basic Code

```
Public Shared Function GetAllShippers() As DataTable
Public Shared Sub InsertShipper(ByVal companyName As String, ByVal phone As String)
Public Shared Sub UpdateShipper(ByVal shipperId As Integer, _
  ByVal companyName As String, ByVal phone As String)
Public Shared Sub DeleteShipper(ByVal shipperId As Integer)
```

Sample of C# Code

```
public static DataTable GetAllShippers()
public static void InsertShipper(string companyName, string phone)
public static void UpdateShipper(int shipperId, string companyName, string phone)
public static void DeleteShipper(int shipperId)
```

You can map an ObjectDataSource control to each of these methods. In doing so, you need to define the parameters each method expects. The following markup shows an example.

```
<asp:ObjectDataSource ID="ObjectDataSource1" runat="server" TypeName="Shipper"
    SelectMethod="GetAllShippers" InsertMethod="InsertShipper"
    UpdateMethod="UpdateShipper" DeleteMethod="DeleteShipper">
    <DeleteParameters>
        <asp:Parameter Name="ShipperId" Type="Int32" />
    </DeleteParameters>
    <UpdateParameters>
        <asp:Parameter Name="shipperId" Type="Int32" />
        <asp:Parameter Name="companyName" Type="String" />
        <asp:Parameter Name="phone" Type="String" />
    </UpdateParameters>
    <InsertParameters>
        <asp:Parameter Name="companyName" Type="String" />
        <asp:Parameter Name="phone" Type="String" />
    </InsertParameters>
</asp:ObjectDataSource>
```

You can then use this ObjectDataSource control with a data-bound control such as a DetailsView. The following markup is an example. In this case, the fields are bound individually. This allows granular control over the ShipperId field because it is an auto-generated primary key (identity) in a Microsoft SQL Server database. Therefore, you set the InsertVisible property to false, to make sure that the DetailsView does not try to pass a value for ShipperId to the InsertMethod of the ObjectDataSource. You also set the ReadOnly attribute of the same field to true, to indicate that the value should not be available to change during an edit operation.

```
<asp:DetailsView ID="DetailsView1" runat="server" AllowPaging="True"
    DataSourceID="ObjectDataSource1" AutoGenerateRows="False" Width="450px"
    DataKeyNames="ShipperID">
    <Fields>
        <asp:BoundField DataField="ShipperID" HeaderText="ShipperId"
            ReadOnly="true" InsertVisible="false" />
        <asp:BoundField DataField="CompanyName" HeaderText="CompanyName" />
        <asp:BoundField DataField="Phone" HeaderText="Phone" />
        <asp:CommandField ShowInsertButton="True" ShowDeleteButton="True"
            ShowEditButton="True" />
    </Fields>
</asp:DetailsView>
```

Defining a Filter

You can also apply filters to an ObjectDataSource. Filters apply to data returned from the object's methods as a DataSet or DataTable. This is because the filter is a valid filter expression as defined by the ADO.NET DataColumn class.

To define a filter for an ObjectDataSource control, you set the FilterExpression attribute to a valid filter. This filter will be applied after the data is retrieved from the database. You can also use FilterParameters to map values from the page to the filter expression by defining a filter expression that contains parameter mappings as numbers enclosed in braces. You then add the appropriate filter parameters.

The following code shows an example. Here, the Customer.GetAllCustomers method is bound to an ObjectDataSource control. When the data is returned, the filter expression city='{0}' is applied to the result. The query string value for city is then passed as the {0} parameter to the filter expression.

```
<asp:ObjectDataSource
    ID="ObjectDataSource1"
    runat="server"
    TypeName="Customer"
    SelectMethod="GetAllCustomers"
    FilterExpression="city='{0}'">
    <FilterParameters>
        <asp:QueryStringParameter
            Name="city"
            QueryStringField="city"
            Type="String" />
    </FilterParameters>
</asp:ObjectDataSource>
```

Sorting and Paging

The data-bound controls that work with an ObjectDataSource control can be configured to page and sort the data returned by the data source control. However, it is often better to sort and page this data when the data is requested from the database. Doing so can reduce the consumption of resources on your server.

The ObjectDataSource control defines specific attributes for managing sorting and paging. You set these attributes to parameters of your SelectMethod. The SelectMethod must also define these properties and use them for sorting and paging. In addition, by using these specific properties, data-bound controls such as GridView can automatically work with your data source to provide input for sorting and paging.

As an example, suppose you want to provide a business object method to control how customer data is sorted and paged as it is retrieved before it is shown to the user. You could define a business method as follows.

Sample of Visual Basic Code

```
Public Shared Function GetPagedCustomersSorted( _
    ByVal sortCol As String, ByVal pageStart As Integer, _
    ByVal numRecords As Integer) As DataTable

    If numRecords <= 0 Then numRecords = 10
    If sortCol = "" Then sortCol = "CompanyName"

    Dim cnn As New SqlConnection(_cnnString)

    Dim sql As String = "SELECT * FROM customers"

    Dim cmd As New SqlCommand(sql, cnn)

    Dim adp As New SqlDataAdapter(cmd)
    cnn.Open()
```

```
    Dim ds As New DataSet("customers")
    adp.Fill(ds, pageStart, numRecords, "customers")

    Dim dsSort = From cust In ds.Tables("customers").AsEnumerable()
                 Order By cust.Field(Of String)(sortCol)
                 Select cust

    return dsSort.CopyToDataTable()

End Function
```

Sample of C# Code

```
public static DataTable GetPagedCustomersSorted(
    string sortCol, int pageStart, int numRecords)
{
    if (numRecords <= 0) numRecords = 10;
    if (sortCol == "") sortCol = "CompanyName";

    SqlConnection cnn = new SqlConnection(_cnnString);

    string sql = "SELECT * from customers";

    SqlCommand cmd = new SqlCommand(sql, cnn);

    SqlDataAdapter adp = new SqlDataAdapter(cmd);
    DataSet ds = new DataSet("customers");
    cnn.Open();
    adp.Fill(ds, pageStart, numRecords, "customers");

    var dsSort = from cust in ds.Tables["customers"].AsEnumerable()
                 orderby cust.Field<string>(sortCol)
                 select cust;

    return dsSort.CopyToDataTable();
}
```

Notice that this business method defines three parameters: one for sorting the data, one for setting the starting record (or page), and one for setting the number of records in a page. You can then use these parameters when defining an ObjectDataSource. You set the control's SortParameterName attribute to the parameter of your business object that is used for sorting data. You set the StartRowIndexParameterName to the parameter that defines the row number at which you want to start retrieving data. You then set the MaximumRowsParameterName to the parameter that is used to define the number of rows you want to include in a data page. The following markup shows an example.

```
<asp:ObjectDataSource
    ID="ObjectDataSource1"
    runat="server"
    TypeName="Customer"
    SelectMethod="GetPagedCustomersSorted"
    SortParameterName="sortCol"
    EnablePaging="true"
    StartRowIndexParameterName="pageStart"
    MaximumRowsParameterName="numRecords">
</asp:ObjectDataSource>
```

You can then bind this data source to a control such as a GridView. The following markup shows an example.

```
<asp:GridView ID="GridView1" runat="server"
    DataSourceID="ObjectDataSource1"
    AllowPaging="True" PageSize="10" AllowSorting="true">
</asp:GridView>
```

When the page is run, the GridView control passes sorting and paging information to the data source. However, because the paging is happening before the GridView is bound, the GridView does not know the number of pages to display. Therefore, you need to implement your own custom paging in this scenario to advance the PageIndex property of the GridView control on the user's request. After you reset this value, the GridView will pass the value on to the ObjectDataSource.

Caching Data

You can tell ASP.NET to cache your ObjectDataSource control. This will keep the data in memory between page calls and can increase the performance and scalability of your application if the data is to be shared and accessed often.

To indicate caching of an ObjectDataSource, you set the EnableCaching attribute to true. You then set the CacheDuration property to the number of seconds you want to have ASP.NET cache the data. The following shows an example of these settings.

```
<asp:ObjectDataSource
    ID="ObjectDataSource1"
    runat="server"
    TypeName="Shipper"
    SelectMethod="GetAllShippers"
    EnableCaching="true"
    CacheDuration="30">
</asp:ObjectDataSource>
```

The first call to this page will call the object and return its data. Subsequent calls within 30 seconds (such as moving through data pages) will use the cached data (and not call the underlying object).

Creating a DataObject Class

There are not many restrictions on which objects you can use as the source of ObjectDataSource controls. If you know that your business object will be used as an ObjectDataSource, you can define attributes on your class that make consuming your class inside an ObjectDataSource easier in the designer. These attributes are used to predefine which methods to use as Select, Insert, Update, and Delete methods.

To get started, you set the DataObject attribute at the top of your class. This simply indicates that your class is meant to be a DataObject. Again, this is not required for use with ObjectDataSource controls but simply makes things easier. The following shows an example of the class declaration and attribute.

Sample of Visual Basic Code

```
<System.ComponentModel.DataObject()> _
Public Class Shipper
```

Sample of C# Code

```
[DataObject()]
public class Shipper
```

You then add the DataObjectMethod attribute to the top of each method you intend to use as a data object method. You pass a DataObjectMethodType enum value to this attribute to indicate Delete, Insert, Update, or Select. The following code shows an example of the method signature and attribute.

Sample of Visual Basic Code

```
<System.ComponentModel.DataObjectMethod(ComponentModel.DataObjectMethodType.Select)> _
Public Shared Function GetAllShippers() As DataTable
```

Sample of C# Code

```
 [DataObjectMethod(DataObjectMethodType.Select)]
public static DataTable GetAllShippers()
```

By defining these attributes, you make the designer aware of your business object's intentions. This can ease the burden of configuring an ObjectDataSource control when large business objects with many methods are involved.

Connecting to Relational Databases by Using SqlDataSource

The SqlDataSource control is used to configure access to relational databases such as SQL Server and Oracle. It can also be configured to work with Open Database Connectivity (ODBC) and Object Linking and Embedding (OLE) Db data connections. You configure the control to connect to one of these database types. The code inside the control will then use the appropriate data provider based on your configuration settings, including ADO.NET provider classes for SqlClient, OracleClient, OleDb, and Odbc.

You configure the SqlDataSource control by first setting its ID property to a unique identifying string value. This property is similar to any other web control ID property. However, the value is used when referring to the data source during data binding (which will be discussed later in this section). You then set the ConnectionString property either to a valid connection string or to page script that reads the connection string from the Web.config file (as shown in the next code example).

You then set various command properties, including commands for selecting, inserting, updating, and deleting data. The command properties you set are based on how you intend to use the control. For example, you use the SelectCommand to define an SQL statement that can be used to retrieve data from a database. In this case, you would use the Text SelectCommandType (which is the default). You can also set the SelectCommandType to StoredProcedure and then provide a stored procedure name for the SelectCommand attribute.

The DataSourceMode attribute is used to define how the SqlDataSource control should retrieve your data. You have two options: DataSet and DataReader. The former connects to the database and returns all records as a DataSet instance. It then closes the database connection before continuing to process the page. The latter, DataReader, keeps an open connection to the database while it reads each row into the data source control.

The following markup shows an example of connecting to a Microsoft SQL Server Express Edition database by first reading the connection string from the Web.config file. It uses a text-based SQL statement and a DataReader. It then binds the data source to a GridView control for display.

```
<asp:SqlDataSource
    ID="SqlDataSource1"
    runat="server"
    ConnectionString="<%$ ConnectionStrings:NorthwindConnectionString %>"
    SelectCommandType="Text"
    SelectCommand="SELECT * FROM [products]"
    DataSourceMode="DataReader">
</asp:SqlDataSource>

<asp:GridView
    ID="GridView1"
    runat="server"
    DataSourceID="SqlDataSource1">
</asp:GridView>
```

You can also work with the data source controls from code. When doing so, you replace the markup attribute settings with object property settings. You first create the data source control inside the Page_Init method. You then add the data source control to the page to ensure that it is available to be bound to other controls. The following code shows the preceding markup example translated as code in a code-behind page.

Sample of Visual Basic Code

```
Partial Class _Default
    Inherits System.Web.UI.Page

    Protected Sub Page_Init(ByVal sender As Object, _
        ByVal e As System.EventArgs) Handles Me.Init

        Dim sqlDs As New SqlDataSource
        sqlDs.ConnectionString = _
            ConfigurationManager.ConnectionStrings("NorthwindConnectionString").ToString
        sqlDs.ID = "SqlDataSource1"
        sqlDs.SelectCommandType = SqlDataSourceCommandType.Text
        sqlDs.SelectCommand = "SELECT * FROM [products]"
        sqlDs.DataSourceMode = SqlDataSourceMode.DataReader
        Me.Controls.Add(sqlDs)
    End Sub

    Protected Sub Page_Load(ByVal sender As Object, _
        ByVal e As System.EventArgs) Handles Me.Load
        GridView1.DataSourceID = "SqlDataSource1"
    End Sub

End Class
```

Sample of C# Code

```csharp
public partial class DefaultCs : System.Web.UI.Page
{
    protected void Page_Init(object sender, EventArgs e)
    {
        SqlDataSource sqlDs = new SqlDataSource();
        sqlDs.ConnectionString =
            ConfigurationManager.ConnectionStrings[
            "NorthwindConnectionString"].ToString();
        sqlDs.ID = "SqlDataSource1";
        sqlDs.SelectCommandType = SqlDataSourceCommandType.Text;
        sqlDs.SelectCommand = "SELECT * FROM [products]";
        sqlDs.DataSourceMode = SqlDataSourceMode.DataReader;
        this.Controls.Add(sqlDs);
    }

    protected void Page_Load(object sender, EventArgs e)
    {
        GridView1.DataSourceID = "SqlDataSource1";
    }
}
```

Working with data source controls in code is less common than working with them in markup. Declaring your data source in markup is very straightforward;, the attributes you define in markup are the same as the properties you set in code. Therefore, the majority of this lesson assumes that you are working with markup only, and will not provide examples in code.

Using Parameters

The SqlDataSource control can also be configured to use parameters for Select, Insert, Update, Filter, and Delete commands. This is done by defining parameters inside your SQL statements by using the @ param syntax. You then map parameter values to these parameter definitions by using parameter declarations.

As an example, suppose that you are creating a SqlDataSource control to return products based on their category ID. The category ID will be passed to the page as a value from the query string. You can define this parameter inside the SelectParameters collection as a QueryStringParameter. The following shows the markup of this example.

```
<asp:SqlDataSource
    ID="SqlDataSource1"
    runat="server"
    ConnectionString="<%$ ConnectionStrings:NorthwindConnectionString %>"
    SelectCommandType="Text"
    SelectCommand="SELECT * FROM [products] WHERE CategoryID=@CategoryId"
    DataSourceMode="DataSet">
    <SelectParameters>
        <asp:QueryStringParameter
            Name="CategoryId"
            QueryStringField="catId"
            Type="Int16" />
    </SelectParameters>
</asp:SqlDataSource>
```

You can then bind this control to a GridView (or similar control). When the page is accessed, the data is filtered based on the query string parameter. The following shows an example Uniform Resource Locator (URL) for this call:

```
http://localhost:5652/DataSourceSamples/Products.aspx?catId=2
```

You use the same method for defining InsertParameters, UpdateParameters, and DeleteParameters. These parameters are mapped to the respective InsertCommand, UpdateCommand, and DeleteCommand commands. Controls such as GridView and DetailsView work to trigger update, insert, and delete actions and, in doing so, pass parameter values to the appropriate command. This is similar to what was demonstrated previously in the ObjectDataSource section.

Filtering Data with SqlDataSource

As with the ObjectDataSource control, you can also filter data inside a SqlDataSource control. Again, the data must be a DataSet because the filter is applied to the ADO.NET DataColumn or DataView.RowFilter property.

To define a filter, you set the FilterExpression attribute to a valid filter. This filter will be applied after the data is retrieved from the database. You can also use FilterParameters to map values from the page to the filter expression by defining a filter expression that contains parameter mappings as numbers enclosed in braces. You then add the appropriate filter parameters.

The following code shows an example of a SqlDataSource control that first selects all products from the database. It then applies a FilterExpression to show only those products that have been discontinued.

```
<asp:SqlDataSource
    ID="SqlDataSource1"
    runat="server"
    ConnectionString="<%$ ConnectionStrings:NorthwindConnectionString %>"
    SelectCommandType="Text"
    SelectCommand="SELECT * FROM [products]"
    DataSourceMode="DataSet"
    FilterExpression="Discontinued=true">
</asp:SqlDataSource>
```

Caching SqlDataSource Data

As with ObjectDataSource, you can also configure a SqlDataSource control to be cached by the server. When doing so, however, you must set the DataSourceMode property to DataSet. DataReader sources cannot be cached, because they would hold open a connection to the server.

You indicate the caching of a SqlDataSource control the same way you would an ObjectDataSource control: by setting the EnableCaching and CacheDuration attributes. The following shows an example.

```
<asp:SqlDataSource
    ID="SqlDataSource1"
    runat="server"
    ConnectionString="<%$ ConnectionStrings:NorthwindConnectionString %>"
    SelectCommandType="Text"
    SelectCommand="SELECT * FROM [products]"
    DataSourceMode="DataSet"
    EnableCaching="True"
    CacheDuration="30">
</asp:SqlDataSource>
```

Working with Access Data Files and AccessDataSource Controls

The AccessDataSource control is meant to connect to and work with Microsoft Access file-based databases (.mdb files). This control is very similar to the SqlDataSource control. In fact, it derives from the SqlDataSource class. Therefore, you can expect to work with the AccessDataSource control in a very similar manner when passing parameters, caching, filtering data, and calling Access stored procedures.

> **NOTE THE NEW ACCESS DATABASE ENGINE**
>
> The Access database engine has been changed in recent versions from Microsoft Jet to one based on SQL Server. The AccessDataSource control is used to work with Jet-based databases. These can be identified by the .mdf file extension. Newer Access files have the .accdb extension. You can connect to these database files by using the SqlDataSource control (not the AccessDataSource control).

One of the main differences between the AccessDataSource control and the SqlDataSource control is how they connect to the database. The AccessDataSource control replaces the SqlDataSource.ConnectionString property with the DataFile property. You pass a path to a database file to this property to define a connection to an Access database. The following markup shows how you configure the AccessDataSource control to connect to an .mdb file in the App_Data folder.

```
<asp:AccessDataSource
    ID="AccessDataSource1" runat="server"
    DataFile="~/App_Data/AccessNorthwind.mdb"
    SelectCommand="SELECT * FROM [Products]">
</asp:AccessDataSource>
```

The code inside this data source control uses the ADO.NET System.Data.OleDb provider for connecting to an Access data file. Of course, this code is abstracted for you by the control itself. You need only define the markup to begin accessing and working with data in the Access file.

Connecting to an Entity Model by Using EntityDataSource

The EntityDataSource control works much like the SqlDataSource control. However, the SqlDataSource control is tied to a specific database model, whereas the EntityDataSource control works with an Entity Data Model that gets mapped to an actual data store (see Chapter 11, "Connecting to and Querying Data with LINQ," for more information on creating and working with Entity Framework's Entity Data Model).

You configure the EntityDataSource control to provide a connection to the entity model's underlying data store, which is done through the ConnectionString property. This value is set to a named entity model connection string that uses the System.Data.EntityClient provider. The connection string is generated and stored in the Web.config file when you set up your entity model (EDMX file).

You can then indicate an EntitySetName to point to the data you want to select and expose through the data source control. This entity set is a named collection of data in your model. Alternatively, you can use the CommandText attribute to define a custom LINQ query to define your selection (more on this later in this section).

The following markup shows an example. This assumes that an entity model named NorthwindEntities has been created. Notice the connection string reference. This string is stored in the Web.config file. Also, notice that the EntitySetName is set to Orders. This is used to establish a default entity set and will return all orders in the data store. Finally, the results are bound to a GridView control for display.

```
<asp:EntityDataSource ID="EntityDataSource1"
    runat="server"
    ConnectionString="name=NorthwndEntities"
    DefaultContainerName="NorthwndEntities"
    EnableFlattening="False"
    EntitySetName="Orders">
</asp:EntityDataSource>

<asp:GridView ID="GridView1" runat="server"
    DataSourceID="EntityDataSource1">
</asp:GridView>
```

Selecting Data to Return

You saw in the previous example that you can return the entire collection for an entity by using the EntitySetName attribute. The EntityDataSource allows you to get more specific with your selection. You can do so through the Select attribute. You define a string in this attribute that will be passed to ObjectQuery<T>. In this way, you can write LINQ to Entities code against the data source for the Select, Where, and Order By attributes.

For example, suppose you want to return only specific fields from the OrderDetails collection in an entity model. You might also want to rename some of these fields and even generate a field based on a calculation. As with a LINQ to Entities query, you can specify a Select statement that will do just that. Recall from Chapter 11 that this is called a *projection*, because you are projecting the results into a collection of a new, anonymous type. The following markup shows an example.

```
<asp:EntityDataSource ID="EntityDataSource1"
    runat="server"
    ConnectionString="name=NorthwndEntities"
    DefaultContainerName="NorthwndEntities"
    EnableFlattening="False"
    EntitySetName="OrderDetails"
    Select="it.OrderId as Id, it.UnitPrice, it.Quantity, it.UnitPrice * it.Quantity as
  LineItemTotal">
</asp:EntityDataSource>
```

SPECIFYING A CUSTOM QUERY

You can specify an entire query (and not just the Select) by using the CommandText property of the EntityDataSource. In this case, you need not set the EntitySetName. The query will indicate the data to select. This query is written as an Entity SQL expression, which uses different syntax than LINQ for Entities. The following markup shows an example (line breaks in the CommandText property are added for clarity.

```
<asp:EntityDataSource ID="EntityDataSource1" runat="server"
    ConnectionString="name=NorthwndEntities"
    DefaultContainerName="NorthwndEntities"
    CommandText =
    "Select o.OrderId as Id, o.UnitPrice, o.Quantity,
            o.UnitPrice * o.Quantity as LineItemTotal
    from OrderDetails as o
    where o.Discount > 0
  order by o.ProductId">
</asp:EntityDataSource>
```

Note that you can write the same query by using the independent Select, Where, and OrderBy properties of the EntityDataSource control. You will see more on this in upcoming sections.

SPECIFYING OBJECTS TO RETURN

You can specify that additional object collections be returned in the result (in addition to the collection being queried). These additional objects are added to your collection by using the Include attribute. These objects should exist as a navigation property in the entity data model. For example, the following markup returns all Orders. For each order object, the results will also include the OrderDetails collection.

```
<asp:EntityDataSource ID="EntityDataSource1" runat="server"
    ConnectionString="name=NorthwndEntities"
    DefaultContainerName="NorthwndEntities"
    EntitySetName="Orders"
    Include="OrderDetails">
</asp:EntityDataSource>
```

Ordering Results

You can use the OrderBy property of the EntityDataSource control to specify an order by statement that will be passed to ObjectQuery<T>. The following markup shows an example of ordering the OrderDetails entity by ProductId.

```
<asp:EntityDataSource ID="EntityDataSource1" runat="server"
    ConnectionString="name=NorthwndEntities"
    DefaultContainerName="NorthwndEntities"
    EntitySetName="OrderDetails"
    OrderBy="it.ProductId">
</asp:EntityDataSource>
```

Filtering Data

You can use the Where property of the EntityDataSource control to specify a Where statement that will be passed to ObjectQuery<T> without modification. The following markup shows an example of filtering orders for only those that have a discount applied.

```
<asp:EntityDataSource ID="EntityDataSource1" runat="server"
    ConnectionString="name=NorthwndEntities"
    DefaultContainerName="NorthwndEntities"
    EntitySetName="OrderDetails"
    OrderBy="it.ProductId"
    Where="it.Discount > 0">
</asp:EntityDataSource>
```

Defining Parameters

The EntityDataSource control allows you to define several parameters that can be used with the @ paramName syntax inside various properties, including Select, Where, and CommandText. These ParameterCollection objects include CommandParameters, DeleteParameters, OrderByParameters, SelectParameters, UpdateParameters, and WhereParameters.

Each of these parameter collections might contain an ASP.NET parameter control such as ControlParameter, FormParameter, QueryStringParameter, CookieParameter, and similar parameters. This allows you to pass values from your website dynamically to the EntityDataSource control.

As an example, suppose you want to filter orders based on their value. You might ask a user to enter a value into a TextBox control. You could then create a <ControlParameter/> in the WhereParameters collection of an EntityDataSource control to map the TextBox.Text field to the Where clause. The following is an example; the parameter is defined as @ OrderValue, which aligns with the parameter name, OrderValue.

```
<asp:EntityDataSource ID="EntityDataSource1" runat="server"
    ConnectionString="name=NorthwndEntities"
    DefaultContainerName="NorthwndEntities"
    EntitySetName="OrderDetails"
    OrderBy="it.ProductId"
    Where="(it.Quantity * it.UnitPrice) > @OrderValue">
    <WhereParameters>
    <asp:ControlParameter
        ControlID="TextBoxValue" Name="OrderValue"
        DbType="Int32" PropertyName="Text"
        DefaultValue="0" />
    </WhereParameters>
</asp:EntityDataSource>

Enter an order value on which to filter:<br />
<asp:TextBox ID="TextBoxValue" runat="server"></asp:TextBox>
<asp:Button ID="ButtonUpdate" runat="server" Text="Button" />

<asp:GridView ID="GridView1" runat="server"
    DataSourceID="EntityDataSource1">
</asp:GridView>
```

Note that you can set the AutoGenerateWhereClause or AutoGenerateOrderByClause attributes to true if you want to have the EntityDataSource control automatically map a parameter to a field in the results. The parameter and field must have the same name for this to work.

Paging, Sorting, Editing, and Updating Data

The EntityDataSource control supports a few additional attributes that you can use to enable specific scenarios. These attributes include AutoPage, AutoSort, EnableInsert, EnableUpdate, and EnableDelete. These are all Boolean properties that, if set to true, will enable these features for your EntityDataSource. Of course, the features are provided by the underlying entity model; they then need to be exposed via a visible control such as a GridView.

The following markup shows an example of both a fully enabled EntityDataSource control and a GridView control that leverages all of these features. A user can access this page and view, sort, edit, update, and delete data.

```
<asp:EntityDataSource ID="EntityDataSource1" runat="server"
    ConnectionString="name=NorthwndEntities"
    DefaultContainerName="NorthwndEntities"
    EntitySetName="OrderDetails"
    AutoPage="true"
    AutoSort="true"
    EnableDelete="true"
    EnableInsert="true"
    EnableUpdate="true">
</asp:EntityDataSource>

<asp:GridView ID="GridView1" runat="server"
    DataSourceID="EntityDataSource1"
    AllowPaging="True"
    AllowSorting="True">
    <Columns>
        <asp:CommandField
            ShowDeleteButton="True"
            ShowEditButton="True"
            ShowSelectButton="True" />
    </Columns>
</asp:GridView>
```

Connecting to XML Data by Using XmlDataSource

The XmlDataSource control provides a means to create a binding connection between controls on your page and an XML file. The XmlDataSource control is best used when you want to bind to XML data that is represented as hierarchical. In these cases, the outer elements of the XML represent data records. The child elements can themselves be subrecords related to the outer records. In addition, the child elements and attributes of these outer "record" elements are typically bound to as fields. You can think of these fields as columns of data on the record. Due to this hierarchical nature, the XmlDataSource control is typically bound to controls that show data in a hierarchical manner, such as the TreeView control. However, XmlDataSource controls can be used to display data in tabular formats, too.

You configure the XmlDataSource control at design time to point to an XML file. XML data in your project is typically stored in your project's App_Data folder. To bind to a file, you set the DataFile attribute on the data source control to point to the path of the XML file. The following code shows an example of defining an XmlDataSource control that points to a file containing product data.

```
<asp:XmlDataSource
    ID="XmlDataSource1"
    runat="server"
    DataFile="~/App_Data/products.xml" >
</asp:XmlDataSource>
```

You can also bind directly to a string value that represents XML. The XmlDataSource class provides the Data property for connecting to a string value in your code-behind page.

Transforming XML with the XmlDataSource Control

You can use the XmlDataSource control to define an Extensible Stylesheet Language (XSL) transformation to change the shape and content of your XML data. You do so by setting the TransformFile attribute to a valid XSL file. The XSL file will be applied to your XML data after your XML is loaded into memory and before the XML is bound for output.

As an example, consider the following XML file that defines a set of products across varied categories.

```
<?xml version="1.0" standalone="yes"?>
<Products>
    <Product>
        <Category>Beverages</Category>
        <Name>Chai</Name>
        <QuantityPerUnit>10 boxes x 20 bags</QuantityPerUnit>
        <UnitPrice>18.0000</UnitPrice>
    </Product>
    <Product>
        <Category>Condiments</Category>
        <Name>Aniseed Syrup</Name>
        <QuantityPerUnit>12 - 550 ml bottles</QuantityPerUnit>
        <UnitPrice>10.0000</UnitPrice>
    </Product>
    <Product>
        <Category>Condiments</Category>
        <Name>Chef Anton's Cajun Seasoning</Name>
        <QuantityPerUnit>48 - 6 oz jars</QuantityPerUnit>
        <UnitPrice>22.0000</UnitPrice>
    </Product>
    <Product>
        <Category>Produce</Category>
        <Name>Uncle Bob's Organic Dried Pears</Name>
        <QuantityPerUnit>12 - 1 lb pkgs.</QuantityPerUnit>
        <UnitPrice>30.0000</UnitPrice>
    </Product>
    <Product>
        <Category>Beverages</Category>
        <Name>Guaraná Fantástica</Name>
        <QuantityPerUnit>12 - 355 ml cans</QuantityPerUnit>
        <UnitPrice>4.5000</UnitPrice>
    </Product>
    <Product>
        <Category>Beverages</Category>
        <Name>Sasquatch Ale</Name>
        <QuantityPerUnit>24 - 12 oz bottles</QuantityPerUnit>
        <UnitPrice>14.0000</UnitPrice>
    </Product>
    <Product>
        <Category>Beverages</Category>
        <Name>Steeleye Stout</Name>
        <QuantityPerUnit>24 - 12 oz bottles</QuantityPerUnit>
        <UnitPrice>18.0000</UnitPrice>
    </Product>
</Products>
```

Suppose that you have to transform this data by first sorting it and then adding descriptive text to each field to help a user when viewing the data in a TreeView control. In this case, you can write an XSL transform file. The following code represents an example.

```
<xsl:stylesheet version="1.0"
    xmlns:xsl="http://www.w3.org/1999/XSL/Transform">
    <xsl:template match="Products">
        <Products>
            <xsl:for-each select="Product">
                <xsl:sort select="Name" order="ascending" />
                <Product>
                    <Name>
                        <xsl:value-of select="Name"/>
                    </Name>
                    <Category>
                        <xsl:text>Category: </xsl:text>
                        <xsl:value-of select="Category"/>
                    </Category>
                    <QuantityPerUnit>
                        <xsl:text>Quantity: </xsl:text>
                        <xsl:value-of select="QuantityPerUnit"/>
                    </QuantityPerUnit>
                    <UnitPrice>
                        <xsl:text>Price: </xsl:text>
                        <xsl:value-of select="UnitPrice"/>
                    </UnitPrice>
                </Product>
            </xsl:for-each>
        </Products>
    </xsl:template>
</xsl:stylesheet>
```

Next, you set the TransformFile attribute of the XmlDataSource control to point to the XSL file. The following shows an example of how the configured data source control would look in your markup, followed by an example of how the XmlDataSource control is bound to a TreeView control in markup.

```
<asp:XmlDataSource
    ID="XmlDataSource1"
    runat="server"
    DataFile="~/App_Data/products.xml"
    TransformFile="~/App_Data/ProductTransform.xsl" >
</asp:XmlDataSource>

<asp:TreeView
    id="TreeView1"
    runat="server"
    DataSourceID="XmlDataSource1">
    <DataBindings>
        <asp:TreeNodeBinding DataMember="Name" TextField="#InnerText" />
        <asp:TreeNodeBinding DataMember="Category" TextField="#InnerText" />
        <asp:TreeNodeBinding DataMember="QuantityPerUnit" TextField="#InnerText" />
        <asp:TreeNodeBinding DataMember="UnitPrice" TextField="#InnerText" />
    </DataBindings>
</asp:TreeView>
```

When the page is rendered, ASP.NET loads the XML file into memory. It then applies the XSL file to the XML data. Finally, the result is bound to the TreeView and embedded in the HTTP response. Figure 12-4 shows this data as it would look in a browser window. Notice that the data is sorted and the additional descriptive text has been added to several nodes.

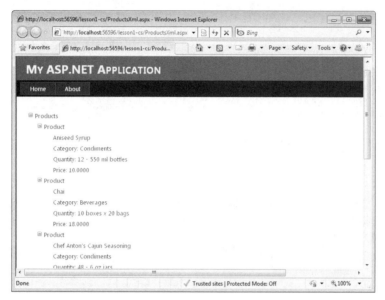

FIGURE 12-4 The transformed file displayed in a browser window.

Filtering XML with the XmlDataSource Control

The XmlDataSource control also allows you to set a data filter to define a subset of your XML. This is done via the XPath attribute. You set this attribute to a valid XPath expression that represents a filter expression. For example, to retrieve a subset of the product data in the XML file defined in the previous section, you could set the XPath attribute as in the following markup.

```
<asp:XmlDataSource
    ID="XmlDataSource1"
    runat="server"
    DataFile="~/App_Data/products.xml"
    TransformFile="~/App_Data/ProductTransform.xsl"
    XPath="/Products/Product[Category='Category: Beverages']" >
</asp:XmlDataSource>
```

In this example, the data is filtered for only those products with a category value set to "Beverages." Notice that the value is actually set to "Category: Beverages." This is because the XPath expression is applied following any XSL transformations. Recall that in the previous example, the "Category: " text was added to data. Therefore, you have to account for it in the XPath expression.

Connecting to LINQ-Based Data by Using LinqDataSource

You can use the LinqDataSource control to easily connect to data supplied by any data source that represents a collection of data. This includes lists, arrays, LINQ to SQL objects, and more. In this way, it is the most flexible data source control and typically requires the least amount of supporting code.

The LinqDataSource control uses the ContextTypeName attribute to define the database context of your LINQ-based data. This attribute can be set to point to the name of the class that represents your database context. As an example, suppose you have created a DBML DataContext file to represent the Northwind database by using LINQ to SQL (see Chapter 11). This file would include the NorthwindDataContext class, which represents the tables in your database. The following markup shows how you would connect to this class by using the LinqDataSource control.

```
<asp:LinqDataSource
    ID="LinqDataSource1"
    runat="server"
    ContextTypeName="NorthwindDataContext"
    EnableDelete="True"
    EnableInsert="True"
    EnableUpdate="True"
    OrderBy="CompanyName"
    TableName="Suppliers"
    Where="Country == @Country">
    <WhereParameters>
        <asp:QueryStringParameter
            DefaultValue="USA"
            Name="Country"
            QueryStringField="country"
            Type="String" />
    </WhereParameters>
</asp:LinqDataSource>
```

The LinqDataSource control is similar to other data source controls. It allows you to define parameters, indicate sorting, enable paging, and more. However, its LINQ-style declarative syntax makes it unique. Consider the preceding markup. Notice that the TableName attribute is set to Suppliers. You then use attributes to define a query that indicates both a Where clause and an OrderBy clause. The Where clause uses the WhereParameters parameter, which represents a query string that filters the data based on the value of country on the query string.

You can use LINQ language constructs in the markup of your LinqDataSource control. For example, by default, if no Select attribute is specified, the data source will return all fields in the collection. However, you can use a LINQ expression to indicate a new anonymous type. You can even create calculated fields as you would with any Select statement in a LINQ query. The following markup shows an example. Notice that the Location field is made up of three different fields from the data source.

```
<asp:LinqDataSource ID="LinqDataSource1" runat="server"
    ContextTypeName="NorthwindDataContext"
    EntityTypeName=""
    TableName="Suppliers"
    Where="Country == @Country"
    Select="new(SupplierId As Id,
            CompanyName As Name,
            Address + ' ' + City  + ' ' + PostalCode As Location)">
    <WhereParameters>
        <asp:QueryStringParameter DefaultValue="USA" Name="Country"
            QueryStringField="country" Type="String" />
    </WhereParameters>
</asp:LinqDataSource>
```

You can also bind a LinqDataSource control to a data-bound control, as you would with any other data source. You can set values on the LinqDataSource to indicate whether to allow deleting, inserting, and updating of data. The data-bound control will then work with the LinqDataSource as appropriate.

Connecting to Site Navigation Data by Using SiteMapDataSource

The SiteMapDataSource control is used to connect to site navigation data for your website. The data for this control is defined in a special XML file called a web.sitemap. You can define one sitemap file in the root of your website. The file includes information about the pages in your site and their hierarchy. It also includes page names, navigational information, and a description of each page. It is meant as a central place for managing the navigational data of your site; it is used by controls such as Menu and TreeView to allow users to easily navigate your application.

As an example, suppose that the following web.sitemap file is defined at the root of your web application.

```
<?xml version="1.0" encoding="utf-8" ?>
<siteMap xmlns="http://schemas.microsoft.com/AspNet/SiteMap-File-1.0" >
    <siteMapNode url="" title="Home" description="">
        <siteMapNode url="products.aspx" title="Products" description="">
            <siteMapNode url="productDetails.aspx"
                title="Product Details" description="" />
        </siteMapNode>
        <siteMapNode url="services.aspx" title="Services" description="" />
        <siteMapNode url="locations.aspx" title="Locations" description="" />
        <siteMapNode url="about.aspx" title="About Us" description="" />
    </siteMapNode>
</siteMap>
```

You can connect to this data by using a SiteMapDataSource control. You simply add the control to your page. You cannot configure it to point to a specific file. Instead, it automatically picks up the web.sitemap file defined at the root of your web application. The following markup shows an example. You bind to this data the same way you bind to the other data source controls. The following code also demonstrates binding to a Menu control.

```
<asp:SiteMapDataSource
    ID="SiteMapDataSource1"
    runat="server" />

<asp:Menu ID="Menu1"
    runat="server"
    DataSourceID="SiteMapDataSource1">
</asp:Menu>
```

The result of this binding is shown in Figure 12-5.

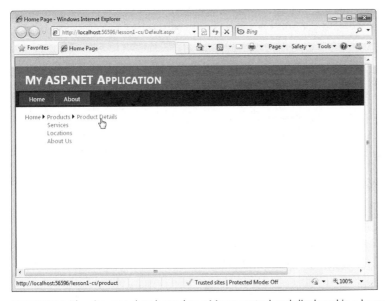

FIGURE 12-5 The site map data bound to a Menu control and displayed in a browser.

Filtering the Data Shown in the SiteMapDataSource

Sometimes, you might want to display only a portion of the data in your sitemap data file. The SiteMapDataSource control provides a couple of attributes that you can use to control the data that is provided to a visual control for display. The first, StartingNodeUrl, is used to indicate the node in the sitemap file that should be used as the root of the data source.

As an example, consider the sitemap file discussed previously. Suppose you need to display only the Products node and its subnodes. You can do so by setting the SiteMapDataSource control's StartingNodeUrl property to product.aspx, as shown in the following sample markup.

```
<asp:SiteMapDataSource
    ID="SiteMapDataSource1"
    runat="server"
    StartingNodeUrl="products.aspx" />
```

You can also use the ShowStartingNode attribute to indicate whether to display the node where the SiteMapDataSource control is set to start. You set this value to false if you want to hide the starting node. This property works with the other properties of the SiteMapDataSource control, such as StartingNodeUrl.

You might find that you want your navigation controls to display navigation data based on the current active page in the browser. You can do so by setting the StartFromCurrentNode attribute to true. This evaluates the name of the current page, finds it in the sitemap, and uses it as the start node for any bound controls on that page. This setting is especially useful if you embed your navigation and SiteMapDataSource controls inside a master page.

Finally, the StartingNodeOffset attribute is used to move the starting node up or down the sitemap data tree. You set the value to a negative number to move the start node up the tree from its current evaluated position. A positive number moves it deeper into the tree hierarchy.

 Quick Check

1. Which attribute of the SqlDataSource control do you use to define a connection to the database?

2. How do you define an ObjectDataSource to connect to a business object?

3. Which attribute of the LinqDataSource control do you use to indicate the O/R class used for connecting to and working with LINQ-based data?

4. Which attribute of the EntityDataSource control do you set to indicate a default entity set for your control to expose?

Quick Check Answers

1. You use the ConnectionString attribute.

2. You use the TypeName attribute.

3. You use the ContextTypeName attribute.

4. You use the EntitySetName attribute.

In this practice, you work with Visual Studio to create a website to work with an EntityDataSource control that exposes data from the Northwind database.

> **ON THE COMPANION MEDIA**
>
> If you encounter a problem completing an exercise, you can find the completed projects in the samples installed from this book's companion CD. For more information about the project files and other content on the CD, see "Using the Companion Media" in this book's Introduction.

EXERCISE 1   Creating the Website and Defining the Entity Model

In this exercise, you create a new website and define the Entity Model.

1. Open Visual Studio and create a new website called **DataSourceLab** by using your preferred programming language.

2. Add the northwnd.mdf file to your App_Data directory. You can copy the file from the sample files installed from this book's CD.

3. Add a new ADO.NET Entity Data Model to your website. Name this model **Northwind.edmx**. When prompted, allow Visual Studio to add the model to the App_Code directory.

4. Using the Entity Data Model Wizard, select Generate from database on the first step and click Next.

5. On the next page, select the northwnd.mdf data file. Make sure to select the check box to save the connection string in the Web.config file. Name this connection string **NorthwndEntitiesCnn** and click Next.

6. On the next page, select the Customers, Order Details, and Orders tables. Make sure that both check boxes are selected, and set the Model Namespace to **NorthwndModel**. Click Finish to complete the wizard and generate your database model.

7. Rename items in the model to better identify them. First, select the Order_Detail entity in the model, right-click it, and choose Rename. Rename the entity to **OrderDetail**. Then select the Order_Details navigation property from the Order entity and rename it to **OrderDetails**.

8. Save and close the model.

EXERCISE 2   Binding to the EntityDataSource Control

In this exercise, you create a webpage that defines an EntityDataSource that will be used to work with the entity model created in the previous exercise.

1. Continue editing the project you created in the previous exercise. Alternatively, you can open the completed Lesson 1, Exercise 1 project in the samples installed from the CD.

2. Open the Default.aspx page. Set the title over the grid (<h2>) to **Customers**, and delete the default markup content. In Design view, drag an EntityDataSource control onto the page from the Data tab of the Toolbox. This control will be used to expose a list of customers in the database.

3. Click the smart tag in the upper-right corner of the EntityDataSource control to open the EntityDataSource Tasks list. Select Configure Data Source to open the Configure Data Source Wizard.

   a. On the first page of the wizard, from the Named Connection list, select NorthwndEntitiesCnn.

   b. On the second page of the wizard, select the Customers EntitySetName. Set the Select fields to CustomerID, CompanyName, City, Region, Country, and Phone.

   c. Finish the wizard, and switch to Source view for your page. Edit the EntityDataSource markup to include AutoPage and AutoSort. Also, include an OrderBy statement to order the results by CompanyName (you can do so inside markup or use the Properties window). Your markup should look similar to the following.

   ```
   <asp:EntityDataSource ID="EntityDataSource1" runat="server"
       ConnectionString="name=NorthwndEntitiesCnn"
       DefaultContainerName="NorthwndEntitiesCnn"
       EnableFlattening="False"
       EntitySetName="Customers"
       AutoPage="true"
       AutoSort="true
       OrderBy="it.CompanyName"
       Select="it.[CustomerID], it.[CompanyName], it.[City], it.[Region],
   it.[Country], it.[Phone]">
   </asp:EntityDataSource>
   ```

4. Add a GridView control to the page. Set the DataSourceID property to point to the EntityDataSource created previously.

5. Define bound columns and change the HeaderText for each field in the result set.

6. Enable AllowPaging and AllowSorting.

7. Add a HyperLinkField to the GridView to call orders.aspx and pass the customer ID as a query string parameter.

Your GridView markup should look as follows.

```
<asp:GridView ID="GridViewCustomers" runat="server" AllowPaging="True"
    AllowSorting="True" AutoGenerateColumns="False"
    DataSourceID="EntityDataSource1">
    <Columns>
        <asp:BoundField DataField="CustomerID" HeaderText="ID"
            ReadOnly="True" SortExpression="CustomerID" />
        <asp:BoundField DataField="CompanyName" HeaderText="Company"
            ReadOnly="True" SortExpression="CompanyName" />
        <asp:BoundField DataField="City" HeaderText="City"
            ReadOnly="True" SortExpression="City" />
        <asp:BoundField DataField="Region" HeaderText="Region"
            ReadOnly="True" SortExpression="Region" />
        <asp:BoundField DataField="Country" HeaderText="Country"
            ReadOnly="True" SortExpression="Country" />
        <asp:BoundField DataField="Phone" HeaderText="Phone"
            ReadOnly="True" SortExpression="Phone" />
        <asp:HyperLinkField DataNavigateUrlFields="CustomerID"
            DataNavigateUrlFormatString="orders.aspx?custId={0}"
            HeaderText="Orders" Text="view orders" />
    </Columns>
</asp:GridView>
```

8. Run the page. Your page should look similar to that shown in Figure 12-6.

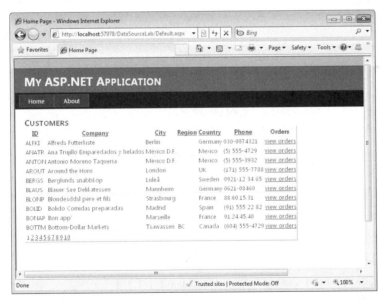

FIGURE 12-6 The EntityDataSource control bound to a GridView.

9. Add an Orders.aspx page to your site.

10. Add an EntityDataSource control to the page. Set attributes to connect to the Customers entity. Define a Where clause to select a customer by a specific ID. Set the ID as a QueryStringParameter. Finally, indicate that the results should include the customer's Orders collection. The following markup shows an example.

```
<asp:EntityDataSource ID="EntityDataSourceCust" runat="server"
    ConnectionString="name=NorthwndEntitiesCnn"
    DefaultContainerName="NorthwndEntitiesCnn"
    EnableFlattening="False"
    EntitySetName="Customers"
    Where="it.CustomerID=@custId"
    Include="Orders">
    <WhereParameters>
    <asp:QueryStringParameter
        QueryStringField="custId"
        Name="custId"
        DbType="String"/>
    </WhereParameters>
</asp:EntityDataSource>
```

11. Next, add a DetailsView control to the page and name it **DetailsViewCust**. In Design view, use the smart tag to set the data source to the EntityDataSource set previously. Select Refresh Schema from the same smart tag task list to generate columns bound to the data source.

12. Add a GridView control under the DetailsView and name it **GridViewOrders**. This will be used to show custom orders. You cannot, at present, bind this to the included collections of the EntityDataSource by using markup. Instead, you must write some code.

13. Add an event handler for the DetailsViewCust DataBound event. This event fires when the DetailsView control has been bound to data. You can use it to pull the bound Customer from the control and use its Orders collection for the GridView control. Your code should read as follows.

```
Sample of Visual Basic Code
Protected Sub DetailsViewCust_DataBound( _
    ByVal sender As Object, ByVal e As System.EventArgs) _
    Handles DetailsViewCust.DataBound

    Dim cust As NorthwndModel.Customer =
        CType(DetailsViewCust.DataItem, NorthwndModel.Customer)

    Me.GridViewOrders.DataSource = cust.Orders
    Me.GridViewOrders.DataBind()

End Sub
```

Sample of C# Code

```csharp
protected void DetailsViewCust_DataBound(object sender, EventArgs e)
{
    NorthwndModel.Customer cust =
        (NorthwndModel.Customer)DetailsViewCust.DataItem;
    this.GridViewOrders.DataSource = cust.Orders;
    this.GridViewOrders.DataBind();
}
```

14. Run the application. Select different customers. Click the view orders link and view the results. You should see something similar to the screen shown in Figure 12-7.

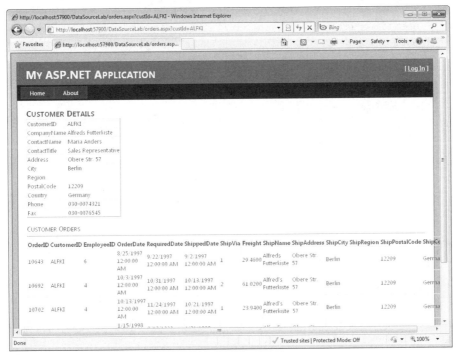

FIGURE 12-7 The orders.aspx page has two controls that are bound to two different collections exposed by the same EntityDataSource control.

Lesson Summary

- ASP.NET provides several data source controls (LinqDataSource, ObjectDataSource, SqlDataSource, AccessDataSource, EntityDataSource, XmlDataSource, and SiteMapDataSource) that allow you to easily work with various types of data. These controls allow you to bind to data by using data-bound web server controls.

- You can pass parameters to most data source controls. A parameter can be bound to a value in a cookie, in the session, in a form field, in the query string, or in a similar object.

- Many of the data source controls allow you to cache data. Those that do include the ObjectDataSource, SqlDataSource, and AccessDataSource controls.

Lesson Review

You can use the following questions to test your knowledge of the information in Lesson 1, "Connecting to Data with Data Source Controls." The questions are also available on the companion CD in a practice test, if you prefer to review them in electronic form.

> **NOTE ANSWERS**
>
> Answers to these questions and explanations of why each answer choice is correct or incorrect are located in the "Answers" section at the end of the book.

1. You have a data context map for your SQL Server database defined inside a class file. You need to connect to this data by using a data source control. Which data source control should you use?

    A. ObjectDataSource

    B. SqlDataSource

    C. SiteMapDataSource

    D. LinqDataSource

2. You are using an ObjectDataSource control to connect to a business object. Which attributes of the control must you set to return data for the data source? (Choose all that apply.)

    A. TypeName

    B. SelectMethod

    C. DataSourceId

    D. SelectParameters

3. You want to apply caching to your data source control to increase your scalability for frequently used data. You want to set the cache to expire every 60 seconds. Which attributes of your data source control should you set to do so? (Choose all that apply.)

    A. CacheTimeout

    B. CacheDuration

    C. EnableCaching

    D. DisableCaching

4. You are using an EntityDataSource control on your page. You need to write a custom query that uses a parameter in the Where clause. What actions should you take? (Choose all that apply.)

    A. Set the command by using the EntitySetName property.

    B. Set the command by using the CommandText property.

    C. Add a WhereParameters section to the EntityDataSource control markup.

    D. Add a CommandParameters section to the EntityDataSource control markup.

Lesson 2: Working with Data-Bound Web Server Controls

Lesson 1 showed you how to connect to various data sources by using the data source controls. After it has been accessed, the data needs to be displayed to users so that they can interact with it. ASP.NET provides a large set of controls for doing so. These controls are referred to as *data-bound controls*. Data-bound controls are controls that provide web-based UI output (HTML and JavaScript) and also bind to data on the server.

This lesson presents an overview of data binding in ASP.NET. It then presents the many data-bound controls found inside ASP.NET.

> **After this lesson, you will be able to:**
> - Understand the basics of how data-bound controls operate.
> - Use simple data-bound controls such as DropDownList, ListBox, CheckBoxList, RadioButtonList, and BulletedList.
> - Use composite data-bound controls such as GridView, DetailsView, FormView, DataList, Repeater, ListView, DataPager, and Chart.
> - Use hierarchical data-bound controls such as TreeView and Menu.
> - Use the data visualization control, Chart.
>
> **Estimated lesson time: 60 minutes**

Introducing Data-Bound Controls

The data-bound controls in ASP.NET can be classified as simple, composite, hierarchical, or visualization controls. Simple data-bound controls are the controls that inherit from ListControl. Composite data-bound controls are classes that inherit from CompositeDataBoundControl, such as GridView, DetailsView, FormView, and similar controls. Hierarchical data-bound controls are the Menu and TreeView controls. Finally, the Chart control is a data visualization control that inherits directly from DataBoundControl.

The Microsoft .NET Framework provides several base classes that are used to provide common properties and behavior for the concrete data-bound controls. These classes form the basis of many of the data-bound controls. In this way, all of the data-bound controls work in a similar manner. Figure 12-8 shows the hierarchy of the base classes used for data-bound controls in ASP.NET.

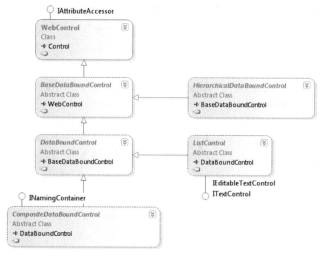

FIGURE 12-8 The base data-bound class hierarchy.

The BaseDataBoundControl is the first control in the hierarchy (inheriting from WebControl). This class contains the DataSource and DataSourceID properties used in data binding. The DataSource property gets or sets the object that the data-bound control uses to retrieve its data items. This property is most often used when binding to data in code, and it was the default binding property in early versions of ASP.NET. However, the DataSourceID property was introduced later to provide a declarative means of binding to data. You use the DataSourceID property to get or set the ID of a data source control that contains the source of the data, such as the data source controls discussed in Lesson 1. You typically set either the DataSource or the DataSourceID property (not both). If both properties are set, the DataSourceID takes precedence.

You can bind a data-bound web control to any data that implements IEnumerable, IListSource, IDataSource, or IHierarchicalDatasource. The data-bound control will automatically connect to the data source at run time by calling the DataBind method (which also raises the DataBound event). You can also call this method yourself in code to force a rebinding of data to the control.

The next control in Figure 12-8, HierarchicalDataBoundControl, inherits from the BaseDataBoundControl. It is the parent class for controls that display hierarchical data such as the Menu and TreeView controls.

The DataBoundControl inherits from the BaseDataBoundControl and is the parent class to the CompositeDataBoundControl, ListControl, and Chart. These classes are the parent classes to controls that display tabular data such as the GridView and DropDownList controls. The DataBoundControl control's DataMember property is a string data type that is used when the DataSource contains more than one tabular result set. In this scenario, the DataMember property is set to the name of the tabular result set that is to be displayed.

Mapping Fields to Templates

Templated binding can be used on controls that support templates. A *template control* is a control that has no default UI. The control simply provides the mechanism for binding to data. The developer supplies the UI in the form of inline templates. The template can contain declarative elements such as HTML and Dynamic Hypertext Markup Language (DHTML). The template can also contain ASP.NET data-binding syntax to insert data from the data source. Controls that support templates include GridView, DetailsView, and FormView, among others. A typical control might allow the following templates to be programmed:

- **HeaderTemplate**   This is an optional header, which is rendered at the top of the control.
- **FooterTemplate**   This is an optional footer, which is rendered at the bottom of the control.
- **ItemTemplate**   The item template is rendered for each row in the data source.
- **AlternatingItemTemplate**   This is an optional template; if it is implemented, every other row is rendered with this template.
- **SelectedItemTemplate**   This is an optional template; if implemented, the template is used to render a row that has been selected.
- **SeparatorTemplate**   This is an optional template that defines the markup used to indicate the separation of items from alternate items.
- **EditItemTemplate**   This is an optional template that is used to render a row that is in edit mode. This usually involves displaying the data in a TextBox instead of a Label control.

Some of the upcoming examples look at defining these templates for specific controls. For the most part, this process is similar regardless of the control with which you are working.

Using the DataBinder Class

In addition to automatically binding data with data-bound controls, you sometimes will need to have more granular control over which fields get bound to which controls on your page. For this, ASP.NET provides the DataBinder class. This class can be used to define code inside your script that controls how a data source is bound.

The DataBinder class provides the static Eval method to help bind data in this manner. The Eval method uses reflection to perform a lookup of a DataItem property's underlying type by looking at the type metadata that is stored in the type's assembly. After the metadata is retrieved, the Eval method determines how to connect to the field. This makes writing data binding syntax on your page an easy task. For example, the following shows binding to the Vin property of a Car object:

```
<%# Eval("Vin") %>
```

The Eval method also provides an overloaded method that allows a format string to be assigned as part of the data binding. As an example, if you were to bind to a field called Price, you can modify the display of this field by providing currency formatting, as shown here.

```
<%# Eval("Price", "{0:C}") %>
```

The Eval method is great for one-way (or read-only) data binding. However, it does not support read-write data binding and thus cannot be used for insert and edit scenarios. The Bind method of the DataBinder class, however, can be used for two-way data binding. This makes Bind preferable when you need to edit or insert records.

Just like the Eval method, the Bind method has two overloads: one without a format and one with the format parameter. The code for the Bind method looks the same as that for the Eval method. However, the Bind method does not work with all bound controls. It only works with controls that support read, insert, update, and delete scenarios, such as GridView, DetailsView, and FormView.

Simple Data-Bound Controls

Several controls in ASP.NET provide basic, list-based data binding. These controls are not meant to work with pages of data or provide elaborate editing scenarios. Instead, they allow you to provide a list of data items with which a user can operate. Figure 12-9 shows these simple data-bound controls, including their common base class, ListControl.

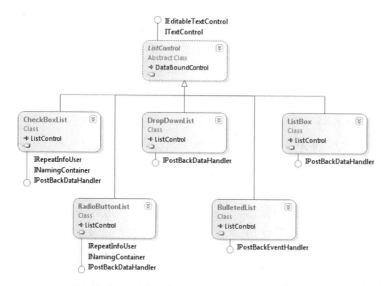

FIGURE 12-9 The ListControl class hierarchy.

The ListControl class is an abstract base class that provides common functionality for the classes that derive from it. This functionality includes an Items collection, which is a collection of ListItem data objects. Each ListItem object contains a Text property that is displayed to the user and a Value property that is posted back to the web server.

You can add items to the ListItems collection in code or declaratively in markup. You can also bind data to the controls that inherit from ListControl by setting the DataSource property (or the DataMember property if the source data has more than one table). You can also declaratively data-bind a ListControl-derived object by setting the DataSourceID property to the ID of a valid data source control on your page.

You can also choose the fields in your results that you will bind to the ListItem.Text and ListItem.Value properties. You can do so in code or through declarative markup by using the DataTextField and DataValueField properties, respectively. The text displayed for each item in the list control can also be formatted by setting the DataTextFormatString property. As an example, the following shows the declarative syntax for a ListBox bound to a SqlDataSource that provides the Northwind shipper table data.

```
<asp:ListBox
    ID="ListBox1"
    runat="server"
    DataSourceID="SqlDataSource1"
    DataTextField="CompanyName"
    DataValueField="ShipperID">
</asp:ListBox>
```

The SelectedIndex property lets you get or set the index of the selected item in the ListControl. By using the SelectedItem property, you can access the selected ListItem object's properties. If you only need to access the value of the selected ListItem, use the SelectedValue property.

The ListControl also contains the property called AppendDataBoundItems, which can be set to true to keep all items that are currently in the ListControl, in addition to appending the items from the data binding. Setting this property to false clears the Items property prior to binding the data.

The ListControl also provides the SelectedIndexChanged event, which is raised when the selection in the list control changes between posts to the server. Recall that you need to set a control's AutoPostback property to true if you intend it to post back to the server for this type of event.

The DropDownList Control

The DropDownList control is used to display a list of items to users to allow them to make a single selection. The Items collection contains the child ListItem objects that are displayed in the DropDownList control. To determine the item that the user has selected, you can retrieve the SelectedValue, SelectedItem, or SelectedIndex property.

In the following example, a DropDownList control is bound to a SqlDataSource control that returns data from the Territories database table in the Northwind database. Notice that the DataTextField and DataValueField attributes are set to fields in the database table.

```
<asp:DropDownList runat="server" Width="250px"
    ID="DropDownList1"
    DataSourceID="SqlDataSource1"
    DataTextField="TerritoryDescription"
    DataValueField="TerritoryID" >
</asp:DropDownList>
```

Suppose that this page also contains a button with an event that captures the selected item from the DropDownList and displays it on a label. This button control's event code might look as follows.

Sample of Visual Basic Code

```
Label1.Text = "You selected TerritoryID: " & DropDownList1.SelectedValue
```

Sample of C# Code

```
Label1.Text = "You selected TerritoryID: " + DropDownList1.SelectedValue;
```

When the page is run and the user makes a selection in the DropDownList control and then clicks the button, the results are displayed in the label.

The ListBox Control

The ListBox control is used to select and display items from a longer list rather than one at a time as done in the DropDownList. With the ListBox control, users can see more data at once. You can also configure the control to allow the selection of a single item or multiple items. To do so, you set the SelectionMode property. The ListBox control also has the Rows property, which is used to specify the number of items displayed on the screen. The following shows an example of a ListBox that is set to allow multiple selections and show up to 13 rows.

```
<asp:ListBox runat="server" Height="225px" Width="275px"
    ID="ListBox1"
    Rows="13"
    DataSourceID="SqlDataSource1"
    DataTextField="TerritoryDescription"
    DataValueField="TerritoryID"
    SelectionMode="Multiple">
</asp:ListBox>
```

The Items collection contains the collection of ListItem objects in the ListBox control. To determine which items the user has selected, you can enumerate the ListItem objects in the Items collection by examining the Selected value for each ListItem element. The following code shows an example of processing the selected items and displaying them inside a Label control.

Sample of Visual Basic Code

```
For Each i As ListItem In ListBox1.Items
    If i.Selected Then
        Label1.Text = Label1.Text & "You selected TerritoryID: " & i.Value & "<br />"
    End If
Next
```

Sample of C# Code

```
foreach (ListItem i in ListBox1.Items)
{
    if(i.Selected)
        Label1.Text = Label1.Text + "You selected TerritoryID: " + i.Value + "<br />";
}
```

The CheckBoxList and RadioButtonList Controls

The CheckBoxList and RadioButtonList controls are very similar. Both are used to display lists of items to users to allow them to make selections but use a check box or button to make the selection. The RadioButtonList control is used to make a single selection. The CheckBoxList control allows users to make multiple selections.

These controls contain a RepeatColumns property that is used to indicate the number of columns to be displayed horizontally. In addition, the RepeatDirection can be set to Horizontal or Vertical (the default) to indicate whether the data should be rendered across by rows or down by columns.

The following shows a CheckBoxList control configured to work with the Territory data and show data across five columns.

```
<asp:CheckBoxList runat="server"
    ID="CheckBoxList1"
    DataSourceID="SqlDataSource1"
    DataTextField="TerritoryDescription"
    DataValueField="TerritoryID" RepeatColumns="5">
</asp:CheckBoxList>
```

The Items collection contains the ListItem objects that are inside the CheckBoxList and the RadioButtonList controls. Use the SelectedValue property to determine the item that has been selected for the RadioButtonList. To find the selected CheckBoxList item or items, you can enumerate the ListItem objects in the Items collection by examining the value of the Selected property for each ListItem element.

The BulletedList Control

The BulletedList control displays an unordered or ordered list of items that renders as HTML <ul> or <ol> elements, respectively. The BulletedList control inherits from the ListControl control. This control renders as either bulleted or numbered, depending on the BulletStyle property.

If the control is set to render as bulleted, you can select the bullet style to Disc, Circle, or Square. Note that the BulletStyle settings are not compatible with all browsers. A custom image can also be displayed instead of the bullet.

If the BulletedList control is set to render numbered, you can set the BulletStyle to LowerAlpha, UpperAlpha, LowerRoman, and UpperRoman fields. You can also set the FirstBulletNumber property to specify the starting number for the sequence.

The DisplayMode property can be set to Text, LinkButton, or HyperLink. If set to LinkButton or HyperLink, the control performs a postback when a user clicks an item to raise the Click event.

The following example shows a data-bound BulletedList control. The control is bound to a data source control that selects the Shippers table data from the Northwind database.

```
<asp:BulletedList runat="server"
    ID="BulletedList1"
    DataSourceID="SqlDataSource1"
    DataTextField="CompanyName"
    DataValueField="ShipperID" BulletStyle="Circle">
</asp:BulletedList>
```

Composite Data-Bound Controls

There are several data-bound controls that use other ASP.NET controls to display bound data to the user. For this reason, these controls are referred to as *composite data-bound controls*. These controls inherit from the CompositeDataBoundControl base class. This class implements the INamingContainer interface, which means that an inheritor of this class is a naming container for child controls.

The classes that inherit from CompositeDataBoundControl directly are FormView, DetailsView, and GridView, as shown in Figure 12-10. These controls are covered in this section, along with the related ListView, DataPager, Repeater, Chart, and DataList data-bound controls.

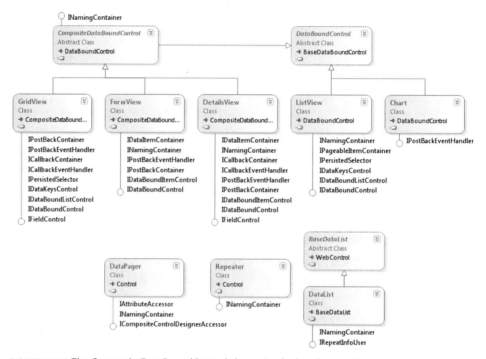

FIGURE 12-10 The CompositeDataBoundControl classes (and related controls).

The GridView Control

The GridView control is used to display data in a tabular format (rows and columns). The control renders in the browser as an HTML table. The GridView control makes it easy to configure features such as paging, sorting, and editing data without having to write much code.

The basic structure of the GridView is shown in Figure 12-11. The GridView control consists of a collection of GridViewRow (row) objects and a collection of DataControlField (column) objects. The GridViewRow object inherits from the TableRow object, which contains the Cells property. This property is a collection of DataControlFieldCell objects.

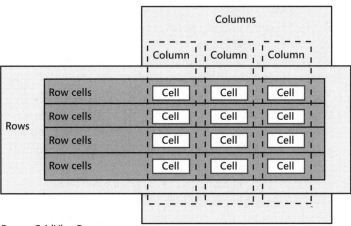

Row = GridViewRow
Column = DataControlField
Cell = DataControlFieldCell

FIGURE 12-11 The basic GridView control structure.

Although the GridViewRow object holds the collection of cells, each DataControlField (column) object provides the behavior to initialize cells of a specific type in the DataControlField object's InitializeCell method. The column classes that inherit from DataControlField override the InitializeCell method. The GridView control has an InitializeRow method that is responsible for creating a new GridViewRow and the row's cells by making calls to the overridden InitializeCell method when the row is being created.

The DataControlField class hierarchy is shown in Figure 12-12. The derived classes are used to create a DataControlFieldCell with the proper contents. Remember that you don't define cell types for your GridView control; you define column types and your column object supplies a cell object to the row by using the InitializeCell method. The DataControlField class hierarchy shows the different column types that are available in a GridView control.

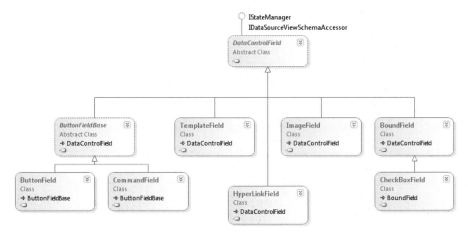

FIGURE 12-12 The DataControlField class hierarchy.

USING STYLES TO FORMAT THE GRIDVIEW CONTROL

You use styles to format the GridView. There are several styles available for you to manage, including an overall GridViewStyle and a HeaderStyle, FooterStyle, RowStyle, AlternatingRowStyle, SelectedRowStyle, EditRowStyle, and more. You can set these styles declaratively at design time. In addition, the RowCreated and RowDataBound events can also be used to control the style programmatically. In these event handlers, the Cells collection on the newly created row can be used to apply a style to a single cell in the row. The difference between the two events is that the RowCreated event takes place first, before the data is available. You can use the RowDataBound event when you need to apply a different style to a cell based on the data in the cell. These events fire after the styles are applied, which means that you can override any existing styles. Applying a different style to a cell based on the data in the cell allows you to apply business rules to determine whether a cell should stand out from other cells (such as making negative "quantity on hand" numbers red, but only when an item is shipped more than once per month).

As an example, consider a page that contains a SqlDataSource control bound to the Products table in the Northwind database. Suppose that this data source control provides SQL statements for selecting, updating, inserting, and deleting data. You can use this data source control to configure a GridView control that allows for this editing. The following markup shows an example of how the GridView would look in Source view.

```
<asp:GridView ID="GridView1" runat="server"
    AllowPaging="True"
    AllowSorting="True"
    AutoGenerateColumns="False"
    DataKeyNames="ProductID"
    DataSourceID="SqlDataSource1">
    <Columns>
        <asp:CommandField ShowDeleteButton="True" ShowEditButton="True"
            ShowSelectButton="True" />
        <asp:BoundField DataField="ProductID" HeaderText="ProductID"
            InsertVisible="False" ReadOnly="True" SortExpression="ProductID" />
        <asp:BoundField DataField="ProductName" HeaderText="ProductName"
            SortExpression="ProductName" />
        <asp:BoundField DataField="SupplierID" HeaderText="SupplierID"
            SortExpression="SupplierID" />
        <asp:BoundField DataField="CategoryID" HeaderText="CategoryID"
            SortExpression="CategoryID" />
        <asp:BoundField DataField="QuantityPerUnit" HeaderText="QuantityPerUnit"
            SortExpression="QuantityPerUnit" />
        <asp:BoundField DataField="UnitPrice" HeaderText="UnitPrice"
            SortExpression="UnitPrice" />
        <asp:BoundField DataField="UnitsInStock" HeaderText="UnitsInStock"
            SortExpression="UnitsInStock" />
        <asp:BoundField DataField="UnitsOnOrder" HeaderText="UnitsOnOrder"
            SortExpression="UnitsOnOrder" />
        <asp:BoundField DataField="ReorderLevel" HeaderText="ReorderLevel"
            SortExpression="ReorderLevel" />
        <asp:CheckBoxField DataField="Discontinued" HeaderText="Discontinued"
            SortExpression="Discontinued" />
    </Columns>
</asp:GridView>
```

Notice the Columns collection in the markup. Each column is defined along with the DataField and the text to be displayed as the column header (HeaderText). When this web-page is executed and displayed, each row is shown to the user along with action buttons for editing, deleting, and selecting the row. A user can click the Edit link on one of the rows to place the row into edit mode. Figure 12-13 shows an example.

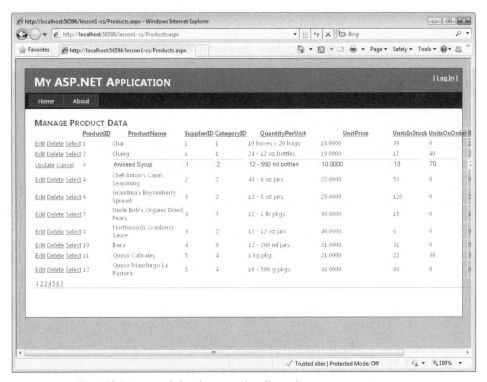

FIGURE 12-13 The GridView control showing a row in edit mode.

The DetailsView Control

The DetailsView control is used to display the values of one record at a time from a data source in an HTML table. The DetailsView control allows you to edit, delete, and insert records. If the AllowPaging property is set to true, the DetailsView can be used by itself to navigate the data source. However, the DetailsView can also be used in combination with other controls such as the GridView, ListBox, or DropDownList, for scenarios in which you want to display a master-detail form.

The DetailsView control does not directly support sorting, whereas the GridView control does. However, you can use the DataSource control, as discussed in Lesson 1, to manage data sorting. You should also note that the GridView does not automatically support inserting new records, whereas the DetailsView does support this feature.

The DetailsView supports the same formatting options that are available with the Grid-View control. You can format the DetailsView control by using the HeaderStyle, RowStyle, AlternatingRowStyle, CommandRowStyle, FooterStyle, PagerStyle, and EmptyDataRowStyle properties.

As an example, again consider a page that has a SqlDataSource control used for defining selection, insertion, updates, and deletion of product data in the Northwind database. You can configure a DetailsView to show this product data as pages and allow users to edit this data, insert new records, and delete existing ones. The following markup shows an example.

```
<asp:DetailsView runat="server" Width="300px"
    ID="DetailsView1"
    AllowPaging="True"
    AutoGenerateRows="False"
    DataKeyNames="ProductID"
    DataSourceID="SqlDataSource1">
    <Fields>
        <asp:BoundField DataField="ProductID" HeaderText="ProductID"
            InsertVisible="False" ReadOnly="True" SortExpression="ProductID" />
        <asp:BoundField DataField="ProductName" HeaderText="ProductName"
            SortExpression="ProductName" />
        <asp:BoundField DataField="SupplierID" HeaderText="SupplierID"
            SortExpression="SupplierID" />
        <asp:BoundField DataField="CategoryID" HeaderText="CategoryID"
            SortExpression="CategoryID" />
        <asp:BoundField DataField="QuantityPerUnit" HeaderText="QuantityPerUnit"
            SortExpression="QuantityPerUnit" />
        <asp:BoundField DataField="UnitPrice" HeaderText="UnitPrice"
            SortExpression="UnitPrice" />
        <asp:BoundField DataField="UnitsInStock" HeaderText="UnitsInStock"
            SortExpression="UnitsInStock" />
        <asp:BoundField DataField="UnitsOnOrder" HeaderText="UnitsOnOrder"
            SortExpression="UnitsOnOrder" />
        <asp:BoundField DataField="ReorderLevel" HeaderText="ReorderLevel"
            SortExpression="ReorderLevel" />
        <asp:CheckBoxField DataField="Discontinued" HeaderText="Discontinued"
            SortExpression="Discontinued" />
        <asp:CommandField ShowDeleteButton="True" ShowEditButton="True"
            ShowInsertButton="True" />
    </Fields>
</asp:DetailsView>
```

Notice that each column in the data table is set inside the Fields collection. The DataField attribute maps to the name of the column in the data source. The HeaderText property is used as the label that describes the data field. When the page is executed and displayed, the DetailsView shows Edit, Delete, and New buttons. When users click the Edit button, they are taken to edit mode for the selected record, as shown in Figure 12-14.

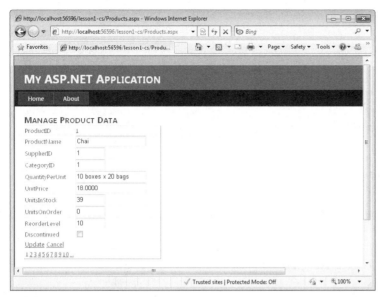

FIGURE 12-14 The DetailsView control in edit mode after the user has clicked the Edit button.

The FormView Control

Like DetailsView, the FormView control is used to display a single record from a data source. However, the FormView control does not automatically display the data in a predefined HTML table. Instead, it allows developers to create templates that define how the data should be displayed. You can define different templates for viewing, editing, and updating records. Creating your own templates gives you the greatest flexibility in controlling how data is displayed.

The FormView contains the following template definitions: ItemTemplate, EditItemTemplate, InsertItemTemplate, EmptyDataTemplate, FooterTemplate, HeaderTemplate, and PagerTemplate. You define a template by placing markup inside it and adding binding code within this markup. You then set the appropriate mode of the FormView control to switch to the specified template.

As an example, consider a page that defines a data source control for selecting the shipper data from the Northwind database. You can configure a FormView control to work with this data. For display, you can define the ItemTemplate. Here you set the controls and HTML used to lay out this data. You use the binding syntax (Eval and Bind) to connect data from the SqlDataSource to the FormView. The markup on the next page shows an example.

```
<asp:FormView runat="server"
    ID="FormView1"
    AllowPaging="True"
    DataSourceID="SqlDataSource1">
    <ItemTemplate>
        Shipper Identification:
        <asp:Label runat="server" Font-Bold="True"
            ID="Label1"
            Text='<%# Eval("ShipperID") %>'>
        </asp:Label>
        <br />
        <br />
        Company Name<br />
        <asp:TextBox runat="server" Width="250px"
            ID="TextBox1"
            Text='<%# Bind("CompanyName") %>'>
        </asp:TextBox>
        <br />
        Phone Number<br />
        <asp:TextBox runat="server" Width="250px"
            ID="TextBox2"
            Text='<%# Bind("Phone") %>'>
        </asp:TextBox>
    </ItemTemplate>
</asp:FormView>
```

When you run the page, the custom template is used with the FormView to display data as defined. Figure 12-15 shows the results in a browser window.

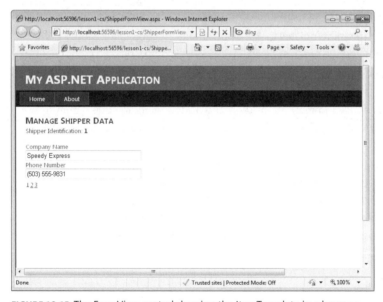

FIGURE 12-15 The FormView control showing the ItemTemplate in a browser.

The Repeater Control

The Repeater control also uses templates to define custom binding. However, it does not show data as individual records. Instead, it repeats the data rows as you specify in your template. This allows you to create a single row of data and have it repeat across your page.

The Repeater control is a read-only template. That is, it supports only the ItemTemplate. It does not implicitly support editing, insertion, and deletion. You should consider one of the other controls if you need this functionality, otherwise you will have to code this yourself for the Repeater control.

The following markup is similar to that for the FormView control example. It displays shipper data from the Northwind database as bound to a Label and two TextBox controls.

```
<asp:Repeater runat="server"
    ID="Repeater1"
    DataSourceID="SqlDataSource1">
    <ItemTemplate>
        <br /><br />
        Shipper Identification:
        <asp:Label runat="server" Font-Bold="True"
            ID="Label1"
            Text='<%# Eval("ShipperID") %>'>
        </asp:Label>
        <br />
        <br />
        Company Name<br />
        <asp:TextBox runat="server" Width="250px"
            ID="TextBox1"
            Text='<%# Bind("CompanyName") %>'>
        </asp:TextBox>
        <br />
        Phone Number<br />
        <asp:TextBox runat="server" Width="250px"
            ID="TextBox2"
            Text='<%# Bind("Phone") %>'>
        </asp:TextBox>
    </ItemTemplate>
</asp:Repeater>
```

When this data is displayed, however, it is repeated down the page. Figure 12-16 shows the results in a browser window.

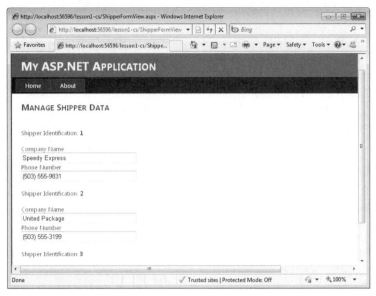

FIGURE 12-16 The Repeater control showing the ItemTemplate in a browser.

The ListView Control

The ListView control also uses templates for the display of data. However, it supports many additional templates that allow for more scenarios when working with your data. These templates include the LayoutTemplate, which allows you to indicate an overall layout inside of which rows of your data will be displayed. The rows themselves are defined with the ItemTemplate. At run time, rows are placed within the LayoutTemplate placeholder identified by a control that has its ID attribute set to itemPlaceholder.

Another template is the GroupTemplate, which allows you to define groups of data. You can then set the GroupItemCount value to indicate the number of items in a group, and you can set the control to lay out groups of data and allow users to page through them.

The ItemSeparatorTemplate allows you to define content that should be placed between rows of items. This allows you to put graphic separators or other data between rows.

The ListView control (unlike DataList and Repeater) also implicitly supports the ability to edit, insert, and delete data by using a data source control. You can define individual templates for each of these scenarios. You can then change the mode of the ListView control through a server-side call and thus invoke the template for the user.

As an example, consider a page that includes a data source control that exposes the Product table from the Northwind database. You can create a ListView control to work with this data. The following markup shows such an example. In this example, a LayoutTemplate defines a <div> tag that includes the itemPlaceholder setting. The ItemTemplate is then defined by a <div> tag. At run time, each row will be added as a <div> tag in the placeholder.

```
<asp:ListView runat="server"
    ID="ListView1"
    DataKeyNames="ProductID"
    DataSourceID="SqlDataSource1">
    <LayoutTemplate>
        <div id="itemPlaceholder" runat="server"></div>
        <br />
        <div style="text-align: center">
            <asp:DataPager ID="DataPager1" runat="server" PageSize="4">
                <Fields>
                    <asp:NextPreviousPagerField
                        ButtonType="Button"
                        ShowFirstPageButton="True"
                        ShowLastPageButton="True" />
                </Fields>
            </asp:DataPager>
        </div>
    </LayoutTemplate>
    <ItemTemplate>
        <div style="text-align: center">
            <b>ProductName:</b>
            <asp:Label ID="ProductNameLabel" runat="server"
                Text='<%# Eval("ProductName") %>' />
            <br />
            <b>QuantityPerUnit:</b>
            <asp:Label ID="QuantityPerUnitLabel" runat="server"
                Text='<%# Eval("QuantityPerUnit") %>' />
            <br />
            <b>UnitPrice:</b>
            <asp:Label ID="UnitPriceLabel" runat="server"
                Text='<%# Eval("UnitPrice") %>' />
            <br />
        </div>
    </ItemTemplate>
    <ItemSeparatorTemplate>
        <hr />
    </ItemSeparatorTemplate>
</asp:ListView>
```

Notice also that the ListView control uses the ASP.NET DataPager control. This control allows you to provide custom data pagers for your data lists. Here the control is embedded at the end of the LayoutTemplate. The ListView control automatically uses the DataPager to move the user through data.

Finally, notice the use of the ItemSeparatorTemplate. This is used to put a horizontal rule between data rows. Figure 12-17 shows the results in a browser window.

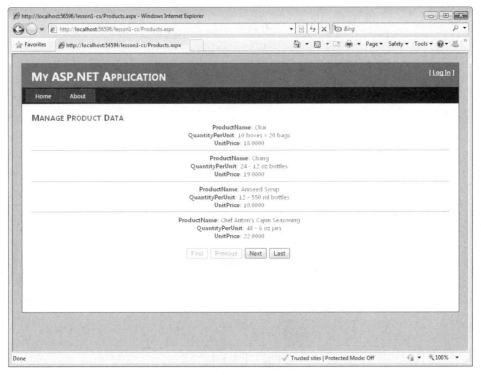

FIGURE 12-17 The ListView control rendered in the browser.

The Chart Control

The Chart control allows you to display data by using chart visualization. You bind a data source to this control much like you do for the other data-bound controls. The big difference is that you then indicate fields from the data source that should be bound to an axis or data series in a chart.

There are more than 25 different chart types for displaying data. When the chart control runs on the server, it generate a graphic file (which is a PNG file by default, but you can change this setting) and then sends this to the browser as part of the response.

There are hundreds of properties you can set to define your chart and how it displays data. The chart definition typically includes the Series and ChartAreas elements. A Series represents a group of data to be shown on a chart. A Series element has a ChartType that defines the visualization of the data (choices are Bar, Area, Bubble, Line, Column, Pie, Radar, Range, and many more). A ChartArea element is used to indicate specifics about areas on your chart, such as an x and y axis. Here you can set intervals, formatting, and related visual items.

As an example, suppose you have the following SqlDataSource control that exposes sales by region.

```
<asp:SqlDataSource ID="SqlDataSource1" runat="server"
    ConnectionString="<%$ ConnectionStrings:NorthwindConnectionString %>"
    SelectCommand="SELECT SUM([Order Details].UnitPrice * [Order Details].Quantity) AS
Total, Orders.ShipCountry FROM Orders INNER JOIN [Order Details] ON Orders.OrderID =
[Order Details].OrderID GROUP BY Orders.ShipCountry Order By Total"></asp:SqlDataSource>
```

You could then bind this to a Chart control to display each country and the total sales for that country. The following markup shows an example.

```
<asp:Chart ID="Chart1" runat="server"
    DataSourceID="SqlDataSource1"
    Width="702px" Height="581px">
    <Series>
        <asp:Series Name="Series1"
            XValueMember="ShipCountry"
            YValueMembers="Total"
            ChartType="Bar"
            XValueType="String"
            IsValueShownAsLabel="True"
            LabelBackColor="White"
            LabelFormat="{c}">
            <SmartLabelStyle CalloutBackColor="White" />
        </asp:Series>
    </Series>
    <ChartAreas>
        <asp:ChartArea Name="ChartArea1">
            <AxisY>
                <LabelStyle Format="{c}" />
            </AxisY>
            <AxisX Interval="1">
            </AxisX>
        </asp:ChartArea>
    </ChartAreas>
</asp:Chart>
```

Running this page will produce results similar to those shown in Figure 12-18.

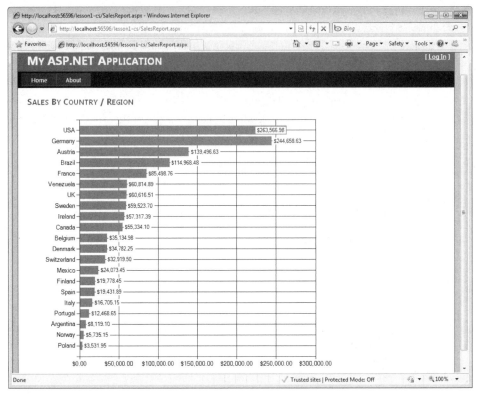

FIGURE 12-18 The Chart control rendered in the browser.

The DataList Control

The DataList control works like the Repeater control. It repeats data for each row in your data set, and it displays this data according to your defined template. However, it lays out the data defined in the template within various HTML structures. This includes options for horizontal or vertical layout, and it also allows you to set how the data should be repeated, as flow or table layout.

The DataList control does not automatically use a data source control to edit data. Instead, it provides command events in which you can write your own code for these scenarios. To enable these events, you add a Button control to one of the templates and set the button's CommandName property to the edit, delete, update, or cancel keyword. The appropriate event is then raised by the DataList control.

The following markup shows an example of a DataList control configured to show product data from the Northwind database. This control's RepeatDirection is set to show data vertically by using a RepeatLayout of flow. The product data is bound to the DataList control inside the ItemTemplate code.

```
<asp:DataList runat="server"
    DataSourceID="SqlDataSource1"
    RepeatDirection="Vertical"
    ID="DataList1"
    RepeatLayout="flow">
    <ItemTemplate>
        <asp:Label ID="Label1" runat="server"
            Text='<%# Eval("ProductName") %>'
            Font-Bold="True">
        </asp:Label>
        <asp:Label ID="Label2" runat="server"
            Text='<%# Eval("UnitPrice", "{0:C}") %>'>
        </asp:Label>
        <br />
    </ItemTemplate>
</asp:DataList>
```

Hierarchical Data-Bound Controls

The HierarchicalDataBoundControl control serves as a base class for controls that render data in a hierarchical fashion. The classes that inherit from HierarchicalDataBoundControl are TreeView and Menu, as shown in Figure 12-19.

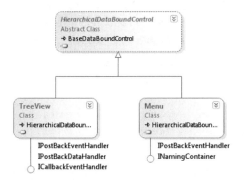

FIGURE 12-19 The HierarchicalDataBoundControl class hierarchy.

The TreeView Control

The TreeView control is a data-bound control that is used to display hierarchical data, such as a listing of files and folders, or a table of contents in a tree structure. Each entry in the tree is called a *node*. The nodes of this control can be bound to XML, tabular, or relational data. This control can also provide site navigation when used with the SiteMapDataSource control.

You can programmatically access and control the properties of the TreeView control. The TreeView can also be populated via client-side script by using modern browsers. In addition, nodes can be displayed as either plaintext or hyperlinks, and you can opt to display a check box next to each node.

Each node is represented by a TreeNode object. A node that contains other nodes is called a *parent node*. A node that is contained by another node is called a *child node*. A node can be both a parent node and a child node. A node that has no children is called a *leaf node*. A node that is not contained by any other node but is the ancestor to all the other nodes is the *root node*.

The typical TreeView tree structure has only one root node, but you can add multiple root nodes to the tree structure. This means that you can display a tree hierarchy without being forced to have a single root node.

The TreeNode has a Text property that is populated with the data that is to be displayed. The TreeNode also has a Value property that is used to store the data that is posted back to the web server.

You can configure a node to be a selection node or a navigation node by setting the NavigateUrl property. If the NavigateUrl property is set to an empty string (string.Empty), it is a selection node, and clicking the node simply selects it. If the NavigateUrl property is not set to an empty string, the node is a navigation node, and clicking it navigates to the location specified by the NavigateUrl property.

POPULATING THE TREEVIEW CONTROL

The TreeView control can be populated by using static data or by using data binding. To populate the TreeView control with static data, you can use declarative syntax by placing opening and closing <Nodes> tags in the TreeView element and then creating a structure of nested <TreeNode> elements within the <Nodes> element. Each <TreeNode> has properties that you can set by adding attributes to the <TreeNode> element.

To use data binding to populate the TreeView control, you can use any data source that implements the IHierarchicalDataSource interface, such as an XmlDataSource control or a SiteMapDataSource control. Simply set the DataSourceID property of the TreeView control to the ID value of the data source control, and the TreeView control automatically binds to the specified data source control.

You can also bind to an XmlDocument object or a DataSet object that contains DataRelation objects by setting the DataSource property of the TreeView control to the data source and then calling the DataBind method.

The TreeView control contains a DataBindings property that is a collection of TreeNodeBinding objects that define the binding between a data item and the TreeNode. You can specify the binding criteria and the data item property to display in the node. This is useful when binding to XML elements when you are interested in binding to an attribute of the element.

Assume that you want to use a TreeView control to display customer data from a file called Customers.xml, which contains a list of customers, their orders and invoices, and the items for each order. This data is stored in a hierarchical format in the XML file. The Customers.xml file looks like the following.

```
<?xml version="1.0" encoding="utf-8" ?>
<Customers>
    <Customer CustomerId="1" Name="Northwind Traders">
```

```xml
    <Orders>
        <Order OrderId="1" ShipDate="06-22-2006">
            <OrderItems>
                <OrderItem OrderItemId="1" PartNumber="123"
                    PartDescription="Large Widget" Quantity="5"
                    Price="22.00" />
                <OrderItem OrderItemId="2" PartNumber="234"
                    PartDescription="Medium Widget" Quantity="2"
                    Price="12.50" />
            </OrderItems>
        </Order>
        <Order OrderId="2" ShipDate="06-25-2006">
            <OrderItems>
                <OrderItem OrderItemId="5" PartNumber="432"
                    PartDescription="Small Widget" Quantity="30"
                    Price="8.99" />
                <OrderItem OrderItemId="4" PartNumber="234"
                    PartDescription="Medium Widget" Quantity="2"
                    Price="12.50" />
            </OrderItems>
        </Order>
    </Orders>
    <Invoices>
        <Invoice InvoiceId="6" Amount="99.37" />
        <Invoice InvoiceId="7" Amount="147.50" />
    </Invoices>
</Customer>
<Customer CustomerId="2" Name="Tailspin Toys">
    <Orders>
        <Order OrderId="8" ShipDate="07-11-2006">
            <OrderItems>
                <OrderItem OrderItemId="9" PartNumber="987"
                    PartDescription="Combo Widget" Quantity="2"
                    Price="87.25" />
                <OrderItem OrderItemId="10" PartNumber="654"
                    PartDescription="Ugly Widget" Quantity="1"
                    Price="2.00" />
            </OrderItems>
        </Order>
        <Order OrderId="11" ShipDate="08-21-2006">
            <OrderItems>
                <OrderItem OrderItemId="12" PartNumber="999"
                    PartDescription="Pretty Widget" Quantity="50"
                    Price="78.99" />
                <OrderItem OrderItemId="14" PartNumber="575"
                    PartDescription="Tiny Widget" Quantity="100"
                    Price="1.20" />
            </OrderItems>
        </Order>
    </Orders>
    <Invoices>
        <Invoice InvoiceId="26" Amount="46.58" />
        <Invoice InvoiceId="27" Amount="279.15" />
    </Invoices>
</Customer>
</Customers>
```

An XmlDataSource and a TreeView control are added to the webpage and configured. The following shows the markup for the TreeView control.

```
<asp:TreeView ID="TreeView1" runat="server"
    DataSourceID="XmlDataSource1"
    ShowLines="True" ExpandDepth="0">
    <DataBindings>
        <asp:TreeNodeBinding DataMember="Customer"
            TextField="Name" ValueField="CustomerId" />
        <asp:TreeNodeBinding DataMember="Order"
            TextField="ShipDate" ValueField="OrderId" />
        <asp:TreeNodeBinding DataMember="OrderItem"
            TextField="PartDescription" ValueField="OrderItemId" />
        <asp:TreeNodeBinding DataMember="Invoice"
            TextField="Amount" ValueField="InvoiceId"
            FormatString="{0:C}" />
    </DataBindings>
</asp:TreeView>
```

In this example, the configuration is kept to a minimum, but configuration is required to display information that is more important than the XML element name, such as the customer's name instead of the XML element name (Customer). The following code is added to the code-behind page to simply display the value of the selected node.

Sample of Visual Basic Code

```
Partial Class TreeView_Control
    Inherits System.Web.UI.Page

    Protected Sub TreeView1_SelectedNodeChanged(ByVal sender As Object, _
        ByVal e As System.EventArgs) Handles TreeView1.SelectedNodeChanged
            Response.Write("Value:" + TreeView1.SelectedNode.Value)
    End Sub

End Class
```

Sample of C# Code

```
public partial class TreeView_Control : System.Web.UI.Page
{
    protected void TreeView1_SelectedNodeChanged(object sender, EventArgs e)
    {
        Response.Write("Value:" + TreeView1.SelectedNode.Value);
    }
}
```

When the webpage is displayed, the Customers node is visible. You can also click the plus (+) sign to expand the nodes, as shown in Figure 12-20.

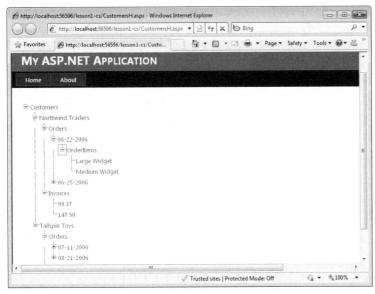

FIGURE 12-20 The TreeView displays the nodes as configured.

The Menu Control

The Menu control is a data-bound control that is used to display hierarchical data in the form of a menu system. The Menu control is often used in combination with a SiteMapDataSource control for navigating a website.

The Menu control can be populated by using static data or by using data binding. To populate the Menu control with static data, you can use declarative syntax by placing opening and closing <Items> tags in the Menu element, and then you can create a structure of nested <MenuItem> elements within the <Items> element. Each <MenuItem> has properties that you can set by adding attributes to the <asp:MenuItem> element.

To use data binding to populate the Menu control, you can use any data source that implements the IHierarchicalDataSource interface, such as an XmlDataSource control or a SiteMapDataSource control. Simply set the DataSourceID property of the Menu control to the ID value of the data source control, and the Menu control automatically binds to the specified data source control.

You can also bind to an XmlDocument object or a DataSet object that contains DataRelation objects by setting the DataSource property of the Menu control to the data source, and then calling the DataBind method.

The Menu control contains a DataBindings property that is a collection of MenuItemBinding objects that define the binding between a data item and the menu item it is binding to in a Menu control. You can specify the binding criteria and the data item properties to display in the items. This is useful when binding to XML elements when you are interested in binding to an attribute of the element.

Assume that you want to use a Menu control to display menu data from a file called MenuItems.xml, which contains a list of the menu items to be displayed. The data is stored in a hierarchical format in the XML file. The MenuItems.xml file looks like the following.

```
<?xml version="1.0" encoding="utf-8" ?>
<MenuItems>
    <Home display="Home"  url="~/" />
    <Products display="Products" url="~/products/">
        <SmallWidgets display="Small Widgets"
            url="~/products/smallwidgets.aspx" />
        <MediumWidgets display="Medium Widgets"
            url="~/products/mediumwidgets.aspx" />
        <BigWidgets display="Big Widgets"
            url="~/products/bigwidgets.aspx" />
    </Products>
    <Support display="Support"  url="~/Support/">
        <Downloads display="Downloads"
            url="~/support/downloads.aspx" />
        <FAQs display="FAQs"
            url="~/support/faqs.aspx" />
    </Support>
    <AboutUs display="About Us" url="~/aboutus/">
        <Company display="Company"
            url="~/aboutus/company.aspx" />
        <Locations display="Location"
            url="~/aboutus/locations.aspx" />
    </AboutUs>
</MenuItems>
```

An XmlDataSource, a Menu, and a Label control are added to the webpage. The XmlDataSource is configured to use the XML file. The Menu control is configured to use the XmlDataSource. The following is the webpage markup.

```
<asp:Menu runat="server"
    ID="Menu1"
    DataSourceID="XmlDataSource1"
    OnMenuItemClick="Menu1_MenuItemClick">
</asp:Menu>
```

The following code is added to the code-behind page to simply display the ValuePath property of the selected MenuItem. When the webpage is displayed, the Menu appears and you can point to a menu item to see its child menu items.

Sample of Visual Basic Code

```vb
Partial Class Menu_Control
    Inherits System.Web.UI.Page

    Protected Sub Menu1_MenuItemClick(ByVal sender As Object, _
        ByVal e As System.Web.UI.WebControls.MenuEventArgs) _
        Handles Menu1.MenuItemClick
            Label1.Text = e.Item.ValuePath
    End Sub
End Class
```

Sample of C# Code

```csharp
public partial class Menu_Control : System.Web.UI.Page
{
    protected void Menu1_MenuItemClick(object sender, MenuEventArgs e)
    {
        Label1.Text = e.Item.ValuePath;
    }
}
```

✔ Quick Check

1. What method should you call on a data-bound control when the data is ready to be read from the data source?
2. What method is used in a FormView to perform two-way data binding?
3. What GUI object can provide a data source that allows you to connect middle-tier objects to data-bound controls?

Quick Check Answers

1. You should call the DataBind method.
2. The Bind method is used to perform two-way data binding.
3. The ObjectDataSource control can provide a data source that allows you to connect middle-tier objects to data-bound controls.

PRACTICE **Using the GridView and DetailsView Controls**

In this practice, you use the GridView and DetailsView data-bound controls together to create a master-detail page.

> **ON THE COMPANION MEDIA**
>
> If you encounter a problem completing an exercise, you can find the completed projects in the samples installed from this book's companion CD. For more information about the project files and other content on the CD, see "Using the Companion Media" in this book's Introduction.

EXERCISE Creating the Website, Adding Controls to the Page, and Configuring the Controls

In this exercise, you create a new website and add the database and data source control. You then add the data-bound controls and configure them accordingly.

1. Open Visual Studio and create a new website called **UsingDataBoundControls** by using your preferred programming language.

2. Add the northwnd.mdf file to your App_Data directory. You can copy the file from the samples installed from the CD.

3. Open Default.aspx. Delete the default content on the page. Add a SqlDataSource control to the page from the Toolbox; name it **SqlDataSourceReadList**. This control will read data for display by the GridView control.

4. In Design view of the Default.aspx page, click the smart tag in the upper-right corner of the SqlDataSource control to launch the Configure Data Source Wizard.

   a. On the first page, set the connection to the northwnd.mdf file in the App_Data directory and click Next.

   b. When prompted, save the connection string as **ConnectionStringNorthwind**, and then click Next again.

   c. On the Configure Select Statement page, select the Customers table from the Name list box. Select the CustomerID, CompanyName, ContactName, City, Country, and Phone fields. Click Next, and then click Finish to close the wizard.

   Your SqlDataSource markup should look similar to the following.

   ```
   <asp:SqlDataSource ID="SqlDataSource1" runat="server"
       ConnectionString="<%$ ConnectionStrings:ConnectionStringNorthwind %>"
       SelectCommand="SELECT [CustomerID], [CompanyName], [ContactName], [City],
       [Country], [Phone] FROM [Customers]">
   </asp:SqlDataSource>
   ```

5. Drag a GridView control onto the Default.aspx page. Using either Design or Source view, configure the GridView control as follows:

   - Set the DataSourceId to SqlDataSourceReadList, created previously.
   - Set Enable Paging (AllowPaging property) to true.
   - Set Enable Sorting (AllowSorting property) to true.
   - Set AutoGenerateColumns to false.
   - Configure the CustomerID, CompanyName, ContactName, City, Country, and Phone fields to be displayed.
   - Add a CommandField to allow a user to select a row of data (you can do so in Design view by clicking Enable Selection).

Your markup should look similar to the following.

```
<asp:GridView ID="GridView1" runat="server"
    AllowPaging="True" AllowSorting="True"
    AutoGenerateColumns="False"
    DataKeyNames="CustomerID"
    DataSourceID="SqlDataSource1"
    width="700px">
    <Columns>
        <asp:CommandField ShowSelectButton="True" />
        <asp:BoundField DataField="CustomerID" HeaderText="ID"
            ReadOnly="True" SortExpression="CustomerID" />
        <asp:BoundField DataField="CompanyName" HeaderText="Company"
            SortExpression="CompanyName" />
        <asp:BoundField DataField="ContactName" HeaderText="Contact"
            SortExpression="ContactName" />
        <asp:BoundField DataField="City" HeaderText="City"
            SortExpression="City" />
        <asp:BoundField DataField="Country" HeaderText="Country"
            SortExpression="Country" />
        <asp:BoundField DataField="Phone" HeaderText="Phone"
            SortExpression="Phone" />
    </Columns>
</asp:GridView>
```

6. If you want, select the GridView in Design view and click the AutoFormat link on the task pane (from the smart tag). Select Professional or another formatting option.

7. Run the website; you should be able to page through data, sort data, and select a row.

8. Next, add another SqlDataSource control to the Default.aspx page; name it **SqlDataSourceUpdate**. Configure this control as before, by using the Configure Data Source Wizard.

   a. On the first page, select ConnectionStringNorthwind and click Next.

   b. The next step is to configure the SELECT statement to pick up the CustomerID parameter from the selected row on the GridView control. On the Configure The Select Statement page, select the Customers table. This time, select each field in the table. Then click the Where button to launch the Add WHERE Clause dialog box. Set the column to CustomerID. Set the Operator to = (the equal sign). Set the Source to Control. Under Parameter Properties, set the Control ID to GridView1. Click the Add button, and then click OK to close the dialog box.

   c. Click the Advanced button. In the Advanced Sql Generation Options dialog box, select the Generate INSERT, UPDATE, And DELETE Statements option. Click OK to close this dialog box. Click Next, and then click Finish to close the wizard.

Your SqlDataSource control's markup should look as follows.

```
<asp:SqlDataSource ID="SqlDataSourceUpdate" runat="server"
    ConnectionString="<%$ ConnectionStrings:ConnectionStringNorthwind %>"
    DeleteCommand="DELETE FROM [Customers] WHERE [CustomerID] = @CustomerID"
    InsertCommand="INSERT INTO [Customers] ([CustomerID], [CompanyName],
 [ContactName], [ContactTitle], [Address], [City], [Region], [PostalCode],
 [Country], [Phone], [Fax]) VALUES (@CustomerID, @CompanyName, @ContactName,
 @ContactTitle, @Address, @City, @Region, @PostalCode, @Country, @Phone, @Fax)"
    SelectCommand="SELECT [CustomerID], [CompanyName], [ContactName],
 [ContactTitle],
 [Address], [City], [Region], [PostalCode], [Country], [Phone], [Fax] FROM
 [Customers] WHERE ([CustomerID] = @CustomerID)"
    UpdateCommand="UPDATE [Customers] SET [CompanyName] = @CompanyName,
 [ContactName] = @ContactName, [ContactTitle] = @ContactTitle, [Address] =
 @Address,
 [City] = @City, [Region] = @Region, [PostalCode] = @PostalCode, [Country] =
 @Country, [Phone] = @Phone, [Fax] = @Fax WHERE [CustomerID] = @CustomerID">
    <DeleteParameters>
        <asp:Parameter Name="CustomerID" Type="String" />
    </DeleteParameters>
    <InsertParameters>
        <asp:Parameter Name="CustomerID" Type="String" />
        <asp:Parameter Name="CompanyName" Type="String" />
        <asp:Parameter Name="ContactName" Type="String" />
        <asp:Parameter Name="ContactTitle" Type="String" />
        <asp:Parameter Name="Address" Type="String" />
        <asp:Parameter Name="City" Type="String" />
        <asp:Parameter Name="Region" Type="String" />
        <asp:Parameter Name="PostalCode" Type="String" />
        <asp:Parameter Name="Country" Type="String" />
        <asp:Parameter Name="Phone" Type="String" />
        <asp:Parameter Name="Fax" Type="String" />
    </InsertParameters>
    <SelectParameters>
        <asp:ControlParameter ControlID="GridView1" Name="CustomerID"
            PropertyName="SelectedValue" Type="String" />
    </SelectParameters>
    <UpdateParameters>
        <asp:Parameter Name="CompanyName" Type="String" />
        <asp:Parameter Name="ContactName" Type="String" />
        <asp:Parameter Name="ContactTitle" Type="String" />
        <asp:Parameter Name="Address" Type="String" />
        <asp:Parameter Name="City" Type="String" />
        <asp:Parameter Name="Region" Type="String" />
        <asp:Parameter Name="PostalCode" Type="String" />
        <asp:Parameter Name="Country" Type="String" />
        <asp:Parameter Name="Phone" Type="String" />
        <asp:Parameter Name="Fax" Type="String" />
        <asp:Parameter Name="CustomerID" Type="String" />
    </UpdateParameters>
</asp:SqlDataSource>
```

9. Add a DetailsView control to the page; place it under the GridView control.

10. Switch to Design view and configure the DetailsView control by using the smart tag and related task list.

11. Set the control's data source to SqlDataSourceUpdate.

12. Enable inserting and editing. (Deleting requires management of a foreign key constraint, so leave that cleared for this example.)

13. Click Edit Templates from the task list of the DetailsView control.

14. Select the EmptyData Template from the Display list in the task list.

15. In the template, type **No customer is currently selected**.

16. Add a LinkButton control to the template. Set the LinkButton control's CausesValidation property to false (from the Properties pane). Set its CommandName property to **New**, and set its Text property to **New**.

17. In the DetailsView Tasks window, click End Template Editing.

Your DetailsView markup should look as follows.

```
<asp:DetailsView ID="DetailsView1" runat="server" Height="50px" Width="125px"
    AutoGenerateRows="False" DataKeyNames="CustomerID"
    DataSourceID="SqlDataSourceUpdate">
    <EmptyDataTemplate>
        <b>No customer is currently selected<br />
        <asp:LinkButton ID="LinkButton1" runat="server"
            CausesValidation="False"
            CommandName="New">New</asp:LinkButton>
        </b>
    </EmptyDataTemplate>
    <Fields>
        <asp:BoundField DataField="CustomerID" HeaderText="ID"
            ReadOnly="True" SortExpression="CustomerID" />
        <asp:BoundField DataField="CompanyName" HeaderText="Company"
            SortExpression="CompanyName" />
        <asp:BoundField DataField="ContactName" HeaderText="Contact"
            SortExpression="ContactName" />
        <asp:BoundField DataField="ContactTitle" HeaderText="Contact Title"
            SortExpression="ContactTitle" />
        <asp:BoundField DataField="Address" HeaderText="Address"
            SortExpression="Address" />
        <asp:BoundField DataField="City" HeaderText="City"
            SortExpression="City" />
        <asp:BoundField DataField="Region" HeaderText="Region"
            SortExpression="Region" />
        <asp:BoundField DataField="PostalCode" HeaderText="Postal Code"
            SortExpression="PostalCode" />
        <asp:BoundField DataField="Country" HeaderText="Country"
            SortExpression="Country" />
        <asp:BoundField DataField="Phone" HeaderText="Phone"
            SortExpression="Phone" />
        <asp:BoundField DataField="Fax" HeaderText="Fax"
            SortExpression="Fax" />
        <asp:CommandField ShowEditButton="True"
            ShowInsertButton="True" />
    </Fields>
</asp:DetailsView>
```

18. If you want, select the DetailsView control in Design view and click the AutoFormat link in the task pane (from the smart tag). Select Professional or another formatting option.

19. Next, add code to update the GridView when a record has been inserted or edited in the DetailsView control. To do so, add event handlers for both the ItemUpdated and ItemInserted events of the DetailsView control. Inside each event, rebind the GridView control. The following code shows an example.

Sample of Visual Basic Code

```vb
Protected Sub DetailsView1_ItemInserted(ByVal sender As Object, _
  ByVal e As System.Web.UI.WebControls.DetailsViewInsertedEventArgs) _
  Handles DetailsView1.ItemInserted

  GridView1.DataBind()

End Sub

Protected Sub DetailsView1_ItemUpdated(ByVal sender As Object, _
  ByVal e As System.Web.UI.WebControls.DetailsViewUpdatedEventArgs) _
  Handles DetailsView1.ItemUpdated

  GridView1.DataBind()

End Sub
```

Sample of C# Code

```csharp
protected void DetailsView1_ItemUpdated(object sender,
    DetailsViewUpdatedEventArgs e)
{
    GridView1.DataBind();
}

protected void DetailsView1_ItemInserted(object sender,
    DetailsViewInsertedEventArgs e)
{
    GridView1.DataBind();
}
```

20. Add a title to the top of the page for **Manage Customers**. Add another title for **Customer Details**.

21. Run the webpage. Notice that the empty DetailsView control allows you to add a new record. Select a row from the GridView. Notice that it appears in the DetailsView section, as shown in Figure 12-21. Click the Edit link (which will appear when a row is selected in the GridView), and then edit a record.

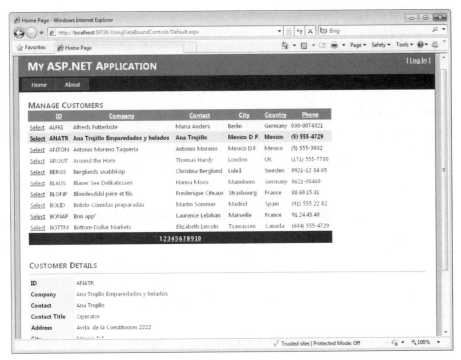

FIGURE 12-21 The master-detail form shown in the browser window.

Lesson Summary

- Simple data-bound controls consist of controls that inherit from the ListControl, such as DropDownList, ListBox, CheckBoxList, BulletedList, and RadioButtonList. For these controls, you set the DataTextField to the name of the column that contains the data you want to display to the user. You set the DataValueField to the column that contains the value or values you want to return to the server for a selected item.

- Composite data-bound controls consist of the GridView, DetailsView, FormView, Repeater, ListView, and DataList controls. The GridView and DetailsView controls show data as tables. The other controls allow you to define templates for laying out your data.

- Hierarchical data-bound controls consist of the Menu and TreeView controls. These controls are used for displaying data that contains parent-child relationships.

Lesson Review

You can use the following questions to test your knowledge of the information in Lesson 2, "Working with Data-Bound Web Server Controls." The questions are also available on the companion CD in a practice test, if you prefer to review them in electronic form.

> **NOTE   ANSWERS**
>
> Answers to these questions and explanations of why each answer choice is correct or incorrect are located in the "Answers" section at the end of the book.

1. You are creating a data-bound CheckBoxList control that allows a user to select options for configuring a vehicle. When the data is displayed to the user, you want the OptionName column to display. When the data is posted back to the server, you need the OptionId column value for all selected items. Which of the following attribute definitions would you set? (Choose all that apply.)

   A. DataTextField=OptionId

   B. DataTextField=OptionName

   C. DataValueField=OptionId

   D. DataValueField=OptionName

2. You want to display a list of suppliers on a webpage. The supplier list must display 10 suppliers at a time, and you require the ability to edit individual suppliers. Which web control is the best choice for this scenario? (Choose all that apply.)

   A. The DetailsView control

   B. The Repeater control

   C. The GridView control

   D. The ListView control

3. You want to display a list of parts in a master-detail scenario so that users can select a part number from a list that takes a minimum amount of space on the webpage. When the part is selected, a DetailsView control displays all the information about the part and allows users to edit the part. Which web control is the best choice to display the part number list for this scenario?

   A. The DropDownList control

   B. The RadioButtonList control

   C. The FormView control

   D. The TextBox control

Lesson 3: Working with ASP.NET Dynamic Data

ASP.NET Dynamic Data is a set of user interface templates and controls for creating data-driven websites. You attach a data context to a Dynamic Data MetaModel object and can then work with that data to read, filter, insert, update, and delete. Dynamic Data does not generate code specific to a particular data schema. Rather, it is a series of extensible templates that can work with any LINQ to SQL, Entity Framework, or custom data context. If you need to customize a template to change the way data is displayed or behaves, you can do so by following the conventions of ASP.NET Dynamic Data.

This lesson helps you get started with using ASP.NET Dynamic Data to either create a new website or add these capabilities to an existing one. The lesson covers creating the scaffolding for using Dynamic Data and customizing the technology, including creating custom routes, fields, pages, and business logic.

> **After this lesson, you will be able to:**
> - Create the scaffolding for using Dynamic Data against a data context.
> - Create custom routing, field templates, page templates, and business logic.
> - Add Dynamic Data scaffolding and/or features to an existing website.
>
> **Estimated lesson time: 40 minutes**

 REAL WORLD

Mike Snell

I have personally written a number of custom web store fronts using ASP and ASP.NET. In each case, most of the work actually involved creating screens to allow administrators to manage the data in the site. This meant adding and editing products, orders, customer information, sales, and more. Dynamic Data would have cut what was weeks (often months) of work down to days.

Getting Started with Dynamic Data Websites

ASP.NET Dynamic Data works at run time to extract information from your data context and apply that information to template pages for handling CRUD operations against your data source. Recall that a data context is created by using LINQ to SQL or LINQ to Entities (see Chapter 11 for more details).

Dynamic Data uses the information from your model, such as table relationships and field data types, to create meaningful pages. For example, if you are showing data in a list, Dynamic Data will use foreign-key relationships to allow you to filter that data (into product categories, for example). It will also allow you to link to related data from a specified data record (such as customer orders). In addition, fields will be shown based on their underlying data type, and when users update or insert data, validation rules will be enforced based on the model.

To start creating a new website with Dynamic Data, you typically follow these steps:

1. Create a scaffold site that includes the default presentation layer templates used by ASP.NET Dynamic Data.

2. Define a data context that represents your data source and model by using either LINQ to SQL, LINQ to Entities, or a custom model.

3. Register your data context with the website's MetaModel instance inside the Global.asax file.

4. Customize the URL routing, page and field templates, business logic, and validation in the website. (This step is optional.)

You will walk through each of these steps in the upcoming sections.

Creating a Dynamic Data Website

You can create a new ASP.NET Dynamic Data website or add Dynamic Data features to an existing site. This section covers the former; you will see how to add these features to existing sites later in the lesson.

Visual Studio ships with two ASP.NET Dynamic Data project templates: ASP.NET Dynamic Data Entities Web Site and ASP.NET Dynamic Data LINQ to SQL Web Site. The first is used to create sites that use the Entity Framework as the data context; the second is for sites that connect to a LINQ to SQL data context. You must choose between the two, because the templates only support a single data context in a site (as it is defined within the application's Global.asax file).

Figure 12-22 shows the structure of a newly created Dynamic Data website. Note that you do not select a data source when you create the website. Instead, you can connect to a data source as a later step. The website only contains templates that use your data context information at run time. The next section covers this website structure in detail.

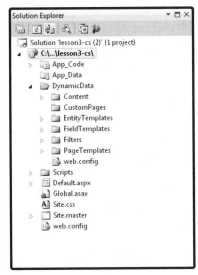

FIGURE 12-22 The structure of an ASP.NET Dynamic Data website.

DYNAMIC DATA WEBSITE STRUCTURE

The Dynamic Data website contains the DynamicData folder and several files in the root of the site. You will look at the contents of the DynamicData folder soon. First, the files in the root of the site are listed here, along with a brief description of each:

- **Default.aspx**   This file is used to display all tables in the data context. It includes a GridView control that is bound to the MetaModel.VisibleTables collection. The MetaModel is exposed through an application variable (from the Global.asax file) called DefaultModel. It is referenced as follows:

```
ASP.global_asax.DefaultModel.VisibleTables.
```

- **Global.asax**   This file contains code that is run for application events, including Application_Start. Dynamic Data uses this file to call RegisterRoutes at Application_ Start. This method connects your data context to a meta-model and uses ASP.NET routing to handle page requests for tables and actions (such as List, Details, Edit, and Insert).

- **Site.css**   This file represents a style sheet used by the master page and related page templates. You can customize this style sheet to change the look of your Dynamic Data site.

- **Site.master**   This is the master page for the Dynamic Data site. By default, it defines navigation for the site, a ScriptManager control, and the main ContentPlaceHolder control. The Site.master page is used by the page templates.

- **Web.config**   This is a less verbose version of the Web.config file that is created for standard ASP.NET websites.

The DynamicData folder contains several subfolders and another Web.config file. The Web.config file registers an HTTP handler for System.Web.HttpNotFoundHandler. The folders and their naming convention define a pattern that is used by Dynamic Data to route requests accordingly. Each folder is listed here, along with a brief description of its contents:

- **Content**   This folder contains content used by Dynamic Data, including images for the pager control and a custom GridViewPager user control.

- **CustomPages**   By default, this folder is empty. You use this folder if you need to create custom templates for displaying or editing data. The convention is to create a new folder under CustomPages with the name of the item in your data model that you want to customize (such as Customers). You then typically copy a page template (from the PageTemplates directory) to this new folder, customize it, and save it. The Dynamic Data routing will look in this CustomPages folder first for items that are named with this convention (and thus use those instead of the default templates).

- **EntityTemplates**   This folder contains user controls that are used by the page templates for displaying and editing data. These user controls include Default.ascx, Default_Edit.ascx, and Default_Insert.ascx.

- **FieldTemplates**   This folder contains a set of user controls (ASCX files) that define the UI for displaying table fields in either a view or edit mode. There are user controls based on the type of data being worked with, including Boolean, DateTime, Text, Url, Decimal, Email, and more. These fields are rendered based on the data type in the data context or on additional attributes that you add to extend the meta-model. You can also create custom field templates to display or edit data with other controls (including third-party controls).

- **Filters**   This folder contains user controls to define the UI that is used to filter data that is displayed in a list. These controls include Boolean.ascx, Enumeration.ascx, and ForeignKey.ascx.

- **PageTemplates**   This folder contains the default templates for working with data. These template pages can show a table in a list (List.aspx), allow you to create a new record (Insert.aspx), edit an existing record (Edit.aspx), view the details of a record (Details.aspx), and show a list of data and a selected record's details on the same page (ListDetails.aspx).

Defining a Data Context

You create a data context by adding either a LINQ to SQL Classes (DBML) file or an ADO.NET Entity Data Model (EDMX) file to your project (see Chapter 11 for more details). You can also create a custom model through code.

As an example, suppose that the Northwind database is in the App_Data directory of your site. You can then create a LINQ to SQL DBML file based on tables found inside this database. Figure 12-23 shows an example.

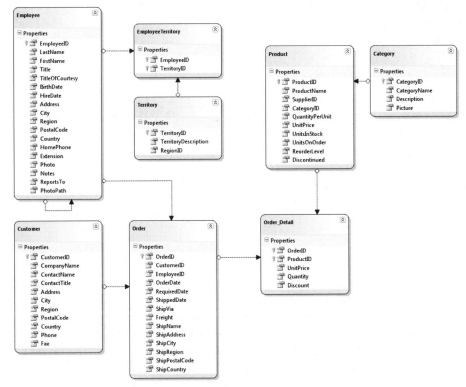

FIGURE 12-23 An example LINQ to SQL DBML model.

Registering Your Data Context with the MetaModel

The next step is to register your data context with System.Web.DynamicData.MetaModel. The MetaModel defines the connectivity or mapping between the scaffold templates and your data layer.

You register your data context inside the Global.asax file. Here you will notice that, at the top of the file, the MetaModel is actually defined as a private application variable and exposed as a read-only property. The following code shows an example.

Sample of Visual Basic Code

```
Private Shared s_defaultModel As New MetaModel
Public Shared ReadOnly Property DefaultModel() As MetaModel
    Get
        Return s_defaultModel
    End Get
End Property
```

Sample of C# Code

```csharp
private static MetaModel s_defaultModel = new MetaModel();
public static MetaModel DefaultModel {
    get {
        return s_defaultModel;
    }
}
```

Further down in the file, notice that the RegisterRoutes method is called at application start. The following code shows an example.

Sample of Visual Basic Code

```vb
Private Sub Application_Start(ByVal sender As Object, ByVal e As EventArgs)
    RegisterRoutes(RouteTable.Routes)
End Sub
```

Sample of C# Code

```csharp
void Application_Start(object sender, EventArgs e) {
    RegisterRoutes(RouteTable.Routes);
}
```

The RegisterRoutes method is used to connect your data source to the MetaModel. You do so through the DefaultModel.RegisterContext method and pass the type name of your data context. You might also want to set the ScaffoldAllTables property to true to make sure that the site will return all tables in the data context by default. The following code shows an example of registering the NorthwindDataContext LINQ to SQL object with the MetaModel.

Sample of Visual Basic Code

```vb
Public Shared Sub RegisterRoutes(ByVal routes As RouteCollection)

    DefaultModel.RegisterContext( _
        GetType(NorthwindDataContext), New ContextConfiguration() _
        With {.ScaffoldAllTables = True})

    routes.Add(New DynamicDataRoute("{table}/{action}.aspx") With {
    .Constraints = New RouteValueDictionary(New _
        With {.Action = "List|Details|Edit|Insert"}),
    .Model = DefaultModel})

End Sub
```

Sample of C# Code

```csharp
public static void RegisterRoutes(RouteCollection routes) {

    DefaultModel.RegisterContext(typeof(NorthwindDataContext),
        new ContextConfiguration() { ScaffoldAllTables = true });

    routes.Add(new DynamicDataRoute("{table}/{action}.aspx") {
        Constraints = new RouteValueDictionary(
            new { action = "List|Details|Edit|Insert" }),
        Model = DefaultModel
    });
}
```

That is all that is required to create a basic Dynamic Data website. You can now run the site and view, edit, insert, and delete data by using the template user interface. Figure 12-24 shows an example of the Products table in a web browser. Notice the URL, Products/List.aspx. This table/action convention is defined in the routing. It simply indicates that the List.aspx template page should be called and the Product data should be displayed from the model.

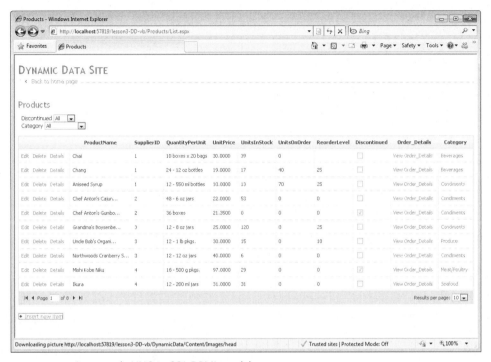

FIGURE 12-24 An example LINQ to SQL DBML model.

Notice also the default filters created for this list. The Discontinued filter is based on a Boolean field in the data. The Category filter is based on the relationship between Product and Category. In fact, relational IDs won't be displayed in the table, but related data will be. You can see that this was possible for the Category, because it exposed the CategoryName field. However, this was not possible for SupplierID because this table does not include a SupplierName field.

You can also see that the form allows you to page the data; select how many rows to show in a page; edit, delete, and view the details of an item; insert a new item; and connect to data related to a particular row (View Order_Details). Figure 12-25 shows an example of inserting a product. Notice that here you again get the Category drop-down list. You can also see that default data validation is being used. The validation is based on stored data types.

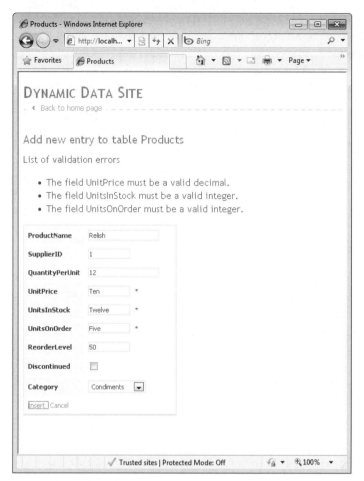

FIGURE 12-25 Automatic data validation in insert mode.

This site behavior is the default behavior with the template scaffolding. You can see that there was no code or customization done to this site. In upcoming sections, you will see how to customize the routing, create new page and field templates, and add custom business logic to validate data.

The Dynamic Data Classes

ASP.NET Dynamic Data relies on several classes inside the System.Web.DynamicData namespace. These classes include controls for defining custom field user controls, managing the routing, and using Dynamic Data inside a webpage. The MetaModel classes are found in the System.Data.Linq.Mapping namespace. Figure 12-26 shows some of the key classes used by Dynamic Data. Many of these classes will be discussed in upcoming sections.

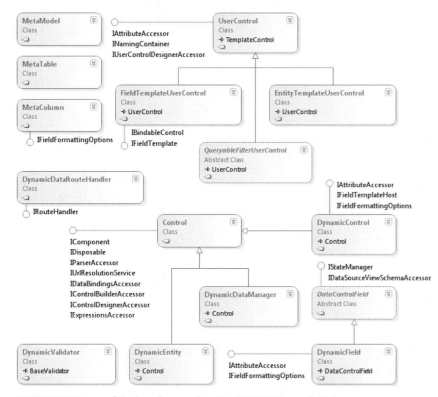

FIGURE 12-26 Some of the key classes related to ASP.NET Dynamic Data.

Extending and Customizing Dynamic Data

ASP.NET Dynamic Data is fully extensible. You can customize how fields are edited, how data is displayed, the look of the pages, the URL routing, data validation, and more. You can create customizations to existing templates that will be applied to all data elements. You can also create new, entity-specific templates for customizations that are specific to a particular entity. This section walks you through common customizations you might want to make when using ASP.NET Dynamic Data.

Defining Custom Routing

Dynamic Data uses the same routing features from System.Web.Routing that are used by ASP.NET model-view-controller (MVC) (see Chapter 14, "Creating Websites with ASP.NET MVC 2"). This routing engine maps intelligent Uniform Resource Identifiers (URIs) that are defined based on user actions to actual pages in your site, which makes the URIs easier to understand for users and search engines.

For example, Dynamic Data exposes the List.aspx, Edit.aspx, Insert.aspx, and Details.aspx page templates for working with data. These pages are called by the routing engine based on the user's action: List, Edit, Details, or Insert. A DynamicDataRoute class is created and added to the RouteTable.Routes collection inside the Global.asax file. This DynamicDataRoute indicates that a URI should be mapped as *table/action*.aspx. The following shows the code from the Global.asax file that does this.

Sample of Visual Basic Code

```
routes.Add(New DynamicDataRoute("{table}/{action}.aspx") With {
    .Constraints = New RouteValueDictionary( _
    New With {.Action = "List|Details|Edit|Insert"}), .Model = DefaultModel})
```

Sample of C# Code

```
routes.Add(new DynamicDataRoute("{table}/{action}.aspx") {
    Constraints = new RouteValueDictionary(
    new { action = "List|Details|Edit|Insert" }), Model = DefaultModel
```

This code ensures that a call to http://mysite/products/Edit.aspx?ProductID=1 will be routed to the /DynamicData/PageTemplates/Edit.aspx page. When accessed, the page will know the right table to edit (Products) and right record to edit (ProductID=1).

EDITING THE URI STRUCTURE

You can customize this routing by editing this code. For example, you might want to change the structure of the URL or even add a custom action. You can switch the table and action in the route definition to read {action}/{table}.aspx and get the same results but a different URL. New requests will be made as http://mysite/Edit/Products.aspx?ProductID=1. In this case, the table is used for the ASPX page name, and the action precedes the table name.

EDITING THE ROUTE TABLE TO SHOW A LIST AND DETAILS ON THE SAME PAGE

The Dynamic Data page templates include the ListDetails.aspx file. This page supports viewing a table in a list and selecting an item from the list to view its details. You can also edit the item or delete it, and you can insert a new item into the list by using this page. However, by default, requests are not routed to this page. You can change this behavior by removing the existing routing and adding entries for the action's List and Details that both point to the ListDetails.aspx page. The following code shows an example.

Sample of Visual Basic Code

```
routes.Add(New DynamicDataRoute("{table}/ListDetails.aspx") With {
    .Action = PageAction.List,
    .ViewName = "ListDetails",
    .Model = DefaultModel})

routes.Add(New DynamicDataRoute("{table}/ListDetails.aspx") With {
    .Action = PageAction.Details,
    .ViewName = "ListDetails",
    .Model = DefaultModel})
```

Sample of C# Code

```
routes.Add(new DynamicDataRoute("{table}/ListDetails.aspx")
{
    Action = PageAction.List,
    ViewName = "ListDetails",
    Model = DefaultModel
});

routes.Add(new DynamicDataRoute("{table}/ListDetails.aspx")
{
    Action = PageAction.Details,
    ViewName = "ListDetails",
    Model = DefaultModel
});
```

The result is that all calls to view a record's details or show a table in a list will be routed to the ListDetails.aspx page. From there, users can do everything they need to with the data. Note that ListDetails.aspx also handles inline editing in the GridView control.

CREATING A CUSTOM ROUTE TO A SPECIFIC PAGE

ASP.NET Dynamic Data can already route to custom pages you create. You simply need to follow the conventions already set up. You do not need to add custom routes. Instead, you create a new folder in the CustomPages folder and name this new folder with the name of an entity from your model. You then place appropriate action pages inside this folder (List.aspx, Edit.aspx, Insert.aspx, and so on). The default routing will look for pages in CustomPage first. You will walk through an example of creating a custom template page in an upcoming section.

Adding Metadata to Your Data Context

The classes in your data context are partial classes that include partial methods. This allows you to add to these classes and their methods outside the generated code. Doing so ensures that your changes are not overwritten if the model's code gets regenerated when the database changes.

You create partial classes so that you can add metadata that defines how your fields are to be displayed and validated (see "Creating Custom Field Templates," later in this lesson). You can also add custom business logic inside a partial method (see "Adding Custom Validation," also later in this lesson).

To start, you simply add a class to the App_Code directory and give it the same name as the class in your data context. Of course, you mark this class as partial. You then create a related metadata class (typically added to the same file). You can name this class by using the *Entity*Metadata convention.

Inside this metadata class, you redefine the properties contained in your data context class (but as simple object types, because the underlying type already has strongly typed properties). You then mark your partial class with the MetadataType attribute from the System.ComponentModel.DataAnnotations namespace. This attribute should pass the metadata class type as a parameter.

You can then add attributes to your metadata class to change how your fields are rendered by Dynamic Data. As an example, if you want to exclude a field from display, you can add the ScaffoldColumn attribute and pass in false. Additionally, if you want to format a value for display, you can use the DisplayFormat attribute. This attribute allows you to indicate whether to only format the value when it is displayed or also when it is being edited. You can also use the Display attribute to change the name of a column.

The following shows an example from the Products entity partial class and metadata class. Notice the use of ScaffoldColumn, Display, and DisplayFormat.

Sample of Visual Basic Code

```vb
Imports Microsoft.VisualBasic
Imports System.ComponentModel.DataAnnotations

<MetadataType(GetType(ProductMetadata))> _
Partial Public Class Product

End Class

Public Class ProductMetadata

    Public Property ProductID As Object
    Public Property ProductName As Object
    Public Property SupplierID As Object
    Public Property CategoryID As Object

    <ScaffoldColumn(False)> _
    Public Property QuantityPerUnit As Object

    <DisplayFormat(ApplyFormatInEditMode:=False,
        DataFormatString:="{0:c}")> _
    <Display(Name:="Price")> _
    Public Property UnitPrice As Object

    <ScaffoldColumn(False)> _
    Public Property UnitsInStock As Object

    <ScaffoldColumn(False)> _
    Public Property UnitsOnOrder As Object

    <ScaffoldColumn(False)> _
    Public Property ReorderLevel As Object

    Public Property Discontinued As Object

End Class
```

Sample of C# Code

```csharp
using System;
using System.Collections.Generic;
using System.Linq;
using System.Web;
using System.ComponentModel.DataAnnotations;

[MetadataType(typeof(ProductMetadata))]
public partial class Product
{
}

public class ProductMetadata
{
    public object ProductID { get; set; }
    public object ProductName { get; set; }
    public object SupplierID { get; set; }
    public object CategoryID { get; set; }

    [ScaffoldColumn(false)]
    public object QuantityPerUnit { get; set; }

    [DisplayFormat(ApplyFormatInEditMode=false,
        DataFormatString="{0:c}")]
    [Display(Name = "Price")]
    public object UnitPrice { get; set; }

    [ScaffoldColumn(false)]
    public object UnitsInStock { get; set; }

    [ScaffoldColumn(false)]
    public object UnitsOnOrder { get; set; }

    [ScaffoldColumn(false)]
    public object ReorderLevel { get; set; }

    public object Discontinued { get; set; }
}
```

When you run the application, this metadata is added to the Product class. Dynamic Data then picks up on this metadata and displays your fields accordingly. Figure 12-27 shows the results in a browser. Notice the missing fields, formatted UnitPrice column, and changed name.

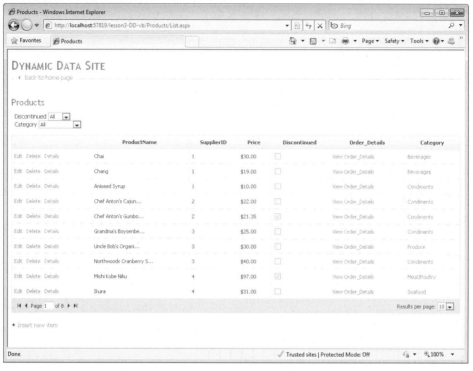

FIGURE 12-27 Using metadata and partial classes to indicate field display options.

There are many additional annotations you can add to your metadata from the System. ComponentModel.DataAnnotations namespace. You will see some of these in the upcoming sections. Table 12-1 provides a partial list of these classes (note that all are attribute classes).

TABLE 12-1 Commonly Used Metadata Annotation Classes

CLASS	DESCRIPTION
Association	Used to mark a property as a data relationship, such as a foreign key.
CustomValidation	Used to indicate a custom validation method to use for validating a property.
DataType	Used to indicate the data type to associate with the field.
Display	Allows you to indicate many things about the display of a field, including its order and its name.
DisplayFormat	Allows you to change how the data in a field is displayed. You can apply the formatting to affect only the view mode (and not the edit mode) if you want.
Editable	Used to indicate whether a property can be edited.
EnumDataType	Allows you to set an enum data type for a property.

CLASS	DESCRIPTION
Key	Allows you to set one or more properties as unique keys for a collection of objects.
MetadataType	Used to set the metadata class to associate with a type from your data context.
Range	Allows you to add a numeric range constraint to a property. You can also set an error message to be shown if the range is not valid.
RegularExpression	Used to add a regular expression constraint to a property.
Required	Used to indicate that a property is required when inserting or editing.
ScaffoldColumn	Indicates whether the column should be part of the scaffold (shown).
ScaffoldTable	Indicates whether an entire table should be part of the scaffold (shown).
StringLength	Allows you to set a constraint on a property based on the specified minimum and maximum number of characters for a property.
UIHint	Used to specify a custom field user control that should be used to display the property.

Adding Custom Validation

You can see from Table 12-1 that you can use attributes to mark your metadata with specific constraints. These constraints will then be enforced by Dynamic Data, and ASP.NET validation controls will be rendered and invoked.

The validation attributes include Range, StringLength, Required, and RegularExpression (among others). You use these controls to enforce additional constraints on your data. For example, suppose you want to add the Range validator to the ReorderLevel property to indicate that users can only reorder stock in quantities of 1 to 144 units. You could do so with the following code.

Sample of Visual Basic Code

```
<Range(1, 144, ErrorMessage:="Quantity must be between 1 and 144")> _
Public Property ReorderLevel As Object
```

Sample of C# Code

```
[Range(1, 144, ErrorMessage = "Quantity must be between 1 and 144")]
public object ReorderLevel { get; set; }
```

This business logic is then processed by Dynamic Data. You can see the results of a row edit in Figure 12-28. Here the user set the ReorderLevel to a value that is out of range (0). You can follow this same construct for other validation attributes, including StringLength and Required. Of course, you can apply more than one attribute to any property.

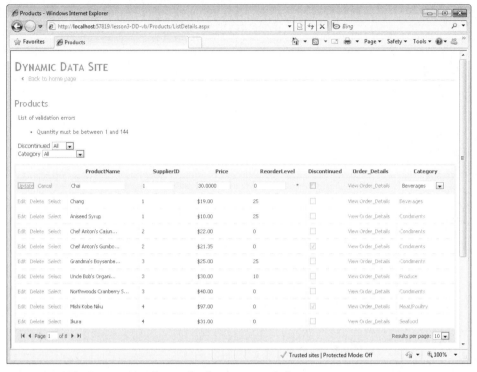

FIGURE 12-28 The Range constraint running in a browser window.

CUSTOM VALIDATION WITH PARTIAL METHODS

The data content model includes partial methods that allow you to add custom code that will be added to the method when the partial class is assembled. In fact, you can see these partial methods inside the Extensibility Method Definitions region of the generated code for a LINQ to SQL model. There are partial methods for OnChanging and OnChanged for each property in the data context. This means that the Product table has an OnUnitPriceChanging and OnUnitPriceChanged partial method. In fact, when you type "partial" into your partial class, Visual Studio's IntelliSense provides you with a list of all partial methods that you can extend.

You can use these partial methods to write customized validation rules. Remember, your partial class is an instance of the actual class representing the entity. Therefore, you have access to all fields on the record. The OnChanging partial method is also passed the value to which the property is being changed. You can use these fields and this value to write custom business logic. If you encounter an error, you throw a ValidationException from System.ComponentModel.DataAnnotations. Dynamic Data will present the exception to the user as an ASP.NET validation error.

As an example, suppose you want to write custom business logic that processes when the Product.UnitPrice is being changed. This logic might prevent a user from lowering the price of an object if there are items still in stock and the product has not been discontinued. You would add this code to the Product partial class as follows.

Sample of Visual Basic Code

```vb
Private Sub OnUnitPriceChanging(ByVal value As System.Nullable(Of Decimal))

    'rule: can only lower the price if product is discontinued
    If (Me.UnitsInStock > 0 And Me.UnitPrice > value) _
        And (Me.Discontinued = False) Then

        Throw New ValidationException( _
            "Cannot lower the price of an item that is not discontinued.")

    End If

End Sub
```

Sample of C# Code

```csharp
partial void OnUnitPriceChanging(decimal? value)
{
    //rule: can only lower the price if product is discontinued
    if ((this.UnitsInStock > 0 && this.UnitPrice > value)
        && (this.Discontinued == false))
    {
        throw new ValidationException(
            "Cannot lower the price of an item that is not discontinued.");
    }
}
```

Figure 12-29 shows an example of this logic processing. Notice that the validation message is shown as part of the validation summary controls in ASP.NET.

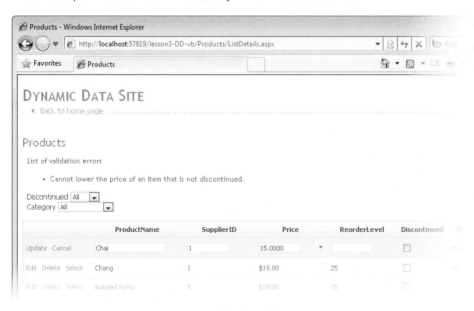

FIGURE 12-29 The custom business logic being processed in the browser.

Creating Custom Field Templates

Recall that the Dynamic Data templates include the FieldTemplates folder. Inside this folder is a set of user controls that inherit from FieldTemplateUserControl. These controls are used to render the appearance and functionality of your data context properties when they are displayed on a details or edit page (or page section).

Field template controls are named as either display controls or edit controls for a specific data type and functionality. For example, the controls used to render DateTime values are DateTime.ascx and DateTime_Edit.ascx. The former is simply a Literal control that is used when a DateTime value is rendered for display. The edit version includes a TextBox, a RequiredFieldValidator, a RegularExpressionValidator, a DynamicValidator, and a CustomValidator control. This composite user control is used whenever a DateTime value is displayed for editing.

You can edit the field template controls or create new ones in order to provide additional behavior in your website. Edits to an existing control will apply to all uses of that control within your website. When you create a new control, you use metadata to specify which properties in your data model use the new control. You will look at both examples next.

CUSTOMIZING AN EXISTING FIELD TEMPLATE

You can customize an existing field template user control as you would any other user control. This means adding client-side script, changing the appearance, and modifying the processing logic.

For example, you could modify the code-behind file for each of the core edit controls (Text_Edit.ascx, DateTime_Edit.ascx, Decimal_Edit.ascx, Integer_Edit.ascx, and MultilineText_Edit. ascx) to change the background color of the control if a different background color is required. To do so, you would add code to the OnDataBinding event. At this point, the SetupValidator methods have already run and any validation controls, including the RequiredFieldValidator, will already be set as either enabled or disabled. You could then add the following code to this event to set the background color accordingly.

Sample of Visual Basic Code

```
Protected Overrides Sub OnDataBinding(ByVal e As System.EventArgs)

    MyBase.OnDataBinding(e)
    If Me.RequiredFieldValidator1.Enabled = True Then
        TextBox1.BackColor = System.Drawing.Color.SandyBrown
    End If

End Sub
```

Sample of C# Code

```
protected override void OnDataBinding(EventArgs e)
{
    base.OnDataBinding(e);
    if (this.RequiredFieldValidator1.Enabled == true)
        TextBox1.BackColor = System.Drawing.Color.SandyBrown;
}
```

You can then add the RequiredAttribute class to any properties in your metadata class that you want to be required. When the control is rendered, Dynamic Data will mark the edit versions for these properties with the color if they are required fields.

CREATING A NEW FIELD TEMPLATE CONTROL

You can create your own custom field template user controls. You can do so by copying an existing user control in Dynamic Data/FieldTemplates or by selecting the Dynamic Data Field template from the Add New Item dialog box.

When you use the Dynamic Data Field item template, Visual Studio will actually generate two controls: one for display (ControlName.ascx) and one for editing (ControlName_Edit.ascx). The display version by default is just a Literal control. The edit version will include a TextBox control and the various validation controls used by DynamicData, some of which were shown in Table 12-1. You can then customize these controls to your needs.

As an example, suppose you want to create a new user control to allow users to use a Calendar control when picking a date in edit mode. To do so, you can add a new Dynamic Data Field to your project named CalendarPicker.ascx. Again, this will create two controls. You can leave the display version as is. You might then modify the markup in the CalendarPicker_Edit.ascx control to use a Calendar control, as follows.

```
<%@ Control Language="VB" CodeFile="CalendarPicker_Edit.ascx.vb"
    Inherits="DynamicData_FieldTemplates_CalendarPicker_EditField" %>

<asp:Calendar ID="Calendar1" runat="server"
    CssClass="DDTextBox"></asp:Calendar>
```

You would then add code to the code-behind page for the control to set the value of the Calendar control when data binding occurs. This code might look as follows.

Sample of Visual Basic Code

```
Protected Overrides Sub OnDataBinding(ByVal e As System.EventArgs)
    MyBase.OnDataBinding(e)
    Dim dte As DateTime = DateTime.Parse(Me.FieldValue)
    Calendar1.SelectedDate = dte
    Calendar1.VisibleDate = dte
End Sub
```

Sample of C# Code

```
protected override void OnDataBinding(EventArgs e)
{
    base.OnDataBinding(e);
    DateTime dte = DateTime.Parse(this.FieldValue.ToString());
    Calendar1.SelectedDate = dte;
    Calendar1.VisibleDate = dte;
}
```

The last step is to mark your metadata properties to indicate that they should use this new control. You do so with the UIHint attribute. You pass the name of your control to this attribute. Dynamic Data will then find your control and use it for all display and edits (including GridView edits) that involve this field. As an example, the following metadata marks the HireDate and BirthDate properties of the Employee class to use the custom CalendarPicker control.

Sample of Visual Basic Code
```
<MetadataType(GetType(EmployeeMetadata))> _
Partial Public Class Employee

End Class

Public Class EmployeeMetadata

    <UIHint("CalendarPicker")> _
    Public Property HireDate As Object

    <UIHint("CalendarPicker")> _
    Public Property BirthDate As Object

End Class
```

Sample of C# Code
```
[MetadataType(typeof(EmployeeMetadata))]
public partial class Employee
{
}

public class EmployeeMetadata
{
    [UIHint("CalendarPicker")]
    public object HireDate { get; set; }

    [UIHint("CalendarPicker")]
    public object BirthDate { get; set; }
}
```

Figure 12-30 shows the control in use on a webpage.

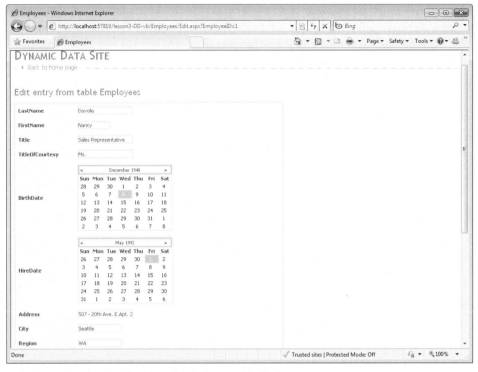

FIGURE 12-30 The custom field template being used in the browser.

Creating Custom Page Templates

Recall that the Dynamic Data templates are not specific to an object in your data context. Rather, they are generic templates that get information about the data they display from your data context at run time. You can customize how these templates display your data by using a metadata partial class and the data annotation attributes. However, you might find scenarios in which you need to create an entity-specific version of a page to control exactly how that entity is rendered to the browser. In this case, you need to create a custom page template.

Custom page templates are specific to a single entity in your data context. You create them by first creating a new folder inside the CustomPages folder. This folder should have the same name as your entity object. To create custom pages for working with products, for example, you would create a Products folder inside CustomPages. You then copy one or more of the page templates from the PageTemplates directory into your new folder. The Dynamic Data routing will look first in the CustomPages/EntityName folders for action pages such as Edit.aspx, Insert.aspx, and List.aspx. If the file it is looking for is there, it will use this custom page for display. If not, it will use the default action page inside the PageTemplates directory.

As an example, suppose you want to create a custom version of the List.aspx page for use with Products. You would create a Products folder in CustomPages. You would then copy the List.aspx page to that folder. You can then open this page and edit the markup and code-behind accordingly. A common edit is to bind the GridView control more tightly with the specific product. You can do so by setting the AutoGenerateColumns property to false. You can then add a series of DynamicField properties to represent your bound data. The following markup shows an example.

```
<asp:GridView ID="GridView1" runat="server"
    DataSourceID="GridDataSource" EnablePersistedSelection="true"
    AllowPaging="True" AllowSorting="True" CssClass="DDGridView"
    RowStyle-CssClass="td" HeaderStyle-CssClass="th" CellPadding="6"
    AutoGenerateColumns="false">
    <Columns>
        <asp:DynamicField DataField="ProductID" HeaderText="ID" />
        <asp:DynamicField DataField="ProductName" HeaderText="Name" />
        <asp:DynamicField DataField="UnitPrice" HeaderText="Price" />
        <asp:DynamicField DataField="UnitsInStock" HeaderText="Stock" />
        <asp:TemplateField>
            <ItemTemplate>
                <asp:DynamicHyperLink runat="server" Action="Edit" Text="Edit"/>
                 <asp:LinkButton runat="server"
                CommandName="Delete" Text="Delete" OnClientClick=
                    'return confirm("Are you sure you want to delete this item?");'/>
                 <asp:DynamicHyperLink runat="server" Text="Details" />
            </ItemTemplate>
        </asp:TemplateField>
    </Columns>
    <PagerStyle CssClass="DDFooter"/>
    <PagerTemplate>
        <asp:GridViewPager runat="server" />
    </PagerTemplate>
    <EmptyDataTemplate>
        There are currently no items in this table.
    </EmptyDataTemplate>
</asp:GridView>
```

Figure 12-31 shows this custom page running in a browser.

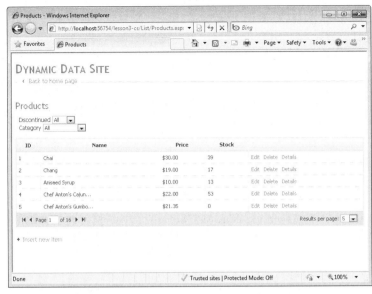

FIGURE 12-31 The custom page template being displayed in the browser.

Using Dynamic Controls in Existing Sites

You can use the features of Dynamic Data in existing sites. For example, you can add the full scaffolding and connect to a data context for CRUD operations, and you can create custom webpages (or customize existing ones) to take advantage of the lower code, lower markup solution that Dynamic Data offers.

Adding Dynamic Data Scaffolding to an Existing Website

You can add Dynamic Data scaffolding to an existing website. To do so, you must have a data context defined in your site (or you must create one). Remember, Dynamic Data works with either LINQ to SQL classes, the ADO.NET Entity Framework, or a custom data context.

You then edit the Global.asax file to register your context and enable custom routing. This code can be copied from the Global.asax file for a blank Dynamic Data site. Refer back to "Getting Started with Dynamic Data Websites" earlier in this lesson for details.

Finally, you copy the DynamicData folder from a blank Dynamic Data site into your existing site. You can then make customizations and use Dynamic Data features as discussed in prior sections.

Enabling Dynamic Data Inside a Webpage

You can use Dynamic Data inside completely custom webpages that do not use the scaffolding or routing common to Dynamic Data. For this scenario, you can create pages that use data-bound controls such as GridView, DetailsView, ListView, and FormView, and use Dynamic Data for displaying, editing, and validating data. In this case, you get the default behavior of Dynamic Data, including data validation. You can then customize this behavior by adding more information to your meta-model as described previously.

As an example, suppose you have a standard ASP.NET website (not one built with the Dynamic Data template). Suppose that this site has an ADO.NET Entity Data Model for working with the Northwind database.

You can then add an EntityDataSource control to the Default.aspx page for the site. This control can be set to use the entity model for selecting, inserting, updating, and deleting. Recall that you set EntitySetName to indicate the entity used by the data source. The following markup shows an example.

```
<asp:EntityDataSource ID="EntityDataSource1" runat="server"
    ConnectionString="name=northwndEntities"
    DefaultContainerName="northwndEntities" EnableDelete="True"
    EnableFlattening="False" EnableInsert="True" EnableUpdate="True"
    EntitySetName="Products">
</asp:EntityDataSource>
```

Next, you can add a data display control to the page. In this example, assume you add a GridView to the page. You would then configure this control to auto-generate columns and enable editing. The following markup shows an example.

```
<asp:GridView ID="GridView1" runat="server"
    DataSourceID="EntityDataSource1"
    AllowPaging="True" AllowSorting="True"
    AutoGenerateColumns="true">
    <Columns>
        <asp:CommandField ShowEditButton="True" />
    </Columns>
</asp:GridView>
```

The final step is to add code to the Page_Init event to enable the Dynamic Data. The following code shows an example.

Sample of Visual Basic Code

```
Protected Sub Page_Load1(ByVal sender As Object, _
    ByVal e As System.EventArgs) Handles Me.Load

    GridView1.EnableDynamicData(GetType(northwndModel.Product));

End Sub
```

Sample of C# Code

```
protected void Page_Init()
{
    GridView1.EnableDynamicData(typeof(northwndModel.Product));
}
```

Figure 12-32 shows the results. Notice that the attempt to edit the first record failed. You can see the asterisk next to the ProductName field. This is because this field cannot be blank, as defined in the model. You can further customize this page to use even more features from Dynamic Data.

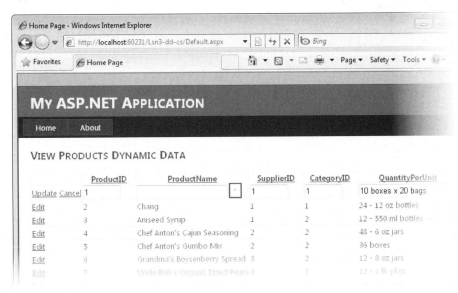

FIGURE 12-32 Dynamic Data being used on a standard webpage.

 **Quick Check**

1. What data models can you use with Dynamic Data?

2. Where do you register your data model with the site's MetaModel?

3. Which of the data annotation classes would you use to define metadata to change the display format of a property?

Quick Check Answers

1. Dynamic data must use a data model based on DataContext or ObjectContext. This includes LINQ to SQL classes and ADO.NET Entity Framework models.

2. You register your data context inside the Global.asax file.

3. You would use the DisplayFormatAttribute.

In this practice, you create a Dynamic Data website and edit the default routing.

EXERCISE **Creating a Dynamic Data Website and an Entity Model**

In this exercise, you create a new Dynamic Data website, add a database to the site, and define an Entity Data Model. You then configure the site to work with the model and customize the routing.

1. Open Visual Studio and create a new ASP.NET Dynamic Data Entities Web Site. Name the site **DynamicDataLab**. Select your preferred programming language.

2. Add the northwnd.mdf file to your App_Data directory. You can copy the file from the samples installed from the CD.

3. Add an ADO.NET Entity Data Model to your site. Name the model **Northwind.edmx**. When prompted, allow Visual Studio to add this to your App_Code directory. Use the Entity Data Model Wizard to connect to all tables in the database; use the default settings throughout the wizard.

4. Open the Global.asax file. Inside RegisterRoutes, uncomment the line that calls RegisterContext. Change this code to register your new entity model and set ScaffoldAllTables to true. Your code should look as follows.

   ```
   Sample of Visual Basic Code
   'VB
   DefaultModel.RegisterContext(GetType(northwndModel.northwndEntities), _
       New ContextConfiguration() With {.ScaffoldAllTables = True})
   ```

   ```
   Sample of C# Code
   DefaultModel.RegisterContext(typeof(northwndModel.northwndEntities),
       new ContextConfiguration() { ScaffoldAllTables = true });
   ```

5. Run the application and view the results. Select Products. Click to edit a product. Notice the URL routing. On the product editing page, clear the name field and click update. Notice the validation that is displayed.

6. Return to the Global.asax file to enable routing to ListDetails.aspx. This page allows you to edit a row directly in the GridView as well as in a DetailsView on the same page. To enable row editing, comment out the routes.Add call for {table}/{action}. Then uncomment both routes.Add calls at the bottom of the method. Notice that these routes indicate that the List and Details actions should route to ListDetails.aspx. This page handles all other actions inline with the page.

7. Rerun the site. Select the Products table. Notice the new URL. Click the Edit link for a product in the GridView control. Notice the inline editing and data validation.

Lesson Summary

- There are two Dynamic Data website templates in ASP.NET: one for working with the Entity Framework and one for working with LINQ to SQL models. Both create a set of page and field template files inside the DynamicData folder. Both allow you to connect your data context to the site inside the Global.asax file.

- You can use the System.Web.Routing inside the Global.asax file to indicate how your Dynamic Data site maps entity requests and actions formatted in a URI to page templates.

- You use partial classes to extend the metadata of your data context. This metadata includes attributes from the DataAnnotations namespace that define display formatting properties and validation rules.

- You can write additions to the OnChanging partial methods from your data context model to extend individual properties to include additional business logic.

- You can create custom field templates that change how properties are displayed and edited. These field templates inherit from FieldTemplateUserControl. You apply a custom field template as metadata to a property in your partial entity class by using the UIHintAttribute.

- You can create custom page templates that are entity specific inside the CustomPages folder. You add a folder with the same name as your entity. You then define custom action pages such as List.aspx and Edit.aspx.

- You can use the EnableDynamicData method of the data view controls (such as GridView) to add Dynamic Data features to existing websites that do not contain the standard scaffolding.

Lesson Review

You can use the following questions to test your knowledge of the information in Lesson 3, "Working with ASP.NET Dynamic Data." The questions are also available on the companion CD in a practice test, if you prefer to review them in electronic form.

> **NOTE ANSWERS**
>
> Answers to these questions and explanations of why each answer choice is correct or incorrect are located in the "Answers" section at the end of the book.

1. You need to add metadata to your data context object, Invoice, in order to change how invoices are handled by Dynamic Data. Which actions should you take? (Choose all that apply.)

   A. Create a new partial class called Invoice in the App_Code directory.

   B. Create a new class called InvoiceAnnotations in the App_Code directory.

   C. Decorate the Invoice class with the MetadataTypeAttribute class.

   D. Decorate the InvoiceAnnotations class with the ScaffoldTableAttribute class.

2. You have defined a custom field template user control for changing the way an Invoice number is edited. You want to apply this control to the Invoice.Number property. Which data annotation attribute class would you use to do so?

   A. MetadataType

   B. Display

   C. Editable

   D. UIHint

3. You want to implement custom business logic that should run when the InvoiceNumber property is modified. What actions should you take? (Choose all that apply.)

   A. Add a CustomValidator control to the DynamicData/FieldTemplates/Integer_Edit.asax file. Set this control to process custom logic to validate an invoice number.

   B. Extend the OnInvoiceNumberChanged partial method inside the Invoice partial class to include additional validation logic.

   C. Extend the OnInvoiceNumberChanging partial method inside the Invoice partial class to include additional validation logic.

   D. If the logic fails, throw a ValidationException instance.

Case Scenarios

In the following case scenarios, you apply what you've learned in this chapter. If you have difficulty completing this work, review the material in this chapter before beginning the next chapter. You can find answers to these questions in the "Answers" section at the end of this book.

Case Scenario 1: Choosing Data Source Controls

You are a developer at Contoso, Ltd, a car insurance company. You have been asked to write an application that allows a customer service agent to provide an insurance quote to a customer over the phone. However, there are many factors that go into pricing the insurance policy. Each of these factors contains data from different sources. This data is displayed to the agent for selection. Based on his or her selection, a price is generated.

You identify most of the data sources as follows:

- **Location premium markup data**   Provided as XML from a web service.
- **Year, make, and model rates**   Provided inside a SQL Server database.
- **Driver history**   Provided through an XML web service.
- **Existing customer information**   Provided through a shared customer object to which the application has a reference.

Thinking about how you will access the data, answer the following questions:

1. Which data source control would you use for accessing the data returned by the location and driver history web services? How would you configure the data source control to receive this data?

2. Which data source control would you use for accessing the year, make, and model rate data?

3. How would you access the data provided by the customer object?

Case Scenario 2: Implementing a Master-Detail Solution

You are a developer who is creating a webpage for displaying customers and their orders in a master-detail scenario. The top of the webpage will provide a list of customers that contains the customer numbers and names. The bottom of the webpage will provide a list of the orders containing the order numbers, the order dates, the order amounts, and the ship dates. The orders will be displayed for the customer that is selected.

Thinking about how you will display your data, answer the following questions:

1. What controls would you use to display the customer and orders?

2. If you want to use this webpage to add customers and orders, what are some ways that you can provide this functionality?

Case Scenario 3: Adding ASP.NET Dynamic Data to a Website

You are a developer working on an existing website. There are several core tables in the database that users cannot edit. This is becoming a problem, because maintenance is needed. You have been asked to quickly enable this editing for some of these tables not already exposed by the functionality of your website.

Answer the following questions about how you would enable this functionality using Dynamic Data.

1. How can you add Dynamic Data scaffolding to this existing site?

2. How would you indicate which tables to expose through Dynamic Data?

Suggested Practices

To help you successfully master the exam objectives presented in this chapter, complete the following tasks.

Create Pages by Using Each of the Controls

For this task, you should complete Practice 1 for the data source controls. Practice 2 should be completed for additional use of the data-bound web controls. If attempting Practice 2, you should complete Practice 1 first. Practice 3 provides experience with using the insert, update, and delete parts of a data source control.

- **Practice 1**   Create a new website and add a new page for each of the data source controls in this chapter, especially those not defined in the practice for Lesson 1. Configure these controls to access data.

- **Practice 2**   Add the ability to display the data defined in the pages in Practice 1. For each data source, select a different display control. Use the Menu control for XML data. Also, be sure to define a layout control that uses templates.

- **Practice 3**   Return to the practice for Lesson 1. Edit the site to enable customer editing.

Create a Master-Detail Solution by Using the Data-Bound Server Controls

This practice gives you experience with using data-bound server controls.

- Create a new website that uses a domain familiar to you, such as customers and orders, owners and vehicles, employees and sick days, or albums and songs. Add a webpage that is configurable as a master-detail page to provide access to related data.

Work with Dynamic Data Websites

For this task, you should complete Practices 1 and 2 to gain experience creating custom field and page templates. Complete Practice 3 for experience with using Dynamic Data outside a Dynamic Data website.

- **Practice 1**   Return to the practice from Lesson 3. Create a custom field template for selecting dates. Use the CalendarPicker example from the chapter. Apply this control to date values in the site.

- **Practice 2**   Return to the practice from Lesson 3. Create a custom page template for displaying only portions of an Employee object.

- **Practice 3**   Create a new, standard ASP.NET website. Define a data context connected to a database. Enable Dynamic Data for a single page within the site (without adding the scaffolding support).

Take a Practice Test

The practice tests on this book's companion CD offer many options. For example, you can test yourself on just the lesson review questions in this chapter, or you can test yourself on all the 70-515 certification exam objectives. You can set up the test so it closely simulates the experience of taking a certification exam, or you can set it up in study mode so you can look at the correct answers and explanations after you answer each question.

> **MORE INFO**   **PRACTICE TESTS**
>
> For details about all the practice test options available, see the "How to Use the Practice Tests" section in this book's Introduction.

CHAPTER 13

Implementing User Profiles, Authentication, and Authorization

Most websites require users to authenticate to gain access to private information, custom settings, and role-based features. Developers need to be able to securely authenticate a user, determine his or her authorization, and manage his or her site membership information. This is true for both internal websites that use role-based security and for public sites whose developers want to allow user-level customizations, data storage, security, and basic user profile information.

Microsoft ASP.NET includes several components, classes, and controls that allow you to manage the security and authorization of your sites. You can use these features to implement security based on a Windows or form-driven account. You can then identify user information through profiles. You can also use the ASP.NET membership features to help manage users. Finally, there is a set of controls that work with the security, profile, and membership features. These include Login, LoginStatus, ChangePassword, PasswordRecovery, and more. These controls allow developers to quickly add basic security, profile, and membership features to their sites.

This chapter explores how developers can take advantage of the many features of ASP.NET user management, including profiles, membership, and security.

Exam objectives in this chapter:
- Configuring and Extending a Web Application
    - Configure providers.
    - Configure authentication and authorization.

Lessons in this chapter:

Before You Begin

To complete the lessons in this chapter, you should be familiar with developing applications with Microsoft Visual Studio 2010 by using Microsoft Visual Basic or Microsoft Visual C#. In addition, you should be comfortable with all of the following:

- The Visual Studio 2010 Integrated Development Environment (IDE)
- Using Hypertext Markup Language (HTML) and client-side scripting
- Creating ASP.NET websites and forms

 REAL WORLD

Tony Northrup

'I've spent time as both a developer and a systems administrator. Each role has different responsibilities. Typically, systems administrators should be responsible for configuring Windows security for a website. This doesn't require them to write any code, because they can configure it by using the Internet Information Services (IIS) Manager and the ASP.NET Web Site Administration Tool (WSAT).

So if you're creating an application that should use Windows authentication, it's okay to leave it up to the systems administrator to configure security. Not all systems administrators know how to properly configure it, however, so you should be familiar with the process and be able to demonstrate how it's done when you hand off application support. And you do need to configure forms authentication, because that requires application-specific configuration settings, such as specifying the logon page. Typically, you would provide all the configuration information as part of your Web.config file.

Lesson 1: Working with User Profiles

A *user profile* in ASP.NET is a set of properties that you define on a per-user basis for your site. This might include color preferences, address information, or other information you want to track for each user. Users set up a profile with your site. You store their profile information between site visits, and ASP.NET will automatically load a user's profile information based on his or her identification. You can then use this profile information in your application to make decisions, prefill data entry boxes, set customizations, and perform similar actions.

This lesson describes how you set up, define, configure, and use ASP.NET user profiles.

User Profile Basics

The ASP.NET user profile feature allows you to quickly and easily create a means to define, store, retrieve, and use user profile information in your site. You can configure most of the setup inside Web.config. This includes defining a storage mechanism and the actual fields to use to define a user profile. ASP.NET and the related user profile classes will then take care of storing your data (without requiring you to create a specific schema), retrieving it, and providing it to you in a strongly typed class.

The following list details the steps involved in setting up a user profile for an ASP.NET website:

1. **Configure a user profile provider.** The profile provider class is used to store and retrieve user profile information to and from a database. There is a default provider for Microsoft SQL Server. You can also create your own custom profile providers.

2. **Define the user profile.** Set up the fields you want to track for a user profile by using the Web.config file. These fields are used by ASP.NET to store data and return it to you in a strongly typed class.

3. **Uniquely identify users.** You can identify both anonymous and authenticated users of your site. You use a unique value to return a user's profile from the data storage.

4. **Set and save a user profile.** You must provide a means that allows users to set their profile information. This information will then be saved by the configured profile provider.

5. **Recognize a returning visitor.** When a user returns to your site, you can retrieve his or her user profile information as a strongly typed class. Your code can then use the profile information to set customizations, prefill data entry fields, and make other decisions related to the application.

These steps represent the basic elements you need to set up to use the ASP.NET profile feature. Each step is covered in detail in the following sections.

Configuring a User Profile Provider

You store and retrieve user profiles in a database by using a provider class. This class abstracts the storage and retrieval of the profile information from the actual profile itself. In this way, you can always configure a new provider (and data store) without having to change any of your code.

ASP.NET provides a default, configured provider for use with user profiles. This provider is the SqlProfileProvider class found in the System.Web.Profile namespace. When ASP.NET is installed, a setting is added to the Machine.config file that connects the SqlProfileProvider class to an instance of a Microsoft SQL Server database on the local machine. This setting is AspNetSqlProfileProvider and is set to work with a local configured version of SQL Server. By default, this is Microsoft SQL Server Express Edition. However, you can change this. The following shows an example of the provider's configuration.

```
<profile>
  <providers>
    <add name="AspNetSqlProfileProvider"
      connectionStringName="LocalSqlServer" applicationName="/"
      type="System.Web.Profile.SqlProfileProvider, System.Web, Version=2.0.0.0,
        Culture=neutral, PublicKeyToken=b03f5f7f11d50a3a"/>
  </providers>
</profile>
```

Notice that in the preceding markup, the provider is configured to use the LocalSqlServer connection string. This connection string is also found in Machine.config. By default, it points to a SQL Server Express Edition version of a database named aspnetdb. The following markup shows an example.

```
<connectionStrings>
  <add name="LocalSqlServer" connectionString="data source=.\SQLEXPRESS;
      Integrated Security=SSPI;AttachDBFilename=|DataDirectory|aspnetdb.mdf;
      User Instance=true" providerName="System.Data.SqlClient"/>
</connectionStrings>
```

In fact, if your web server includes SQL Server Express Edition, ASP.NET will automatically create the profile database when this feature is used. It does so inside the configured DataDirectory (or App_Data). You can, of course, override these settings.

> **NOTE SOLVING PERSONALIZATION PROBLEMS**
>
> If personalization begins to fail during development, it might be caused by a corrupted database. Though you'll lose any saved personalization data, you can quickly get personalization working again by deleting the personalization database; simply stop the website and delete the ASPNETDB.mdf and ASPNETDB_log.ldf files from the App_Data directory. ASP.NET will automatically recreate these databases the next time you use personalization.

Configuring a New Profile Database

In most cases, you can rely on this database to exist in your development environment and therefore you will need to do nothing to configure a user profile provider or database. However, you might want to configure a provider to use a standard version of SQL Server, which can use more processor cores and memory than SQL Server Express Edition and thus might perform better if you have a very busy website and a large number of users. To do so, you must first generate the database schema on the database server. ASP.NET provides the Aspnet_regsql.exe tool to help.

The Aspnet_regsql.exe tool can be found on your development machine at %windir% \Microsoft.NET\Framework\%version%. For example, on a standard installation of a Windows 7 development machine, you can find this tool at C:\Windows\Microsoft.NET\Framework \v4.0.30319.

When you run the tool, you have the option of running it in command-line mode or using the user interface to walk through a wizard that allows you to set up the profile schema database. In command-line mode, you have the option to set the database name (-d), the server name (-S), and other important information such as login (-U) and password (-P). There are a large number of other options, which are described in detail at *http://msdn.microsoft.com /en-us/library/x28wfk74.aspx*.

For example, this tool can be used to set up more than just the profile table. It is also used to define the role, membership, and Web Part tables. To define the tables you want to set up, you use the -A command and append another letter(s) based on the table you want to set up. For example, -A all sets up all the tables, whereas -A p only sets up the Profile table and -A c only sets up the Personalization table.

The following example configures the profile table (-A p) for the server (-S) of localhost by using Windows credentials (-E).

```
aspnet_regsql.exe -E -S localhost -A p
```

Running Aspnet_regsql.exe without parameters launches the setup wizard, which walks you through the process of both configuring ASP.NET application services and removing them. Figure 13-1 shows the Select The Server And Database page in the wizard. By default, the profile database is named aspnetdb. After the database is configured, add the proper connection string to your application's Web.config file.

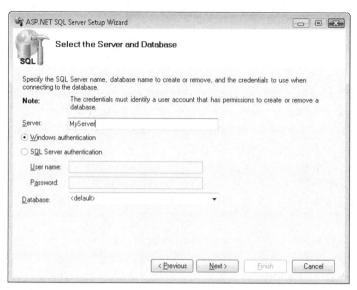

FIGURE 13-1 Defining an ASP.NET Application Services database.

Defining the User Profile

You define a user profile by determining the individual fields you want to track for each user in your site. For instance, you might want to track the user's first and last name, the date and time of his or her last visit, preferred font and color settings, and so on. Each value to be tracked is defined as a profile property. Profile properties can be of any type, such as string, DateTime, and even custom types that you create.

You define user profile fields inside the Web.config file by adding a <profile> element to the configuration file followed by a <properties> element. Inside the <properties> element, you use the <add> child element to indicate a new field. You name the field by using the name attribute. Unless otherwise specified, property fields are of type string. However, you can use the type attribute to specify another specific type. The following is an example of a user profile defined in a Web.config file.

```
<configuration>
  <system.web>
    <profile>
      <properties>
        <add name="FirstName" />
        <add name="LastName" />
        <add name="LastVisit" type="System.DateTime" />
      </properties>
    </profile>
  </system.web>
</configuration>
```

Anonymous User Profiles

By default, a user profile and its properties are enabled only for authenticated users—those users who provide logon credentials for your site and then are authenticated against a user data store. However, you might want to allow anonymous users (those who do not have logon credentials to your site) to use features of a user profile. To do so, you start by defining properties as anonymous by using the allowAnonymous attribute. You set this attribute value to true for each property for which you want to allow anonymous profiles.

Next, you must add the <anonymousIdentification> element to your Web.config file and set the enabled attribute to true. The <anonymousIdentification> element has several other attributes that you can define to control how cookies are used. However, the default settings are typically sufficient.

The following shows an example of both the anonymousIdentification element and the allowAnonymous attribute.

```
<anonymousIdentification enabled="true" />

<profile>
  <properties>
    <add name="FirstName" allowAnonymous="true" />
    <add name="LastName" allowAnonymous="true" />
    <add name="LastVisit" type="System.DateTime" allowAnonymous="true" />
  </properties>
</profile>
```

In this case, anonymous profiles are enabled and ASP.NET creates a unique identification for each user the first time he or she visits your site. This value is stored and tracked with a browser cookie. By default, this cookie is set to expire 70 days after the user's most recent site access. If a browser does not support cookies, user profiles can also function without them by storing unique identifiers in the URL of the page request; however, the profile is lost when the user closes his or her browser.

Profile Property Groups

You can group profile properties together under a group name. For example, you might want to define an Address group that contains Street, City, and PostalCode properties. Adding these items to a group allows you to access them through the profile class much like you would encapsulate data in a class (Profile.Address.Street).

The following markup demonstrates defining a grouped profile property in a Web.config file.

```
<profile enabled="true">
  <properties>
    <group name="Address">
      <add name="Street" />
      <add name="City" />
      <add name="PostalCode" />
    </group>
  </properties>
</profile>
```

Custom Profile Property Types

You can create your own custom class and use it as a profile property. For example, you might have a class that defines a user's position in your organization, that user's reports-to information, and his or her direct reports. You could use this type as a profile property. To do so, you need to make sure your custom class is marked as serializable by using the Serializable attribute. You then reference the custom type by using the type attribute of the <add> element. The following markup shows an example of adding a custom type called OrgPosition.

```
<profile>
  <properties>
    <add name="Position" type="MyNamespace.OrgPosition" serializeAs="Binary" />
  </properties>
</profile>
```

Identifying Users

As discussed previously, user profiles can be used with either authenticated or anonymous users. If your website requires and implements user authentication, you can immediately begin using profiles because they are automatically enabled for authenticated users. For more information on implementing user authentication, see Lesson 2, "Using ASP.NET Membership," later in this chapter.

If your site does not authenticate users, you must explicitly enable user profiles through the <anonymousIdentification> Web.config element, setting its enabled attribute to true, as discussed previously. In this case, users are identified by either a cookie setting or a URL value.

You might also want to implement a scenario whereby users of your site have anonymous profiles to start. However, at some point they might want to create an account and thus make their anonymous profile one that requires authentication. Fortunately, ASP.NET supports this scenario.

Migrating Anonymous User Profiles

If you enable anonymous user profiles but later allow a user to create authentication credentials, ASP.NET creates a new profile for the user. To avoid losing the user's anonymous profile information, you respond to the MigrateAnonymous event that ASP.NET raises when a user logs on to your site. The following code demonstrates how to migrate information when a user is first authenticated with his or her new credentials.

Sample of Visual Basic Code

```vb
Public Sub Profile_OnMigrateAnonymous(sender As Object, args As ProfileMigrateEventArgs)
  Dim anonymousProfile As ProfileCommon = Profile.GetProfile(args.AnonymousID)

  Profile.ZipCode = anonymousProfile.ZipCode
  Profile.CityAndState = anonymousProfile.CityAndState
  Profile.StockSymbols = anonymousProfile.StockSymbols

  ' Delete the anonymous profile. If the anonymous ID is not
  ' needed in the rest of the site, remove the anonymous cookie.
  ProfileManager.DeleteProfile(args.AnonymousID)
  AnonymousIdentificationModule.ClearAnonymousIdentifier()
End Sub
```

Sample of C# Code

```csharp
public void Profile_OnMigrateAnonymous(object sender, ProfileMigrateEventArgs args)
{
  ProfileCommon anonymousProfile = Profile.GetProfile(args.AnonymousID);

  Profile.ZipCode = anonymousProfile.ZipCode;
  Profile.CityAndState = anonymousProfile.CityAndState;
  Profile.StockSymbols = anonymousProfile.StockSymbols;

  // Delete the anonymous profile. If the anonymous ID is not
  // needed in the rest of the site, remove the anonymous cookie.
  ProfileManager.DeleteProfile(args.AnonymousID);
  AnonymousIdentificationModule.ClearAnonymousIdentifier();
}
```

Notice that in this code, the user's anonymous profile information is actually copied into his or her new profile. After this action, the user's anonymous profile is deleted from the system.

Setting and Saving a User Profile

You can save a user profile by simply setting the values of individual properties and then calling the Profile.Save method. This method will use the configured profile provider to write the profile data out to the configured database.

Typically, you set user profile information in response to a user's selection, such as his or her preferred color or font size for your website. You might also allow users to enter and edit their profile information by using a web form. You do so in a way similar to how you might code any web form. You add controls to the page, validation, a Save button, and an event in your code-behind file to write the data to the data store.

For example, suppose that you have a user profile that contains both first and last name along with the most recent time the user visited your site. In this case, you might start by creating a form to allow users to edit their name information. This form would contain a couple of TextBox controls, a Button control, and perhaps some validation controls. When the user clicks the Save button, you simply set the profile information and call the Save method. The following code shows an example.

Sample of Visual Basic Code

```vb
Protected Sub Button1_Click(ByVal sender As Object,
  ByVal e As System.EventArgs) Handles Button1.Click

  Profile.FirstName = TextBoxFirst.Text
  Profile.LastName = TextBoxLast.Text
  Profile.Save()

End Sub
```

Sample of C# Code

```csharp
protected void Button1_Click(object sender, EventArgs e)
{
  Profile.FirstName = TextBoxFirst.Text;
  Profile.LastName = TextBoxLast.Text;
  Profile.Save();
}
```

To set the time of the user's most recent site access, you could add code to the Global.asax file to override the Session.End event. The following shows an example.

Sample of Visual Basic Code

```vb
Sub Session_End(ByVal sender As Object, ByVal e As EventArgs)

  Profile.LastVisit = DateTime.Now
  Profile.Save()

End Sub
```

Sample of C# Code

```csharp
void Session_End(object sender, EventArgs e)
{
  Profile.LastVisit = DateTime.Now;
  Profile.Save();
}
```

Note, however, that the Session.End event does not run if the server is unexpectedly shut down; for example, by a power outage.

Recognizing a Returning Visitor

ASP.NET automatically loads a user's profile based on his or her identification. Again, if you allow anonymous authentication, this identification is passed as a cookie setting. Otherwise, identification happens at the time of authorization. Either way, after the profile is loaded, you can access the data to make decisions such as setting color and font preferences.

In the previous example, a web form was used to allow a user to set his or her profile information. You could add code to the Load method of this form to initialize the form fields with profile data. This code would look as follows.

Sample of Visual Basic Code

```vb
Protected Sub Page_Load(ByVal sender As Object, ByVal e As System.EventArgs) _
  Handles Me.Load
  If Not IsPostBack Then
    TextBoxFirst.Text = Profile.FirstName
    TextBoxLast.Text = Profile.LastName
    LabelLastVisit.Text = Profile.LastVisit.ToString()
  End If
End Sub
```

Sample of C# Code

```csharp
protected void Page_Load(object sender, EventArgs e)
{
  if (!IsPostBack)
  {
    TextBoxFirst.Text = Profile.FirstName;
    TextBoxLast.Text = Profile.LastName;
    LabelLastVisit.Text = Profile.LastVisit.ToString();
  }
}
```

Using profiles in this way is extremely easy compared to the alternatives, because you do not need to explicitly determine who the user is or perform any database lookups. Simply referring to a profile property value causes ASP.NET to perform the necessary actions to identify the current user and look up the value in the persistent profile store.

PRACTICE Applying User Profiles

In this practice, you define and configure user profiles. You also create a form that allows a user to modify his or her profile information.

> **ON THE COMPANION MEDIA**
>
> If you encounter a problem completing an exercise, you can find the completed projects in the samples installed from this book's companion CD. For more information about the project files and other content on the CD, see "Using the Companion Media" in this book's Introduction.

EXERCISE Working with ASP.NET User Profiles

In this exercise, you enable user profiles for anonymous users and track information for website visitors.

1. Open Visual Studio. Create a new, file-based website by using the ASP.NET Empty Web Site template.

2. Open the Web.config file for your project. Navigate to the <system.web> element. Inside this element, add markup to configure anonymous user profiles. The following shows an example.

   ```
   <anonymousIdentification enabled="true" />
   ```

3. Add user profile information to the Web.config file under <system.web>. Add fields for name, postal code, and color preference, as in the following.

   ```
   <profile>
       <properties>
           <add name="Name" allowAnonymous="true" />
           <add name="PostalCode" type="System.Int16" allowAnonymous="true" />
           <add name="ColorPreference" allowAnonymous="true" />
       </properties>
   </profile>
   ```

4. Add a master page to your site. Right-click the site and choose Add New Item. Use the default page name of **MasterPage.master**.

5. Add markup to the master page to include a HyperLink control to both show the name of the user and to link to the user profile edit page you will create in a later step.

6. Surround your markup with a Panel control. This control will be used to set the user's preferred color for the site. The contents of the <body> element for your page should look similar to the following.

```
<body>
    <form id="form1" runat="server">
    <asp:Panel ID="Panel1" runat="server">
        <h1>My Site</h1>
        <hr />
        <div style="float: right">
            <asp:HyperLink ID="UserProfileHyperLink" runat="server"
            NavigateUrl="UserProfile.aspx"></asp:HyperLink>
        </div>
        <asp:ContentPlaceHolder id="ContentPlaceHolder1" runat="server">
        </asp:ContentPlaceHolder>
    </asp:Panel>
    </form>
</body>
```

7. Add a Page_Load event handler to the master page's code-behind file. In this handler, add code to set the HyperLink control's text and the Panel control's background based on the user's profile. Your code should look similar to the following.

Sample of Visual Basic Code

```
Protected Sub Page_Load(ByVal sender As Object, _
    ByVal e As System.EventArgs) Handles Me.Load

    If Profile.Name.Length > 0 Then
        UserProfileHyperLink.Text = "Welcome, " & Profile.Name
    Else
        UserProfileHyperLink.Text = "Set Profile"
    End If

    If Profile.ColorPreference.Length > 0 Then
        Panel1.BackColor = System.Drawing.Color.FromName(Profile.ColorPreference)
    End If
End Sub
```

Sample of C# Code

```
protected void Page_Load(object sender, EventArgs e)
{
    if (Profile.Name.Length > 0)
    {
        UserProfileHyperLink.Text = "Welcome, " + Profile.Name;
    }
    else
    {
        UserProfileHyperLink.Text = "Set Profile";
    }

    if (Profile.ColorPreference.Length > 0)
    {
        Panel1.BackColor =
            System.Drawing.Color.FromName(Profile.ColorPreference);
    }
}
```

8. Add a new web form called Default.aspx. When doing so, select the Select Master Page check box in the Add New Item dialog box and select your master page. In Solution Explorer, right-click the Default.aspx page and set it as the startup page for the solution.

9. Inside the new Default.aspx page, add text within the second asp:Content control to indicate that the user is on the home page. Your markup might look as follows.

```
<asp:Content ID="Content1" ContentPlaceHolderID="head" Runat="Server">
    <title>Home</title>
</asp:Content>

<asp:Content ID="Content2" ContentPlaceHolderID="ContentPlaceHolder1" Runat="Server">
    <h2>Home</h2>
</asp:Content>
```

10. Add another new form to your page. Name it **UserProfile.aspx**. Be sure to select MasterPage.master as its master page.

11. Edit the markup of the UserProfile.aspx page to include form fields to allow a user to manage his or her profile. Your markup might look similar to the following.

```
<asp:Content ID="Content1" ContentPlaceHolderID="head" Runat="Server">
    <title>User Profile</title>
</asp:Content>

<asp:Content ID="Content2" ContentPlaceHolderID="ContentPlaceHolder1" Runat="Server">

    <h2>User Profile</h2>

    Name<br />
    <asp:TextBox ID="NameTextBox" runat="server"></asp:TextBox>
    <br /><br />
    Postal Code<br />
    <asp:TextBox ID="PostalTextBox" runat="server"></asp:TextBox>
    <br /><br />
    Background Preference<br />
    <asp:DropDownList ID="ColorsDropDownList" runat="server">
        <asp:ListItem Text="White" Value="White"></asp:ListItem>
        <asp:ListItem Text="Yellow" Value="Yellow"></asp:ListItem>
        <asp:ListItem Text="Green" Value="Green"></asp:ListItem>
    </asp:DropDownList>
    <br /><br />

    <asp:Button ID="SaveButton" runat="server" Text="Save" />
</asp:Content>
```

12. Add an event handler for the UserProfile.aspx page's SaveButton click event. Add code to this event handler to set the user's profile, save it, and redirect the user back to the home page (Default.aspx). Your code should look similar to the following.

Sample of Visual Basic Code

```vb
Protected Sub ButtonSave_Click(ByVal sender As Object, _
  ByVal e As System.EventArgs) Handles ButtonSave.Click

    Profile.Name = NameTextBox.Text
    Profile.PostalCode = PostalTextBox.Text
    Profile.ColorPreference = ColorsDropDownList.SelectedValue.ToString()

    Profile.Save()

    Response.Redirect("Default.aspx")
End Sub
```

Sample of C# Code

```csharp
protected void ButtonSave_Click(object sender, EventArgs e)
{
    Profile.Name = NameTextBox.Text;
    Profile.PostalCode = short.Parse(PostalTextBox.Text);
    Profile.ColorPreference = ColorsDropDownList.SelectedValue.ToString();

    Profile.Save();

    Response.Redirect("Default.aspx");
}
```

13. Add another event handler to the UserProfile.aspx page for the Page.Load event. Add code to this event to initialize the form fields if user profile values exist. Your code should look as follows.

Sample of Visual Basic Code

```vb
Protected Sub Page_Load(ByVal sender As Object, _
  ByVal e As System.EventArgs) Handles Me.Load

    If Not IsPostBack Then
        NameTextBox.Text = Profile.Name
        If Profile.PostalCode > 0 Then
            PostalTextBox.Text = Profile.PostalCode
        End If
        If Profile.ColorPreference.Length > 0 Then
            ColorsDropDownList.SelectedValue = Profile.ColorPreference.ToString()
        End If
    End If
End Sub
```

```csharp
protected void Page_Load(object sender, EventArgs e)
{
    if (!IsPostBack)
    {
        NameTextBox.Text = Profile.Name;
        if (Profile.PostalCode > 0)
        {
            PostalTextBox.Text = Profile.PostalCode.ToString();
        }
        if (Profile.ColorPreference.Length > 0)
        {
            ColorsDropDownList.SelectedValue = Profile.ColorPreference.ToString();
        }
    }
}
```

14. Run the application and go to the Default.aspx page. Notice that the first time you run the application, it takes a little time, as ASP.NET generates the ASPNETDB.mdf file for your site.

15. Click the Set Profile link, edit your profile, and then view the results. Close the application and run it again and notice that ASP.NET stores your information between requests.

16. In Solution Explorer, click the Refresh button. Notice that the App_Data subdirectory now exists and contains an ASPNETDB.mdf database file.

Lesson Summary

- You can configure user profiles by using the Web.config file and the <profile> element. You add fields to this element based on which data elements you intend to track for users of your site.

- ASP.NET automatically creates a strongly typed object based on your profile field settings in the Web.config file. You can access this class and its properties through the Profile.<*FieldName*> syntax in your code.

- You call the Profile.Save method to save a user's profile to a database.

- By default, ASP.NET uses the SqlProfileProvider to store and retrieve user profile information to a SQL Server Express database called ASPNETDB.mdf. You can change the provider and the database by using configuration files.

Lesson Review

You can use the following questions to test your knowledge of the information in Lesson 1, "Working with User Profiles." The questions are also available on the companion CD in a practice test, if you prefer to review them in electronic form.

1. Which of the following Web.config files correctly enables the website to track the age of anonymous users in a variable of type Int32?

   A.
   ```
   <anonymousIdentification enabled="true" />
   <profile>
       <properties>
           <add name="Age" type="System.Int32" allowAnonymous="true" />
       </properties>
   </profile>
   ```

   B.
   ```
   <anonymousIdentification enabled="true" />
   <profile>
       <properties>
           <add name="Age" allowAnonymous="true" />
       </properties>
   </profile>
   ```

   C.
   ```
   <anonymousIdentification enabled="true" />
   <profile>
       <properties>
           <add name="Age" type="System.Int32" />
       </properties>
   </profile>
   ```

   D.
   ```
   <profile>
       <properties>
           <add name="Age" type="System.Int32" />
       </properties>
   </profile>
   ```

2. You want to create a user profile that uses a custom type as one of the profile properties. What actions must you take? (Choose all that apply.)

   A. Mark your class as serializable.

   B. Set the type attribute of the profile property to the fully qualified name of your custom type.

   C. Add the group element to your profile property. Add one element to the group element for each property in your custom type. Set each element's name to match that of a property in your custom type.

   D. Add your custom type in the Machine.config file in the <customTypes> element.

Lesson 2: Using ASP.NET Membership

One key feature of nearly every enterprise website is the ability to manage users and their access to the features of a site. This includes creating and editing users, managing their passwords, authenticating users based on role, and much more. In the past, this code was written by nearly every website team out there (sometimes more than once). Fortunately, ASP.NET now includes membership features that reduce the amount of code you have to write. ASP.NET membership features include all of the following:

- Wizard-based configuration of user management capabilities
- Browser-based user management and access control configuration
- A set of ASP.NET controls that provides users with the ability to log on, log off, create new accounts, and recover lost passwords
- The Membership and Roles classes, which you can use to access user management capabilities within your code

ASP.NET membership is related to the user profiles that you learned about in Lesson 1. User profiles store data about unique users. Membership is meant to uniquely identify users. This lesson describes how you take advantage of the ASP.NET membership features in your own websites to manage user accounts and authorization.

> **After this lesson, you will be able to:**
> - Understand the features of the ASP.NET logon controls and use them in a site.
> - Configure an ASP.NET website to support user management.
> - Use the Membership class to manage user information.
> - Use the Roles class to define authentication groups for your site.
>
> **Estimated lesson time: 45 minutes**

Using the WSAT to Configure Security

You can use the Web Site Administration Tool (WSAT) to define and manage users, roles, and security on your site. Administrators and developers can use the tool to manage security settings from a web browser. This tool allows you to configure authentication, create and manage users, and create and manage role-based authorization.

Creating Users

Recall that you launch the WSAT tool in Visual Studio by choosing ASP.NET Configuration from the Website menu. This takes you to the administration page for your site. The user configuration information is found on the Security tab. The first step is to click the Select Authentication Type link. Here you choose Windows-based, local Active Directory security authentication (From A Local Network), or web-based forms that use a database authentication (From The Internet). After the type of authentication has been selected, you can create users, manage users, define their roles, and control their access. Figure 13-2 shows an example of creating a new user with the WSAT.

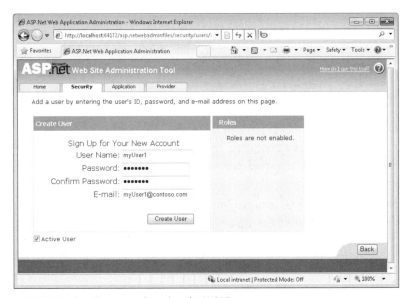

FIGURE 13-2 Creating a user by using the WSAT.

When you select web-based security by using the WSAT, ASP.NET automatically creates the ASPNETDB.mdf file for your site and stores it in the App_Data directory (see Lesson 1 for information on configuring a different database). It also updates your site's Web.config file to enable this security feature. It adds the authentication element, as shown here, if it did not previously exist.

```
<configuration>
  <system.web>
    <authentication mode="Forms" />
  </system.web>
</configuration>
```

The WSAT is a great tool for administrators and developers. You can use it to edit configuration settings and manage the data found inside ASPNETDB. However, it does not allow users to create or manage their own accounts. For this, you need to use the logon controls to create pages on which users can set up and manage their information.

Creating Roles

You can also use the WSAT to create, configure, and manage user roles, which are simply groups of users that you define. You can then apply authorization at the role level rather than at the individual user level. This makes management easier because roles do not change, but the users assigned to them do.

To enable roles by using the WSAT, on the Security tab, click the Enable Roles link. This will edit your Web.config file to enable roles, as shown in the following.

```
<configuration>
  <system.web>
    <roleManager enabled="true" />
  </system.web>
</configuration>
```

On the Security tab, you can now use the Create Or Manage Roles link. To create a new role, you start by assigning it a name. You then click Manage for the role to assign users to or remove users from the role.

Roles, by themselves, do not enforce security on your site. Instead, you need to do one of two things (or both). First, you can use the Roles class in your code to determine whether a user has access to a specified page or feature. You can query the IsUserInRole method (described later in this lesson) to do so. Second, you can use the WSAT to create role-based access rules for your site.

Creating Access Rules

You create role-based access rules on the Security tab in the WSAT. An access rule allows you to define folder-level access to items in your site on either a per-user or role basis. You start by clicking the Create Access Rules link. This takes you to the Add New Access Rule page, as shown in Figure 13-3. From here, you can apply a rule to a role, an individual user, all users, or anonymous users. You select a folder for the rule, choose to whom the rule applies, and specify whether you intend to allow or deny permission.

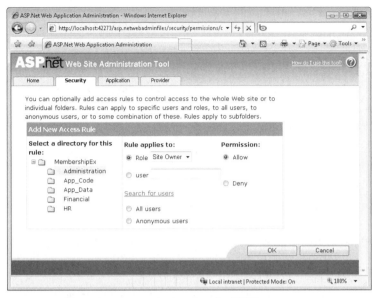

FIGURE 13-3 Managing access rules by using the WSAT.

The WSAT adds a Web.config file to any folder to which you apply an access rule (or it edits the existing Web.config file if the folder already contains this file). This configuration file applies only to the content of that folder. In the example shown in Figure 13-3, the role of Site Owner is being allowed for the Administration folder. The following represents the content of the Web.config file found inside the Administration folder after this operation.

```
<configuration>
  <system.web>
    <authorization>
      <allow roles="Site Owner" />
    </authorization>
  </system.web>
</configuration>
```

Logon Controls

ASP.NET provides a set of controls, classes, and management tools for authenticating users with web forms and storing user information in a database. These controls allow you to track, manage, and authenticate users without creating your own schema, relying on the Active Directory user database, or managing users by other means. Prior to version 2.0 of the Microsoft .NET Framework, custom user authentication required creation from scratch of many complex components, such as user database schemas, logon pages, password management pages, and user administration. Creating these components yourself is time-consuming and risky to your application's security. ASP.NET helps you minimize this risk.

The Login Control Classes

There are seven controls in ASP.NET for managing the logon information of a user. These seven controls are grouped together as the logon controls. They provide user interface elements for managing the logon features related to users. Like the profile features, these controls are configured to work with the ASPNETDB.mdf SQL Server Express Edition database by default.

Each of these controls provides a specific feature required of most user-driven websites. The following is a list of each of these controls and their purpose:

- **CreateUserWizard** This control gathers information from a new user, such as user name and password, and creates a new user account. You can use the user profile features in conjunction with the CreateUserWizard.

- **Login** This control defines a user interface for prompting users for their user name and password and enables users to select whether they want to be automatically authenticated the next time they visit your site. You can use the Login control with ASP.NET membership without writing any code, or you can write your own authentication code by adding a handler for the Authenticate event.

- **LoginView** This control is used to display different information if a user is logged onto your site. For example, you could use this control to provide links to features that are available only to authenticated users.

- **LoginStatus** You use this control to allow users to link to your logon page if they haven't been authenticated. It displays a link to log off for users who are currently logged on.

- **LoginName** This control displays the current user's user name (if logged on).

- **PasswordRecovery** This control enables password retrieval or reset for a user by sending an email message or by having the user answer a security question.

- **ChangePassword** This control enables a user who is logged on to change his or her password.

With the functionality built into these controls, you can create—without writing any code— a website that enables users to create their own accounts, change and reset their passwords, and log on and log off. You can, of course, create your own custom providers or migrate to a higher version of SQL Server.

Creating a User Account Creation Page

Most public websites allow users to create their own accounts. This simplifies user creation and takes the burden off of the administrator. If you create a site by using the ASP.NET Web Site template, Visual Studio generates a page named Register.aspx in the Account folder specifically for this purpose. This page is preconfigured to work with the default logon database.

You use the CreateUserWizard control to create a custom page that allows users to create their own accounts by using the standard ASP.NET membership. This control can be added to a page and automatically works with the provider that works with the ASPNETDB.mdf file.

The CreateUserWizard control, by default, prompts a user for a user name, password, email address, security question, and security answer. Figure 13-4 shows an example of the control on a page inside Visual Studio. The CreateUserWizard control is also capable of validating required fields, ensuring a strong password, and confirming a password.

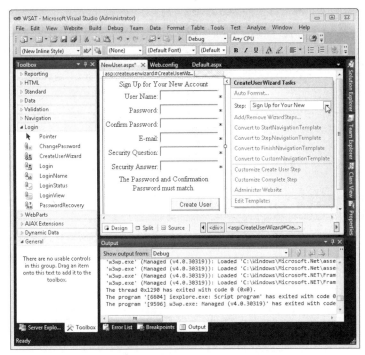

FIGURE 13-4 The ASP.NET CreateUserWizard control in Visual Studio.

There is nothing additional that you need to do to configure, set up, or use a CreateUserWizard control. However, you will most likely want to set the ContinueDestinationPageUrl property. This property should be set to the page to which you want users to go after they have completed their account creation process. In addition, you can add your own code to the ContinueButtonClick event to add processing when the user clicks the final step in the wizard.

The CreateUserWizard control is a composite, template-driven control. Therefore, you have access to edit the templates that are defined by the control. You can even change and add to the steps defined by the wizard. These features are useful if you want to add information to the user registration process or change the layout of the interface.

As an example, suppose you want to add controls to allow a user to define additional profile information as part of the account creation process. You can do so by clicking the Customize Create User Step link from the CreateUserWizard Tasks pane (refer back to Figure 13-4). This will render the entire markup to create a user form inside your page. You can then edit this markup to include your own controls as necessary. Figure 13-5 shows an example of a CheckBox control added to the page.

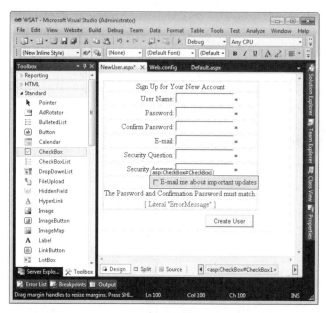

FIGURE 13-5 A customized version of the CreateUserWizard control.

You can store this additional information by handling the CreatedUser event. In this event, you use the Membership class (discussed later in this lesson) to get the user and update the Comment property of the MembershipUser class. This property is used to store custom values for a user. However, a better method is to use the Profile object, as discussed in Lesson 1.

Unfortunately, you cannot easily set the user's profile information inside the CreatedUser event because the user is not considered identified and authenticated to the site until after this event completes. To help with this issue, the CreateUserWizard control exposes the properties EditProfileText and EditProfileUrl. You can use these properties to create a link that appears on the final page for the created user. This link can take users to a page that allows them to edit their profile (as discussed in Lesson 1). This profile will be associated with the newly created user. However, without deeper customizations, you will have to maintain both a profile page and a create user page.

By default, new user accounts do not belong to any roles. To add a new user to a role (such as a default Users role), add a handler for the CreateUserWizard.CreatedUser event, and then call the Roles.AddUserToRole method as described later in this lesson.

Creating a Logon Page

A logon page allows a user to present his or her credentials to your site and then be authenticated. In most cases, a logon page will include logon information, a link to create a new account, and a link to retrieve a password for an existing account. If you create a site by using the ASP.NET Web Site template, Visual Studio generates a page named Login.aspx in the Account folder specifically for this purpose. It is preconfigured to work with the default logon database.

To create a custom logon page, edit the Web.config file to point nonauthenticated requests to your logon page by adding the loginUrl attribute to the <forms> element as follows.

```
<authentication mode="Forms">
  <forms loginUrl="Login.aspx" />
</authentication>
```

On the logon page, you start by adding a Login control. This control is used to prompt a user for his or her credentials. The Login control also includes features for validation to ensure that the user types a user name and password. However, to get the actual error messages to the page (instead of just asterisks indicating incomplete information), you should add a ValidationSummary control to your logon page. You configure this control to work with the Login control by setting the ValidationGroup property to the ID of your Login control. Figure 13-6 shows an example of both controls added to a page.

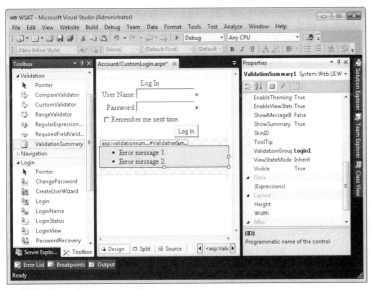

FIGURE 13-6 The Login control prompts the user for credentials.

You do not need to write any code to use the Login control. It works automatically with the site configuration to authenticate users by using forms-based authentication.

Adding Password Recovery

To complete your logon page, you might want to add a PasswordRecovery control. This control assists users if they forget their password. This control enables users to type their user name and receive a new, random password via email. Email messages are sent based on the configured email provider in the Web.config file. You can also require users to answer a security question before their password is sent.

> **NOTE CONFIGURING AN EMAIL SERVER**
>
> You can configure an email server for your site manually in the Web.config file, or you can use the WSAT. When using the WSAT, you set up a Simple Mail Transfer Protocol (SMTP) server from the Application tab.

Figure 13-7 shows an example of the PasswordRecovery control in Visual Studio. Notice that there are three template views: UserName, Question, and Success. The UserName view allows a user to enter his or her user name; the Question view allows your application to ask for and validate the user's secret question, and the Success view indicates a successful lookup.

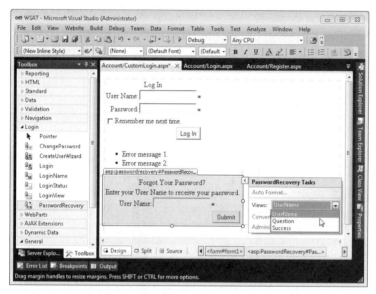

FIGURE 13-7 The PasswordRecovery control can send email messages to users who request their passwords.

If the user provides valid credentials, the user is logged in to your site. The membership controls such as LoginStatus will then automatically reflect that. If the user does not provide valid credentials, the Login control prompts the user to retype his or her password. You should create a handler for the Login.LoginError event and perform security auditing by adding an event to the Security event log. Similarly, you should handle (log) the PasswordRecovery.UserLookupError and PasswordRecovery.AnswerLookupError events. This ensures that administrators can discover excessive attempts to look up and recover a password.

Creating a Password Change Page

Another important form is the change password form, which allows a user to enter his or her current password and create a new one. If you create a site by using the ASP.NET Web Site template, Visual Studio generates pages named ChangePassword.aspx and ChangePasswordSuccess.aspx in the Account folder specifically for this purpose.

You can create a custom change password page by using the ChangePassword control, as shown in Figure 13-8. On completion, you can either show a success message or automatically navigate to another page. To enable the latter scenario, set the SuccessPageUrl property of the ChangePassword control to the name of the page to which you want to redirect the user following a successful password change. The control also exposes other useful properties, such as EditProfileUrl and EditProfileText to create a link to allow the user to edit other portions of his or her profile.

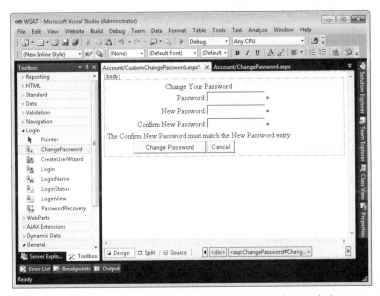

FIGURE 13-8 The ChangePassword control allows users to change their passwords.

The FormsAuthentication Class

The FormsAuthentication class is the basis for all forms authentication in ASP.NET. The class includes the following read-only properties, which you can use to programmatically examine the current configuration:

- **FormsCookieName**   This property returns the configured cookie name used for the current application.
- **FormsCookiePath**   This property returns the configured cookie path used for the current application.
- **RequireSSL**   This property gets a value indicating whether the cookie must be transmitted by using SSL (that is, over HTTP Secure [HTTPS] only).

> **IMPORTANT**   **IMPROVING SECURITY IF THE WEB SERVER HAS AN SSL CERTIFICATE**
>
> Enable RequireSSL for best security. This will ensure that forms authentication is encrypted.

- **SlidingExpiration** This property gets a value indicating whether sliding expiration is enabled. If sliding expiration is enabled, the user's authentication timeout is reset with every web request.

> **IMPORTANT** **IMPROVING SECURITY (AT THE COST OF CONVENIENCE)**
>
> Disable SlidingExpiration for the highest level of security. This prevents a session from remaining open indefinitely.

Additionally, you can call the following methods:

- **Authenticate** This method attempts to validate the provided credentials against those contained in the configured credential store.
- **Decrypt** This method returns an instance of a FormsAuthenticationTicket class, given a valid encrypted authentication ticket obtained from an HTTP cookie.
- **Encrypt** This method produces a string containing an encrypted authentication ticket suitable for use in an HTTP cookie, given a FormsAuthenticationTicket object.
- **GetAuthCookie** This method creates an authentication cookie for a specified user name.
- **GetRedirectUrl** This method returns the URL for the original request that caused the redirect to the logon page.
- **HashPasswordForStoringInConfigFile** Given a password and a string identifying the hash type, this routine produces a hash password suitable for storing in a configuration file. If your application stores user credentials in the Web.config file and hashes the password, build this method into a management tool to enable administrators to add users and reset passwords.
- **RedirectFromLoginPage** This method redirects an authenticated user back to the originally requested URL. Call this method after verifying a user's credentials with the Authenticate method. You must pass this method a string and a Boolean value. The string should uniquely identify the user, and the method uses the string to generate a cookie. The Boolean value, if true, allows the browser to use the same cookie across multiple browser sessions. Generally, this unique piece of information should be the user's user name.
- **RenewTicketIfOld** This method conditionally updates the sliding expiration on a FormsAuthenticationTicket object.
- **SetAuthCookie** This method creates an authentication ticket and attaches it to the cookie's collection of the outgoing response. It does not perform a redirect.
- **SignOut** This method removes the authentication ticket, essentially logging the user off.

The Membership Class

The logon controls discussed previously use the methods of the System.Web.Security.Membership class to implement their functionality. This is, for the most part, abstracted from developers. However, there are many cases in which you might want to use these methods yourself. For instance, you might want to create your own custom user interface outside of the logon controls, intercept logon control events, and implement other security-related code on your site. In each case, you use the Membership class. It provides capabilities that allow you to add, remove, and find users. The following are the important static methods in this class, along with each method's capability:

- **CreateUser**   This method adds a user to the database. Use this method if you create a custom page to enable users or administrators to add new accounts.

- **DeleteUser**   This method removes a user from the data store. Use this method if you create custom user management tools.

- **FindUsersByEmail**   This method gets a collection of membership users with the specified email addresses.

- **FindUsersByName**   This method gets a collection of membership users with the specified user names.

- **GeneratePassword**   This method creates a random password of the specified length. Use this if you are implementing custom controls to generate or reset passwords.

- **GetAllUsers**   This method returns a collection of all users in the database.

- **GetNumberOfUsersOnline**   This method returns the number of users currently logged on.

- **GetUser**   This method returns a MembershipUser object representing the current logged-on user. Call this method any time you need to access the current user's account.

- **GetUserNameByEmail**   This method gets a user name with the specified email address.

- **UpdateUser**   This method updates the database with the information for the specified user. Use this method if you create a page to enable users or administrators to modify existing accounts.

- **ValidateUser**   This method verifies that the supplied user name and password are valid. Use this method to check a user's credentials if you create your own custom logon controls.

The Roles Class

Role management consists of a set of classes and interfaces that establish roles for the current user and manage role information. In ASP.NET user management, roles function as user groups, enabling you to assign access rights to all users who are part of a specific role. The most useful of these classes is System.Web.Security.Roles, which provides the ability to add users to or remove users from roles, create new roles, and determine to which roles a user belongs.

The Roles class provides many static methods, including the following:

- **AddUserToRole, AddUserToRoles, AddUsersToRole, and AddUsersToRoles**   These methods add a user or users to a role or roles.
- **CreateRole**   This method creates a new role.
- **DeleteRole**   This method deletes an existing role.
- **FindUsersInRole**   This method returns a collection of users in a role.
- **GetAllRoles**   This method returns a collection of all roles that currently exist.
- **GetRolesForUser**   This method returns a collection of roles for the current user.
- **IsUserInRole**   This method returns true if the user is a member of a specified role.
- **RemoveUserFromRole, RemoveUsersFromRole, RemoveUserFromRoles, and RemoveUsersFromRoles**   These methods remove a user or users from a role or roles.

For example, if you want to assign the user being created as part of the CreateUserWizard control to a role named Users, you could use the following code:

Sample of Visual Basic Code

```
Roles.AddUserToRole(CreateUserWizard1.UserName, "Users")
```

Sample of C# Code

```
Roles.AddUserToRole(CreateUserWizard1.UserName, "Users");
```

You cannot use the Roles class to manage Windows user groups when using Windows authentication. Windows authentication is discussed in more detail in the next section.

 Quick Check

1. Which control would you use to provide a logon link?
2. Which logon controls are useful only to authenticated users?

Quick Check Answers

1. Use the LoginStatus control to provide a logon link.
2. The LoginName and ChangePassword controls are useful only to authenticated users. LoginView is also useful to unauthenticated users when you set the LoginView.AnonymousTemplate property.

Configuring Websites to Require Windows Authentication

If your application is targeted for use inside an organization in which users have existing user accounts within a local user database or Active Directory repository, then you should authenticate users with Windows authentication. You can configure Windows authentication in two ways: within IIS and within your ASP.NET application. To provide stronger security, you should configure your site to use both techniques.

When a website requires Windows authentication, the application rejects any request that does not include a valid user name and password in the request header. The user's browser then prompts the user for a user name and password. Because the browser prompts the user for credentials, you do not have to have pages to request the user's user name and password. Some browsers, such as Windows Internet Explorer, automatically provide the user's current user name and password when the server is located on the intranet. This seamlessly authenticates the user, eliminating the need to retype the password for intranet site visits.

With that said, most public websites use forms-based authentication; Windows authentication is primarily useful for intranet sites in an Active Directory domain environment.

To configure an ASP.NET application for Windows authentication, edit the <authentication> section of the Web.config file. This section, like most sections related to ASP.NET application configuration, must be defined within the <system.web> section. The <system.web> section, in turn, must exist within the <configuration> section. This example shows the <authentication> section of the Web.config file configured to use Windows authentication.

```
<configuration>
  <system.web>
    <authentication mode="Windows" />
      <authorization>
        <deny users="?" />
      </authorization>
  </system.web>
</configuration>
```

The <authorization> section simply requires all users to be successfully authenticated. Specifying <deny users="?" /> within <authorization> requires users to be authenticated, whereas specifying <allow users="*" /> within <authorization> bypasses authentication entirely. The question mark (?) represents unauthenticated users, and the asterisk (*) represents all users, both authenticated and unauthenticated.

You can also configure Windows authentication in your application's Web.config file by following these steps, which are more user friendly:

1. Create an ASP.NET website by using Visual Studio.

2. From the Website menu, select ASP.NET Configuration.

3. Click the Security tab, and then click Select Authentication Type.

4. Under How Will Your Users Access The Site, select From A Local Network, and then click Done.

EXAM TIP

The exam objectives specifically exclude Windows authentication, so don't put too much of your time into understanding how it works. In the real world, however, Windows authentication is commonly used in intranet Active Directory environments.

Restricting Access to ASP.NET Websites, Files, and Folders

Authentication determines a user's identity, whereas *authorization* defines what the user is allowed to access. Before the .NET Framework, administrators controlled web user authorization entirely with Windows permissions. Although Windows permissions are still a key part of configuring security for ASP.NET applications, these permissions are now complemented by ASP.NET's authorization capabilities. Authorization is now controlled with Web.config files, just like authentication is. This enables authorization to work with any type of authentication—even if the authorization doesn't use the local user database or Active Directory directory service on which NTFS permissions are based. The use of Web.config files also makes copying file permissions between multiple web servers as easy as copying files.

In the sections that follow, you will learn how to restrict access according to user and group names, how to restrict access to specific files and folders by using either a .config file or file permissions, and how to use impersonation in an ASP.NET application.

Restricting Access to Users and Groups

The default Machine.config file contains the following authorization information.

```
<authorization>
  <allow users="*"/>
</authorization>
```

Unless you modify this section of the Machine.config file, or override the Machine.config file by adding this section to your application's Web.config file, all users permitted by your authentication configuration are allowed to interact with all parts of your ASP.NET website. The <allow users="*"> subsection of the <authorization> section tells ASP.NET that all users who pass the authentication requirements are allowed access to all ASP.NET content.

To configure an ASP.NET application to provide access only to the users whose user names are Eric and Sam, override the Machine.config security settings by editing the Web.config file in the root of the ASP.NET application and add the following lines within the <system.web> section:

```
<authorization>
  <allow users="Eric, Sam"/>
  <deny users="*"/>
</authorization>
```

The <allow> and <deny> subsections contain users and roles attributes. The users attribute should be set to a list of user names separated by commas, an asterisk (*) to indicate all authenticated and unauthenticated users, or a question mark (?) to indicate anonymous users. If Windows authentication is used, the user names should match names in the local user database or Active Directory service and need to include a domain name (that is, *DOMAIN\user* for domain accounts or *COMPUTERNAME\user* for local user accounts).

The roles element contains a comma-separated list of roles. When Windows authentication is used, roles correspond to Windows user groups. In this case, the names must exactly match group names in the local user database or Active Directory repository. Provide the domain name for groups in the Active Directory repository, but do not specify the computer name for local groups. For example, to specify the IT group in the CONTOSO domain, use CONTOSO\IT. To specify the local users group, use Users.

If you are using Windows authentication, you must disable the roleManager element in your Web.config file to use role security to authorize Windows user groups. The roleManager element is disabled by default, so removing it from your Web.config file is sufficient to disable it. You can authorize Windows users with roleManager enabled, but it must be disabled to authorize Windows groups.

Controlling Authorization for Folders and Files by Using .config Files

The previous techniques are useful for controlling user access to an entire ASP.NET application. To restrict access to specific files or folders, add a <location> section to the <configuration> section of the Web.config file. The <location> section contains its own <system.web> subsection, so do not place it within an existing <system.web> section.

To configure access restrictions for a specific file or folder, add the <location> section to your Web.config file with a single path section. The path section must be set to the relative path of a file or folder; absolute paths are not allowed. Within the <location> section, include a <system.web> subsection and any configuration information that is unique to the specified file or folder. For example, to require forms authentication for the ListUsers.aspx file and allow access only for the user named admin, add the following text to the <configuration> section of the Web.config file.

```
<location path="ListUsers.aspx">
  <system.web>
    <authentication mode="forms">
      <forms loginUrl="AdminLogin.aspx" protection="All"/>
    </authentication>
    <authorization>
      <allow users="admin"/>
      <deny users="*"/>
    </authorization>
  </system.web>
</location>
```

When multiple <location> sections are used, files and subfolders automatically inherit all settings from their parents. Therefore, you do not need to repeat settings that are identical to the parents' configurations. When you are configuring authorization, inheritance has the potential to lead to security vulnerabilities. Consider the following Web.config file.

```
<configuration>
  <system.web>
  <authentication mode="Windows" />
  <authorization>
    <deny users="?" />
  </authorization>
  </system.web>

  <location path="Protected">
  <system.web>
    <authorization>
    <allow roles="CONTOSO\IT" />
    </authorization>
  </system.web>
  </location>
</configuration>
```

In this example, there are actually *three* layers of inheritance. The first is the Machine.config file, which specifies the default <allow users="*"/>. The second layer is the first <system.web> section in the example, which applies to the entire application. This setting, <deny users="?"/>, denies access to all unauthenticated users. By itself, this second layer denies access to any user. However, combined with the Machine.config file, this layer allows access to all authenticated users and denies access to everyone else.

The third layer is the <location> section, which grants access to the CONTOSO\IT group. However, this section also inherits the <deny users="?"/> and <allow users="*"/> settings. Therefore, the effective settings for the Protected subfolder are the same as for the parent folder: All authenticated users have access. To restrict access to *only* users in the CONTOSO\IT group, you must explicitly deny access to users who are not specifically granted access, as the following code demonstrates.

```
<location path="Protected">
  <system.web>
  <authorization>
    <allow roles="CONTOSO\IT" />
    <deny users="*" />
  </authorization>
  </system.web>
</location>
```

Configuring Impersonation by Using .config Files

By default, ASP.NET applications make all requests for system resources from the ASPNET account (in IIS 5.0) or the Network Service account (in IIS 6.0, IIS 7.0, and IIS 7.5). This setting is configurable and is defined in the <processModel> item of the <system.web> section of the Machine.config file. The default setting for this section is as follows.

```
<processModel autoConfig="true" />
```

You can change autoConfig to false and set the userName and password attribute to define the account that ASP.NET impersonates when requesting system resources on behalf of a web user.

Automatic configuration is sufficient for most ASP.NET implementations. However, in many cases, administrators need to configure ASP.NET to impersonate the client's authenticated user account, IIS's anonymous user account, or a specific user account. This configuration is done by setting the impersonate attribute of the <identity> element of the Machine.config file (for server-wide settings) or the Web.config file (for application-specific or directory-specific settings). To enable impersonation of the client's authenticated Windows account, or the IIS IUSR_*MachineName* account for anonymous access, add the following line to the <system.web> section of the Web.config file.

```
<identity impersonate="true" />
```

When IIS is configured for anonymous access and impersonation is enabled, ASP.NET makes requests for system resources by using the IUSR_*MachineName* account. When a user authenticates directly to IIS by using a Windows logon, ASP.NET impersonates that user account. To enable ASP.NET to impersonate a specific user account, regardless of how IIS authentication is handled, add the following line to the <system.web> section of the Web.config file and replace the *DOMAIN*, *UserName*, and *Password* placeholders with the account logon credentials.

```
<identity impersonate="true" userName="DOMAIN\UserName" password="Password"/>
```

REAL WORLD

Tony Northrup

If you create Internet applications, you'll never need to use Windows authentication or impersonation. Those concepts are vital to understand if you create intranet applications for enterprises with an Active Directory infrastructure, however.

One of the biggest selling points of Active Directory directory services is centralized control of user credentials and roles. Active Directory directory services allow an enterprise to create a single user account for each employee and grant those accounts access to just about any network resource, including files, printers, applications, databases, and even specific data within a database. If an enterprise has 5,000 users, managing those users is time consuming enough. If dozens of different applications were to require users to have separately managed accounts, each with different management techniques, it would not only be exceedingly time consuming to manage, but security vulnerabilities would begin to appear as user accounts that should be removed or updated are overlooked.

Windows authentication and impersonation allow you to take advantage of the Active Directory user database for your own application. It's not any easier or harder to program than using forms authentication, but it's definitely easier to manage. Not only will users not need a separate account, but you can rely on systems administrators to manage the user accounts and control permissions each user receives.

PRACTICE **Configuring Authentication in ASP.NET Applications**

In this exercise, you create an ASP.NET website and then configure it to restrict access by using roles.

ON THE COMPANION MEDIA

If you encounter a problem completing an exercise, you can find the completed projects in the samples installed from this book's companion CD. For more information about the project files and other content on the CD, see "Using the Companion Media" in this book's Introduction.

EXERCISE Creating and Configuring an ASP.NET Site to Use Membership Features

In this exercise, you create a new ASP.NET website and add support for ASP.NET memberships.

1. Open Visual Studio. Create a new, file-based website by using the ASP.NET Web Site template.

2. Create two subfolders in your site. Name one **Members** and the other **Admin**. You can do so by right-clicking the project and choosing New Folder.

3. To each subfolder, add a blank ASP.NET web form named **Default.aspx**. Later, you'll access these pages to verify that ASP.NET requires proper authentication.

4. From the Website menu in Visual Studio, select ASP.NET Configuration. This launches the WSAT in a browser.

5. Click the Security tab to get started. In the Users section, click the Select Authentication Type link. On the next page, select From The Internet, and click Done. This enables forms-based authentication (though it was already enabled as part of the Visual Studio ASP.NET Web Site template).

6. On the Security tab, click the Enable Roles link to enable roles for the site.

7. In the Roles section, click the Create Or Manage Roles link. On the next page, add a role called **Users**. Repeat this process to add another role called **Administrators**.

8. Click the Security tab to return to the main security page. Use the Create User link to add two users.

   a. Create a user named **StandardUser**. In the Roles section, select the Users role.

   b. Add another user named **Admin**. In the Roles section, select the Administrators role.

   c. For both users, you can set the password, security question, and email address as you like. (The code provided in the samples installed from the CD uses the password *password!*.)

9. Click the Security tab to return to the main security page. In the Access Rules section, click the Create Access Rules link. Create the following rules:

   ■ Create a rule that denies all anonymous users access to the root of the site.

   ■ Create a rule that grants all users (other than those who are anonymous) access to the root of the site.

   ■ Create a rule that grants users in the Administrators role access to the Admin directory.

   ■ Create a rule that denies all users access to the Admin directory.

   Note that the order of the rule creation is important, because each rule is processed in order. You can move rules up or down by clicking Manage Access Rules on the Security tab of the WSAT interface.

10. Return to Visual Studio. Click the Refresh button at the top of Solution Explorer. Notice the inclusion of the ASPNETDB.mdf file in your site. Also notice the additional Web.config file inside the Admin folder. Open both Web.config files for your site and examine the new settings.

11. Open the Default.aspx page in the site root. Add the following controls:

   ■ A HyperLink control with the text set to **Members only** and NavigateUrl set to **Members/Default.aspx**

   ■ A HyperLink control with the text set to **Administrators only** and NavigateUrl set to **Admin/Default.aspx**

12. Run Default.aspx in a web browser. Notice that you are redirected to the Account/ Login.aspx page. Log in as **StandardUser**. (The code provided in the samples installed from the CD uses the password *password!*.) You should now be able to view the page.

- Click the Members Only link. You should have full access.
- Click the Administrators Only link. You should be redirected to the Login page. Notice that the URL includes a parameter named ReturnUrl that contains the page you were attempting to access.
- Log on as Admin and notice that you are redirected to the Administrators Only page.

Lesson Summary

- ASP.NET provides several logon controls to enable you to easily build pages that support creating user accounts, logging on, logging off, and resetting passwords. These controls include Login, LoginView, LoginStatus, LoginName, PasswordRecovery, CreateUserWizard, and ChangePassword.
- Use the Membership class when you need to perform user management tasks from within your code, such as creating, deleting, or modifying user accounts. This class enables you to create custom forms that provide similar functionality to that provided by the standard ASP.NET logon controls.
- Use the Roles class when you need to perform role management tasks from within your code, such as adding users to roles, removing users from roles, creating new roles, or examining to which roles a user belongs.
- To control which users can access folders and files in a website, you can use either NTFS file permissions or Web.config files.

Lesson Review

You can use the following questions to test your knowledge of the information in Lesson 2, "Using ASP.NET Membership." The questions are also available on the companion CD in a practice test, if you prefer to review them in electronic form.

> **NOTE ANSWERS**
>
> Answers to these questions and explanations of why each answer choice is correct or incorrect are located in the "Answers" section at the end of the book.

1. Which of the following controls provides a link for unauthenticated users to log on?
    A. Login
    B. LoginView
    C. LoginStatus
    D. LoginName

2. You are creating a web form that enables users to log on to your website. Which of the following ASP.NET controls should you add to the page? (Choose two answers.)

   A. Login

   B. CreateUserWizard

   C. LoginName

   D. PasswordRecovery

3. You have created an ASP.NET web form that enables users to create accounts with a CreateUserWizard control. After a new user creates an account, you want to redirect the user to a page listing the rules for your website. To which of the following events should you respond?

   A. CreateUserWizard.Unload

   B. CreateUserWizard.ContinueButtonClick

   C. CreateUserWizard.CreatedUser

   D. CreateUserWizard.Init

4. Which of the following Web.config segments correctly requires that all users be authenticated by using a Windows user account?

   A.
   ```
   <authentication mode="Windows" />
   <authorization>
       <deny users="*" />
   </authorization>
   ```

   B.
   ```
   <authentication mode="Windows" />
   <authorization>
       <allow users="*" />
   </authorization>
   ```

   C.
   ```
   <authentication mode="Windows" />
   <authorization>
       <deny users="?" />
   </authorization>
   ```

   D.
   ```
   <authentication mode="Windows" />
   <authorization>
       <allow users="?" />
   </authorization>
   ```

5. Given the following Web.config file, what permissions do users have to the Marketing folder?

   ```
   <configuration>
     <system.web>
       <authentication mode="Windows" />
       <authorization>
         <deny users="?" />
       </authorization>
     </system.web>
   ```

```
    <location path="Marketing">
      <system.web>
        <authorization>
          <allow roles="FABRIKAM\Marketing" />
          <deny users="*" />
        </authorization>
      </system.web>
    </location>
</configuration>
```

   A. Authenticated users and members of the FABRIKAM\Marketing group have
         access. All other users are denied access.

   B. Members of the FABRIKAM\Marketing group have access. All other users are
         denied access.

   C. All users, authenticated and unauthenticated, have access.

   D. All users are denied access.

6. You are configuring NTFS file permissions for a website with the following
   Web.config file:

```
<configuration>
  <system.web>
    <authentication mode="Windows" />
    <authorization>
      <deny users="?" />
    </authorization>
  </system.web>

  <location path="Marketing">
    <system.web>
      <authorization>
        <allow roles="FABRIKAM\Marketing" />
        <deny users="*" />
      </authorization>
    </system.web>
  </location>
</configuration>
```

   For the Marketing folder, you remove all file permissions, and then grant read access
   to the FABRIKAM\John and FABRIKAM\Sam user accounts. John is a member of the
   FABRIKAM\Domain Users and FABRIKAM\Marketing groups. Sam is only a member
   of the FABRIKAM\Domain Users group. Which of the following users can access web
   forms located in the Marketing folder?

   A. Unauthenticated users

   B. Authenticated users

   C. Members of the FABRIKAM\Domain Users group

   D. FABRIKAM\John

   E. FABRIKAM\Sam

Case Scenarios

In the following case scenarios, you apply what you've learned about how to authenticate users and control access by using authorization. If you have difficulty completing this work, review the material in this chapter before beginning the next chapter. You can find answers to these questions in the "Answers" section at the end of this book.

Case Scenario 1: Configuring Website Authorization

You are a developer for Southridge Video, a business that creates instructional videos. The business is deploying a new ASP.NET intranet application, and the administrators need some help configuring the security. The website has several subfolders, and each subfolder is managed by a different organization within Southridge. You meet with each of the managers and review the technical requirements to determine how you should configure security for each organization's subfolder.

Interviews

Following is a list of company personnel interviewed and their statements:

- **Wendy Richardson, IT Manager**   My web experts have created an ASP.NET intranet application in the /Southridge/ virtual folder of our web server's default website. The application should be accessible only to users who have valid accounts in the SOUTHRIDGE Active Directory domain. Several of the internal groups have their own subfolders in the application, including IT. Check with each of the managers to determine how he or she wants security configured. For the IT subfolder, I just want members of the IT group in the SOUTHRIDGE domain to be able to access it.

- **Arif Rizaldy, Systems Administrator**   Hey, I hear you're configuring a new website. Can you do me a favor and put all the configuration in a single Web.config file? I had to troubleshoot a security problem the other day and spent hours trying to figure out what it was because I forgot that there might be a Web.config file in any of the folders. One Web.config file is just easier for me to manage.

- **Anders Riis, Production Manager**   For now, I'd like our Production subfolder to be accessible to members of the Production group. Oh, also, give Thomas access to it. Thomas is the Sales Manager. I don't know what his user account name is.

- **Catherine Boeger, Customer Service Manager**   Anyone who is an employee should be able to open the CustServ folder.

- **Thomas Jensen, Sales Manager**   For now, only I should have access to the Sales folder. I'll probably change this later, but there's confidential information in there now. My user account is TJensen. Sometimes I have to enter it as Southridge-backslash-TJensen.

Technical Requirements

Create a single Web.config file for the application that configures permissions for each of the subfolders according to the requirements outlined in Table 13-1. Require Windows authentication for every file in the application.

TABLE 13-1 Application Authorization Requirements for Southridge Video

FOLDER	AUTHORIZED USERS
/Southridge/	All authenticated users
/Southridge/IT/	All members of the SOUTHRIDGE\IT group
/Southridge/Production/	All members of the SOUTHRIDGE\Production group plus the SOUTHRIDGE\TJensen user account
/Southridge/CustServ/	All authenticated users
/Southridge/Sales/	Only the SOUTHRIDGE\TJensen user account

Questions

Configure security for Southridge Video, and then answer the following questions.

1. What does the Web.config file that you created look like?

2. Besides creating a Web.config file, how can you further protect the folders?

Case Scenario 2: Configuring Website Authentication

You are a developer for Northwind Traders. Your manager has asked you to create a simple ASP.NET webpage to display the contents of a text file. The text files are generated by a legacy system to report on various aspects of your company's financial status, so they are protected by using NTFS file permissions. The IT Manager, Nino Olivotto, describes the problem:

"The financial people want to be able to view these text reports from our intranet, so it would be nice if you could create an ASP.NET web form to allow that. Here's the catch, though. I don't want to change the permissions on the file so that just anyone can read it. The web server doesn't have the file permissions to access the files by default, and I don't want it to. Instead, I'd like to have the user provide Windows credentials, and have your application use those credentials to show the file. Oh—and name the project ShowReport. You can place it in the C:\Inetpub\Wwwroot\ShowReport\ folder."

You review the company's technical requirements before creating the ASP.NET website.

Technical Requirements

Create an ASP.NET website in the C:\Inetpub\Wwwroot\ShowReport\ folder by using either C# or Visual Basic .NET. Create several text files in the ShowReport folder, remove all default NTFS permissions, and then add permissions so that only specific users can access the files. Use impersonation to take advantage of the user's Windows credentials to display the contents of the files.

Questions

Create the ASP.NET website and then answer the following questions to explain to the IT manager how you created the application and why you did what you did.

1. What authentication method did you use? Why?
2. What XML code did you add to the Web.config file?

Suggested Practices

To successfully master the exam objectives presented in this chapter, complete the following tasks.

Configure Authentication and Authorization

For this task, you should complete Practices 1, 2, and 3 to gain experience creating custom logon pages. To gain experience configuring Web.config files for authentication, complete Practices 4 and 5. To gain experience working with Windows authentication, complete Practices 6 and 7.

- **Practice 1**   Respond to the CreateUserWizard.CreatedUser event to automatically send an email to the new user welcoming him or her to your website.

- **Practice 2**   Create a custom web form that provides common user management features, such as displaying a list of users, deleting users, and adding users to roles. Though this duplicates the functionality of the WSAT, it will give you experience working with important user management classes and methods.

- **Practice 3**   Create an ASP.NET website and implement custom forms authentication. For simplicity, store user names and passwords in a collection. Use the Web.config files to restrict access to specific files and folders and verify that the authorization features work properly. Extend the website to store user credentials in a database. Store the passwords by using hashes so that they are less vulnerable to attack.

- **Practice 4**   Using the website you created in Lesson 2, delete the Web.config files in the Admin folder. Then use <location> elements in the root Web.config file to configure identical access rules in a single file.

- **Practice 5** Use a browser that supports cookies to go to an ASP.NET website that you created that uses forms authentication. Then disable cookies in the browser and attempt to go to the site. Change the cookieless attribute of the <forms> element to AutoDetect and test the website again.

- **Practice 6** Create an ASP.NET website that uses Windows authentication. Then create several different groups and user accounts on the web server. Write code that examines the user's account and displays the user name and whether the user is a member of built-in groups such as Users and Administrators.

- **Practice 7** Create an ASP.NET website that uses Windows authentication. Then create several different groups and user accounts on the web server. Experiment with NTFS file permissions and Web.config access rules to determine how ASP.NET behaves when one or both denies access to a user.

Configure Profiles

For this task, you should complete at least Practices 1 and 2. If you want experience with the raw data stored by user profiles, complete Practice 3 as well.

- **Practice 1** Using the ASP.NET website you created in the exercise for Lesson 2, create a template to modify the colors and fonts used by the controls based on a user selection.

- **Practice 2** Using a copy of a real-world application that you created, add personalization capabilities for elements of the website that users might want to change.

- **Practice 3** Configure user profiles to store information in a custom SQL Server database. Examine the data contained with the database tables.

Take a Practice Test

The practice tests on this book's companion CD offer many options. For example, you can test yourself on just the lesson review questions in this chapter, or you can test yourself on all the 70-515 certification exam objectives. You can set up the test so it closely simulates the experience of taking a certification exam, or you can set it up in study mode so you can look at the correct answers and explanations after you answer each question.

> **MORE INFO PRACTICE TESTS**
>
> For details about all the practice test options available, see the "How to Use the Practice Tests" section in this book's Introduction.

CHAPTER 14

Creating Websites with ASP.NET MVC 2

The Microsoft ASP.NET model-view-controller (MVC) represents an alternative architecture to the standard ASP.NET web form model. This alternative is based on the common MVC software design pattern that separates the layers of your website into user interface (view), data and business logic (model), and input handling (controller). This separation through MVC results in loosely coupled objects that are highly testable, can be developed independently from one another, and offer granular control of your application code.

ASP.NET MVC 2 is not meant to replace web forms; it is simply an alternative you can take advantage of based on your specific needs. In fact, you can combine both models in a single website.

Lesson 1 provides an introduction to the MVC architecture. This includes a definition of MVC and coverage of the execution life cycle of an ASP.NET MVC application and the project structure of the ASP.NET MVC template. You create a simple ASP.NET MVC application at the completion of this lesson. Lesson 2 digs more deeply into MVC. Here you see how to create custom models, views, and controllers. The lesson also discusses MVC routing, application areas, and other MVC topics.

Exam objectives in this chapter:

- Developing a Web Application by Using ASP.NET MVC 2
    - Structure an ASP.NET MVC application.
    - Create custom routes.
    - Create controllers and actions.
    - Create and customize views.

Lessons in this chapter:

Before You Begin

To complete the lessons in this chapter, you should be familiar with developing applications with Microsoft Visual Studio 2010 by using Microsoft Visual Basic or Microsoft Visual C#. In addition, you should be comfortable with all of the following:

- The Visual Studio 2010 Integrated Development Environment (IDE)
- Using Hypertext Markup Language (HTML) and client-side scripting
- Creating ASP.NET websites and forms
- Adding web server controls to a webpage
- Working with generic types in C# or Visual Basic
- Using Microsoft ADO.NET, the Entity Framework, and LINQ to SQL to work with data
- Writing Microsoft Language-Integrated Query (LINQ) queries and working with LINQ data–specific providers

 **REAL WORLD**

Mike Snell

I see some real advantages to using ASP.NET MVC. It is great for teams that have a high separation of tasks between UI, database, and web developers (or those teams with similar aspirations). It also offers many benefits in terms of creating test-driven code. The greater control of your output is also nice. However, developers need to understand it, review the tradeoffs, and migrate only if they see real advantages. It is tempting to jump to ASP.NET MVC because it is new and gets a lot of buzz. However, the web form model is tested and provides a much more Rapid Application Development (RAD) experience for most web developers. ASP.NET MVC typically involves a lot more code and requires a good understanding of pattern-based development. My advice is to make sure you are comfortable with the model before making such a switch.

Lesson 1: Understanding ASP.NET MVC Applications

If you are accustomed to building ASP.NET applications, you need to rethink that approach to understand how an ASP.NET application running under MVC operates. The model that uses postback and ViewState is nonexistent with ASP.NET MVC. Instead, MVC uses a routing engine and a set of controllers that provide you with deeper control over your processing and output, at the expense of some automation. There are, however, a few familiar items that are preserved in ASP.NET MVC, such as master pages, style sheets, membership, and standard page markup. But almost everything else is different, including the process of a page through its life cycle. This lesson gets you started with using this very different web application architecture.

The ASP.NET MVC Architecture

An ASP.NET MVC application has a different architecture, page processing model, conventions, and project structure than an ASP.NET web form site. Requests to an ASP.NET MVC application are handled by the UrlRoutingModule HttpModule. (See Chapter 10, "Writing and Working with HTTP Modules and Web Services," for more information regarding HttpModules.) This module parses the request and selects a route for that request based on a configuration that you define. Ultimately, the request is routed to one of the many controller classes that you write to manage request processing. It is the selected controller's job to access your data and business logic (the model), connect it for display (the view), and send the response back to the user. The controller handles all requests—view and updates (posts).

This is considerably different than the basic architecture of an ASP.NET application, in which requests are handled by ASP.NET: it calls your page; it executes your events in order; those events affect the response; and ASP.NET ultimately returns the response. With ASP.NET MVC, you write the model, create the views, and code the controllers; thus you have finer control over how each request is handled and each response is rendered. With ASP.NET MVC, there is less "hidden" from you (and thus less work done automatically for you).

Figure 14-1 shows the high-level architecture of the components you write to manage a request with ASP.NET MVC. As you can see, requests are routed to controllers. The controller works with the data model, selects a view (based on an action), and returns the results.

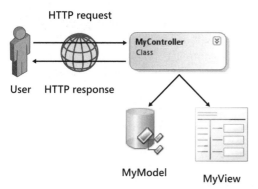

FIGURE 14-1 The architecture of an ASP.NET MVC application.

These components should be familiar to you as a web developer. A controller is a class; the model is either made up of custom classes or generated classes that use the Entity Framework or LINQ to SQL; and the views are ASPX webpages. The following list provides a more detailed definition of these components:

- **Model**   The model is the data and related business logic or validation rules in your application. The model objects typically can retrieve, update, and add records to an underlying data store such as a Microsoft SQL Server database. A model can be a LINQ to SQL layer, an Entity Framework layer, or some other layer that provides access to your data and the business rules.

- **View**   The view indicates how data from the model will be displayed. It is a set of webpages and user controls that define layout for model data based on user actions such as read, edit, and insert. For example, you might have a view that defines specific layout information for a page that allows a user to edit a Customer object from your model. View tasks do not include the input logic or the processing of user actions; these are managed inside the controller. This separation is what makes the input logic more test-ready for unit testing.

- **Controller**   This is code you write to handle the user interaction (often called *input logic*) and the connection between the model and the view. A controller is a class that inherits from System.Web.Mvc.Controller. It includes logic for processing user events or actions. HTTP requests are routed to individual controllers; the controller responds to the request by calling the model and selecting a view for displaying results.

The ASP.NET MVC Request Life Cycle

Much of the request processing that makes ASP.NET MVC work is found in the System.Web. Routing namespace. This is because much of what happens with requests is done through routing. The UrlRoutingModule HttpModule is found in this namespace; it acts as a front-controller for your website. UrlRoutingModule takes a request and looks up a Route object in the RouteTable collection. You add routes to this collection inside the Global.asax file's RegisterRoutes method (which is called by Application_Start). These routes are added to the table when your application starts. The request is then mapped to a route, and RouteData and RequestContext objects are created to represent the route and the request, respectively.

Processing of the RequestContext object is then passed to classes in the System.Web.Mvc namespace. The MvcRouteHandler class handles the routing to your MVC controller class. It creates an instance of MvcHandler to actually call the controller and run its Execute method. The controller that the MvcHandler calls is a controller class that you write to handle the processing of requests to your application. Of course, there are several examples later in the chapter.

Your controller then uses ControllerActionInvoker to determine which action to run based on the request. Your action method accepts the user input and prepares a response (by using your model and views). Figure 14-2 illustrates this life cycle.

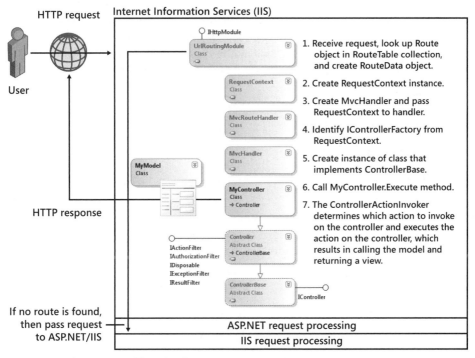

FIGURE 14-2 The execution life cycle of an ASP.NET MVC HTTP request.

EXAM TIP

Be sure to know how the execution life cycle of ASP.NET MVC applications differs from that of ASP.NET.

Understanding Routing Basics

As you can see, the routing engine routes requests to one of your controller classes. The URL of the request determines the appropriate controller and action to invoke. As an example, suppose that a request is made to *http://myMvcApplication/Employees/Detail/5*.

In this case, the portion of the request beyond the domain (myMvcApplication) is parsed by the routing engine based on routing rules defined in your Global.asax file. By default, the routing rules would parse this request as *controller/action/id*. Therefore, the employees section would map to an EmployeesController controller class (all controllers by convention include the suffix *Controller*). The action would map to Detail in the URL, so the routing would invoke the Detail method of the EmployeesController object. The value, 5, would be passed as a parameter to the Detail method. The Detail method would then return an ActionResult instance as a response. Your controller class would look similar to the following:

Sample of Visual Basic Code

```
Public Class EmployeesController
    Inherits System.Web.Mvc.Controller

    Function Details(ByVal id As Integer) As ActionResult
        Return View()
    End Function

End Class
```

Sample of C# Code

```
public class EmployeesController : Controller
{
    public ActionResult Details(int id)
    {
        return View();
    }
}
```

> **NOTE ASP.NET AND ASP.NET MVC**
>
> Your website can respond to both ASP.NET and ASP.NET MVC requests. If no route is found for a request, the request passes to ASP.NET for processing.

Controller Action Methods

Your controllers can define as many action methods as required. These methods typically correspond to individual user actions such as saving data or navigating to another page. In the previous code example, you can see that the controller action method (Details) returns an instance of a class that inherits from System.Web.Mvc.ActionResult. This is the case for most action methods. The most commonly used ActionResult is the ViewResult class, which simply returns a webpage.

There is a predefined set of ActionResult objects that can be returned from an action method (see Lesson 2 for a complete list). The base Controller class includes a helper method for returning these results. For instance, to return a ViewResult, you can call View() from your controller class (as shown in the code example). You will learn more about action methods and using the ActionResult objects in Lesson 2.

The Structure of an ASP.NET MVC Application

The ASP.NET MVC application template in Visual Studio is a project template, not a website. This means that you create it by using the Add New Project dialog box. When you do so, Visual Studio asks you to create a related Unit Test Project. Recall that one of the goals for ASP.NET MVC is to increase the testability of your application. This unit test project is created so that you can define tests for your controller classes. Therefore, it is recommended that you create this testing project; in fact, Visual Studio will generate some basic tests for the Account controller (which is used for ASP.NET membership) and the home page controller.

The actual ASP.NET MVC application has a different structure than that of a traditional ASP.NET website. Models, views, and controllers are grouped into a series of folders. In addition, the project template uses different item templates for creating controller classes and views. Figure 14-3 shows the general structure of an ASP.NET MVC project (along with its related testing project).

FIGURE 14-3 The structure of an ASP.NET MVC application.

Many of the files and folders are the same as those you would find in a standard ASP.NET website (such as App_Data, Web.config, and Scripts). However, some of the other folders are specific to ASP.NET MVC. The following describes these folders inside this project template:

- **Content**   Use this folder for static files in your site, such as images. You can also place style sheets and standard HTML files here.

- **Controllers**   This is where you put your controller classes. In general, each entity in your model has a single controller. You might also define additional controllers for other types of processing, such as LoginController, HomeController, and NavigationController. Controller classes are named with the *Entity*Controller convention.

- **Models**   This is where you put code that represents your business model. In most sites, this code interacts with the database and processes business rules. If your model is an Entity Framework or LINQ to SQL model, you can put the DBML or EDMX file and its related code here. Your model can also be a separate DLL file or class library that is referenced by the project (in which case this folder would be empty).

- **Views**   This folder is where you put the views for your application (ASPX pages, ASCX user controls, and master pages). The convention is to create a folder for each controller in your application. Therefore, if you have a controller called EmployeeController, you would have a folder called Employee in the Views folder. The Employee folder would contain pages used for rendering different user activity related to an Employee in your model. The routing engine uses this convention to search for views.

    The Views folder also contains a Shared folder. This is used for views that are shared across controllers (such as a master page).

Defining Application Areas

You can use the default project structure for most websites without having any problems. However, there are some sites that are very large; keeping all the models, views, and controllers in this single folder set can be difficult to manage. For such cases, you can define different MVC project areas in your application.

An *area* in ASP.NET MVC is a subset of the project structure based on a logical grouping. Each area contains area-specific models, views, and controllers. The root of the site contains the sitewide models, views, and controllers. This type of partitioning can make it easier to manage your application files.

You create an area in ASP.NET MVC by right-clicking the project and choosing Add | Area. You give each area a name and Visual Studio generates a separate set of folders for storing the MVC files in your area. Figure 14-4 shows an ASP.NET MVC site with two additional areas: DataAdministration and SecurityManagement.

FIGURE 14-4 The ASP.NET MVC project structure, including two additional areas.

You add models, views, and controllers to these individual areas in the same way you do to the site root. One difference, however, is that items added to an area have a different namespace distinction, which further assists with organizing your project structure. For example, adding a controller to the DataAdministration project creates the MyApplicationName.Areas.Data-Administration.Controllers namespace.

Each area also includes an AreaRegistration class file (see Figure 14-4). These files map your area with the routing engine by using the *AreaName/controller/action/id* format. The Application_Start method in the Global.asax file then includes the AreaRegistration. RegisterAllAreas() call to ensure that the area mapping is carried out.

Running Your First ASP.NET MVC Webpage

Many applications actions do not require a model. Instead, you might need to write controller methods to handle navigation or to simply display a view. In these cases, the model is optional. In this section, you look at a simple example designed to familiarize you with the project model and the ASP.NET MVC execution life cycle. Lesson 2 will cover more involved examples that include models.

When you first create an ASP.NET MVC application, Visual Studio generates a HomeController class and a Home folder in the Views folder. The HomeController class has two action methods: Index and About. These methods simply return a ViewResult instance. The Index method also adds a message, System.Web.Mvc.ViewDataCollection, to the ViewData collection. These methods look as follows.

Sample of Visual Basic Code

```vb
<HandleError()> _
Public Class HomeController
    Inherits System.Web.Mvc.Controller

    Function Index() As ActionResult
        ViewData("Message") = "Welcome to ASP.NET MVC!"

        Return View()
    End Function

    Function About() As ActionResult
        Return View()
    End Function
End Class
```

Sample of C# Code

```csharp
[HandleError]
public class HomeController : Controller
{
    public ActionResult Index()
    {
        ViewData["Message"] = "Welcome to ASP.NET MVC!";
        return View();
    }
    public ActionResult About()
    {
        return View();
    }
}
```

The routing engine maps requests for the *http://mySite/home/index* URL to this controller. There is also a special route (*http://mySite*) mapped for the home page to allow it to display when the user requests the default page for your site.

The line of code, return View(), in the controller tells ASP.NET MVC to look in a folder with the same name as the controller (Home) and to look for a view with the same name as the action method (Index.aspx), and to return it as the response.

The Views/Home/Index.aspx page is built from a master page and includes MainContent, whose markup is shown below. Notice that ViewData is pulled from the dictionary and displayed in the view; this is how you move data from the controller (and often the model) to the view.

```
<asp:Content ID="Content2" ContentPlaceHolderID="MainContent" runat="server">
    <h2><%: ViewData["Message"] %></h2>
    <p>
        To learn more about ASP.NET MVC visit <a href="http://asp.net/mvc"
            title="ASP.NET MVC Website">http://asp.net/mvc</a>.
    </p>
</asp:Content>
```

Figure 14-5 shows the result of running this page. The request is routed to the HomeController based on the URL. The action method, Index, is then called based on the URL and routing rules (*controller/action*). The Index method adds data to the view by using the ViewData dictionary collection. The method then returns a ViewResult object. The view is then found by looking in the folder with the same name as the controller (Home) and returning a view with the same name as the action method (Index.aspx). You will create a custom controller and view in the practice for this lesson.

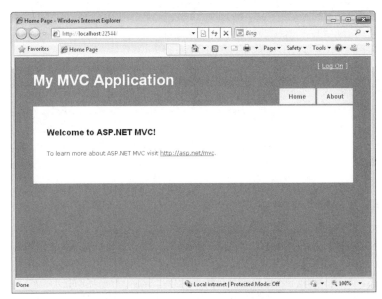

FIGURE 14-5 The home page of an ASP.NET MVC application running in the browser.

✔ **Quick Check**

1. What is the ASP.NET MVC convention for naming controller classes?

2. What is the ASP.NET MVC convention for storing views?

3. What is the ASP.NET MVC convention for naming views?

Quick Check Answers

1. You name your controller classes after entities in your model and add the Controller suffix, as in *Entity*Controller.

2. A view should be stored in a folder with the same name as the controller (minus the suffix), as in *Entity*.

3. A view should be named after the action method in the controller, such as Index.aspx or Create.aspx.

PRACTICE **Creating an ASP.NET MVC Web Application**

In this practice, you create an ASP.NET MVC 2 web application, a custom controller, and a custom view.

ON THE COMPANION MEDIA

If you encounter a problem completing an exercise, you can find the completed projects in the samples installed from this book's companion CD. For more information about the project files and other content on the CD, see "Using the Companion Media" in this book's Introduction.

EXERCISE 1 Creating the ASP.NET MVC Web Application

In this exercise, you create a new ASP.NET MVC 2 web application.

1. Open Visual Studio. Select File | New Project (not New Web Site). From the New Project dialog box, select your preferred programming language and the web node from the Installed Templates area (on the left side of the dialog box). Select the ASP.NET MVC 2 Web Application template. Name the project and solution **MyMvcSite**.

2. When prompted to create a unit test project, click Yes. Use the default name, **MyMvcSite.Tests**, and click OK.

3. Open the Global.asax file and examine the Application_Start and RegisterRoutes methods. Notice the default routing scheme.

```
{controller}/{action}/{id}
```

4. Open the Controllers folder in Solution Explorer and double-click HomeController. Notice the two action methods, Index and About, and their return types.

5. Navigate to the Views/Home folder in Solution Explorer and double-click Index.aspx. Notice the use of the master page (which is stored in Views/Shared/Site.master). You can also open the MyMvcSite.Tests project in Solution Explorer and examine the Controllers folder to find the HomeControllerTest class. Notice that there are tests for both Index and About. The Index test validates the result of the call to Controller.Index and the related ViewData.

6. Run the tests. Right-click the test project and choose Set As StartUp Project. Notice that all tests pass by default. You can also set breakpoints in the tests and step through the controller code.

7. Run the website and view the results. If you ran the tests in the previous step, you will have to right-click the MyMvcSite project and choose Set As Startup. Notice the URL. Click the About and Home links.

EXERCISE 2 Creating a Controller and a View

In this exercise, you add a controller and a view to the ASP.NET MVC 2 application created in the previous exercise.

1. Continue editing the project created in the previous exercise. Alternatively, you can open the completed Lesson 1, Exercise 1 project in the samples installed from the CD.

2. Add the Northwnd.mdf database to the App_Data directory of your site. You can get this database from the CD for this book.

3. Right-click the Models folder in Solution Explorer and select Add | New Item. Add a LINQ to SQL Classes file. Name this file **Northwind.dbml**.

4. Open Northwind.dbml and add the Customer table to the design surface from Server Explorer. Save and close the file. You now have a basic model with which to work.

5. Open the Site.Master file (which is in the Views/Shared folder). Here you will notice two ActionLink HTML helpers, one for Home and one for About. These form the rudimentary menu you saw when you ran the application in the previous lesson. To the unordered list (<ul/>), add a new menu ActionLink called **Customers**. This will create a new menu tab on the master page. The ActionLink is an ASP.NET MVC HTML helper method that lets you define a hyperlink that will work with ASP.NET MVC. This method takes a display name, the name of an action method to invoke when selected, and the route to your controller. Your code should look as follows.

```
<li><%: Html.ActionLink("Customers", "Index", "Customer")%></li>
```

6. Right-click the Controllers folder and choose Add Controller. Name the controller **CustomerController**.

7. Open CustomerController. Add code to the Index action method to create an instance of the data model (NorthwindDataContext). Next, return a View and pass the model as a parameter. The following code shows an example.

Sample of Visual Basic Code

```
Function Index() As ActionResult
    Dim nwd As New NorthwindDataContext()
    Return View(nwd.Customers.ToList())
End Function
```

Sample of C# Code

```
public class CustomerController : Controller
{
    public ActionResult Index()
    {
        Models.NorthwindDataContext nwd = new Models.NorthwindDataContext();
        return View(nwd.Customers.ToList());
    }
}
```

8. Add the new folder, Customer, to your Views folder.

   a. Right-click it and choose Add View.

   b. In the Add View dialog box, set the view name to **Index**.

   c. Select the **Create a strongly-typed view** option. This will generate a view based on part of your model.

   d. In the View data class list, select MyMvcSite.Models.Customer. (If this list item doesn't appear, compile the application and try again.)

   e. In View content, select List.

   f. Make sure to select the master page, and click the Add button.

9. Examine the view that is created. In this case, the Customer table, as accessed via the model, is queried and the results are displayed in a table. Note that the Edit, Delete, Details, and Add New ActionLink items are added to the grid to allow users to interact with the data. Delete them for now (and delete the related <th/> tag). You might also want to trim some of the columns for display or edit the column names.

10. Run the application. Select the Customers tab in the navigation area. Figure 14-6 shows sample results.

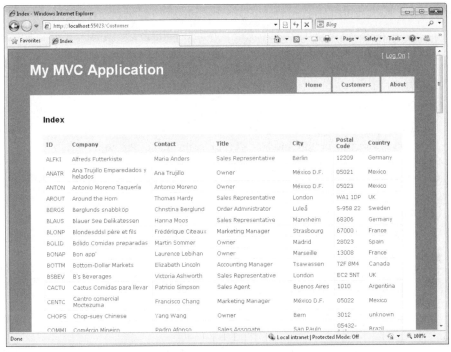

FIGURE 14-6 The Customer Index view showing the related model data in a browser.

Lesson Summary

- An ASP.NET MVC 2 application does not use the standard ASP.NET life cycle that includes the postback model, ViewState, and most of the ASP.NET controls. Instead, it emphasizes separation of tasks, testability, and fine control of output.

- Requests to an ASP.NET MVC application are handled by the UrlRoutingModule. This module creates a RequestContext and a Route object based on routing rules defined in the Global.asax file. The request is then routed to a controller class that you write.

- Your controller classes contain action methods that return ActionResult instances. Each action method represents some user action, such as Index (view page), Edit, or Insert. You add code in the action method to work with your model and return the appropriate view.

- Views are ASPX pages that you write to render the display of model data. By default, a view is returned based on the matching of its name with a corresponding action method; for example, Index matches Index.aspx.

Lesson Review

You can use the following questions to test your knowledge of the information in Lesson 1, "Understanding ASP.NET MVC Applications." The questions are also available on the companion CD in a practice test, if you prefer to review them in electronic form.

> **NOTE** ANSWERS
>
> Answers to these questions and explanations of why each answer choice is correct or incorrect are located in the "Answers" section at the end of the book.

1. You need to define a page that allows a user to add a new product to the product catalog. You are using ASP.NET MVC and the default structure and routing. Which actions do you take? (Choose two.)

   A. Add a class to the Controllers folder and name it Catalog. Add a method called AddProduct to this class.

   B. Add a class to the Controllers folder and name it ProductController. Add a method called Add to this class.

   C. Add a new folder to the Views folder and name it Product. Create a view inside this new folder and name it Add.aspx.

   D. Add a new folder to the Views folder and name it AddProduct. Create a view inside this new folder and name it Catalog.aspx.

2. You have a very large website and you want to structure the files in this site logically so that they are easier to manage. What actions should you take? (Choose all that apply.)

   A. Create separate area folders inside the Models, Views, and Controllers folders. Name these folders based on the logical grouping in your site folder.

   B. Ensure that the RegisterAllAreas() method is defined in your Application_Start method.

   C. Create separate Controllers, Models, and Views folders within your area folders.

   D. Create an Areas folder and add individual area folders based on the logical grouping in your site.

3. You are writing an action method inside your controller. You want to pass string data to the view and display that data inside the view. You are using the default MVC templates. What actions should you take? (Choose all that apply.)

   A. In your action method, add your string value to the ViewData collection.

   B. In the view, reference the string value by using this inline code: <%: *object* %>.

   C. Create a constructor for your view that takes a string value.

   D. Reference the string value in the code-behind file for your view, and write it to the page.

Lesson 2: Creating Models, Views, and Controllers

The first lesson oriented you to the ASP.NET MVC project structure and page execution model. In this lesson, you build on what you learned in Lesson 1 and dig deeper into creating webpages that are built on this pattern. Coverage includes defining the model through custom classes as well as adding rules to generated models such as LINQ to SQL models. You will also look closely at building views (and partial views) and using the HTML helper classes inside ASP.NET MVC. In addition, you will look more closely at controllers and their action methods and related results. The lesson concludes with a deeper look at the ASP.NET MVC routing engine.

> **After this lesson, you will be able to:**
> - Define a model that includes business rules to be processed by ASP.NET MVC.
> - Create new views, strongly typed views, and partial views.
> - Use the HTML helper classes to ease the rendering of code that you write in views.
> - Use the many ActionResult classes inside your controller.
> - Customize the ASP.NET routing engine to meet specific development scenarios.
>
> **Estimated lesson time: 40 minutes**

 REAL WORLD

Mike Snell

I have the opportunity to attend a lot of developer events such as local code camps, user group meetings, and the occasional TechEd or PDC. Over the last couple of years, all these events have really ramped up on the ASP.NET MVC talks. Developers are excited about this technology and eager to learn. Microsoft, too, is committed. In fact, at the time of this book's publication, Microsoft has already released the first preview of ASP.NET MVC 3. You can check it out at *http://www.asp.net/mvc* or take a look at the roadmap for the technology at *http://aspnet.codeplex.com /wikipage?title=Road%20Map*. You will want to be sure to keep up with this fast-moving technology.

Defining a Model and Business Rules

The ASP.NET MVC model can be written in any form that makes sense to your application. There are no constraints or requirements put on it by ASP.NET MVC. This means that you can create custom classes, use generated code, work with a mix of classes, or use an existing model. Models do, however, have many attributes in common: they work with data in a data store (such as SQL Server); they contain business rules and validation that are executed when users insert, update, and take action on elements within the model; and they provide features for selecting individual items or lists of items and other actions. As an example, the Northwind model might include a Customer object that allows you to get a customer, get a list of customers, add a new customer, check a customer's orders, and more.

Creating a Custom Model

You typically put the models for your application in the Models folder. However, you can also put them in the App_Code directory or in another class library project altogether, especially if you need to share the model with another application. As discussed, a model can be a custom class file or partially generated and partially customized code.

The custom class approach typically involves creating a class for each entity in your model. You then define properties for that entity and methods to work with that entity and the data store. The following code shows an example of a custom model for the Customer entity. Note that the methods are just stubbed out but would ultimately include code to work with the data store. In addition, business logic would be added as either code or annotations (more on this in the next section).

Sample of Visual Basic Code

```vbnet
Public Class CustomerModel

    Public Property Id As Integer
    Public Property Name As String
    Public Property Address As String
    Public Property City As String
    Public Property State As String
    Public Property PostalCode As String
    Public Property Phone As String

    Public Shared Function Insert( _
        ByVal customer As Customer) As Integer

    End Function

    Public Shared Sub Delete(ByVal id As Integer)

    End Sub

    Public Shared Sub Update(ByVal customer As Customer)
```

```
    End Sub

    Public Shared Function GetAllCustomers() _
        As List(Of Customer)

    End Function

    Public Shared Function GetCustomer(ByVal id As Integer) _
        As Customer

    End Function

End Class
```

Sample of C# Code

```csharp
public class CustomerModel
{
    public int Id { get; set; }
    public string Name { get; set; }
    public string Address { get; set; }
    public string City { get; set; }
    public string State { get; set; }
    public string PostalCode { get; set; }
    public string Phone { get; set; }

    public static int Insert(Customer customer)
    {
    }
    public static void Delete(int id)
    {
    }
    public static void Update(Customer customer)
    {
    }
    public static List<Customer> GetAllCustomers()
    {
    }
    public static Customer GetCustomer(int id)
    {
    }
}
```

Creating a Partially Generated Model

Recall that in Lesson 3, "Working with ASP.NET Dynamic Data" in Chapter 12, "Working with Data Source Controls and Data-Bound Controls," you read about creating a data context by using LINQ to SQL or the Entity Framework. You then used the partial class and partial method concepts to provide additional metadata and validation logic to your generated model. The ASP.NET MVC framework can work in a similar way. You can generate your model and then create a simple class that can be used to provide metadata to that model.

For example, assume that you create an Entity Framework model (EDMX) for the Northwind database. You then create a partial class for adding metadata to the Customer class that gets generated by the model. This partial class would include the MetadataType attribute from DataAnnotations, which would point to your metadata class, as shown in the following code.

Sample of Visual Basic Code

```vb
Imports System.ComponentModel.DataAnnotations

<MetadataType(GetType(CustomerMetadata))> _
Partial Public Class Customer

End Class

Public Class CustomerMetadata
    Public Property CustomerId As Object
    Public Property CompanyName As Object
    Public Property Address As Object
    Public Property City As Object
    Public Property PostalCode As Object
    Public Property Country As Object
    Public Property Phone As Object
End Class
```

Sample of C# Code

```csharp
using System.ComponentModel.DataAnnotations;

[MetadataType(typeof(CustomerMetadata))]
public partial class Customer
{
}

public class CustomerMetadata
{
    public object CustomerId { get; set; }
    public object CompanyName { get; set; }
    public object Address { get; set; }
    public object City { get; set; }
    public object PostalCode { get; set; }
    public object Country { get; set; }
    public object Phone { get; set; }
}
```

You can use this partial class and its metadata counterpart to extend your model by adding validation logic, UI display hints, and formatting.

Model Validation Rules

One of the easiest ways to add validation and business rules to your model is to use the DataAnnotations classes. Recall from Chapter 12 that these classes allow you to define required fields, acceptable values, formatting, and UI display information to your model. For example, the following attribute marks the CustomerId property as required in the data model.

Sample of Visual Basic Code

```
<Required(ErrorMessage:="Customer id is required.")> _
Public Property CustomerId As Object
```

Sample of C# Code

```
[Required(ErrorMessage = "Customer id is required.")]
public object CustomerId { get; set; }
```

> *NOTE* **USING DATAANNOTATIONS**
>
> The DataAnnotations attribute classes are discussed at length in Chapter 12, Lesson 3.
> Refer to Table 12-1 in that chapter for a quick refresher.

The rules you define for your model will automatically be processed by the ASP.NET MVC validation engine. Prior to executing a method such as Update or Insert, you should check your controller class's ModelState.IsValid property to determine whether your model has thrown any validation errors (you will look at verifying that model data is valid in the upcoming section, "Creating Controllers"). If it has, you then might redisplay the view and use a Validation-Summary control (see "Using the HTML Helper Classes," later in this lesson) to display any error messages.

Of course, you can take advantage of these attribute classes in both your custom models and your partially generated ones. You can also use the ValidationException object to throw an exception that will be caught by ASP.NET MVC as part of the model validation. Recall there is also an example of doing this back in Chapter 12, Lesson 3.

Creating Controllers

Recall from Lesson 1 that you create controllers for each item in your model by using the *Entity*Controller naming convention, as in CustomerController. Controllers are stored in the Controllers folder. Each controller inherits from the Controller base class (which itself inherits from ControllerBase).

Each controller has a set of action methods that are based on user activity, such as adding, updating, inserting, viewing, or deleting one or more entity objects; clicking a link; or submitting a form. There is typically a 1:1 mapping from user action to action method. Action methods are often passed values from the request (as parameters in either the URL or HTTP post). The action methods typically work with the model by instantiating it and calling appropriate methods. Action methods are also responsible for handling errors and validation that occurs within the model. Action methods return a selected ActionResult (typically a view) as a result of the request. The result might pass data to the view from the model. Finally, a WebFormViewEngine class is used to render the results to the user.

The Controller Template

Visual Studio includes a template that is used for creating controllers. If you right-click the Controllers folder, you will see the Add | Controller option. This brings up the Add Controller dialog box, as shown in Figure 14-7. This template allows you to name your controller and generate method stubs for common scenarios such as create, read, update, and delete (CRUD) activities.

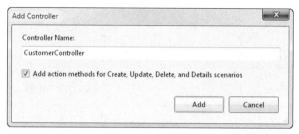

FIGURE 14-7 The Add Controller dialog box for the controller item template in Visual Studio.

By default, this controller template generates code with the following methods (note that you can change these method names as you see fit): Index, Details, Create, Edit, and Delete. Each of these methods is intended to be used as the method name describes. (Index is used to view a single item.)

As an example, suppose that you are using an Entity Framework model tied to the Northwind database. You might opt to define a CustomerController class. This class could include a Details method that is designed to get a customer from the model based on the customer's ID. You would then display those details by using the default details view (Details.aspx), passing the Customer instance as a parameter to the view. The following code is an example.

Sample of Visual Basic Code

```
Function Details(ByVal id As String) As ActionResult

    Dim nw As New northwndEntities()
    Dim custQuery = From c In nw.Customers
                    Where c.CustomerID = id
                    Select c

    Dim cust As Customer = custQuery.FirstOrDefault()

    Return View(cust)

End Function
```

Sample of C# Code

```
public ActionResult Details(string id)
{
    northwndEntities nw = new northwndEntities();
    var custQuery = from c in nw.Customers
                    where c.CustomerID == id
                    select c;
    Customer cust = custQuery.FirstOrDefault();
    return View(cust);
}
```

This action method would then be called based on the URL routing. By default, a call to *http://mySite/customer/details/ALFKI* would invoke the CustomerController.Details method and pass the customer ID (ALFKI) as a parameter. The view would then be returned as the Detail.aspx page inside the Views/Customer folder. The view would then use the Customer object sent to it to display information (as you will see in the "Creating Views" section later in this lesson).

Returning Different ActionResult Objects

The return type for most action methods is ActionResult. The ActionResult class is actually a base class that can be used to define several different result types. Each result type does something different as a result of your action method. Possible types include a ViewResult to show a webpage and a RedirectResult to redirect to another controller.

Each action result class has an associated helper method that is exposed by the Controller class. You can use these helper methods in your controller to indicate the appropriate ActionResult, as in using *View* to indicate *ViewResult*. These action result classes and their helper methods (in parentheses) are listed here:

- **ViewResult (View)**   Used to return a webpage from an action method.
- **PartialViewResult (PartialView)**   Used to send a section of a view to be rendered inside another view.
- **RedirectResult (Redirect)**   Used to redirect to another controller and action method based on a URL.
- **RedirectToRouteResult (RedirectToAction, RedirectToRoute)**   Used to redirect to another action method.
- **ContentResult (Content)**   Used to return a custom content type as the result of the action method. This is an HTTP content type, such as text/plain.
- **JsonResult (Json)**   Used to return a message formatted as JSON.
- **JavaScriptResult (JavaScript)**   Used to return JavaScript code that will be executed in the user's browser.
- **FileResult (File)**   Used to send binary output as the response.
- **EmptyResult**   Used to return nothing (void) as the result.

You can also return simple types, such as string or integer, from your action methods. In this case, the results will be wrapped in an ActionResult object for you. Finally, you can indicate that a method inside your controller does not return an ActionResult. To do so, you mark it with the NonAction attribute to indicate that it is not an action method.

Passing Data to Action Methods

Data is passed to action methods from a request as a series of name-value pairs. These name-value pairs include form data, query string values, and cookie contents. ASP.NET MVC will try to automatically map data values sent in the request to action method parameters by name. For example, suppose that a request is routed to the Customer controller's Search action method and that this method takes the customerName and companyName parameters. Suppose that the request is formatted as *http://mySite/customer/search /?customerName=test&companyName=test*.

This request would automatically map to the Customer.Search(customerName, companyName) action method. Because of this behavior, you do not have to write code to pull the parameter values out of the request.

Of course, you can also rely on routing to map common parameter values such as ID. Recall from Lesson 1 that the default routing is set to *controller/action/id*. Therefore, requests that look like *http://mySite/customer/details/5* will automatically map to the Customer.Details(id) method and parameter.

HTTP POST PARAMETERS

You can also call an action method as part of an HTTP post. To do so, you mark the action method with the HttpPost attribute. This indicates that the action method should be called when the page is sent as a post (typically in response to a submit button action).

In this case, you define a parameter to your action method by using the FormCollection name-value collection. ASP.NET MVC will then map the posted form data to this collection. You reference each form element by name within the collection. The following code shows an example.

Sample of Visual Basic Code

```vb
<HttpPost> _
Function Create(ByVal collection As FormCollection) As ActionResult
    Try
        Dim cust As New Customer()
        cust.CompanyName = collection("CompanyName").ToString()
        ' ... map remaining customer properties

        Dim nw As New northwndEntities()
        nw.AddToCustomers(cust)
        nw.SaveChanges()

        Return RedirectToAction("Index")
    Catch
        Return View()
    End Try
End Function
```

Sample of C# Code

```csharp
[HttpPost]
public ActionResult Create(FormCollection collection)
{
```

```
try
{
    Customer cust = new Customer();
    cust.CompanyName = collection["CompanyName"].ToString();
    // ... map remaining customer properties

    northwndEntities nw = new northwndEntities();
    nw.AddToCustomers(cust);
    nw.SaveChanges();

    return RedirectToAction("Index");
}
catch
{
    return View();
}
}
```

REQUEST AND RESPONSE DATA

You can also get at additional data in the request (HTTP get) or response (HTTP post). If, for instance, your data is not passed or mapped to a parameter, you can use the Controller class's Request and Response properties. These properties follow the HttpRequest and HttpResponse semantics you are familiar with in ASP.NET. Therefore, to get a query string value in your action method, you can call Request.QueryString("name"). To add to the response, you can call Response.Write("Hello World").

Passing Data to Views

There are two principal means for passing data from a controller class to a view: a ViewDataDictionary and a strongly typed view. The System.Web.Mvc.ViewDataDictionary is a collection of objects that are referenced by string keys. Both the Controller base class and the ViewPage base class (used for views) implement a property named ViewData, which is of type ViewDataDictionary. In this scenario, you add items to the ViewData property inside your controller. These items are then passed to the ViewData property of the selected view.

You can add any type of object, including a list, to ViewData. For example, the following code adds a list of countries or regions to the ViewData collection from within a controller. Notice that this list is converted to a System.Web.Mvc.SelectList. This class makes it easier to display a single-select list by using the HTML helper classes (more on these classes later in this lesson).

Sample of Visual Basic Code
```
Dim countries As New List(Of String)
countries.Add("USA")
countries.Add("Canada")
countries.Add("India")
countries.Add("China")
countries.Add("Mexico")
ViewData("countries") = New SelectList(countries)
```

Sample of C# Code

```
List<string> countries = new List<string>();
countries.Add("USA");
countries.Add("Canada");
countries.Add("India");
countries.Add("China");
countries.Add("Mexico");
ViewData["countries"] = new SelectList(countries);
```

The ViewData can then be referenced inside a view. The following markup shows a page that uses the HTML helper object to create a drop-down list control from the list data in the view:

Sample of Visual Basic Code

```
<%: Html.DropDownList("countries", CType(ViewData("countries"), SelectList))%>
```

Sample of C# Code

```
<%: Html.DropDownList("countries", (SelectList)ViewData["countries"])%>
```

You can also pass data to views that are strongly typed. In this case, you pass the type from the controller to the view as a parameter, as in Return View(cust). You will see an example of this in the upcoming section, "Creating Strongly Typed Views."

Using Action Filters

The ASP.NET MVC framework allows you to run code both before an action method is called or after it has run. You do so by using action filters. Action filters are applied by using attributes to action methods. Action filters allow you to define pre-execution and post-execution actions to your action methods.

Action filters are attribute classes that implement the FilterAttribute base class. You can create your own custom action filters. You apply these attribute classes to your action methods. ASP.NET MVC also includes several predefined action filters, including Authorize, OutputCache, and HandleError. The Authorize filter allows you to check security before executing an action method. OutputCache allows you to cache the results of an action method. The HandleError action filter allows you to wrap an action method to an error view page (by default this page is Views/Shared/Error.aspx).

Creating Views

You create views to render the user interface. Views are stored in the Views folder; you create a subfolder in the Views folder for each controller. You then add views to this folder based on your core action method names, such as Edit, Index, Create, Details, and similar names. Recall that, by default, ASP.NET MVC will render the view that matches the executed controller action method. You can also pass a specific view name to the View function in the controller, as in Return View("SomeView").

All processing of input logic should be done by the controller. All data storage and manipulation is handled by the model. Therefore, views do not require, and therefore typically do not have, code-behind classes. Instead, they use inline code inside the markup to reference data sent to them for display. User actions are then passed to the controller for processing.

Standard views (pages with the .aspx extension) inherit from the System.Web.Mvc.ViewPage class, which is based on the ASP.NET Page class. You can also have master pages (pages with the .master extension) in ASP.NET MVC; these inherit from ViewMasterPage. User controls (those with the .ascx extension) are also supported; they are called *partial views* and inherit from ViewUserControl.

You can create a view by using the Visual Studio View item template. You do so by right-clicking a folder in the Views directory and choosing Add | View. This brings up the Add View dialog box. Here you set the view name and can choose to select a master page.

A view page uses the @ Page directive; this works like the standard @ Page directive in ASP.NET pages. You can use it to set a page title, language, master file, and inheritance. The following markup shows an example.

Sample of Visual Basic Code

```
<%@ Page Title="Customer Details" Language="VB"
    MasterPageFile="~/Views/Shared/Site.Master" Inherits="System.Web.Mvc.ViewPage" %>
```

Sample of C# Code

```
<%@ Page Title="Customer Details" Language="C#"
    MasterPageFile="~/Views/Shared/Site.Master"
    Inherits="System.Web.Mvc.ViewPage<dynamic>" %>
```

The markup inside your view is similar to that of standard ASP.NET pages. If you are using a master page, you put your content inside ContentPlaceholder controls. You then use inline syntax to call code within your markup. For example, the following markup writes the customer name from the ViewData property to the page output.

Sample of Visual Basic Code

```
<asp:Content ID="Content2" ContentPlaceHolderID="MainContent" runat="server">
    <h2>Customer Details</h2>
    <%: ViewData("CustomerName")%>
</asp:Content>
```

Sample of C# Code

```
<asp:Content ID="Content2" ContentPlaceHolderID="MainContent" runat="server">
    <h2>Customer Details</h2>
    <%: ViewData["CustomerName"]%>
</asp:Content>
```

Using the HTML Helper Classes

The ASP.NET MVC framework provides the System.Web.Mvc.HtmlHelper class to make generating repetitive and sometimes tricky HTML easier. This includes a set of form helpers for creating user input items such as drop-down lists, text boxes, buttons, validation summaries, and more; a set of URL helpers for creating route-driven URLs; and helpers for encoding, formatting, and rendering HTML strings. You can also create your own custom HTML helpers.

You saw an example of an HtmlHelper action method in the previous section's code. In that case, a call was made inside the view to Html.DropDownList. This call populated a <select> input element from a collection. Without the HTML helper, you would have to write the markup for the select HTML and define a loop for adding each element to the option list. The helper simply generates this markup for you and gives the element the name you specify as a parameter to the method call.

An HtmlHelper instance is exposed through the ViewPage.Html property. This instance contains many action methods, each of which includes many overloads. You use these methods strictly to ease the creation of your MVC views. Table 14-1 lists many common helper methods and their usage.

TABLE 14-1 Some HtmlHelper Class Methods

HELPER METHOD	DESCRIPTION
ActionLink	Used to create an anchor tag inside the webpage.
BeginForm	Used to write out the form tag for the page.
CheckBox	Used to create a check box input element.
DropDownList	Used to create a select list based on a set of values.
Editor	Used to create an input text box or multiline text box (depending on the data type and the UIHint attribute).
Hidden	Used to create a hidden input element.
Label	Used to create an HTML label.
ListBox	Used to create a multiselect select element.
Password	Used to create a password input element.
RadioButton	Used to create a radio button input element.
RenderAction	Used to call an action method of a child controller. The action method will then return the appropriate view to be rendered from within the parent.
RenderPartial	Used to render a partial view (user control) from the parent. You pass the view name and an HtmlHelper to this method to indicate how to render the child view.
RouteLink	Used to create an anchor tag based on a route to an action.

HELPER METHOD	DESCRIPTION
TextArea	Used to create a <textarea> element.
TextBox	Used to create a text input element.
Validate	Used to apply rules to data fields.
ValidationMessage	Used to display validation messages for individual fields.
ValidationSummary	Used to display a list of all validation rules in the ModelStateDictionary.

Creating Strongly Typed Views

A strongly typed view is one that expects a certain object to be passed to it from the model as a parameter rather than as general information stored in ViewData, the data for which is based on simple name-value pairs. Recall that a view page inherits from the ViewPage class, as shown in the following @ Page attribute markup:

Sample of Visual Basic Code

```
... Inherits="System.Web.Mvc.ViewPage"
```

Sample of C# Code

```
... Inherits="System.Web.Mvc.ViewPage<dynamic>"
```

This class also supports a generic version, to which you can pass a strong type. This allows you to strongly type the ViewPage, indicating that the page works with a class defined in your model. The following markup shows an example.

Sample of Visual Basic Code

```
... Inherits="System.Web.Mvc.ViewPage(Of Customer)"
```

Sample of C# Code

```
... Inherits="System.Web.Mvc.ViewPage<Customer>"
```

This strong type is then mapped to the Model property of the page. You can use this Model property inside your view code to reference the type, as in the code shown next. This code writes out the Customer.CustomerID from the instance passed to the page.

```
<div class="display-field"><%: Model.CustomerID%></div>
```

Visual Studio provides support for helping you generate strongly typed views. In the Add View dialog box, you have the option to create a strongly typed view. Selecting this option allows you to indicate both a view data class and a primary view content control, such as a list or grid. The view data class is a class from your model (such as Customer). The view content indicates a page type that should be generated, such as Create, Delete, Details, Edit, List, or Empty. Figure 14-8 shows an example of creating a Details content page based on the Customer class.

FIGURE 14-8 The Add View dialog box allows you to define a strongly typed view.

Markup and inline code is then generated based on the selected type and content. For example, if you select List in the view content drop-down, Visual Studio will create a view that receives an IEnumerable list of Customer objects as the type. This view will then include an HTML table for displaying the list, to include a For...Each loop for writing out each row in the table. You will see an example of this in the practice at the end of this lesson.

Using Data Scaffolding and Model Validation in Views

You saw in the defining models section of this lesson how you can use the DataAnnotations scaffolding to provide metadata about your model, indicating required fields, range valida-tion, regular expression validation, and more. This scaffolding will impact how your strongly typed views are generated, validated, and processed by the controller.

As an example, suppose you have created a model based on the Northwind database by using the Entity Framework. That model might include a Customer object. You could use the scaffolding features to add validation attributes to your model. The following code shows an example of doing so. In this example, the Required, StringLength, and RegularExpression attributes are used.

Sample of Visual Basic Code

```vb
<MetadataType(GetType(CustomerMetadata))> _
Partial Public Class Customer
End Class

Public Class CustomerMetadata

    <Required(ErrorMessage:="Customer id is required.")> _
    Public Property CustomerID As Object

    <Required(ErrorMessage:="Company name is required.")> _
    Public Property CompanyName As Object

    <StringLength(125, ErrorMessage:="City must be 125 characters or less")> _
    <Required(ErrorMessage:="City name is required.")> _
    Public Property City As Object

    <RegularExpression("((\(\d{3}\) ?)|(\d{3}-))?\d{3}-\d{4}", _
        ErrorMessage:="Phone number should be in the format, 123-123-1234.")> _
    Public Property Phone As Object

End Class
```

Sample of C# Code

```csharp
[MetadataType(typeof(CustomerMetadata))]
public partial class Customer
{
}

public class CustomerMetadata
{
    [Required(ErrorMessage = "Customer id is required.")]
    public object CustomerID { get; set; }

    [Required(ErrorMessage = "Company name is required.")]
    public object CompanyName { get; set; }

    [StringLength(125, ErrorMessage = "City must be 125 characters or less")]
    [Required(ErrorMessage = "City name is required.")]
    public object City { get; set; }

    [RegularExpression(@"((\(\d{3}\) ?)|(\d{3}-))?\d{3}-\d{4}",
        ErrorMessage = "Phone number should be in the format, 123-123-1234.")]
    public object Phone { get; set; }

}
```

This metadata can be used by your controller to handle business rule processing. These rules can then be displayed inside the view as both validation summary and individual, field-level validation messages.

As an example, consider the Customer class defined previously. Assume that you are creating a strongly typed view based on the Edit option in the view content drop-down. This will generate a view that inherits from ViewPage<Customer>. This view will use the Html.ValidationSummary and Html.ValidationMessageFor helper classes, as shown here.

Sample of Visual Basic Code

```
<% Using Html.BeginForm() %>
    <%: Html.ValidationSummary(True) %>
    <fieldset>
        <legend>Fields</legend>

        <div class="editor-label">
            <%: Html.LabelFor(Function(model) model.CustomerID) %>
        </div>
        <div class="editor-field">
            <%: Html.TextBoxFor(Function(model) model.CustomerID) %>
            <%: Html.ValidationMessageFor(Function(model) model.CustomerID) %>
        </div>
...
```

Sample of C# Code

```
<% using (Html.BeginForm()) {%>
    <%: Html.ValidationSummary(true) %>

    <fieldset>
        <legend>Fields</legend>

        <div class="editor-label">
            <%: Html.LabelFor(model => model.CustomerID) %>
        </div>
        <div class="editor-field">
            <%: Html.TextBoxFor(model => model.CustomerID) %>
            <%: Html.ValidationMessageFor(model => model.CustomerID) %>
        </div>
...
```

When a user submits this form, the Edit action method is called in the controller. Note that the typical view would contain two Edit action methods: one for get and one for post. The get version of the method takes an ID parameter, looks up the entity object in the model, and selects the Edit.aspx view page, to which it provides the entity object instance (such as a Customer object). The following code shows an example.

Sample of Visual Basic Code

```
Function Edit(ByVal id As String) As ActionResult

    Dim nw As New northwndEntities()
    Dim custQuery = From c In nw.Customers
                    Where c.CustomerID = id
                    Select c

    Dim cust As Customer = custQuery.FirstOrDefault()

    Return View(cust)

End Function
```

Sample of C# Code

```csharp
public ActionResult Edit(string id)
{
    Models.northwndEntities nw = new Models.northwndEntities();
    var custQuery = from c in nw.Customers
                    where c.CustomerID == id
                    select c;
    Models.Customer cust = custQuery.FirstOrDefault();
    return View(cust);
}
```

The post version of the method is called when the user submits the result of his or her edits. This method can take a FormCollection object or a strong type if strongly typed views are being used. In the case of the latter, the view data is automatically provided as a parameter (ASP.NET MVC will convert the data into the strongly typed value as required). Any rules that are not valid can then be checked by calling ModelState.IsValid. If this call returns false, you typically redisplay the view. Any field-level validation messages will then be rendered to the screen. If data validation succeeds, the user will be directed to the index (main) page. The following code shows an example of the post version of the Customer.Edit method inside the controller class.

Sample of Visual Basic Code

```
<HttpPost()> _
Function Edit(ByVal id As String, _
    ByVal c As Customer) As ActionResult

    If ModelState.IsValid = False Then
        Return View("Edit", c)
    Else
        'add code to update the model

        Return RedirectToAction("Index")
    End If

End Function
```

Sample of C# Code

```csharp
[HttpPost]
public ActionResult Edit(string id, Models.Customer c)
{
    if (ModelState.IsValid == false)
    {
        return View("Edit", c);
    }
    else
    {
        //add code to update the model
        return RedirectToAction("Index");
    }
}
```

When a user posts his or her changes to the server, this Edit method is called. If the form is not valid, the editing page is returned. Any validation errors are then shown on the form, as shown in Figure 14-9.

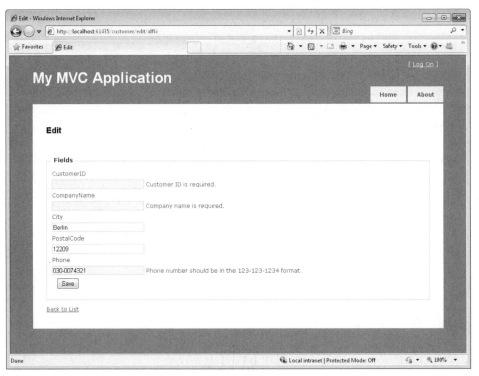

FIGURE 14-9 You can use DataAnnotation classes to validate your model and pass that validation down to the controller and view.

Creating Partial (Child) Views

There are times when you need to break up your view into smaller parts. For example, you might have a page that presents a dashboard of both sales order data and inventory data. In this case, you would have a parent view for the dashboard; the parent view would bring together the two child views (order and inventory).

A child (partial) view in ASP.NET MVC is a user control (ASCX file). These user controls are considered to be views (albeit partial). Therefore, each can be accessed by a controller.

For example, suppose you have a Dashboard folder inside the Views folder. This folder would contain an Index.aspx page for the main view. It would also contain both the OrdersSummary.ascx and InventorySummary.ascx partial views. Figure 14-10 shows an example from Solution Explorer.

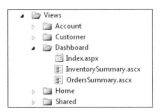

FIGURE 14-10 You can place both view pages and view user controls (partial views) inside a view folder.

Note that you can create partial views either by selecting the MVC 2 View User Control template from the Add New Item dialog box or by selecting Create A Partial View in the Add View dialog box.

Next, you would create a DashboardController class for rendering the views. This class would contain action methods called Index, OrdersSummary, and InventorySummary. Each of these methods would return a view as ActionResult. The following code shows an example.

Sample of Visual Basic Code

```
Public Class DashboardController
    Inherits System.Web.Mvc.Controller

    Function Index() As ActionResult
        Return View()
    End Function

    Function OrdersSummary() As ActionResult
        Return View()
    End Function

    Function InventorySummary() As ActionResult
        Return View()
    End Function

End Class
```

Sample of C# Code

```csharp
public class DashboardController : Controller
{

    public ActionResult Index()
    {
        return View();
    }

    public ActionResult OrdersSummary()
    {
        return View();
    }

    public ActionResult InventorySummary()
    {
        return View();
    }

}
```

Users would request the Index page (as in *http://mySite/dashboard/index*). You then render the parent view (Index.aspx); it is up to the parent view to know how to render its children by using HTML helper methods.

The HTML helper methods you would use include Action and RenderAction. The Html.Action method returns a child view as a string. You can then determine how to render the string output inside your view. The Html.RenderAction method renders the child view inline inside the parent. If you use these methods to simply write out the results on a page, they are functionally equivalent. The following markup shows the Index.aspx page rendering its child views.

```
<asp:Content ID="Content2" ContentPlaceHolderID="MainContent" runat="server">

    <h2>Index</h2>

    <%= Html.Action("OrdersSummary")%>
    <%= Html.Action("InventorySummary")%>

</asp:Content>
```

When the page is requested, a call is made to DashboardController.Index. The Index view then calls out to DashboardController.OrdersSummary and DashboardController.InventorySummary. Both of these methods return a partial view (user control) that is rendered to the page.

Note that partial views have access to the ViewData from their parent. Therefore, in the example, you could add to the ViewData inside the Index method. This data could be used by either user control. However, the instance of ViewData provided to the partial view is a copy of that data. Any changes made to this copy belong to the partial view only.

Customizing MVC Routing

You saw previously that routes are registered in the Global.asax file by following the *controller /action/id* pattern. The ASP.NET MVC framework maps this routing pattern to your controllers and their action methods. For the most part, you should not have to modify this routing setup in your ASP.NET MVC application. However, it is important to know more about routing in ASP.NET, in case you do need to make customizations.

Route Segments and Placeholders

Recall that requests to ASP.NET MVC applications are handled by the UrlRoutingModule HTTP module. These requests are passed to the MvcRouteHandler to determine the controller and action method to call. This is determined by parsing the URL pattern in the request.

A URL pattern is a defined set of segments delimited by a slash (/), as in Customer/Index/5. In this case, there are three segments in the URL pattern. When the request is received, the URL is broken into segments and placeholders. These segments are stored as key-value pairs, in which the key is the placeholder defined in the routing definition and the value is the value from the URL. In ASP.NET MVC, these placeholder keys are defined as {controller}/{action}/{id}. This routing is established by calling routes.MapRoute in the Global.asax file. Routes is a RouteCollection instance. The values (such as Customer/Index/5) are then mapped accordingly to these keys when passed in the request.

You can define a placeholder by putting it in braces, as in {route}. You can also define multiple placeholders in a segment by using a literal delimiter, as in {language}-{country}/{route}. In this case, there are two segments (separated by the slash), and the first segment has two placeholders that would act as keys in the route collection.

Setting Default Route Parameters

These route placeholders are also referred to as *route parameters*. They are used to pass named parameters (named with the key) to the routing engine. You can also set default values for your route parameters. These defaults are used if a parameter is omitted from the URL.

You define a default route parameter by using a RouteValueDictionary object. By using this object, you can pass route parameter names and default values. In fact, the default routing setup uses default parameter values. The following code shows an example. Notice that the {controller}, {action}, and {id} are all mapped to default values. In this case, if you omit all segments of the URL, users will be routed to Home/Index by default. In addition, the {id} parameter is set to optional for all routes.

Sample of Visual Basic Code

```
routes.MapRoute("Default", _
    "{controller}/{action}/{id}", _
    New With {.controller = "Home", .action = "Index", .id = UrlParameter.Optional} )
```

Sample of C# Code

```
routes.MapRoute("Default",
    "{controller}/{action}/{id}",
    new { controller = "Home", action = "Index", id = UrlParameter.Optional } );
```

Defining Route Constraints

You can also specify that a particular route segment's value must match a constraint that you define. This might be the length of the segment, a date range, or any string data validation that you can define. If a URL does not meet the constraint, the route is not used to process the request.

You define route constraints with regular expressions or by using objects that implement the IRouteConstraint interface. You then add each constraint to a RouteValueDictionary object and pass that to routes.MapRoute().

As an example, suppose you want to add a route definition that searches for the month/year numeric pattern in the URL (as in 12/2012). You could do as shown in the following code. This code creates default values for month and year based on the current month and year. It then sets a route constraint for each segment by using regular expressions.

Sample of Visual Basic Code

```vb
routes.MapRoute("MonthYear", _
    "{month}/{year}", _
    New RouteValueDictionary(New With {.month = DateTime.Now.Month,
        .year = DateTime.Now.Year}), _
    New RouteValueDictionary(New With {.month = "\d{2}", .year = "\d{4}"}))
```

Sample of C# Code

```csharp
routes.MapRoute("MonthYear",
    "{month}/{year}",
    new RouteValueDictionary(new { month = DateTime.Now.Month,
        year = DateTime.Now.Year}),
    new RouteValueDictionary(new { month = @"\d{2}", year = @"\d{4}" }));
```

Preventing Route Handling

There are scenarios in which routing does not handle the request. One such scenario is when a request actually maps to a physical file. In this case, the physical file on your server is returned and the route is ignored. For example, a call to *http://mySite/customer/edit.aspx* would return the edit.aspx page, if it exists in the customer folder on your site.

You can prevent physical files from circumventing routing. You do so in an ASP.NET MVC application by setting the RouteCollectionExtension object's RouteExistingFiles property to true, as in routes.RouteExistingFiles = true, inside the Global.asax file.

You can also turn off routing explicitly for certain requests. You do so in an ASP.NET MVC application through the RouteCollectionExtensions.IgnoreRoute method. This method creates a StopRoutingHandler that will block routing for a specified request. You pass a route pattern to this method to indicate which request patterns you want routing to ignore.

By default, ASP.NET MVC includes the following line of code in the Global.asax.

```
routes.IgnoreRoute("{resource}.axd/{*pathInfo}")
```

This indicates that calls for files with the .axd extension will not be routed, because ASP.NET uses this HTTP handler to serve embedded resources such as JavaScript for a page.

 Quick Check

1. What are the restrictions placed on defining a model for ASP.NET MVC?

2. How would you return a specific view from an action method?

3. How do you indicate that an action method should be called as part of an HTTP post?

Quick Check Answers

1. There are no restrictions on creating a model. You can create any set of custom classes or use generated code such as an Entity Framework model.

2. You can do so by passing the view name in the View method, as in return View("Edit").

3. You add the HttpPostAttribute class to the action method signature.

PRACTICE Creating a Full-Featured ASP.NET MVC Application

In this practice, you create an ASP.NET MVC 2 web application and a model. You then create views and controller methods to work with the data in the model so that users can view, add, edit, and delete model items.

ON THE COMPANION MEDIA

If you encounter a problem completing an exercise, you can find the completed projects in the samples installed from this book's companion CD. For more information about the project files and other content on the CD, see "Using the Companion Media" in this book's Introduction.

EXERCISE 1 Creating the ASP.NET MVC Web Application and the Model

In this exercise, you create a new ASP.NET MVC 2 web application and define a data model.

1. Open Visual Studio. Select File | New Project (not New Web Site). From the New Project dialog box, select your preferred programming language and the web node from the Installed Templates area (on the left side of the dialog box). Select the ASP.NET MVC 2 Web Application template. Name the project and solution **EmployeeMgrMvc**. When prompted to create a unit test project, you can select either yes or no. This practice does not create tests.

2. Add the northwnd.mdf database to the App_Data directory of your site. You can get this database from the CD for this book.

3. Right-click the Models folder in Solution Explorer and select Add | New Item. Select the Data node on the left side of the Add New Item dialog box. Select an ADO.NET Entity Data Model template. Name this file **Northwind.edmx**.

4. Step through the Entity Data Model Wizard and connect to the Northwind database. Select the Employees table.

5. Add a new class to the Models folder and name it **Employee**. This class will allow you to define metadata validation rules for your model.

6. At the top of this class, add a using (imports in Visual Basic) statement for System.ComponentModel.DataAnnotations.

7. Next, define a class called **EmployeeMetadata**. Add rules for some of the fields in your model (see the code shown for step 8).

8. Finally, define a partial class called **Employee**. Assign the MetedataType attribute to this class. This will be used to add the rules to your generated model.

The following code shows an example.

```
Sample of Visual Basic Code
Imports System.ComponentModel.DataAnnotations

<MetadataType(GetType(EmployeeMetadata))> _
Partial Public Class Employee

End Class

Public Class EmployeeMetadata

    <Required(ErrorMessage:="Employee id is required.")> _
    Public Property EmployeeID As Object

    <Required(ErrorMessage:="First name is required.")> _
    Public Property FirstName As Object

    <Required(ErrorMessage:="Last name is required.")> _
    Public Property LastName As Object
```

```
        <StringLength(60, ErrorMessage:="Address must be 60 characters or less")> _
        Public Property Address As Object

        <RegularExpression("((\(\d{3}\) ?)|(\d{3}-))?\d{3}-\d{4}", _
            ErrorMessage:="Phone number should be in the format, 123-123-1234.")> _
        Public Property HomePhone As Object

End Class
```

Sample of C# Code
```
using System.ComponentModel.DataAnnotations;

namespace EmployeeMgrMvc.Models
{
    [MetadataType(typeof(EmployeeMetadata))]
    public partial class Employee
    {
    }

    public class EmployeeMetadata
    {
        [Required(ErrorMessage = "Employee id is required.")]
        public object EmployeeID { get; set; }

        [Required(ErrorMessage = "First name is required.")]
        public object FirstName { get; set; }

        [Required(ErrorMessage = "Last name is required.")]
        public object LastName { get; set; }

        [StringLength(60, ErrorMessage="Address must be 60 characters or less")]
        public object Address { get; set; }

        [RegularExpression(@"((\(\d{3}\) ?)|(\d{3}-))?\d{3}-\d{4}",
            ErrorMessage = "Phone number should be in the format, 123-123-1234.")]
        public object HomePhone { get; set; }
    }
}
```

You now have your site and your model. You can build the code and even run the application to verify.

EXERCISE 2   Creating the Controller and Views

In this exercise, you add the controller and related views to the ASP.NET MVC 2 application created in the previous exercise.

1. Continue editing the project created in the previous exercise. Alternatively, you can open the completed Lesson 2, Exercise 1 project in the samples installed from the CD.

2. Right-click the Controllers folder and choose Add | Controller. Set the controller name to EmployeeController. Select the check box to create the default set of action methods.

3. Open the EmployeeController. Remove the Delete methods because this practice will not implement these. Add code to each action method to work with the model based

on the action. This includes the Index method (which returns a list of Employees) and the Details, Create, and Edit methods. Assume that each of these pages will be created as a strongly typed view. Be sure to add a using (Imports in Visual Basic) statement for EmployeeMgrMvc.Models. The following code shows an example.

```vbnet
Sample of Visual Basic Code
Namespace EmployeeMgrMvc
    Public Class EmployeeController
        Inherits System.Web.Mvc.Controller

        Function Index() As ActionResult
            Dim nw As New northwndEntities()
            Return View(nw.Employees)
        End Function

        Function Details(ByVal id As Integer) As ActionResult
            Return View(GetEmployee(id))
        End Function

        Function Create() As ActionResult
            Return View()
        End Function

        <HttpPost()> _
        Function Create(ByVal emp As Employee) As ActionResult
            If ModelState.IsValid Then
                Try
                    Dim nw As New northwndEntities()
                    nw.AddToEmployees(emp)
                    nw.SaveChanges()
                    Return RedirectToAction("Index")
                Catch
                    Return View()
                End Try
            Else
                Return View("Create")
            End If
        End Function

        Function Edit(ByVal id As Integer) As ActionResult
            Return View(GetEmployee(id))
        End Function

        <HttpPost()> _
        Function Edit(ByVal emp As Employee) As ActionResult
            If ModelState.IsValid Then
                Try
                    Dim nw As New northwndEntities()
                    Dim origEmp As Employee = GetEmployee(emp.EmployeeID)
                    nw.Employees.Attach(emp)
                    nw.ApplyOriginalValues("Employees", origEmp)
                    nw.SaveChanges()
                    Return RedirectToAction("Index")
                Catch
                    Return View()
                End Try
            Else
                Return View("Edit", emp.EmployeeID)
            End If
        End Function
```

```
        <NonAction()> _
        Function GetEmployee(ByVal id As Integer) As Employee

            Dim nw As New northwndEntities()
            Dim empQuery = From e In nw.Employees
                    Where e.EmployeeID = id
                    Select e

            Dim emp As Employee = empQuery.FirstOrDefault()

            Return emp

        End Function

    End Class
End Namespace
```

Sample of C# Code

```csharp
using System;
using System.Collections.Generic;
using System.Linq;
using System.Web;
using System.Web.Mvc;
using EmployeeMgrMvc.Models;

namespace EmployeeMgrMvc.Controllers
{
    public class EmployeeController : Controller
    {
        public ActionResult Index()
        {
            northwndEntities nw = new northwndEntities();
            return View(nw.Employees);
        }

        public ActionResult Details(int id)
        {
            return View(GetEmployee(id));
        }

        public ActionResult Create()
        {
            return View();
        }

        [HttpPost]
        public ActionResult Create(Employee emp)
        {
          if (ModelState.IsValid)
          {
            try
            {
                northwndEntities nw = new northwndEntities();
                nw.AddToEmployees(emp);
                nw.SaveChanges();
                return RedirectToAction("Index");
```

```
        }
        catch
        {
            return View();
        }
    }
    else
    {
    return View("Create");
    }
}


public ActionResult Edit(int id)
{
    return View(GetEmployee(id));
}

[HttpPost]
public ActionResult Edit(Employee emp)
{
    if (ModelState.IsValid)
    {
        try
        {
         northwndEntities nw = new northwndEntities();
         Employee origEmp = GetEmployee(emp.EmployeeID);
         nw.Employees.Attach(emp);
         nw.ApplyOriginalValues("Employees", origEmp);
         nw.SaveChanges();
         return RedirectToAction("Index");
        }
        catch
        {
            return View();
        }
    }
    else
    {
        return View("Edit", emp.EmployeeID);
    }
}

[NonAction]
private Employee GetEmployee(int id)
{
    northwndEntities nw = new northwndEntities();
    var empQuery = from e in nw.Employees
                    where e.EmployeeID == id
                    select e;
    Employee emp = empQuery.FirstOrDefault();
    return emp;
}
    }
}
```

4. Next, add a subfolder to the Views folder and name it **Employee**.

5. Right-click the Employee folder and choose Add | View. Name this view page **Index**. Check the Strongly Typed View check box. Select EmployeeMgrMvc.Models.Employee from the View Data Class list. Select List from the View Content list. Leave the other settings as defaults, and click Add. If you want, inside the Index.aspx page, remove some of the fields from the display grid to show only pertinent information.

   Notice that the ActionLink HTML helper class is used inside the markup to create links for editing, viewing, deleting, and creating new employees. These action links will create requests bound for the EmployeeController by using the appropriate action method and passing an ID.

6. Remove the ActionLink for Delete from the table.

7. Open the Shared/Site.Master page. Add an ActionLink to the menu to call the Employee-Index.aspx page, as in the following.

   ```
   <li><%: Html.ActionLink("Employees", "Index", "Employee")%></li>
   ```

8. Add view pages for Details.aspx, Edit.aspx, and Create.aspx to the Employee folder. Make each page strongly typed. Be sure to remove the EmployeeID field information from the Create.aspx page, because the ID is generated by the database. If you want, remove some of the fields from each page so that you will only work with pertinent information (such as EmployeeID, LastName, FirstName, Address, and HomePhone).

9. Run the site. You should be able to create new employees and edit existing ones. Be sure to notice how your model validation rules are processed when data is being updated.

Lesson Summary

- You can create models to work with ASP.NET MVC by using any class you like. You can also generate your models by using the Entity Framework or LINQ to SQL. If you do, you can attach metadata and business rules to your model by using the DataAnnotations classes.

- Controllers include action methods that work with the model, process user input, and return different ActionResult objects. The ActionResult value you can return includes a view or a file, redirecting to another controller, and more.

- You can pass data from a controller to a view by using the ViewDataDictionary object. You can also create strongly typed views that are based on entity classes in your model.

- The HtmlHelper classes ease writing HTML that works with data sent to a view from a controller. Helper methods include ActionLink, TextBox, and ValidationMessage (and many others).

- You create partial (child) views by using user controls (ASCX files). Each user control has its own action method in a controller. The parent view can render any child views (user controls) by using the Html.Action helper method.

- You can customize the ASP.NET MVC default routing to provide additional routes, parameter constraints, and default values for route parameters.

Lesson Review

You can use the following questions to test your knowledge of the information in Lesson 2, "Creating Models, Views, and Controllers." The questions are also available on the companion CD in a practice test, if you prefer to review them in electronic form.

> **NOTE ANSWERS**
>
> Answers to these questions and explanations of why each answer choice is correct or incorrect are located in the "Answers" section at the end of the book.

1. You are writing an action method called ShipOrder inside the Order controller. The logic in your code indicates that you need to call the Shipment controller's Status method as a result of your controller's action method. Which line of code would accomplish this? (Choose all that apply.)

    A. `return View("Shipment.Status")`

    B. `return Redirect("Shipment/Status")`

    C. `Response.Redirect("Shipment.aspx?action=Status")`

    D. `return Content("Shipment.Status")`

2. You want to add a default route for when requests are made to your site without the controller and action parameters in the URL. This default route should point to Default.aspx inside the view folder named Main. You create a controller named DefaultController. Which code would you write? (Choose all that apply.)

    A.

    Visual Basic Code

    ```
    routes.MapRoute("HomePage", _
        "{controller}/{action}", _
        New With {.controller = "DefaultController", .action = "Default"} )
    ```

    C# Code

    ```
    routes.MapRoute("HomePage",
        "{controller}/{action}",
        new { controller = "DefaultController", action = "Default"} );
    ```

B.

Visual Basic Code

```
routes.MapRoute("Default", _
    "{DefaultController}/{Default}", _
    New With {.controller = "Default", .action = "Default"} )
```

C# Code

```
MapRoute("Default ",
    "{ DefaultController }/{ Default }",
    new { controller = "Default", action = "Default"} );
```

C.

Visual Basic Code

```
routes.MapRoute("Default", _
    "{DefaultController}/{Default}")
```

C# Code

```
routes.MapRoute("Default ",
    "{ DefaultController }/{ Default }");
```

D.

Visual Basic Code

```
routes.MapRoute("HomePage", _
    "{controller}/{action}", _
    New With {.controller = "Default", .action = "Default"} )
```

C# Code

```
routes.MapRoute("HomePage",
    "{controller}/{action}",
    new { controller = "Default", action = "Default"} );
```

3. You want to create a strongly typed view. What actions should you take? (Choose all that apply.)

   A. Mark your @ Page directive to inherit from ViewPage<TModel>.

   B. Add a strong type as a parameter to the View method inside your action method.

   C. Add a strong type to the ViewData collection inside your action method.

   D. Mark your @ Page directive to include the ViewDataClass attribute and point to an entity inside your model.

Case Scenarios

In the following case scenario, you apply what you've learned in this chapter. If you have difficulty completing this work, review the material in this chapter before beginning the next chapter. You can find answers to these questions in the "Answers" section at the end of this book.

Case Scenario: Creating an ASP.NET MVC Application

You are a developer working at Contoso, Ltd. You are creating a new application to manage your division's inventory. Quality has been a big issue in the past; therefore, you plan to take advantage of the testability of ASP.NET MVC applications.

You meet with subject-matter experts and gather requirements. You realize that this application will have to display products obtained from an existing product database (exposed to you as a web service). It will then have to define a new database and a functionality that allows users to view and update current inventory; provide functionality for viewing, editing, and adding suppliers; and create a restock page that allows a user to order a product from an approved supplier.

You expect this application to grow very large over time. You also anticipate a large team of developers working to extend the application as Contoso, Ltd. grows.

1. What controllers would you create to handle the requirements for this application?
2. What views would you create to allow users to interact as required?
3. How would you define your model?
4. How would you get data from the model to the views?
5. How might you consider structuring your application?

Suggested Practices

To successfully master the exam objective presented in this chapter, complete the following tasks.

Work with Controllers, Views, and Routing

For this task, you should complete Practice 1 to gain experience with using partial views. Practice 2 will help you understand routing and route constraints. Practice 3 will add to your understanding of the HTML helper classes.

- **Practice 1**   Return to the practice in Lesson 2. Create a partial view as a user control for displaying the total number of employees. Add a method to the EmployeeController to render this view. Add code to the Index page to show this user control as part of its view.

- **Practice 2**   Return to the practice in Lesson 2. Add a route constraint inside the Global.asax file to restrict route controller names to 10 characters or less. Test the results.

- **Practice 3**   Return to the practice in Lesson 2. Use the HTML helper classes to change the way data is displayed and edited. You can add date formatting. You might also display a list of employee territories as check boxes in the Create and Edit views.

Take a Practice Test

The practice tests on this book's companion CD offer many options. For example, you can test yourself on just the lesson review questions in this chapter, or you can test yourself on all the 70-515 certification exam objectives. You can set up the test so it closely simulates the experience of taking a certification exam, or you can set it up in study mode so you can look at the correct answers and explanations after you answer each question.

> **MORE INFO**   **PRACTICE TESTS**
>
> For details about all the practice test options available, see the "How to Use the Practice Tests" section in this book's Introduction.

Answers

Chapter 1: Lesson Review Answers

Lesson 1

1. Correct Answer: D

   A. **Incorrect:** IsCallback is generated by client-side scripts and does not involve reloading a page.

   B. **Incorrect:** IsReusable is a standard property that indicates whether an object can be reused.

   C. **Incorrect:** IsValid indicates whether page validation succeeded. IsValid is discussed in more detail in Chapter 5, "Input Validation and Site Navigation."

   D. **Correct:** If IsPostBack is true, the page loading is the result of a form being submitted by the user. IsPostBack is discussed in more detail in Chapter 5.

2. Correct Answer: C

   A. **Incorrect:** The PUT command is used to add a file to a web server.

   B. **Incorrect:** The CONNECT command is not frequently used. It is reserved for use with proxy servers under very specific conditions.

   C. **Correct:** The POST command is used when a browser submits the results of a form. The form data is stored as part of the response packet.

   D. **Incorrect:** The GET command is used to submit a form with the form data included as part of the URI.

Lesson 2

1. **Correct Answer: C**

    A. Incorrect: Although the remote HTTP option would create a site on a remote server, it requires Front Page Server Extensions.

    B. Incorrect: The file system option for a web project creates the project on the local computer, rather than on a remote web server. If you chose the file system option, you would need to connect to an IIS 7.5 server using WebDAV or deploy the site to the remote server after development.

    C. Correct: FTP allows you to publish a website to a remote server that does not support Front Page Server Extensions. However, your ability to debug the site is limited.

    D. Incorrect: You can use the local HTTP option to create a website by using IIS installed on your local computer. However, the question requires you to create the website on a remote computer.

2. **Correct Answer: A**

    A. Correct: Unlike ASP.NET Web applications, ASP.NET websites can contain pages that use different languages. In practice, however, this makes the site very difficult to maintain, because developers would need to be familiar with both Visual Basic and C#. Therefore, although you can simply add the Visual Basic page to the existing C# site, a better option would be to use a Visual-Basic-to-C# converter to convert the page to C#.

    B. Incorrect: Joe does not need to rewrite the code-behind file by using C#. However, he might want to do this to make the site easier to maintain.

    C. Incorrect: The ASPX page is not language specific, and thus would not need to be rewritten even if the code-behind page were converted from Visual Basic to C#. Additionally, Joe could add the Visual Basic page to the existing C# site without problem.

    D. Incorrect: Joe can simply add the Visual Basic page to the website.

Lesson 3

1. **Correct Answer: C**

    A. Incorrect: The Global.asax file is used to define application-level events, but not settings.

    B. Incorrect: Application Web.config files will only define settings for a single web application, and changing that file will not change settings for Windows applications.

    C. Correct: You can use the Machine.config file to manage settings for both web and Windows applications at the machine level.

    D. Incorrect: The root Web.config file will define settings for all web applications, but not Windows applications. Instead, you should edit the Machine.config file.

2. **Correct Answer: B**

    A. Incorrect: Changes to the Web.config file that is in the same folder as Machine.config will apply to all websites on the machine, not just a single web application.

    B. Correct: Changes to the Web.config file at the web application root will apply only to that web application.

C. **Incorrect:** The Machine.config file is used to set global settings on the machine. As a result, changes to the Machine.config file would impact all .NET Framework applications.

D. **Incorrect:** The Global.asax file is used to define application-wide events. It does not define application settings.

Chapter 1: Case Scenario Answers

Case Scenario 1: Creating a New Website

1. Have each developer create a new website on their local computer, and use that during debugging. When a developer has created a stable version of a component, have the developer copy it to the development server.

2. The development server will host an IIS website. Individual developers can perform development and debugging by using IIS on their local computers or on file-system–based websites.

Case Scenario 2: Placing Files in the Proper Folders

1. You will place the ShoppingCart.dll file in the Bin folder. You will place the data-base files in the App_Data folder. The wrapper file (ShoppingCartWrapper.cs or ShoppingCartWrapper.vb) will be placed in the site's App_Code directory.

2. A primary benefit to adhering to the ASP.NET folder structure is that these folders are secured. A user who attempts to browse to any of these folders will receive an HTTP 403 Forbidden error.

Chapter 2: Lesson Review Answers

Lesson 1

1. **Correct Answers: B, C, and D**

    A. **Incorrect:** Private properties are never available from other objects.

    B. **Correct:** You can access public properties from a content page. For example, you can access the Boolean property Master.EnableViewState to get or set whether the master page uses view state.

    C. **Correct:** You can access public methods from a content page. For example, you can access the method Master.FindControl to get a control located on the master page.

    D. **Correct:** You can use the public Master.FindControl method to create an object representing a control on the master page.

2. **Correct Answers: A and C**

    A. Correct: The @ MasterType declaration is required to access the properties in the master page. As an alternative to using the declarative syntax, you can specify the master page at runtime.

    B. Incorrect: You only need to add the @ Master declarations to the master page, not the content pages.

    C. Correct: A content page must have a MasterPageFile attribute in the @ Page declaration that points to the master page.

    D. Incorrect: The master page, not the content pages, uses the ContentPlaceHolder control. Content pages will replace the ContentPlaceHolder control with their own content.

3. **Correct Answer: D**

    A. Incorrect: Page_Load occurs after the content page has bound to the master page. If you attempt to change the master page, the runtime throws an exception.

    B. Incorrect: Page_Render occurs after the content page has bound to the master page. If you attempt to change the master page, the runtime throws an exception.

    C. Incorrect: Page_PreRender occurs after the content page has bound to the master page. If you attempt to change the master page, the runtime throws an exception.

    D. Correct: Page_PreInit is the last opportunity to change the master page. After this event, the content page binds with the master page, preventing you from changing it.

Lesson 2

1. **Correct Answers: A and C**

    A. Correct: Themes specified by using the page's Theme attribute override control attributes because they are applied after control attributes are applied.

    B. Incorrect: Themes specified by using the StyleSheetTheme attribute do not override control attributes because they are applied before control attributes are applied.

    C. Correct: Themes specified by using the page's Theme attribute override control attributes because they are applied after control attributes are applied.

    D. Incorrect: Themes specified by using the StyleSheetTheme attribute do not override control attributes because they are applied before control attributes are applied.

2. **Correct Answer: C**

    A. Incorrect: Skin files should not include the ID attribute, and skin files must include the runat="server" attribute.

    B. Incorrect: Skin files should not include the ID attribute. The ID attribute is reserved for controls themselves.

    C. Correct: Skin files must include the runat="server" attribute but should not include the ID attribute.

    D. Incorrect: Skin files must include the runat="server" attribute.

3. **Correct Answer: D**

   A. **Incorrect:** Page_Load occurs too late in the rendering process to change the theme.

   B. **Incorrect:** Page_Render occurs too late in the rendering process to change the theme.

   C. **Incorrect:** Page_PreRender occurs too late in the rendering process to change the theme.

   D. **Correct:** Page_PreInit is the proper method in which to specify the theme because the page theme property has not already been set by ASP.NET. After Page_PreInit executes for the page, you can no longer change the theme property without causing a run time exception.

Lesson 3

1. **Correct Answer: A**

   A. **Correct:** In this example, your primary concern is that a different copy of the page is cached for each state that the user might select. The state would be provided as a parameter; therefore, configuring the VaryByParam attribute with the name of the control containing the state input provides optimal caching.

   B. **Incorrect:** The VaryByHeader attribute is used to dynamically generate the page if an item in the page's header varies. In this case, the header is not unique for different states, and you cannot use the attribute to configure the correct type of caching.

   C. **Incorrect:** The SqlDependency attribute might seem like the correct attribute because the webpage is based on a SQL query. However, in this scenario, you are not concerned about updating the page if the database is updated. You are only concerned with updating the page output if the user chooses to filter the customer list, which is provided by a parameter, not the database.

   D. **Incorrect:** The VaryByCustom attribute enables you to implement custom control over how pages are cached. Although you could implement a custom method to meet your requirements, this would be time consuming and inefficient. The capability you need is provided by the VaryByParam attribute.

2. **Correct Answer: B**

   A. **Incorrect:** The Request object contains methods and parameters that describe the user's request. To configure page output caching, you must use the Response object instead.

   B. **Correct:** The Response object contains methods such as Response.Cache.SetExpires and Response.AddCacheDependency that enable you to configure page output caching programmatically.

   C. **Incorrect:** The Application collection allows you to share data across all pages and processes in your application. Page output caching is configured on a per-page basis by using the Response object.

   D. **Incorrect:** The Server object contains methods such as UrlDecode and UrlEncode that are useful for processing server file paths. To configure page output caching, you must use the Response object instead.

3. **Correct Answer: C**

   A. **Incorrect:** You can directly define Cache items. However, this technique does not provide for automatic expiration. When you directly define a Cache item, it stays cached until you remove it manually.

   B. **Incorrect:** The Cache.Get method allows you to retrieve cached items, not define them.

   C. **Correct:** You can use the Cache.Insert method to add an object to the cache and specify one or more dependencies, including an expiration time span.

   D. **Incorrect:** Although you would use DateTime.Now.AddMinutes(10) to specify an expiration time 10 minutes in the future, you cannot directly cast it to the Cache type.

4. **Correct Answers: B, C, and E**

   A. **Incorrect:** You can configure page output caching to vary with an HTTP header. However, the Cache object cannot use HTTP headers as dependencies.

   B. **Correct:** You can create file dependencies for Cache objects.

   C. **Correct:** You can make a Cache object expire after a specific time span or at a specific time.

   D. **Incorrect:** You cannot configure a Cache object to expire when a registry key is changed.

   E. **Correct:** You can configure a Cache object to expire when a different cached object expires.

Chapter 2: Case Scenario Answers

Case Scenario 1: Providing Consistent Formatting for an External Web Application

1. Use a master page to implement the layout. Use content pages only to add content to the master page.

2. You can use themes and add a .skin file that defines fonts for different controls.

3. If you apply a theme by using the <pages Theme="*themeName*"> element in the Web.config file, it overrides control attributes.

4. To enable users to change colors on a website, use programmatically applied themes and set a session variable or user cookie to remember a user's selection.

Case Scenario 2: Improving the Performance of a Public Website

1. Yes. You can use the Cache object to store a copy of database query results, and then quickly retrieve those results the next time they are required.

2. The database administrator mentioned that you are using SQL Server, so you could configure a dependency on the database table that contains the list of movies.

3. Yes. If you create user controls for cacheable components, such as the portion of the page that displays a list of movies, those user controls can be cached while the rest of the page is dynamically generated.

Chapter 3: Lesson Review Answers

Lesson 1

1. **Correct Answer: C**

   A. **Incorrect:** You cannot respond to the Application_Start event within a webpage.

   B. **Incorrect:** You cannot write code to respond to any event inside the Web.config file.

   C. **Correct:** The Global.asax file allows you to handle special events such as the Application_Start event.

   D. **Incorrect:** These pages represent code-behind files to webpages. You cannot respond to application-level events from a webpage.

2. **Correct Answer: D**

   A. **Incorrect:** Application_Start is called when the application loads. You cannot access the Session object from the Application_Start event handler.

   B. **Incorrect:** Application_End is called when the application shuts down. You cannot access the Session object from the Application_End event handler.

   C. **Incorrect:** Session_Start is called when a user first connects.

   D. **Correct:** The Session_End event handler is called when a user's session times out. However, this event will not fire if the server is shut off unexpectedly or if the SessionState mode is not set to InProc.

3. **Correct Answer: A**

   A. **Correct:** To indicate that a control's default event should cause a postback, you set the AutoPostBack property of the control to true.

   B. **Incorrect:** ASP.NET does not define a method called ForcePostBack.

   C. **Incorrect:** An ASP.NET webpage does not have a property called PostBackAll.

   D. **Incorrect:** The client makes no attempt to communicate with the server for the CheckBox click event until you set the AutoPostBack property to true.

4. **Correct Answer: A**

   A. **Correct:** The PreInit event is where you want to create (and re-create) your dynamically generated controls. This ensures that they will be available for initialization, ViewState connection, and code inside other events such as Load.

   B. **Incorrect:** The Init event is meant to be raised after all controls have been initialized. You can also use this event to initialize additional control properties. Adding a control here will technically work, but it will not follow the prescribed life cycle.

   C. **Incorrect:** Prior to the Load event, ASP.NET ensures that there is an instance of each control and that each control's view state has been connected. Adding a control here will technically work, but it will not follow the prescribed life cycle.

   D. **Incorrect:** The PreRender event is used to make final changes to the page prior to its rendering. If you add your controls here, they will appear on the form. However, user input will not be available during postback, and view state will not work.

Lesson 2

1. **Correct Answer: B**

   A. **Incorrect:** Client-side state management requires the client to transmit the user name and password with each request. It also requires the client to store the information locally, where it might be compromised. This is not a secure solution.

   B. **Correct:** Server-side state management provides better security for confidential information by reducing the number of times the information is transmitted across the network.

2. **Correct Answer: A**

   A. **Correct:** Client-side state management is an excellent choice for storing nonconfidential information. It is much easier to implement than server-side state management when multiple web servers are involved, and it minimizes load on the servers.

   B. **Incorrect:** You could use server-side state management; however, it would require a server-side database to synchronize information among multiple web servers. This would increase the load on your servers.

3. **Correct Answer: A**

   A. **Correct:** View state is the simplest way to store this information. Because it is enabled by default, you might not need to write any code to support state management for your form.

   B. **Incorrect:** You can use control state; however, it requires extra coding and is only necessary if you are creating a control that might be used in a webpage that has view state disabled.

   C. **Incorrect:** You can store the information in hidden fields; however, that requires writing extra code. View state supports your requirements with little or no additional code.

   D. **Incorrect:** Cookies require extra coding and are only required if you need to share information between multiple web forms.

   E. **Incorrect:** You can use query strings to store user preferences. However, you need to update every link on the page that the user might click. This is very time consuming to implement.

4. **Correct Answer: D**

   A. **Incorrect:** View state can only store information for a single web form.

   B. **Incorrect:** Control state can only store information for a single control.

   C. **Incorrect:** Hidden fields can only store information for a single web form.

   D. **Correct:** Unless you specifically narrow the scope, the user's browser submits information stored in a cookie to every page on your site. Therefore, each page processes the user preference information. If you configure the cookie expiration to make it persistent, the browser submits the cookie the next time the user visits your site.

   E. **Incorrect:** You can use query strings to store user preferences. However, you need to update every link on the page that the user might click. This is very time consuming to implement.

5. **Correct Answer: E**

   A. **Incorrect:** View state information is not stored in the URL, and therefore is lost if the URL is bookmarked.

   B. **Incorrect:** Control state information is not stored in the URL, and therefore is lost if the URL is bookmarked.

   C. **Incorrect:** Hidden fields are not stored in the URL, and therefore are lost if the URL is bookmarked.

   D. **Incorrect:** Cookies are not stored in the URL, and therefore are lost if the URL is bookmarked.

   E. **Correct:** Query strings are stored in the URL. Although they are not the easiest type of client-side state management to implement, they are the only technique that allows state management data to be easily bookmarked and sent via email.

Lesson 3

1. **Correct Answer: B**

   A. **Incorrect:** The Session object is user specific and therefore is not available to all users and pages in the site.

   B. **Correct:** The Application object allows you to store data that is scoped at the application level and therefore is available to all users. The Application object never expires, which is not the case with caching.

   C. **Incorrect:** The Cookies collection is client and user specific.

   D. **Incorrect:** The ViewState collection is client and user specific.

2. **Correct Answer: A**

   A. **Correct:** Storing this value in the Session object will prevent the client from tampering with the value. It will also ensure that this user-specific data is only available for the specified session and user.

   B. **Incorrect:** The Application collection represents global data available to all users.

   C. **Incorrect:** Storing authentication information in the user's cookie file exposes the site to a potential security risk.

   D. **Incorrect:** The ViewState is sent to the client and therefore would pose a security risk.

3. **Correct Answers: A and D**

   A. **Correct:** You must manage session state on a central server in this case. StateServer or SqlServer allows you to do so.

   B. **Incorrect:** You cannot set the SessionState mode attribute to InProc, because this would store each user's session on the individual web servers. The load balancer might then route different requests to different servers and thus break your application.

   C. **Incorrect:** Turning sessions off for your application will break the application in this case.

   D. **Correct:** You must manage session state on a central server in this case. StateServer or SqlServer allows you to do so.

Chapter 3: Case Scenario Answers

Case Scenario 1: Selecting the Proper Events to Use

1. You should place the code to dynamically create the controls in the Page_PreInit event handler. After the Page_PreInit event handler has been executed, all dynamically created controls should be instantiated. Following the Page_Init event, all controls on the page should be initialized.

2. You should place the code to set the control properties in the Page_Load event handler. When the Page_Load event handler fires, all controls should already be instantiated. Here you can check whether the page is a postback, and set control properties appropriately. The controls should already have been initialized in the Page_PreInit event.

Case Scenario 2: Remembering User Credentials

1. You should use client-side state management in the form of cookies. You should not, however, store the user's credentials in this cookie (see question 2). Cookies, however, will allow you to identify the user between requests and between sessions, because they can be persisted on the client.

2. First, you should not store the users' actual credentials in the cookie. Instead, you should store a token that proves the user has authenticated. Second, you can require Secure Sockets Layer (SSL) for your web application so that all communications are encrypted. Third, you can narrow the scope of the cookies so that the browser only submits them to the SSL-protected portion of your website. Finally, you should maintain the user's session. However, if you are relying on a cookie, you should ask the user to reauthenticate before doing anything of consequence on the site, such as making a purchase or accessing private information.

3. You should not use state management techniques to store previous orders. Instead, you should retrieve that information directly from the database.

Case Scenario 3: Analyzing Information for Individual Users and for All Users

1. You can use the Application object to log data related to all users. You can update a collection that tracks the number of users currently viewing certain pages in your site. Of course, you would want to periodically reset this collection, because it should be a snapshot of a certain time period.

2. You can use the Session object to track where a user has gone on the site and what navigational path he or she has followed. For each page view, you could add the page that the user visits to a custom collection in the Session object. You can log this information and allow the marketing department to watch and analyze this information to make advertisement decisions.

Chapter 4: Lesson Review Answers

Lesson 1

1. **Correct Answer: C**

   A. **Incorrect:** The correct attribute to indicate that an HTML server control should be run on the server is the runat attribute (not run).

   B. **Incorrect:** Double-clicking an HTML control will not convert it to run on the server. Instead, it will generate a client-side event handler (in JavaScript) for the control.

   C. **Correct:** To convert an HTML element to a server control, you add the runat="server" attribute and value to the element.

   D. **Incorrect:** Visual Studio does not allow you to modify this attribute from the Properties window. You must set this value in Source view.

2. **Correct Answers: A and B**

   A. **Correct:** A single RadioButtonList control can allow users to select one of multiple choices that you define.

   B. **Correct:** You could add a RadioButton control for each choice: Small, Medium, and Large. To ensure that the user can only select one at a time, you would need to set the GroupName property of all controls to the same value. The specific value does not matter.

   C. **Incorrect:** A CheckBoxList control allows users to select as many or as few of a list of options as necessary. In this scenario, you need users to select exactly one choice, which is what radio buttons should be used for.

   D. **Incorrect:** The CheckBox control allows users to select multiple choices. It does not have a GroupName property like the RadioButton control because CheckBox controls always function separately from each other.

3. **Correct Answers: A and D**

   A. **Correct:** If you need to handle clicks for multiple buttons with a single method, the Button.Command event is the most convenient way to do it. You could also handle Button.Click, but it would require extra code to determine which button had been clicked.

   B. **Incorrect:** The Button.Load event fires when the page is initially loaded, not when the button is clicked.

   C. **Incorrect:** Button.CommandName must be unique for different controls because you will use this value to determine which button was clicked.

   D. **Correct:** The value you set Button.CommandName to is available in the ComandEventArgs. CommandName parameter in the Button.Command event handler. You can use this value to determine which button the user pressed.

Lesson 2

1. **Correct Answer: B**

   A. **Incorrect:** Unless you intend to use the Table control on the server, you should consider using a standard HTML table.

   B. **Correct:** If you need to populate an HTML table with data generated at run time, you should use the Table server control.

   C. **Incorrect:** In this case, a standard HTML table will work because the data is static. No server-side processing is required.

   D. **Incorrect:** You should not use tables for layout. Instead, use <div> and <span> tags.

2. **Correct Answer: D**

   A. **Incorrect:** Although you could employ this method, it could be difficult to execute and certainly is not the best way to accomplish this task.

   B. **Incorrect:** The product lines are not rectangular, so this would not be an option.

   C. **Incorrect:** The MultiView control only shows one View at a time, so this would not be a solution.

   D. **Correct:** The ImageMap control provides the ability to define hot spot areas, and the PostBackValue can be used to determine the area that was clicked.

3. **Correct Answer: C**

   A. **Incorrect:** The View control requires a MultiView control to work properly. Even if you did include a MultiView control, this would not be the easiest solution to the problem.

   B. **Incorrect:** The TextBox control will not provide multiple-page data collection.

   C. **Correct:** The Wizard control will solve this issue by providing an easy-to-implement solution for collecting multiple pages of data from users.

   D. **Incorrect:** The Panel control is a useful container for storing other controls. However, it does not provide a mechanism for developing pages that span multiple controls.

Chapter 4: Case Scenario Answers

Case Scenario 1: Determining the Type of Controls to Use

- For this application, consider using web server controls. These controls provide a more consistent programming model for developers and often provide a better user experience for users.
  - Use TextBox controls to capture the customer names and addresses. The text associated with these controls can be simple HTML text.
  - Use a CheckBox control for the active indicator.
  - Use multiple CheckBox controls for the vertical market categories. This allows the user to select multiple categories.
  - Use RadioButton controls to allow the user to select a single, mutually exclusive quantity of computers.

Case Scenario 2: Determining How to Prompt for Data

- You could divide the prompts by category and create a separate webpage for each category. This solution splits your code and data over several pages and can add to the overall complexity of the website.

  Alternatively, you could implement a solution that uses the MultiView control and create a separate View for each category. The MultiView and View controls do not have a user interface, so you have complete flexibility with regard to the graphical interface of the webpage.

  As a third alternative, you could implement the Wizard control and create a WizardStep control for each category. The Wizard contains the behavior for moving between steps and offers a more complete solution.

Case Scenario 3: Implementing a Calendar Solution

1. This solution can use the Calendar control in every situation in which the user must enter a date or dates, and in every situation in which a schedule is being displayed to a user. The following list describes some of the situations in which you can use the Calendar control:

   - To prompt for a class start date

   - To prompt for a class end date

   - To display a training provider's class schedule

   - To display a contractor's schedule

2. Although you could use the Table control in these situations, you would need to write lots of code to get the functionality that the Calendar control provides natively, so the Calendar control is the best solution.

Chapter 5: Lesson Review Answers

Lesson 1

1. **Correct Answer: C**

   A. **Incorrect:** The RegularExpressionValidator control does string pattern matching. It should not be used to look up database values.

   B. **Incorrect:** The RangeValidator control validates data in a specified range. In addition, the control does not define a DbLookup operation.

   C. **Correct:** The CustomValidator control can be used to call server-side code to validate the vendor ID.

   D. **Incorrect:** The CompareValidator control does not define a feature as described. It is used to compare two values.

2. **Correct Answer: A**

   A. Correct: You need to test the IsValid property of the webpage before executing code in your event handler methods.

   B. Incorrect: The IsValid property is not set yet; exiting the Load event handler method still allows the event handler methods to execute.

   C. Incorrect: Although this will appear to correct the problem, a malicious user could disable client-side validation, and the server-side problem would still exist.

   D. Incorrect: This is the default setting and does not correct the problem.

3. **Correct Answer: B**

   A. Incorrect: The Text property should be an asterisk and the ErrorMessage property should be set to the detailed error message.

   B. Correct: Setting the Text property to an asterisk places the asterisk next to the control, and setting the ErrorMessage property to the detailed error message causes the detailed errors to be placed into the ValidationSummary control at the top of the webpage.

   C. Incorrect: The Text property should be an asterisk, and the ErrorMessage property should be the detailed error message.

   D. Incorrect: The Text property should be an asterisk, and the ErrorMessage property should be the detailed error message.

Lesson 2

1. **Correct Answer: C**

   A. Incorrect: The Redirect method is available on the HttpResponse class, and it causes a round trip back to the client.

   B. Incorrect: The MapPath method returns the physical path of a specific virtual path.

   C. Correct: The Page.Server.Transfer method transfers the page processing to another page without calling back to the client.

   D. Incorrect: The UrlDecode method decodes a string that was encoded before being transmitted over HTTP.

2. **Correct Answer: D**

   A. Incorrect: The Menu control requires a data source.

   B. Incorrect: The TreeView control requires a data source.

   C. Incorrect: The SiteMapDataSource control is a data source and does not have a visual display for a user.

   D. Correct: The SiteMapPath control will automatically pick up a site map file and display its contents to a user.

3. **Correct Answer: C**

   A. **Incorrect:** The SiteMapPath control connects to the site map file and displays the user's current, breadcrumb-trail navigation path.

   B. **Incorrect:** The SiteMapDataSource control is used to provide data binding from a site map file to a navigation control.

   C. **Correct:** The SiteMap class will allow you to load the site map file and work with the data contained inside.

   D. **Incorrect:** The HttpServerUtility class does not provide such functionality.

Lesson 3

1. **Correct Answers: A, B, and C**

   A. **Correct:** A user control can be used as a Web Part by placing it into a Web Part zone.

   B. **Correct:** ASP.NET will automatically define a Web Part when you place a standard control, such as a Label, into a Web Part zone.

   C. **Correct:** You can create Web Parts by defining custom controls based on the WebPart class.

   D. **Incorrect:** A master page defines a common interface for your application and is not used as a Web Part.

2. **Correct Answers: B and D**

   A. **Incorrect:** The LayoutEditorPart control enables users to change the chrome state and zone of a control. It does not provide the ability to change the Web Part's title.

   B. **Correct:** You must add an EditorZone container to the webpage. Then add an AppearanceEditorPart control to the EditorZone.

   C. **Incorrect:** The CatalogZone control enables users to add new Web Parts to a page, but it does not enable them to change Web Part titles.

   D. **Correct:** The AppearanceEditorPart control enables users to set the titles of Web Parts.

3. **Correct Answers: B and C**

   A. **Incorrect:** The LayoutEditorPart control enables a user to change the chrome state and zone of a control. It does not provide the ability to add Web Parts.

   B. **Correct:** The DeclarativeCatalogPart control enables a user to add Web Parts when the page is in catalog mode.

   C. **Correct:** The CatalogZone container is required to hold the DeclarativeCatalogPart control, which enables a user to add Web Parts.

   D. **Incorrect:** The AppearanceEditorPart control enables the user to edit the appearance of existing Web Parts, but it does not enable a user to add new Web Parts.

4. **Correct Answer: B**

   A. Incorrect: The ConnectionConsumer attribute should be applied to the method that receives the provider Web Part's data.

   B. Correct: You should apply the ConnectionProvider attribute to a public method to allow consumers to access the method.

   C. Incorrect: You cannot use properties for connections between Web Parts.

   D. Incorrect: You cannot use properties for connections between Web Parts.

Chapter 5: Case Scenario Answers

Case Scenario 1: Determining the Proper Validation Controls to Implement on a User Name

1. The RequiredFieldValidator control ensures that data has been entered. The RegularExpressionValidator can be used, and the ValidationExpression can be set to Internet Email Address.

2. Use a RequiredFieldValidator control to ensure that data has been entered. Use a CustomValidator control, and write code to check for the character types and length as specified by the requirements, or use a RegularExpressionValidator control with an appropriate regular expression.

3. Use a RequiredFieldValidator control to ensure that data has been entered. Optionally, use a RegularExpressionValidator control to verify that the user enters the account number in the correct format on the client. Use a CustomValidator control, and write code to the database to determine whether the account number is correct.

Case Scenario 2: Implementing a Site Map

- You can use the TreeView control with the SiteMapDataSource control, and a SiteMapPath control to display the breadcrumb path.

Case Scenario 3: Meeting Customization Requirements for an Internal Insurance Application

1. You can use a combination of user profiles and customizable Web Parts to meet the requirements.

2. Connected Web Parts can provide what you need. You can have a provider Web Part that enables the Underwriter to choose a claim type, and consumer Web Parts that retrieve the currently selected claim type and display related statistics.

Chapter 6: Lesson Review Answers

Lesson 1

1. **Correct Answers: B and C**

   A. **Incorrect:** The language abbreviation must come before the .resx extension.

   B. **Correct:** The default language extension should not have a language extension. This way, both English users and all others will be given the settings in this file.

   C. **Correct:** To create a German language resource file, you add the language extension (de) between the file name and the .resx extension.

   D. **Incorrect:** You do not need to add a language-specific resource file for the default language. In addition, this site should have a default resource file specified.

2. **Correct Answers: B and C**

   A. **Incorrect:** The Page.Culture property is used to define cultural formatting (such as how numbers are formatted), not language.

   B. **Correct:** The Page.UICulture property is used to define the language for the page. ASP.NET will load the appropriate resource file based on this setting.

   C. **Correct:** You should override the page's InitializeCulture method to set the Page.UICulture property.

   D. **Incorrect:** The Page.ReadStringResource method is not related to defining a language.

3. **Correct Answer: A**

   A. **Correct:** You do not need to reference the class / file name as Resources:<filename> when explicitly binding to a local resource.

   B. **Incorrect:** This syntax is not valid for local resources. You would use the class / file name as Resources:<filename> when explicitly binding to a global resource.

   C. **Incorrect:** The resource file / class name should come before the resource name when using explicit localization in markup.

   D. **Incorrect:** The resource file / class name should come before the resource name when using explicit localization in markup. In addition, you only reference an actual file / class name when using global resources.

4. **Correct Answer: A**

   A. **Correct:** ASP.NET will automatically create a strongly typed object for your global resources. This object can be referenced as Resources.ResourceFileName.Resource (or Resources.Resource.Login in this case).

   B. **Incorrect:** You can create global resources by using strings. However, you need to call the GetGlobalResourceObject method to load these.

   C. **Incorrect:** You can create global resources by using strings. However, you need to call the GetGlobalResourceObject method to load these.

   D. **Incorrect:** ASP.NET does not create strongly typed properties inside the Resources class. Instead, you must use the Resources.Resource object.

Lesson 2

1. **Correct Answers: B and C**

   A. **Incorrect:** ASP.NET uses the Image.AccessKey parameter to provide a keyboard shortcut for an image.

   B. **Correct:** ASP.NET uses the Image.AlternateText parameter to create the alternative text for an image. Screen readers typically describe images by using the alternative text.

   C. **Correct:** DescriptionUrl links to an HTML page that provides a long description of an image. ASP.NET uses this link to create the longdesc HTML attribute.

   D. **Incorrect:** ToolTip is not related to accessibility. ToolTip defines data that Internet Explorer displays when you point to an image.

2. **Correct Answers: A and C**

   A. **Correct:** Controls such as Image provide properties that you can use to provide a description for those who cannot see the image.

   B. **Incorrect:** ASP.NET controls are not displayed in high contrast by default. However, they are designed to support high-contrast mode by default.

   C. **Correct:** Controls such as CreateUserWizard, Menu, SiteMapPath, TreeView, and Wizard support skipping links.

   D. **Incorrect:** ASP.NET controls do not display text in large font sizes by default. However, they are designed to support browsers configured to display large font sizes.

3. **Correct Answers: A, B, and D**

   A. **Correct:** Visual Studio can automatically test web applications for compliance with WCAG Priority 1 guidelines.

   B. **Correct:** Visual Studio can automatically test web applications for compliance with WCAG Priority 2 guidelines.

   C. **Incorrect:** ADA, the Americans with Disabilities Act, provides accessibility guidelines for facilities, transportation, and more. However, it does not provide web application accessibility guidelines.

   D. **Correct:** Visual Studio can automatically test web applications for compliance with Section 508 guidelines.

Chapter 6: Case Scenario Answers

Case Scenario 1: Upgrading an Application for Multiple Languages

1. You can use local and global resources to provide translations for your website. Use local resources to provide page-specific translations, and use global resources to provide phrases that are used on multiple pages.

2. Translators need to update the local and global resource files. These are standard XML files, so any XML editor can be used. You can also create an application to facilitate the translations.

3. Web browsers often are configured for language preferences. ASP.NET can automatically detect this preference and use the preferred language if the resource is available. Additionally, you should allow a user to specify a language.

4. Specific cultures distinguish both languages and regional requirements, as opposed to neutral cultures, which only distinguish the language.

Case Scenario 2: Making a Web Application Accessible

1. Visual Studio includes tools to test individual web pages. Additionally, you can configure Visual Studio to automatically test an entire web application for Section 508 compliance during the build process.

2. Accessible applications can be used with alternative input and display devices.

3. No, accessible applications do not require users with traditional input and display devices to make any sacrifices. Most accessibility features take the form of hidden textual descriptions and access keys, which users who do not need them will probably not notice.

4. You need to provide textual descriptions for all visual elements, such as forms, tables, and images. Additionally, you should make the web application usable without a mouse.

Chapter 7: Lesson Review Answers

Lesson 1

1. **Correct Answers: B and D**

   A. Incorrect: An ASPX page is a webpage in ASP.NET and not a user control. In addition, you use the @Register directive to register a user control on a page, not to create one.

   B. Correct: A user control's associated code should inherit from the UserControl class.

   C. Incorrect: A user control should inherit from the UserControl class. A webpage inherits from the Page class.

   D. Correct: An ASCX file with the @Control directive indicates to ASP.NET that the markup contained in the file is a user control.

2. **Correct Answers: B and D**

   A. Incorrect: This will not add the controls to the form. User controls must be added to a form to operate.

   B. Correct: Each control must be added to the form.

   C. Incorrect: The form object does not support a LoadControl method.

   D. Correct: You can load a user control dynamically by using the LoadControl method of the page object.

3. **Correct Answer: C**

   A. Incorrect: Although you could use this method, it would be difficult to do and certainly is not the best way to accomplish this task.

   B. Incorrect: Although you could use this method, it would be difficult to do and certainly is not the best way to accomplish this task.

   C. Correct: The templated user control exposes the data to the webpage designer, who can then specify the format of the data in a template.

   D. Incorrect: This user control does not natively expose the style property, and if you choose to expose the property, you can only set an overall format for the user control, not a format for each of the data elements that is being exposed.

4. **Correct Answer: B**

   A. Incorrect: This will not allow a user to read and modify the user control's TextBox control's Text properties as required.

   B. Correct: This will ensure that a user is able to read and modify the values stored in the TextBox control.

   C. Incorrect: Controls inside a user control are, by default, private to the user control.

   D. Incorrect: This will not allow a user to read and modify the user control's TextBox control's Text properties as required.

Lesson 2

1. **Correct Answers: B and C**

   A. Incorrect: Inheriting directly from WebControl will not allow you to extend the ASP.NET Button control.

   B. Correct: You inherit directly from a base control such as Button to extend its features.

   C. Correct: You add your HTML to the output for the control by using the Render method. You also must call the base render method to ensure that the control's base rendering gets sent to the page.

   D. Incorrect: The RenderChildren method is used to render multiple child controls of your custom web server control.

2. **Correct Answers: B and D**

   A. Incorrect: There is no need to set a reference to this namespace.

   B. Correct: This namespace is required for the ToolboxBitmap class.

   C. Incorrect: The ToolboxData attribute is used to influence the markup when your control is added to the page.

   D. Correct: The ToolboxBitmap attribute allows you to define an image for your custom control inside the Toolbox.

3. **Correct Answer: D**

   A. **Incorrect:** This method does not send output to the browser.

   B. **Incorrect:** This method does not send output to the browser.

   C. **Incorrect:** This method does not send output to the browser.

   D. **Correct:** The Render method must be overridden, and you must provide code to display your control.

4. **Correct Answer: A**

   A. **Correct:** The CreateChildControls method must be overridden with code to create the child controls and set their properties.

   B. **Incorrect:** This method is not used for creating child control properties.

   C. **Incorrect:** This method is not used for creating child control properties.

   D. **Incorrect:** This method is not used for creating child control properties.

Chapter 7: Case Scenario Answers

Case Scenario 1: Sharing Controls Between Applications

1. You should consider developing a custom web server control. You should also make this a composite control, because these types of controls can easily contain other controls and the layout of the control is always consistent.

2. You would exclude creating a user control because it would not be reusable across websites. A templated control is ruled out, because the goal is to keep the layout of the control consistent.

Case Scenario 2: Providing Layout Flexibility

1. You should consider creating a user control, because this control is only within one site. This can provide easier development and additional flexibility in change and deployment.

2. You should consider creating the control as a templated control. This will allow the users of the control to manage the many layouts required by the site.

3. A user control inherits from the System.Web.UI.UserControl class.

Chapter 8: Lesson Review Answers

Lesson 1

1.   **Correct Answer: C**

   A. **Incorrect:** This will turn on debugging for the entire site.

   B. **Incorrect:** Setting debug to false inside the compilation element of Web.config will turn off debugging for the entire site.

   C. **Correct:** Setting the debug attribute of the @ Page directive to true will turn on debugging just for the selected page.

   D. **Incorrect:** This will turn off debugging for the selected page.

2.   **Correct Answers: B and D**

   A. **Incorrect:** This action is used to define error-specific pages (not a sitewide default error page).

   B. **Correct:** The defaultRedirect attribute of the customErrors element will set a default sitewide error page.

   C. **Incorrect:** You use statusCode to define an attribute of the error element to set specific error pages based on HTTP status codes.

   D. **Correct:** You can use the aspxerrorpath query string parameter to retrieve the requested page to display on the default error page.

3.   **Correct Answers: B and C**

   A. **Incorrect:** You need to run the Remote Debugging Monitor on the server, not the debug host computer.

   B. **Correct:** Running the Remote Debugging Monitor on the server allows remote debugging for a specified user with the appropriate rights.

   C. **Correct:** You need to attach to the process on the server that is hosting the application.

   D. **Incorrect:** Attaching to the browser's process is valid only if you are debugging client-side script. To debug the server-side code, you need to attach to the server process running your application.

Lesson 2

1.   **Correct Answer: A**

   A. **Correct:** You can use ASP.NET tracing to view page life-cycle timings.

   B. **Incorrect:** This might get the results, but it is a time-consuming effort and will not be as accurate or as easy to maintain.

   C. **Incorrect:** This attribute does not exist in the Web.config file.

   D. **Incorrect:** There is no such setting in the website properties.

2. **Correct Answer: D**

   A. **Incorrect:** In this option, tracing is disabled. The localOnly attribute is also set wrong.

   B. **Incorrect:** This option has the wrong values for pageOutput and localOnly.

   C. **Incorrect:** This option has the wrong value for mostRecent.

   D. **Correct:** This option matches the requirements defined in the question.

3. **Correct Answer: C**

   A. **Incorrect:** The Control Tree section shows information about each control on the webpage, but not the posted data.

   B. **Incorrect:** The Headers Collection section does not contain the posted data.

   C. **Correct:** The Form Collection section contains the posted data.

   D. **Incorrect:** The Server Variables section does not contain the posted data.

4. **Correct Answer: D**

   A. **Incorrect:** This is a base web event class that includes request data.

   B. **Incorrect:** This is a base web event class for logging audit events.

   C. **Incorrect:** This class sends an event when the website starts, stops, or processes another significant event.

   D. **Correct:** This class sends an event when a user successfully authenticates with the website.

Lesson 3

1. **Correct Answer: A**

   A. **Correct:** Any installation changes you make should occur in the Install phase.

   B. **Incorrect:** If you can divide an aspect of setup into separate installation and commit phases, you should do so. However, registry entries are simple changes that can be made entirely in the Install phase.

   C. **Incorrect:** The Rollback phase is used to remove changes made during the Install phase if setup is cancelled or otherwise fails.

   D. **Incorrect:** The Uninstall phase is called when a user removes an application from Add Or Remove Programs.

2. **Correct Answer: C and D**

   A. **Incorrect:** You would perform the initial change in the Install phase and record the previous value so that it could be removed later. However, you do not undo your registry modification in this phase.

   B. **Incorrect:** The Commit phase finalizes setup changes and should not be used for undoing setup modifications.

   C. **Correct:** The Rollback phase is used to remove changes made during the Install phase if setup is cancelled or otherwise fails. Therefore, you should undo your registry modification here if the change has already taken place.

   D. **Correct:** The Uninstall phase is called when a user removes an application with Add Or Remove Programs. Therefore, you should undo your registry modification here.

3. **Correct Answer: C**

   A. **Incorrect:** Setup projects are used to deploy Windows Forms applications, not websites.

   B. **Incorrect:** Web Setup Projects package websites in executable setups and Windows Installer files. You can use a Web Setup Project to deploy a website to a web server. However, it does not assist the development process by detecting versioning conflicts.

   C. **Correct:** The Copy Web tool detects when a version of a file has been modified on the web server after it is synchronized with the local copy of a file. Therefore, it can detect versioning conflicts when multiple developers work on a single site.

   D. **Incorrect:** The Publish Web Site tool is used to precompile and deploy websites. It does not have the ability to detect versioning conflicts.

4. **Correct Answer: D**

   A. **Incorrect:** Setup Projects are used to deploy Windows Forms applications, not websites.

   B. **Incorrect:** Web Setup Projects package websites in executable setups and Windows Installer files. You can use a Web Setup Project to deploy a website to a web server; however, it does not precompile the website.

   C. **Incorrect:** The Copy Web tool detects when a version of a file has been modified on the web server after it was synchronized with the local copy of a file. It does not enable you to precompile the website, however.

   D. **Correct:** The Publish Web Site tool is used to precompile and deploy websites. Precompiling reduces the delay when the first user to visit the website requests a webpage, improving initial responsiveness of a site.

Chapter 8: Case Scenario Answers

Case Scenario 1: Debugging

1. Edit the Web.config file and set debug to false for the compilation element.

2. Create a default error page. Add a customErrors element to the Web.config file. Set the defaultRedirect attribute to the name of the default error page.

3. Set the mode attribute of the customErrors element to RemoteOnly.

4. Run the Remote Debugging tool (msvsmon.exe) on the staging server. Connect to the ASP.NET process on the staging server from Visual Studio.

5. You can use Web.config transformations (if you use the Publish Web dialog box) or Web.config replacements (if you use a Web Deployment Project) to automatically update the development environment's Web.config file for production use.

Case Scenario 2: Troubleshooting

1. Turn tracing on for the site by setting the enabled attribute of the trace element to true inside the Web.config file. In addition, set the localOnly attribute to true to enable tracing only for local users.

   Note that you cannot set tracing on at the page level in this scenario. Doing so will override any settings in the Web.config file and output trace information on the page for any users who display the page.

2. Add child rule elements to the <healthMonitoring> element in the Web.config file. Also set the <healthMonitoring> element's enabled attribute to true.

Case Scenario 3: Deploying a Website

1. You can use either the Copy Web tool or the Publish Web Site tool to update the staging server. However, the Copy Web tool is more bandwidth-efficient because it only copies changed files.

2. The Publish Web Site tool is the best tool for the quality assurance people to use to update the production web server. It enables the site to be precompiled, which can improve performance.

Chapter 9: Lesson Review Answers

Lesson 1

1. **Correct Answers: A and C**

   A. **Correct:** The UpdatePanel control will enable the portion contained inside the panel to update independently of the rest of the page.

   B. **Incorrect:** The AsyncPostBackTrigger control is used to allow a control outside the UpdatePanel to trigger an update to the UpdatePanel. This is not a requirement of this scenario.

   C. **Correct:** Every AJAX page must have a ScriptManager control to manage the JavaScript files sent to the client and the communication between client and server.

   D. **Incorrect:** The ScriptManagerProxy control is used for creating AJAX-enabled child pages of a master page or user controls. Neither is a requirement of this scenario.

2. **Correct Answers: A, B, and D**

   A. **Correct:** An UpdatePanel control can be used to update only the portion of the page.

   B. **Correct:** A Timer control can be used to retrieve updates from the server on a periodic basis.

   C. **Incorrect:** Using a ScriptManager control on a user control prevents the user control from being added to a page that already contains a ScriptManager control.

   D. **Correct:** The ScriptManagerProxy control is used to avoid conflict with a ScriptManager control that is already on a containing page.

3. **Correct Answer: D**

   A. Incorrect: The UpdatePanel control does not have an AsyncPostBackTrigger attribute.

   B. Incorrect: A Button control does not have an AsyncPostBackTrigger attribute.

   C. Incorrect: An AsyncPostBackTrigger control should be added to the Triggers collection, and not the other way around.

   D. Correct: An AsyncPostBackTrigger control should be added to the Triggers collection of the UpdatePanel. You then set the ControlID property to the Button control's ID.

4. **Correct Answer: B**

   A. Incorrect: A nested UpdatePanel control will be shown to the user at all times. It will not be simply a part of the progress indicator.

   B. Correct: An UpdateProgress control is used to display text or graphics during a partial-page update. The DisplayAfter attribute controls how long the page waits from the start of the request until it displays the progress indicator. If the request returns during this time, the progress indicator is not shown.

   C. Incorrect: A ProgressBar is a Windows (not web) control.

   D. Incorrect: You cannot set two controls to have the same ID on the page. This will cause an error. In addition, the UpdatePanel does not have an Interval property.

Lesson 2

1. **Correct Answer: D**

   A. Incorrect: You derive from the Sys.UI.Control class to create an AJAX UI control (not a DOM extension).

   B. Incorrect: This call simply indicates that you intend to implement the IDisposable interface. It does not indicate proper inheritance for extending a DOM element.

   C. Incorrect: This call creates your class without inheritance. To extend a DOM element, you should inherit from Sys.UI.Behavior.

   D. Correct: This call creates a control that extends a DOM element.

2. **Correct Answer: B**

   A. Incorrect: The endRequest event fires when the postback has completed (and is over).

   B. Correct: The pageLoading event fires when the postback first comes back from the server.

   C. Incorrect: The pageLoaded event fires when the postback comes back from the server and the content has been updated in the browser (after pageLoading).

   D. Incorrect: The beginRequest event fires as the postback is being sent to the server.

3. **Correct Answer: C**

   A. Incorrect: You need a ScriptManager control on the page to use the Microsoft AJAX Library. In addition, your scripts must be registered with the ScriptManager control.

   B. Incorrect: You must explicitly register your .js files with the ScriptManager.

C. Correct: To use a .js file that targets the Microsoft AJAX Library, you set a reference to it inside a ScriptManager control. You do so through the <asp:ScriptReference /> element.

D. Incorrect: The ScriptReference class is used from a custom control (and not a page) to reference and embed a .js file.

4. **Correct Answers: B and D**

A. Incorrect: A behavior is meant to extend multiple controls. Therefore, it is not specific to a single control as this would imply.

B. Correct: A behavior is implemented by inheriting the ExtenderControl class.

C. Incorrect: The IScriptControl interface is implemented for custom UI controls. It is not used for a behavior control.

D. Correct: The TargetControlType attribute is used by a behavior control to allow users to attach a behavior to a control.

Lesson 3

1. **Correct Answers: B and D**

A. Incorrect: The example does not tell you the ID of the <h2> tag. Also, the .fadeIn() method does not take numeric values.

B. Correct: You can use the :first keyword to indicate the first instance of a tag. You can then pass the name "slow" to the .fadeIn() method to handle the animation.

C. Incorrect: This dot notation is used for selecting elements based on cascading style sheet class names.

D. Incorrect: The .fadeIn() method can also take numeric values indicating the duration (in milliseconds) of the fade.

2. **Correct Answers: A and B**

A. Correct: You can use the .bind() method to bind code to a selected element's event.

B. Correct: The .ready() event indicates the DOM has been loaded.

C. Incorrect: The .load() event indicates that an element (and not the DOM) has been loaded.

D. Incorrect: The .add function allows you to add elements to found items. This would not bind an event.

3. **Correct Answer: A**

A. Correct: This code looks up the city code by state, by using the ASPX page.

B. Incorrect: This code uses an ASMX service (not the page). It also uses the state variable and not the data variable for the results.

C Incorrect: This code appends the state name to the URL rather than passing this value through the data setting.

D Incorrect: This code does not correctly pass the data setting. It is missing single quotes and braces.

4. **Correct Answer: D**

   A. **Incorrect:** The $.post() method will send an HTTP POST request to the server.

   B. **Incorrect:** The $.getScript() method is used to load a JavaScript file.

   C. **Incorrect:** The $.getJSON() method is used to get a JSON formatted message from the server.

   D. **Correct:** The $.get() method sends an HTTP GET request to the server to retrieve HTML, text, XML, script, and JSON files.

Chapter 9: Case Scenario Answers

Case Scenario 1: Using the ASP.NET AJAX Extensions

1. The UpdatePanel control will allow you to encapsulate the grid control and execute its updates independent of the rest of the page. This will speed up these updates and keep the user's context within the page.

2. You must add a ScriptManager control to the page to use ASP.NET AJAX.

3. The UpdateProgress control can be used to notify the user as to the progress of the partial-page update.

Case Scenario 2: Using the Microsoft AJAX Library

1. The clock should be implemented as a Sys.UI.Control class so that it can be used across pages of the site and provide a UI for a single control. The highlight object should be written as a Sys.UI.Behavior class because it extends the behavior of multiple controls. The validation logic does not have a UI. Therefore, you can implement it as a Sys.Component class.

2. The highlight control should be implemented as a custom server control. if you do so, it would inherit the ExtenderControl class. You could also consider wrapping the clock control as a custom server control. If you do, it would inherit from a control such as the Label control (or similar). You would also implement the IScriptControl interface.

Case Scenario 3: Using jQuery

1. To bind to the click event for the image control, you should find it by ID and then create a function bound to the click event, as in $("#ImageBike").click(function (){... . To ensure that the DOM has been loaded, wrap your code inside the document's ready event, as in $(document).ready(function() {... . You can use the event.pageX and event.pageY parameters inside the click event to determine the location of the mouse click. The following shows an example of using these methods:

```
$("#ImageBike").click(function (ev) {
    alert("x:" + ev.pageX + ", y:" + ev.pageY);
});
```

2. You can use the $.ajax() jQuery method to call the web service. You would set the dataType to JSON, type to POST, and pass the url and data parameters to the service. You should ensure that the web service has the System.Web.Script.Services.ScriptService attribute so it can be called from jQuery.

3. You have many options here, including .show(), .animate(), .slideDown(), and .fadeIn().

Chapter 10: Lesson Review Answers

Lesson 1

1. Correct Answer: C

   A. **Incorrect:** You need to capture the request for the custom MIME type within your application. The IPartitionResolver interface has nothing to do with that process.

   B. **Incorrect:** An HTTP module will respond to all requests sent to the application for application events to which you subscribe. In this scenario, you need only respond to requests based on the file type, .docx.

   C. **Correct:** You create a custom HTTP handler to respond to specific file types such as .docx.

   D. **Incorrect:** This is a factory class. It is used to create classes that dynamically manufacture new instances of classes that implement the IHttpHandler interface.

2. Correct Answers: B and D

   A. **Incorrect:** You use the <httpHandlers/> section when configuring an HTTP handler to work with IIS 6.0 or the classic mode of IIS 7.0.

   B. **Correct:** You use the <handlers/> section when configuring an HTTP handler to work with IIS 7.0 running in integrated mode.

   C. **Incorrect:** You add an <httpHandlers/> section to the <system.Web/> section when configuring an HTTP handler to work with IIS 6.0 or the classic mode of IIS 7.0.

   D. **Correct:** You add a <handlers/> section to the <system.WebServer/> section when configuring an HTTP handler to work with IIS 7.0 running in integrated mode.

3. Correct Answers: B and D

   A. **Incorrect:** The IHttpHandler interface is used to create HTTP handlers. In this case, you need an HTTP module to handle each request for the application.

   B. **Correct:** You implement the IHttpModule.Init method to indicate which application events to intercept.

   C. **Incorrect:** The ProcessRequest method is used to send a response for an HTTP handler. In this case, an HTTP module is required.

   D. **Correct:** You implement the IHttpModule interface to create an HTTP module for handling application events for each request.

Lesson 2

1. **Correct Answer: B**

   A. **Incorrect:** The WebServiceAttribute class is used to mark a class as a web service. It does not provide a base class and does not allow for access to ASP.NET features.

   B. **Correct:** The WebService class is a base class that will allow your web service to have access to session state and more.

   C. **Incorrect:** The WebMethodAttribute class is used to tag public methods as web services.

   D. **Incorrect:** To get easy access to the ASP.NET objects, you should inherit from WebService. This will give you access similar to the access you get when inheriting from the Page object for webpages.

2. **Correct Answers: B and D**

   A. **Incorrect:** The Add Reference dialog box is used for referencing DLL files.

   B. **Correct:** The Add Web Reference dialog box will find the web service and its description and generate a proxy for use by your website.

   C. **Incorrect:** To call a web service, you simply call the generated proxy class.

   D. **Correct:** The proxy class will provide access to the web service.

3. **Correct Answer: C**

   A. **Incorrect:** Windows Basic would send unencrypted passwords over the Internet. This would invite tampering.

   B. **Incorrect:** Windows Digest works only with systems based on Windows.

   C. **Correct:** Client certificates can be secured and verified by a third party.

   D. **Incorrect:** A custom SOAP header might be a viable option. However, it is not, by default, verifiable as trusted.

4. **Correct Answers: A, B, C, and D**

   A. **Correct:** The ScriptService class indicates that the web service can be called from client script.

   B. **Correct:** You write client-side JavaScript to call the service proxy created by the ScriptManager class, which in turn calls your service directly.

   C. **Correct:** You set a reference to the ASMX service from the ScriptManager. This tells the ScriptManager to generate a client proxy for calling the web service.

   D. **Correct:** If you intend to use ASP.NET AJAX for calling a web service from client script, both the client and the service must be in the same domain.

Lesson 3

1. **Correct Answer: B**

   A. **Incorrect:** The WCF Service library creates a DLL for your service. You can still reference this from a website and therefore host in IIS. However, you are not taking advantage of the ASP.NET programming model in this case.

   B. **Correct:** A WCF service application is an ASP.NET website that is set up to define and expose WCF services.

   C. **Incorrect:** The ASP.NET Web Service application project is used for creating XML web services with ASP.NET (and not WCF services).

   D. **Incorrect:** A Windows Service application is used to create a Windows service (and not a WCF service). A Windows service can, however, host a WCF service outside of IIS.

2. **Correct Answers: A and D**

   A. **Correct:** The DataContract attribute class indicates that your class can be serialized with WCF.

   B. **Incorrect:** ServiceContract is used to define a WCF service class.

   C. **Incorrect:** OperationContract is used to define a service method.

   D. **Correct:** The DataMember attribute indicates public members that should be serialized as part of the DataContract.

3. **Correct Answers: A and C**

   A. **Correct:** You create a WCF data service by inheriting from DataService.

   B. **Incorrect:** The DataContract class is used to indicate a class that can be serialized to work with WCF.

   C. **Correct:** You set access rules to govern how your data is used inside the InitializeService method of the data service.

   D. **Incorrect:** The Init method is applicable to HTTP modules that implement IHttpModule (and not data services).

4. **Correct Answers: B, C, and D**

   A. **Incorrect:** A web reference is used for XML web services (and not WCF services).

   B. **Correct:** A service reference will generate a proxy to call the data service.

   C. **Correct:** You pass a URI object as a parameter to the data service proxy. This URI should point to your service.

   D. **Correct:** The System.Data.Services.Client namespace includes classes such as DataServiceQuery that are used to access the data exposed by the service.

Chapter 10: Case Scenario Answers

Case Scenario 1: Working with HTTP Requests

1. You should create an HTTP handler. This class would implement the IHttpHandler interface, which includes the ProcessRequest method. You would add code to the ProcessRequest method to generate the XPS document and transmit it as part of the response. You would then register the handler in the Web.config file to indicate that it should be called for all requests made for files of type XPS.

2. You should implement the custom security and logging feature inside an HTTP module. This module would be called for all requests made to the site. You would register application events inside the module's Init event. You would then register the module in the Web.config file.

Case Scenario 2: Selecting a Service Model

1. Both ASMX and WCF services can be configured to work with this scenario. The current requirements do not dictate that you need the features of WCF (such as multiple endpoints for communicating across multiple channels). Therefore, you might lean toward building these services with ASMX. Of course, you can also add WCF services to the same site.

2. All access to the services is done over the web. In addition, the application would benefit greatly from the scalability of IIS, the caching in ASP.NET, session state management, and more. Therefore, you should consider hosting the services in IIS.

3. You should consider exposing this data as WCF Data Services. This will ensure that partners are able to easily work with this data with a wide variety of clients.

4. The user information can be stored by using ASP.NET sessions (in memory, in a proxy caching server, or inside a Microsoft SQL Server database).

Chapter 11: Lesson Review Answers

Lesson 1

1. Correct Answers: A, B, C, and D

    A. **Correct:** You can write LINQ queries against any object that implements IEnumerable or a derivative. This includes the DataSet class.

    B. **Correct:** You can write LINQ queries against any object that implements IEnumerable or a derivative. This includes the List<T> class.

    C. **Correct:** You can write LINQ queries against any object that implements IEnumerable or a derivative. This includes the Array class.

    D. **Correct:** You can write LINQ queries against any object that implements IEnumerable or a derivative. This includes the Dictionary<TKey, TValue) class.

2. **Correct Answers: A and D**

   A. Correct: In this query, the data is sorted first by county and then by city. These results are then properly grouped by county.

   B. Incorrect: This is a valid LINQ query. However, it actually sorts the groups by those with the cities in ascending order. It does not sort the cities within the group (just the groups themselves by their cities).

   C. Incorrect: This is a valid LINQ query. However, it sorts the list twice by the same value (County), because County is the key in the group collection.

   D. Correct: This will produce the intended result of a list grouped by county, sorted by county, and then sorted within the groups by city.

3. **Correct Answer: D**

   A. Incorrect: The ToList method allows you to execute a LINQ query into a IEnumerable list.

   B. Incorrect: The DataContractJsonSerializer object allows you to serialize and deserialize objects into JSON formatted messages.

   C. Incorrect: The XElement class allows you to work with XML and LINQ.

   D. Correct: The Concat method allows you to join two lists together to form a single list.

Lesson 2

1. **Correct Answer: B**

   A. Incorrect: You are using a strongly typed DataSet. Therefore, you would code against the University.Property value directly.

   B. Correct: You can write the query directly against the property because you are using a strongly typed DataSet.

   C. Incorrect: The DataTable represented by "u" is not a collection class of fields.

   D. Incorrect: The strongly typed DataSet does not expose a Fields collection for working with column properties.

2. **Correct Answer: D**

   A. Incorrect: A DataSet object is used to represent in-memory versions of data tables.

   B. Incorrect: The XElement class is used by LINQ to XML to work with XML data.

   C. Incorrect: The ObjectContext class is used by the Entity Framework and LINQ to Entities.

   D. Correct: DataContext is the class from which LINQ to SQL O/R models derive.

3. **Correct Answers: A, B, and C**

   A. **Correct:** The ObjectContext can be generated with a default constructor that connects to the database by using a default connection string.

   B. **Correct:** You can pass a connection string to the Entity Data Model to work with a specific database connection.

   C. **Correct:** You can pass an EntityConnection object to the Entity Data Model.

   D. **Incorrect:** The ObjectContext does not include an overloaded constructor that takes a DataContext in the constructor.

Chapter 11: Case Scenario Answers

Case Scenario 1: Writing LINQ Queries

1. You can use LINQ to XML to return all students from the XML web service. You can do the same to load the XML files from a directory; you can put this data into a common XML schema so that both data sources can be appended and queried together.

2. You can query the data as IEnumerable<XElement>. You can use the XElement Descendants and Element properties to query against the XML nodes.

Case Scenario 2: Working with LINQ and ADO.NET

- You should consider LINQ to Entities. This way, you can write your application against a common application model that is independent of the database technology. You can then update the database schema and map when installing at each subsidiary.

Chapter 12: Lesson Review Answers

Lesson 1

1. **Correct Answer: D**

   A. **Incorrect:** The ObjectDataSource control is used to connect data defined in a middle-tier business object and not in an O/R map.

   B. **Incorrect:** The SqlDataSource control can be used to connect to a SQL Server database. However, in this case, it would ignore the O/R map.

   C. **Incorrect:** The SiteMapDataSource control is used to connect to data found in a sitemap file.

   D. **Correct:** The LinqDataSource can be used to connect to a context map that is defined for your database.

2. **Correct Answers: A and B**

    A. **Correct:** TypeName is used to indicate the name of the class you intend to use for your object-based data source control.

    B. **Correct:** SelectMethod is used to indicate a method on your object to be used for selecting data.

    C. **Incorrect:** The DataSourceId property is not part of the ObjectDataSource control. Instead, it is used by a data-bound control to connect to a data source control.

    D. **Incorrect:** The SelectParameters attribute is used to define parameters for your ObjectDataSource select method. These parameters are optional and are not mentioned in the question.

3. **Correct Answers: B and C**

    A. **Incorrect:** There is no CacheTimeout attribute defined for data source controls.

    B. **Correct:** The CacheDuration attribute defines the length of time that the data of the control should be cached.

    C. **Correct:** The EnableCaching attribute is used to turn on caching for a data source control.

    D. **Incorrect:** There is no DisableCaching attribute defined for data source controls.

4. **Correct Answers: B and D**

    A. **Incorrect:** EntitySetName defines a table only (not a custom query) for the EntityDataSource control.

    B. **Correct:** The CommandText property can be used to define an entity SQL expression as a custom query. You can use the parameter in the CommandText as @ParamName.

    C. **Incorrect:** You define the parameters used by CommandText inside the CommandParameters collection.

    D. **Correct:** You use a CommandParameters section to define a parameter to use inside the CommandText query. You reference the parameter in the query using the construct @ParamName.

Lesson 2

1. **Correct Answers: B and C**

    A. **Incorrect:** The DataTextField is used to set the data displayed to the user. This would display IDs to the user (and not names).

    B. **Correct:** The DataTextField is used to display text to the user.

    C. **Correct:** The DataValueField is used to return values for selected items.

    D. **Incorrect:** The DataValueField is used to set the value returned for selected items. This would return names, not IDs.

2. **Correct Answers: C and D**

    A. **Incorrect:** The DetailsView control is used to show only one record at a time.

    B. **Incorrect:** The Repeater control does not implicitly support the ability to edit data with a data source control.

    C. **Correct:** The GridView control allows for the display of multiple rows of data and allows users to update that data.

    D. **Correct:** The ListView implicitly supports displaying data in a list and updating that data.

3. **Correct Answer: A**

    A. **Correct:** The DropDownList control can display a list that uses a minimum amount of space.

    B. **Incorrect:** The RadioButtonList control does not provide a list in a minimum amount of space.

    C. **Incorrect:** The FormView control does not provide a list in a minimum amount of space.

    D. **Incorrect:** The TextBox control does not provide a list.

Lesson 3

1. **Correct Answers: A, B, and C**

    A. **Correct:** You use a partial class to extend auto-generated code for your data context.

    B. **Correct:** You create a metadata class to be used for marking specific fields in your data context with attributes. You use this class to decorate the Invoice partial class by using MetadataType.

    C. **Correct:** You use this class to indicate that InvoiceAnnotations defines the metadata to be attached to the Invoice class.

    D. **Incorrect:** You do not add this attribute to the class used to define the metadata. This attribute can be used to indicate whether an individual entity should be included in the scaffold.

2. **Correct Answer: D**

    A. **Incorrect:** The MetadataType attribute is used to indicate a metadata class to associate with your data context type.

    B. **Incorrect:** The Display attribute allows you to customize how a property is displayed—for instance, by setting its name or order.

    C. **Incorrect:** The Editable attribute class is used to indicate whether a property can be edited by a user.

    D. **Correct:** The UIHint attribute takes a name of a field template. Dynamic Data will use this name to find your control in the FieldTemplates folder and render it accordingly.

3. **Correct Answers: C and D**

    A. **Incorrect:** The field templates are used by all fields of type Integer within the site (and is not limited to the InvoiceNumber field).

B. **Incorrect:** This event fires after the InvoiceNumber has already been changed. This is too late for validation.

C. **Correct:** The OnInvoiceNumberChanging partial method allows you to validate the invoice number before it is changed. To prevent the change, you need to throw an exception.

D. **Correct:** The ValidationException allows you to indicate a message to be displayed by Dynamic Data if validation fails.

Chapter 12: Case Scenario Answers

Case Scenario 1: Choosing Data Source Controls

1. The data is returned as XML. You could therefore configure an XML data source control to work with this data. You can use the DataFile property to connect to the data.

2. A SqlDataSource control can be configured to provide access to this data.

3. You can configure an ObjectDataSource control to access the customer object.

Case Scenario 2: Implementing a Master-Detail Solution

1. A GridView is probably best suited to display the customers and orders, because the ability to display this data as a list is a requirement.

2. The GridView does not natively support the ability to add new data records, but you can modify the GridView to provide this functionality. You can also supply a Button control that simply adds an empty data record and then places the record in edit mode.

   Another solution is to provide a DetailsView control in addition to the GridView control for the customers and orders. The DetailsView provides the ability to add new rows, and you can edit all of the fields.

Case Scenario 3: Adding ASP.NET Dynamic Data to a Website

1. Because it is an existing site, you should copy the DynamicData folder from a blank Dynamic Data site into your existing site. You should then create a DataContext or ObjectContent for your database (if one does not already exist). Finally, you should edit the Global.asax file to register a MetaModel and your DataContext.

2. You have a couple of options. First, you could add just those tables you want to expose to your data context. You could then turn on scaffolding for all tables in the data context from within the Global.asax MetaModel.RegisterContext code.

   Alternatively, you could create partial classes to add metadata to your data context classes. In these classes you could decorate each entity with the ScaffoldTable attribute and indicate which tables to expose.

Chapter 13: Lesson Review Answers

Lesson 1

1. **Correct Answer: A**

    A. **Correct:** User profiles are disabled by default for anonymous users. To enable anonymous user profiles, add the <anonymousIdentification enabled="true" /> element to the <system.Web> section of the Web.config file. Then in the <profile><properties> section, add the variables you want to track and set allowAnonymous="true" for each variable.

    B. **Incorrect:** You must specify the type of all variables except strings.

    C. **Incorrect:** You must set allowAnonymous="true" for each variable that anonymous users will access.

    D. **Incorrect:** You must add the <anonymousIdentification enabled="true" /> element to the <system.Web> section of the Web.config file. Additionally, you need to set allowAnonymous="true" for each variable that anonymous users will access.

2. **Correct Answers: A and B**

    A. **Correct:** Custom types that you want to use as profile properties must be marked as serializable.

    B. **Correct:** When you use a custom type, you must qualify it by namespace and class in the type attribute of the profile property.

    C. **Incorrect:** The group element is used to create a profile property group. It has nothing to do with custom types.

    D. **Incorrect:** You do not need to register a custom type with the Machine.config file in any way.

Lesson 2

1. **Correct Answer: C**

    A. **Incorrect:** The Login control prompts the user for a user name and password.

    B. **Incorrect:** The LoginView control enables you to display custom content for authenticated or unauthenticated users.

    C. **Correct:** The LoginStatus control displays "Login" with a link to a logon page if the user is unauthenticated, or "Logout" to authenticated users.

    D. **Incorrect:** The LoginName control displays the user's name when he or she is authenticated. The control is not visible when a user is not authenticated.

2. **Correct Answers: A and D**

   A. **Correct:** The Login control is required on a logon page, because it prompts the user for a user name and password.

   B. **Incorrect:** The CreateUserWizard control enables a user to create an account. However, it is a very large control, and a user should only need to access it once. Therefore, it should be placed on its own page.

   C. **Incorrect:** The LoginName control is not a good choice for a logon page because it displays an authenticated user's name. Because the user is not yet logged on when accessing the logon page, there would not be a user name to display, and the control would not be visible.

   D. **Correct:** The PasswordRecovery control is a good choice for a logon page because it can be used to recover a password if the user forgets his or her password.

3. **Correct Answer: B**

   A. **Incorrect:** The Unload event is called when the control is unloaded and does not allow you to redirect the user after a successful account creation.

   B. **Correct:** After a user creates an account, he or she is notified of the successful account creation and prompted to click Continue. The ContinueButtonClick event is called when the user clicks that button.

   C. **Incorrect:** The CreatedUser event is called when a user account is successfully created. However, it is called before the user has been notified of the account creation. Therefore, you should respond to ContinueButtonClick instead.

   D. **Incorrect:** The Init event is called when the page is initialized, which would occur before the user account had been created. Therefore, redirecting the user in response to this event prevents him or her from being able to create an account.

4. **Correct Answer: C**

   A. **Incorrect:** The asterisk (*) refers to all users, authenticated or unauthenticated. Therefore, this Web.config file blocks all users.

   B. **Incorrect:** The asterisk (*) refers to all users, authenticated or unauthenticated. Therefore, this Web.config file grants access to all users without prompting them for credentials.

   C. **Correct:** The question mark (?) refers to all unauthenticated users. Therefore, this Web.config file correctly blocks unauthenticated access.

   D. **Incorrect:** The question mark (?) refers to all unauthenticated users. Therefore, this Web.config file grants access to unauthenticated users without prompting them for credentials.

5. **Correct Answer: B**

   A. Incorrect: Authenticated users who are not members of the FABRIKAM\Marketing group are denied access, because the <deny users="*" /> element overrides the <allow users ="?" /> default element in the Machine.config file.

   B. Correct: Only members of the FABRIKAM\Marketing group are allowed access, because the settings in the <location> element override the settings in the parent folders.

   C. Incorrect: The <deny users="*"> element in the <location> element blocks users who are not members of the FABRIKAM\Marketing group.

   D. Incorrect: The <allow roles="FABRIKAM\Marketing" /> element takes precedence over the <deny users="*"> element, granting members of the FABRIKAM\Marketing group access.

6. **Correct Answer: D**

   A. Incorrect: Unauthenticated users do not have access because the Web.config file denies them access. Additionally, NTFS permissions also deny them access.

   B. Incorrect: Authenticated users do not have access because the Web.config file denies them access to the Marketing folder. Additionally, NTFS permissions deny them access, because the NTFS permissions grant access only to John and Sam.

   C. Incorrect: Members of the Domain Users group do not have access because the Web.config file denies them access to the Marketing folder. Additionally, NTFS permissions also deny them access, because the NTFS permissions grant access only to John and Sam.

   D. Correct: John has access because he is granted permissions through ASP.NET because of his membership in the FABRIKAM\Marketing group. Additionally, he is granted NTFS permission to access the folder.

   E. Incorrect: Sam does not have access because the Web.config file denies him access to the Marketing folder. However, he can access the webpages from a shared folder, because NTFS permissions grant him access. Only ASP.NET blocks access.

Chapter 13: Case Scenario Answers

Case Scenario 1: Configuring Website Authorization

1. Your Web.config file should resemble the following.

```
<configuration>

  <system.web>
    <authentication mode="Windows" />
    <authorization>
        <deny users="?" />
    </authorization>
  </system.web>
```

```
    <location path="IT">
      <system.web>
        <authorization>
          <allow roles="SOUTHRIDGE\IT" />
          <deny users="*" />
        </authorization>
      </system.web>
    </location>

    <location path="Production">
      <system.web>
        <authorization>
          <allow roles="SOUTHRIDGE\Production" />
          <allow users="SOUTHRIDGE\TJensen" />
          <deny users="*" />
        </authorization>
      </system.web>
    </location>

    <location path="Sales">
      <system.web>
        <authorization>
          <allow users="SOUTHRIDGE\TJensen" />
          <deny users="*" />
        </authorization>
      </system.web>
    </location>
  </configuration>
```

You also could have explicitly created a <location> section for the CustServ folder. However, because its permissions are identical to those of the parent folder, creating the <location> section is unnecessary.

2. You can use NTFS file permissions to further restrict access to the folders. This would provide multiple layers of protection, a security technique known as *defense-in-depth*.

Case Scenario 2: Configuring Website Authentication

1. You should use Windows authentication, because you need the user to provide Windows credentials that the application can use to access the file.

2. You should configure the <authentication> and <authorization> sections as follows.

```
<configuration>
    <system.web>
        <authentication mode="Windows" />
        <authorization>
            <deny users="?" />
        </authentication>
    </system.web>
        <identity impersonate="true" />
</configuration>
```

Chapter 14: Lesson Review Answers

Lesson 1

1. **Correct Answers: B and C**

   A. Incorrect: The default routing for ASP.NET MVC is based on naming conventions. You need to create the controller, action method, view folder, and view according to convention. Answer A creates a controller and action method, but these do not match another answer in the list.

   B. Correct: This naming convention would be the most logical for the controller and action method. A better choice (not shown as an answer) would be to use the RedirectToAction method which does not rely on routing conventions that can change. For example, RedirectToAction("Status", "Shipment").

   C. Correct: This naming convention would be the most logical for the view folder and view. A better choice (not shown as an answer) would be to use the RedirectToAction method which does not rely on routing conventions that can change. For example, RedirectToAction("Status", "Shipment").

   D. Incorrect: The default routing for ASP.NET MVC is based on naming conventions. You need to create the controller, action method, view folder, and view according to convention. This answer creates a view folder and view, but this view would not be located when the ASP.NET MVC routing handler tried to match the desired view to the controller. Routing is based on file location and name, and this answer uses an incorrect name.

2. **Correct Answers: B, C, and D**

   A. Incorrect: You need to define an Areas folder. This folder should contain subfolders, each based on a logical area in your site.

   B. Correct: The RegisterAllAreas() method ensures that each area's routes are registered by ASP.NET MVC.

   C. Correct: Each area folder contains its own Controllers, Models, and Views folders.

   D. Correct: You add subareas to the Areas folder in the root of your site.

3. **Correct Answers: A and B**

   A. Correct: You can use the ViewData collection to pass data to be read by the view.

   B. Correct: You use inline code to work with data passed to the view. In this case, you would write the following to display the view data.

   ```
   <%: ViewData("ItemName") %>
   ```

   C. Incorrect: You do not instantiate views and pass constructors by using standard ASP.NET MVC.

   D. Incorrect: By default, ASP.NET MVC views use the single-page model, and thus would use an inline code and markup style, not a code-behind file.

Lesson 2

1. **Correct Answer: B**

    A. **Incorrect:** You can return a different view by passing its name. However, you cannot call a controller and an action method in this way.

    B. **Correct:** The redirect helper method uses the RedirectResult ActionResult to redirect to another action method based on the URL.

    C. **Incorrect:** You cannot use Response.Redirect to call a controller and action method by using the query string and page name.

    D. **Incorrect:** The Content helper method uses ContentResult to return a different content type as a result of an action method.

2. **Correct Answer: D**

    A. **Incorrect:** The controller name should not include the Controller suffix in the route table.

    B. **Incorrect:** The default values do not match the parameter key names.

    C. **Incorrect:** This route does not define default parameter values.

    D. **Correct:** This will create a route that includes the default values for calling DefaultController and the Default action method (which will return the Default.aspx view).

3. **Correct Answers: A and B**

    A. **Correct:** You indicate that your view page inherits from the generic ViewPage<TModel>, as in ViewPage<Customer>.

    B. **Correct:** You pass the type as a parameter to the ViewResult, as in View(cust).

    C. **Incorrect:** This will pass the data. However, it will not make the view strongly typed to an element from your model.

    D. **Incorrect:** There is no such attribute. However, this is an option (View Data Class) in the Add View dialog box for creating strongly typed views.

Chapter 14: Case Scenario Answers

Case Scenario: Creating an ASP.NET MVC Application

1. You should create a controller for each entity in the requirements: ProductController, InventoryController, SupplierController, and OrderController.

2. You should create the following subfolders and views.

```
Views
    Product
        Index.aspx
        Details.aspx
    Inventory
        Index.aspx
        Details.aspx
        Edit.aspx
    Supplier
        Index.aspx
        Details.aspx
        Edit.aspx
        Create.aspx
    Order
        Restock.aspx
```

3. You should consider a mix of custom classes and a generated model. You might use a custom class to work with the product database web services. You might then generate a model by using the ADO.NET Entity Framework for your new database tables.

4. You should consider strongly typing your views. This will allow you to more rapidly build your application.

5. You might implement ASP.NET MVC areas to subdivide your application, given the anticipated size of the project and the development team.

Index

Symbols

@ Control directive, 332
@ Page directive
  Debug attribute, 391
  MVC views and, 857
@ Register directive, 265, 339, 378
$.ajax() method, 535–537
$create method, 498

A

About method of HomeController class, 840
absolute positioning, avoiding, 304
ACCDB files, 702
Access
  connecting to, 702
  database engine, 702
access rules
  creating, 806–807
  creating (practice), 822–824
AccessDataSource control
  configuring, 702
  explained, 702
accessibility
  benefits of, for all users, 318
  controls and, 313–314
  guidelines for, 313
  keyboard shortcuts, 316–317
  practice for, 322–324
  Rehabilitation Act standards, 313
  testing, 318–320
  visual, 314–315
Accessibility Validation dialog box, 319
AccessKey property of controls, 166, 167, 316

action filters (MVC), 856
ActionLink method of HtmlHelper class, 858
ActionResult class, 853
ActionResult objects, 836
ActiveViewIndex property of View control, 208
Add method of Datatable.Rows object, 652
AddUserToRole method of Roles class, 816
administrative privileges, setting launch condition
    for, 431
ADO.NET Entity Data Model. *See* Entity Framework (EF);
    LINQ to Entities
AJAX
  advantages of, 454
  calling REST services from, 606–607
  class libraries, creating, 513
  client components, 495–492, 495–496
  client components, creating (practice), 504–505
  client life cycle events, 493–494
  jQuery and, 535–539
  in master pages, 459
  Microsoft AJAX Library, 456, 458
  overview of, 455
  user control functionality, 459
  uses for, 457
  web services and, 583–585
AJAX applications
  debugging, 409
  tracing, 409
AJAX client controls
  connecting with DOM elements, 498–499
  creating, 496–498, 502–503, 505
  creating (practice), 507–510
  embedding as custom controls, 512–517
  implementing on webpages, 498–499, 510–512,
    517–518
AJAX Control Toolkit, 456

C

E

L

roles *(continued)*
  enabling (practice), 822–824
  finding users in, 816
  managing, 816
  removing users from, 816
  returning list of, 816
Roles class, 816
Roles.AddUserToRole method, 816
Roles.CreateRole method, 816
Roles.DeleteRole method, 816
Roles.FindUsersInRole method, 816
Roles.GetAllRoles method, 816
Roles.GetRolesForUser method, 816
Roles.IsUserInRole method, 816
Roles.RemoveUserFromRole method, 816
RootNode property of SiteMap class, 253
RouteLink method of HtmlHelper class, 858
RouteValueDictionary object, 867
rows, table. *See* TableRow control
RowUpdated event of DbDataAdapter object, 654

S

Save method of Profile object, 796
SaveAs method of FileUpload control, 203
SaveStateComplete event, 106
ScaffoldColumn class, 769
ScaffoldTable class, 769
scavenging settings, 77
screen readers. *See* accessibility
script blocks, 472
ScriptManager control, 409, 458
  vs. ClientScriptManager object, for registering
    scripts, 479
  markup for, 458
  partial-page updates, enabling, 458
  referencing client controls with, 498, 505
  referencing jQuery with, 523
  registering classes with, 492
  registering client scripts with, 478–479, 479
ScriptManagerProxy control, 459
ScriptReference class, 479
scripts, client. *See also* JavaScript; jQuery
  accessibility considerations, 315
  adding to websites (practice), 504, 507
  binding to client-side events, 530–533

calling web services from, 583–585
creating, with script blocks, 472–475
debugging, 396
debugging (practice), 400
dynamically adding, 475–478
embedding in custom controls, 499–502, 516
jQuery references in, 523
overview of, 472
referencing ASP.NET controls in, 475
registering on page submission only, 478
registering with ScriptManager control, 478–479
search engine optimization, 127
security. *See also* authentication; authorization
  of debugging, 390
  of FileUpload control, 203
  of settings inheritance, 820
  SSL, requiring for cookies, 813
  of tracing, 407
  of view state, 124
  web-based, 805
SelectedDate property of Calendar control, 198
SelectedDates property of Calendar control, 198
SelectedDayStyle property of Calendar control, 198
SelectedIndexChanged event of DropDownList
    control, 175, 725
SelectionChanged event of Calendar control, 199
SelectionMode property of Calendar control, 197, 198
SelectMonthText property of Calendar control, 198
selectors, jQuery
  advanced, 524–525
  examples of, 525–526
  overview of, 524
SelectorStyle property of Calendar control, 198
SelectWeekText property of Calendar control, 198
Serializable attribute class
  overview of, 580
  for profile properties, 794
server controls. *See also* custom web server controls;
    data source controls; data-bound controls; HTML
    controls
  accessibility, 313–314
  adding (practice), 217–223
  adding in Source view, 164
  adding in Source view (practice), 181–184
  adding to forms, 106–107
  advantages of, 162
  AJAX. *See* AJAX server controls

About the Authors

TONY NORTHRUP, MCSE, MCTS, and CISSP, is a consultant and author living in New London, Connecticut. Tony started programming before Windows 1.0 was released but has focused on Windows administration and development for the past 15 years. He has written more than 25 books covering Windows development, networking, and security. Among other titles, Tony is author of *MCTS Self-Paced Training Kit (Exam 70-536): Microsoft .NET Framework— Application Development Foundation, Second Edition*, and co-author of *MCTS Self-Paced Training Kit (Exam 70-562): Microsoft .NET Framework 3.5—ASP.NET Application Development*. You can learn more about Tony by visiting his personal website at *http://www.northrup.org* and his technical blog at *http://vistaclues.com*.

MIKE SNELL spends his work life helping teams build great software that exceeds the expectations of end users. Mike runs the consulting practices at CEI (*www.ceiamerica.com*). He is also a Microsoft Regional Director (*www.theregion.com*); Regional Directors act as community liaisons between developers and Microsoft. Mike has written several books on programming the .NET Framework, including books in the Microsoft Press Training Kit series and the Microsoft Visual Studio Unleashed series. You can learn more by visiting Mike's blog at *http://www.visualstudiounleashed.com*. You can also follow him on Twitter *@mksnell*.

For Web Developers

Microsoft® ASP.NET 4 Step by Step
George Shepherd
ISBN 9780735627017

Ideal for developers with fundamental programming skills—but new to ASP.NET—who want hands-on guidance for developing Web applications in the Microsoft Visual Studio® 2010 environment.

Microsoft Silverlight® 4 Step by Step
Laurence Moroney
ISBN 9780735638877

Teach yourself essential tools and techniques for Silverlight 4—and begin creating interactive UIs for the Web and the latest version of Windows® Phone.

Programming Microsoft ASP.NET 3.5
Dino Esposito
ISBN 9780735625273

The definitive guide to ASP.NET 3.5. ASP.NET expert Dino Esposito guides you through the core topics for creating innovative Web applications, including Dynamic Data; LINQ; state, application, and session management; Web forms and requests; security strategies; AJAX; and Silverlight.

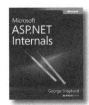

Microsoft ASP.NET Internals
George Shepherd
ISBN 9780735626416

Make Web pages more efficient—and speed development—by understanding how ASP.NET works in depth. This book delves into architecture and provides established patterns.

Programming Microsoft ASP.NET MVC
Covers ASP.NET MVC 2 and Microsoft Visual Studio 2010
Dino Esposito
ISBN 9780735627147

Author Dino Esposito leads you through the features, principles, and pillars of the ASP.NET MVC framework, demonstrating how and when to use this model to gain full control of HTML, simplify testing, and design better Web sites and experiences.

Programming Microsoft LINQ
Paolo Pialorsi and Marco Russo
ISBN 9780735624009

With LINQ, you can query data—no matter what the source—direct from Microsoft Visual Basic® or C#. Guided by two data-access experts, you'll learn how Microsoft .NET Framework 3.5 implements LINQ and how to exploit it for faster, leaner code.

Microsoft ASP.NET and AJAX: Architecting Web Applications
Dino Esposito
ISBN 9780735626218

Rethink the way you plan, design, and build Web applications. Whether updating legacy sites or architecting RIAs from the ground up—you'll learn pragmatic approaches to AJAX development you can employ today.

System Requirements

We recommend that you use a test workstation, test server, or staging server to complete the practice exercises in each lesson. However, it would be beneficial for you to have access to production-ready data in your organization. If you need to set up a workstation to complete the practices and use the companion CD, the minimum system requirements follow:

- Personal computer with at least a 1-GHz 32-bit (x86) or 64-bit (x64) processor
- At least 1 GB of RAM (x86 systems) or 2 GB of RAM (x64 systems)
- At least a 40-GB hard disk
- DVD-ROM drive
- Super VGA (800 × 600) or higher resolution video adapter and monitor
- Keyboard and Microsoft mouse or compatible pointing device

The computer must also have the following software:

- A web browser, such as Windows Internet Explorer
- An application that can display PDF files, such as Adobe Acrobat Reader, which can be downloaded at *http://www.adobe.com/reader*
- Microsoft Visual Studio 2010 Professional, a trial version of which can be downloaded at *http://www.microsoft.com/visualstudio/en-us/products/2010-editions/professional*

These requirements support your use of the companion CD-ROM. To perform the practice exercises in this training kit, you might require additional hardware or software. See the Introduction to the book for detailed hardware requirements.

What do you think of this book?

We want to hear from you!
To participate in a brief online survey, please visit:

microsoft.com/learning/booksurvey

Tell us how well this book meets your needs—what works effectively, and what we can do better. Your feedback will help us continually improve our books and learning resources for you.

Thank you in advance for your input!